W0246609

The Magnificent
DIWAN

ALSO BY THE SAME AUTHOR

A Dictionary of Dates
A Book of Cricket Days
Jeh: A Life of J.R.D. Tata
Sugar in Milk: Lives of Eminent Parsees
Barons of Banking: Glimpses of Indian Banking History
Zubin Mehta: A Musical Journey

The Magnificent DIWAN

The Life and Times of
SIR SALAR JUNG I

BAKHTIAR K. DADABHOY

VINTAGE
An imprint of Penguin Random House

VINTAGE

USA | Canada | UK | Ireland | Australia
New Zealand | India | South Africa | China | Singapore

Vintage is part of the Penguin Random House group of companies
whose addresses can be found at global.penguinrandomhouse.com

Published by Penguin Random House India Pvt. Ltd
4th Floor, Capital Tower 1, MG Road,
Gurugram 122 002, Haryana, India

First published in Vintage by Penguin Random House India 2019

Copyright © Bakhtiar K. Dadabhoy 2019

All rights reserved

10 9 8 7 6 5 4 3 2

The views and opinions expressed in this book are the author's own and the
facts are as reported by him which have been verified to the extent possible,
and the publishers are not in any way liable for the same.

ISBN 9780670092529

Typeset in Adobe Caslon Pro by Manipal Technologies Limited, Manipal
Printed at Replika Press Pvt. Ltd, India

This book is sold subject to the condition that it shall not, by way of trade
or otherwise, be lent, resold, hired out, or otherwise circulated without the
publisher's prior consent in any form of binding or cover other than that in
which it is published and without a similar condition including this condition
being imposed on the subsequent purchaser.

www.penguin.co.in

This is a legitimate digitally printed version of the book and therefore might not
have certain extra finishing on the cover.

For Nawsha and Noshir Jalnawala
and in memory of Feroz Shapurji

Contents

Genealogical Trees

The Nizams of Hyderabad

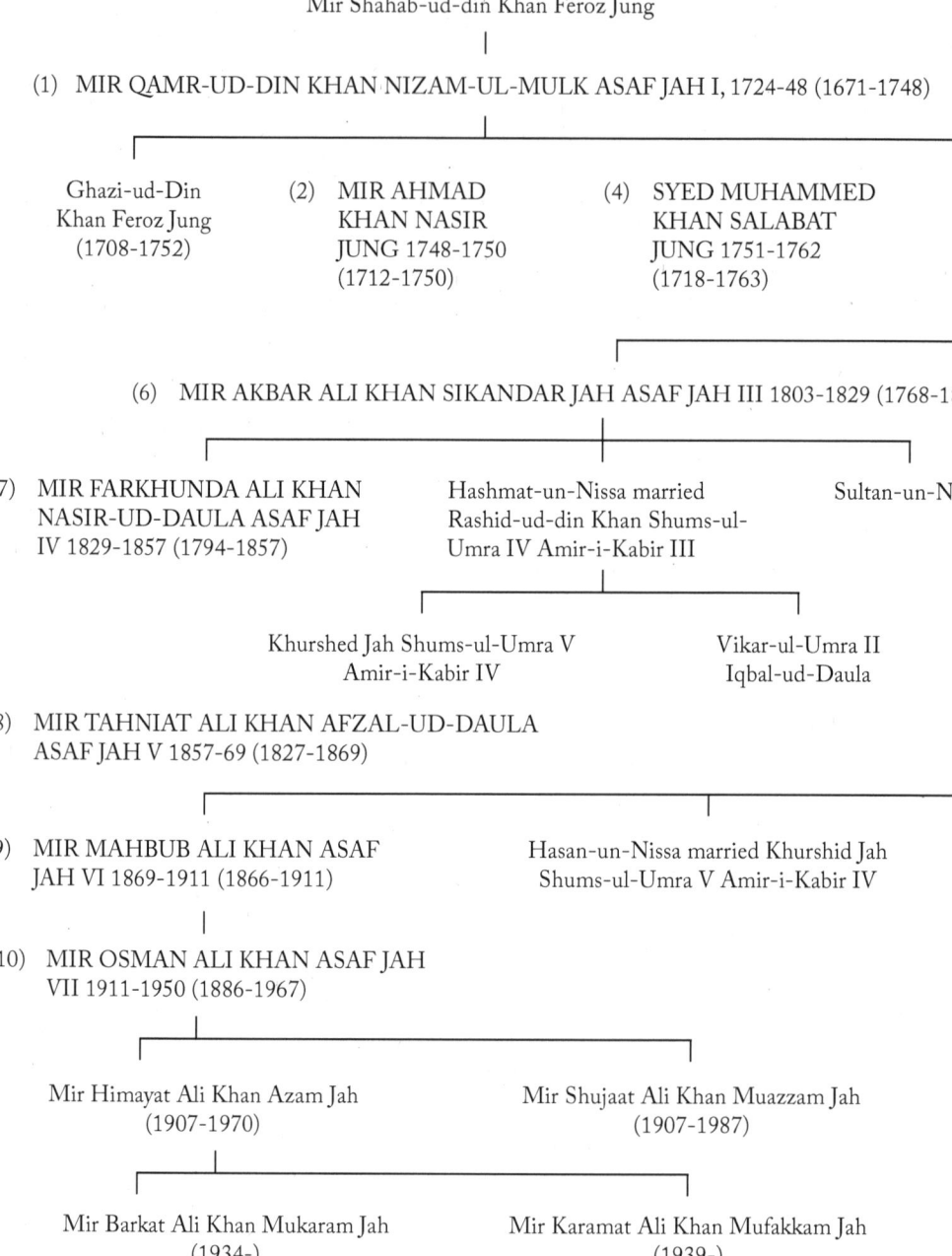

Khwaja Abid Qilich Khan

Mir Shahab-ud-din Khan Feroz Jung

(1) MIR QAMR-UD-DIN KHAN NIZAM-UL-MULK ASAF JAH I, 1724-48 (1671-1748)

Ghazi-ud-Din Khan Feroz Jung (1708-1752)

(2) MIR AHMAD KHAN NASIR JUNG 1748-1750 (1712-1750)

(4) SYED MUHAMMED KHAN SALABAT JUNG 1751-1762 (1718-1763)

(6) MIR AKBAR ALI KHAN SIKANDAR JAH ASAF JAH III 1803-1829 (1768-182

(7) MIR FARKHUNDA ALI KHAN NASIR-UD-DAULA ASAF JAH IV 1829-1857 (1794-1857)

Hashmat-un-Nissa married Rashid-ud-din Khan Shums-ul-Umra IV Amir-i-Kabir III

Sultan-un-Niss

Khurshed Jah Shums-ul-Umra V Amir-i-Kabir IV

Vikar-ul-Umra II Iqbal-ud-Daula

(8) MIR TAHNIAT ALI KHAN AFZAL-UD-DAULA ASAF JAH V 1857-69 (1827-1869)

(9) MIR MAHBUB ALI KHAN ASAF JAH VI 1869-1911 (1866-1911)

Hasan-un-Nissa married Khurshid Jah Shums-ul-Umra V Amir-i-Kabir IV

(10) MIR OSMAN ALI KHAN ASAF JAH VII 1911-1950 (1886-1967)

Mir Himayat Ali Khan Azam Jah (1907-1970)

Mir Shujaat Ali Khan Muazzam Jah (1907-1987)

Mir Barkat Ali Khan Mukaram Jah (1934-)

Mir Karamat Ali Khan Mufakkam Jah (1939-)

MIR NIZAM ALI
KHAN ASAF JAH
II 1762-1803
(1734-1803)

Mir Muhammed
Sharif Khan
Basalat Jung

Mir Mughal Ali Khan
Humayun Jah

Khair-un-Nissa
Begum

(3)   MUZAFFAR JUNG Dec
1750-Feb 1751
(d. 1751)

Bashir-un-Nissa Begum married Fakhr-ud-din Khan
Shams-ul-Umra II Amir-i-Kabir

Farid-ud-din Khan
Khurshid Jung
(1802-1815)

Rafi-ud-din Khan
Shams-ul-Umra III
Amir-i-Kabir II
(1805-1877)

Sultan-ud-din Khan
Bashir-ul-Mulk
(1814-1853)

Parwarish-un-Nissa
married Asman Jah

Jahandar-un-Nissa married
Vikar-ul-Umra II Iqbal-ud-Daula

Note: The ten rulers of Hyderabad are shown in capitals (Nos. 2, 3 and 4 were never formally
recognized by the Mughal emperor and therefore were never given the title of Asaf Jah.)

The Paigah Family

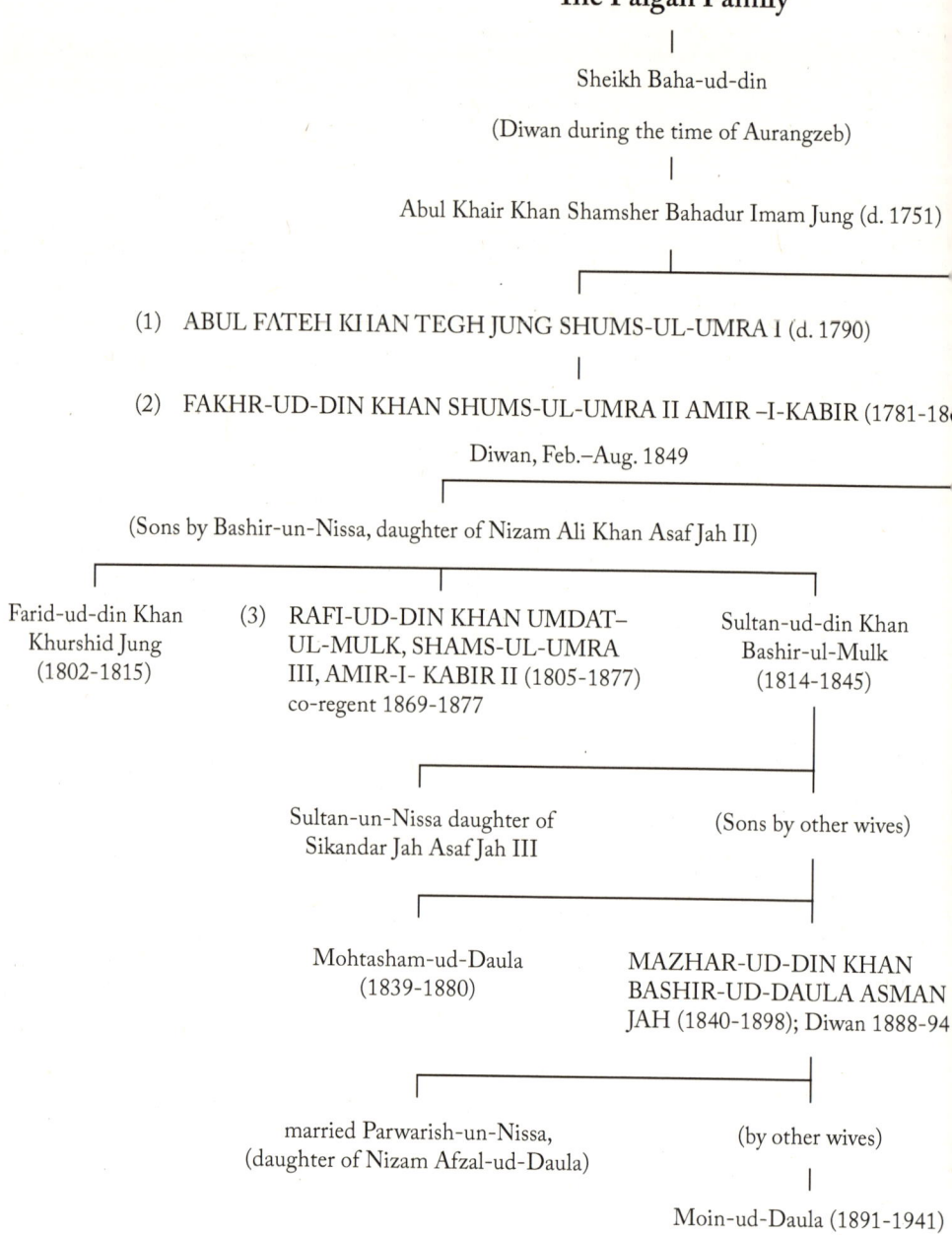

Sheikh Baha-ud-din

(Diwan during the time of Aurangzeb)

Abul Khair Khan Shamsher Bahadur Imam Jung (d. 1751)

(1) ABUL FATEH KHAN TEGH JUNG SHUMS-UL-UMRA I (d. 1790)

(2) FAKHR-UD-DIN KHAN SHUMS-UL-UMRA II AMIR –I-KABIR (1781-18...

Diwan, Feb.–Aug. 1849

(Sons by Bashir-un-Nissa, daughter of Nizam Ali Khan Asaf Jah II)

| Farid-ud-din Khan Khurshid Jung (1802-1815) | (3) RAFI-UD-DIN KHAN UMDAT–UL-MULK, SHAMS-UL-UMRA III, AMIR-I- KABIR II (1805-1877) co-regent 1869-1877 | Sultan-ud-din Khan Bashir-ul-Mulk (1814-1845) |

Sultan-un-Nissa daughter of Sikandar Jah Asaf Jah III

(Sons by other wives)

Mohtasham-ud-Daula (1839-1880)

MAZHAR-UD-DIN KHAN BASHIR-UD-DAULA ASMAN JAH (1840-1898); Diwan 1888-94

married Parwarish-un-Nissa, (daughter of Nizam Afzal-ud-Daula)

(by other wives)

Moin-ud-Daula (1891-1941)

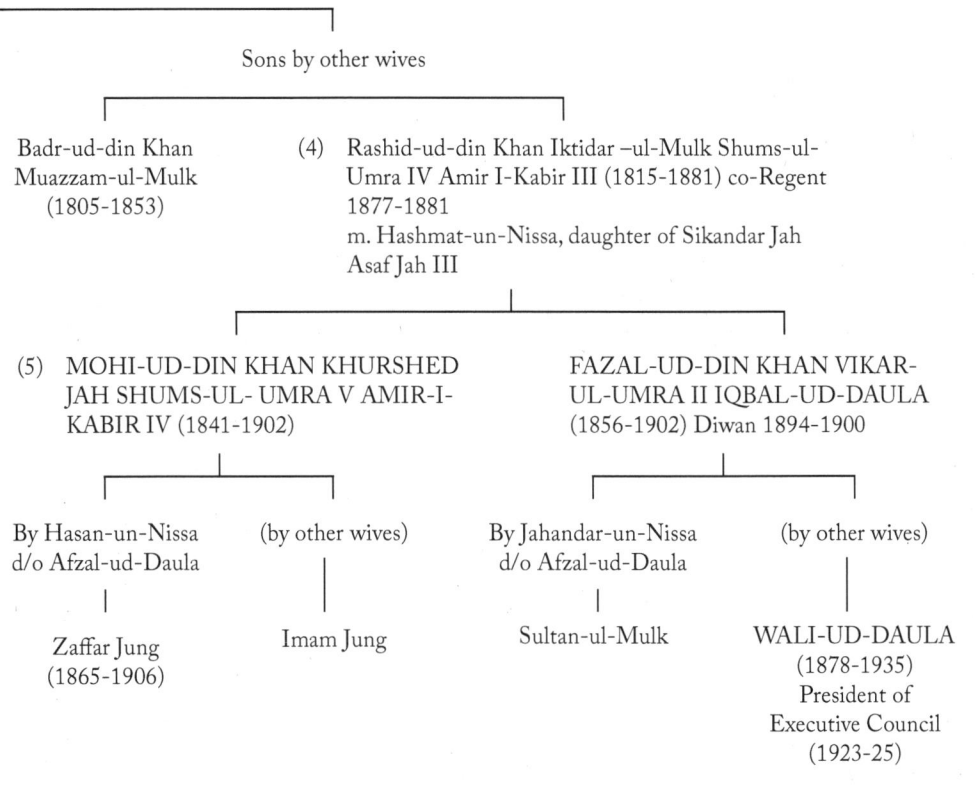

Abul Barkat Khan Imam Jung

Sons by other wives

Badr-ud-din Khan
Muazzam-ul-Mulk
(1805-1853)

(4) Rashid-ud-din Khan Iktidar –ul-Mulk Shums-ul-
Umra IV Amir I-Kabir III (1815-1881) co-Regent
1877-1881
m. Hashmat-un-Nissa, daughter of Sikandar Jah
Asaf Jah III

(5) MOHI-UD-DIN KHAN KHURSHED
JAH SHUMS-UL- UMRA V AMIR-I-
KABIR IV (1841-1902)

FAZAL-UD-DIN KHAN VIKAR-
UL-UMRA II IQBAL-UD-DAULA
(1856-1902) Diwan 1894-1900

By Hasan-un-Nissa
d/o Afzal-ud-Daula

(by other wives)

By Jahandar-un-Nissa
d/o Afzal-ud-Daula

(by other wives)

Zaffar Jung
(1865-1906)

Imam Jung

Sultan-ul-Mulk

WALI-UD-DAULA
(1878-1935)
President of
Executive Council
(1923-25)

Note: Diwans and holders of the titles Shums-ul-Umra and Amir-i-Kabir are shown in capitals.

The Salar Jung Family

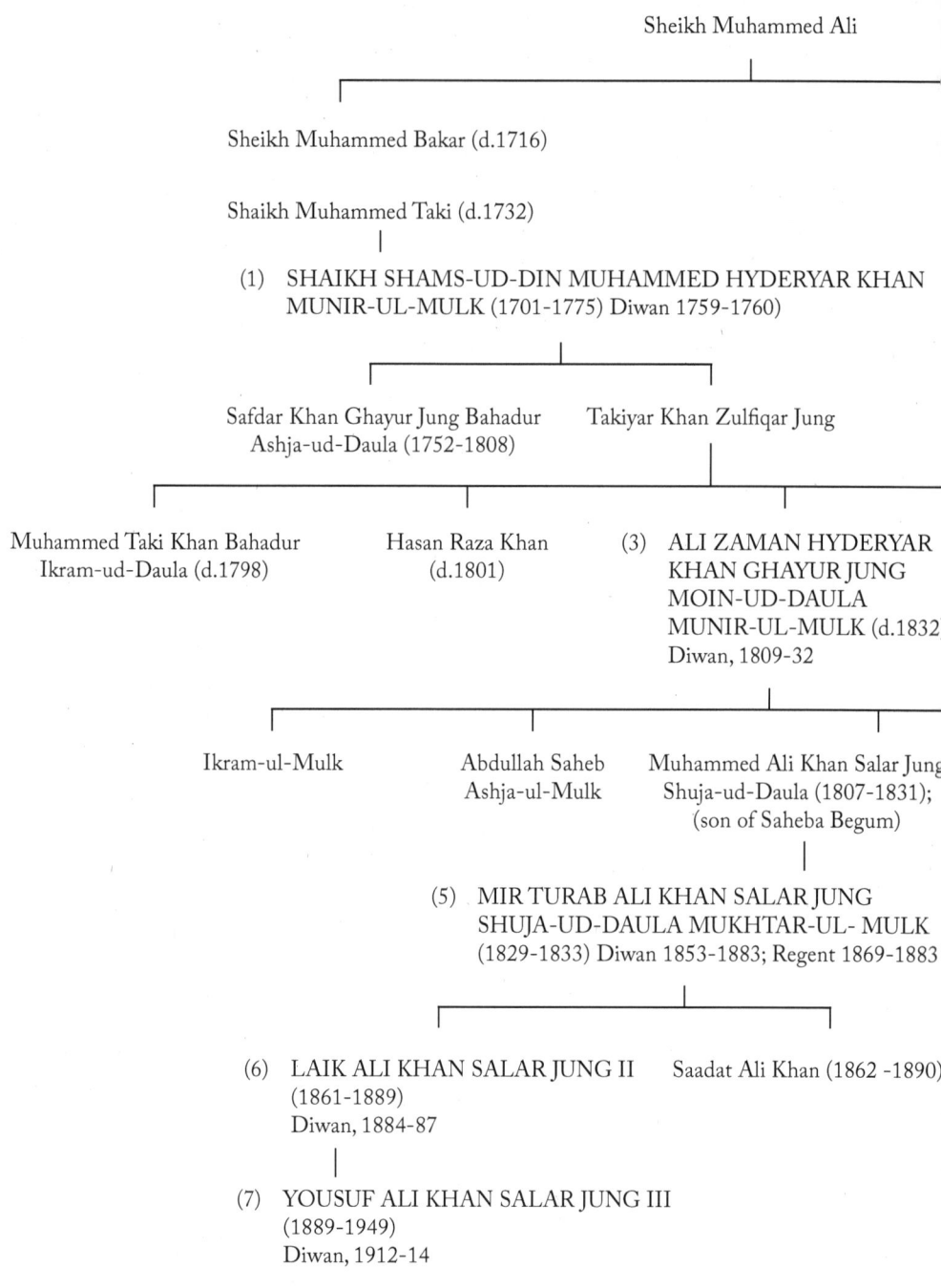

Sheikh Muhammed Ali

Sheikh Muhammed Bakar (d.1716)

Shaikh Muhammed Taki (d.1732)

(1) SHAIKH SHAMS-UD-DIN MUHAMMED HYDERYAR KHAN
MUNIR-UL-MULK (1701-1775) Diwan 1759-1760)

Safdar Khan Ghayur Jung Bahadur   Takiyar Khan Zulfiqar Jung
Ashja-ud-Daula (1752-1808)

Muhammed Taki Khan Bahadur   Hasan Raza Khan   (3) ALI ZAMAN HYDERYAR
Ikram-ud-Daula (d.1798)   (d.1801)   KHAN GHAYUR JUNG
                                                                MOIN-UD-DAULA
                                                                MUNIR-UL-MULK (d.1832)
                                                                Diwan, 1809-32

Ikram-ul-Mulk   Abdullah Saheb   Muhammed Ali Khan Salar Jung
                     Ashja-ul-Mulk   Shuja-ud-Daula (1807-1831);
                                             (son of Saheba Begum)

(5) MIR TURAB ALI KHAN SALAR JUNG
SHUJA-UD-DAULA MUKHTAR-UL- MULK
(1829-1833) Diwan 1853-1883; Regent 1869-1883

(6) LAIK ALI KHAN SALAR JUNG II   Saadat Ali Khan (1862 -1890)
(1861-1889)
Diwan, 1884-87

(7) YOUSUF ALI KHAN SALAR JUNG III
(1889-1949)
Diwan, 1912-14

Sheikh Muhammed Hyder

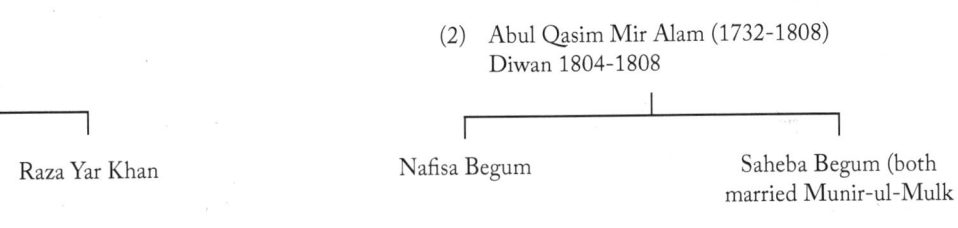

(2) Abul Qasim Mir Alam (1732-1808)
Diwan 1804-1808

Raza Yar Khan   Nafisa Begum   Saheba Begum (both
                                                      married Munir-ul-Mulk

(4) ALAM ALI KHAN SIRAJ-UL-MULK (1809-1853)
Diwan, 1846-48; 1851-53; (son of Saheba Begum)

Note: Diwans are shown in capitals

The Peshkar Family

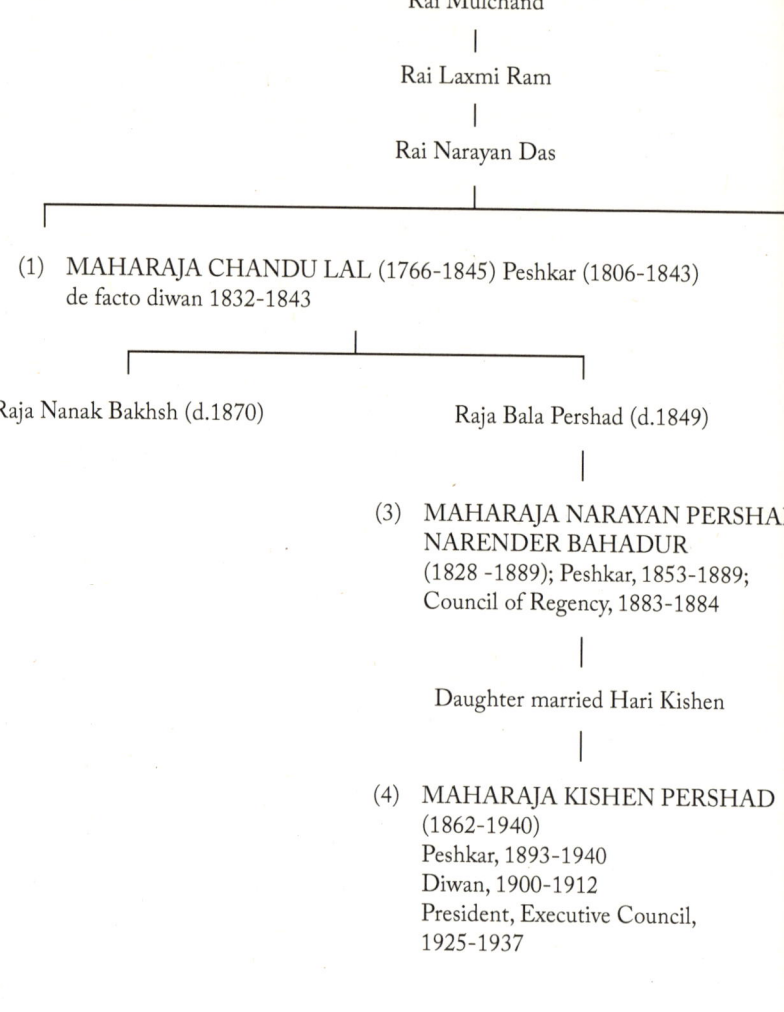

Rai Mulchand

|

Rai Laxmi Ram

|

Rai Narayan Das

|

(1) MAHARAJA CHANDU LAL (1766-1845) Peshkar (1806-1843)
de facto diwan 1832-1843

Raja Nanak Bakhsh (d.1870)   Raja Bala Pershad (d.1849)

|

(3) MAHARAJA NARAYAN PERSHAD
NARENDER BAHADUR
(1828 -1889); Peshkar, 1853-1889;
Council of Regency, 1883-1884

|

Daughter married Hari Kishen

|

(4) MAHARAJA KISHEN PERSHAD
(1862-1940)
Peshkar, 1893-1940
Diwan, 1900-1912
President, Executive Council,
1925-1937

Raja Govind Bakhsh (d.1835)

(2)   RAJA RAM BAKHSH (d 1871)
      Peshkar, 1843-1846; de facto diwan,
      1849-1851

Author's Note

Histories and biographies give us a picture of the past, and the good ones rest on a solid base of facts that nobody disputes. There is nothing personal about facts; what is personal is their choice and grouping. The events may not be new but it is akin to turning a kaleidoscope—the pieces remain the same but they fall differently each time, forming ever-changing patterns. A biography is a form of creative non-fiction which allows the writer the freedom to select the stories and anecdotes to be related or highlighted, and set the pace and the tone of the telling. As American author Brenda Ueland has observed, 'You have to hold your audience in writing to the very end—much more than in talking, when people have to be polite and listen to you.' I can only hope that the stories I have selected are interesting, and the pace unflagging. The idea was to write an entertaining book concise enough to appeal to the general reader who has neither the time nor the inclination to go into too many details but yet detailed and nuanced enough to provide an accurate and complete picture. Despite my best efforts, concision has eluded me. This book has ballooned to double the size it was intended to be and it is hoped that at the end of it the reader feels suitably rewarded.

It is said that the principal task of a historical biography is to use the life as a window to the times. This book is not merely a chronicle of Salar Jung's life but also a history of Hyderabad—both social and governmental—and gives the reader an encompassing view of the man and his world, using his life and work to illumine the period. History is not epitomized in an individual; it is the interplay of socio-economic forces and new ideas, but no one can deny that individuals are significant and representative figures in history, the subject of this biography being one such personality. This account of Salar Jung's life is more in the nature of a political biography; his personal life finds mention in passing. This is because a lot less is known about his personal life, and more importantly, it is his political career which is by far the more interesting one. Inevitably, it is Salar Jung the statesman, and not so much Salar Jung the man, who comes into sharper focus.

A biographer is often confronted by the paucity of material but in this case I was faced with an embarrassment of riches. The problem was not what to include, but what to keep out. What is included and what left out is necessarily a subjective choice. Since significance is subjective I may have been influenced in my selection by what is in fact a personal judgement or even a prejudice. I have taken the material available to me and tried to weave an interesting narrative.

A challenge that every biographer faces is the distribution of periods and phases—the right proportion among varied fields of public and personal activities, and the right scale for the many episodes of a subject's life. If certain moments in history like the Mutiny of 1857 occupy more space, it is because they are interesting as well as significant. Other incidents may not be as important but are worth discussing in some detail because they are illustrative of society at a particular point of time. One example, of many, in this book, is the detailed discussion on shoes and discalceation.

Those who know a lot more about Salar Jung than I do may be disappointed at some of my omissions, but I leave the general readers, to whom this book is chiefly addressed, to form their own judgement of the man. I have tried to paint Salar Jung against his proper background, much of which was his own creation, and to set him in the context of his time. It is also equally important for a biographer to temper admiration with discernment given that in most cases it is admiration, at least initially, which makes a biographer invest his time, energy and resources in writing someone else's life-story.

I have tried my best to be impartial and it is for the reader to decide how far I have succeeded. My bias apart, the biases and prejudices of the writers of the numerous books from which I have drawn must also be allowed for. Though I have made attempts to read between the lines it would do well to remember that objectivity was rarely a part of the job description: each writer had an agenda, be it political, religious or merely sycophantic.

The writing is based on well-researched history and the wide scope of the work means that not all the primary research is mine; much of it is based on the works of others available to me through published writings. My own primary research is reflected particularly in the use of newspaper articles which provide a fertile primary source for the writing of history and have generally remained an underutilized resource. The sources of my information are clearly set out in the reference notes and give the interested reader an opportunity to follow up with further reading. They are, however, not essential to an enjoyment of the book.

Introduction

Mir Turab Ali Khan Bahadur Sir Salar Jung Shuja-ud-Daula Mukhtar-ul-Mulk, G.C.S.I., D.C.L., better known as Sir Salar Jung I, diwan (prime minister) of the nizam's dominions from 1853 to 1883, was arguably the foremost statesman and diplomat that India produced since the establishment of the British supremacy. In his lifetime, his fame transcended the limits of not only Hyderabad, but also of India, but today there are no crossroads or avenues named in memory of the founder of modern Hyderabad. This lack of civic memorialization can hardly be said to be mitigated by the fact that, ironically, the name Salar Jung is remembered in connection with a museum in Hyderabad which houses the collection of art and artefacts of his grandson, Mir Yousuf Ali Khan Salar Jung III.

Details about Salar Jung's early life are few, and provide little material to trace the development and formation of a character which, for a generation, exercised a commanding influence over the destiny of Hyderabad. His life and character form an inseparable part of the history which he himself enacted since early manhood. A man with a broad and enlightened mind and a strong will, Salar Jung applied his rare energies to the improvement of Hyderabad and the amelioration of the condition of its people. His long and illustrious career was also distinguished by his efforts to promote friendly relations between the nizam and the British government. The unexampled prosperity of Hyderabad since it fell under the administration of Salar Jung was a subject of much comment.

An Arab by descent, two of his family before him had filled the post of diwan, but he was by far the most distinguished representative of his family, becoming diwan when he was only twenty-four on the death of his uncle, Siraj-ul-Mulk. As a boy, he was taught English, and was closely associated with the family of the British resident in his formative years. His opinion of the British as a just and honourable people must have been formed at this time, and it was something he believed in all his life, only to be greatly disillusioned towards the end.

Salar Jung had an enviable command of English and an intimate acquaintance with English ideas and with Western statesmanship. Though he was very comfortable in European society—often referred to as the Anglophile minister of Hyderabad, and contemptuously called '*firanghi bachcha*' (foreign boy) by the nizam—he never ceased to be Indian. He did much to bring together the European and the Oriental in friendly social intercourse. Salar Jung's refined manners, enlightened views and generous hospitality made him a great favourite with Englishmen.

His palace was also furnished in English style—perhaps with more ostentation than taste, but he also stubbornly fought to preserve the old Mughlai ways in social intercourse, and to preserve old customs, mistakenly believing that changes and reforms in the administrative and political spheres could be kept separate from the religious and social. At the Delhi durbar in 1877, he was the only Indian who made a speech in English. But though he adopted much of Western culture, he was never a denationalized Indian, remaining faithful to the traditions of his creed and country.

When Salar Jung became diwan, the economy and the finances of the government were in a shambles. There was discord among the nobles, and the authority of the nizam was little more than a farce. The roads were patrolled by bands of robbers, and each nobleman's palace was a nest of brigands. And with the Governor General, Lord Dalhousie, just waiting to annex as much territory as he could, Salar Jung, when he assumed office, was faced with dangers both from within and without. Many thought that the days of Hyderabad as an independent principality were numbered. It was Salar Jung's great achievement that he disappointed these expectations, and showed in the most remarkable manner, that in his person the hour had indeed produced the man.

Salar Jung first turned his attention to the restoration of law and order and to 'rescue Hyderabad from its embarrassment'. At that time, there were a large number of Arab mercenaries employed in the nizam's army. They were amenable only to their own chiefs, and subject only to the laws and customs of their own country. They were outside the pale of the justice system (or whatever passed for it) of Hyderabad. The 'laxity of the desert soon became the license of the town', and the Arabs soon terrorized the very people they were supposed to protect. Salar Jung, by a combination of coercion and concession, succeeded in taming the Arabs before devoting his energies to the other evils that clamoured for his attention.

He had inherited a Hyderabad which was almost a wilderness, one in which anarchy and lawlessness reigned without a check. His uncle's legacy included an empty treasury, heavy debts, large arrears to the city troops and no credit. The credit of the government was so low that his uncle could have borrowed Rs 10,000 from bankers, if at all, with great difficulty. Money could not be obtained from sahukars, except under the guarantee of the military chiefs and that too at extortionate rates. Salar Jung, by his personal character, restored credit to the government such as it had never possessed before.

The idea of an organized system of government in Hyderabad owed its birth to the vision of Salar Jung. Before him, all power was centralized in the diwan: there was no concept of a regular and systematic form of government with separate departments and secretariats. Salar Jung reduced Hyderabad to order and settled government; he restored its prosperity and developed its resources to such an extent that the nizam's dominions were as orderly as any other part of India.

He established courts and reorganized the police. The Arab chiefs were restrained, the irregular troops suppressed, and the Rohillas[1] disbanded. He overhauled the system of land revenue, built roads and tanks, dug wells, and renewed or created irrigation works. He founded schools and introduced the railways. His labours brought the nizam's government from a condition of 'organized brigandage' to one of the most enlightened in India. As a result of the improvement in law and order, trade prospered and the finances of the government improved. He was not spared the vituperation of his many detractors, but his results spoke for themselves: his opponents were silenced before facts which did not admit of any dispute.

Devoted to the nizams he served, he was inspired at the same time with the best traditions of British administration in India, and contributed perhaps more than any native statesman to the establishment of friendly and cordial relations between the two powers, the maintenance of which became one of the settled principles of British policy in India. That the British supported him when he was found useful and pliant, but thought nothing of encouraging his great rival Rashid-ud-din Khan Amir-i-Kabir III, when they found themselves discomfited by his petitions for the restoration of Berar, is a different matter.

When Salar Jung took office in 1853, the policy of annexation was still in the ascendant. Hyderabad escaped absorption only by the cession of the fertile cotton-cultivating province of Berar,[2] an assignment of territory which rankled with successive nizams, and whose restoration was Salar Jung's idée fixe throughout his life. Salar Jung realized that what remained to the nizam could only be preserved by showing that native statesmen could administer as efficiently as the British rulers who surrounded them. Accordingly, he devoted his life to making Hyderabad a model state and lived long enough to see it prosper.

For long, the native princes had lived under the threat of annexation. But they were now aware that so long as their governments were just and stable, their independence was secure. Salar Jung was the man who typified this policy and was its most conspicuous representative, at least in the eyes of the British. He reorganized Hyderabad and remained loyal to the British at the time of the Mutiny of 1857. By so doing, he did as much as any man to save the native states from absorption.

The native princes, inspired by Salar Jung's example, showed themselves ready to promote the well-being of their subjects and foster prosperity so as to make their states no different from a British-administered province. For this change in sentiment and policy, credit must go to Salar Jung, who set an example for the others. The early part of his career was spent in disheartening struggles to reform the administration, an endeavour in which he had to encounter the opposition of the nobility, and also endure frequent humiliation at the hands of the nizam.

During the Mutiny of 1857, Salar Jung rendered signal service to the English in a moment of great peril. It was his prudence and courage which prevented the fanaticism of Hyderabad from being given free play. Resisting all the temptations to which sympathies of race and creed exposed him, he cast his lot with the British power, which, though under momentary eclipse at the time, he saw destined to permanence. It was expedience, rather than any romantic preference for English supremacy, which made Salar Jung support the British. He realized that peace and order in Hyderabad depended on the stability of British rule, and was also the best pledge of its prosperity. If Hyderabad remained faithful, it was due to the foresight of its young diwan. The loyalty and cooperation of Hyderabad had been one of the strongest buttresses of the British in India, and it had a major role in the building of the British Empire in India. While the foundations of the Empire were laid at Plassey and Arcot, it was Hyderabad who provided them with the finance they needed to complete the structure of the Empire.[3]

By the time the Mutiny ended, Salar Jung's reforms were already showing results. In fact, his reforms continued without a diminution of excellence or zeal (save for a brief period when he was battling a hostile resident and viceroy), down to the hour of his death. This was all the more creditable since he did not always receive the support, recognition or gratitude he deserved from the nizams he served. Both the fourth and the fifth nizams, Nasir-ud-Daula and Afzal-ud-Daula, were apprehensive of change or innovation. During the reign of the fifth nizam, Afzal-ud-Daula, Salar Jung was all but a prisoner in Hyderabad. He dared not leave his palace without the nizam's express permission, and his smallest actions were reported to his master through spies. In the presence of the nizam, he was in a state of terrified submission. This greatly restricted his capacity for guiding beneficial change. With more liberty, and the support of his sovereign, he would have achieved much more, and perhaps more quickly.

To understand Salar Jung, we must understand that his most dominant sentiment was devotion to the nizam. He did not hesitate to oppose the nobles of the court, and to reform every department of the disorganized administration, because he realized that the strength of the ruler lay in the firmness of the administration. His loyal attitude during the Mutiny was but a part of this well-considered policy. Throughout his career, the mainspring of his policy was the interest of his master, the nizam.

His loyalty to the British, notwithstanding his childhood influences, sprang from a deliberate conviction that the maintenance of British authority was the best pledge of safety to the dynasty he served so faithfully. At the risk of his own popularity, and often at the risk of his own life, he refused to align with fanatics. For the nizam's sake, he bore the humiliation he received from the British which resulted from his persistence on the restoration of Berar. He bore with meekness the frequent indignities to which he was exposed in the palace, and waged a constant and unequal battle against fanatics and other malcontents.

Till Afzal-ud-Daula's death, Salar Jung had never left Hyderabad, a fact which makes his administrative reforms still more remarkable, since they were accomplished in spite of the opposition of a capricious nizam, and hostile nobility. His strong individuality, firmness and caution gave him an ascendancy in Hyderabad which no previous diwan had attained.

The difficulties he faced, unusually trying and complicated in themselves, were compounded by the fact that he was never able to rely on the support of the court because he was identified with a policy of reform which threatened vested interests.

Imbued with a liberal education and outlook thanks to the English influence in his formative years, Salar Jung honestly believed in the superiority of British administration. He adopted the fundamentals of British principles of administration in his reforms which covered almost every sphere of activity: land revenue, police, judiciary, administration and education. Sir Richard Temple, who was resident in 1867, believed that Salar Jung, as a man of business and in matters of finance, had no rival among Indian ministers. European influences had greatly moulded his thinking, and Temple recognized that he was a great imitator. Whatever improvement the British government introduced, he would sooner or later adopt, to good effect.[4] It is no surprise that British influence preponderated, since apart from his own predilections, he was encouraged and advised by successive residents who wanted to foster good government, not only in Britain's own interest, but for a principle as well. Carrying 'civilization' to India was both an imperial necessity and a mission of pride in the nineteenth century.

As long as Afzal-ud-Daula was nizam, Salar Jung depended very heavily on the cooperation of the resident, Sir George Yule, to push through his reforms. Yule also provided effective support when the nizam, in his periodic fits of pique, wanted to dismiss Salar Jung. With the arrival of Sir Richard Temple as resident, his schemes for reform received a further fillip. Temple kept himself in the background, and gave his advice privately which was intended only for Salar Jung's ears. Salar Jung's famous *zillabandi* system was introduced in 1867 after consulting Temple and obtaining his approval. To Temple's encouragement and advice could also be attributed a system of municipal administration on the lines of British India which was introduced in 1869, a year after Temple left Hyderabad.

After Afzal-ud-Daula's death, Salar Jung's reforms proceeded apace. Untrammelled by the nizam, he made various changes in the administrative structure which were dominated by Western concepts of centralized administration. The pernicious system of farming out the revenue was abolished: graded revenue authorities now collected revenue in the diwani districts. Land revenue increased by more than 200 per cent in twenty-five years. The impact on trade too was positive, though the reduction in custom duties operated chiefly in favour of the British. The extension of cotton cultivation gave an impetus to the foundation of textile mills. All this was facilitated by the introduction of the railways and the construction of roads which made the movement of goods and labour easier.

Salar Jung's personal interest in education led to the encouragement of both Western and Oriental systems of learning. In 1856, the Dar-ul-Uloom, or Oriental College, was established. In 1873, Salar Jung founded the Madrasa-i-Aliya to give Western education to the sons of the nobles. The City Anglo-Vernacular School, which later came to be known as Hyderabad College, was founded in the capital, and two schools, one Persian and the other vernacular, were established in each taluka. A medical school for transmitting Western medical knowledge had already started in 1846, and in 1869, a civil engineering college was set up at the prodding of Temple. All these institutions acted as a westernizing influence in the state.

Salar Jung's reforms needed efficient personnel which was scarce in Hyderabad. Rising above parochial considerations, he had no hesitation in importing men of talent and education to man official posts in his administrative hierarchy. Indians with British training and experience were inducted into the administration after 1869. The bias seems to have been in favour of recruiting Muslims from north India. Salar Jung took personal interest in this endeavour, and many were personally selected by him.

In 1872, Salar Jung had written to Sir Syed Ahmed Khan to obtain the services of civil servants from north India. Aligarh became a major source of recruitment in the 1870s, with many of those who took jobs in Hyderabad being associated with Sir Syed Ahmed Khan and the fledgling Aligarh Muslim University. The term 'non-*mulki*' was applied to these, though they were also called 'Hindustani' since the majority were from north India. Apart from these, there were Parsis and Hindus and some Europeans as well.[5] This initiated a process where the mulkis (old residents of Hyderabad) started resenting the fact that the non-mulkis deprived them of the loaves and fishes of office.

While Salar Jung wanted to improve the administration by the introduction of personnel from outside, he was equally keen to preserve the old Mughlai political traditions and culture. He realized that the importing of British practices and personnel from outside Hyderabad could have a serious cultural and political impact on Hyderabadi society. In order to ensure that this did not happen, he developed policies which were designed to isolate the new administrators and the British officials, not only from each other, but also from the nizam and other important nobles in Hyderabad. The diwans preceding Salar Jung had denied the resident access to the nobles of Hyderabad to prevent intrigue, and Salar Jung continued with this policy till his death in 1883. He sought to prevent access to traditional sources of power and tried not to draw too many recruits from the same source. The diwani employees had no status in court, being mere paid employees.

Salar Jung encouraged Parsis, Kayasthas and Maharashtrians to join the civil service. In later years, prosperous agriculturists from coastal Andhra came to set up businesses. Hyderabad blended all these communities into a harmonious whole, distinguished by the adoption, each in their own manner, of the Hyderabadi *tehzeeb*, a composite of civility, grace and courtesy in speech and manners which conveys respect and consideration. The old Hyderabad was all about etiquette and courtesy, and old Hyderabadis were acutely conscious of their tehzeeb, and resented any dilution of it by newcomers. The manner of sitting in the presence of elders, proper dress and salutation were all part of this tehzeeb.

It was this tehzeeb that Salar Jung was trying to protect, but with so many changes and innovations, it was only natural that Western ideas and values would impact Hyderabad society. Old customs were either rendered obsolete or were synthesized with Western ideas. In other fields, they were superimposed on existing customs and laws, all leading to a hybrid culture and a new cosmopolitanism. The elite began to take an active interest in public affairs, and the seeds of a new Hyderabad were also nurtured by the press.

Hyderabad witnessed a multidimensional transformation in the second half of the nineteenth century, with many features of modern civilization emerging at this time. No doubt the inspiration for all these was British, but Salar Jung's role as a catalyst cannot be underestimated. 'The transformation was primarily brought about by the leaven of western ideas and British influence, but Salar Jung intensified the process by encouraging the flow of liberal and progressive ideas associated with the West. By the time of his death, the dawn of a new era had arrived in Hyderabad.'[6] Still, it must be remembered that imperial and pragmatic considerations dictated British action in each state: paramountcy was sustained, both by siding with the forces of modernization and also supporting reactionary elements when necessary.

The warm relationship with the British, which lasted while Afzal-ud-Daula lived, suffered a setback when Salar Jung developed ambitions for his state and for his nizam. The assignment of Berar had been an injustice done to Hyderabad, and he now wanted the province to be returned. This strained his relationship with the paramount power since his ambitions were now in opposition to British aims and policies. At one time their principal collaborator, he now became, in a sense, their chief adversary. The concern over Berar was basically one of land and its revenue, but it also had to do with an issue of symbolic importance, namely, the nizam's sovereignty. During the time of the Mutiny, when Salar Jung had remained loyal, the British lauded him as a man of principle and an able administrator. But when Salar Jung started using his talents for the restoration of Berar, this opposition to the imperial purpose caused great resentment.

Salar Jung took to increasingly devious and secretive measures to press for the restoration of Berar: he hired confidential agents as lobbyists who cost him huge sums of money, and paid them by accounting jugglery which accorded ill with his principles. This was the only blot on Salar Jung's probity. He ended up falsifying the accounts to the extent of Rs 41 lakh, and when the matter was brought to the knowledge of the nizam, Mahbub Ali Khan, by his son Salar Jung II after his father's death, the nizam granted a pardon, and asked that all those records be destroyed. It was his way of saying that whatever Salar Jung had done was for the good of Hyderabad.

If there was one leitmotif running through Hyderabad's history from 1858 onwards, it was the consolidation of British paramountcy over the state. One of the petty ways used by the British for asserting this paramountcy was by controlling the English versions of titles permitted to Indian rulers. Indigenous rulers were known as 'chiefs', with a few important ones being called 'princes'. Terms such as 'throne' or 'royal' were prohibited since they implied independence or attributes of sovereignty. Similarly, Salar Jung was never referred to as prime minister but only as minister, since in the British view, there was only one prime minister, and he was in London.[7]

This attitude was also responsible for the wholly unnecessary unpleasantness which resulted from Salar Jung's refusal to allow the young nizam, Mahbub Ali Khan, to travel to Bombay to welcome the Prince of Wales in 1875. The young, excitable ruler was almost always in delicate health, and Salar Jung wanted to prevent him from being exposed to the risks of such a long journey. The doctors too attested to the weak constitution of the young boy. But the British took umbrage at the absence of the nizam, which was perceived as a slight. In the end, the nizam did not attend but the atmosphere was unnecessarily vitiated.

In 1876, Salar Jung travelled to England with the hope of obtaining the restoration of Berar. It proved to be a futile attempt, and politically speaking, the visit was a failure. But it was a great social success and convinced him that his past services had not been forgotten. The city of London gave him its freedom and Oxford University, the degree of Doctor of Civil Law honoris causa. He had already been made Knight Grand Commander of the Order of the Star of India in 1867.

For a long time, the restoration of Berar was the search for a chimera, but after the trip to England, Salar Jung seems to have had the impression that he had come within measurable distance of its realization. But the glimmer of hope given by the secretary of state, Lord Salisbury, on the Berar restoration proved to be a false dawn. Yet he never allowed himself to lose sight of the fact that the one way to obtain the recovery of the lost provinces was to show that Hyderabad was as well-governed as any British territory. Adequate justice can only be done to his long and illustrious career if one realizes how different Hyderabad was thirty years after he first took up the reins of office.

Back in Hyderabad, he realized that he had lost the confidence of the viceroy, Lord Lytton, who was out to 'tame' him. (The equine analogy to describe Salar Jung seems to figure prominently in the correspondence between Lord Lytton and others.) The viceroy made it his business to treat him with distrust and, almost, with scorn. The appointment of his political rival and enemy, Rashid-ud-din Khan Amir-i-Kabir III, as co-regent was the viceroy's way of neutralizing Salar Jung. The dispute over the dismissal of his private secretary, Arthur Oliphant, only served to further embitter relations between Calcutta and Hyderabad.

At one time, Lytton had intended to make Salar Jung's position so uncomfortable that he would be forced to resign. Though his frustration may have led him to contemplate such a move on more than one occasion, Salar Jung, who had outlived much opposition, was in no mood to oblige. He reasserted his position, but his usefulness, at least while the co-regent was alive, was impaired by the rivalry and opposition introduced into the administration by the British. This must have been all the more distasteful to Salar Jung, for few men had done better work or done it with greater single-mindedness of purpose.

Crippled and fettered by the open encouragement given to his political rival, this was the most trying period of his life, and his conduct during this time only proved the calibre of his statesmanship. Identified on the one hand with reforms that sparked resentment in the old nobility, and on the other with claims on Berar which Lytton considered preposterous, he could only look for support to his loyal adherents, and more importantly, his own strength of character. But some of his best administrative work was conceived at this time, and his political marginalization, if it can be called that, resulted in much good.

In carrying out his beneficent schemes, Salar Jung had had to encounter the most formidable opposition. The support of the British enabled him to withstand the gloomy and sullen hostility of the nizam. On occasion, Salar Jung was threatened with dismissal by the nizam, and he owed his survival as diwan to the intervention of the resident at Hyderabad. This obligation which he incurred towards the British for preserving him during his early career must have no doubt operated in restraining his impatience at this time when he had reason to resent their behaviour.

Regardless of the validity of his claim on the restoration of Berar, it is impossible not to admire the single-mindedness with which he made it the one thought and effort of his life, even though personally he had nothing to gain by the change, apart from restoring family pride. So persistently did he identify himself with this subject that for a time, his very name, at least in official circles, became synonymous with this troublesome demand. It was undoubtedly his aim to crown his services to the nizam by restoring to him the territory assigned to Lord Dalhousie in 1853, but this was not to be. The British 'opposed him with increasing bitterness and, often, plain deviousness and dishonesty, quite contrary to the gentlemanly qualities Salar Jung saw—and persisted in seeing—in them, layer by upward layer to his very last'.[8]

Lytton's departure, and Ripon's arrival, heralded better times for Salar Jung. He regained the government's trust, and in 1881 when the co-regent died, Salar Jung was once again left in single and unmolested possession of administrative power. For Ripon too, British paramountcy was an article of faith, but unlike his predecessors, particularly Lytton, he realized that British aims could be more easily achieved with a pacified Salar Jung. This policy proved to be successful, for Salar Jung returned to his old policy of subordinate cooperation with the British, and an atmosphere of trust, friendship and cordiality once again prevailed. Despite Salar Jung's determined challenge in the later years, there is little doubt that British paramountcy was repeatedly asserted over Hyderabad, with both the nizam and Salar Jung continuously under the influence, if not following the orders, of the British. In the last few years of his life, Salar Jung was a beaten man and made no effort to confront the British.

A man of strong intellect, highly cultivated intelligence and cultured aesthetic tastes, no person had a greater capacity for work. He was a hard-working, self-denying man, wholly immersed in work from dawn to night. Not for him idle days or the enervating pleasures of the zenana. Blessed with a wonderfully retentive memory and a highly subtle and comprehensive understanding, he was able to analyse an argument or a character with equal ease. He was a shrewd judge of character and made use of this ability with almost unerring accuracy. As Temple has noted in his memoirs, 'He discharged his duties with unwearying assiduity, entire integrity and efficiency unprecedented in the Deccan. He was a gentleman in the highest sense of the term; the quality of his mind was indicated in his discreet manner and refined aspect.'[9]

A good conversationalist, he was able to enjoy a good joke as well as any other man. He had a quiet humour of his own but he never indulged in ridicule. Moderately fond of poetry and an avid collector of paintings, he also appreciated music but often remarked that he was tone-deaf. He enjoyed a game of billiards in the evening, but his greatest passion was riding, and his stables housed some magnificent Arab horses. He was fond of history, but was fonder still of any study leading to practical results connected with statecraft. He, however, had little time to spare for reading, being occupied in official work from early morning till 11 p.m. The entire administration revolved around him, with centralization being the distinguishing feature of his administration.

Regal in his charity and hospitality, Salar Jung was simple in his tastes. His tall, spare figure and the distinguished plainness of his white dress and turban stood out in any company. He wore his small white turban with more dignity than many princes wore their bejewelled headgear. He was very upright and had a dignified deportment, and his face, which was thoughtful and calm, would light up in a most pleasant manner when he smiled, but otherwise his countenance betrayed little of what he was thinking. He spoke English with ease and elegance, and his manners were so engaging that an English official who was opposed to Salar Jung's claims on Berar thought that 'Englishmen of influence and rank should not be encouraged to go to Hyderabad as Salar Jung was sure to make converts of them'. A distinguished official once said that Salar Jung's charm of manner was so great that one could not speak to him for ten minutes without becoming his friend for life.

In his personal relations, he was just, humane and truthful. Kind and affectionate to his family and friends, he showed the same consideration to his subordinates. By taking a friendly interest in their private affairs, and by extending to them his sympathy and help, he succeeded in winning their loyalty and affection. He was fond of society, and nothing gave him greater pleasure than to have a few English friends meet him at the breakfast or dinner table and share his hospitality.

Despite the rivalry and intrigues of the court, he retained office under three nizams continuously, until the day he died. It was a strong testimony to the permanence of Salar Jung's reforms that the shock of his sudden demise was not followed by the slightest disorder or lawlessness. To those who remembered the many elements of mischief which had to be guarded against not so long ago, it was nothing short of a miracle that there was no recrudescence of disorder when death suddenly removed him from the scene. This was because the Hyderabad of 1883 was an altogether different place from the Hyderabad of 1853.

Salar Jung was equally remarkable in his liberality of thought. In no place in India were benevolent institutions of other religions and denominations aided so generously and with such catholic impartiality. (Salar Jung even received the thanks of the Pope when he visited the Vatican.) Perhaps of all modern statesmen, he made the greatest allowance for the religious and social prejudices of those whom he governed. Salar Jung was a Shia, but given his general outlook, it is hardly surprising that there was nothing of the bigot in him: he was a thorough liberal with respect to religion and perfectly free from all sectarianism. He did follow, however, the more binding injunctions of his religion, seldom neglecting his daily prayers or the fasting observed in the month of Ramadan.

Nothing with Salar Jung was ever hurried; no reform, however important, was carried out in haste. He never forced a reform down the throats of his people. His policy was one of a 'wise and wary conservatism', and though he greatly disliked extreme measures and revolutionary schemes, he was equally willing to forsake old systems once he was convinced of their inefficacy. He was often accused of undue lenity, something which could be attributed as much to this policy as to the kindness of his disposition. He advocated and practised a system of government by compromise and conciliation, which he carried almost to an extreme. Given the opposition he faced, perhaps there was no other way. One great advantage of this, however, was that his changes and reforms did not jar on the senses of the people as an innovation.

Salar Jung was also a man of many contradictions and dichotomies. He was a man of honour but was guilty of transferring money to his estate. A man of courage, who was undeterred by threats to his own life, he was terrified of the nizams as also of opposing the British in the last part of his life. A man of sound judgement, he was the ready dupe of his confidential agents in England who had an axe to grind in keeping alive the Berar issue. He firmly believed in the British as just and fair, but faced great disappointment in persisting in this belief, particularly with reference to Berar.

Salar Jung believed at the start of his career that the relationship with the British was a collaborative one. In the early days, he used the resident as a sounding board, and was happy to take his advice on the reforms he was contemplating. Later, as the British became more powerful, they felt entitled to demand and expected to receive. Salar Jung now responded less willingly, and towards the end, the relationship became an adversarial one. Salar Jung believed that reciprocity was normative, and in this belief too, he was to face great disappointment since relationships in Western society tended to be more contractual.

He was an amalgam of tradition and modernity even in his personal life. He had one nikah marriage, through which he had two daughters. But he also had numerous concubines, and his two sons, Mir Laik Ali Khan, the elder son and his successor, and Mir Saadat Ali Khan, the younger son, were the offspring of two of his concubines. The daughters were educated by a French governess, and were proficient in both Persian and English. Salar Jung's was the first instance in India of a Muslim noble giving his daughters a European-style upbringing. He wanted the benefits of modernization while retaining the grace of the old culture. The sons were for some years taught by a private tutor until they commenced to attend the Nobles' School established in Chaderghat by Salar Jung himself a few years before his death. They continued to be pupils of the institution until their departure for England. They were both accomplished and well-bred young men, and made a most favourable impression in England during their visit there.

There still remains an air of mystery associated with Salar Jung's death. Though it was officially declared to be caused by cholera, the French governess of his daughters was convinced he was poisoned. One oral tradition suggests suicide. Whatever the reasons for the unexpected termination of his life, the anxiety experienced after his death was perhaps the best tribute to his worth.

Proofs of Salar Jung's many achievements were to be found everywhere at the time of his death. Salar Jung's reform of the medieval oligarchy that was Hyderabad took many forms: the history of Hyderabad during his thirty years as diwan is little more than the history of Salar Jung's reforms. In the case of Salar Jung, we may apply Thucydides's famous saying of antiquity: 'For the whole earth is the tomb of famous men.' Hyderabad was in a very real sense the tomb of its great diwan.

Like many others, from childhood, I associated the name Salar Jung with a museum in Hyderabad. That the Salar Jung whose collection it houses had 'III' suffixed to his name did not particularly arouse my curiosity. I didn't know who 'I' and 'II' were, and nor did I care. Being a mulki by birth, this was unpardonable, and the only defence I can offer is that though I was born in Secunderabad, I was never a resident till midlife, thanks to the peregrinations of my father which ensured that we relocated every few years. Thus, while I was fully aware of the 'Great Collector', I was only dimly aware of the existence of the grandfather, the 'Great Diwan', and that too because his bust was displayed in the Secunderabad Club. (The building was his bequest to the club.) Sandwiched between the 'Great Diwan' and the 'Great Collector' is Salar Jung II, a fleeting character on the political stage, as indeed, on the stage of life itself.

In 2008, I was asked to contribute an article for an anthology on Hyderabad. The brief was open-ended, and it was left to me to choose my subject. I accepted but had to indicate the subject in advance so that there would be no duplication in the collection. I chose to write on the Salar Jungs and the museum, and the article was appropriately, if somewhat unimaginatively, called 'Three Salar Jungs and a Museum'.

It was while researching for this article that I made my acquaintance with Turab Ali Khan Sir Salar Jung I, and it is possible that the seed for this biography was sown at this time. I scouted around for a biography in English, but was surprised to find that apart from Harriet Ronken Lynton's excellent *My Dear Nawab Saheb*, which is in the nature of a political biography based on his vast correspondence, and V.K. Bawa's *The Nizam between Mughals and British: Hyderabad under Salar Jang I*, again a political account based on his doctoral thesis, there were none. Syed Hossain Bilgrami's *A Memoir of Sir Salar Jung G.C.S.I.*, a slim volume on his life, also proved to be useful, but I am sure that Salar Jung's former secretary had no pretensions about it being a definitive biography of the man he had served. Since my needs at the time were limited, I gave no further thought to this lacuna in the literature on Salar Jung. But whatever I had read on the former prime minister of Hyderabad had made me an admirer; it was a remarkable life by any standards, even if it ended somewhat prematurely, a dissolution made more interesting by the hint of mystery associated with his passing.

Somewhere deep down within me there lurked a desire to write a full-length biography of arguably Hyderabad's greatest statesman. That there was an enormous amount of material which one could draw from was a happy thought: I would have to labour to use the material but not toil to locate it. The Telangana State Archives and Research Centre which houses his immense correspondence, and the National Archives in New Delhi, are both fertile sources of archival material. If ever I was looking for a subject to write on, then here it was.

I was working on my biography of Zubin Mehta at the time, and whatever weak resolve I had to pursue research on Salar Jung soon disappeared. Due to a variety of reasons, the Zubin Mehta biography was put on the back-burner, and the writing of another book intervened. At around this time, I was invited to write a book on the history of banking and *Barons of Banking: Glimpses of Indian Banking History* was published in 2013. When Zubin Mehta's biography finally saw the light of day in 2016, my attention was once again drawn to Salar Jung and his remarkable life. Visits to Hyderabad rekindled the old desire to narrate the story of his life, and soon after the publication of the maestro's biography, I decided that I would spend the next few years in the company of Mukhtar-ul-Mulk Sir Salar Jung I. Researching for this book has been a highly rewarding and deeply enriching experience, one I would have cherished even if the book the reader holds in his hand (or the soft copy on his Kindle, phone or tablet) had not become a reality.

An autobiography, it has been said, is a pre-emptive attack on a future biographer.[10] From that perspective, it is an advantage that Salar Jung's multifarious activities did not include indulging a desire for confidential expansion. 'It does not much matter what people think of a man after his death,' wrote Rudyard Kipling at the end of his life, with a view to discouraging future biographers. He destroyed many of his personal papers and wrote an autobiography which was absurdly deficient in its description of the events of his life. But Salar Jung was no Kipling, and we can be almost sure that he would have cared about the opinion of posterity. His vast correspondence available in the archives in Secunderabad gives us a very good idea of the man: it is his own story that emerges from the remarkable collection he left behind.

This book is divided into nineteen chapters, and the narrative unfolds as a story in what is largely a chronological scheme. However, there is some unavoidable back and forth, given the concurrence of events, since for the purposes of readability, the narrative proceeds subject-wise. Thus, what follows is a largely linear account, but with a thematic quality, dwelling on topics because of the interest they hold, or because of their importance to the narrative.

A detailed prologue sets the background, traces the history of the Asaf Jah dynasty from the time of its founder, and touches upon the rivalry between the French and the English, and the process by which the British established their paramountcy, the role of various diwans, and much else. A separate chapter describes in some detail Salar Jung's seminal role during the Mutiny of 1857 and how his support of the British saved the British Empire in India. His relations with successive nizams, residents and viceroys are also narrated in detail, along with the intrigues involved. The controversy over the nizam being unable to receive the Prince of Wales at Bombay, Salar Jung's enmity with Rashid-ud-din Khan Amir-i-Kabir III (the powerful Paigah noble who opposed and troubled him as long as he was alive), and his trip to England and the Continent are also covered in detail.

The assigning of Berar to the British and his persistent petitions for its restoration to the nizam, and his role in the Nizam's State Railway also find elaborate mention. His ill-treatment at the hands of the viceroy, Lord Lytton, Lytton's grand durbar in 1877, and Salar Jung's subsequent humiliation, all examples of the consolidation of British paramountcy in Hyderabad, are narrated in detail. A separate chapter describes the diwan deodi (palace) and Salar Jung's daily routine, among other things. There was an air of mystery associated with his passing, and a narration of his death and the events leading up to it mark the end of the book. A long Epilogue covers the events after Salar Jung's death and gives a brief picture of his son, Salar Jung II, and grandson, Salar Jung III. It also briefly describes the genesis of the Salar Jung Museum and its subsequent development.

And now a word about the names in the book. People in Hyderabad were given one name at birth, but when they were granted a title, they became known by that title. When they received more titles, they came to be known by the more recent one. I have retained the personal name or the name by which the personality was introduced throughout the book. Many titles were hereditary, and this added to the confusion by having to keep track of the generations. Thus, Rashid-ud-din Khan became Ikhtidar-ud-Daula, then Ikhtidar-ul-Mulk, Shums-ul-Mulk, Shums-ul-Umra IV, Vikar-ul-Umra I, Amir-i-Kabir III. When one of his titles is used, it is prefaced with his given name so as to avoid confusion in the reader's mind.

Another source of potential confusion is in the transliteration of names, which has been done by different people. Persian was the court language, and Urdu that of the people. Thus Rashid-ud-din is sometimes spelt Rasheed-ood-Din and ul Mulk as ool Mulk, and Shums-ul-Umra as Shamsul Umra or Umrah and even Omrah. In this case, the safest guide is phonetic: if they are pronounced similarly, they are, in all probability, the same. I have also retained the old names of places, so we have Bombay, Calcutta, Madras, Simla, Baroda, Shorapore, Poona, and so on.

I have chosen to write for a general readership, and this book, it is hoped, will appeal to a wide range of aims and interests. For those interested in the history of the Deccan generally, a study of Hyderabad history and its famous prime minister is definitely of interest. For those exploring Hyderabad as it is now, an understanding of its history and the people who made it what it is today will certainly enhance their experience. It will also appeal to all those who simply like a good story.

This biography is intended to be a popular account of a man who deserves to be rescued from his present-day obscurity; it does not purport to be a scholarly work, but I believe I have not compromised on the rigour of scholarship. I will have considered my labours rewarded if this account of Salar Jung's life and work increases the readers' knowledge of an unusual personality who was one of the greatest statesmen of nineteenth-century India. Salar Jung's name carries little resonance for today's generation, but this tome would have served its purpose if it serves as an introduction—and perhaps a little more—to one of the great Indians of yesteryear, even as it rekindles the memory of a man who has become the victim of collective amnesia.

Prologue

In February 1739, the Mughal Emperor Muhammad Shah 'Rangila' suffered a humiliating defeat at Karnal at the hands of the Persian invader Nadir Shah. Nearly a month later, on 20 March, Nadir Shah entered Delhi in a grand procession astride a grey charger surrounded by the elite Qizilbash troops in their distinctive red headgear. The defeated emperor had preceded him by a day, in order to give the conqueror a befitting welcome. Nadir Shah occupied what was once Shah Jahan's own imperial suite near the Diwan-i-Khas. His army encamped round the fort, on the banks of the Jamuna, and the remaining soldiers found accommodation in houses throughout the city.

The next day was the festival of Eid-ul-Zuha, and the name and titles of Nadir Shah were proclaimed as sovereign in the sermon, or *khutba*, at the Jama Masjid and other mosques in the city. Coins were struck in his name which remained current for two months. Nadir Shah made a show of graciously allowing Muhammad Shah to retain the throne, and the Mughal emperor, for his part, laid out a vast treasure as an offering. This was in effect the indemnity demanded by the invader to leave India.

But if all was civility inside the palace, outside it, trouble was brewing. Nadir Shah had entered the city with 40,000 of his soldiers, and grain was in great demand. When the Persian mounted police ordered the granaries in Paharganj to be opened and fixed a price of corn which was unacceptable to the merchants, a mob assembled. A scuffle followed in which the Persian horsemen were killed. At around 4 p.m., a rumour was spread that Nadir Shah had been killed by a female palace guard. Persian soldiers were attacked, and by dawn, the uprising had gained considerable momentum. The underworld joined in the mayhem. An incredulous Nadir at first refused to believe that his men had been killed, but later events convinced him that the situation was indeed alarming.

At sunrise on 22 March, the tumult broke out afresh. When Nadir Shah, dressed in armour, rode through the streets the next day, he found hundreds of his soldiers lying dead, some of their bodies horribly mutilated. From the terrace of the golden mosque of Roshan-ud-Daula, near the Kotwali Chabutra in the middle of Chandni Chowk, in what is today Old Delhi, he saw the populace hurling stones and missiles from the rooftops on his soldiers below. After ascertaining which wards and classes of men had been responsible for the massacre of his troops, he unsheathed his sword, and waving it above his head, gave the signal for a general massacre (*qatle-aam*) of the population, supervising the carnage himself.

That day proved to be the saddest and bloodiest day in Delhi's history. The indiscriminate slaughter began at 9 a.m. and continued unchecked till about 2 p.m. The Persians laid violent hands on everything and everyone. The soldiers moved from house to house, killing people, plundering property and abducting wives and daughters. Many women committed suicide, and even Muslim citizens were reported as resorting to a kind of *jauhar*, killing their own women and children. Houses were set on fire, and the stench from thousands of unburied bodies infected the air of the entire city. Some 20,000 people were killed, and 10,000 taken as slaves. The town was reduced to ashes, and the streets remained strewn with corpses. There was scarcely a spot left in Delhi which was not stained with human blood.

The hapless Muhammad Shah, desperate to end the pogrom, called on the services of one of his oldest and most capable generals who was famous for both his bravery and tact. The old general then went bareheaded to the Persian invader with his hands tied with his turban and with a sword hanging around his neck. He begged Nadir Shah on his knees to stop the killing, appealing to his sense of pity by reciting a couplet by the Persian poet Hafiz:

> The roar of your anger has killed so many men,
> If you want to kill some more, bring the dead back to life again.[1]

Another version holds that it was, 'If the beloved kills all his lovers, then whom will he rule?' Impressed with the nobility of the old general, and moved by the couplet, Nadir Shah agreed to stop the killing. He told the venerable *demandeur* before him, 'I grant pardon to these rascals because of your white beard.'[2] The plunder continued but the killing stopped. The general was Nizam-ul-Mulk Asaf Jah I, the founder of the Asaf Jahi dynasty of Hyderabad, and also its most distinguished member.

NIZAM-UL-MULK ASAF JAH I

In 1687, Golconda had fallen to Aurangzeb after a long siege of eight months. The imperial forces were under the command of Ghazi-ud-din Khan Feroz Jung. Leading the Turkish troops at the same siege, and under the overall command of his own son, was Ghazi-ud-din's father, Khwaja Abid, who had been given the title of Qilich Khan by Aurangzeb in 1680. One day, while storming the walls of the Golconda fort, a musket ball ripped off his right arm at the shoulder. The old warrior refused to dismount and rode all the way back to camp despite the grievous injury. On hearing of the injury to his faithful general, Aurangzeb sent his personal surgeons to treat him.

His prime minister, Asad Khan Jumdat-ul-Mulk, followed the next day. When he reached camp, he was surprised to find Qilich Khan calmly sipping a cup of coffee with his left hand, while the surgeons were ministering to his right shoulder. He told the prime minister that he hoped to be well soon and resume his service to the emperor. But the best physicians could not save him, and he died three days later. He was buried near Himayatsagar, about 4 miles from Golconda fort. His right arm, which had been carried away by a musket ball, was recognized by his signet ring and was buried in the village of Qismatpur.

Qilich Khan was born in the neighbourhood of Samarqand in the kingdom of Bukhara. He first came to India in 1654–55 on his way to Mecca at the end of Shah Jahan's reign. In 1657, he joined the service of Aurangzeb, who soon formed a very high opinion of his abilities. He received many honours and held many high posts under Aurangzeb, including the governorship of Bidar. In 1680, he was awarded the title of Qilich Khan. He had five sons, of whom the eldest, Shihab-ud-din Khan, later known as Ghazi-ud-din Khan Feroz Jung, was the most famous.

Ghazi-ud-din Khan Feroz Jung arrived in India in 1669 when he was barely twenty years of age. The son of his favourite general was bound to be well received by Aurangzeb, who conferred the rank of 300 *zat* and seventy horse[3] on the young man. Impressed by the youth, he got him married to Safia Khanam, the daughter of the chief minister of

Shah Jahan, who bore him Mir Qamr-ud-din, whom history knows as Nizam-ul-Mulk Asaf Jah I.

Qamr-ud-din, who received his name from Aurangzeb, was born on 11 July 1671, in all probability, in Agra. History is silent as to his birthplace, but his father had lived in Agra at that time, and it is very probable that this is where he was born. Asad Khan Jumdat-ul-Mulk used to say to Feroz Jung, 'The star of destiny shines on the forehead of your son.'⁴ At the age of six, Qamr-ud-din was awarded a *mansab*. He received the rank of 400 zat, 100 horse, when he was barely thirteen years old. He continued to receive honours and gifts from the emperor, and in 1691, he received the title of Chin Qilich Khan, and a female elephant as a gift. Eight years and many expeditions later, he was promoted to the rank of 3500 zat, 3000 horse. In 1702, he was raised to the governorship of Bijapur and was awarded a *sarpech* (head ornament) and a steed.

When Aurangzeb died in 1707, Shah Alam Bahadur Shah became the emperor after winning the struggle for succession. He was born as Muazzam, the third son of Aurangzeb by his wife Nawab Bai. Aurangzeb died without nominating an heir. At the time of his father's death, Muazzam was governor of Kabul, and his half-brothers, Muhammad Kam Baksh and Muhammad Azam Shah, were the governors of the Deccan and Gujarat respectively. Muhammad Azam Shah, who harboured ambitions of becoming emperor, was defeated by Muazzam at the battle of Jajau in June 1707. He and his son were killed, and Muazzam ascended the throne under the title of Bahadur Shah.

When Aurangzeb died, Feroz Jung was at Ellichpur as the governor of Berar. Bahadur Shah invited all the leading nobles, including Feroz Jung, to the court. The latter had reason to be wary of the new sovereign because it was on his report that Aurangzeb had disgraced Bahadur Shah on the charge of disloyalty during the siege of Golconda. Feroz Jung was sent assurances on behalf of the new emperor, but his fears prevented him from coming to the court. He had been rendered blind by an attack of small pox many years ago and sought exemption from court attendance on the grounds of this disability. Even Aurangzeb, out of regard for his past services, had excused him from waiting on him in person. Bahadur Shah made Feroz Jung the subedar of Gujarat. In 1710, he was sent to quell the revolt of Raja Ajit Singh of Jodhpur who was in open rebellion. It was on this campaign that he took ill and had to return to Ahmedabad. He expired soon after at the age of sixty-two, and was buried in a tomb he had built in his lifetime near Ajmeri gate in New Delhi.

After Aurangzeb's death, Qamr-ud-din gave his support to Azam Shah, who as we have seen, was defeated by Bahadur Shah at the battle of Jajau. The victorious Bahadur Shah thought it prudent to keep Qamr-ud-din on his right side and appointed him subedar of Awadh. But developments at the imperial court so disgusted Qamr-ud-din that he resigned and started living the life of a recluse in Delhi. When Bahadur Shah died in 1712, his son Muiz-ud-din ascended the throne as Jehandar Shah.

A dissolute man with dissipated tastes, he cared little for the duties of ruling and was seen in public with a common courtesan as his companion. He was under the influence of his favourite concubine, Lal Kunwar who enjoyed great power. Under Jehandar Shah, 'the imperial court adopted a culture of extreme frivolity, extravagance, drunkenness and debauchery'.[5]

Not content with holding drunken orgies in his palace, he even frequented brothels in the bazaar. Qamr-ud-din, disgusted at the profligacy of the court, kept himself in even stricter retirement, biding his time to make his next move.

Jehandar Shah reigned for only nine months. He was defeated in battle at Samugarh near Agra, by Farrukh Siyar, a grandson of Bahadur Shah, who became emperor. Farrukh Siyar's principal supporters were the two Syed brothers, Syed Abdullah and Hussein Ali, who played the role of kingmakers. Many of the chief generals of his defeated rival joined him, among whom was Qamr-ud-din who had cause for resentment against Jehandar Shah, and who it seems certain had entered into a private arrangement with the Syeds to hold aloof during the military engagement.

Farrukh Siyar welcomed Qamr-ud-din, and in 1713, rewarded him with a mansab of 7000 horse and the appointment of subedar of the Deccan, with the title of Nizam-ul-Mulk Fateh Jung. Nizam-ul-Mulk (by which name he will be designated in future) was one of the strongest personalities to emerge from the chaos that resulted after the death of Aurangzeb in 1707. His rise to power marked the dawn of a new era in the south in the early eighteenth century.

The elder Syed was appointed vizier, with the title of Qutub-ul-Mulk and a mansab of 7000 horse, and the younger, Hussein Ali, was given the title of Amir-ul-Umra with a similar mansab. The new emperor was a man of low mind and lower manners who was extremely jealous of the two Syeds, but dared not oppose them openly.

In 1714, Nizam-ul-Mulk was victorious in a few engagements with the Marathas at Paithan and Jalna. Shortly after his return to Aurangabad, he set out for Delhi. The emperor now appointed him subedar of Muradabad, where he stayed till 1718 when he was again recalled to Delhi. Farrukh Siyar was keen to rid himself of the Syed brothers and enlisted the nizam's aid for this purpose, promising him the prime minister's post if he assisted him. But the prime minister's post was given to a low-born favourite of the emperor, and Nizam-ul-Mulk bided his time awaiting the course of events.[6] He retreated into seclusion once again, watching the many intrigues at court in silent agony.

Farrukh Siyar was deposed, blinded and then murdered by the Syed brothers in 1719. His successors were two effeminate, consumptive young princes, who died within a span of only nine months. Rafi-ud-Darajat, was followed by his older brother Rafi-ud-Daulah, and both died from the effects of opium addiction.[7] It was during this interregnum that he was offered the governorship of Bihar but preferred to stay on in Delhi.

The unexpected death of their puppets disconcerted the plans of the Syeds, who knew it was necessary to place a scion of the royal family on the throne, but at the same time, select a candidate who would not interfere with their plans. They finally selected Muhammad Roshan Akhtar, a great-grandson of Aurangzeb, who was proclaimed emperor under the title of Muhammad Shah in September 1719. The Syeds had, in the meanwhile, ensured that the nizam was removed from the scene of action in Delhi by sending him to Malwa as governor. The nizam, meanwhile, was quietly strengthening his position by gathering around him a body of loyal followers, who, when the time came, would be ready to give up their lives for him.

Syed Hussein Ali was not slow in noticing this fact, and brought charges against him to which the nizam gave clear answers. This was merely a ploy because Hussein Ali wanted Malwa for himself, and asked the nizam to choose from Agra, Allahabad, Multan or Burhanpur. This brought matters to a head, and the nizam decided to break with the Syeds. The emperor and his mother secretly looked to the nizam to rid themselves of the Syeds and sent word to him that there was no time to be lost if the Syeds were to be unseated.

In the military engagements which followed, the nizam won decisive victories. Marching from Ujjain to Agra, he then turned towards the Deccan. Burhanpur surrendered immediately, as did many other towns and forts. Soldiers flocked to his standard from all parts of the Deccan. The nizam defeated an army under Dilawar Ali Khan in May 1720 some 30 miles from Burhanpur. He followed it up with a victory against Alam Ali Khan, the acting subedar of the Deccan, in August 1720. Mubariz Khan, the subedar of Hyderabad, joined the nizam with some 6000 horse. When news of this second defeat reached the Syeds, they were greatly alarmed. It was decided that the emperor, accompanied by Hussein Ali, should do battle against Nizam-ul-Mulk. Meanwhile, a conspiracy had been hatched to murder Hussein Ali in which the emperor and his mother connived. Hussein Ali was murdered in 1720, and the conspirators immediately placed the emperor at the head of such troops as they could muster, and proclaimed their intention of freeing him from the tyranny of the Syeds.[8]

Syed Abdullah at once prepared to avenge his brother's death. He assembled a large army in a few days' time and marched to avenge his brother's murder. The armies met at Shahpur, and a long and bloody encounter ended with Syed Abdullah's capture. Rewards were distributed by Muhammad Shah to those who had supported him. Nizam-ul-Mulk was allowed to keep his subedarship of the Deccan and that of Malwa. When the recently appointed prime minister, Muhammad Amin Khan, died, Nizam-ul-Mulk was invited to take his place.[9] After witnessing the intrigues of the court, this was a post he was not anxious to occupy, but given the prevailing situation, he deemed it advisable to consent. After settling his affairs in the Deccan, he marched in leisurely fashion towards Delhi, arriving in the middle of 1721.

Muhammad Shah was nicknamed 'Rangila', or Colourful, and the 'Merry Monarch' by his subjects. The effete ruler was, however, also an aesthete much given to wearing ladies' *peshwaz* (long outer garment) and shoes embroidered with pearls. A discerning patron of music and painting, he was responsible for bringing the sitar and tabla into his court. He also revived the Mughal miniature atelier. Delhi, after Aurangzeb's harsh puritanism, saw a veritable explosion of sensual art, dance, music and literary experimentation. It was also the age of the great courtesans, and this sensuality was reflected in the painting of the period which depicted images of pleasure and lovemaking. One painting even showed the emperor making love to one of his concubines.

Nizam-ul-Mulk, with a reputation for great boldness, but tempered at the same time with shrewdness and caution, was now the most prominent personality in the empire. It was unlikely that such a man would be without enemies for long, and almost on his arrival, the intrigues against him started. On every side, he found himself thwarted and opposed. Muhammad Shah's courtiers were hostile to him and poked fun at his old-world values and ways. The emperor had no interest in administration, and the discipline of the court was very lax. His mornings were occupied with watching partridge and elephant fights; in the afternoon, he was amused by jugglers, conjurors and the like. He paid little or no attention to affairs of state which were left in the hands of venal and incompetent people who curried favour with him or his powerful mother, Qudsiya Begum.

MAKING THE DECCAN HIS OWN

Nizam-ul-Mulk was too shrewd to throw away the substance of power, which he had already won in the Deccan, for its shadow, which depended on the fickleness of a pleasure-loving monarch. He resolved to leave at the earliest opportunity and never return to Delhi as a subject. He appointed his son Ghazi-ud-din as his deputy, and, taking the opportunity provided by an uprising of the Marathas in Malwa, advanced towards Ahmedabad. Here, he received news from both Delhi and the Deccan. Ghazi-ud-din had been removed by the intrigues of his enemies, and Mubariz Khan, who was deputizing for him in the Deccan, had declared himself subedar of the Deccan. It appears that this had the blessings of the emperor, who on the instigation of his coterie, had appointed Mubariz Khan in his place. Apparently, the feeble occupant of the nominal throne in Delhi resented the accretions to Nizam-ul-Mulk's power. Nizam-ul-Mulk decided to leave Delhi forever and marched rapidly towards Aurangabad. He sent conciliatory messages to Mubariz Khan, but to no avail. The two armies met near Shakar Kheda in 1724, and Mubariz Khan and his two sons were killed in battle.

Muhammad Shah knew when he was beaten, and accepted the fait accompli with as much grace as possible. He conferred the title of Asaf Jah[10] on him, the name by which the dynasty he founded is identified, and the word nizam came to designate his descendants, the rulers of Hyderabad. The kingdom also came to be known as the nizam's dominions. It is from this time on, that the independence of Hyderabad can be dated.

Realizing that Delhi was no longer a stable repository of imperial power, Nizam-ul-Mulk prudently selected the distant Deccan for pursuing his ambitions. Given the chaotic conditions prevailing in India at the time, it was only natural that he should aspire to be independent. His association with the imperial court was increasingly effected on his own terms, and in his own interest. However, he was shrewd enough to recognize the inadvisability of breaking the imperial connection in a peremptory manner. In fact, the imperial connection was never broken, since he continued to pay nominal allegiance to the Mughal emperor in Delhi while he waged wars, concluded treaties, conferred titles, granted jagirs and behaved in every way like an independent ruler. He, however, stopped short of formally proclaiming his independence and assuming the usual attributes of sovereignty. (Successive nizams were virtually independent rulers but refused to adopt the title of king even when it was offered to them by the British in 1810. It was only in 1947 that Osman Ali Khan, the seventh nizam, formally claimed to be a ruler in his own right. It was too late by then, and Hyderabad soon became a part of India.)

Nizam-ul-Mulk had brought with him from Delhi a band of devoted adherents. A vast cavalcade had set out from the capital which included the army and its commanders; four noblemen from the Mughal court and their families; various administrators, both Muslim and Hindu; clerks and accountants, and learned and holy men. Merchants and moneylenders, singing girls, prostitutes and eunuchs also came with him in the hope of building new fortunes. All the people he needed to fill a whole range of posts that would form the nucleus of a new government were there.

To his devoted adherents, and these included both Muslims and Hindus, he bestowed large gifts of land. The former provided military service: in return for the jagirs, they furnished large bodies of soldiers, horse and artillery. So great was his dependence on them for support that he divided his territory into three types of lands. One-third was reserved for his own privy purse and was called *sarf-i-khas*; another one-third was for the expenses of government and was called *diwani*; and the remaining one-third was for distributing as jagirs, or feudal estates.

The original jagirdars were Nizam-ul-Mulk's followers who had accompanied him from Malwa. Among them were military commanders who were granted jagirs on military tenure. Apart from these, the nizam also granted jagirs for carrying on administrative work in the department of revenue and finance to a Kayastha family, which was entrusted with the working of the Daftar-i-Mal (the revenue office) and were also in charge of the eastern *suba*s of the Deccan. One of the oldest Hindu families who came with Nizam-ul-Mulk were the Mathurs, a Kayastha family of northern India. Family members held high government positions with the post of *daftardar* becoming hereditary. Their family mansion, the ornate Malwala Palace, was built not far from the Charminar. The Maratha Brahmin family of Raja Rai Rayan was given charge of four western subas. Also, a large number of indigenous chieftains who held grants from earlier rulers and exercised semi-independent powers were recognized as rulers on payment of tribute.

Of the military fiefs, the most important were known as the Paigah estates. Abul Khair Khan's eldest son, Abul Fateh Khan, was awarded the titles of Shums-ul-Umra (The Sun among the Nobles) and Tegh Jung (The Sword of the Battlefield) and granted large jagirs. It is Tegh Jung who is considered the founder of the Paigah, interpreted variously as meaning 'the place where the foot of the ruler is kept' or 'stable'. The Paigah were linked to the Asaf Jahs by marriage since princesses of the royal family were married exclusively into the Paigah family. When Fakhr-ud-din Khan, the son of Tegh Jung, married the daughter of the second Asaf Jah, Nizam Ali Khan, he was given the added title of Amir-i-Kabir (Grand Amir). The Paigah family was second only to the nizam in power and importance.

The Salar Jungs, another influential family who were originally from Arabia, achieved prominence in Bijapur politics. When that kingdom crumbled, they transferred their allegiance to the Mughals, settling in Aurangabad with Emperor Aurangzeb. They then gained favour with the Asaf Jahs, eventually providing diwans from their ranks, the most famous of whom was Mir Turab Ali Khan, the subject of this biography. The title of Umra-i-Uzzam (premier nobles) was given only to four families: Salar Jung, Chandu Lal, the Khan-e-Khanan and the Fakhr-ul-Mulk families. Their family estates were referred to as *ilaqa*s and were exempt from paying tax or revenue.

Seventeen of the major jagirs had been declared exempt from the jurisdiction of the *khalsa* or diwani administration. Apart from the ilaqas and Paigah jagirs, these included five Hindu *samasthan*s. The samasthans were small principalities which had come up with the collapse of the Warangal kingdom. Local chiefs declared their independence and divided the territory among themselves. The Muslim rulers of the Bijapur, Qutub Shah and the Mughal dynasties maintained them as buffer states along the Krishna river. As peace came to the Deccan, the original requirement of military assistance to the overlord was now satisfied by the payment of an annual tribute called *peshkash*. There were sixteen samasthans till independence. They were known as Poligars and their territories, Palayams.

THE LEGEND OF THE KULCHAS

The most famous legend associated with Nizam-ul-Mulk is that of the seven kulchas (dry, baked bread) offered to him by a holy man. There appears to be no unanimity on when, where, and which holy man he met. One version holds that the meeting took place before he left Delhi for the last time, and another maintains that he met the Sufi, Nizam al-Din, in Aurangabad when he was appointed subedar of the Deccan. Another maintains that it was on one of his hunting expeditions while returning to the Deccan that he lost his way and encountered a hermit who gave him kulchas and water.

In a different version of the story the Sufi was Shah Inayat. Regardless of the details, in summary, the story is as follows: the holy man offered him kulchas and water. After the nizam had eaten his fill, the hermit counted the remaining loaves in the basket. He found that the nizam had eaten seven. He then said: 'You have eaten seven loaves. Your family will rule for seven generations.' (There were actually ten nizams but three of them, collectively termed the 'Pretenders', were not considered to be nizams since they were not granted the title of Asaf Jah by the Mughal emperor. This is certainly very convenient since it accommodates the legend.)

It is commonly believed that for his flag, he chose a kulcha set on a yellow background. Above it were the words '*Azmutul Illah*'—'The Greatness of God'—and below it his name. This was the flag for all the seven nizams with only the name below the kulcha changing from ruler to ruler. Even the pips which the Hyderabad police wore on their shoulders to designate rank were in the shape of kulchas.

The nizam, however, always maintained that it was not the kulcha on the Asaf Jahi flag but the mark of the moon.

I remember events since the age of three. At that age I put the mark of the moon on the standard of my army. My name was Qamr-ud-din, which means the 'moon of my faith'. Though the mark on my standard represented the moon, people thought that it represented a round piece of bread. This has been continuing from the time of my grandfather, the late Abid Khan, and my father, Feroz Jung. This legend about the representation of bread on the flag is not true, though commonly believed.[11]

Nizam-ul-Mulk may himself have helped to perpetuate this belief, for in his last testament he advised his heirs: '. . . and if you follow in my footsteps, the present expenditure remaining the same, they will suffice for the next seven generations, but if you want to have your way in this matter, it would not take more than a year or two before everything is squandered away.'[12] The kulcha story, however, remains fixed in the memory with all the tenacity of a popular legend.

NADIR SHAH'S INVASION

It was Muhammad Shah's misfortune to have as his neighbour the Persian-speaking warlord Nadir Shah known for his barbarity and cruelty, a man who was at once 'admired, feared and execrated'. A ruler of remarkable military ability, he was a ruthless fighting machine. In 1732, he seized the Persian throne, and in May 1738, he marched into Afghanistan and captured Kabul. On 24 February 1739, he won a major victory at Karnal, defeating three merged Mughal armies. The Mughal army, while numerically large, was little more than an undisciplined rabble. The nizam was in Bhopal at the time, negotiating a settlement with the Marathas, when he rushed back to assist the emperor in his conflict with the Persian invader.

The rivalry between Saadat Khan, the nawab of Awadh, and Nizam-ul-Mulk, the emperor's two principal generals, also made things easier for the invader. Saadat Khan, who had been summoned from Awadh, arrived at the imperial camp on 23 February after a long march. As the plans for the battle were being drawn, Saadat Khan received the news that Persian skirmishers had fallen on his baggage and were carrying off 500 loaded camels. The khan wanted to immediately engage with the Persians despite the wise counsel of Nizam-ul-Mulk who advised delay, given the fact that Saadat Khan's army, exhausted after a month of incessant marching, was not battle worthy at the time.

Saadat Khan ignored the advice and decided to ride straight into battle. As he took the field, the Persian skirmishers pretended flight; he gave chase and was lured away to a distance of 2 miles from the camp. He led his forces straight into the trap Nadir Shah had planned for him. The Persian army was entirely composed of cavalry, and their artillery consisted of long muskets or swivel guns, 7 or 8 feet in length, with a prong to rest on. Each of these was mounted on a camel which lay down on command, with the guns being fired from the backs of these animals.[13]

The Persian skirmishers had successfully screened Nadir's main position where 3000 of his best troops lay waiting, ready to discharge their deadly muskets. As Saadat Khan gave chase, the screen of the Persian skirmishers drew aside and Nadir Shah's mounted musketeers fired at point-blank range at his cavalry. Within a few minutes, the Mughal forces were decimated. A similar fate befell the army commander and Mir Bakshi, Khan Dauran's division, which was massacred by continuous fire from the swivel guns without a chance of reply. The murderous fire from Nadir's guns continued for two hours, but 'arrows cannot answer bullets', and the flower of the Mughal army perished in a hopelessly one-sided battle. The nizam, the ablest general on the Indian side, did absolutely nothing to help. He probably hoped to take the places of his rivals if they perished. Khan Dauran died of wounds sustained in the battle; Saadat Khan fought bravely but was captured.

On being questioned by Nadir about the resources of the emperor, Saadat Khan was able to convince Nadir that Muhammad Shah was still in a position to fight on equal terms. When Nadir wanted to know how he could get a handsome indemnity from the emperor, Saadat Khan advised him to summon the nizam, whom he described as 'the Key of the State of India' for negotiations. The day after the battle, the nizam left for Nadir's camp with full powers to negotiate. Impressed with the nizam, Nadir asked why, if there were nobles like him on the emperor's side, the Marathas had the temerity to take ransom from him. The nizam replied, 'Since new nobles rose to influence, His Majesty did whatever he liked. My advice was not acceptable to him. Therefore, in helplessness I left him and retired to the Dakhin.'[14]

After a long negotiation, it was agreed that the Persian army would return on payment of an indemnity of Rs 50 lakh, out of which the first instalment of Rs 20 lakh was to be paid immediately, and subsequent payments of Rs 10 lakh each on reaching Lahore, Attock and Kabul. The nizam returned from the negotiation, and Nadir sent the emperor an invitation to dine with him the next day which was duly accepted. When Muhammad Shah came to know of Mir Dauran's death, he gave the office of Mir Bakshi (Paymaster of the Empire) to Nizam-ul-Mulk.

When Saadat Khan came to know that this post which had been promised to him had now been given to Nizam-ul-Mulk, he was blinded with rage and envy. He took revenge by revealing to Nadir Shah the immense wealth held in the Mughal treasury, hinting that he would be greatly benefited by raising the demands of the indemnity. He also advised the Persian warlord to take Muhammad Shah and Nizam-ul-Mulk into custody and march on Delhi. This suggestion was after Nadir's heart, and he sent for Nizam-ul-Mulk immediately. Suspecting no treachery, the latter went to the camp where he was taken into custody and told that now the price of Nadir's return was Rs 20 crore and 20,000 troopers to serve as auxiliaries under the Persians. He was forced to send a letter to the emperor to the effect that he had settled final terms of peace and that his presence was required for confirmation. Muhammad Shah soon found himself Nadir Shah's prisoner as well.[15] His wives, children and servants were also brought from Karnal and lodged close to Nadir Shah's tents.

Nadir Shah ordered Saadat Khan to march to Delhi at the head of 4000 horse and establish his authority in Delhi. Later, the two rulers, as we have noted in the beginning of this narrative, entered Delhi a day apart. But the traitor soon found himself in trouble with his new overlord when the enormous indemnity he had promised was not forthcoming. Nadir Shah threatened him with personal chastisement, and Saadat Khan, stung by the insult, committed suicide by consuming poison on the night of 20 March itself, the day Nadir entered Delhi.

As already noted, a rumour that Nadir Shah had been killed sparked off widespread violence. The Persian overlord Shah ordered a mass massacre of the population, ending the killing, as we have seen, on the request of the nizam, but the robbing and plunder continued. The city was divided into five divisions with collections being made in a systematically remorseless manner. Nizam-ul-Mulk now had to loot his own capital to pay the indemnity: the accumulated wealth of nearly three and a half centuries changed hands in a matter of days. But Nizam-ul-Mulk, instead of trying to exact money from the people as the other nobles had done, paid the greater portion of the sum allotted to him for collection from his own money.

The Persians marvelled at the incredible riches offered to them over the next few days: oceans of pearls, heaps of other gems, gold and silver vessels encrusted with gems, and other luxurious objects in such vast quantities that it was impossible for them to even make an inventory of them. Workers laboured for a month to melt the gold and silver articles into ingots to facilitate their transport. The booty included the Peacock Throne on which had once been set the famous Koh-i-Noor diamond and the Timur ruby. There is a story that Nadir Shah came to know that Muhammad Shah had hidden the Koh-i-Noor diamond in his turban and won it by offering to swap turbans as a lasting memento of their friendship. It is a pretty story, but uncorroborated by any contemporary sources. In all probability, both the Koh-i-Noor and the Timur ruby were still embedded in the Peacock Throne when he carried it away.[16]

On 16 May, Nadir Shah finally left Delhi, carrying with him the wealth of eight generations. The total indemnity secured was estimated at Rs 15 crore by Nadir's secretary though some sources have put it as high as Rs 70 crore.[17] The spoils were loaded on 700 elephants, 4000 camels and 12,000 horses, and consisted of gold, silver and precious stones. Before his departure, he had reinstated Muhammad Shah as emperor but annexed all his northern provinces to the west of the Indus. Nadir Shah's son, Nasrullah, had married a great-great-granddaughter of Shah Jahan, with Nadir promising to send a force from Kandahar if the emperor needed help against any enemy.

When he was leaving Delhi, Nadir Shah summoned Nizam-ul-Mulk and offered him the throne of Delhi, saying that it was he, and not the sybarite Muhammad Shah, who deserved to be emperor. He promised to leave 10,000 of his soldiers to serve him. But Nizam-ul-Mulk refused, saying that he did not want to acquire the stigma of a traitor.

Nizam-ul-Mulk reported the encounter in the following manner:

> Thus when Nadir Shah, with an overwhelming force, reached Delhi and, in his extreme graciousness, cast his eye on me, he offered me personally the sovereignty of the Indian Empire. I at once answered, 'By this command no benefit will accrue to either of us except that I, as a servant, will merit the notoriety of not being true to my salt, and your August self the odium of breach of faith.' He was greatly pleased with my reply and honoured me with his praise.[18]

While Nizam-ul-Mulk was in Delhi, his son, Nasir Jung, who officiated for him in the Deccan, declared his independence. The father cautioned his son but he was in no mood to relent. The battle between the two was

joined near Daulatabad in 1741, and Nasir Jung was easily defeated. He
was captured and brought before his father who forgave him, but kept him
under close watch.

The first nizam passed away in May 1748. When the time to pass
on to higher realms arrived, he dictated his last will and testament.
Surrounding his deathbed were his son, Nasir Jung, the superintendent of
posts, the head of religious endowments, and his chief secretary, Munshi
Mansa Ram. The seventeen articles of this document encapsulated
the collective wisdom of the experiences of his long and eventful life.
He had seen the reign of eight Mughal emperors, had actively served
four, and taken part in eighty-seven battles. A brilliant military leader,
accomplished diplomat, and a shrewd statesman, he was also a poet who
wrote under the pen-name of 'Shakir'.

He warned his heirs to beware of the Marathas and not trust the people
of Burhanpur, Bijapur, Gujarat and Kashmir. He wanted them to be always
grateful to the Mughal emperor and remain subservient to him. He had a
very poor opinion of the Brahmins of the Deccan who he thought were
fit only to be hanged and quartered. In the end, he exhorted his heir to
appoint his own men to look after the affairs of state.[19] Having unburdened
himself of such wide-ranging wisdom, the first nizam, the greatest leader
of eighteenth-century India, and the first and most outstanding member
of the dynasty founded by him, passed away on 19 June 1748 in Burhanpur
at the age of seventy-eight.

Henry Briggs's assessment of the first nizam is less than glowing, but
he has to be judged in the context of his times. Briggs himself admits
as much.

If pliableness of will, unparalleled duplicity and utter unscrupulousness
constitute the necessary elements to greatness, Nizam-ul-Mulk possessed
them in a degree passing belief. But it must be remembered that Nizam-
ul-Mulk lived at a time and in a country where men gloried in excelling
in these qualities . . . Nurtured and trained at the court of Aurangzeb,
it is not strange that Nizam-ul-Mulk should have been both wily and
unscrupulous; nor yet that, like his royal master, he should have exercised
his devotions to austerity; but unlike Aurangzebe, he was an affectionate
parent and his attachment to his friends was both sincere and steady. He
left a legacy to his posterity which the rebellion of 1857 has made 'the
greatest Mohammadan power in India'.[20]

THE PRETENDERS

Nizam-ul-Mulk's advice fell on deaf ears. His successors were weak men with vaulting ambition but little or no ability. On his death, he left six sons and five daughters. His eldest son, Ghazi-ud-din, was at the court in Delhi as prime minister, and Nasir Jung succeeded him in the Deccan. His grandson from his daughter, Muzaffar Jung, was appointed governor of Balaghat (upper part of Karnataka) with his headquarters at Bijapur. The nizam had been astute enough not to get involved in the affairs of the English and French trading companies, who were fighting for commercial supremacy in the Coromandel coast. Unfortunately, his successors were less discerning and soon became embroiled in the politics of the south. The fratricidal wars of succession which followed had the involvement of rival powers, with each candidate invoking the help of either the French or the British.

The nawab of Arcot, an appointee of the nizam, died without an heir. There was a contest between Chanda Saheb, a representative of the earlier ruling family, and Anwar-ud-din, the nominee of the nizam. Muzaffar Jung, who dreamt of becoming nizam, allied with the French. The understanding was that he would become nizam, and Chanda Saheb would be made nawab of Arcot. The French would gain commercial and political ascendancy over their rivals, the English. In the first engagement at Ambur, the nizam and his allies were defeated, and Anwar-ud-din was killed.

It was now time for the English to enter the fray. They promised to help Nasir Jung and Anwar-ud-din's son, Mohammed Ali. Nasir Jung, assisted by the Marathas and a small force of the English, marched upon the fort of Ginjee, near Pondicherry, with an army estimated at 3,00,000 soldiers. The huge army, combined with overtures made by his uncle, played a role in Muzaffar Jung's surrender. He gave himself up on the promise of pardon, but was imprisoned. However, his career was not yet over: a sudden and unexpected reversal of fortune was soon to take place. This action of Nasir Jung did not go down too well with the nawabs of Kurnool, Cuddapah and Savanur who had been instrumental in convincing Muzaffar Jung to surrender. They were loyal to the first nizam and wanted to bring about a reconciliation.

When the French governor of Pondicherry, Joseph François Dupleix, heard of their discontent, he started a correspondence with them. He also sent ambassadors to Nasir Jung, ostensibly to obtain lenient terms for

Muzaffar Jung and Chanda Saheb, but in reality, to gain time to enter into a conspiracy with the discontented nawabs. In a daring move, Dupleix decided to attack the fort of Ginjee since Nasir Jung, thinking that the engagement had ended, had departed with the greater part of his army.

Dupleix sent a small force of 250 Europeans and 4200 sepoys under the command of his general, Charles Joseph Patissier de Bussy, to attack the fort. Bussy, who had the advantage of surprise, managed to take the fort with some difficulty. Nasir Jung then reassembled as many forces as he could and marched on Ginjee. But the rainy season greatly slowed his progress, and the army could march only 4 miles a day with great difficulty. Meanwhile, Dupleix had opened negotiations for peace, his conditions being that Muzaffar Jung should be released and Chanda Saheb be appointed nawab of the Carnatic.

Nasir Jung was reluctant at first, but his hand was forced by the fact that disease had broken out in his army, and supplies were running short. He agreed on the condition that Dupleix and Chanda Saheb acknowledge his sovereignty. Dupleix was at the same time corresponding with the discontented nawabs and had hatched a conspiracy. He came to an understanding with the nawabs by which it was agreed that on receipt of a message from them, the French forces would attack the Mughal camp in case an agreement was not reached. It was decided that the conspirators would withdraw and station themselves with their armies at a short distance from the main camp and hoist the French flag at an opportune time.[21]

Dupleix, who was assured of success in both cases, was content to let chance take its own course. On the one hand, he sought ratification of the treaty with Nasir Jung, and on the other, sent instructions to his troops to attack the Mughal camp on a signal from the conspirators. Nasir Jung agreed to free Muzaffar Jung and to appoint Chanda Saheb nawab of the Carnatic, and also restore the port of Masulipatnam to the French. But the nawabs, alarmed at the prospect of an amicable settlement, gave the signal to attack. Dupleix had sent a message to suspend hostilities, but it reached his troops commanded by La Touche too late. La Touche, unaware of the latest developments, attacked the Mughal camp. Nasir Jung, who only the day before had concluded the treaty with the French, could scarcely believe what had happened. When he became convinced of the truth, he ordered the execution of Muzaffar Jung, but Ramdas Pandit, who was a partisan of Muzaffar Jung, bribed the executioners to delay the execution.[22]

Nasir Jung, when he was informed of the inactivity of the nawabs, rode unarmed on his elephant to the camps of the nawab of Kurnool, Himmat Khan, and the nawab of Cuddapah, Abdul Nabi Khan, asking them to take the field against the French. The nawab of Cuddapah said that he was not aware of any enemy. An enraged Nasir Jung ordered his soldiers to fire on the troops of the nawab. In the ensuing melee, the nawab of Kurnool shot Nasir Jung, killing him instantly. His head was severed from his body, and the nawabs then hailed Muzaffar Jung as the nizam on 14 December 1750. Amidst great pomp, they arrived in Pondicherry on 26 December 1750. Dupleix entered Pondicherry seated in the same palanquin as Muzaffar Jung. Muzaffar Jung, suspicious of the nawabs who he suspected might betray him too, confided in Dupleix.

A grateful Muzaffar Jung heaped riches and awards on Dupleix, including appointing him as his deputy for the territories which lay to the south of the River Krishna. He was made nawab of the Carnatic and Mysore, while Chanda Saheb, who was given the title of the nawab of Arcot, was made his deputy. The Pondicherry currency was made legal tender throughout the Carnatic, and Dupleix was empowered to collect its revenues. He was given the title of Zaffar Jung and a mansab of 7000 was conferred on him. The French were also given Masulipatnam, Yanam and Karaikal.[23] Ramdas Pandit was given the title of Raja Raghunath Das, and Nasir Jung's brothers, Salabat Jung, Nizam Ali Khan and Basalat Jung, were elevated to the rank of 7000 horse, while Nasir Jung's sons were imprisoned. But the nawabs remained dissatisfied even after receiving a handsome share of the spoils, and plotted against Muzaffar Jung.

Muzaffar Jung now expressed a desire to return to Hyderabad, and was given an escort led by Bussy. In early February 1751, the party reached Rayachoti, a village some 25 miles to the south of Cuddapah. The Mughal officers set fire to some neighbouring villages. The nawab of Cuddapah, who was waiting for an opportunity to make trouble, retaliated by attacking the party in the rear. The nawabs conveyed their willingness to Bussy to come to terms, but Muzaffar Jung, angered by their arrogance, marched against them despite opposition from Bussy. The French forces were left far behind, and this proved to be disastrous for Muzaffar Jung. Instead of waiting for his cavalry, he followed on his elephant and was killed by a spear thrown by the nawab of Kurnool. Before expiring, Muzaffar Jung cut down the nawab with his sword at about the same time. The conspiracy involving all three nawabs ended with the death of the nawabs of Kurnool and Savanur, and grievous injury to the nawab of Cuddapah Cuddapah. Within only six weeks of becoming nizam, Muzaffar Jung too was killed.

Bussy wasted no time in declaring Salabat Jung, Nizam-ul-Mulk's third son, as nizam. French influence in the Deccan peaked in the 1750s, and Bussy became the kingmaker in the state. It was his power that kept Salabat Jung on the throne. Even though the capital was at Aurangabad, Bussy's troops were headquartered in Hyderabad, and it was the seat of power. Hyderabad's Troop Bazaar, which housed the barracks of Bussy's troops, still bears that name. Bussy had been allotted large personal jagirs as a reward for the defence of Salabat Jung's *gaddi* with almost the entire Northern Circars (provinces on the north-eastern edge of the nizam's dominions) being under his control.

In 1756, the Seven Years' War between France and England broke out. Bussy was recalled by Comte de Lally in May 1758, and never returned to Hyderabad. In the same year Nizam Ali Khan marched from Aurangabad to Hyderabad with a large body of troops and forced his brother to accept him as diwan. Bussy's successors were defeated by the English led by Colonel Francis Forde, and the French lost control of the Northern Circars. The French, who were unable to recover their lost territories after the Seven Years' War, had to content themselves with providing outside support to Indian rulers who were enemies of the British, the most important being Hyder Ali and his son Tipu Sultan, both of whom played a major role in south Indian politics from the 1760s to the end of the century. Nasir Jung, Muzaffar Jung and Salabat Jung were never recognized formally by the Mughal emperor and are therefore referred to as 'the Pretenders'.

NIZAM ALI KHAN ASAF JAH II

In 1762, Nizam Ali Khan deposed and imprisoned his elder brother Salabat Jung in the dungeons at Bidar (where he was later strangled), and declared himself nizam. Unlike his brothers, he was able to obtain the formal sanction of the Mughal emperor for his appointment, and is therefore referred to as the second nizam, although in reality, he was the fourth ruler from the family. Without the dynamic Bussy, Hyderabad now had to look for other allies in the rulers of Mysore and in the British. It appeared that the state of Hyderabad was on the brink of extinction. It is to Nizam Ali Khan's credit that at his death four decades later, he had turned Hyderabad from 'the Sick Man of late Mughal India into the vital strategic asset of the eighteenth-century Cold War, without whose friendship and support no power could gain dominance in India'.[24]

Contemporary observers give more credit to the nizam's wily diwan, Aristu Jah, for the skilful manoeuvring in Deccan politics than to the nizam. Aristu Jah was a ruthless politician, but he was also a civilized man whose extensive patronage of poets and painters led to a revival of both the arts which had declined during the austere rule of Nizam-ul-Mulk. Another key figure was Mir Alam, who went on to become diwan in 1804. A former private secretary of Aristu Jah, he had become quite influential at court.

Mir Alam, whose real name was Mir Abul Qasim, was the son of Syed Reza who was descended from the Syeds of Shustar. In 1730, Syed Reza, a young Shustari *mujtahid*, left Shustar to seek his fortune under the Mughals. He soon found his way to Delhi and got employment under a fellow Persian exile, Abul Mansur Khan Khorasani, who happened to be the prime minister of the Mughal emperor and was famous as Safdar Jung. Syed Reza stayed in Delhi for many years, but when the Mughal Empire descended into chaos, he decided to return to Shustar. Since the land route to Kabul was blocked by fighting, he decided to head towards the Deccan from where he hoped to catch a ship to the Gulf of Persia. He met Nizam-ul-Mulk by chance in Hyderabad and so impressed him with his learning that the first nizam persuaded him to stay on under his patronage. He accepted and settled in Hyderabad, and it was here that Abul Qasim, famous as Mir Alam, was born in 1752. A second son Zeinul-Abidin Shustari followed.

Nizam Ali Khan Asaf Jah II, bestowed on Syed Reza a jagir of Rs 10,000. The latter used to visit the nizam every Tuesday, having been bestowed the favour of recommending one person for the nizam's patronage on each visit. On Tuesdays, his residence was besieged by persons seeking his recommendation, and he is said to have always promised his patronage to the person who arrived first.[25]

Syed Reza gave up worldly attachments in his old age and dedicated his life to prayer. He died in 1780, and it was during the period of mourning that the young Mir Alam met Aristu Jah, diwan to Nizam Ali Khan, and the most powerful official in Hyderabad. From his earliest years, Mir Alam had showed great intelligence and ability. Under the tutelage of his father and uncle, he became a proficient Arabic scholar. Aristu Jah realized that he was a man of uncommon talents, and before long had appointed him his private secretary. In 1787, he sent him on an important embassy to

Calcutta to the East India Company's headquarters. He was the nizam's official vakil to the Company, effectively his minister for British affairs. Mir Alam struck up an enduring friendship with the Governor General, Lord Cornwallis. He stayed in Calcutta for three years and made a wide variety of contacts. His visit to the military arsenals at Fort William convinced him that the British were invincible in India. More importantly, he realized that it was in Hyderabad's best interest—as indeed his own—to closely ally with the British. Cornwallis gave Mir Alam a diamond-encrusted walking stick as a farewell gift.

In 1766, the nizam assigned the five Northern Circars to the British on the understanding that the Company would assist the nizam with a body of troops whenever he required it, and when he did not, pay him a quit-rent or peshkash of Rs 9 lakh per annum. This was the origin of the Subsidiary Force which pledged to uphold the nizam's power and also preserve internal peace. ('The Honourable East India Company do hereby promise and engage to have a body of their troops ready to settle the affairs of His Highness's Government in everything that is right and proper, whenever required.') The terms of this treaty were quite favourable in comparison with the ones that followed. Nizam Ali Khan had yet to commit the tactical mistakes which would strengthen the Company's stranglehold on Hyderabad.

Even as he was negotiating the terms of the treaty with the British, Nizam Ali Khan was conducting secret talks with his old enemies, the Marathas. The reason for this change of heart was that Mysore was now under the control of a Muslim military adventurer, Hyder Ali, and his son Tipu Sultan. They had built up a formidable army with the help of French mercenaries, and were looking at territorial expansion. Having secured the support of the Marathas, the nizam invited the British to also join the alliance which was to attack Mysore.

Nizam Ali Khan set out from Hyderabad at the head of 17,000 of his own troops and 10,000 Maratha soldiers, paid for out of his own treasury. Rather than engage in a battle he could well have lost, Hyder Ali resorted to bribery. He bought off the Marathas for Rs 35 lakh; the nizam wanted much more, but as it turned out, settled for much less.[26] It was March 1767, and the troops promised by the British, which should have arrived in December 1766, had not yet arrived. When the British troops from Madras under Lt Col. Charles Tod finally arrived in April 1767, they were shocked to find that the Marathas were nowhere to be found. What was worse, the nizam had changed sides and was now preparing to fight the Company's forces alongside Hyder Ali, who had bought off the nizam quite cheaply for only Rs 6,00,000 a month, for the duration of the war.

The Mysore forces reached Madras, but were badly beaten at Tiruvannamalai. The furious British decided to teach the turncoat nizam a lesson—their plan was to invade a largely undefended Hyderabad. Faced with the loss of his capital, Nizam Ali Khan again switched sides, and sent his emissaries to Madras to negotiate a new treaty. Unsurprisingly, the terms of the treaty of 'Perpetual Friendship and Alliance' signed in February 1768 were less generous. The peshkash was reduced to Rs 7 lakh, and the nizam agreed to pay war expenses of Rs 25 lakh which was to be deducted from the peshkash over six years. (Later the British stopped this payment of peshkash altogether, labelling it as tribute.) The nizam now also had to pay for the upkeep of the Subsidiary Force, whether he needed it or not. In case of another war with Mysore, the nizam undertook to provide a force of not less than 25,000 to 'seriously and vigorously' prosecute the war. Hyder Ali was declared a usurper and a rebel, and all treaties with him were revoked.

The Company's promise of help was little more than a sham. Over the next two decades, whenever the nizam applied for the assistance of the Subsidiary Force, it was never forthcoming. To make matters worse, the payment of peshkash was in arrears. The nizam was understandably upset since he had been denied both the benefits of the treaty. But external factors came to his aid when the threat of Tipu Sultan forced the Governor General, Lord Cornwallis, to write a letter to the nizam in July 1789 in which he promised to pay the arrears of peshkash but rejected the demand for a mortgage on the portion of the Circars as guarantee since 'the faith of the English nation [is] pledged for the due payment of it'.[27] In addition, a new exception that the Force 'is not to be employed against any power in alliance with the Company' was added.

The nizam, wanting protection against the Marathas, tried to revert to the older interpretation which would guarantee him British help against any threat to his dominions. The Marathas, realizing that this meant protection to the nizam against them, objected to its inclusion in the Tripartite Treaty of 1790. Lord Cornwallis, who was keen that this treaty be signed, assured the nizam that he would 'always find me in the best disposition to endeavour to save His Highness from the necessity of submitting to mortification or injury'.[28] Taking the Governor General at his word, the nizam sent troops to join the British against Tipu Sultan. Tipu was defeated in 1792, and the nizam gained Gooty, Cuddapah and other areas, apart from a tribute of Rs 10 lakh.

But the alliance with the Marathas was too fragile to last. The Marathas had been a constant source of trouble for the nizam and the other players competing for control of the Deccan. They were essentially predators whose main source of income was their practice of demanding *chauth* (one-fourth of all revenue) from their conquered subjects. The Maratha army has been described as being 'more indefatigable and destructive than myriads of locusts' and the Marathas as possessing an 'insensibility of heart with which other nations are unacquainted'.[29]

In 1794, the nizam decided to eradicate the menace once and for all by attacking the Marathas at Poona. His army was now a more disciplined force, thanks to the training it had received at the hands of Michel Joachim Marie Raymond, popularly known as François Raymond or Monsieur Raymond, an enterprising French adventurer who came to Pondicherry in 1775 with the intention of setting up a business.

When Pondicherry fell to the British in 1778, Raymond went to Mysore where he served in the army under Hyder Ali. After Hyder Ali's death, he did not want to serve under his son Tipu, and moved to Hyderabad, where with just 300 men and guns taken on hire from a French merchant, he promised the nizam that under his command, Hyderabad's army could defeat any force. He earned the nizam's trust and was appointed a commander of a contingent of 900 men, which in time swelled to 11,000 men, all the officers being Frenchmen.

Raymond trained the troops on Western lines, and the regiment under his control was called the 'Corps of François'. It became a model army, and Raymond was assigned territories yielding Rs 16 lakh a year for their maintenance. In order to provide arms of good quality, Raymond established a gun foundry for the manufacture of cannons and guns, the ruins of which still exist in Hyderabad, and the area around it is still called Gunfoundry. Raymond was one of the offspring of that stirring time who were disparagingly classified as adventurers, but exhibited the highest administrative abilities.

Nizam Ali Khan sent his diwan, Aristu Jah, to ask the new resident, William Kirkpatrick, for help in his campaign against the Marathas. He was turned down on the grounds that the treaty of 1768 enjoined British neutrality. The real reason was the need to stay on good terms with the

Marathas and isolate Tipu Sultan. Aristu Jah boasted (rather unwisely) that the peshwa would be sent with a brass pot in his hand and a cloth round his loins to pray on the banks of the Ganges at Benares.[30]

William Kirkpatrick realized that the nizam's army would be no match for the forces of Nana Phadnavis. The Marathas, apart from having a large pool of mercenaries, also had four brigades of European-led troops under the command of Benoit de Boigne, a Frenchman and soldier of fortune like Raymond. Boigne had started his career with the king of Sardinia and is today considered an important military figure in eighteenth-century India. The nizam, overconfident about the abilities of his army, marched his 1,10,000-strong force towards Poona in December 1794. The Marathas despatched an army of 1,30,000, and the battle was joined on 14 March 1795, near the half-ruined fort of Kharda, with the two compatriots Raymond and de Boigne facing each other in battle. Despite continuous firing from the Marathas, the nizam's army made some progress on the first day.

But the nizam was soon to face a humiliating defeat. It was brought on by his insistence of travelling with his oversized zenana and his favourite wife, Bakshi Begum, something the historian Herbert Compton described as 'the imbecile infatuation of an Oriental Potentate'. The begum was so frightened by the booming of the cannon and death all around her, that she threatened to 'expose herself to public gaze' unless he took her and the rest of the zenana to shelter inside the fort.[31] A Maratha night patrol stumbled upon the nizam and his unit of female bodyguards while looking for water. During the ensuing skirmish, the nizam tried to escape but found himself trapped in the fort. His troops panicked and retreated to the fort, leaving their ammunition and stores on the battlefield. The Marathas quickly surrounded the fort, and after a siege of twenty-two days, the nizam was forced to sue for a humiliating peace.

In the treaty that followed, the nizam was forced to cede Daulatabad, Ahmednagar and Shorapore, and pay an indemnity of Rs 3 crore. To add salt to his wounds, Nana Phadnavis forced him to hand over Aristu Jah as a hostage. No campaign could have ended with results so contrary to the avowed objective. The battle was a disaster for British foreign policy as well. Furious at his humiliation, and thoroughly alienated by what he considered a serious breach of faith by the British, the nizam decided that henceforth he would depend on the French rather than the British. He gave approval for the expansion of Raymond's troops and permission to set up arsenals and foundries to manufacture weapons. By 1795, Raymond was in command of 15,000 men, divided into twenty battalions under the command of 124 Europeans. The nizam grew exceedingly fond of Raymond and treated him as his own son. He was given the titles of Mutwar-ul-Mulk, and Azdhar-i-Jung. The nizam ceded the districts of Cumbum and Cuddapah to pay for the maintenance of the troops. Raymond was also very popular with the people of Hyderabad. The Muslims called him Musa Rahim, and the Hindus, Musa Ram.

In February 1796, Nizam Ali Khan suffered a stroke from which he never fully recovered. The rival factions in the court now had full freedom to plot and scheme. One faction supported the nizam's eldest son, Sikander Jah. Feridun Jah, another contender, had the support of the Paigah nobles. Both factions courted Raymond's favour, who it appeared would play the role of kingmaker.

In the late summer of 1797, Aristu Jah, who had been imprisoned at Poona for over two years, announced to the nizam that he had been freed. Not only that, in what was nothing short of a miracle, he had also successfully negotiated the return of almost all the land and fortresses that had been ceded after the disaster at Kharda. The Marathas had even waived the enormous indemnity owed to them by the nizam. What made this remarkable achievement even more astounding was that it had been negotiated from confinement. It was widely believed that Aristu Jah was a master of the dark arts, and his achievement was the result of his mastery of the occult. Whatever the means by which he had achieved this diplomatic coup, Aristu Jah returned to Hyderabad a hero. He was reinstated as diwan and showered with honours, estates and jewels.

Raymond's success, and his complete ascendancy over the nizam, greatly alarmed the British, who realized the grave threat to their power. In Lord Mornington (later Marquess Wellesley), who became Governor General in April 1798, they found the man who would restore them to their former power. Wellesley was an empire builder, who between 1798 and 1804 expanded the Company's territories to include most of southern India, the entire eastern strip, all of Bengal and parts of northern India.

Luckily for Wellesley, his task was made easier by the fact that Raymond had died suddenly in March 1798, in circumstances that suggested that he may have been poisoned. His death marked the decline of French influence in Hyderabad. Raymond's shining black granite tomb had an attractive pavilion based on the Palladian style on it. There was also a tall obelisk on the face of which was a black marble tablet inscribed with 'JR' in calligraphic style.

The nizam ordered that an annual Urs be conducted at the tomb to mark his death anniversary, an event in which both Hindus and Muslims participated. The graves of his dog and horse are also near his tomb. This entire area bears the name Musaram Bagh after him. No European, before or after him, had succeeded in gaining to such an extent the love and admiration of the natives of the country. Raymond left behind 15,000 disciplined soldiers under the command of his deputy Jean-Pierre Peron. Peron had less influence over the nizam than his former commander, and this may be one of the reasons that he could not prevent the subsequent disbanding of his troops.

Wellesley was a hard-core imperialist whose first aim was to rid the country of the French. To achieve this, it was essential to destroy the power of Tipu Sultan who had allied himself with the French, and was the most formidable enemy of the British in the south. In 1798, when Tipu again gathered his French allies, the British were desperate for support. Wellesley asked James Achilles Kirkpatrick who had taken over as resident from his brother, William, to open negotiations with the nizam on a new treaty under which the British government would protect him against the Marathas, provided he dismissed the French forces and agreed to an increase in the Subsidiary Force.

JAMES ACHILLES KIRKPATRICK: THE WHITE MUGHAL

There had been a British resident at Hyderabad since 1779, but it was only after Raymond's death that the resident was able to acquire an ascendancy which continued for the next one and a half centuries. The resident was the political officer controlling the conduct of state affairs. He was also the head of the Secunderabad and Bolarum cantonments, and later, the judicial and civil chief of Berar. He was consulted on all important matters by the diwan; and the nobles, merchants and bankers all curried favour with him. It must be remembered that the nizam was regarded in treaties as an ally or an equal, and though he became, in reality, a dependant, the appearance of equality was maintained.

The nizam's obligation to govern according to the advice of the resident was vague, but in practice, it became impossible to govern without the assistance of the British, given the deplorable condition of the government.

'Thus although the Resident had not, either in the wording of the treaties or the terms of his credentials any declared right of interference, yet he was the Atlas on whose shoulders rested the government of the State.'[32] It was the highest of the political or diplomatic appointments under the Government of India, and was considered a preparation for the post of foreign secretary since it furnished the best example of the diplomatic and political duties which fell to the lot of British officers in India. Sir Richard Temple, who was resident in 1867, did in fact become foreign secretary immediately after.

One of the most colourful characters to occupy this post was James Achilles Kirkpatrick, who was resident from 1798 to 1805, having succeeded his brother, William, in that post. The most famous of the 'White Mughals', he was a favourite of Nizam Ali Khan who treated him like his son and bestowed on him the title of Hashmat Jung. He had taken to wearing what Arthur Wellesley described as 'a Mussulman's dress of the finest texture', smoked a hookah, wore Indian-style 'mustachios' and dyed his fingers with henna. He spoke fluent Persian, and by wearing Islamic dress and using Mughal styles of address, was able to participate in Hyderabadi court ritual in a way which had no precedent in the past, and was never repeated in the future. He gave nazars and accepted *khillat*s, and by mastering the finer points of court etiquette, gained a trust not reposed in any resident of the past.

Kirkpatrick, for his part, was fond of the ailing nizam and referred to him affectionately, if somewhat irreverently, as 'old Nizzy'. He even ordered a special quilt to keep him warm during the winter. The nizam was losing strength, his condition made worse by the quack remedies to which he submitted. Kirkpatrick uncovered a plot to kill the nizam using black magic. He reported to his superiors in Calcutta that images made out of paste had been found in the palace with powdered glass in their bodies and dog's hair.

Kirkpatrick, with Aristu Jah's help, managed to convince the nizam that a subsidiary alliance was the answer to all his problems. He succeeded in negotiating another treaty in September 1798 under which the Subsidiary Force (created by an earlier treaty) was made permanent, with an increase in its strength to 6000 sepoys at a cost of a little over Rs 24 lakh a year. The British also won the right to mediate in disputes between the nizam and the peshwa. The French forces were disbanded in October after some initial reluctance. The nizam's order sparked a mutiny in the French forces, and

Peron was made a prisoner. It was left to John Malcolm, the commander of the British forces, and later, deputy to Kirkpatrick, to quell the revolt, which was ultimately achieved without a single shot being fired.

The Subsidiary Force was to lend real military aid to the nizam 'at all times ready to execute services of importance, such as the protection of the person of His Highness, his heirs, and successors from race to race, and overawing and chastising all rebels or exciters of disturbance in the dominions of this State'. The number of troops to be maintained is significant. Many years later, Salar Jung attempted to use it as a bargaining chip when it was discovered that for many years the force had been kept at only a quarter of its strength but the nizam had continued to pay for the full strength of the Force.

With Raymond and his French troops out of the way, Wellesley now turned his attention to neutralizing the threat from Tipu Sultan. In early 1799, he began making detailed plans for an attack on Tipu's well-fortified river island of Seringapatam. From captured correspondence, he now had enough proof that Tipu was seeking French troops and supplies from the governor of Mauritius, and was actively plotting with Napoleon Bonaparte to end British rule in India. The nizam was asked to send his troops to assist his British allies as had been agreed in the newly signed treaty. In February 1799, the nizam sent 6000 of his finest cavalry, under the command of Mir Alam, to assist in the war against Tipu. Four battalions of Hyderabadi sepoys under John Malcolm, and six East India Company battalions under Lieutenant Colonel James Dalrymple, also joined the main force under the command of Major General Arthur Harris.

By mid-April, the siege of Seringapatam had begun. Tipu defended with tenacity and ingenuity, but by 3 May, a substantial breach was made. The next day in the afternoon, a storming party entered the breach, and within a few hours the city had fallen to the British. Tipu was found dead amid a heap of dead and wounded, his eyes still open and body so warm that it was thought that he was still alive. The victorious Hyderabadi army reached home five months later to rapturous applause, the hero of the hour being Mir Alam.

Ironically, his own younger brother, Zeinul-Abidin Shustari, was Tipu's private secretary and a senior courtier in the Mysore court. Tipu was defeated and killed on 4 May 1799, but it took the victorious army five months to return to Hyderabad. Mir Alam made a triumphal entry into Hyderabad on the nizam's personal elephant. As an additional honour, the nizam had ordered the nobility to come out of the city to welcome him. With him, came the orphaned children of his younger brother. (It is unclear if his brother died during the assault or a little before it.)

Mir Alam returned from his nine-month campaign in triumph, but physically he was much weaker than when he had left Hyderabad. He had been so ill in Madras that his formal audience with Lord Wellesley had to be delayed. This severe illness was the first sign that he had contracted the leprosy that would slowly eat away at him in the next decade. But apart from his ill health, there was a new confidence, even arrogance, about him. There were rumours that he was eyeing his mentor and benefactor, Aristu Jah's post, that of the diwan.

Regardless of the honours given to him when he entered Hyderabad, both the nizam and Aristu Jah had reason to be put out with Mir Alam. The first had to do with the way Mysore was carved up after the victory over Tipu. The nizam quite rightly thought that he would be entitled to half the territory since he had provided half the army. But it was not a simple two-way division. The British decided to keep some land for themselves and gave some to the nizam, with the major part going to the ancient Wadiyar dynasty, thereby ensuring that the reinstated raja would be utterly beholden to them. The nizam was upset when he came to know that Mir Alam had agreed to the division, and especially angry when he learnt that the latter had put his own seal on the partition treaty rather than sending it to him (the nizam) for ratification. His anger increased further when he came to know that Mir Alam had also accepted a large pension from the British which appeared suspiciously to be a reward for his acquiescence and cooperation in the matter.

Another reason had to do with the fate of Tipu's captured treasure. It appears to have been distributed between the commanders and the soldiers. In India, there was no equivalent to this European tradition, and the nizam was extremely annoyed at his spoils of war being distributed in such a manner. Rumours were also rife that Mir Alam had got hold of some of Tipu's finest jewels, and though he had presented the nizam jewels worth Rs 11 lakh, these were mere baubles compared to what he had retained. It was also rumoured that Mir Alam had embezzled much of the state treasure carried with him to the war. Clearly Mir Alam knew how to look out for himself. Also of concern to Aristu Jah was the close relationship between Wellesley and Mir Alam, a connection the latter made no effort to hide.

The tension between Aristu Jah and his protégé was building, and in early November 1799, a point of no return was reached. Mir Alam had appealed to the resident, James Achilles Kirkpatrick, to take his side, but he got no support from him. The wedding of the nizam's son and heir apparent, Sikandar Jah, and Jahan Pawar Begum, the granddaughter of Aristu Jah, had been fixed. At one of the prenuptial parties thrown by Aristu Jah, he challenged Mir Alam as to the whereabouts of Tipu's state jewels. Mir Alam denied all knowledge of them. It was now universal knowledge that the two had become enemies.

Mir Alam left Hyderabad soon after to take up his post as governor of the newly conquered territories of Mysore, little realizing that Aristu Jah was plotting his downfall. How this was achieved can only be understood against the background of the famous liaison between James Achilles Kirkpatrick and Khair-un-Nissa, a grand-niece of Mir Alam. Aristu Jah realized that if he wished to disgrace Mir Alam, he would first have to alienate him from his British supporters. He leaked the news of the affair to a Hyderabadi news writer in a deliberately exaggerated form.[33]

The resulting newsletters accused the resident of not just sleeping with Khair-un-Nissa but, in fact, raping her. There were also gossipy titbits about Kirkpatrick's past dalliances. Aristu Jah then wrote an anonymous letter to Mir Alam, giving all the sordid details of the liaison.[34] Already upset with Kirkpatrick for failing to take his side against the diwan, Mir Alam fell for the story and wrote an angry letter to Wellesley demanding punishment (in fact execution) for Kirkpatrick. Wellesley wrote to the nizam and Aristu Jah demanding to know the truth about the charges. This was exactly what Aristu Jah had hoped for, and he now cut a deal with Kirkpatrick. He outlined to him what his fate would be if he chose to corroborate the charges against him. He told the resident that he would clear his name by personally telling the nizam to write to the Governor General that the charges were little more than Mir Alam's creative malice with no basis in fact, provided he sacked Mir Alam as the Company's vakil and agreed to work with him (Aristu Jah) in the best interest of Hyderabad.[35]

Mir Alam was dismissed from his post of vakil and also lost the lucrative post of overseeing the newly acquired territories. He was imprisoned in isolation in Rudrur fort from where he was released after six months but remained under house arrest on his country estates.

With Tipu dead, the East India Company found itself thinking about the Maratha threat. This brought the nizam and the British closer, and the Treaty of Perpetual and General Defensive Alliance signed on 12 October 1800 was a reflection of this. The size of the Subsidiary Force was increased, and the nizam was made responsible for its upkeep, something which was achieved by the cession to the Company of all the territories he had acquired by the treaties of 1792 and 1799 with Mysore. The British placed a value of £630,000 per annum on these territories, averring that the sum would pay for the augmented Subsidiary Force, comprising eight battalions and two regiments of cavalry. In return, this force was to be available to the nizam for internal and external protection at the Company's expense. That this was an empty promise became obvious when in 1802, the services of the Subsidiary Force were denied him. The force, it was asserted, was stationed in Hyderabad as a psychological deterrent, and not to quell internal disturbances.

During war, the nizam was to not only spare the services of the Subsidiary Force but also provide 6000 infantry and 9000 horse from his own troops. This treaty was a master stroke of British diplomacy. In a step which effectively made Hyderabad a protected state, from an equal ally, the nizam was forbidden to negotiate with foreign powers without consulting the Company. However, it recognized the rights of the nizam over his children, subjects and servants. This right too 'became subject over the years to increasingly intrusive interpretations, quite in line with the shrinking power of His Highness and increasing encroachments by the Paramount Power'.[36]

In June 1803, Nizam Ali Khan suffered another stroke. He died two months later, on 6 August, and was buried on the same day at the Mecca Masjid, Hyderabad's main mosque. Briggs observed, 'He is the first of his family who sought the English; and that he did not make more out of his connection was—whatever may be asserted to the contrary—in consequence of his unbounded faith in his ally.'[37] He was succeeded by his son, the thirty-two-year-old Akbar Ali Khan, who assumed the title of Sikander Jah, and became Asaf Jah III.

A tall, melancholy man, who indulged in wine and women, and mixed in disreputable company, Sikander Jah was at best semi-literate and could neither write nor speak Persian well. He spent most of his time in seclusion while his government plumbed new depths.

It was at this time that Mir Alam's luck turned. Aristu Jah died in 1804, some nine months after Nizam Ali Khan. British interference in the internal affairs of the state came into sharper focus when they insisted on Mir Alam being made diwan. Sikander Jah had wanted to take personal control of the government, but the British rejected his request. Mir Alam, who had Wellesley's support, now became a front runner for the diwan's post. This decision seems to have been taken when Mir Alam was still under house arrest and had yet to return to Hyderabad. This was just as well, because had any of them been aware of how Mir Alam looked at this time, the decision may have been different. His leprosy was in a far advanced stage, with his nose having fallen off, and the disease having also hideously deformed other parts of his body. Secretions oozed from his suppurating sores, but the doctors, both British and Indian, could do nothing to help him. The die had been cast, and Mir Alam was confirmed in his post in July 1804. He immediately set out on a quest for vengeance, ransacking the house of Aristu Jah's widow, Sarwar Afza Begum. The nizam, instead of helping, added to her woes by publicly humiliating his wife who was the begum's granddaughter. He also turned a blind eye as Mir Alam targeted each of the former diwan's associates, ransacking their properties by turn.

Mir Alam, who in the words of Henry Russell, 'aggravated many abuses, and never redressed one' was a creature of the British. He specially raised the land revenue assessment by one anna per rupee so that he could give himself an enormous salary. His term in office was passed in a series of struggles to reduce the nizam to a cipher with the active support of the British. The nizam retired from the unequal contest in disgust, and in the words of Sir Charles Metcalfe, led a life of 'gloomy retirement and sullen discontent'. Not content with reducing him to complete impotence, the British even doubted his sanity. According to Metcalfe, Sikander Jah was not mad but was suffering from the effects of long depression and seclusion. He said that he could hardly imagine a situation more entitled to pity, for here was a ruler held in complete subjection by his servant with the support of an irresistible foreign power.

James Kirkpatrick's tenure as resident was a milestone in the history of the English in Hyderabad. We have noted that it included seminal events such as the disbanding of the French troops and the negotiations of important treaties. He was also responsible for the construction of the residency. It was thanks to James Kirkpatrick that the British resident had an official residence which was so grand that comparisons were drawn with Government House at Madras and the Governor General's residence in Calcutta.

Sir John Malcolm, a military officer and diplomat who was governor of Bombay from 1827 to 1830, in a journal-letter to his wife in 1817, described the residency which resembled the newly constructed White House in Washington: 'You may conceive my surprise to approach a palace—for such the present mansion of the British Resident of Hyderabad may well be termed. It is only surpassed in splendour and magnitude by the Government House in Calcutta.'[38]

There is an amusing story connected with the approval given for building the residency. When Kirkpatrick first submitted the plan to the nizam, it was rejected. When the crestfallen resident asked Mir Alam the reason, he was told that the nizam, alarmed by the size of the paper on which the plans were submitted, had thought that he was being asked to part with vast tracts of land. Kirkpatrick reduced the scale, and the same plan for the proposed 64-acre property was resubmitted on a piece of paper the size of a visiting card. This, the nizam was happy to sanction, confirming to Kirkpatrick that the mir had been correct in his guess as to the cause of his former failure. He also agreed to bear the expenses of maintaining the residency which was constructed on the north side of the Musi river.

Kirkpatrick is famous in Hyderabad lore for his love affair with the teenage Khair-un-Nissa, who was Mir Alam's grand-niece, whom he later married after he himself had converted to Islam. It became a cause célèbre of the times, and Lord Wellesley ordered an inquiry (on Mir Alam's complaint) which was finally dropped. The union produced two children, a boy and a girl. The boy, William George, died young, but the girl, Catherine, who was known for her beauty and wit, married into a good English family and was the inspiration for Thomas Carlyle's Blumhilde in his novel *Sartor Resartus*.

Kirkpatrick was suddenly taken ill in 1805 and left for Calcutta for a change of air. But his health deteriorated, and on 15 October 1805, the flamboyant resident passed into history. He was only forty-one and had been married for six years. His residency now houses the University College for Women. The property has now shrunk to 34 acres, the remaining having been made over to the Osmania Medical College. In close proximity is the bazaar known as Hashmat Ganj. Few realize that it was named after an Englishman.

THE HYDERBAD CONTINGENT AND CHANDU LAL'S MALADMINISTRATION

Mir Alam died of his leprosy in January 1809. His name is associated with the Mir Alam Tank and the Mir Alam Mandi, the former, it is said, built from the spoils of his Seringapatam campaign against Tipu. Sikander Jah wanted to appoint Mir Alam's son-in-law, Munir-ul-Mulk, as diwan. This time the two sides reached a compromise. Munir-ul-Mulk was appointed as the nominal diwan but was forced to sign a declaration abnegating all part in the administration. The real power was with the *peshkar*, Chandu Lal, who became the de facto diwan.

Mir Alam was succeeded as diwan by his son-in-law, Munir-ul-Mulk, in 1809. Munir-ul-Mulk was a dummy diwan, and the real power was vested in his peshkar, Chandu Lal, who was a favourite of the English. They had forced Mir Alam on Sikander Jah who had been obnoxious to his master. On his death, it was thought advisable to let the nizam select his own diwan. Two candidates were in the field—Shums-ul-Umra, whom the nizam held in high esteem, and Munir-ul-Mulk whom he detested. With a curious mixture of cunning and perversity (which justified to some extent the doubts about his mental stability held by some), he postponed making a choice till he discovered whom the British favoured. When he realized that they were inclined to side with his own favourite, Shums-ul-Umra, he immediately announced the appointment of Munir-ul-Mulk as diwan. The British did not consider Munir-ul-Mulk wholly trustworthy and therefore gave all the power to Chandu Lal, forcing the nizam to accept the fact that the man he had selected would only be a nominal diwan.

Munir-ul-Mulk bound himself by a written undertaking given to the nizam in the presence of the resident that he would take no part in the administration of the dominions nor make any effort to obtain power. Chandu Lal would continue to administer as before, and Munir-ul-Mulk was made to give an undertaking in writing to that effect. Lord Minto's letter to Munir-ul-Mulk gives us an idea of what the terms and conditions of his appointment were:

... To this system of conduct, indeed, you will recollect that you solemnly and specifically bound yourself at the time, when you were soliciting the appointment of Minister, having called Raja Chandoo Lal privately at night and assured him that his authority and influence should not suffer in the event of your nomination, swearing upon the Koran and the head of your son Abdoola that you would give the Raja entire authority in the administration of the country.[39]

Notwithstanding any undertaking given by him, Munir-ul-Mulk spent much of his time and money on intrigues to obtain that authority he had sworn never to aspire for. If he failed in acquiring power, he succeeded in widening the breach between the nizam and Chandu Lal, sowing dissension among government officials and obstructing public business. Munir-ul-Mulk remained diwan till his death in 1832, after which Chandu Lal, long the de facto diwan, was formally appointed to the post, which he held till 1842.

Chandu Lal had come to Hyderabad from Punjab and started life as a stamp vendor and copyist. His social graces, financial acumen, and a capacity for hard work saw him rise to the position of peshkar (a minister of finance reporting to the diwan), under Mir Alam. Said to be weak, hesitant and lacking self-confidence due to his low social status, he gave the appearance of being physically infirm. He was dark complexioned, bent over, thin and toothless, and had a very subservient air about him. Chandu Lal made up for his low social status by becoming a master of intrigue. He bribed the nobility and palace officials, and between his appointment as de facto diwan in 1809, until his resignation as diwan in 1843, Chandu Lal exerted more influence over Hyderabad than any other individual ever had. A man of intelligence and indefatigable industry, he was also thoroughly corrupt, and retained his position by his fidelity to the British and subservience to the British residency. His reckless expenditure was also responsible for bankrupting the state, though he himself became a fabulously rich man.

According to the treaty of 1800, the nizam was to assist the Company with troops in times of war. Henry Russell, who became resident, succeeding T. Sydenham in 1811, had served as assistant to James Kirkpatrick. A vain, ambitious and corrupt man, he took Kirkpatrick's widow Khair-un-Nissa to Calcutta, seduced her, and then abandoned her in Masulipatnam before returning to Hyderabad. Russell had no time or sympathy for the nizam, who presided over a rotten system where nothing seemed to flourish except corruption. He was quick to reject the nizam's last feeble attempt to remove Chandu Lal, and Sikander Jah, stung by the rebuke, responded by taking no further part in the governance of his state.

He withdrew to the Chowmahalla Palace, and his seclusion was so complete that he did not leave his palace for four years continuously. He made indolence a virtue and intrigues a policy. His strange conduct and language led to doubts about his sanity. He spent his time sitting alone in his palace or in the company of a few personal attendants of low habits and poor character who would flatter him and plot and scheme. The nizam's seclusion only made Chandu Lal's position stronger. It also allowed Russell to enrich himself by the expedient of what came to be known as the Hyderabad Contingent.

In 1812, two battalions of the nizam's army mutinied. They tied their commanding officer to a cannon and threatened to blow him away unless they were paid on time, and their offences pardoned. Russell saw in this episode the need to put the nizam's troops, a badly armed rabble, on a more professional footing. With the help of the ever-obliging Chandu Lal, Russell established a force which the diwan later called the Russell Brigade. It initially consisted of 2000 soldiers and was located in the old French gun foundry. Keeping a cut for himself, Russell kept on creating fresh posts for new applicants, and it ballooned in size over the years.

These troops were trained and equipped like the East India Company's troops and were like a part of the Company's army. The nizam never got to use this force but paid for it. To acquire the money for this newly formed force which was referred to variously as the Nizam's Army, the Nizam's Contingent, the Hyderabad Contingent and later the Contingent, Chandu Lal became involved in a disreputable financial arrangement with Palmer & Company, a commercial firm, which was established by William Palmer in 1811 to open up the state for economic exploitation. Russell connived with Chandu Lal to allow the establishment of this firm, and what the duo saw as a solution only drew the nizam further into debt.

In 1816, the firm was allowed to lend money to the nizam who used those funds to ensure regular payments to the Russell Brigade. Chandu Lal paid the Company in cash or by assignment of land. Districts were leased out to the highest bidder, mortgaging the entire revenue of the state to outsiders. When Sir Charles Metcalfe became resident in 1820, he soon realized the drain on the Hyderabad finances caused by the baleful connection with Palmer & Co. and took steps to end the exploitation, a subject which is discussed in some detail in Chapter 7.

Sikander Jah died in May 1829, and few mourned his passing. His reign had nothing to recommend it. As Edward Thompson has observed, 'No state can ever have combined such material importance with so undistinguished a record and so fictitious an independence.'[40] He was succeeded by the illegitimate Nasir-ud-Daula, the eldest of nine sons. Nasir-ud-Daula was a large, powerfully built, overweight man, with blue Afghan eyes and pleasing features. Although unlettered like his father, he was a quick learner. But his hands-off approach encouraged corruption. He showed no willingness to rein in extravagant expenditure, and Chandu Lal continued to flourish. By the mid-1830s, the nizam's government's credit rating was so poor that local bankers refused to grant it loans.

Under the patronage of the resident and Chandu Lal, the Contingent ballooned in size. In fact, Chandu Lal's greatest service to his masters, the British, was the support he gave to Russell in the organization and maintenance of the Russell Brigade which subsequently became the Hyderabad Contingent. Chandu Lal ruled Hyderabad, neither in the people's nor the ruler's interest, but in the interest of the British. When Siraj-ul-Mulk became diwan, one of his main concerns was to find ways to pay for the upkeep of the Contingent which had become an outrageously expensive force.

In April 1846, it consisted of 2592 cavalry and 6835 infantry and was officered by ninety-five Europeans appointed by the Governor General. A few years later, it grew to 8000 men under the command of as many as five brigadiers and five brigade majors, with numerous subordinate officers and supporting staff. The force in question was 'enormously in excess of any conceivable need and so egregiously over-officered as to constitute an oppressive and intolerable burden upon the Nizam's resources, in which the germ of his subsequent embarrassments is plainly enough discernible'.[41]

Since the nizam was footing the bill, no attempt was made to curtail expenditure, and 'poor Nizzy pays for all' became the proverbial expression in Hyderabad. These troops were supported at the nizam's expense at a cost of Rs 40 lakh per annum, approximately a third of the revenue of the state, the nizam becoming the passive instrument of an ally's exorbitant behests. The officers' salary bill had bloated to £130,000 a year. It was discovered later that the same salary bill could have been reduced to a mere £35,000.

Since the nizam had no money to pay the Contingent, he farmed out districts, pawned state jewels and borrowed money from the Company. He became more and more indebted as time passed, and in 1847 he was in debt to the tune of Rs 37 lakh. The Contingent was an unbearable burden for the nizam and became the millstone around his neck. But it suited both the British and Chandu Lal for Hyderabad to hurtle towards financial doom. Sir Charles Metcalfe, who was resident during 1820–25, observed in a note dated 1832 that Chandu Lal 'was the creature of our ascendancy' who saw in the existence of the force a way of maintaining his own power against rival nobles as well as refractory subjects. It was in his personal interest to maintain the force.

General J.S. Fraser, who became resident in 1838, also noted the nizam's continuing opposition to the Contingent. The correspondence reveals that British officers at various stages of their careers protested that there was no legal basis for the nizam to pay for the Contingent, but Calcutta chose to ignore these pleas. The reasons for this are not difficult to understand. The Contingent provided them an efficient army at no cost, apart from offering a substantial field of patronage. It gave the British control over the nizam's internal administration and put him at their mercy militarily. Dalhousie, who 'represented a particularly aggressive form of his government's policy of annexation and imperialism',[42] knew Hyderabad was in dire straits but chose to ignore Fraser's recommendation to save the state from financial ruin, since he 'appeared not to care about certain fundamental requirements of social and political morality'.[43]

Under Chandu Lal, the financial condition of the state steadily deteriorated. As we have noted, he resorted to tax-farming, selling the rights to collect taxes from the stipulated areas to the highest bidder. Chandu Lal made grants of land so recklessly that in later years documents issued during his time were not accepted as proof of title unless supported by other evidence. The story goes that he once spied a man sitting on a donkey with his face to the tail of the animal. On being questioned, the man answered that he had just been appointed talukdar of a district and wanted to ensure that no one else had bribed the diwan and been appointed to the same post.

This system led to the oppression of the farmers, not only because of the excessive tax demands, but also the rapidity with which they had to be paid, since the tax farmers wanted to recoup their investment as quickly as possible before their successors arrived to dispossess them. The tyranny of the Arabs was another problem. They and their followers exacted payment in coin or kind from the villagers in lieu of payments due to them as arrears of pay for service in the irregular troops or other reasons. Many ryots fled their lands, leaving the land uncultivated, and therefore unproductive of any revenue.

Sir Richard Temple, who was resident in 1867, had made a thorough perusal of General Fraser's correspondence and notes, and was struck at the extraordinarily defective character of Chandu Lal's administration. 'I knew . . . that in those days lawlessness prevailed . . . but I had no idea until I read these papers, how utterly the very foundations of good Government were poisoned at their source—and so much of the blame, too, is traceable to Chandu Lal personally!'[44] A native banker told Temple that Chandu Lal had 'plundered the people, and then spent the proceeds in almsgiving'.[45] A man devoid of any principles and with no aptitude to manage a country, he was also without any feeling for the people. Profuse in almsgiving in the hope of conciliating, and equally profuse in expenditure for the purposes of corruption, he was timid before the violent, and fierce and abusive to the weak. His mismanagement was responsible for virtually handing the country over to the moneylenders.[46]

Chandu Lal took no steps to increase the revenue or to reduce the expenditure of the state. As a result, from his time onwards, the problem of balancing the budget became a chronic one. He has been stigmatized with perpetual contempt in a Hyderabad legend for his promise to pay tomorrow—Chandu Lal *ka kal*—a tomorrow which never came. Chandu Lal was forced to resign in September 1843 when the payments of the Hyderabad Contingent fell into arrears and his appeal for a loan of Rs 1 crore was ignored by the British. And since charity begins at home, he did not fail in the noble task of granting himself a generous pension of Rs 1000 per day. His immediate successor was his nephew, Raja Ram Bakhsh, who was appointed peshkar. The post of diwan was kept vacant for three years before it was filled by Siraj-ul-Mulk in 1846.

Astonishing abuses existed in the nizam's government even during the time of Siraj-ul-Mulk. Temple discovered that some 30,000 men of an irregular army existed only on paper, and Rs 20–30 lakh was embezzled annually. The diwan wanted to get rid of the paper army, but Nasir-ud-Daula insisted on its continuance. The forgery of government documents was also rampant, and on one occasion, hundreds of such documents were found and seized. It was again the nizam who wanted to continue the corrupting system of *nazarana*s.[47]

In the last part of Siraj-ul-Mulk's first administration (1846–48), Nasir-ud-Daula took the government into his own hands and exacted large sums in this manner, auctioning offices to the highest bidder. Many of the troubles of those troubled times, including the cession of Berar, were largely due to Nasir-ud-Daula's perversity.[48] General Fraser remonstrated but to no avail. Nor did the government in Calcutta pay heed to his request for intervention which could have saved the day. As Temple put it, 'The Nizam's infatuated perversity at that time was quite astonishing, even for an Asiatic prince . . .'[49] He persisted in trying to govern without the slightest notion of how to do it. Fraser was so disgusted that when he retired from service, he left without bidding goodbye to the nizam.

The nizam contributed a large sum from his personal finances, but the finances of the state remained in a critical condition. For the first time in Asaf Jahi history, a ruler was forced to dip into his personal treasury to prevent the financial bankruptcy of his kingdom. Nasir-ud-Daula withdrew Rs 1 crore in cash and another Rs 8,00,000 in gold to help tide over the crisis. But this provided only temporary relief, and in April 1845, Lord Hardinge sent him a strongly worded letter regarding the arrears of payment of the Hyderabad Contingent and general maladministration. Another raid on his own treasury yielded Rs 1.2 crore, but soon the debt started mounting, and in September 1846 it stood at around Rs 38 lakh. It was at this time that Siraj-ul-Mulk was made diwan. He had the support of General Fraser, but since the nizam did not like him, there was little that he could achieve.

Siraj-ul-Mulk remained diwan till he was replaced in November 1848. A succession of four diwans followed, after which he was appointed to that post once again in 1851, holding it till his death in 1853. He made a sincere effort to reform the administration but his efforts did not receive the support of the British, largely because of the attitude of Lord Dalhousie. General Fraser, who supported his efforts, had to face criticism from Lord Dalhousie for exceeding his brief.

According to Dalhousie, it was not the responsibility of the British government if the nizam mismanaged his affairs. Dalhousie set a deadline of 31 December 1850 for the discharge of the nizam's entire debt and issued a threat that if the Governor General's expectations were disappointed, it would be his duty to 'take such decided steps as the interests of the British Government demanded'. Although it was not spelled out, the implied threat was that this would involve the ceding of territory as security for the payment of principal and interest. The territory in question was Berar, the jewel in the nizam's crown, containing, as it did, the finest cotton tracts in India.

Fraser resigned (or was bullied into resigning) in 1852, and was replaced by the subservient Colonel John Low who had been sent to Hyderabad with the specific mandate of ensuring that the nizam ceded Berar, a territory which Dalhousie had been eyeing for some time as a security for the payment of usurious arrears and the upkeep of the Contingent. This was achieved by the treaty of 1853, after the signing of which Siraj-ul-Mulk passed away.

The scene was now set for Salar Jung, whose entry inaugurated an era of unprecedented prosperity and progress in Hyderabad. It was not something which anyone could have predicted.

1

The Heritage

Since the last days of the Bahmani kingdom, the family to which Salar
Jung belonged had taken a leading part in the affairs of the Deccan.
They owed their allegiance first to the Adil Shahis and then to the Mughal
emperors and lastly to the Asaf Jah dynasty. Salar Jung's ancestors belonged to
a noble family of Medina and were descended from the famous Sheikh Ovais
Karani of Medina. Sheikh Ovais III, an ancestor in the ninth generation,
was the first of the line to leave Arabia and settle in India. He came to
India in the middle of the seventeenth century, accompanied by his son,
Sheikh Muhammed Ali, and settled in Bijapur. Muhammed Ali married the
daughter of Mulla Ahmed Nait, a nobleman of the Bijapur court, and Ali
Adil Shah the ruler of Bijapur appointed him to the post of *dabir* (secretary).
Muhammed Ali's two sons, Sheikh Muhammed Bakar and Sheikh Hyder,
were appointed as chief steward and auditor respectively.[1]

Later, the two brothers left the Bijapur court and took up service
under Aurangzeb who gave them mansabs and high posts. Bakar was
made diwan of Shahjahanabad and Kashmir, and later was transferred to
the Deccan as diwan, where he died in 1715 at Aurangabad. He was an
Arabic scholar and had written books on rhetoric and philosophy which
were well regarded.

Bakar's son, Sheikh Muhammed Taki, also held a high rank, first under
Aurangzeb and then under Bahadur Shah. During the reign of Farrukh
Siyar, he was appointed *amil* or collector of toll tax at Aurangabad. The
first nizam, when he became subedar, appointed him commander of the
garrisons of all ports in the Deccan. He died in 1772, survived by his only
son, Sheikh Shams-ud-din Muhammed Hyder.

Shams-ud-din was appointed master of the elephant stables by
Nizam-ul-Mulk, and he later became *arzbegee* when he accompanied the

nizam to Delhi. He was a close confidant of the first nizam and was given the titles of Hyderyar Khan and later Munir-ul-Mulk, and was appointed as chief steward. His mansab rank was 7000 zat and 7000 sawar. He became diwan of the subas of the Deccan, and in Nizam Ali Khan's time, he was appointed subedar of Aurangabad, where he died in 1775 aged seventy-eight.[2]

Shams-ud-din was survived by his two sons, Safdar Khan Bahadur Ghaiyur Jung and Takiyar Khan Zulfiqar Jung. The former was born in 1732 and received a mansab from Nizam-ul-Mulk and was appointed deputy master of the elephant stables. Muzaffar Jung raised his rank and gave him the title of 'Khan'. He received the title of Ghaiyur Jung Bahadur Ashja-ud-Daula in 1760, and with it, a fringed palanquin and command of 4000 soldiers, which was soon extended to a division of troops with a strength of 5000 soldiers and 4000 horse. In 1782, he was appointed to the office of diwan for the subas of the Deccan with the title Ashja-ul-Mulk. Eight years later, he was given the title of Khan Khanan. He died in 1790 and was buried in the tomb of his father at Aurangabad.

Ghaiyur Jung Bahadur left behind four sons who were born of the daughter of Dargah Quli Khan Salar Jung. They were Muhammed Taki Khan Bahadur, Hasan Raza Khan Bahadur, Ali Zaman Hyderyar Khan Bahadur Ghaiyur Jung Moin-ud-Daula Munir-ul-Mulk and Raza Baz Khan Bahadur Amin-ul-Mulk.

The Salar Jungs were the direct descendants of the third son, Ali Zaman Hyderyar Khan Bahadur Ghaiyur Jung Moin-ud-Daula Munir-ul-Mulk,[3] who was the diwan of Hyderabad from 1809 to 1832. He was married to Nafisa Begum, daughter of Mir Alam, who had preceded him as diwan, and who was a descendent of the Nuria Syeds of Persia. She died in 1799, and Munir-ul-Mulk then married her sister, Sahiba Begum, who bore him two sons Muhammed Ali Khan Shuja-ud-Daula Salar Jung and Alam Ali Khan Siraj-ul-Mulk, who was diwan from 1846–48, and again from 1851–53.

The eldest son, Shuja-ud-Daula, married the daughter of Saiyid Qasim Ali Khan Bahadur, a nobleman descended from the Naishapur Syeds of Persia. Turab Ali Khan (the future Salar Jung I), the offspring of this union, was born on 2 January 1829 at Bijapur (modern-day Vijaypura in Karnataka). It was also the year in which the nizam, Sikander Jah, died. He was succeeded by Nasir-ud-Daula, who became the fourth nizam. By now, the British stranglehold on Hyderabad was complete. The resident had an important say in the appointment of the diwan. The diwans were beholden to him and ensured that British interests were well protected.

The period 1842–53 saw the vacillating nizam appoint as many as six diwans, three of whom had tenures which ranged from two to five months. Munir-ul-Mulk's other son through Sahiba Begum, Siraj-ul-Mulk, was first appointed as diwan in 1846. He was replaced by Saif Jung in 1848. In 1851, when the British pushed the nizam, he was obliged to appoint him once more to that post. Siraj-ul-Mulk was a man of great learning and did not covet the post of diwan. It was during his tenure that Berar was ceded to the British, and he was blamed by both the nizam and the populace for the loss.

SALAR JUNG'S EARLY YEARS

Little is known of Salar Jung's early life, forcing the biographer to spin thin facts into whole cloth. What is known is that his childhood coincided with a period of misfortune for his family. His father had died when he was two years old, and he was brought up by his uncle, Siraj-ul-Mulk. Before he had turned four, his grandfather, Munir-ul-Mulk, also passed away. Just before his grandfather's death the young Salar Jung was taken dangerously ill with high fever. He was unconscious for seven days. The concerned grandfather was very distressed at this, and it is said that at midnight on the seventh day, he came to the boy's bedside and prayed that whatever calamity was to befall the child should be transferred to him. The Muslims term this *tassaduq,* and two centuries ago, the first Mughal ruler of India, Babur, had similarly offered himself as a substitute for his dying son, Humayun. Humayun recovered and Babur passed away. Similarly, Munir-ul-Mulk died after a few days, and the young Salar Jung recovered. As a child, he had a weak constitution, and his health remained delicate till his twelfth year. It was around this time that he was given the title of Salar Jung Bahadur. He also had a younger sister Najeeba Begum, who went on to marry Khaisar-ud-Daula and was the mother of Mukaram-ud-Daula, of whom we will hear more later in the narrative.

Munir-ul-Mulk left a legacy of debt to his successors. He owed nearly Rs 25 lakh to Palmer and Company and some Arab chiefs. Many nobles seem to have lived beyond their means, with little or no thought for posterity. Even Salar Jung owed Rs 26 lakh when he died.[4] The nizam, Nasir-ud-Daula, had established the custom of paying off the debts of his nobles. He did so in this case as well, paying off Munir-ul-Mulk's chief creditors. While discharging these liabilities, the nizam took possession of all the assets of the family, including several jagirs and Mir Alam's Tank in satisfaction of the loan he had made. He even seized the family jewels and sold them.

The only source of income left to the family was a small property known as the Tarbund Bazaar which yielded about Rs 700 per month and a monthly allowance of Rs 1500 granted to the family by Chandu Lal. The income from the property went to pay the family's armed retainers, with the balance barely sufficing for the needs of a large family. The only means of conveyance, if it could be called that, was an old female elephant which had been with the family for long. It wasn't the most conducive environment for a future prime minister of Hyderabad, and unsurprisingly, the young boy's education too was of a middling nature.

His uncle, Siraj-ul-Mulk, the only male member of the family, was far too busy with affairs of state to worry about Salar Jung's education, and it was under his paternal grandmother's supervision (who alone seemed interested in his future) that he was privately educated. The care she bestowed on him bore abundant fruit. When he was seven years old, the Bismillah ceremony was performed. Given the family's finances it was an unostentatious affair. However, the nizam graced the occasion with his presence, and it was in front of the nizam that he opened the book and read from it. Even before that, Salar Jung had been receiving instruction from a moulvi who was teaching his sister. The young boy had insisted on being taught, and so for a year before his own ceremony, he received instruction from the moulvi.

Now a regular pupil, he continued to study under private tuition for the next seven years. But he was a sickly child, constantly falling prey to some ailment or the other, and it is hardly surprising that he showed no fondness for his studies, trying to escape from them as much as possible. It is said that when he was about ten or eleven years old, he missed his studies for six weeks due to ill health. When his grandmother wanted him to continue his studies, he played truant and hid himself in the house. He was ferreted out by his grandmother, but her attempts at summary chastisement with a stick were less than successful since the young boy made her chase him all around the house.

In a fit of rage, she cursed him, saying that if he disliked studies, it would be much better he were dead. This imprecation seems to have done its work; it is said that after this incident, Salar Jung became an industrious student.[5] His frequent ill health may also explain his lack of affinity for any sport. He was, however, a good rider in his adult life; he rode every day and had some magnificent horses in his stables. Syed Hossain Bilgrami, his biographer, tells us that as a boy, he would mount his uncle's giraffe, much to the consternation of his attendants.[6] Riding was a passion with him, and his recklessness resulted in his having many narrow escapes.

It was by all accounts an ordinary education. A tutor was engaged to teach him Persian and Arabic, and he soon acquired a tolerable knowledge of the former. He conversed in Persian with a native of that country and soon acquired enough knowledge to speak and write it fluently. He understood Arabic but never mastered it sufficiently to speak or write it. He received lessons in logic and theology, and was also taught calligraphy. From 1847 to 1852, he learnt English from Henry Bowen, who later became his private secretary, but that was only for half an hour a day, which makes his great fluency in the language in later life all the more remarkable.

From the age of fifteen to nineteen, his education was desultory. Nor did he receive any training which would equip him for public life. His only exposure to public administration was when his grandmother gave him the accounts of her jagir villages and asked him to study them with the help of clerks and then explain them to her. He missed out on the company of boys of his own age and had no pocket money to speak of. This was in a way a blessing in disguise, for it prevented him from falling into the dissolute ways of young nobles with money at their command.[7]

A benevolent influence on him during his formative years was that of the British resident, General James Stuart Fraser, and his family. Their role in the enlightened views which Salar Jung held as an adult can hardly be underestimated. The *Times of India* correspondent observed:

We have hitherto entirely failed in our duty to the various native princes, in not having raised up, from among the sons of the leading men, statesmen like Salar Jung, who but for General James Stuart Fraser and his family would humanly speaking have been like the rest of his countrymen. We want more real noble-mindedness and humanity about us; and this Salar Jung—unfortunately at Hyderabad only Salar Jung—possesses in a wonderful degree.[8]

In 1847, when he was eighteen years old, Salar Jung made his entry into public life. He was appointed talukdar of certain talukas in the Telangana districts, including Khammam, replacing Henry Dighton. Europeans had been appointed to administer certain districts, but when the nizam decided that this should stop, Salar Jung took Dighton's place. Though he was unable to visit the districts or make any changes in the administration, he soon mastered all the details of the land revenue system introduced by his predecessor. When the lands and other estates attached by the nizam in satisfaction of the debt owed by Munir-ul-Mulk were released and reverted to the family in 1848, Siraj-ul-Mulk appointed Salar Jung to look after them. He managed them efficiently, and in 1853, inherited them on the death of his uncle.

Salar Jung received no systematic instruction in administration from his uncle, picking up knowledge of public affairs in a desultory way. Siraj-ul-Mulk entrusted his nephew with some work of minor importance occasionally, and at times consulted him on ordinary matters. Siraj-ul-Mulk's thinking and morals accorded with the times in which he lived, and were not marked by any great degree of wisdom or rectitude. Salar Jung, who had imbibed much of the British sense of fair play and justice from his association with the Fraser family, was straightforward and honest. Unsurprisingly, there was friction between the uncle and his nephew as regards the conduct of public affairs.

Notwithstanding their divergent views, Siraj-ul-Mulk had asked Lala Bahadur, the influential daftardar, to consult Salar Jung on all important matters. On one occasion, Siraj-ul-Mulk was pressed for a loan and was inclined to resort to the Arabs for it at a high rate of interest. Lala Bahadur agreed, but Salar Jung thought otherwise. He indignantly protested against the prevailing method of administration in which money borrowed at high rates of interest was squandered without any corresponding benefit to the public. His protests fell on deaf ears, and he angrily told Lala Bahadur that in future he should never consult him again.

It was the norm at that time to borrow money from the Arabs or the Pathans at extortionate rates of interest and to assign them talukas or districts as security for payment. Since the credit of the government was so low, this was the only way of raising money to meet the current expenditure of the state. Salar Jung always protested vigorously against it, and one of his first administrative acts after becoming diwan was to discontinue this method of raising funds by re-establishing the credit of the government in the eyes of the sahukars or moneylenders.

Although he had no say in matters of state, from the beginning, Salar Jung had evinced anxiety about the state of the administration and openly spoke out against it, advocating the need for reforms. His uncle, amused at the gratuitous advice, used to quote the well-known Urdu proverb in jest: 'Why is the Kazi lean? Because he is anxious about the city.'[9] Salar Jung was never taken to any private durbar of the nizam, and therefore the latter never had any chance of forming his own judgement of Salar Jung's abilities.

Salar Jung was a fairly tall, well-built man, very upright of stature with a rather small head well set back on the shoulders. He had a pleasing presence. Of wheat complexion, 'on his broad face there shone the prestige and dignity of his position'.[10] His heavily lidded eyes had a sad, dreamy look, and his thin, compressed lips almost always had the hint of a smile playing across them. The somewhat heavy jowl displayed both energy and resolve. Even so, it is difficult to detect the exceptional man behind such features. However, he exuded a compelling magnetic quality which enlivened the power of his personality and attracted the fond admiration of almost all those whose lives he touched.

It is said that it took just ten minutes to become his friend; and his friendships once made were lifelong. In his younger days, he had a tendency to be short-tempered, but with age, it had mellowed down into 'constant affability and all-prevailing good humour'. He was a master at concealing his feelings, and it was impossible to discover from his words, manner or expression the real state of his temper. It was said that he could read a person's thoughts at a glance; he also never forgot a face he had once seen.

The *Athenaeum* observed,

It was a face which you would look at twice wherever you met it—a noble face, thoughtful, calm and deep—a face which in repose would baffle the most acute physiognomist, but which lights up wonderfully when it smiles. His dress is plain and quiet, and he wears a small closely fitting turban. He speaks English remarkably well, although he has only learnt it lately. As he talks with you, you feel that he is learning all about you, and that he is reading your thoughts, while you are learning nothing whatever about his.[11]

Salar Jung shaved his beard and had his hair closely cropped but indulged in the luxury of a long moustache. He dressed simply, usually wearing a long Persian coat of *jamawar*, of different colours. It had a closed collar and hung below the knees. He sometimes wore English trousers but generally wore native white pyjamas. He never wore a complete suit of English clothes. His long coats of tweed, silk or cashmere were cut in the Oriental fashion. Collars and ties found no place in his wardrobe. He generally wore a gold brocade cap of a pattern peculiar to his family, but on ceremonial occasions wore a white turban and cummerbund. He wore socks at all times but shoes only when he was outdoors. A double-chained watch and a ring was the only jewellery he wore. Though his attire was simple and understated, it gave him a distinctive appearance: sartorial elegance was very much a part of his personality.

On occasions like the nizam's birthday, however, he dressed in full regalia. He wore a red muslin gown embroidered with gold, and his neck and arms were adorned with necklaces and bracelets of gold set with diamonds and pearls. When on a visit to the resident or nobles equal in rank, he put on a turban. At the durbar, he wore the *neema jama*, the old Mughlai costume whose prominent feature was an overdress of muslin with yards and yards of billowing shirt. The muslin, it was said, was so fine that 40 yards of it could be pulled through a finger ring.

On 26 May 1853, Siraj-ul-Mulk passed away after a long illness. He was on a visit to the Parsi banker Pestonjee's house at Chaderghat for a change of air and died there in the evening. He had been afflicted by an incurable disease, and his demise, while expected, seems to have come sooner than anticipated. Some attribute this to the strain and the heartache caused by the cession of Berar only five days prior to his death. Salar Jung, in a letter to Henry Dighton, described his uncle's demise:

> The present mail brings you the sad tidings of the death of my uncle which occurred on the 26th ultimo. He had been suffering from fever and other complaints a short time previously, but on Friday, the 20th ultimo, he had a very severe attack of illness, and was so weak that he could hardly stand; notwithstanding which, feeling slightly better, he attended Darbar on Saturday, and had a new Treaty with the British Government

executed by His Highness the Nizam. He grew worse after this, and on Tuesday, the 24th, was removed to Pestonjee's House at Chadarghat by Dr. MacLean's advice, but he rapidly declined, and expired on Thursday evening (26th) at 7 o'clock.[12]

He may not have guessed it at the time, but Salar Jung's life was about to undergo a dramatic change. For Hyderabad too, a new era was about to be inaugurated.

2

The Diwan and His Deodi

After Siraj-ul-Mulk's death, the nizam, Nasir-ud-Daula, toyed with the idea of being his own diwan but Colonel Low, the resident, quickly disabused him of this notion and urged him to appoint a minister at once. Beneficent and kindly, Nasir-ud-Daula, it was said, never witnessed distress without a desire to alleviate it. Unfortunately, he lacked the firmness and ability needed for good administration. He was surrounded by sycophants and cronies whose only aim was to feed his pleasures and his vanity. His dislike of the English and their habits was well known, and it was a prejudice his minions took good care to keep alive. He was consistent in nothing but his opposition to the views of the resident.

The nizam reminded the resident that Lord Dalhousie, in a minute, had confirmed his right to appoint his own minister without consulting the British. Low complained that the lack of a minister interfered with the Company's government, and it was therefore necessary to appoint one immediately. The nizam told the resident that he required a month to deliberate on the matter. He was asked to expedite the appointment so as 'not to impede public business'. The treaty of 1853 had just been concluded, and the resident wanted to avoid delay at this critical juncture. Low told the nizam that if maladministration were to ensue during the interregnum, and if this adversely affected the Company's business, the Governor General would view the matter with great displeasure. It was also in the nizam's own interest not to postpone the appointment 'as he will otherwise be personally exposed to the expostulations and clamour of those persons who will be displaced from their former position by the new arrangements'.[1]

SELECTION OF A NEW DIWAN

The palace rumour mill went into overdrive. Rumours were rife as to who the next diwan would be. The press reported that it could be Raja Bal Mukund but also added a caveat that it was not possible to read the nizam's mind. 'Whom the Nizam will appoint his Minister no man can tell, but of this every man makes sure that he will disappoint the general expectation.'[2] The same report also said that it would not be surprising if the partisans of the late diwan made a push to 'obtain the succession to the office for his nephew Salar Jung, and success is not impossible'. These proved to be prescient words as the course of events showed. Salar Jung was twenty-four at the time, and largely an unknown entity, and it is no surprise that the reports about his abilities were less than sanguine. 'There is nothing against this young gentleman, which is not a little to say of a man of his years, but to assert that there is any positive excellence upon which any expectation could be built, would be to advance a problem not easy to be solved. We cannot in every man expect to find a Pitt.'[3]

The nizam for his part played his cards very close to his chest, giving no clue as to whom he would appoint to the post. Raja Bal Mukund was at one time a front runner, but there were forces who were strongly advocating the candidature of the young Salar Jung. The fact that Rafi-ud-din Khan Umdat-ul-Mulk, the eldest son of Fakhr-ud-din Khan Shums-ul-Umra II, the premier noble of the realm, had been meeting the nizam for two or three hours every day gave rise to the supposition that he would be appointed to the post. But such hopes were belied. In a sudden and inexplicable turnaround, Rafi-ud-din Khan lost favour with the nizam, who instructed him to come to the durbar only when sent for.

A coterie close to the nizam consisting of Burhan-ud-din, Mama Jamila and Lala Bahadur were using all their influence to secure the appointment of Salar Jung whom they thought would be a puppet in their hands. Burhan-ud-din was an attendant who decided whom the nizam would see, and when. Even the diwan was granted an audience through him, and many official proposals were approved by the nizam on the recommendations of this flunkey. Chandu Lal had often complained to the resident about Burhan-ud-din and his influence on the nizam.

Mama Jamila was a maid-in-waiting. Mamas were often wet nurses or simply maids to royal ladies. They played an important role in palace affairs in Mughal history and later with the Asaf Jahs. The royal children often grew up under their influence and could seldom shake it off. Mama Jamila was an influential figure in court intrigues. She would often announce the nizam's decision to supplicants, and this included the allotment and cancellation of jagirs. Her word could not be cross-checked because the nizam could only be met by appointment, which usually took two weeks to get, while Mama Jamila met the nizam many times in a day. Often, she was the last one he saw before retiring to bed, and so hers was quite literally the last word.[4] The last of the triumvirate, Lala Bahadur, was the influential daftardar, and it was said that if the three got together to achieve a common aim, there was every chance that they would succeed.

Securing Salar Jung's appointment was an uphill task. The nizam held Salar Jung's family responsible for the cession of Berar, and he was not predisposed to appointing another minister from the same family who had 'done him an injury'. The coterie importuned their sovereign: 'It is not a Minister, but your prestige [ekbal], which governs. Suraj-ool-Moolk conducted the administration through the subordinate departments. Lala Bahadoor, who did everything, will as before conduct the affairs of the administration for Salar Jung. He is in every respect superior to his uncle.'[5] Their suggestions were met with disgust, personal reasons being cited for the nizam's disapproval. The coterie argued that since the post was a sinecure, it may as well be bestowed upon Salar Jung as upon any other person.

The *Madras Spectator* wrote:

A strong party near the Nizam, at the head of which are these— Burhan-ood-Deen, Mama Jemela and Lala Bahadoor—is putting forth all its energies, all its influence, and all its contrivances to procure the appointment for Salar Jung, the nephew of Suraj-ool-Moolk, a mere youth of under twenty-five years of age. The young gentleman who bears a fair reputation, is reluctant, with a judgement beyond his years, to accept the office, and although the Nizam has expressed strong objection to his employment, on the express ground of his having sustained injury from his relation the late Minister, his party has not relaxed its exertions, and pursue their object with an eagerness unrestrained by any fears of their master's resentment only to be accounted for by their knowledge of his caprice and the impressible power of repeated solicitations upon his Highness's mind.[6]

In the end, the coterie had its way. On 31 May 1853, the nizam appointed Salar Jung and Maharaja Narayan Pershad Narender Bahadur, Chandu Lal's grandson, as diwan and peshkar respectively. The peshkar was an Arabic scholar, and was also fully conversant with Sanskrit, Marathi and Telugu. Also present on the occasion were the resident and the assistant resident, Major Cuthbert Davidson, who would succeed Colonel Low in that post. It was expected that Salar Jung would act under the pupilage of Lala Bahadur, and Narender Pershad would be mentored by Raja Bal Mukund. By all accounts, the decision was the nizam's own, the resident not being taken into confidence. Before the nizam presented Salar Jung with his khillat, he obtained from Lala Bahadur his pledge and surety for the good conduct of the young diwan.

Writing about his elevation in a letter dated 1 June 1853 to Henry Dighton, Salar Jung observed:

On Monday evening, 30th May, I was unexpectedly ordered by His Highness to attend the Darbar the next day and to bring two *surpainches*, and also to write to the Resident and ask him to attend at the same time; and without any solicitation on my part or my grandmother's His Highness was pleased to confer the office of Dewan on me at the Darbar the day before yesterday and that of Peshkar on Rajah Narindher. I should have been quite content to remain in unmolested possession of my uncle's jaghirs, were it possible, without the cares which such an office would impose upon me, especially in the present critical state of affairs here, but I was advised by friends, European and Native, and with too much appearance of truth to reject the advice, that if I declined the office, myself and my family would be utterly ruined . . . I shall nevertheless, do my best with God's help to restore some order in the affairs of this country and endeavour to extricate the Government from its embarrassments.[7]

It was rumoured that Lala Bahadur had promised the nizam Rs 13 lakh in two months' time if he appointed Salar Jung as diwan. Another story was that Salar Jung had agreed to pay the nizam Rs 11 lakh in repayment of a debt taken by his uncle Siraj-ul-Mulk, and Rs 2.25 lakh as thanks for appointing him diwan. Lala Bahadur had been tasked with raising the latter amount for which he was forced to borrow the money from a local moneylender. The *Englishman* reported that the nizam had demanded Rs 11 lakh as a condition of his appointment.[8]

But these were just rumours. Salar Jung, in a memorandum written ten years after he had become diwan, explained the circumstances under which he obtained his office. After the death of his uncle, Salar Jung tells us that he had neither hopes of obtaining the diwani, nor was he anxious to get it. In any case, he was only twenty-four years old at the time. He also seems anxious to clarify that there was no way he could have lobbied for the position, given the circumstances.

> In other countries high appointments may have been conferred on young men, but such an idea as regards myself was far from my thought. However, on the following Saturday, His late Highness agitated the subject of my appointment, and while I was reflecting on the course I should pursue, most of my advisers here, as well as General Low, who was then Resident . . . recommended me to accept the office as a means for upholding the position of my family, which it was thought would otherwise be much impaired. I was therefore constrained to accept the offer, and on the Tuesday following, after the Durbar for the Resident, I was appointed. It will thus be clear from the above that in the space of three days, between Saturday and Tuesday, it was not possible that I could have succeeded by my own endeavours in obtaining the appointment.[9]

It was widely expected that Salar Jung would be a pliable puppet in the hands of the coterie. Observers cautioned against the perils of expecting a person invested with power to refrain from using it. They cited the example of Siraj-ul-Mulk's father, Munir-ul-Mulk, who was appointed diwan so as to preclude the vacant office from becoming an object of constant competition and intrigue. But the coterie had miscalculated in their choice of Salar Jung. He asserted himself almost from the start, a story which is told in the next chapter.

In 1854, Salar Jung married through a nikah ceremony, Hayat-un-Nissa Begum, daughter of Nawab Mir Ghulam Hussain Khan Fakhr-ul-Mulk I, one of the Umra-e-Uzzam, or one of the eleven chief nobles of the highest rank in the state. After marriage, she was given the name of Aziz-un-Nissa Begum Dulhan Pasha. In August 1854, the nizam presented Salar Jung with jewels to mark his marriage. He had two daughters by his nikah wife,

Noor-un-Nissa Begum, who was born in 1861 and who married Nawab Mukaram-ud-Daula, and Sultan Bakht Afroz Begum, who married Mir Dawar Ali Khan Bairam-ud-Daula, son of Mir Bahadur Ali Khan Satwant Jung. (There is some confusion about her date of birth. She was born either in 1865 or 1869.) There was none of the usual bias for a male child. Writing to an English friend, Captain Taylor, in 1856, Salar Jung said that he had not been blessed with a son but hoped that he would be the father of a son or daughter, and 'either would be equally agreeable to me'.[10]

Salar Jung's two sons, Laik Ali Khan (Salar Jung II) and Saadat Ali Khan, were not born of nikah marriages. They were born of different mothers, his concubines, six months apart in 1861 and 1862 respectively. Like many others, Salar Jung combined in himself contradictory elements of tradition and modernity, but this was an arrangement that was not regarded as exceptional at the time. It was perfectly normal for nobles to have mistresses, and this was the norm rather than the exception. He had nineteen concubines who were listed by his mother, Janaba Hazrata Zinat-un-Nissa Begum, when she wrote to the government asking for enhanced pensions. They included Wazir-un-Nissa Khanum, Salar Jung II's mother, and Amir-un-Nissa Khanum who was mother to Saadat Ali Khan, his younger brother. The other concubines had names like Nurafza Buwa, Dilruba Buwa, Khushkadam Buwa and Nanhi Bi.[11] Salar Jung was the first Muslim nobleman in India to educate his daughters in a manner which Europeans would consider a proper young woman's education. They had a French governess and could speak and write in both English and French. As we shall see later, his daughter and his wife sent him chatty letters when he visited Europe.

THE DIWAN DEODI

In the eighteenth and nineteenth centuries, nobles and wealthy men in Hyderabad lived in traditional fortified residences called *deodi*s. They were distinguished by their prominent main entrances, high enclosing walls and inner courtyards. There were a series of courtyards set apart for the public and private activities of the residents, ranging from the public enclosures for men, to the private quarters of the family, and the zenana of the women. Behind the deodi, lived a large number of servants and retainers.[12]

An important feature in Hyderabad was the large entrance which reflected the power and influence of its owner. The bigger and more elaborate the gate, the higher the status of its lord. Over a period of time, structures like a *khazana, toshakhana, mezkhana, farshkhana* and *bawarchikhana* were added. The deodis of Hyderabad were like self-contained townships in which the nobles lived with their extended families and a large retinue of servants, all guarded by armed men.[13] Chandu Lal, Maharaja Kishen Pershad and the hereditary daftardars, the Rai Rayans, had their large deodis in Shah Ali Banda, close to the Panch Mahalla Palace. The Malwalas, another hereditary daftardar family, lived close to Alijah Kotla.

Salar Jung resided in the diwan deodi which had been home to other diwans from his family as well. The red-and-white double-storey building was an important landmark in the walled city from the time it was built in the last quarter of the eighteenth century. Situated on the Charminar thoroughfare, on the south bank of the Musi river, its construction was started by Mir Alam when he became diwan. Successive diwans added buildings and structures, and the size and opulence of the deodi reflected the growing influence of the family. In its final form, the deodi occupied a whole block on the Paththargatti high road. It stretched from Chatta Bazaar to Mir Alam Mandi, and from the Charminar to the Purani Haveli.[14]

Though practically nothing remains of the deodi today apart from an imposing gate painted in white, the deodi was a hub of activity and the epicentre of power and influence, especially when Salar Jung was diwan. He worked from his deodi, and at any time of the day, elephants, horses and palanquins could be seen at the entrance. Vakils carried dispatches to and from the residency, and anxious petitioners and powerbrokers all waited in different parts of the deodi depending on their status. Busy arzbegees carried petitions back and forth, and the *chobdar*s with their long staffs announced visitors.

The sprawling palace complex had many gates, but the entrance on the side of Paththargatti was the one used regularly. A narrow passage connected the deodi from the Charminar thoroughfare. To the right, as one entered, were the reception rooms, screened from public view by red velvet curtains with green borders. Beyond the curtain was a formal courtyard which served as the main reception area. A large marble fountain played in the courtyard, and there were goldfish in the cisterns. Exquisite marble statuary stood all around. In its heyday, the apartments of the deodi were luxuriously furnished and full of rare objets d'art.

On one side of the courtyard was the famous *ainakhana* (Hall of Mirrors), the formal reception room of the deodi. Its columns and walls were covered with small coloured glass arranged in different shapes in the Persian style. True to its name, the walls of the hall had large mirrors. It had a number of gilt chairs upholstered in crimson velvet which had once belonged to George IV of England. Opposite the main hall was another room which was a smaller version of the ainakhana, and the two were connected by a banquet hall.[15] The ainakhana also housed a billiard table. Salar Jung played a fair game, and sometimes had a game with the resident and other visitors. Normally, he played with the marker before dinner. John Roberts Jr, the celebrated billiards player, visited Hyderabad in 1877 and received Rs 4000 from Salar Jung. William Cook and S.W. Stanley also played exhibition matches for an audience drawn from the residency and Secunderabad. Carlotta Patti, the famous soprano, sang here in 1880 and received Rs 1000 for her labours.

Close to the ainakhana to the east was a small room called *chinikhana*, or Chinese room, whose walls were covered with antique china plates and cups and saucers all arranged in various designs. Silver plates were displayed on the shelves, and it was this unique room that housed the famous marble sculpture, the *Veiled Rebecca*, which Salar Jung acquired in Rome during his visit to the Continent in 1876. Beyond the chinikhana, to the east was the treasury and next to this was the *diwankhana*, arranged in traditional style with a gold embroidered masnad and takhts worked in gold thread and canopies of silver. This was where Salar Jung held court.[16]

Lady Isabel Burton, wife of the famous explorer Sir Richard Burton, gives us a description of the deodi:

After inspecting the town we proceeded to the palace of Sir Salar Jung. We found him a noble, chivalrous, large-hearted Arab gentleman, of the very best stamp; and throughout our stay at Hyderabad he was most kind to us. His palace contained about seven courts with fountains, and was perfectly magnificent; but unfortunately, instead of being furnished with oriental luxury, which is so grand and rich, it was full of European things—glass, porcelain, and bad pictures. One room, however, was quite unique: the ceiling and walls were thickly studded with china—cups, saucers, plates, and so forth—which would have aroused the envy of any china-maniac in London. Sir Salar entertained us to a most luxurious breakfast, and when that was over showed us a splendid collection of weapons, consisting of swords, sheaths, and daggers, studded with gorgeous jewels. After that we inspected the stables, which reminded me somewhat of the Burlington Arcade, for they were open at both ends, and the loose boxes, where the shops would be, opened into a passage running down the centre. There were about a hundred thorough-bred Arab and Persian horses. When we left Sir Salar, he presented me with four bottles of attar of roses.[17]

To the west of the ainakhana was the library which had many rare books and manuscripts in Persian, Arabic, Turkish and Urdu. Salar Jung's grandson, Yousuf Ali Khan Salar Jung III, inherited some very rare and old books and manuscripts from his grandfather. There was a copy of the Koran dating back to AD 1283 which had the autographs of the Mughal emperors, Jehangir, Shah Jahan and Aurangzeb, and is today part of the Salar Jung Museum Library.

Monier Williams,[18] the Boden professor of Sanskrit at Oxford University who visited Hyderabad in 1875 and again in 1876, met Salar Jung and came away much impressed by his English. While praising both Sir T. Madhava Rao, the diwan at Baroda, and Salar Jung, he remarked: 'I conversed with both these great ministers not long since in their own houses [one at Hyderabad, and the other at Baroda], and found them capable of talking on all subjects in as good English as my own.'[19] He noted that Salar Jung had an extensive library, but his private study was small and plainly furnished with a few bookcases containing modern books of reference, chiefly in English. He also narrated how Salar Jung, on hearing that a deserving young Indian at Oxford was in need of assistance, assigned an annual allowance for his support, stipulating that he should be trained for the nizam's educational service. Other Indians studying in London received similar support.[20]

Above the chinikhana were the bedrooms which Salar Jung built. Though all the rooms were luxuriously appointed, one room in particular stood out. Furnished in white and gold, it had a cut-glass hand basin and toilet fittings. It was here that Mahbub Ali Khan, the sixth nizam, stayed for three days when he came to attend the wedding of Salar Jung's daughter. These rooms comprised the mardana, exclusively meant for men. Set apart from the mardana to the west was the zenana which comprised a series of two-storey apartments, sometimes joined together but each with its own courtyard meant exclusively for the ladies of the family. (During his time, Salar Jung III, the last occupant of the deodi, added a theatre to screen silent movies for his entertainment. It was a great novelty at the time.)

The zenana was a very traditional set-up, largely untouched by Western influence. The senior begums held court, received visitors and controlled the household. The women of the Salar Jung household were known for their dignity and strength of character, and had on more than one occasion used their influence to save Salar Jung's job when the nizam wanted to dismiss him.

As European influence increased at court, prominent citizens started to introduce elements of European lifestyle in their residences. Reception rooms with contemporary European furniture were added, and some even had billiards rooms and libraries stocked with English and French books. Suites with Western toilets were also introduced in the deodi, and a European visitor once observed that there was little difference between Salar Jung's deodi and a wealthy Englishman's residence.

Mirza Agha Beg, who was a tutor to Mahbub Ali Khan and later ennobled with the title of Server-ul-Mulk, gives us a glimpse into Salar Jung's daily routine in his autobiography.[21] After performing his morning ablutions, he used to say his morning prayers and recite the Koran. He would then receive the salutation of his servants, guards and other officials. He would appear on the upper veranda whilst his staff would stand in a line in the courtyard below. On a signal from the head chobdar, they would bow and touch their foreheads thrice with their right hand. After accepting the morning salutation, he would go to the garden where horses would be kept ready for his morning ride. A few of his favourite companions, and, at times, his two sons would accompany him. On occasion, he went out of the city towards Sarurnagar. Salar Jung owned some outstanding horses, many of them Arabs. (When the poet and famous traveller in the Middle East, Wilfrid Scawen Blunt visited Hyderabad, Salar Jung's son, Laik Ali Khan Salar Jung II, showed him his late father's horses. A vociferous opponent of imperialism, Blunt is famous today for introducing the Arab horse into England.)

Although Salar Jung had six shikar elephants which he loaned to Europeans fond of the sport, he himself never considered that pastime worth the candle. His personal elephant was called 'Khudadad', and Salar Jung's guests were allowed to ride it to get a good view of Hyderabad over the crowds. What he did take great interest in was horticulture, and he showed visitors his gardens with great pride.

The diwan deodi hummed with activity, and from morning till midnight, nobles, officials, mansabdars and aspirants to offices and other petitioners came and went in a steady stream. Depending on the time available, an hour or half an hour was allotted for each interview. Those who came from the districts and talukas were also given a time on which to call. In case a person came on a different day, or at a time other than that allotted to him, Fakir Mohamed, the head chobdar, would turn him away. A dark-complexioned man who was bent almost double with age, he wore a turban and carried a staff in his hand. He ruled despotically and many resented his overbearing attitude, but he had Salar Jung's full support.

Any breach of etiquette or improper behaviour, of which he was the sole judge, would evoke a public rebuke which was both vocal and sharp. On occasion, he also used his staff to point out to a person the error of his ways. Status was no bar for him, and on one occasion, he rebuked Rafik-Yar-ud-Daula, an eminent officer and jagirdar, when he removed his turban, telling him that he was at the minister's palace and not his grandmother's house![22] The chobdars, including Fakir Mohamed, were not above having their palms greased, and Server-ul-Mulk had to part with Rs 50 on two occasions before he got his interviews with Salar Jung. It is difficult to believe that Salar Jung did not know what was going on. Presumably, he chose to turn a blind eye.

Whenever Salar Jung went for an official visit to the royal court or to meet the resident, it was in an elaborate procession. The convoy was led by eight to ten camel riders in red uniforms. The cavalry unit in red livery with a pennant and a band followed them. Next, there were white-uniformed cavalry. Drummers and hundreds of Arabs armed with muskets were behind them. Salar Jung was accompanied by his close companions on horseback, and the party was followed by men with lances and matchlocks. If Salar Jung chose to ride an elephant, spear-bearing soldiers covered both flanks.[23]

The ainakhana served as a reception room for those of higher rank; the gallery accommodated the secretaries and heads of departments who were waiting for an interview. The members of the nobility generally met the diwan by appointment. Learned men from various religious denominations were allotted a special time, and Salar Jung used to leave the masnad whenever he received such visitors. He received numerous visitors, all differing in status and position, but the treatment given to them all was such that each one of them left believing that he had been specially favoured.

A rule which Salar Jung followed was that officials and other servants who served from father to son in the palace were retained so that they might not be deprived of their hereditary rights. He was also very particular that those servants whose domicile was outside the Deccan should have nothing to do with his private dealings or with the nizam's palace. While he was fully aware of the talent available outside Hyderabad, he thought it impossible for an outsider to have the 'same sympathy as those who, from father to son were serving the State'. He, as we shall see later, was more than willing to utilize their knowledge and experience in administrative matters. Another rule that was strictly followed was that no diwani official was allowed to see the resident or any other noble of the Paigah family without special permission. This was just as well, given the scheming and intriguing which bedevilled Salar Jung's entire tenure as diwan.

Despite the despotic Fakir Mohamed, Salar Jung remained accessible to all, irrespective of rank. Petitioners were free to seek an audience and place their requests before him. The Persian language was always used in all official matters. With the exception of private correspondence which was in English, Persian was used in all administrative matters and in official correspondence with the resident. An English office was kept for ordinary private and friendly correspondence under the charge of Henry Bowen, an Anglo-Indian, who was called the private secretary, and two copyists. This office was mainly concerned with such matters as requests for elephants, horses and carriages, with making appointments for interviews or issuing invitations for banquets and giving permission for shikar.[24] It had nothing to do with administrative affairs. The Persian office was called *Daftar-e-Mulki* (Home Affairs), and its secretary was Munshi Mohamed Siddeek. He was a master of Persian prose and had daily interviews with the diwan.

Salar Jung zealously protected the dignity of the sovereign, sometimes even going to absurd lengths for this purpose. On one occasion, when a mansabdar called the nizam a 'big child', Salar Jung inflicted a fine and the man was banned from the durbar. Tahniyat Yavar-ud-Daula, a noble, and the arzbegee were specially empowered to remove anyone from the court on grounds of misbehaviour, regardless of rank or position. Salar Jung never sat before the nizam unless specifically told to do so. He also ensured that no European or Anglo-Indian official behaved impolitely or even freely in his presence. All such persons, with the exception of military officers, were allowed in his presence without shoes and with bared heads. Initially, no European was allowed to sit: requests were made standing and then the petitioner left.

Salar Jung also made it a point to converse only in Urdu with all officials. Even when he discussed political affairs with the resident, it was only in Urdu. In his thinking, the resident would get the upper hand of him in any discussion held in English, but in Urdu he thought that the advantage lay with him. Also, Salar Jung was known to take his own decisions with regard to appointments, especially when the appointment was of a European. While he gave credence to the views of the resident and assistant resident, he was a little chary of accepting the views of the Government of India. When the regular force was formed, he selected Colonel Neville over the recommendation of the government. Similarly, when a tutor was needed for the young nizam, Mahbub Ali Khan, he sent for Captain John Clerk from England to oversee his education and selected Arthur Oliphant to succeed Henry Bowen as his private secretary.

However, in all important matters connected with the nizam or the royal palace, Salar Jung always consulted the Paigah noble Fakhr-ud-din Khan Shums-ul-Umra II Amir-i-Kabir. Narsing Rao played the part of vakil (confidential intermediary) and was in constant touch with the diwan. The Amir-i-Kabir was a very likeable and popular figure in Hyderabad, and was affectionately called 'Manjlay Mian'. A learned man who was well versed in mathematics, he was also a master of Arabic and Persian literature. His interest in the natural sciences and in astronomy led him to build an observatory with modern instruments, which it was said, he himself could operate. Generous and polite, he was universally loved and admired.

As far as the central treasury and accounts were concerned, only Hindus having members of families who were connected to the state for generations were employed to work there. Among the Hindus, it was the kayasthas who were generally entrusted with this responsibility. Every night as the clock struck the midnight hour, Pattapi Rama Rao, and before him his father, would present the register of the central treasury to Salar Jung who would put his signature on the last item of the day, thus closing the accounts for the day.

Salar Jung brought the same efficiency to the running of his household. Every department had a statement prepared of the monthly expenditure and a strict watch kept on budgeted expenditure. Siddi Ambar, his Sudanese housekeeper, managed the household apart from the *mahallat* (ladies' apartment) which was managed by Salar Jung's mother herself. There is an interesting story associated with Siddi Ambar, who had been with the family since he was a child. He became a trusted aide, and Salar Jung's sons called him 'bhai' (brother).

After Salar Jung's death, his eldest son, Laik Ali Khan, was concerned about where he would get the money to buy the jewellery for his younger sister's wedding. The legend goes that Siddi Ambar asked him to take care of the ceremonies and he would produce the jewels. Sure enough, he brought a tray full of jewels and asked Laik Ali to select what he wanted. Not a word was said as to from where the jewels had been procured or about the payment to be made for them. Not long after, Laik Ali died, leaving a very young son, Yousuf Ali Khan, who was barely a month old at the time. When Siddi Ambar lay dying, he sent for Yousuf, who by then was a young boy, saying he had something to give him, but his mother Zainab Begum Saheb refused to send him. Siddi Ambar then sent a set of keys to Yousuf and died soon after. No one knew what the keys fit, and the jewels were never seen again. The family believed that the keys secured the jewels.[25]

Salar Jung was a generous man which explains why he was often in debt. Even though the running of the household was based on principles of sound economy, the dignity of his position was never compromised. Server-ul-Mulk gives us an example of noblesse oblige related to him by Salar Jung himself.

> One day when I attended on him, I perceived a basket made of coconut leaves placed close to the 'Masnad', which contained a few marble curios of Agra workmanship. Noticing signs of astonishment on my face, he smiled and said that that was the fine which he had to pay for his position as Minister. An Englishman had come to see him, and had brought these curios as presents, and had then sent a bill for Rs. 5,000 which he had to pay.[26]

Server-ul-Mulk also narrates an incident which shows that Salar Jung found it difficult to raise large sums of money for his personal use. The nizam was in residence at the Golconda fort, and Salar Jung too was in residence at his ancestral home there. Server-ul-Mulk noticed that the house was in a dilapidated condition and observed that it needed repairs. The diwan's reply surprised him since he 'asked where he was to get the money, for the *Darogah* [manager] had put in an estimate of Rs. 3,000'.[27]

It is said that Salar Jung fed a number of people every day, and people flocked to him with requests for jobs, quick justice and financial help. No one who asked for help was ever turned down, with, it is said, one notable exception. Ghalib, the famous poet of Delhi, once wrote to him asking for financial help. The poet, who lived beyond his means, was always deep in debt. Ghalib wrote a *qasida* in honour of Salar Jung, expecting a large donation. But his request came at a time when Salar Jung was in mourning. His father-in-law, Nawab Fakhr-ul-Mulk I, had passed away, and a whole year of mourning had just been announced. After the mourning period ended, Salar Jung forgot about the request.[28] In the end, poor Ghalib received nothing. It was possibly the only occasion when Salar Jung had failed to respond to a call for help.

THE LAKKAD KOT

An interesting addition to the deodi was the *baradari*, which was unique to Hyderabad. The word 'baradari' literally means twelve doors, and has its origins in the Qutub Shahi period. An example of a baradari built during that period is the Taramati baradari which is a single large room built on a hillock with arches on all sides. Nobles like Chandu Lal and Salar Jung built their baradaris outside city limits, either in a garden or overlooking a waterbody. Chandu Lal's baradari was set in a garden, and Salar Jung's baradari, the Lakkad Kot, was built on the banks of the Musi river. Chandu Lal's baradari was said to have been specially built to entertain Nizam Ali Khan. Maha Laqa Bai Chanda, the famous dancer and poetess of Hyderabad, is said to have danced here for the minister and the nizam.[29] In later years, the baradaris were built next to the deodis in the city itself; the baradari of the Paigah noble, Khurshed Jah, and the baradari of Erram Manzil built by Salar Jung's brother-in-law, Nawab Fakhr-ul-Mulk II, being two good examples.

The Lakkad Kot was Salar Jung's favourite haunt. To the east of the diwan deodi was the Chatta Bazaar, and over the bazaar was an arch which acted as a bridge connecting the deodi to a garden. It was in this garden overlooking the Musi river that the structure called Lakkad Kot was situated. It was a three-storey wooden structure, set in a terraced garden with fountains and a large reservoir. Its carved wooden arches, delicately patterned *jharokha*s, airy rooms and spacious halls made it an ideal place to relax and entertain. It was cool throughout the year, and it was this charming structure that Salar Jung repaired to when he wanted to escape the hustle and bustle of court affairs. His prospect was all light and air and pleasure, with the sky reflected in the water.

The Lakkad Kot was used extensively for both private and public entertaining. It was the venue for many banquets which Salar Jung threw on behalf of the nizam. Salar Jung was a connoisseur of good food and enjoyed all types of cuisine. Darogah Abdul Wahab was the manager of his kitchen. His private invitations were infrequent and given to a select few (usually to his special English friends whom he invited to breakfast). But his official dinners were marked with a lavishness and pomp which astounded his guests.

Salar Jung took his entertaining seriously and was an attentive host. A table for his English guests was beautifully decorated and could seat as many as 500 guests. Salar Jung sat with the resident at the head of the table. A separate spread for his Indian guests was readied in another hall opposite the first one. All state officials and his personal acquaintances were invited to his parties. At the time of departure, Salar Jung would bid his guests goodbye at the entrance, offering them long attar bottles. Server-ul-Mulk recounts in his autobiography:

At the time of departure the Minister would again go to the door, and standing there, offer long scent-bottles—to some a dozen, to another ten, to another two and to another one, according to rank—and bid his guests good-bye. At first I used to get two [of] these; but later they were increased to five, and finally to nine.[30]

Salar Jung was always dignified, courteous and correct but never familiar or warm in official parties. It was obvious to the discerning that he was performing a duty. An English journalist who happened to attend the official reception in December 1875 to welcome Sir Richard Meade at Salar Jung's residence spoke of Salar Jung:

. . . smiling that pleasant smile of his peculiar to himself among all men . . . [On receiving the guests] when His Excellency shakes hands with you, how is it that he directs his eyes clean over your head? Is it to show that the deed he is performing is an act of official courtesy and not of personal friendship? You individually are nothing, but the uniform you wear shows you to be a servant of the Empress of India, and so you are a welcome guest of her 'Faithful Ally' [the Nizam]![31]

Hyderabadi hospitality was at its best particularly when foreigners were in attendance. It was remarked by English officials that such elaborate banquets were not seen even in Europe. Lady Isabel Burton gives us a glimpse into a party chez Salar Jung:

> Our last recollections of Hyderabad were brilliant, for Sir Salar Jung gave a magnificent evening *fête*. One of the large courts of the palace was illuminated: the starlight was above us, the blaze of wax lights and chandeliers lit up every hall around the court, and coloured lamps and flowers were everywhere . . . We had a most delicious dinner afterwards, at which we were waited on by retainers in wild, picturesque costumes. When that was over, the band played. We walked about and conversed, were presented with attar of roses, and went home.[32]

Mir Moazam Husain, who served as second talukdar in Gulbarga and was in his own words 'a member of the integrated Salar Jung, Khan Khanan and Fakhr-ul-Mulk family',[33] observes:

> Mukhtar-ul-Mulk dispensed hospitality lavishly at Lakerkot, his wooden wonder-lodge ensconced in lush surroundings on the Musi . . . When I used to go to the Lakerkot in the 1920s, it still charmed though on its last legs. The artistry in timber of the finest grain boggled the mind. Its intricately carved ceiling and chiselled pillars and its superbly planned layout would have been the envy of a Kublai Khan.[34]

The English painter, Val Prinsep, visited Hyderabad in 1877, and the young nizam, Mahbub Ali Khan, and Salar Jung sat for him. The Calcutta-born Prinsep seems to have been well acquainted with the goings-on in Hyderabad and wrote knowledgeably about Salar Jung and the Berar question. He also describes his visits to the deodi and his breakfasting with Salar Jung on five consecutive mornings. After his morning session with the nizam, it seems that he was Salar Jung's guest for breakfast, and during these visits also painted his portrait.

> Everybody in London is familiar with that tall sad-looking man, with his small white turban and simple long black or dark cloth coat. Everybody agrees that Sir Salar is the best dressed native in India . . . I must say

that both in appearance and manners he is quite the polished gentleman. To every one he is most polite and courteous, and to me he was most friendly. As I breakfasted with him five consecutive mornings, I saw a great deal of him, and all that I saw I liked.[35]

Prinsep described the deodi as 'an irregular pile of buildings without any architectural elevation whatever'. The place where he painted Salar Jung was entirely English, with pictures, books and furniture which one would find in any wealthy Englishman's home. There was also a gallery of paintings which does not seem to have impressed Prinsep. He was also a little put off with his host constantly soliciting his opinion on the paintings exhibited. 'He has an embarrassing way of saying, "And what do you think of that picture?" otherwise I always enjoyed my visit to him very much.'[36]

This was not, however, the first occasion on which Salar Jung had sat for his portrait. In 1871, the artist of the Portrait Gallery of Western India in Poona, Theodore Jensen, had painted the portraits of not only Salar Jung but also the Paigah nobles, Rashid-ud-din Khan Vikar-ul-Umra who went on to become Amir-i-Kabir III, Khurshed Jah who became Amir-i-Kabir IV, and Bashir-ud-Daula, the future Sir Asman Jah. Salar Jung's example, it can be presumed, must have influenced the more conservative nobles to overcome the old orthodox bias against images.

Salar Jung's period as diwan also marked the golden period of the deodi, which never regained its earlier glory under succeeding residents. Salar Jung's son, Laik Ali Khan Salar Jung II, did add sections to the old deodi but he lived there only for a short period. In his grandson Salar Jung III's time, the deodi started resembling a warehouse with art pieces strewn everywhere.

The Lakkad Kot was pulled down along with the main deodi in the mid-1970s. It had suffered much damage when the Musi was in spate during the great flood of 1908 and had to undergo extensive repairs. By that time, some of the buildings were already in a state of neglect. A small section of the baradari which was used as an outhouse has survived, and its Shah Jahani arches and carved woodwork allow the viewer to form an impression of the beauty of the original building. Unfortunately, nothing has been done to preserve it.

3

Early Reforms

Hyderabad was founded as a military aristocracy with its ruling class being dominated by north Indians who had accompanied the first nizam to the Deccan. By the beginning of the nineteenth century, the state had become a Mughal civil bureaucracy. Later, the British resident and the Hyderabad Contingent also became part of the equation.

THE POLITICAL SYSTEM

The two main territorial divisions of land in Hyderabad were jagir and khalisa. The jagir was a tenure common in Hyderabad in which the public revenue of a given tract of land was made over to a servant of the state, along with the powers to enable him to collect the revenue and administer the territory so assigned. The jagir lands were of different types: Al-Tamgha which were permanent and hereditary grants; zat jagirs which were personal; Paigah which were assigned to the nobility in lieu of levying a certain number of troops;[1] *tankhahi mahalat*, the assignment of villages in lieu of certain state debts or advances made to government or for the pay of offices, establishment and troops; and sarf-i-khas or crown jagirs which were assigned to the nizam.

The second territorial division called khalisa or diwani, where the revenue remained with the government. It was under the administration of the diwan, hence the name diwani. When Salar Jung became diwan, the territory left under the direct management of the diwan was very small. A large part of the khalisa lands were in the possession of the Arab military chiefs in lieu of payments for the troops. These lands were later redeemed from a descendant of the original creditor, and many zat jagirs were resumed, owing either to their possessors not having valid titles or lapsing to the state due to the failure of heirs.

The word khalisa, as applied to lands, consisted of lands paying revenue, peshkash or quit-rent to the government. Bilmakta was a sole tenure in which the quit-rent was fixed and peshkash was a tax, tribute or quit-rent, a kind of present to the ruling power on receiving an appointment or assignment of revenue or on the renewal of a grant or title. The most important of these was the khalisa proper, which yielded land revenue and was characterized by the absence of middlemen.

The sarf-i-khas, or crown lands, consisted of, among others, an entire district surrounding Hyderabad, two talukas in Bidar and Aurangabad, one in Nanded, four in Naldurg and a few villages in Gulbarga, Medak and some other places. These were taken under the immediate management of the nizam. The revenues from these lands were meant exclusively for the nizam and his family. Expenses for the palace and the payment of annuities to the nizam's blood relations were made from these revenues. The nizam's dominions were divided into subas (provinces) which included a number of *circars* (districts), which again were broken up into subdivisions. The diwani was divided into five *simt*s, or divisions; each simt included three or four *zilla*s, and each zilla was in turn divided into talukas.

Before Salar Jung became diwan, the official business of the government was conducted in two offices, the Daftar-i-Mal and Daftar-i-Diwani. Both of these were under the supervision of daftardars who kept the state accounts and registers of grants of jagirs, with the administration being entirely in the hands of the diwan. The Dar-ul-Insha attended to the official correspondence of the diwan. In the districts, there were no public offices of any kind, and it was the talukdars who employed subordinates and clerks to help them collect revenue, but no public records were maintained.

In Hyderabad, there were three courts of justice: the Dar-ul-Qaza and the Sadarat-ul-Aliya were civil courts, whereas the third, the Kotwali, was the police court. There were no courts of justice in the mofussil. During Chandu Lal's time, the Adalat-i-Diwani and the Adalat-i-Faujdari were established. In the time of Raja Ram Bakhsh, a court of justice presided over by four moulvis was established, but its jurisdiction did not extend beyond Hyderabad. During the first ministry of Siraj-ul-Mulk, Salar Jung's uncle, the Adalat-i-Diwankhana was established in the metropolis, and some courts of justice presided over by *munsif*s and *mir adal*s established in the

mofussil areas. Over a period of time, these fell into disuse, and by the time
he was appointed diwan again, they had almost disappeared. As far as the
mofussil was concerned, the talukdars were the only government officers,
and most of the present departments and institutions were established by
Salar Jung.[2]

The land revenue from the state or khalisa lands was collected by revenue
farmers called talukdars. They received contracts from the state record
keepers, the daftardars, to collect the revenue from specified districts, and
paid into the treasury the amount stipulated in their contracts. Lands were
also given to nobles as jagirs for their personal income or the maintenance
of troops. Tributary zamindars who were large landholders also contributed
some income, even though their territories were exempted from direct state
control. Other sources of income included taxes on commercial activities,
market taxes and customs duties.[3]

The disbursements by the government largely consisted of payment of
salaries and allowances to its employees and dependants. Those performing
clerical duties received monthly cash stipends which were usually hereditary
ones. High-ranking nobles received cash allowances to maintain troops or
were given land which provided equivalent revenue. Salary disbursements
to the military men led by their jemadars or commanders, the attendants,
musicians, palace guards and relatives of the nizam comprised some of the
other payments. By the 1830s, the expenses of the Hyderabad Contingent
had also become considerable.[4]

Bankers played an important role in Hyderabad politics, involved as
they were in a complex relationship which went beyond moneylending and
trade. Apart from the Gujaratis and Marwaris, those involved in banking
included Europeans, Eurasians and Parsis. William Palmer and Company
had close links with Gujarati bankers; in fact, William Palmer's partner,
Benkati Das, was a Gujarati. Henry Dighton, an Englishman who started
his career with William Palmer and Company, later became a banker and
revenue contractor in Hyderabad. The firm of Pestonjee Viccajee, headed
by Parsi brothers from Bombay, was a major creditor from 1835 to 1845.

Pestonjee Viccajee's land assignments were reclaimed, and although
Pestonjee fought the state troops by recruiting mercenary Rohillas and
also asked the East India Company for help, his time was up. The firm
went bankrupt in 1848. Puran Mal, another very prominent banker, also
suffered a similar fate, at least temporarily, when he faced a liquidity
problem in 1851.

Since the land revenue only provided seasonal income, the government depended heavily on sahukars to make good the shortfall. The major bankers played an important role in the political system because granting and withholding a loan had a powerful effect on the political standing of an individual or on the viability of a diwan's administration. They also controlled the minting of currency, either through their own mints or those they administered for the government.

According to Karen Leonard, Chandu Lal had come to power with the help of the sahukars, and stayed in power because of his ability to command credit. The political intrigues which followed his resignation produced a financial crisis and resulted in the assigning of Berar. The bankers were heavily involved in these intrigues. Chandu Lal was financed by an informal coalition of bankers called the Panch Bhai, or Five Brothers. The members of this group changed, but two firms which definitely figured in this list were those of Makhdum Seth, a Muslim of Begum Bazaar, and the Gujarati firm of Seth Kishan Das of Karwan Sahu. The famous Palmer and Company, of which we will hear more of in later chapters, was also a major lender to Chandu Lal. Most of these firms were Hindu and from outside Hyderabad. The great firms of the time belonged to three major communities: Gujaratis, Gosain and Marwari, but as already noted, the Europeans, Eurasians and Parsis were also involved in the banking business of Hyderabad.

What is significant is that the bankers were closely involved with high civil and military officials and the talukdars. In fact, government officials in the first half of the nineteenth century did not keep separate independent records of the loans received from the bankers. The bankers kept these records which were signed by the officials and used by the government when necessary. The records of Berar handed over to the British were in fact those kept by the Parsi banker, Pestonjee.

The firms dealt in *hundi*s or bills of exchange payable elsewhere on sight (*darshani*) or after a certain date. They also disbursed cash for local expenses, such as the expenses of the nizam's household, or salaries of the military troops in the city. Loans were also given to talukdars who used the money for an offering (nazarana) to the record keepers or daftardars to secure contracts for revenue collection. As guarantee, the bankers received bonds or guarantees of repayment, diamonds and gold given in mortgage. Land from which they could collect revenue and repay themselves was also given with increasing frequency.

Most bankers employed Arab and Pathan mercenaries as personal bodyguards and to also act as their agents in the collection of revenue. The military commanders also received land grants of their own from the government when it was unable to pay their salaries. The talukdars and the military commanders both collected land revenue, often in excess of what their contract specified, and grew wealthy enough to become major creditors of the state.

While successive diwans repeatedly took loans from these bankers, they were seldom repaid. When land assignments could not be made directly, a coalition of bankers was given an order on a talukdar who would be responsible for quarterly repayments of their loan. Loans were also given 'by discount' where the entire interest was deducted at the time of lending. If repayment was not made on time, the state had to pay the interest again. *Jokhum* chitties (the name itself signifying the risky nature of the loan, jokhum meaning risk) were guarantees of payments by a powerful official on behalf of the government given to a banker, and were used when the creditor was not powerful enough to ensure payment from the government on his own. This official for some time was Lala Bahadur, the influential daftardar, and on one occasion, the bankers even tried to get the British resident to become a guarantor.[5] But by 1850, it was said that three-fourths of the country had been assigned to the Arabs and Pathans, and the bankers had taken a back seat.[6]

THE DAFTARDARS

The financial responsibilities of the diwan were delegated to subordinates called peshkars and daftardars. They handled the diwan's correspondence and kept financial records, particularly those pertaining to land revenue. By the end of the eighteenth century, two daftardar families had assumed control of the land revenue records. They presided over two central records offices. The first was the Daftar-i-Diwani, which was linked to the Maharashtrian Brahmin family called the Rai Rayan family. The second, called Daftar-i-Mal, was held by a Mathur family known as the Malwalas, or 'those of the land revenue'. By the end of the eighteenth century, both these families ranked in the nobility.[7]

The two daftars handled land revenue contracts and other financial arrangements for the nizam. Income came mainly from land revenue from the talukas which had been farmed out to contractors, nazarana or tribute presented to the nizam, and loans and deposits from moneylenders. However, the daftars had no record of the amounts the contractors actually collected. They had on record only the revenue contractors, the area assigned to them and the estimated revenue. The contracts were awarded annually. The contractors kept their own records or none at all. In any case, the figure which the daftardars recorded as the amount of land revenue was quite different from the amounts actually collected.

Since land revenue collection was seasonal in nature and its remittance uncertain, there was also dependence on other sources of revenue. Contracts awarded for the collection of revenue, confirmation of succession to property and other official appointments all required varying amounts of tributes from applicants. While these nazaranas were a steady source of income for the nizam's household establishment, of greater importance were the loans from moneylenders. The daftardars negotiated the terms for the loans and kept records. Thus they were more in the nature of negotiators and brokers between those who controlled or collected resources and those who needed cash.

Over time, the political power of the daftardars grew considerably as record keepers at all levels, and they became key figures because they decided the priority for disbursing money. More importantly, their records were essential to financial juggling. The personal knowledge of the daftardars was also greatly valued, for they knew reclaiming whose land would benefit the state most, or who would make the most efficient revenue collector. By the 1840s, they had become vital intermediaries in financial negotiations. When Chandu Lal resigned in 1843, he took the official records with him as family property, hoping to force the appointment of his son or nephew as diwan. At that time, only the daftardars possessed the financial information which successive diwans needed.[8]

Of all the daftardars, the most remarkable was the Malwala kayastha, Raja Ram Pershad Lala Bahadur.[9] He assumed supervision of the Malwala daftar in the 1830s, and well before Chandu Lal's resignation had assumed control of some of his financial functions. After Chandu Lal's resignation, he emerged as the most powerful figure in the state. It was he who authorized payments and loan arrangements during the period 1843–46 when there was no diwan. When the nizam finally accepted Siraj-ul-Mulk (who had the resident's support) as diwan in

1846, he found Lala Bahadur to be his chief opponent. Those who had dealt with the diwan had now got used to transacting business with the daftardar, and Lala Bahadur came to represent all those who feared the reforms proposed by successive diwans and the resident. These reforms included dismissal of troops, redemption of lands and checks on the authenticity of jagirs.

When Fakhr-ud-din Khan Shums-ul-Umra II Amir-i-Kabir succeeded Siraj-ul-Mulk as diwan in 1849, there was a confrontation with Lala Bahadur. The diwan refused to accept his revenue statements, calling them false. He then discovered, to his chagrin, that revenue contractors accepted contracts only from the daftardars: sources of credit were available only when the daftardars served as intermediaries. Declaring that he could not obtain a satisfactory revenue statement from the principal daftardar, Shums-ul-Umra II reportedly confiscated the Malwala's customary fees and jagirs.[10] But this show of strength ended in failure. No confiscation actually took place, and a little later, it was Shums-ul-Umra II who resigned. In 1850, the nizam tried to be his own diwan and direct the administration himself, but nothing came of it.

When Siraj-ul-Mulk became diwan once again in 1851, his attempt to sideline the daftardars in dealings with the moneylenders failed because the latter declared that they would discuss such matters with Lala Bahadur alone. One moneylender who agreed to lend money on the daftardar's pledge refused to lend money to the diwan.[11] However, there seems to have been some diminution in the power of the daftardars because when two years later the cession of Berar took place, the daftardars were present only to provide details of the land assigned.

But Lala Bahadur was far from being a spent force. He still enjoyed the confidence of the nizam and was able to influence the choice of the next diwan, Salar Jung, who was selected precisely because he was thought to be a weak candidate. Lala Bahadur expected him to be a puppet, entirely under his influence. He was to get a rude shock, for Salar Jung showed from the beginning that he was his own man. Salar Jung had formed his own ideas about administration, and had not been hesitant in communicating them to his uncle. Now at the helm of affairs by the miscalculation of the coterie who placed him there, Salar Jung went on to establish a new political and economic order for Hyderabad in the three decades that he was in charge.

AN UNENVIABLE INHERITANCE

When Salar Jung assumed office, the government was in deep debt. The sahukars extended loans to the government at extortionate rates of interest. The assigning of Berar had created new claims, with those who were dispossessed of their jagirs claiming compensation from the government. This ranged from Rs 5 lakh to Rs 30 lakh. Salaries of the mansabdars and nizam's relatives remained unpaid, and even the nizam himself was a claimant. Salar Jung gradually paid off the sahukars. This was the beginning of a relationship of trust between the sahukars and Salar Jung which resulted in an improvement in the creditworthiness of the government in their eyes.

The trust that the sahukars reposed in Salar Jung can be gauged from the fact that they agreed to release the nizam's large diamond even before the debts had been paid. Afzal-ud-Daula, suspicious as usual, said he had heard that the diamond had been replaced with one of lesser value. Salar Jung assured him that its very size was a guarantee of its safety, since stones a quarter of its size were difficult to find.[12] The total debt of the state at the time was about Rs 2.7 crore. Another serious difficulty was the claims made on the government on forged documents. Even former diwans, Chandu Lal and Ram Bakhsh, had no qualms about antedating and affixing the official seal on documents, which gave its holders a claim on the government which had no foundation in reality.

Perhaps the worst evil, and one from which all the others flowed, was the system of anticipating the public revenue and of farming it from year to year to the highest bidder, thereby producing a succession of collectors of revenue over whom there was no check. In many instances, they appointed irresponsible and inefficient deputies whose only interest was in extorting money from the cultivator in order to be prepared for the exactions which could at any time be levied on them by the government itself.

The misery and oppression of the lower classes, and the insecurity of life and property was all too obvious. Both agriculture and the collection of land revenue suffered under this system, but the nizam was in favour of the status quo. Another pernicious aspect of this system was the *batai* system in which revenue was collected in kind, and which proved to be against the interest of both the cultivator and the government. The farmers were not allowed to harvest the crop until the yield had been inspected and security for payment obtained. Apart from offering great scope for harassment of cultivators, this system was a disincentive for any improvements in cultivation.

Law and order was another problem. The Arab, the Rohilla and the Sikh mercenary bands that were armed to the teeth constituted other power centres. For half a century, the countryside had been dominated by the Arabs and Rohillas, mostly disbanded mercenaries from the Maratha and Pindari armies. Like the other Indian princes during the eighteenth century, the nizams had employed Arab soldiers. As the disorder in the state increased, so did the employment of Arabs. When their numbers and power increased, so did their ability to foment trouble.

In the late eighteenth century, Hyderabad became the centre of large-scale Arab immigration. Most of these Arabs were from Hadhramaut, Yemen. The region had a long history of migration to Asia and Africa, with the people leaving Hadhramaut to engage in trade, to work as soldiers or to spread Islamic learning. It was not uncommon to find Arabs in multiple roles: they were traders, warriors and Sufi saints.[13] By the middle of the nineteenth century, the city attracted Hadhramis both from Yemen and within India, and a large body of Arabs were domiciled in Hyderabad. They enjoyed high positions in the nizam's administration as soldiers, administrators and scholars. The nizam had a large force of Arab soldiery that traced its origin to these parts.

Many Arabs married and settled in Hyderabad, and the word *mowullud* was used for their descendants. The Arabs were of two kinds. The true Arabs, *asal*, who were either born in Arabia or of Arabian parents, possessed many martial qualities, and were known for their courage, endurance and skill in fighting, especially under some kind of cover. Many Arabs married and settled in Hyderabad, and the word mowullud was used for their descendants. The mowullud were those born of Arab fathers and Indian mothers, and had the same characteristics as the asals, though toned down.[14] These Indian Arabs forged strong links with Hyderabad and Hadhramaut, and as we shall see later, this meant that they were also drawn into the factional politics and wars in their homeland. Hyderabad had four different classes of Arabs: those who had undergone military training and were enrolled in the regular levies of the nizam's government; undrilled Arab infantry who worked for the government; private guards of the nobility; and, finally, those who did not work for anyone. There were more than 8000 Arabs in the state, and most were Deccan born.[15] The British called them 'Indian Arabs', a new category coined to describe those who resided in Hyderabad with family and connections in Arabia, a categorization which was accompanied by a negative stereotype which attributed all corruption and lawlessness in society to them.

The men were under the jemadars who paid them regardless of whether the chiefs received their grants from the treasury or were given assignments on the revenue of districts, called in consequence, the *tankhwah* (pay) talukas. The army was raised, paid, mustered, equipped and accounted for by the military chiefs. Between the jemadar and the men was an officer called *chaus*. The British intervened, asking the nizam to control the Arabs, who had become licentious and refractory. The Arabs were then controlled to an extent but still remained very powerful. Successive nizams had allowed the Arab troops to grow in a manner which made the Arab chiefs very wealthy, apart from giving them control over territory. Arab chiefs were contracted for supplying a certain number of men and for paying them. When the pay of these men fell into arrears, they were given a mortgage on the land revenue of a district which was made over to them, and they garrisoned it with their men. This invested them with dangerous power and often inflicted misrule on the districts.

When a capable military chief was entrusted with the management of a district, it resulted in the establishment of a comparatively efficient feudal system, but when he received a lump sum, and settled with his men in his own manner, anything resembling a military organization was destroyed. This practice also encouraged the existence of a paper army. The principal jemadars were Abdulla bin Ali Saif-ud-Daula, an old man who was said to be immensely rich; jemadar Jan-Baz Jung Bahadur Omer-bin-Oud, another elderly chief; his mowullud son, Barak Jung, also very rich, and favourably disposed to the British; and Ghalib-bin-Almas Ghalib Jung, a mowullud leader of advanced age. Some lands had been made over to Omer-bin-Oud as a guarantee for pecuniary obligations. A large part of these tankhwah jagirs which were assignments of villages, parganas or talukas in lieu of state debts or advances made to the government or for the pay of offices, establishment or troops, were subsequently resumed by Salar Jung.

The huge profits made by the Arab chiefs from the military contracts were invested in general business and moneylending. Thus, they controlled not only the army but influenced the money market as well. But unlike the Rohillas, who were 'incorrigible robbers and miscreants, the common enemy of the Deccan people',[16] the Arabs as a class, though ready for armed conflict if so commanded by their chiefs, as a rule were not generally guilty of crime since 'when off duty they were like lordly tigers not condescending to common prey'.[17] The Rohillas, though, were a different matter, and used to prowl the country in bands like hungry wolves. The government realized that the best way of keeping them out of trouble was by employing them, since 'Rohilla guards afforded the best protection against Rohilla outrage'.[18] They also obtained land mortgages like the Arabs but on a much lesser scale.

The Arab military chiefs also loaned money to the government and therein lay the root of much evil. When asked for a pecuniary subsidy, a chief would make it a condition that the number of his forces should be raised, whereby he would be a permanent gainer. The chief then became an opponent of economy, and what was worse, acquired a vested interest in ensuring that his accounts were not settled since this gave him leverage on the government to continue his contracts. Successive diwans were thus forced to keep troops they could well have done without: military accounts became intricate and complex. This often led to disputes between the treasury and the troops, and led to the city *danga*s, common in Hyderabad at the time. A danga was a riot, generally accompanied by at least some bloodshed, which was stirred up by a military chief, or his men, to enforce the payment of salary in arrears.[19]

The Arabs all but overshadowed the government: they had their own law courts, their own officers and held all the important forts including Golconda. They were, to all intents and purposes, a military republic superimposed on the Hyderabad administration. The bankers used the services of these marauders to coerce their debtors, and the revenue farmers utilized their services for similar ends. Little wonder then that Dalhousie told the nizam that the Arab soldiery were his masters and not his servants. There was also reason to believe that the nizam tacitly supported the Arabs as a counterpoise to the diwan.[20]

The Arabs were engaged by nobles to enforce their claims against different groups of people, and the Arab jemadars held almost half the revenue of the state and nearly all its power. By 1850, it was said that three-fourths of the country was held one way or another by Arabs and Pathans. They settled their disputes themselves, and considered themselves outside the purview of the local civil or criminal law. As already noted, the sahukars hired Arab, Rohilla and Sikh mercenaries to realize their dues. The men of the Arab chiefs guarded the houses of their debtors lest they escape.

On occasion, they were imprisoned in the houses of Arab jemadars where they were starved into making payment. One would think that death would be a release in such a case. Not so. If a debtor died, his body was not released for burial till the dues were paid. Often, the members of respectable families kept the death a secret till they had quietly buried the body under cover of darkness.

Salar Jung confided in Sir Richard Temple, who was resident in 1867, that he had difficulty in dealing with the Arabs because of their position of prominence in the city and the nizam's partiality for them. He said that he himself had some 300 inside his own house, not of his appointment but those he had inherited. The nizam had several hundred in his palace, and every important noble in the city also had Arab retainers. Salar Jung admitted that they were afraid of the Arabs mainly because their houses, their persons, and almost their lives were at the mercy of the Arabs. The diwan's household troops, distinct from the Reformed Troops, were under the command of the Arab chief, Ghalib Jung.

As regards the military troops, Salar Jung observed that he was not aware if the troops were ever placed under the command of a man on account of his competence. The troops formerly under the command of Raja Govind Bakhsh and Setul Das were the only regular body of troops under the government, but became disorganized with neglect. Chandu Lal initially favoured the Sikhs, but gradually the Arabs gained his confidence. The Arab chiefs made large advances to Chandu Lal, who always needed money, and for these loans, they secured not only a high rate of interest but also an increase in their strength.

No Arab chief would even stir unless an increase was sanctioned to the numerical strength of his troops. Owing to the arrears of payment, all that the troops would do was to clamour for payment. It was useless ordering any troops into the districts, for they would not go. Since each party of men was under the absolute command of its chief, who drew their pay and enlisted and discharged them at pleasure, the men considered themselves servants not of the government but of the military chief. In their eyes, there was no authority superior to their chief, and even the nizam and the diwan meant nothing to them. The chiefs, whose only aim was to amass wealth, were destitute of any military zeal. They gave only a portion of the pay to their men, appropriating the rest, and therefore were unable to compel the men to do any duty which did not suit their inclination.

Apart from the Arabs, there was a sizeable African presence in Hyderabad. In December 1869, the British political agent in Turkish Arabia reported that many African slaves were allegedly disguised as women in order to pass through customs in Bombay. Dr E.G. Balfour, deputy inspector general of hospitals in Secunderabad, confirmed that a number of Africans were imported into Hyderabad as domestics, and that many Arabs returned from Mecca with one or two Africans who posed as members of the family. The resident, C.B. Saunders, had also noted their presence in 1870 but did not think they were slaves, basing his opinion on Salar Jung's letter to the assistant resident, Tweedie, in which he said that although some Arabs did bring back Africans with them, he did not think they were slaves because soon after their arrival, they were seen working for other 'masters'. He observed: 'Since I have assumed the administration, except for one or two cases, I have not heard of any complaint from any African of oppression having been exercised on him, or any complaint touching slavery.'[21]

SALAR JUNG AND LALA BAHADUR

That Salar Jung was not going to be a cat's paw became obvious from the start. He now had the power to delay or initiate administrative procedures, and he did both. Within two weeks of becoming diwan, he refused to sign certain papers which were presented to him by Lala Bahadur, saying that he could not sign 'till he had satisfied himself by a knowledge of their contents of the propriety of doing so . . .'[22] Lala Bahadur was taken aback at this and more than a little put out. The strained relations between the two manifested themselves almost immediately. They concurred in nothing and pulled in different ways. The English press was fully aware of this division between the diwan and the influential daftardar. The *Madras Spectator* observed on 25 July 1853:

> The young minister and his principal Dufturdar divide the authority of the State and do not pull together . . . The Minister had charged the Dufterdar, Lala Bahadoor, to his Sovereign with perversion of facts, falsifying accounts and gross frauds . . . The Minister declines sanctioning the accounts brought to him by the Dafturdar by refusing his signature to them, and the whole Government is necessarily paralyzed. None of its functions in connection with its receipts and disbursements is discharged.[23]

Lala Bahadur seems to have been extremely upset at this unexpected opposition from the man he had made diwan. The *Englishman* noted that the dissension between the two was common knowledge, and reported that Lala Bahadur had appeared at a wedding at his own house 'unadorned, while the rest of the family are decked out . . . in their richest ornaments'. On being asked to participate in the festivities, he glumly replied that 'there had been no peace for him since Chundoo Lal's resignation of office'.[24]

By the end of August 1853, the two were in direct confrontation with each other, and there was the inevitable showdown. Salar Jung wanted Rs 5–6 lakh to enable him to dismiss the new levies which the nizam had sanctioned during the ministry of his uncle. The nizam refused to provide the money, and Lala Bahadur professed himself incapable of raising it. The latter presented Salar Jung with a statement of the state's finances and 'requested his direction as to the way and means for the supply of money'. Salar Jung responded by sending the nizam *wajeeb-ool-urzis*, documents containing a list of certain propositions which he wanted the nizam to sanction in the interest of reform and better governance, threatening to resign if he did not. The nizam signed the petition, signalling victory for the young diwan. Salar Jung then proceeded to eliminate the daftardars as intermediaries between himself and the sahukars.

Another practice which Salar Jung put an end to was the presentation of nazarana—a gift to the appointing authority, including the nizam—for a position. He declared this to be a corrupt practice. Originally, a nazar was a token presentation from an individual to his social or official superior. It was not to be offered or accepted except on special occasions, and it certainly was not meant to impoverish the donor or enrich the recipient. It was not governed by any law, but long usage had established certain conventions. The nizam would, in all probability, only touch it as a gesture of symbolic acceptance and return it, at times with a counter-gift of a larger amount. Over time, this convention degenerated to iniquitous depths and became a bribe for a position; in Osman Ali Khan's time, it almost became a substitute for taxation.[25]

During the time of Chandu Lal, the daftardars, who were supposed to be only revenue record keepers under the diwan and the peshkar were given undue importance because they became the recognized agents for collecting nazaranas. Succeeding diwans came to depend more and more on these daftardars for information and assistance. They also had the power to appoint talukdars, a privilege which they had arrogated to themselves. They had become powerful intermediaries between the state, the bankers and the talukdars, and this nexus was sapping the treasury. When Salar Jung took charge, he showed the daftardars that he meant business and asked them to clean up the administration. They confessed that they were impotent in this regard, admitting that since they themselves were responsible for the present situation, therefore its amendment was beyond them.

> [After the failure of the daftardars to improve their administrative practices was evident] I gradually . . . made arrangements with certain sahookars quite unconnected with the Duftardars to make advances to meet the exigencies of the Government, and in consequence of the period of the revenue collections being yet eight months distant, I deprived the Duftardars of the power to appoint Talooqdars, a privilege which they had hitherto arrogated to themselves . . . I obtained His Highness the Nizam's guarantee for the first advances from the sahookars . . . he . . . accepted and signed at two different times the sahookar's papers of requisitions, and the two Wajib-ool-Urzis I submitted to him.[26]

The 'certain sahookars' referred to above were almost certainly Lachmi Das and his brother Lachman Das of the banking firm of Lachmi Das Lachman Das. Sir William Temple, who became resident in 1867, noted in his diary on 13 May 1867 that Salar Jung introduced a native banker to him as the first man to assist him when he became diwan.

> During the day I received a visit from a native banker, introduced by the Minister as having been the first to come forward to assist him on his accession to power, when he greatly wanted money to carry on the Government. This man told me that at the outset the Minister's great opponents were the Daftarwalas, or Daftardars . . . who advised the bankers not to advance money to him, saying that his regime would not last, and that the Nizam would soon displace him for some one else.[27]

A court diary entry for 27 August 1853 noted that Salar Jung presented the sahukars Lachmi Das and his brother to the nizam who accepted their nazar and signed the papers submitted to him. Since the final confrontation with Lala Bahadur took place at the end of August, there is little doubt that Temple was referring to Lachmi Das in his account.[28]

Lala Bahadur's fall from grace with the nizam and his loss of influence can be attributed to a number of reasons. Most importantly, his direction of the state's finances had failed to prevent the cession of Berar. Some of the military were turning against him, and the Pathans had threatened to kidnap him in an effort to collect their pay, which had resulted in his becoming housebound. A major banker had refused to loan him money, and a revenue contractor had complained to Salar Jung that Lala Bahadur had favoured Arabs at the expense of other contractors.[29]

If Lala Bahadur's influence was on the wane, Salar Jung's star was certainly on the ascendant. Unlike his predecessors, Salar Jung succeeded in winning significant allies. He secured the backing of the Arab, Ghalib Jung, one of the three most powerful mercenary leaders, by a combination of 'personal diplomacy and political concessions'. Salar Jung emphasized his Arab ancestry in his dealings with the Arab chieftains, and more importantly, recognized their authority by establishing a special Arab court in his own palace, conceding to the Arab leaders the power to arrest and try their own people.[30] He started to resume the state lands held by the Arabs and other military forces. These measures slowly instilled confidence in the nizam as to Salar Jung's abilities, paving the way for support for future reforms.

Though Lala Bahadur was displaced as the key financial figure, it was not as if the new administration suddenly sprang into place. It developed slowly over the decades Salar Jung was in power, and changes continued well after his death. Salar Jung's victory did not immediately impact the fortunes of the Malwala family. The daftardars were not replaced, nor were their hereditary positions abolished. Salar Jung worked slowly towards setting up new financial offices and the installation of new personnel. He appointed two Maharashtrian Brahmins from his own jagirs as head of the new 'accountancy' and 'treasury' office. It was called the Munshi Khana and did the work of the daftardars 'but its ambiguous title was selected to disguise that fact'[31] since this would have been a cause of resentment. The new accounts office was said to be maintaining the diwani accounts. Thus, Salar Jung managed to secure his own set of revenue records through this new office, even though the original state revenue documents continued to remain in the custody of the daftardars.

However, Salar Jung's attempt to reduce the remuneration of the daftardars seems to have failed. He is supposed to have got the sanction of the nizam to confiscate the Malwala jagirs, replacing that revenue with a salary of Rs 15,000 a month—a salary equal to his own—indicating that Lala Bahadur's influence, even though under eclipse, was still considerable. This measure failed, and Salar Jung made no further attempts to reduce the payments made to the two daftardars. While the daftars continued to be the repository of documents of transactions before Salar Jung became diwan, all later documents had copies filed elsewhere. The monopoly of the daftardars on financial information was thus ended. The political power of the daftardars also ebbed, and they became known as the custodians of state records, their chief role being archival. They verified jagir and *inam* claims by reference to the original documents.[32]

The bankers seldom acted jointly as an interest group, and although there were a few coalitions, it was competition rather than cooperation which was the norm. Most of the important bankers had cases in the courts against the government and also had troops sent against them at some point in time. Karen Leonard has enumerated the incidents of violence involving leading Hyderabad bankers in the period 1846–57,[33] and Salar Jung's role in the case of the Gosain banker, Umraogir, is revealing.

The cession of Berar had a silver lining to it. Salar Jung was able to dislodge many powerful military chiefs from their land assignments there. He was able to reduce their troops and also, in some cases, dismiss entire units of Arabs and Pathans. The most notable banker allied with the ousted talukdars of Berar was the Gosain, Umraogir, who was also close to Lala Bahadur and some of the Arab and Pathan leaders. He now became Salar Jung's enemy. The East India Company also supported Salar Jung against the Arabs. An incident, which had occurred in 1854 when Arabs had fired upon the English in Yeshwantpura, had turned the Company against them.[34]

Initially a confidant of Siraj-ul-Mulk, the two had a falling-out when the diwan urged Umraogir's own Arabs to turn against him. Siraj-ul-Mulk imprisoned Umraogir and cancelled or collected for himself most of the debts due to him.[35] After his release, he began raising troops and made common cause with those ousted from their Berar holdings. Salar Jung imprisoned him for conspiracy in 1855 when Umraogir's Arab allies besieged the diwan deodi. Brigadier Colin Mackenzie, who was with the Hyderabad Contingent at the time, noted Umraogir's imprisonment and the Arab siege when he attended a party chez Salar Jung. Mackenzie has dated it 1854. It is possible that he got his dates mixed up, or else Umraogir was imprisoned at that time as well.

So if we had stayed at Salar Jung's a few hours later, we might have all been captured, for just after the company left his house it was invested by the Arabs. They had evidently no intention of annoying us . . . and then seized the chouk or main street of the city, barricaded it, and shot several people . . . Some time before, the Nawab had imprisoned one of the Gosains . . . in whom the Arabs had some interest.[36]

A settlement was negotiated between Salar Jung and Umraogir, but there was trouble again in 1857. Turrebaz Khan, one of the main leaders who led the attack on the residency during the Mutiny of 1857, was said to be an adherent of Umraogir. Umraogir died in 1857, allegedly murdered in the diwan deodi.[37]

ON HIS TERMS

Salar Jung's predecessors had either been incompetent or corrupt, mostly both, and Hyderabad was rescued from ruin by his administrative qualities and love of justice which promised a just and efficient administration. Intrigue was forever in the air in Hyderabad, and for some people was the only occupation. Often, the methods were clumsy and easily seen through; on the other hand, there was 'frequently a delicate touch, a finesse worthy of the trained and cultured brain behind it',[38] the whole constituting a very interesting drama. Salar Jung, who was a man altogether different from the rest of his countrymen, was met at every turn by resistance, both active and passive, from ancient prejudice, local customs, and vested interests and by a distaste and fear of innovation.

Salar Jung faced an uphill task in his reforms, looked upon with suspicion for the most part by his own sovereign, and opposed by all those who had a vested interest in the continuance of the ancien régime. A few years into his tenure, in 1856, he sent an *urzee*, a representation to the nizam, regarding proposals for the improvement in administration as also measures to protect himself from the intrigues of mischief-makers. In his representation, he tells the nizam what he expects from him.

The representations I make regarding the Administration of the affairs of the State should, in view to their improvement be acceded to. If anybody should make misrepresentations regarding me to your Highness which may excite your displeasure, enquiry should immediately be made and the guilty party punished, in order that it may prove a warning to others. Your Highness will be pleased to approve of the measures that I shall give effect to, in matters connected with the Dewanee, and in regard to the removal and appointment of Talookdars and others, in the usual way. In regard to the removals and appointments in offices under the Dewanee, which it has long been the custom for the Dewan to propose and His Highness to sanction, Your Highness will be pleased according to custom to approve of any representations. In regard to affairs connected with the Dewanee of a pecuniary nature, or in issuing new rules, or in any other important matter, it is solicited that your Highness will not give your orders without first questioning me on the subject, and allowing me to give an explanation, as the responsibility of the above matters rests with the Dewanee.[39]

In his memorandum on administration, Salar Jung argued for the affairs of government to be arranged on the basis of rules which the people should be persuaded or even intimidated into following, as a result of which business would be facilitated, authority respected, and at the same time the people protected from the excesses of the government. His admiration of the British in this regard is obvious.

I can assure His Highness that no rules can be established which will not bear some resemblance to those of the British Government, because that Government, after a careful examination and enquiry into all the rules and regulations, the laws and customs of each caste and tribe, have made a selection of those which are most useful and advantageous. These laws have been brought into operation during a long course of years, and when any error was discovered it was immediately corrected; *therefore if any good rules are prepared, such rules can only resemble those of the British Government.* [emphasis added].[40]

He was aware of the resistance he would encounter, and his conclusion, written more than 250 years ago, is still as relevant today as it was at the time.

When we commence a systematic form of government, it is necessary to carry out established rules, with firmness and vigour, as at the outset people will be disinclined to observe them, being naturally disposed to follow their own independent wills. These rules will be a restraint on their inclinations, especially in the case of those who possess power, and as these persons are more independent than others they will feel this restraint the more. They will therefore throw every obstacle in their power against the introduction of such a system, and incline others to join them in doing so. *The best plea they will put forward is that such a system is contrary to Mohamedan laws and by doing so they will try to sow the seeds of discontent among the people.* [emphasis added].[41]

By 1856, Salar Jung's reforms had started to take effect. The credit of the government was now better than it had been in many years, and the fresh loans were raised at a more reasonable rate of 8 to 12 per cent instead of 18 to 24 per cent in the past. The loans taken at this cheaper rate were then used to repay loans taken at a higher rate. The collections of the central treasury showed an improvement of Rs 80 lakh for the year 1855. There were serious attempts to defy the government by the Rohillas and the Arabs, but strong and timely action by Salar Jung ensured that these incidents had no lasting impact on his reforms. A special court for the trial of Rohillas was set up in the city, and those convicted were deported to the Andaman Islands.[42]

FINANCIAL REFORMS

Reform was something which was desperately needed since the government was in the last stage of decay. The administration for the last fifty years had been one of shifts and expedients. Every department was notoriously corrupt, with bribes being given when contracts were to be procured, accounts settled, and when disputes were to be adjudicated. Since personal gain was the only motive, every situation was sold and therefore every position was abused. The treasury was empty, and every department had heavy arrears due to it. It must also be remembered that when Salar Jung became diwan, he had no personal influence with the nizam. He wrote to Colonel Low, the resident, about his position: 'You are aware that Burhan-ud-din is my medium of communication with the Nizam, and he is the only man who has influence enough with His Highness to persuade him to consent to my measures.'[43]

Salar Jung thus inherited an empty treasury, heavy debts, large arrears to the city troops and no credit. When he succeeded to the post of diwan, the credit of the government was so low that his uncle could have borrowed Rs 10,000 from bankers, if at all, with great difficulty, and after prolonged negotiation. Money could not be obtained from sahukars except under the guarantee of the military chiefs and that too at extortionate rates. Interest was paid at 18 to 24 per cent per annum, besides a premium of 4 to 5 per cent. When money was obtained directly from Arab and Pathan chiefs, an increase in troops was sanctioned, generally at the rate of 400 men for Rs 1 lakh, and this increase whether real or only on paper, constituted an actual charge against the government. Salar Jung, by his personal character, restored credit to the government such as it had never possessed before. He realized that the moneylending classes, the Arabs, the Rohillas, and the Marwari sahukars, held the key to the situation, and much of his subsequent success was due to the fact that he enlisted on his side these powerful and influential moneylenders. The sahukars knew that Salar Jung would never borrow money which he could not repay. Also, the rate of interest was reduced from 1.5 per cent to 1 per cent per month.

As far as talukas under military chiefs were concerned, Salar Jung tried his best to minimize the lands in their hands. When the state failed to pay salaries on time, this encouraged the military chiefs and mansabdars to obtain for themselves lands in payment of their salaries. This worked out to their great advantage since they not only realized their salaries but also earned large profits. Gradually, Salar Jung resumed the talukas in the hands of the military, and only those whose claims on the government were very large were left out to be resumed at a later date. One of the most important steps taken by Salar Jung after he became diwan was the disbanding of nearly 1900 Arab troops and his redeeming the districts from mortgage. Of the districts yielding revenue of Rs 75 lakh belonging to the diwani, there was not one when he assumed office that was not mortgaged. Within a year, he had recovered revenue of Rs 40 lakh which was now deposited into the treasury.

There was a catch-22 situation prevailing at the time, and even the courts of justice could do nothing about it. Arab creditors petitioned the court for a claim against a debtor. The debtor submitted to the court an assignment which he held from the government, under the acceptance of the drawee talukdar, unpaid for a period of months, often years. While he held these, he could not be called an insolvent debtor. The court evading a settlement would grant protection of three years to the debtor against his creditor. The debtor accepted this as a pis aller, and the creditor remained wholly dissatisfied. There were a large number of such cases. The Arabs considered themselves ill-used in not being paid; and their debtors who had claims against the government resorted to extorting payment which resulted in great misery to the cultivator.

Salar Jung, in his memorandum, gives us an account of the sorry state of affairs which greeted him on assuming office. There were no accounts of the revenue of the country which were available. The only documents available were the statements of receipts, and that too in a format which was five decades old. The only difference was that the names of the present talukdars were added, and in some cases, there had been a reduction in the revenue of districts held by certain individuals. The accounts of disbursements were similar in nature, with the increased charges of the military and cattle departments being added. When Salar Jung wanted to know the net revenue available with the government, the daftardars said it was Rs 18 lakh, which was not sufficient to even pay the nizam's relatives, the Pathans and other troops. Salar Jung obtained the guarantee of the nizam for the loans he now took from the sahukars. The nizam himself advanced a sum of Rs 15 lakh in cash which was to be repaid when some district was restored by the British or when the revenues started to show a surplus.[44]

To set an example, Salar Jung voluntarily cut his salary from Rs 25,000 to Rs 15,000 per annum soon after he assumed office. He then cut the salary of the military by a third, a decision which caused an uproar, at least initially. But when it was found that salaries were paid regularly and on time, the initial unpopularity of the decision soon gave way to universal approbation, and the credit Salar Jung earned for this particular action far exceeded that of many other more important reforms.

As a young man of eighteen, Salar Jung had served as the talukdar of Khammam, a part of the family estate which had been restored after a period of confiscation for non-payment of debts. It was initially in the charge of Henry Dighton, a former employee of William Palmer and Company, who was replaced because the nizam did not want the districts to be administered by English collectors. In the short time that the districts had been administered by them, they had 'settled' the land revenue and introduced beneficial changes in the system of collection and revenue, and in other aspects of administration.

Finding every department of the state mismanaged, Salar Jung's uncle, Siraj-ul-Mulk, wanted to employ men of integrity and independence to the more important revenue offices and had, to this end, appointed Dighton and Mahomed Azim Ali Khan in charge of some of the talukas and the treasury, but this was not liked by the nizam. The system was discontinued when Nasir-ud-Daula became nizam, and the English collectors were withdrawn. Indian collectors reverted to the old system of collecting revenue on a commission basis, and the benefits of improved yield and increased prosperity to the cultivators became a thing of the past.

Salar Jung abolished the farming out of revenue. The old talukdars were gradually dismissed. The new ones appointed were paid salaries by the government and were provided with a staff of subordinates who were also government employees. Their duties were well defined, and they were directly responsible to the government. The peasant, no longer oppressed by fraudulent and extortionate taxation, returned to his village realizing that he could now make a living by cultivating the land once again. One of the main characteristics of Salar Jung's reforms was the centralization of authority in the talukdar at the district level. Naturally, all these measures were heartily opposed by those used to unlawful gains, and they tried to stir up trouble by saying that these reforms were opposed to sacred Mohammedan law.

Later on, Salar Jung resolved to discontinue all assignments of lands on account of loans. The revenues of all the districts were to be received directly into the treasury from where each sahukar would receive the sums due to him. There was no treasury worth the name when Salar Jung became diwan. Chandu Lal's only preoccupation was how to raise funds, something he did by obtaining advances on districts, by nazaranas for the grant of jagirs or by fines on presumed malpractices. These practices continued even after Chandu Lal, and insolvency was the result. Salar Jung wanted each department to have its own treasury. Similarly, he felt that for the transaction of business, all the principal districts should have their own treasuries. Over time, he resolved to supply this deficiency.

Under Chandu Lal, jagirs were granted to his relatives and others upon making payment. They were also made under orders from the nizam. Since the jagirdars had received the jagirs as gifts, Chandu Lal extracted his pound of flesh whenever he needed money. The nizam had ruled that 25 per cent of the revenue should be paid to the government, but this never happened in practice. The wealthy and influential paid nothing; it was only the few friendless jagirdars, chiefly the poorer class of nobles, who ended up paying. Salar Jung discontinued the practice of levying a fourth or fifth of the value of the holdings and reduced the number of jagirs where no valid right existed. He was of the view that jagirs should be given to ancient nobility, persons who had rendered distinguished service or those had exceptional abilities and talents. He bemoaned the decadence which resulted from this inherited wealth.

> I refer to the division of a jagir among the children or next of kin on the death of a Jaghirdar. The results are detrimental to the members of the family. The dignity attached to this estate is reduced, and as each person obtains a subsistence without any labour or exertion, he leads a life of indolence and ignorance, and has not the usual motive for exertion, and the family in the course of one or more generations, owing to the partitions and subdivisions of the property, is reduced to a state of poverty and destitution.[45]

Replacing debased currency

One of Salar Jung's biggest contributions at this time (1856–57) was the introduction of new currency, to replace the debased *hali sicca*. The base metal of the Hyderabad coin was a continued cause of complaint. In this business of debasing the coin, the samasthans of Gadwal and Wanaparthy seem to have been the chief culprits. They had enjoyed the right of coining for a long time and had not been slow in taking advantage of this privilege.

Since all manner of coins were considered legal tender, the sahukars saw a great opportunity in this. Seeing the profit to be made in lucrative recoinage, they sent good coins from Hyderabad to these places where the coins would be reminted, suffering a debasement of about 6 per cent in the process. This multiplication of mints was Chandu Lal's doing, but this time perhaps not from any corrupt motive, since he had expressly stipulated that the coins issued from these mints should strictly abide by the Hyderabad standard.

Matters deteriorated to such an extent that in May 1855 the raja of Wanaparthy was called by the resident to account for the highly debased coins issuing from his mint at Seegur. A formal trial followed in which the raja was convicted and sentenced to four years' imprisonment.[46]

There were different rates of exchange from the coins issuing from the mints of Govind Bakhsh and the mints at Narainpet, Seegur and Gadwal with the Company's rupee. In August 1855, 100 of the Company's rupees were exchanged for approximately 119 hali sicca and Govind Bakhsh coins. The rates for coins from the mints at Narainpet, Seegur and Gadwal were about 122, 132 and 129 respectively.[47]

Salar Jung abolished the mints both in the districts and in the city. There was a 15 per cent difference between the new coin and the British coin, and it was hoped that once the new coin had obtained a wide enough circulation and the old debased coin had disappeared, this measure would greatly facilitate mercantile transactions and the keeping of accounts. The old coin was not recalled but was replaced by the new and more trustworthy coin in a gradual manner. It took several years for the debased coin to disappear, but by the end of Salar Jung's tenure, the coinage was above suspicion.[48]

JUDICIAL REFORMS

As in other matters, Chandu Lal put himself at the apex of the judicial system as well, except that there was nothing in existence at that time which could be given that appellation. At the beginning of his administration, there were no adalats or courts in existence. There were courts of the Kazee, the Mufti, the Sadarut and the Nizamut, but these took cognizance only of minor points relating to religious matters and the division of property. Subjects of importance from which a profit could be made were settled by Chandu Lal. A military court for the trial of cases between military men was established under Raja Govind Bakhsh, who commanded a large number of troops.

There was no efficient police force in the nizam's dominions prior to 1865. Police duties were performed by the irregular troops, the sebundy peons and village servants. In Hyderabad, the police were under a kotwal, but as in the matter of justice, Chandu Lal became the kotwal in all matters where money could be made. For other crimes, there was the regular kotwal. A famous name in those times was Talib-ud-Daula, who by his individual energy and unflinching severity towards offenders, inspired dread among malefactors. But there was no proper organization, and there were many glaring defects in the system. The police did not have undivided authority in the city. The great nobles exercised jurisdiction within the limits of their own property so that no offender could be arrested if he sought sanctuary there. Several Arab chiefs also followed this example. Salar Jung drew up a set of rules for remodelling the police but was stymied initially by the fact that the kotwal did not have full authority over all parts of the city.

The judicial reforms Salar Jung introduced in the first decade of his administration were essentially of an evolutionary character and did not constitute any radical departure from the system he inherited from his predecessor, Siraj-ul-Mulk. Their main object was to meet the exigencies of the time. The early nizams had kept the Mughal judicial system intact. From 1821 to 1846, successive diwans set up several courts in the city but paid little attention to the judicial administration in the districts. Siraj-ul-Mulk, in his first term in office (1846–48), had attempted a reform of the judicial machinery in the districts, and in his second ministry was able to induce the nizam to abolish the practice of sati. In 1856, Salar Jung followed this push to social reform by forbidding traffic in children.

As we have noted, the Arabs, Rohillas, and others had a free rein when Salar Jung assumed office. He realized that these militant and intractable elements could not be reduced to obedience without raising the power and the prestige of the courts. Following the tradition of his predecessors, he established a number of new courts in the city. The only difference was that these were set up with the definite object of reining in certain classes of society like the Arabs, Rohillas and Sikhs. A significant feature was that the jurisdiction of each court was clearly defined for the first time.

At the time Salar Jung assumed office, violence and sedition on the part of the Arabs who almost ruled the city was rampant. The government did not have the power to reduce them to obedience, and Salar Jung had to persuade the Arab chiefs to submit their claims to the courts instead of recourse to force and violence. Salar Jung realized that the existing courts were unsuited to try cases in which the Arabs and Rohillas were involved. He set up the Adalat-e-Badshahi in 1855, in addition to the existing courts which consisted of a chief justice and four puisne judges. This court was authorized to handle all cases except those which fell under the purview of the Dar-ul-Qaza and the Kotwali. The former was one of the oldest judicial institutions of the city and entertained all cases relating to marriage, divorce, and succession to inheritance in the Muslim community. The Kotwali-e-Balda dealt with all cases of assault, hurt, and petty thefts up to the value of Rs 300. The Kotwali-e-Bairoon-e-Balda was responsible for arresting those guilty of offences on the highways and in the suburban villages.

The Adalat-e-Badshahi functioned under the supervision of the diwan, and in cases of capital punishment, his approval was required. Salar Jung authorized the court to execute its own decrees, and no one could disregard with impunity the summons of the court. The idea behind setting up this new court was to discard the prevalent belief that only the diwan could dispense justice. Since the court was invested with full authority, the practice of bringing cases before the diwan ceased.

Siraj-ul-Mulk had established the Diwan Khana Adalat, which served as a medium for the receiving of petitions. Salar Jung relocated this to the chinikhana in his deodi, and it was popularly known as the Adalat-e-Chinikhana. It tried all civil cases including debt, mortgage and purchase of commodities up to the value of Rs 1000, excluding those falling under the jurisdiction of the Dar-ul-Qaza and Govind Rao's court, the latter being a new court set up in 1860 to try cases in which Hindus were involved and presided over by a Hindu called Govind Rao. All suits above Rs 1000 were transferred to the Adalat-e-Diwani-e-Buzurg. Another new court which Salar Jung set up in 1855 was a court to try cases in which the Sikhs who were employed in the army were parties.

It must be remembered that the judicial administration of Salar Jung was confined only to the diwani territory. The jagirdars exercised almost sovereign power in their own jagirs and naturally resisted surrendering any of their rights or privileges, the exclusive retention of original judicature in their hands being one of their greatest sources of power. Over time, Salar Jung was able to reduce their influence, but they were one of the greatest obstacles to the establishment of a uniform justice system. It was Salar Jung's aim to impress upon the people and the nobility the principle of equality before the law. This was, of course, easier said than done, in the feudal oligarchy that was Hyderabad.

In 1860, Raichur Doab and Naldurg were restored to the nizam after being under British administration for eight years. The system of administration adopted by the British government was continued by the nizam, and two new offices were created for the restored districts. The Kacheri-Azla-e-Mustarida was to supervise the revenue administration, and the Sadar Adalat-e-Mustarida was to act as the court of appeal for the territory. Both these offices were directly under Salar Jung. A special court for the trial of cases arising in this territory known as Sadar Adalat-e-Azla-Mustarida was set up.

In the districts, Siraj-ul-Mulk had appointed mir adals who acted as magistrates, and in the talukas the munsif acted as taluka judges. When Salar Jung assumed office, he did not make any changes in this system except that now the mir adals could decide civil cases to which Hindus were parties. The Adalat-e-Faujdari was the court of appeal for the district and munsif courts in Siraj-ul-Mulk's time. This power of review was given to the Sadar Adalat-e-Azla-Mustarida in Salar Jung's time.

Salar Jung realized that unless strict measures were taken to control the Arab and Rohilla mercenaries, the peace in Hyderabad would always be threatened. Special officers called *zilladars* were appointed in the districts for the suppression of the crimes in which Rohillas were the chief offenders. The zilladars were fully equipped with an armed force sufficiently powerful to deal with any armed resistance. The force under the zilladars was called Jamiat-i-Zilladari and was stationed in different parts of the state, especially in places where such disturbance was common. A board consisting of four members and a president was appointed in Hyderabad to supervise and direct the operations of the zilladars. The zilladars seem to have enjoyed success in their task since large number of Rohillas were either killed or captured and imprisoned. Later, many of them were set free on the orders of the nizam with the concurrence of the resident, Colonel C. Davidson, who appears to have encouraged this system.

An important change introduced by Salar Jung in 1861 was the separation of the civil and criminal jurisdictions of the courts. Later, a notification was issued in which the jurisdiction of each court was clearly defined. This measure had several advantages since it reduced the conflict of jurisdictions and avoided duplication of work, saving both time and money. Salar Jung had done all he could to restore the prestige and position of the courts. He now also emphasized the execution of orders and decrees, and to this end, he established the Mahakma-e-Ijra-was-Amal. The Mahakma was under his direct supervision. The civil courts were directed to submit all decrees and orders passed by them to government which were then forwarded to the Mahakma for execution.

Perhaps one of the most important reforms introduced by Salar Jung had to do with the salaries of the judges. The judges did not receive their salaries on time, and this was a perpetual source of discontent. Salar Jung was aware that unless the judges were kept free of pecuniary temptations, impartial justice was impossible. The salaries of the judges were disbursed not from the treasury but by the talukdars who were in charge of the revenue collection, a clear violation of the principle of the independence of the judiciary. Salar Jung ordered that the salaries would henceforth be paid from the treasury, and the payment of the judges' salaries in land grants was abolished. In 1862, a secretariat was established to assist Salar Jung in his judicial functions. Salar Jung's reforms in this early part of his premiership paved the way for the reorganization which followed from 1864 onwards.

For the sake of readability, the reforms discussed above have reference to the period 1853 to 1864. Salar Jung's reforms, for which his ministry was justly famous, proceeded apace till an event occurred which slowed down the process temporarily. This event, the Mutiny of 1857, one in which Salar Jung played a pivotal role in guiding the destiny of Hyderabad in a time of crisis, is the subject of the following chapter.

4

'Our Faithful Ally'

The year 1857 witnessed an unprecedented military and civil upsurge in India which shook the British Empire to its foundations. It has been described variously as the Revolt of 1857, the Sepoy Mutiny, the Great Rebellion, and for the more patriotic, the National War of Independence. For the sake of convenience, we shall refer to it as the Mutiny.

The Indian sepoy had his grievances. He was constantly abused and discriminated against in a variety of ways. His great forbearance finally gave way, and the initial spark seems to have been the new Lee-Enfield cartridges which contained greased powder-and-shot. Soldiers had to use their teeth to open the wrapping. At first, the British officers denied that the fat, either of cows (sacred to Hindus), or pigs (anathema to Muslims), was used in the cartridge. A later inquiry revealed that the early batches did use prohibited fats but the subsequent ones did not. The sepoys were faced with the choice of rejecting their faith or facing disciplinary action, which could even attract a death penalty. The signs of disaffection soon became more and more apparent, and the first shots of the Mutiny of 1857 were fired in Barrackpore, Bengal. On 29 March 1857, Mangal Pandey, a sepoy of the 34th Light Infantry, shot and wounded two officers and exhorted his fellow sepoys to revolt. He was promptly tried and hanged.

This incident has been seen as a crucial event of the Mutiny but its importance has been greatly exaggerated. In many ways it was irrelevant, since the sepoys marched not to Calcutta, but to Delhi, whose capture turned an army mutiny into the most serious armed challenge to British imperialism. As William Dalrymple has observed: 'Instead of the single coherent mutiny or patriotic war of independence beloved of Victorian or Indian nationalist historiography, there was in reality a chain of very different uprisings and acts of resistance, whose form and fate were determined by local and regional situations, passions and grievances.'[1]

The Mutiny started in Meerut on 10 May 1857 when the Indian soldiers of the 3rd Bengal Light Cavalry rebelled against their British officers. After slaughtering their officers, they rode towards Delhi in the hope of securing the blessings of Bahadur Shah Zafar, the poet-king who had been reduced to pleading for favours from the East India Company. Soon after dawn on 11 May, sawars of the 3rd Cavalry who had ridden all night passed the gates of the Red Fort, approached Zafar's balcony, and called out to him. Though old and powerless, he was still regarded as the emperor and became the rallying point for the mutineers. They wanted the king to bless, in fact, even lead their defiance. Delhi was central to the uprising, and 'despite its diffuse and fractured nature, many of its different elements converged into a single programme: to restore the Mughal Empire.'[2] The Mutiny has been presented as a revolt against British economic and social policies; these certainly played a part, but it is often overlooked that it was equally a defensive action against, and a resistance to, the imposition of Christianity. Queen Victoria may have been thousands of miles away, but she was quick to discern the real reason for the disquiet. Writing to Charlotte Canning, the Governor General's wife, she asserted that 'a fear of their religion being tampered with is at the bottom of it'.[3]

Zafar vacillated for a few hours, during which he heard of the massacre in Delhi. By afternoon he succumbed, and around midnight he authorized the firing of a twenty-one-gun salute to announce that 'Hindustan' had its own ruler again. In north India as a whole, the rebellion involved both Hindus and Muslims, but in Delhi it centred on the 'Last Mughal'. The newly educated intelligentsia, which included both Hindus and Muslims, were, however, not part of the uprising which had strong elements of orthodoxy such as the Wahabis, who led a movement for the restoration of Islam in its pure form.

HYDERABAD AND THE MUTINY

The news spread rapidly throughout India, and memories of the Kabul rout of 1842 were revived. The fall of Delhi, Kanpur and Lucknow reminded the people that the British were not invincible. At Hyderabad, the rulers had never repudiated their allegiance to the Mughal emperor, and in the past, each of the nizams had to secure a firman from the emperor to legitimize his claim to the masnad. The emperor's name appeared on the coins issued by the nizam till 1858 (when it was dropped at the request of the British), and his name was read when the khutba was recited.

As one revolt succeeded another, and a large part of the north and central part of the subcontinent was in open rebellion, it was only natural that men cast their eyes at Hyderabad. The sneeze in Delhi threatened to give Hyderabad a cold. But Hyderabad remained loyal to the British in spite of all attempts to win over the nizam. That Hyderabad remained staunch was in large part due to Salar Jung, whose wise and energetic leadership during this period was responsible for the stability of British rule in south India. But Hyderabad too had its share of revolutionary instability. And although the overt manifestations of the Mutiny were promptly suppressed, the discontent continued to simmer till 1862, when it finally died out.

Just how important it was for Hyderabad to support the British can be appreciated by the telegram which the governor of Bombay, Lord Elphinstone, sent to the resident, Major Davidson: 'If the Nizam goes all is lost.' He was not exaggerating. Hyderabad joining the revolt would have had serious repercussions for British rule, not only in the south, but in the whole of India. Had Hyderabad joined the Mutiny, the flames would have spread to Bombay and Madras. No one knew this better than Salar Jung and Davidson. Salar Jung described the condition of affairs at this time as a 'trial, the tension and force of which can never be understood by a European and Christian'.[4]

Salar Jung, for his part, had a delicate balance to maintain between his loyalties to the nizam and the British. But given his upbringing among British friends, and the support he had received from the British on becoming diwan, Salar Jung's decision is not difficult to understand. He had made up his mind that the cause of England was the cause of good government. He realized that the success of the rebellion would 'only make universal the state of things from which he had been for four years endeavouring to rescue the territories of his master'. He also rightly guessed that with their technical superiority, the British would ultimately emerge as victors. Whatever his reasons, subsequent events showed he had acted wisely. Also, he was only following the example of other princely states that had remained loyal to the British.

Writing about this nearly two decades later, the *Times of India* correspondent recalled the diwan's role in suppressing the Mutiny when Salar Jung had just returned from England.

> It has been invidiously remarked that he was cute enough to perceive that we should win the day in the long run, and so for his own interest he stuck to the winning side. Even granted so, then he deserved every credit for his cuteness, and if a few other highly placed officials had been endowed with equal clearness of perception and judgement we should have been in a position to crumple . . . our own sepoy mutineers with greatly accelerated despatch.[5]

Apart from ensuring the loyalty of the troops in the Subsidiary Force at Secunderabad and the Hyderabad Contingent at Bolarum, Salar Jung also had to keep a watchful eye on the activities of disaffected religious elements among the Muslims who dreamt of a country without foreigners. In a city comprising a large number of turbulent and desperate characters, sympathy for the mutineers who were pursuing unchecked a course of murder and brigandage would not have been hard to find. His reforms had not made him popular with a large section of the nobles, and there were 'malcontents around the Nizam who wished to rid the State of the innovating Minister and return to the old system which they knew how to manipulate . . .'[6] As we shall see later, Salar Jung had to spend a lot of his time and energy in combating the continuous intrigues which aimed at unseating him from his position. Even though Salar Jung had made strenuous efforts to establish law and order in the districts and the city since he assumed office, much remained to be done, and 'lawless elements like Rohillas, Afghans and Arabs used to obtain their dues from officials only by resort to physical force and armed affray'.[7]

The unsettled conditions of the districts also added to the dangers of revolt in the city. Salar Jung suppressed tumults, punished rioters, and his conduct and demeanour inspired the resident with such conviction of his loyalty that the Hyderabad Contingent was ordered to join the British forces in the north and assist them in the task of combating the mutineers. Passionate appeals were made to his patriotism, honour and his faith by his co-religionists. The enraged populace would have stormed his house and murdered him had it not been for his faithful Arab guards. He was exposed to constant menaces and much danger, but he remained undeterred by these threats.

It was said that two men saved India—the maharaja of Patiala in the north, and Salar Jung in the south. But Patiala hardly had to reckon with the obstacles and difficulties which were the lot of Salar Jung. An added threat was the fact that the ruler of Shorapore, a feudatory of the nizam, had joined hands with the rebels. Even after the revolt had been suppressed, the western part of Hyderabad seems to have become a safe haven for people like Tatya Tope, who had fled from the north, and Ram Rao, who travelled from Shorapore to Hyderabad to spread discontent in the nizam's dominions.

On 16 May, six days after the outbreak of the Mutiny in Meerut, the nizam, Nasir-ud-Daula, died aged sixty-six. A humane man, his prejudices had stood in the way of innovation and progress, but his 'inaptitude for public affairs coexisted with a gracious disposition to private charity, and with much bountiful kindness to his dependents'.[8] He was succeeded by his son, the thirty-two-year-old Tahniyat Ali Khan, who ascended the masnad under the title of Afzal-ud-Daula. On his deathbed, the nizam asked his son to remain faithful to the British. The transition was smooth since there was complete agreement between Salar Jung and the resident as to the succession. In fact, prior telegraphic instructions had also been received from the Government of India in this regard.

On returning from the installation ceremony, Davidson was given a telegram from the Governor General announcing the fall of Delhi. When he gave Salar Jung the news, he was told that such information had reached the city three days earlier. 'Even the downfall of Delhi, which at the time was looked upon by those unacquainted with the resources of the English as synonymous with the destruction of the British power in India, never for a moment shook the Minister's loyalty and his confidence in the ultimate success of the British arms.'[9]

Like his father, Afzal-ud-Daula was a man of lofty stature, large and robust, with a passion for outdoor amusements. He rode well, drove a fine team and enjoyed field sports. A popular man who remained away from the limelight during his father's reign, he was neither capricious nor profligate in any way, not even the pleasures of the harem. Nor was he tyrannical, harsh or arrogant, and it was said that he was a truthful man. Later, he became a corpulent figure with a triple chin and 'a chest inflated with the ease of good living', far removed from the soldier-like athleticism of the first nizam. But by then, Hyderabad was also far removed from the Hyderabad of Nizam-ul-Mulk. The intervening century had reduced it to a state of subservience, with succeeding nizams losing their power to act independently.

DISAFFECTION IN THE NIZAM'S DOMINIONS

The mutiny of the troops of the first cavalry of the Hyderabad Contingent at Aurangabad on 12 June 1857 was the first serious incident in the nizam's dominions. The troops were aware of the events in the north and, fearing that they would be marched to Delhi to fight against the Mughal king, revolted. The revolt was put down by Captain Abbot with an iron hand, and the punishments ranged from hanging, being blown up by cannon, to flogging and transportation. About one hundred soldiers were cashiered.

Thirteen soldiers under Jemadar Cheeda Khan deserted and sought shelter in Hyderabad, but found no respite. As soon as he was aware of their presence in the city, Salar Jung had them arrested and handed over to the resident. This greatly angered the disaffected section of the community. A delegation of four moulvis waited on the nizam to plead for their release, threatening to sack the residency if their demands were not met. Salar Jung, and even the nizam, received threatening letters. With the aid of a few trustworthy Arabs and some of the nizam's personal guards, a modicum of order was maintained.

Arab guards were placed at the principal city gates with orders to fire upon anyone who incited the people against the British. People found guilty of preaching sedition were arrested. The moulvis were preaching revolt against the British, and incidents of unrest were frequent. The resident ordered the general at Secunderabad to parade his troops in a show of strength, and Salar Jung stood beside him at the review in an exhibition of solidarity for the British cause. (Secunderabad was a British cantonment, as were Bowenpalli and Bolarum, at some distance beyond Secunderabad.)

There was close contact between the troops and religious elements in the city, and on 10 and 11 June there was unrest among the British Indian troops near Secunderabad. On 12 June, a fakir from Bowenpalli was arrested for preaching sedition. There was a call for jehad, or a holy war, at Mecca Masjid, one of the principal mosques of the city. Within a month of Afzal-ud-Daula's accession, placards and posters appealed for a revolt against the foreigners in the name of Islam, their aim being the re-establishment of the Delhi throne. The posters roundly abused all those who failed to rise in revolt against the infidels.[10] They were crudely worded but left no one in doubt as to their inflammatory intent. They exhorted the nizam to collect all the Muslims, suppress the kafirs and march to Delhi. The poster writers assured the nizam that he had the blessings of the Almighty, and he should not be fearful or apprehensive. 'Not to leave the object of their exhortations in any manner of doubt, it was also helpfully added: "If fearful he should wear bangles and sit at home."'[11]

There was close consultation between Salar Jung and Davidson, and they freely exchanged information, though Davidson 'thought his information more complete than Salar Jung's and attributed this fact to the Minister's known adherence to the British cause'.[12] On the morning of 12 June 1857, Salar Jung wrote to Davidson, approving of the precautionary measures taken by him, and that any excitement that existed among the lower and more ignorant classes could be attributed to the instigation of the sepoys from Secunderabad, and their emissaries, such as the fakir. He told him that the fakir had been sent by the cavalrymen at Bowenpalli to make the populace join them, stating at the same time that the Native Corps at Secunderabad were ready to join the cause. He went on to write:

> I heard also this morning but cannot vouch for its truth that the men of your cavalry escort whilst following you through the City the other day addressed inflammatory language to the people . . . Agreeably to your intimation conveyed by Capt. Thornhill's note of yesterday I have again ordered to prevent any of the Secunderabad sepoys from coming into the City unless they are provided with passports.[13]

THE ATTACK ON THE RESIDENCY

An uneasy peace followed, punctuated by sporadic incidents. On 18 June, Davidson observed in a letter to the Foreign Department that cavalry and infantry sepoys of the Hyderabad Subsidiary Force had been visiting the city without permission and were preaching sedition to the people. He expressed the apprehension that all that was missing was a leader, and an opportunity, to extend the revolt to the Deccan and the entire south. There were rumours of an imminent attack on the residency, and Davidson was urged to move to the safety of Bolarum since the troops were stationed there. The gutsy Davidson reportedly said, 'I have taken a fancy to lay my bones at Hyderabad. If open force be used I will fight to the last.'[14]

Despite all their precautions, the attack on the residency could not be prevented. On 17 July, a large congregation met at the Mecca Masjid to demand the release of the thirteen army deserters who had been arrested by Salar Jung and handed over to the resident. When the imam rose to deliver his khutba, he was heckled. They asked him to stop babbling like a woman and wanted him to exhort the populace to raise the banner of revolt against the foreigners. A riot was about to ensue, but the kotwal had the ringleaders arrested, and he and the imam managed to escape in the ensuing melee.

Salar Jung sent his Arab guards to disperse the crowd, and for a while, peace was restored. That same evening, 500 Rohillas, led by Moulvi Ala-ud-din and Turrebaz Khan, headed for the residency. Salar Jung, who was in constant touch with Davidson (and his assistant, Captain Thornhill) through the day, warned him about the impending attack. His second letter, written in the evening, gave Davidson a half-hour's warning. In his first letter, Salar Jung had warned that some two or three hundred men had managed to get out of the city, and he had ordered his Arab guards to attack them if found within 'our limits'. 'I have ordered the guards at the gates not to allow any people to pass out, and it will be necessary for you to take the necessary measures at the residency.'[15]

In the evening, the letter was again brief, warning the resident of the impending attack. 'I have just heard that 4 or five hundred men are going towards the Residency. I have ordered them to be intercepted by Arabs in the City and, if need be, destroy them.'[16] By the time the insurgents had reached the residency, the mob accompanying them had swelled to several thousand where they converged at Sultan Bazar. Opposite the western wall of the residency were two high-terraced houses which were taken over by the rebels to fire on the residency. The Rohillas seem to have received an assurance that the sepoys inside the residency would join them, and attacked the bullock gate but were repulsed by the forces led by Major Briggs, military secretary to the resident.

The rebels then retreated to two houses facing the residency, which belonged to two merchants, Jaigopal Das and Akbar Sahib. They thus faced the gate of the residency on the Putli Bowli[17] side. They then asked the Indian guards at the residency to bring Jemadar Cheeda Khan and his associates to them. One of the Indian rissaldars, Ismail Khan, tried to convince them to return but was fired at for his pains. He, however, escaped unhurt. Sporadic fire was exchanged with the troops in the residency. Matters became a little more complicated because it was dark by then, and the nizam's men were reluctant to enter the residency for fear of being mistaken for the insurgents.

The correspondence between Salar Jung and Davidson continued through the night till the next morning in an attempt to coordinate the activities of the two groups. They now started recording the hour on their letters. In a letter written at 9.40 p.m., Salar Jung wrote:

> The Chaprassee brought me word that the Resident wishes the Arab Jemadars to wait upon Major Briggs to receive their orders, but as it is now dark I think it is best that the Arabs should be placed in the rear of the Mosque so as to cut off their retreat and to prevent others joining them from the City and I have accordingly so ordered them.[18]

Three hours later, we find an exhausted Salar Jung still on the job, assuring the resident that he would leave no stone unturned to 'have this unfortunate business settled'. In a postscript, he hoped that the resident would allow the local forces to do their job before the British troops were called upon to act.[19] In yet another note, he outlined the plan of action:

> I shall order the Arabs to attack the Rebels in Pestonjee's and Ubban Sahib's gardens. If they leave the gardens and go anywhere within the Residency limits your troops must attack them, and if they come within the reach of the Arabs again, they will be desired to renew the attack.[20]

In his account, written four years later, Henry George Briggs describes the atmosphere prevailing in Hyderabad in 1857.

> As it was, Colonel Davidson was hourly being telegraphed by politicals from the north of Central India to as far south as Travancore to keep them alive of passing occurrences and to hold to the last, conscious that if the capital of the Nizam went, the whole Peninsula would soon rise. The native mind was in a state of ferment, and it merely required some powerful house or great chief to create a flame, to make that flame a blaze from the Bay of Bengal . . . as far south as Cape Comorin.
>
> . . . Colonel Davidson from the very onset had trustworthy information that the fanatical spirit which prevailed in the city was strong against his Government and his country; he knew that a *jehud* . . .

had been taken to repeat at Hyderabad the scene of Cawnpore; he was even made aware that he was specially marked for assassination; and he was told that every Sepoy of our military force had been tampered with, and was ready to turn upon us by joining any successful body of insurgents.[21]

The Rohillas launched a fierce attack on the residency, bringing down the Putli Bowli gate, firing continuously for half an hour. Briggs responded with cannon fire and kept pounding them without interruption till dawn. By early morning, the attack had been repulsed, and the Rohillas evacuated the two houses leaving their dead behind. Turrebaz Khan and the moulvi escaped. Davidson, who seems to have earned his promotion and become Colonel Davidson on the night of the action, in a letter to the nizam the next day, wrote that the Rohillas had fled leaving six dead. In the same letter, he expressed his unhappiness at the Arabs who failed to prevent the escape of the rebels since they had failed to make arrangements to surround them. He went on to add,

> It is unnecessary for me to point out to Your Highness how you should act in this matter for your Highness is I am sure well aware that since friendship has existed between our two governments the English Government has never (till now) been subjected to such an insult. I feel assured that your Highness will issue whatever orders may be necessary in this case.[22]

This letter was a follow-up to one which had been written by Captain Thornhill to Salar Jung on the night of the attack. That letter had been much sharper in its tone, imperious even, and lacking in customary formality.

> I am desired by the Resident to inform you that 200 Rohillas under Toorah Baz Khan have occupied the house of Ubban Sahib in the Residency Bazaar. *They have had the audacity to fire on British Picquets, and in the first instance to attack the Residency. This insult cannot be forgotten.* [Emphasis added.] The Resident only refrains from causing them to be attacked owing to the darkness of the night and he holds the Nizam's Govt responsible that Toorah Baz Khan and the whole of his followers are given up to him tomorrow as prisoners. You will be pleased

to communicate to His Highness the Nizam without delay that this is a demand from the Resident on the part of the British Government.[23]

In his reply, the nizam described the events and the reasons for his troops not making as timely an appearance as expected. He also said that a reward of Rs 4000 for the capture of each of the two leaders had been offered.

> I am sure you will be fully aware that it is the cause of great regret to me that such a sudden outbreak should have taken place solely through the instrumentality of a set of low scoundrels, because our two governments are one, and what is insult to the one is so to the other. Since the commencement of this disturbance every endeavour has been made by me to arrange matters. It will always be my desire that the ancient friendship which has existed between our two governments shall remain and by God's grace I hope it may day by day increase.[24]

Salar Jung had written to Captain Thornhill recounting details of how the moulvi and Turrebaz Khan had acted according to what appeared to be a 'preconcerted plan'. He assured him that no one in government or any of its servants joined in the affair which was the work of Turrebaz Khan and his out-of-work Rohillas.

> I am exceedingly sorry to find Toorah Baz Khan has fled, but sowars [horsemen] have been sent in search of him and every exertion will be made for his apprehension . . . The Arabs were under great apprehension of coming in contact with the British troops by mistake in the darkness of the night, and the consequence was that considerable delay took place in sending out guards and moving out of the City . . . A reward of Rs. 4,000 has been offered for the apprehension of Moulvie All-ood-Deen, and the same sum for Toorah Baz Khan, by the Circar.[25]

A few days after the attack, Davidson gave Salar Jung the names of four suspects whom he thought ought to be interrogated. More importantly, he indicated that the moulvi involved was a servant of Nawab Ikhtidar-ul-Mulk Bahadur, the son of Fakhr-ud-din Khan Shums-ul-Umra II, the head of the Paigah family and the first noble of the state. Rashid-ud-din Khan, for that was the given name of the son, is an important character in this story. At first out of favour with the foreign rulers, he was later used by the British to 'vex and then undercut Salar Jung'. But we are getting a little ahead of our story.

In his account to the Governor General in Calcutta, Davidson said that the nizam had behaved well but was a little upset with Salar Jung at 'having been deceived and had no intelligence'. Davidson did not think that Fakhr-ud-din Khan Shums-ul-Umra II was in any way involved. '"SJ" is of course staunch to us, indeed I attribute his unpopularity, and his want of reliable intelligence to the knowledge by all parties that he is hand and heart with us.'[26] As noted before, so confident was the resident of Salar Jung's abilities and loyalty that he sent the Hyderabad Contingent to the north to assist the British forces against the mutineers, when ironically, their own motives had been suspect back home.

The letters sent home by these troops about their victories in the north, and their safe return home, had a calming effect on the uneasy quiet which had descended on Hyderabad. In his administrative report for 1858–59, Davidson cited the letters of the men of the Contingent cavalry to their friends and families in the city describing desperate encounters and British victories as one of the causes which contributed to the preservation of peace in Hyderabad.

> The letters of the men of the contingent cavalry, mostly Mahommedans of the Deccan, to their friends and families in the city . . . did more as political engines to expose the true state of the contest than all . . . that could be urged by the British authorities. Theirs were considered inventions of the enemy, the braggadocio of the Hyderabad troopers were received as gospel, and satisfied the disaffected that the game to subvert British supremacy in India was already ended.[27]

A few weeks after the attack on the residency, the situation appeared to be tense again. Salar Jung warned Davidson of the Subsidiary Force's route march with its full complement of ammunition which could lead to unnecessary panic and commotion. Davidson wrote to Major General Coffin, the commander of the Secunderabad cantonment, about this, and he agreed to discontinue the practice.

Turrebaz Khan was captured while attempting to flee. His interrogation showed that the uprising was a spontaneous one and without any plot. He did not reveal any names, not even that of Moulvi Ala-ud-din, and seemed proud of his mission. In March 1858, he was sentenced to transportation

to the Andaman Islands by a criminal court consisting of moulvis set up
to try him. Salar Jung was unable to secure a death penalty because of the
nizam's fear of taking life, the advice of his opponents, and the moulvis
of the court themselves who did not want it to become a precedent for
Moulvi Ala-ud-din Khan (who, after all, was one of them), in the event of
his capture.

Davidson realized that any demand for a death sentence would have to
be backed by armed force, and the existing Subsidiary Force was inadequate
for this purpose. Also, Salar Jung's opponents were gaining strength, and
though the British considered the punishment inadequate, they did not
want to press the issue and further weaken the position of the loyal diwan.
In the event, Turrebaz Khan was shot dead while attempting to escape
from the custody of British soldiers near a village called Toopran. The
moulvi was arrested in Bangalore and sentenced to transportation to the
Andamans where he died in 1884.

Davidson maintained that 'letters of the most treasonable and seditious
character were intercepted from Aurangabad, Bhopal, Ahmedabad,
Belgama, Kurnool, and Mysore', and 'Hyderabad would have been speedily
in a state of insurrection as it had already been of sedition, but fortunately
no one of rank, wealth and position could rise after the unsuccessful attack
on the Residency . . .'[28]

Almost a year after the outbreak, Davidson's superiors in Calcutta
wanted him to test the statement that the nizam was 'entirely innocent
of rebellious intentions' since a prisoner's deposition before the judicial
commissioner of Mysore had implicated the nizam. Davidson replied
that the deponent was misusing the nizam's name since 'he had caused
the Nizam to be narrowly watched from quarters and in ways he little
suspected, and although emissaries had come to him, he had after
listening to their stories, refused complicity in any movement against the
British Government'.[29]

THE REBEL RAJA

One of the saddest stories of the Mutiny was that of the young raja of
Shorapore, Venkatappa Naik, the only native chieftain to join the rebels.
A youth who had 'squandered his capital, financial, mental and physical,
in orgies of wild dissipation and debauch',[30] he had joined the uprising
because of a mistaken belief that the British were about to disarm his state.

Egged on by the mutineers, he raised an army of rebels comprising Arab and Rohilla mercenaries. The resident sent Captain Rose Campbell, one of his personal assistants, to try and convince the delinquent of his folly. But the raja was too far gone down the road of sedition and planned a trap for Campbell and his forces. Campbell was attacked in the night, and it took all the resources and courage of his 400 men, armed with just two guns, to defend themselves till reinforcements arrived in the morning and ended the mutineers' hopes.

The raja, realizing that he had overplayed his hand, fled to Hyderabad where he was arrested from a market with just a few of his attendants for company. Salar Jung promptly handed him over to the resident to be tried. A feudatory of the nizam, the raja's father had been unable to fulfil his obligations to the nizam. On his death, the administration passed into the hands of the British during the minority of the young raja. It was subsequently handed over to him when he attained his majority. Colonel Philip Meadows Taylor, who was appointed to administer Shorapore during the long minority of the raja, had established a 'sincere bond of affection' with his ward who called him 'Appa' or father.

Taylor was a popular figure in the nizam's dominions, having imbibed Hyderabadi customs and culture. He entered military service under the nizam and soon moved to administration. He excelled in many fields, but is best remembered for his historical fiction based on Deccan history. His *Confessions of a Thug* (1839) was the most influential novel about India before Kipling's *Kim* and became a bestseller. Taylor's publishers in London asked him to write a novel on Tipu Sultan, and he took the research so seriously that he even met the Duke of Wellington, who as Arthur Wellesley, had defeated and killed Tipu Sultan in May 1799. Taylor married Mary Palmer, a daughter of William Palmer, and his marriage brought him close to the social and ruling elite of Hyderabad. He knew several languages including Hindustani, Persian, Marathi and Telugu.[31]

After Meadows Taylor left Shorapore, the young man fell into bad habits, took alcohol and opium to excess, and 'drifted into zenana intrigues and wild debauch'.[32] When Meadows Taylor came to know what had happened, he obtained permission to meet his former ward, who by then, was suitably contrite. When asked if he would like to meet the resident, he refused, saying that he would be expected to beg for his life which he would not do, for he deserved to die for what he had done. This speech was repeated to Davidson, and it pleased him greatly. In a subsequent meeting with Meadows Taylor, the raja asked him if he was going to die. Taylor said that it was a distinct possibility at which the raja expressed the hope that he would not be hanged like a robber. He then asked Meadows Taylor to leave; his only request to him was to convey to the world that he (the raja) was no coward.

Davidson, when he heard the details of the interview, decided that he would try to save the young man. At the trial, the raja was condemned to death, but Davidson had it commuted to transportation for life. It was decided to imprison him in a fortress in Madras. He was told that if his behaviour showed signs of reform, he would be freed after four years. Meadows Taylor conveyed the happy tidings to the ladies of the harem, and a festive atmosphere prevailed as a result of the reprieve. The only one who seemed unmoved was the old *shastri*, the Brahmin priest. Some years ago, the raja's horoscope had been examined, and it had been predicted that he would not live to see his twenty-fourth birthday. The shastri maintained that as his master's birthday was close at hand, he could not help the feeling of dread till the date had passed.

The ladies were making preparations to visit the raja in Madras when an express runner came with an urgent message for Taylor from the residency. It brought the news which the shastri was dreading. The young raja, when being taken to Madras, at the very first encampment, had somehow got hold of his escort's revolver and shot himself. The verdict was suicide, but Meadows, from his intimate knowledge of the young man, maintained that the raja, driven by curiosity, had examined the weapon and had inadvertently pulled the trigger. Regardless of whether it was a suicide or an accidental death, the prophecy had been fulfilled to the letter.[33]

THE STAUNCH ALLY

On 14 September 1857, the British blew open the Kashmiri Gate and entered the old city. By 20 September, the last remnants of any resistance had been put down, and the entire city and the fort were now in British hands. Bahadur Shah Zafar had agreed to a peaceful surrender on the condition that his life would be spared. He was brought back from Humayun's tomb, where he had sought sanctuary, and imprisoned in the fort. His two sons and a grandson were killed in cold blood near Delhi Gate by Major Hodson who was charged with bringing them back to the city. Bahadur Shah Zafar was found guilty of rebellion and waging war against the government and exiled to Rangoon with his wife, Zeenat Mahal, and sons, Jawan Bakht and Shah Abbas.[34]

Throughout the long and weary months of the Mutiny, Salar Jung held steadfastly to the British alliance. His own life was often in danger, and with the exception of a few faithful followers, there was no one he could trust. It was only his confidence in the power of the British to crush the rebellion that enabled him to remain sanguine about the final outcome. Bilgrami writes, 'But few except the Minister knew how great had been the danger here until the peril was passed.'[35] Salar Jung had to counter not only the patriotic, but also the religious prejudices, of his countrymen. He was denounced as a traitor to his faith, and numerous plots were hatched to overthrow him even as he prevented Hyderabad from being swept into a maelstrom of conspiracy and revolution.

Considering that the inducement to abide by the British alliance at the time was small, it is surprising that even a man as clear-sighted as Salar Jung had unhesitatingly elected to side with the British. There was no city from which the mutineers could have expected more sympathy than from Hyderabad. Many of the nobles were disaffected, and the nizam too had a personal grievance against the British for the sequestration of Berar. The populace were just waiting for a signal from their ruler to join the insurgents. The *Morning Post* put things in their proper perspective.

> It is true that he did no more than was to be expected of a brave, honourable, and high-minded man; but then such men are not very plentiful, in India or elsewhere, and we cannot too much appreciate them when they are found in important and trying positions. Sir Salar Jung could not have done more for England than he did, and he readily might have done less. He has gained our respect and admiration, and earned our gratitude.[36]

Salar Jung, for his part, gave much of the credit to Captain Thornhill (who later became a general). Writing to a friend in England many years later, he explained why he thought so.

> Colonel Davidson was an excellent man . . . but the magnitude of the emergency had taken him so completely by surprise that had it not been for the strong will and stout heart of General Thornhill he would never, in my opinion, have tided over the troubles. As for myself, it was

entirely General Thornhill's constant counsel and support that kept up my courage, and enabled me finally to triumph over the disaffection with which the whole city seemed to be enveloped, to an extent which few British officers have any conception of.[37]

He also had words of praise for Captain Briggs, the military secretary, but did not rate his services as highly as that of Thornhill.

> Next to General Thornhill, though not to be compared with him in point of importance, were the services of General Briggs. His strong arm and undaunted courage were of the greatest service in saving the Residency when it was attacked by the mutinous rabble. I never felt so discouraged in my life as when I saw the services of these two officers passed over without notice.[38]

For his part, Colonel Davidson had nothing but the highest praise for the resolute minister, who by now had been given the new title of Mukhtar-ul-Mulk, when he wrote to the viceroy in Calcutta on 29 March 1858.

> The unhesitating energy and promptitude with which the Nizam's Minister assisted the British was beyond all praise. No Minister of the Dekhan ever before showed himself so strenuously and truly the friend of the English and the British Government . . . His assassination was planned a dozen times, and I believe he was aware of this; but neither dread on that account, nor for a time the continued intelligence of repeated reverses to our arms in the North West shook him for a moment; every contingency and every requisition made to him by me was met with the same firmness and consistency, and the resources of the Nizam's Government were, as far as lay in his power, placed unhesitatingly at my disposal.[39]

Almost twenty years later in 1876, when Salar Jung visited England, Major General William Hill, who had been chief military commander in the nizam's dominions, wrote about Salar Jung's role in a letter to the *Times*:

> . . . These energetic measures saved South India, for had the people of Haiderabad risen against us, the Mahomedan population of Madras would, it was well known at the Presidency, have followed their example, and it is but just to this distinguished man that the people of England

should be informed how entirely the stability of British rule in south India was owing to the wise and energetic measures adopted at this crisis by Salar Jung.[40]

The Mutiny brought out Salar Jung's hitherto untested qualities of firmness, courage and unflappability. Once the ordeal had ended, he resumed his reforms of the administration. Now there was nothing but gratitude in the air. As Lord Canning was generous enough to concede, the states had served as 'breakwaters in the storm which would have swept us in one great wave'. But such open admiration was only forthcoming as long as Salar Jung 'ploughed the straight furrow of fidelity'[41] in assisting and cooperating with British interests in Hyderabad. The moment he tried to adopt a stance of independence (particularly on Berar), the smiles on the faces of the Englishmen were replaced with frowns of disapproval and disbelief. As we shall see later, Salar Jung, who was the hero of the Mutiny in the eyes of the British, in the closing stages of his life, became something of an anathema to the British rulers.

5

After the Mutiny

The unenviable task of suppressing the Mutiny and restoring order fell on Charles John Canning, the Governor General. A son of a former prime minister, he had started his career as a Peelite and was part of Lord Palmerston's cabinet in 1855. He succeeded his friend Dalhousie as Governor General and had to face much of the resentment created by the much-hated Doctrine of Lapse. A capable diplomat and a pragmatic administrator, he was not known for any especial brilliance, but he was able to restore order and proclaim peace within a few months.

He was known for his policy of moderation throughout the Mutiny, and this earned him the sobriquet 'Clemency Canning'. A just man who refused to sully justice with indiscriminate reprisals, he insisted that culprits be treated with justice, and that a distinction be made between the instigators of the revolt and their ignorant followers. Canning, who received little support from Britain where indignant cries were raised against the savagery of the rebels, did all he could to curb the racial feelings that had been aroused. As a result, he was unpopular both in England and with the English in India for a time.

His wife, Charlotte Canning, documented the Mutiny in detail and sent reports directly to Queen Victoria. Of all the vicereines, Charlotte Canning, who had served for thirteen years as a lady of the bedchamber, was the closest to the queen. She kept a detailed diary, and was also a prolific watercolour painter and photographer. Charlotte sent the queen detailed accounts of the Mutiny, its progress, its atrocities and horrors, including the difficulty in separating truth from rumour. These carefully documented reports had a significant impact on Victoria's perception of the grim events unfolding at the time. She asked Charlotte to confirm and expand upon the reports of the defilement of British women by native rebels.

Her letters provided a corrective to the sensational narratives of the events, particularly at Kanpur and Lucknow. She told the queen that the mutilations which had caused the most horror were carried out on the bodies of the dead: there was little to prove that they had been the victims of violent sexual assault when alive.[1] As the months passed, Victoria came to depend more upon Charlotte than her own ministers for accurate information. That Lady Canning was close friends with Sir Colin Campbell, commander-in-chief of the Indian army, who freely discussed military matters with her, must certainly have helped. He showed her letters and telegrams which made the vicereine privy to decisions taken at the highest level.[2]

A bill had been introduced in Parliament to transfer governance from the East India Company to the Crown. Thus, it was Canning's lot to not only suppress the Mutiny but also initiate the peaceful revolution which followed it. His patience, tenacity and courage during the Mutiny earned him the respect of those who knew what risks he had to run. Canning himself realized the nature and seriousness of the rebellion. 'The struggle which we have had has been more like a national war than a local insurrection. In its magnitude, duration, scale of expenditure, and in some of its moral features it partakes largely of the former character.'[3] In Lord Curzon's words, 'He was calm amid the tumult, silent in the face of obloquy, resolute upon the great and crowning lesson of mercy.'[4]

The Mutiny had profoundly shaken the British, and the realization of their vulnerability came as a rude shock. The sepoys, on whom the East India Company had depended, had proved to be unreliable, and historian Sarvepalli Gopal believed that the outbreak took most of the British in India by surprise. None of the officers, civil or military, had expected such an uprising. With hardly any exception, they swore by the fidelity of the men under their command. Back home, statesmen with far less knowledge of the details on the ground had shown more prescience. Canning, on the eve of his departure in 1856, had spoken of such a possibility, and even Palmerston, who was indifferent to Indian affairs, had indicated that the maintenance of the Indian empire might become a military problem.[5]

Canning, before he left for India, put on record his view that a major crisis was imminent: 'I wish for a peaceful term of office. But I cannot forget that in the sky of India, serene as it is, a small cloud may arise, no larger than a man's hand, but which, growing larger and larger, may at last threaten to burst and overwhelm us in ruin.'[6] The Mutiny was not caused by any one single reason. The British, in their arrogance, had failed to read the warning signs. William Dalrymple has observed: 'So removed had the British now become from their Indian subjects, and so dismissive were they of Indian opinion, that they had lost all ability to read the omens around them or to analyse their own position with any degree of accuracy. Arrogance and imperial self-confidence had diminished the desire to seek accurate information or gain any real knowledge of the state of the country.'[7]

The princes, who had been looked upon with suspicion, had turned out to be loyal and a source of strength. The native rulers had been treated shabbily, with successive Governors General nurturing dissent when accommodation was possible. They had been coerced into ceding territories on untenable grounds with alien concepts and doctrines imported from England. Yet, it was the loyalty of these very rulers which ensured that the British survived in India.

It was decided that power would be transferred from the East India Company to the Crown. This initiative was taken by Prime Minister Palmerston himself, who told Canning that a vast territory and a population of 150 million could not continue under the nominal supremacy of a company of merchants and needed to be placed under the direct authority of the Crown. The Company made a last-ditch effort to save its power, and John Stuart Mill drew up a petition on its behalf to Parliament. But Palmerston went ahead with his bill, proposing transfer of the Company's Indian administration to the Crown. The bill failed because of the unexpected fall of his government. His successor was the Earl of Derby, whose first India Bill also failed, but the second was passed with minor amendments.

The Act for the Better Government of India, 1858, mainly the handiwork of Lord Stanley, the president of the Board of Control for India, received royal assent on 2 August 1858. India was now to be governed directly by, and in the name of the Crown, through a Secretary of State. He would be aided by a fifteen-member council of whom at least nine should have served in India for not less than ten years, and have left India not more than ten years before their appointment to the council.

In India, the administration would remain in the hands of the Governor General, who was now given the title of viceroy, a purely ceremonial title since the viceregal duties were never defined. But Canning was pleased with his new designation since it gave the head of the Indian government an exalted status. In the nine decades which followed, it was as viceroy that the head of government was best known. The duties of the council were essentially advisory, and the Governor General could overrule their decision in all but financial matters.

While many believed the change to be merely a change of nomenclature, (which was in a sense true since there was no immediate change in the personnel or traditions of the Government of India), it did have significant psychological and practical implications. A social order was now established with the British Crown at the centre of authority 'capable of ordering into a single hierarchy all its subjects, Indian and British'.[8]

According to the Act, the change of government had to be announced to the Indian people through a royal proclamation. Stanley, who became the first Secretary of State, wanted Canning to make a formal announcement but wanted it to be low-key. Canning too, was not in favour of any ostentation and decided that the proclamation (which was translated into seventeen Indian languages and sent to all the princely states) would be read in his presence at Allahabad on 1 November 1858, and also at Bombay, Madras, and Calcutta and other important centres.

The proclamation was read at 5 p.m. at a dignified ceremony. Queen Victoria, having delivered the last of her nine children, now conveyed some reassurance to India's princes. She promised to be bound by the same obligations to the Indian people as to her other subjects, and to respect the ancient customs and laws of India. The rights of the princes were to be respected and due regard given to their treaties with the East India Company.

Thus, the 'first and most important effect of the change was the establishment and positive recognition of British paramountcy'.[9] After 1858, it was not only a historical fact, but a legal principle capable of interpretation and expansion. Significantly, the princes, who had been erstwhile allies of the East India Company, now became feudatories of the Crown. The concept of the queen as the head of the empire became something which was very tangible and real, and was meant to inspire the princes with a sense of loyalty, a fact which was reiterated by all her representatives.[10]

The proclamation had an immediate impact on Hyderabad, which became a subordinate ally bound by loyalty to the paramount power. The nizam had never been a vassal or feudatory of the British according to any of his treaties with the East India Company, but the proclamation materially changed his position. With Bahadur Shah Zafar exiled to Burma, the nizam, who in theory still owed allegiance to the Mughal emperor, was asked to discard the Mughal coins and strike new ones bearing his own name. The nizam was reluctant, wanting to extend such courtesy to the last Mughal while he was alive, but Canning was adamant.

Salar Jung agreed that it was pointless to retain an inscription which referred to a sovereign who did not exist. New coins in the name of 'Nizam-ul-Mulk Asaf Jah Bahadur' were struck and the figure 92, signifying Prophet Muhammad, was impressed upon them. Also, the khutba was read in the name of the nizam for the first time. He accepted the honour without any enthusiasm. The irony of being able to adopt these two symbols when he had all but lost his freedom to act independently must certainly not have been lost on him. But even in this, he seems to have lost his freedom, since in 1859, when he proposed a change in the inscription of his coins by replacing the digit 92 with the name of the Prophet, Davidson refused permission, suspecting that the change was designed to deny the supremacy of the Crown and to show that the nizam's sovereignty flowed from the Prophet.

The title of viceroy was also conferred by the royal proclamation. Now officially representing the queen, the respect and authority of the Governor General, now also styled as viceroy, was greatly enhanced. The resident, as his political representative, also rose commensurately in status and influence, and 'his powers although necessarily undefined, became omnicompetent for all practical purposes'.[11] While the nobles and the principal traders and bankers vied for influence at the residency, the common people still distrusted the British, and the resident, their representative at the court. The assassination attempt on Salar Jung and Davidson may well have been an expression of this popular sentiment.

THE ASSASSINATION ATTEMPT

On 9 March 1859, Davidson returned from Calcutta, carrying with him a *khareeta*[12] from Canning. Davidson requested for an audience immediately but had to wait for a few days because the nizam was recovering from cholera. It was granted on 15 March when the khareeta was read. It thanked the nizam for his loyalty, but apart from a promise of a reward, there was nothing tangible to lift the spirits of the nizam. It was left to the somewhat embarrassed Davidson to once again assure the nizam that his services were appreciated by the Governor General, and he would eventually receive some material proof of gratitude. Significantly, it congratulated the nizam on removing from the coinage and seals of Hyderabad 'the devices and title of the House of Delhi'. It added, in a more ominous tone, that the ruler of Delhi had by rebellion forfeited his title, and neither his titles nor any of the honours attached to it would ever be revived.

However, this day is noteworthy not so much for the reading of the khareeta from Canning but for an event which occurred soon after the durbar was over. When Salar Jung and Davidson were only a short distance from the nizam's apartments, a man fired at them. A bystander with quick reflexes succeeded in striking the muzzle of the gun downwards, thereby deflecting the shot. It struck Tehvur Khan, a foster-brother of Salar Jung. The man then drew his sword and struck a blow which was warded off by Fateh Ali, Salar Jung's *khansama*, who received it on his arm. By that time, some of Salar Jung's followers stepped in front of him and the resident to shield them from any renewed attacks. After a brief engagement, the assassin was cut down. This ended an assassination attempt, which if it had met with success, had the potential to change the history of Hyderabad.

Captain Hastings Fraser, the son of General Fraser who had been resident in Hyderabad, who was appointed second assistant resident at Hyderabad in January 1859, was an eyewitness to the attack. He narrated how he had drawn his sword and thrown himself before Davidson, but fortunately the assassin was intercepted by the minister's dependants, and cut down.

> Had the man attempted to pass me, I should there and then have cut him down, but seeing that several of the minister's attendants were cutting at him, I refrained from joining them, and Colonel Davidson observed to me afterwards, that it was fortunate I had done so, as most probably the crowd, who were all armed to the teeth, would have become excited at seeing the Feringhee killing a Mohammedan, and would have fallen on the whole of the staff, and thus all our lives might have been sacrificed.[13]

Greatly disturbed by the event, Afzal-ud-Daula sent for Salar Jung and Davidson and asked them to retire to the safety of a private garden next to the hall of audience while he busied himself by listening to reports of the incident and making arrangements for their safety. The nizam was certainly taking no chances: hundreds of people—the nizam's entire retinue—accompanied the party back to the residency.

The *Englishman* reported, 'Whilst the ferment lasted His Highness was firm in mind, vigorous in action. With the cessation of the excitement after the Resident had left him he was quite overcome and exhibited a degree of feeling creditable to his heart and his principles.'[14] Davidson, for his part, set the nizam's mind at rest when he said that he had not the slightest suspicion of his good faith towards his government or of his goodwill towards himself. He reiterated this through Salar Jung when he had safely reached the residency.

Salar Jung mounted an elephant along with Davidson, and as an added precaution requested that Rafi-ud-din Khan and Rashid-ud-din Khan, the two sons of Shums-ul-Umra II, be included in the escort party.

Rashid-ud-din was, as we have already noted, implicated in the attack on the residency. The would-be assassin had been identified as a Pathan from Rampur, Jehangir Khan, the standard-bearer of Khurshed Jah, Rashid-ud-din's son.[15] He had a bad reputation, having previously attempted to stab a judge who had dismissed a case in which he was a plaintiff. Failing to stab the judge, he turned on the defendant whom he was suing. He was also involved, along with some others, on the attack on Brigadier Colin Mackenzie at Bolarum. He had also been involved in violence in the palace some years ago when he, along with two dozen others, had attempted to coerce the late nizam to pay a debt he did not acknowledge.[16] Most of the party were killed but he had escaped with his life. He was also said to be a fanatical supporter of the Mughal emperor. He died of his wounds the next day.

Jehangir Khan was usually clad in complete armour, but on that day wore a thickly quilted *angharka* which 'bore a good deal of slashing before he was wounded'.[17] Salar Jung must have suspected the involvement of at least one of the two brothers, and his request ensured that the party would not be attacked by their adherents.

While on the elephant, Davidson asked Salar Jung if the shot could have been fired by accident, and if otherwise, its intended target. Salar Jung said that it was not an accident since the man's angharka had several layers of clothing, the customary protection against sword injuries. He thought that the resident was the target since they could have despatched him (Salar Jung) more easily elsewhere. The next day, however, Salar Jung seemed to have a change of heart and said that probably the assassin was indifferent as to whom he killed. Sometime later, he maintained that he alone had been the target. Attempts to elicit a confession from the attacker failed. He maintained that he was acting alone, and the shot was accidental. Those of his community anxious to exculpate themselves from complicity cited his past record as proof of his having required no instigation for the deed, forgetting that if one required the services of an assassin, a man of his antecedents would find immediate favour.

Davidson exonerated Rashid-ud-din Khan and his father. In his communication with Calcutta, he attempted to analyse the attacker's motives. He said that apart from gratifying his fanatical feelings and pleasing his immediate master, the expressions in regard to the last Mughal king in the Governor General's khareeta were well known in the city, and all these taken together were enough to ignite an excitable mind.

He ended the despatch by expressing the view that the nizam and Salar Jung should both be warned to be more rigorous in their measures for 'our protection'. Calcutta concurred strongly. The secretary to the viceroy wrote that the nizam should clearly understand that the safety of the British resident within his territory was his responsibility. Nothing could have been more ironic since all the early treaties were based on the fact that the nizam was buying his protection from the British by cession of territories. In a reversal, the British were now claiming protection from the nizam, and insisting that it be firm and vigorous.

The murder attempt was not the only example of resentment. A conspiracy to depose the nizam, attack the residency and proclaim Nana Saheb as the ruler of Hyderabad was also discovered. This plot at the fag end of the Mutiny was the brainchild of Rao Sahib, a Maratha Brahmin who had come to Hyderabad from Baroda. Rao Sahib managed to escape, but some thirty others implicated in the plot were arrested and received prison sentences. The British held the nizam's government responsible for the escape of the chief conspirator. But the rebels enjoyed the sympathy of the masses and the police. The sahukars who had supported Salar Jung in the early part of his tenure were also involved in the scheme. Little surprise then that Rao Sahib managed to escape.

'GRATITUDE' AT LAST

Given the nizam and Salar Jung's support to the British in the dark days of the Mutiny, it was natural for them to expect some mark of gratitude from the British. Unfortunately, this was strangely missing for a long time. As Harriet Ronken Lynton observes, 'That loyalty conferred an obligation was normative in Salar Jung's world. The loyalty which the "Faithful Ally" confidently expected to be returned was mysteriously missing in Calcutta, where the Viceroy was so busy being magnanimous to former enemies that he earned from the European community the derisive nickname "Clemency" Canning.'[18]

The nizam seemed worried about the lack of acknowledgement of Hyderabad's role. On a visit to the residency in June 1858, he had sought reassurance from Davidson about the state of the relationship and if 'anything had occurred to interrupt the amity and alliance of the two governments'. The resident was quick to assure him that all was well. Part of the nizam's apprehension lay in the fact that the British had been silent about his services. Even the press seemed to give more credit to Salar Jung than to the nizam, so jealousy played an important role. It is possible that the suspicious Afzal-ud-Daula was wondering if the Governor General too was 'apportioning credit in the same way'.

Davidson, generous with his praise, and persistent in his efforts, tried his best. On 29 March 1858, he had written a letter to the government noting that the 'unhesitating energy and promptitude with which the Nizam's Minister assisted the English Government were beyond all praise'. Even a year after writing this letter he had yet to receive a reply which satisfied him.

Salar Jung was not unduly worried about the lack of tangible evidence of gratitude from the British. He had received news from his old friend Colonel James Oliphant that 'substantial marks of the obligation felt by the British Govt. will be conferred upon his Highness'.[19] Colonel Oliphant had been in the Madras Engineers and been assigned to Hyderabad where he built the bridge which still bears his name. Salar Jung and he must have become friends at this time. He became a director and then chairman of the East India Company, and had been appointed by Queen Victoria to attend to the young Maharaja Duleep Singh when he first arrived in England, and served him as equerry and comptroller of the household.

In August 1858, Oliphant informed Salar Jung of the despatch to the 'Supreme Govt. calling for a list of those Princes who have distinguished themselves by acts of fidelity to the British Govt. and asking their [the Supreme Govt's] views as to the best means of rewarding them; whether by territorial grants, by pensions, or gratuities, or by Honorary distinctions.'[20] Oliphant assured him that high on the list, along with other worthies like Scindia, Holkar and the king of Nepal, was the nizam.

There is no evidence to suggest that the resident knew about this correspondence or that Salar Jung ever confided in Davidson the information Oliphant had shared with him. However, knowing that some reward or honour was bound to be given, the resident expressed his confidence to the nizam that a mark of British gratitude could certainly be expected.

In early 1860, when still nothing had been heard in the matter of a reward, Oliphant wrote to Salar Jung once again, informing him of his interview with Sir Charles Wood on the subject. Wood said that they were keen to reward the nizam, but Lord Canning had shown little interest in the matter. Oliphant wrote: 'I replied "It is a poor return to the Nizam for all that he has done, that every little petty state and zemindar has had gifts and jagheers and titles bestowed, when our oldest and most faithful ally to whom we owe the safety of Southern India has been left unnoticed."'[21]

In a subsequent letter, Oliphant again inquired from Salar Jung as to why the resident had done nothing to remind the Governor General about the reward. 'They have done what they thought right for the Resident; how is it that they have done nothing for the Native Prince?'[22]

The Treaty of 1860

While the British realized that some reward or tangible form of gratitude was necessary for the princes who had stood by them, they were unsure as to how to reward them. Vernon Smith, president of the Board of Control, was unsure as to how to honour those who had 'behaved well'. Ross Mangles, chairman of the East India Company, recommended some special mark of distinction from the queen. The more pragmatic Canning rightly believed that some accession of territory would go down well with the smaller chiefs. For the more important princes like Scindia and Holkar, he recommended some alteration or relaxation in the treaties. The latter would also benefit the British since many of the treaties were inconvenient to them, there being something to amend in almost all of them.

When these matters were being discussed, Lord Palmerston's government fell in February 1858, as we have already noted, and the Earl of Derby formed his second cabinet. Lord Stanley became president of the Board of Control and later the first Secretary of State for India. A generous man, Stanley wanted Canning to reward the princes with land to show that 'we can recompense as well as punish'. In the end, the smaller chiefs received jagirs and titles, and both Scindia and Holkar were rewarded with territory. A suitable reward for the nizam was, however, proving to be a difficult decision. Stanley had already suggested land, and Canning agreed. In fact, the viceroy went as far as suggesting that the restoration of Berar, even a partial one, was the only reward worth giving the nizam. He was well aware that it was also the one he would appreciate the most. It would not be too extravagant to suggest that one of Salar Jung's reasons for supporting the British during the Mutiny was an expectation of just this reward.

In June 1859, the Derby government fell and gave way to the second Palmerston government. This was distinctly unlucky for the nizam and Salar Jung, for it put Sir Charles Wood at the helm of affairs as Secretary of State. The energetic and experienced Wood had previously been head of the Board of Control and was an expert on Indian affairs, a field he dominated till 1866. He was far less sympathetic to Indian aspirations than Stanley and would be the last person to restore Berar. In fact, he had chafed at two of the provisions of the treaty of 1853: the payment of the Berar surplus and the submission of Berar accounts to the nizam, bemoaning the fact that Dalhousie had not been able to negotiate better terms. In the guise of 'rewarding' the nizam, Wood saw his opportunity to rid himself of these inconvenient provisions of the treaty of 1853.

At that time, Manchester was in need of Indian cotton as a reserve against excessive dependence on supplies from America. They believed that the cotton from Dharwar and Berar could be transported to the eastern coast via the Godavari river. Wood was very keen to make the river navigable, but the problem was that it ran for about 200 miles through the nizam's territory. It was essential for the British to control at least one side of the river. This would also rid them of the annoying 5 per cent duty on all goods in transit on the river which the nizam levied. Wood therefore set out to acquire the left bank of the Godavari and to free the navigation from the duties payable to the nizam. He told Canning that while rewarding the nizam's loyalty, it would be a good idea to get some concessions as well.

Canning required little persuasion. He seems to have changed his views on the restoration of Berar almost immediately on Wood's arrival, abandoning his earlier resolve to restore the districts as part of the nizam's reward. In all probability, he may never have been particularly enthusiastic about the restoration and had suggested it merely to please his previous superior, Stanley.

The viceroy sent his terms for the new treaty to Davidson. The provisions included the following: First, the nizam's debt to the Company of Rs 50 lakh was cancelled and Shorapore was to be given to him. Second, Berar was to be leased in perpetuity. If the nizam protested, the districts would continue to be held in trust. Third, the sarf-i-khas estates (nizam's personal estates) in these districts were to be handed over to the Government of India. Fourth, all accounts of Berar were to be dispensed with. Fifth, the left bank of the Godavari was to be transferred to the Government of India, and the nizam was to abolish all duties on goods transported on the river in lieu of a monthly payment or a cession of territory.

The fair-minded Davidson was quite shocked at receiving these terms from Canning since they were even harsher than those originally proposed by Dalhousie. Salar Jung was dismayed and rejected them as not meeting the views of the nizam. He sent the resident a letter outlining the expectations of the nizam and his government. Berar was to be restored, failing which, at least yearly accounts were to be furnished and surplus paid. Cancellation of the debt and restoration of Shorapore to the nizam were other demands. As regards the cession of the left bank of the Godavari, Salar Jung said that since the subject was a new one, no decision could be given on it without knowing the views of the British on the restoration of Berar.

Salar Jung's letter and Davidson's objections had little effect on a determined Canning. He instructed Davidson to conduct negotiations for a new treaty in which the nizam was to cede the lands on the left bank of the Godavari, abolish customs duties, and dispense with the furnishing of Berar accounts. The Government of India would cancel the debt, and restore the districts of Raichur, Dharaseo and Shorapore. It would keep the east and west districts of Berar, amalgamated by the sarf-i-khas lands and adjoining territory as would make up a gross revenue of Rs 32½ lakh required for the payment of the Contingent and other treaty obligations and the cost of administration.

Salar Jung agreed to hand over the left bank of the Godavari and to abolish the transit duties on the river, but resisted the move to administer Berar from Nagpur. He insisted that the administration of Berar should continue to be with the resident (so as to assure public recognition of the fact that Berar still belonged to Hyderabad), and that the Berar surplus should be paid into the coffers of the nizam. Canning sent the resident four proposals which he wanted to be accepted or rejected in their entirety. They were the restoration of Raichur and Dharaseo, the cancellation of the debt, dispensing of the Berar accounts and transfer of the sarf-i-khas estates. Salar Jung's plea that the Godavari matter was linked to all these fell on deaf ears.

It is significant that when the Government of India asked Davidson for his confidential comments on the draft treaty, he had no hesitation in discussing the provisions with Salar Jung, for his report mentions Salar Jung's responses on several occasions. The two shared a good working relationship—a quality Salar Jung missed with many of the later residents.[23] In fact, Davidson went a step further in trying to convince his superiors in Calcutta of the justice of the nizam's claims. On 12 October 1860, he wrote that with the queen's proclamation, the princes now thought that the regime where their counterclaims were not admitted was a thing of the past and wanted the viceroy to 'succinctly understand some of the pecuniary dealings by which the Nizam's Government considers itself to have been injured and aggrieved by that of the Hon'ble Company'.[24]

Davidson's attempts at putting across the Hyderabadi point of view did not go down well with Calcutta. Canning severely rebuked him, telling him that had he stuck to his mandate, 'negotiations would have been brief and successful'. Left with no choice, Davidson asked Salar Jung to accept the viceroy's terms. The nizam finally consented, only asking that the Berar surplus be paid, and that the administration of Berar be kept in the hands of the resident. Canning agreed to grant him his requests, but it was made clear to the nizam that he could not question the costs of administering Berar.

Happy with his bargains, Canning now proceeded to send presents to the nizam, Salar Jung and other nobles. On 5 October 1860, the government forwarded gifts worth Rs 1 lakh for the nizam, which were presented to him in the durbar by the resident. The treaty of 1860, under which the gifts were to be sent, had been negotiated, and 'presents of English manufacture, valued at one lakh of rupees . . . to be procured in Calcutta' were to be presented to the nizam in recognition of his fidelity. Salar Jung and Shums-ul-Umra II also received gifts of jewellery, as did Raja Rameswar Rao of Wanaparthy and other chiefs.

J. Oliphant sent Salar Jung a newspaper clipping from London which had estimated Salar Jung's gifts to be worth Rs 30,000, but 'which is however not considered equal to his merits'.[25] The nizam communicated his thanks to the Governor General and also announced that he was sending a gift of jewellery to the viceroy, no doubt with a view to freeing himself of any sense of obligation. The nizam was told that while he could send gifts if he wanted, the viceroy could not accept them personally. The gifts, with an estimated value of Rs 1,57,000, were delivered to Canning who sent them to the government treasury.

Although the nizam's letters written in flowery Persian contained the customary protestations of friendship and fidelity, it was obvious that the ruler of Hyderabad still nursed a grievance. Davidson was spot on when he wrote to Calcutta that the nizam would be satisfied with nothing short of the unreserved restoration of the whole of Berar.

The treaty between the nizam and the government was finally concluded on 7 December 1860. The debt of Rs 50 lakh due to the Government of India was cancelled and Raichur, Naldurg and Dharaseo were restored to the nizam, together with the principality of Shorapore, whose raja had joined the Mutiny. The British obtained valuable concessions which included the cession of the left bank of the Godavari in exchange for other land, and the customs duties on the river were abolished; all sarf-i-khas lands in Berar were to be given to the British; and all accounts of receipts and expenditures in Berar, past, present and future, were dispensed with.

The document, which was sent to Canning for his ratification, had the nizam's seal fixed at the top, even though records at Calcutta showed that the nizam's seal and signature had always been placed at the bottom of treaties. In the Indian context, this meant a document addressed to an inferior. Canning refused to sign it. Two copies were sent to Davidson on which were marked the proper places for the resident's and nizam's seals. The nizam objected at first but later gave in.

Canning considered the treaty a personal diplomatic triumph, and Wood congratulated him on its successful conclusion. Always one to strike a hard bargain, Wood regretted the restoration of Raichur and Dharaseo, and the inability to get Berar in full sovereignty. But the British had every reason to crow over their success. The treaty gave them almost everything they wanted, while the 'new arrangement gave the Nizam nothing that was not his own'.[26] The raja of Shorapore was the nizam's subordinate, and the nizam had an undisputed right to Shorapore. The cancellation of a debt the nizam had never considered as one could hardly be termed a reward. Even in the districts restored to the nizam, Salar Jung was made to promise that land for the Madras and Great Indian Peninsular Railway would be given to the British when it was required.

The view in Hyderabad was that the treaty was not so much a reward but a further exaction from the state, with the British gaining some lands they preferred in exchange for lands which were of no real value to them. As for the British, they felt that restoration of some of the assigned districts and the waiver of the debt of Rs 50 lakh was sufficient reward to the nizam. This was corroborated thirteen years later by Lord Salisbury when, as Secretary of State, he was being pressured about a Berar petition. He said that the nizam had been well rewarded for his loyalty by the restoration of a quarter of the assigned districts and the waiver of the debt of Rs 50 lakh. Salar Jung's acceptance of the gifts made it easier on the British conscience each time they denied the petitions for the restoration of Berar, and it is possible that he may just have regretted giving them that sense of closure.

KNIGHT COMMANDER OF THE STAR OF INDIA

Another type of reward, though not exclusively for the nizam, also fell flat and produced resentment on all sides. On 25 November 1861, the nizam was created a Knight Commander of the Star of India, a newly created order for Indian princes and nobility. It was, according to J. Oliphant, who wrote to Salar Jung about it in June 1861, intended to be bestowed on twenty-five princes and chiefs of India, and the nizam was one of them.

In December 1857, Lord Palmerston had suggested to the queen that an Indian order of knighthood be established as a means of rewarding the loyal princes. Eighteen months later, Queen Victoria informed Canning of her desire to institute a high order of chivalry for the princes of India. The institution of the Order of the Star of India, as it came to be called, was a subject in which both the queen and Prince Albert took personal interest. The idea was to join the princes in a fraternity and attach them by personal ties to the queen. The Order which Canning proposed was both for Indian princes and English officers. This would enhance the self-esteem of the princes and convey to the world that the princes and English officers were equally amongst the 'first members and officers of her Indian empire'. The princes would also be closely identified with the Crown's government, something which suited Canning well, since it was in consonance with his own policy of friendship with, and reliance on, the princes. The queen approved of Canning's idea and asked Wood to expedite its execution. Canning initially intended it to be exclusively for Indians but was told that

Indian elites would not favour an honour set aside just for them. It was then decided that both Indians and Europeans would be eligible.

The appurtenances of the Order, the star, the collar, the badge, the riband and the motto were all decided in England after much deliberation. Prince Albert, Victoria's consort, took great personal interest in the matter, even though he did not always see eye to eye with Wood and Canning on the details. 'Morning Star', 'Imperial Star' and 'Celestial Star' were some of the names rejected by the viceroy and the Secretary of State. An exasperated Albert suggested that it should be known as the 'golden impossibility' since no one could agree. Eventually the Star of India was settled on.[27]

The Order, which provided for the queen as sovereign and the viceroy as grand master, was to be restricted to not more than twenty-five recipients. A long list of Indian recipients was drawn up, but it was eventually reduced to eight: five Hindu princes (the maharajas of Gwalior, Kashmir, Indore, Patiala and the Gaekwar of Baroda) and three Muslim rulers (the nizam, the begum of Bhopal and the nawab of Rampur). In London, the first knights were Albert, the Prince of Wales and Maharaja Duleep Singh. The new order was launched on 1 November 1861, simultaneously in Allahabad and London. Four Indian rulers came to Allahabad for the investiture ceremony, while the others were admitted at investiture ceremonies at their own courts.[28]

It was, by and large, well-received in India, with only the nizam being an exception. The Governor General made confidential inquiries from the resident about the possibility or otherwise of the nizam accepting such an award since there had been rumours that he may be reluctant to do so. Wood had informed Canning that he had doubts about how the nizam would react. Since it was offered to the nizam, Davidson's answer must obviously have been in the affirmative. Indeed, the nizam would have been disappointed if he had been passed over, but there were also some difficulties—religious, customary and popular objections—in his accepting the recognition.

Since it was to be suspended around the neck, the Persian word *tauq* was used in the translation of the Governor General's letter to denominate the collar of the order. But in Persian, tauq meant a collar worn by slaves, and it was natural for the nizam to baulk at receiving such an honour. It was only after having received an assurance that Prince Albert was also one of the recipients that he finally accepted it.

The insignia of the Order contained the effigy of Queen Victoria, and to wear the likeness of any created being constituted a serious infringement of the precepts of the Muslim religion. If the nizam did so, the people would 'feel confirmed in their suspicion that the British purpose was actually to make a Christian of their ruler'. The insignia and robes were to be worn at stated times, and if these clashed with dates of religious significance, it would be impossible to wear them. Also, to wear a robe of any other form than that usually worn at the durbar would provoke ridicule. Other objections had to do with the written agreement required by Statute IX and the language of the statutes which was dictatorial and, in some cases, 'peculiarly offensive' in translation. The rule of the Order threatened expulsion for rebellion. The nizam, in an objection that was both amusing and pertinent, asked how he could be a rebel.

It was no surprise, therefore, that the nizam dragged his feet about setting a date for accepting the honour. Davidson discussed the issues with Salar Jung, and when no progress was made, voiced his displeasure with some vehemence, asking the nizam to receive with gratitude the honour the queen was so graciously pleased to confer on him.

The correspondence dragged on till the end of the year and caused much bitterness on all sides. When the nizam was finally invested with the honour, it turned out to be a source of anxiety rather than gratification. It is said that Afzal-ud-Daula was grumpy throughout the elaborate proceedings. When the moment arrived to receive the medal, the nizam, exhibiting childish pique, simply grabbed it from Davidson's hand, deposited it on the masnad, and sat on it![29]

The people in Hyderabad regarded it as a cheap way of undercutting the nizam and the local culture and religion. They expressed their disapproval by putting up placards and posters all over the city, criticizing both Salar Jung and the nizam for accepting the award. The correspondent from the *Englishman*, however, approved, 'For all that, it is satisfactory to see His Highness rising above vulgar prejudices and repudiating popular opinions. I look upon this acknowledgement as progression towards other opinions and a juster conception of the views and motives of his allies.'[30]

Davidson resented what he thought was Salar Jung's intransigence and lack of support on this subject; Salar Jung was caught in a delicate balancing act between the demands of the resident and his own sovereign; the nizam harboured ill will towards his own minister, the resident and the viceroy; and the viceroy was unhappy with the way his resident had handled the whole affair. When Salar Jung later fell out of favour with the British, he was reminded of this delay by the nizam in accepting the honour. As

Harriet Ronken Lynton observed, 'This disparity between points of view widened over the years, subtly expressed at first over a succession of small issues, until even the loyal Salar Jung could no longer gloss it over.'[31]

Canning's five-year tenure ended in 1861, but Wood asked him to stay on for one more year in the public interest. One of the last things he did before he left India in March 1862 was to send the nizam the Adoption Sanad. The sanad assured the nizam that on failure of a natural heir, any succession to the government of Hyderabad which was recognized by Muslim law would be upheld by the British, so long as he was loyal to the Crown and faithful to the treaties signed by him. While this was not the first time that the British had interfered in matters of succession, it was the first time that their ultimate authority in this matter had been formally and officially recognized. Hitherto, the succession had been regulated by acknowledged custom and Muslim law since the nizam had been treated as an independent sovereign. The sanad changed all that. It made the succession conditional on loyalty and subordination, though no treaty had given the British the power to regulate succession.[32]

Canning signed the document on 11 March 1862 on the eve of his departure from India. When the document was placed in the nizam's hand in a durbar, he accepted it in silence and placed it on the cushion beside him, recognizing implicitly the right of the paramount power to settle all questions of succession in Hyderabad.

Lord Elgin succeeded Canning as viceroy. Hard-working and scholarly, if a trifle unglamorous, this Scottish peer could leave little impact on India. Wood's dominance had reduced him to the level of a subordinate officer who was only expected to carry on Canning's general policy. His death in Dharamshala of a heart attack in November 1863 ended a short, unexciting and uneventful tenure. Forty years after his death, the monument over his grave was badly damaged by an earthquake; it was as if even the elements were trying to obliterate the name of this least remembered of all viceroys.[33]

The next viceroy was Sir John Lawrence, famous as the 'Saviour of the Punjab' during the Mutiny. Even before that uprising, he was well known for his immense energy and industry. With his brother Henry and others, he worked tirelessly to bring order and prosperity to the newly annexed provinces. A trusted lieutenant of Wood, he owed his elevation as viceroy to his mentor. Wood obtained the queen's permission and gave Lawrence the news at Paddington station.

Lawrence arrived in Calcutta in January 1864 to a hero's welcome. He hated the pomp and ceremony associated with the office of the viceroy and was soon shocking the Europeans with his informality. His dislike of banquets, balls and parties made him totally unsuited to the social side of his office, and Government House during his tenure was a trifle dull. But the durbars he held at Lahore, Agra and Lucknow were splendid affairs, and when the occasion demanded, 'he assumed with ease the dignity and circumstance of an Eastern monarch'.[34] But Lawrence, dominated by 'Maharaja Wood' (as Sir Charles Wood was called in India), was reduced to being a mere mouthpiece of the government in England.

6

The Nizam's Perpetual Displeasure

If Salar Jung's role in resisting the Mutiny earned him the goodwill of the British and much adulation both in the press and elsewhere, it did little to endear him to the nizam. The lion's share of the credit went to Salar Jung, and Afzal-ud-Daula was jealous of his success. With no education or training in administration, and no experience of dealing with people outside his court, he was highly suspicious of whatever he couldn't understand. Much of what Salar Jung did fell in this category, and this made the nizam view many of his activities with great suspicion, even prejudice. Like his father before him, he surrounded himself with a coterie whose only occupation was to promote intrigue.

The relations with Nasir-ud-Daula had, in fact, been worse. Salar Jung's presence in power had been distasteful to him because he was the nephew of Siraj-ul-Mulk in whose time Berar had been assigned. It was a matter of constant reproach and sarcasm that he had been unable to recover what another in his family had failed to keep, and he was ordered to retrieve Berar as the price of restored family honour.

Salar Jung confided in his English friends his difficulties with the nizam and the intrigues of a previous diwan, Raja Ram Bakhsh, who was trying to unseat him from his post. One of his closest confidants was, as we have already noted, Colonel J. Oliphant, whom he approached for advice on how best to deal with the nizam and also on delicate political matters. He corresponded with General Fraser and was also close to the resident, G.A. Bushby, and his assistant, Major Davidson (later colonel), who succeeded him in that post.

The nizam's greatest drawback was his extremely suspicious nature. He suspected not just Salar Jung but everybody and everything. If reform in the justice system was attempted, he saw it as an attempt to disgrace the nobility by bringing them to trial before men of lower rank. He once sent a verbal message to Salar Jung suggesting the abolition of the useless (*nikamma*) courts of justice.[1] He was opposed to the regular administration of justice because people told him that it had a levelling effect and brought degradation to the nobles.

The nizam was very partial to the Arabs, even after they had committed acts of violence in his own palace, and would chide Salar Jung when he tried to bring them to book. 'Why do you blacken the character of my Arabs?'[2] Once, in an answer to an inquiry about his health, he had replied to the vakils: 'It is for the Minister and the Amir-i-Kabir to keep me contented by their conduct, and then my health will be all right.'[3] On another occasion, Salar Jung was told: 'You obey the orders of your master, and never you mind whether the kingdom goes well or badly (*riasat sudhare ya bigade*).'[4] Salar Jung confided in Sir Richard Temple, who was resident in 1867, that the nizam thought it fit to trouble him a little now and then to keep him on a tight leash. On one occasion, Afzal had sarcastically said that Salar Jung was descended from British ancestors (*inki aulad mein se hai*). Shortly afterwards, he sent something resembling an apology, asking Salar Jung to excuse the unkind language as his ill health had made him irritable and peevish.[5] The nizam abhorred all innovation, and therefore a lot of the resentment against Salar Jung had its basis in the reforms he had introduced which were based on the English model or, at all events, quite new. Another grouse was that Salar Jung was 'much too familiar with European officers and went too much into society'.[6]

If the resident spoke to some noble near the throne, the nizam saw it as a conspiracy to secure the throne for him. Still, he was less inclined than his predecessors to interfere in matters of state, and Salar Jung told Temple that he could never have carried out his reforms in the reign of Nasir-ud-Daula.[7] Temple, while speaking to a Marwari banker, was told that the nizam felt slighted at not getting the importance he deserved, with Salar Jung taking all the credit and acting on the advice of the residency (*kothi ki salah*). He also said that the nizam would not converse much with anyone, firstly, because it was not the custom of his ancestors, and secondly, he was unsure of his own abilities and did not want to commit a faux pas.[8]

Temple had hinted to Salar Jung that it might be a good idea to do everything nominally in the nizam's name so that he might feel he had a personal share in the success or credit. Salar Jung said that this he fully understood.[9] Salar Jung, it appears, was keen to associate the nizam in public affairs, but the latter was unwilling to shoulder the responsibility. However, he experienced a frisson of envy if things were done without him.[10]

Driven to the wall, Salar Jung even enlisted the help of William Palmer, of Palmer and Company fame who lived on in Hyderabad till he died at the age of eighty-seven. Palmer served as an intermediary with the Paigah nobles, and also advised the young Salar Jung on how to neutralize his enemies and conciliate the nizam. Salar Jung complained to Palmer that most of the influential men in Hyderabad 'endeavoured to injure him with His Highness', and it was only the support of the resident and 'His Highness when left to his unbiased opinion' that had prevented his ruin. Salar Jung seems to have been blamed for almost every occurrence in Hyderabad, and he observed wryly that his only surprise was 'when a concubine of His Highness was found to be with child surreptitiously the other day that he was not in some way or other blamed for it'.[11]

Old William Palmer confirmed to Temple that Salar Jung was the only good minister Hyderabad had ever had. About the nizam, he said that Afzal-ud-Daula feared the British desperately but also clung to them. Despite all appearances to the contrary, he could not rid himself of the fear that the British would depose him and annex his kingdom. Nor would he cease being jealous of Salar Jung, or willingly hold confidential intercourse with the resident, unless he was convinced that he (the resident) would help him to trouble Salar Jung.[12]

It must be remembered that Salar Jung's reforms were carried out in the face of persistent opposition from powerful opponents and the most senseless and vexatious interference from the nizam. He had a jealous master and many enemies, open and concealed, arrayed against him. Considering the circumstances under which he had to act, his accomplishments were all the more remarkable. 'He passed his life, indeed, in the cold shadow of the indiscriminating disapproval of a master to whom he looked for applause almost by hereditary instinct.'[13] While Salar Jung despaired of ever conciliating Afzal-ud-Daula, he said that he was better in many respects than his father and grandfather. Salar Jung thought himself much worse off than any other minister: they had had friends at court and adherents even in the nizam's palace, while he did not have a single friend anywhere near the nizam.

The relations between the nizam and his minister, as indeed the public perception of these relations, also influenced the general tenor of the administration. The police arrested offenders, the moulvis presiding over the courts gave decisions, and the administration worked smoothly, if the minister was perceived to have the support of his sovereign.

Despite all he had done to set Hyderabad in order, Salar Jung received no gratitude for his efforts. On the contrary, he was faced with his sovereign's antagonism which was fanned by those who had the nizam's ear, and who filled it with accusations against him. The nizam often let it be known that his minister did not enjoy his confidence. Part of this annoyance was due to the fact that Salar Jung's reforms had affected the nizam personally. The ban on nazarana had resulted in a big loss to the nizam, and he often complained about 'that firangi bachcha' and his reforming ways. It sounds unbelievable but Salar Jung dared not appear in court unless he was summoned. His enemies and detractors had far greater access to the nizam, and they were not slow in trying to show him down.

Salar Jung was almost a prisoner in his own house and could not go beyond the outer gates of his courtyard without the nizam's permission. And this permission was not a mere formality, but a request which could be refused, or if allowed, would be granted grudgingly. If he wished to entertain in his summer house or attend a parade or even visit the resident, the express permission of the nizam was required.[14] Sir Richard Temple observed in his memoirs that he had much business with Salar Jung, but it was difficult for him to meet Salar Jung often since that would reinforce the nizam's jealousy. Sending him official papers in despatch boxes very frequently, it was feared, would invite a similar response. The reason for this strange conduct, according to Temple, was that the nizam, chafing and fretting at being under the control of his minister in all matters of state, 'revenged himself by punctiliously enforcing supervision in social matters'.[15] The diwan, though, remained perfectly loyal. Temple observes,

> Salar Jung did not seem to regard this in the light of a personal grievance;
> he shared the reverence which his countrymen felt for their master. He
> seldom was admitted to the Nizam's presence; when he was, however, he
> would be almost pale from agitation. He must have been quite hopeless
> of conciliating his master's regard, yet he was perfectly loyal, and would
> have undergone any labour for the welfare of his liege.[16]

Salar Jung's reforms had earned him many enemies, and it was the British who helped him survive in his post. British support, in turn, made him more disliked by the nobles and that much more vulnerable. Salar Jung was appointed by a coterie who thought he would be a puppet. Unfortunately for his supporters, he was his own man from the beginning, and it was not long before he added the coterie and their friends and dependants to his list of enemies. Some of his reforms had resulted in a diminution of the nizam's personal influence, and he publicly bemoaned the fact that after Salar Jung's advent, the old Mughlai ways were no longer good enough. Other reforms had restricted the power of the Arab chiefs and lesser nobles who also felt alienated.

Salar Jung had to contend with constant intrigues at court as well as the simmering, and on occasion, open resentment of nobles and jagirdars who had suffered losses or felt threatened on account of his reforms. There was an undercurrent of constant conflict, and fears of personal attacks on him and his family. He repeatedly offered to resign; an extreme step which usually came in the aftermath of the nizam's open criticism which he felt so undermined his authority that he could not accomplish what he needed to do. On other occasions, he used this threat as a way of getting concessions or orders from the nizam which he felt were in the interest of good administration. This course of action led to another complaint from the nizam that his minister was always threatening to resign. In time, even this ultimate weapon lost its effectiveness through overuse.

It was only a matter of time before the resident of the day became involved in maintaining peace between the nizam and his minister. This became a regular feature over the years, and it was done with Salar Jung's knowledge, and also sometimes, at his request. In some cases, it was done against his protest since the British knew that they could ill-afford the dismissal of the now almost irreplaceable diwan. One cannot say with any surety just how much Salar Jung was responsible for inviting the resident to interfere in what were domestic matters, but in this he was not alone. Other nobles too, when personal interests were involved, appealed to the resident or even the viceroy in the hope of getting a favourable verdict. The resident was seen as 'interfering' only when they had nothing to lose. So Salar Jung was not alone in creating this 'ominous opening', even if at first it was allowed unwittingly or dictated by circumstances.

The British were only too happy to use the numerous opportunities which the nobles and others served up for meddling in the internal affairs of Hyderabad. In the light of general developments, it may not have made much difference either way, since the imperial momentum was picking up. But the role of the resident was not without its dangers. It inculcated a habit of interference and also constituted a precedent cited by others when it suited them. More importantly, it provoked a sullen anger in the nizam, who, chafing at his impotence and dependence on Salar Jung, saw in his minister's success, his own marginalization.

'I WANT TO RESIGN'

The British kept a close watch on relations between the nizam and Salar Jung. As early as mid-1958, Stanley was told that Salar Jung's enemies at court were gaining the upper hand, and he was losing the nizam's support. Stanley wanted Canning to support Salar Jung since they did not have too many Indian friends, and Salar Jung was one of their best. He had also asked the viceroy to reward his services during the Mutiny with a special recognition. This, Canning did not do, but he came to Salar Jung's aid whenever he faced the nizam's displeasure. While Salar Jung used the threat of resignation often, there were at least three serious episodes in which he either threatened to resign, or was threatened with dismissal, by the nizam. The first of these was in May 1859, an incident in which we find Davidson playing an active role in the contretemps for the first time.

In May 1859, Salar Jung told Davidson of his intention to resign and also asked for British protection. Though the nizam had been displeased with him for long—part of that displeasure stemming from jealousy—the immediate trigger for this episode was the fact that Salar Jung, on the urging of the resident, had reported to the nizam that four persons in Hyderabad were openly hostile to the English and were planning an insurrection.

The first was Azmut Jung, the most prominent in rank and influence of the four, who was poisoning the ears of the nizam as to the sinister designs of the British against him (the nizam) and was seen openly distributing ammunition to his men as if preparing for an armed rebellion. The second was Mirdha Chand, the head of one of the two sections of the nizam's chobdars, who was a noted bigot and a friend of Jehangir Khan who had died in the failed assassination attempt. The next was Boz Khan, a burly Pathan, who was openly hostile to all Englishmen and whose residence opposite a boundary wall of the residency was one of the locations earmarked for the use of the insurgents during the Mutiny. The last was Moulvi Ibrahim, a rabid Sunni who hated the Shias and the English in equal measure, and was perhaps more famous for preaching sedition rather than the Koran.[17]

When the nizam was given the names of the persons allegedly involved in the conspiracy, he flew into a rage and accused Salar Jung of targeting his (the nizam's) friends and said that he would behead him! Writing to the Government of India, Davidson reported that Salar Jung had expressed a wish to resign since the nizam was exceedingly jealous of him. He told Davidson that the nizam's sycophantic advisers made it appear that he took all the credit himself, and by poisoning the ears of the sovereign, thwarted him in the beneficial measures he wished to adopt for improving the administration. Salar Jung also wanted to know if Davidson could guarantee his personal safety.

Peace seems to have been restored a little later and Davidson reported further developments to the government. After the incident, Salar Jung told the resident that he had been summoned by the nizam but had expressed his inability to be present at the durbar since he had been publicly disgraced and was therefore useless as his minister. The nizam then ate humble pie and communicated to Salar Jung that everything he desired would be complied with, and that he should not 'mind words spoken in anger, and when I was momentarily incensed'. Davidson reported that after much cajoling and entreaties, Salar Jung visited the palace and was well-received. He was successful in having his representations placed on the annals of government, and the nizam ordered that they should be complied with.

The four persons were exiled from Hyderabad after initial reluctance. They were permitted to return a year later but with the condition that they would not be received by the nizam, privately or publicly. In spite of this injunction, the nizam received these men and restored them to his court and favour, something which earned him a sharp rebuke from the resident. In a letter addressed to Salar Jung, the resident said that it was not advisable for the nizam to be a clandestine friend of those who were enemies of the English. After ignoring the resident's letter for a few days, an order was suddenly issued that the two leading rebels should be expelled immediately. It was Ramzan, and the nizam said that he would not break his fast till the pair had left the city, which indeed they did with the urgency expected of them.

In another incident in 1860, the nizam's uncle, Muzaffar-ud-Daula, seized and imprisoned a sahukar in the Residency Bazaar. This sahukar possessed a garden which was coveted by Muzaffar-ud-Daula who insisted on acquiring it even after it was sold to someone else. Unable to take no for an answer, he abducted the banker and placed him in confinement. When the resident demanded the banker's release, Muzaffar-ud-Daula openly defied the government and surrounded himself with armed Rohillas. For twenty-four hours, the main street leading to the chowk and other parts of the city were completely closed, and a number of persons lost their lives in this incident.[18]

Despite the resident asking the nizam to 'inflict condign punishment' on his uncle and his followers, the nizam, heeding the advice of his coterie not to take strong action against a member of the royal house, allowed the matter to be settled by compromise.[19] Salar Jung had wanted the prince to be punished like a commoner but failed to obtain the nizam's consent. An upset Salar Jung, who viewed the rejection of his advice as a slight, tendered his resignation. The resignation was not accepted, but the incident revealed to the public that the nizam and his diwan did not see eye to eye. This particular crisis ended, and 'Salar Jung retained his head, but not the love of his Master',[20] for in May 1861 there was another serious rift where the nizam told the resident that he was dismissing Salar Jung.

DISMISSAL THREATENED

At the end of May 1861, the nizam invited Colonel Davidson to a conference. What was different on this occasion was that Salar Jung was not there to receive him, and he was 'ushered into a private chamber without the usual formality of being attended by the Minister'. The nizam informed the resident that he had called him to announce to the Governor General that he had removed Salar Jung from office. Davidson expressed regret that the nizam should have any such intention in regard to the man who had rendered exemplary service, and had almost single-handedly saved Hyderabad during the time of the Mutiny.

The nizam, when asked to give a reason, temporized. When pressed for a reason, he gave no answer except that he did not wish to continue with Salar Jung. When the resident told him that a simple expression of his desire, without any reason being assigned for it, would not go down very well in Calcutta, the nizam gave two reasons, both specious, if not entirely laughable. His first objection was that Salar Jung had failed to preserve law and order during the rebellion, an amazing charge against a man who more than anyone else had striven to keep Hyderabad under control in those dark days. The second reason posited was that Salar Jung had mishandled affairs when Mir Fateh Ali, the nizam's uncle, had opposed the nizam.

Davidson replied that the peace which prevailed in Hyderabad, and the services rendered by Salar Jung during the Mutiny, were unequalled by any other in India. As for the Mir Fateh Ali affair, Salar Jung had been given no powers of discretion in the matter, and the nizam's orders were inconsistent and contradictory. Since he had been instructed that the uncle should come to no harm, the nizam's troops could not return the hostile party's fire. When Salar Jung requested leave to withdraw the troops from their positions, this too was not permitted. Davidson told the nizam that the two reasons would cut no ice with the Governor General and dissuaded him from proposing Salar Jung's dismissal on such flimsy grounds. The nizam remained adamant, and when asked if he had any other charge to make against his diwan, replied, 'None.' Davidson said he would write to Calcutta and also promised to draft a written note of what had transpired during their meeting.

Davidson drafted the note the same day and sent it to the nizam who thought nothing of forwarding it to Salar Jung, asking him to comment on his own dismissal. Salar Jung diplomatically said that since he was not present at the meeting, he could not comment on it, and in any case, since the matter related to him, it would not be appropriate for him to answer it. The nizam then ordered the presence of Fakhr-ud-din Khan Shums-ul-Umra II Amir-i-Kabir, and his son Rashid-ud-din Khan Iktidar-ul-Mulk. Shums-ul-Umra II, when asked for his opinion, told the nizam that he had acted unwisely and wished to know what, or who, had prompted the nizam to act in such a manner. The nizam's answer shocked him. He was told that it was none other than his other son, Rafi-ud-din Khan Umdat-ul-Mulk, who was behind the move. The father then told the nizam that his son would have to answer for his own conduct.

While on the face of it, the principal player in this drama appeared to be Rafi-ud-din Khan Umdat-ul-Mulk, in reality, he was incapable of planning any such measure. He was advised by a cabal consisting of Yacoob Ali, a small mansabdar, Mohammed Shakoor, his own minion who was the steward of his private and public establishments, and Lal Mahomed, a minion of the nizam. There was also Vithal Row, who had prepared the financial statements charging Salar Jung with defalcation at the behest of one of the co-conspirators, and who had died a mysterious death, allegedly by his own hand. When the nizam summoned Vithal Row to ascertain the facts, he was presented with his corpse. Had he lived, he would certainly have disclosed the secrets of the cabal, something his murder, or suicide, conveniently prevented. The *Englishman* observed: 'The English Government cannot allow a cabal, the principal agitators in which are vile menials, to prevail against this great and good man. His affairs are in the hands of the Resident, they could not be in better.'[21]

The nizam, realizing that he had been taken for a ride, retracted his proposal and asked Salar Jung to continue as diwan. His questioning of Rafi-ud-din Khan would have made him aware of the conspiracy to get rid of Salar Jung. The nizam told Salar Jung that he was satisfied with him and wrote a letter to the resident conveying the same sentiment.

An amusing episode in connection with this temporary estrangement between the nizam and Salar Jung was a revolt of the harem. The ladies of the zenana threatened to rebel if Salar Jung was dismissed and Rafi-ud-din Khan Umdat-ul-Mulk was appointed in his place. They said that since he (Salar Jung) had been in office, their allowances and pensions had been paid on time, something which had never happened under earlier dispensations. They threatened to quit the purdah, break Rafi-ud-din Khan's palanquin and stone his friends. It was reported that the ladies were 'expert in this style of warfare', and with stones as their weapons, had on two other occasions closed the street passing by the nizam's palace for three days. The zenana, from the time of the second Asaf Jah, Nizam Ali Khan, appears to have been quite influential in deciding matters of state. It is said that Nizam Ali Khan's two senior wives, Bakshi Begum and Tinat-un-Nissa Begum, had a great deal of influence over the 'professional life expectancy of the Nizam's advisers and ministers'.[22]

What is worth noting about this episode is that it transformed the nizam's explicit right to appoint his own minister into the government's right to ratify or reject the appointment. Lord Dalhousie had stated that the nizam could appoint any minister of his choice, and this had been reiterated on several occasions. In this case, when Davidson heard the nizam's decision, he told him that he did not believe that the Governor General would agree. When the nizam reminded him that he had the power to dismiss his minister without permission, Davidson replied that he could not agree to any such proposal.

In the note which Davidson sent the nizam, he summarized the conversation and concluded by telling him that unless instructed otherwise by the Governor General, he would not conduct official business with anyone but Salar Jung. This made things a little more difficult for Salar Jung, and he offered to resign three times in quick succession before peace was finally restored. The nizam demanded an undertaking from Salar Jung that he would be obedient in future. Salar Jung complied by asserting that he had never been deficient in his obedience in the past, and in the future too, he would not be found wanting in obedience and submission.

The Governor General expressed relief when he received Davidson's report on the patch-up between the nizam and his minister. It will be recalled that Salar Jung had also asked for protection in the event he was no longer diwan. In a rather strange explanation, the Governor General, who had just prevented his dismissal, denied the request for protection, saying that such an interposition between the ruler of a native state and his minister was inconsistent with the policy of the Government of India towards native states.

After this episode, the relations between the nizam and Salar Jung improved but the former nursed a grievance about Davidson's interference for a long time, a fact he was not slow in communicating to his diwan. On the occasion of Eid, however, the nizam presented Salar Jung with nine pieces of jewellery (valued at Rs 50,000), the largest number that was bestowed on such occasions, as a khillat. The nizam asked Salar Jung to go and purchase them himself so as to have them ready for Eid. A part of the honour was that the nizam tied the armbands with his own hands. He also transferred to the charge of Salar Jung the districts recently restored by the British. In July 1861, the Governor General wrote to the nizam that he would not permit Salar Jung's removal from office, thereby ensuring that no capricious authority would be allowed to interfere with Salar Jung's administration in the future.

Davidson died of pneumonia in Hyderabad on 2 August 1862. His death removed from the scene a well-wisher of Hyderabad. For Salar Jung, it was a personal loss, for the rapport between the two had been perfect. Davidson had been resident at a most critical time in the history of the state, having weathered the Mutiny during which he showed sterling leadership and courage. A fair-minded man with a sense of justice, he tried his best to present Hyderabad's case to the viceroy. His manifest lack of success in this was due to the policies of the paramount power which he represented, rather than his own shortcomings or lack of effort.

In November 1862, Salar Jung fell from his horse and was severely bruised. The nizam sent him Rs 5000 (tassaduq) to be given in alms as a thanksgiving for his providential escape. What was special about this was the largeness of the amount. In other respects too, the nizam expressed great interest in the welfare of his loyal diwan, and it was noted by all that the sovereign had manifested goodwill towards his minister for a long time.

The *Englishman* reported, 'We do not now hear of the constant misrepresentations to the Nizam, formerly not a little in vogue, of the proceedings of the Minister, of the Resident, and the British Government. This gives us repose in that direction, but I take it to be a mere lull, and do not expect it to last long.'[23] The 'lull' lasted a while though, since the next serious flare-up occurred six years later in 1867, an episode which is discussed later. But before we see just why they were at loggerheads on this particular occasion, a discussion of what came to be known as the Murray case is both interesting and germane.

THE MURRAY CASE

The one man who was a perpetual source of mischief and worry to Salar Jung throughout his career was Rashid-ud-din Khan, son of Shums-ul-Umra II who became Shums-ul-Umra IV Amir-i-Kabir III and co-regent with Salar Jung in 1877. He was actively involved in almost every intrigue, especially those against Salar Jung. Davidson described him as 'that most pernicious and factious intriguer' whose only purpose was to oppose and thwart Salar Jung in everything that he did. Rashid-ud-din was also determined to replace him, and this is where the Murray affair has its origins.

The Murray affair appeared soon after Davidson's death in August 1862. Davidson's first wife had died when he was resident, and in October 1857, he married the daughter of an army officer, who, like Davidson, held a commission in the Bengal Army. After some months of widowhood, Ellen Davidson decided to return to England. When she was still in Hyderabad, a story involving her broke. Major Thornhill, who was Davidson's son-in-law, and was officiating as resident, noted in his account that in the year 1858 a man named Murray, a discharged apothecary, was employed by Rashid-ud-din Khan. Murray was a Eurasian, the term for people of mixed blood, and his wife was putatively British. Murray was the only person in the Paigah noble's household who could read English and was often entrusted with bills of exchange (hundis) for the payment of bills or purchase of goods on behalf of the nawab.

In 1858, Rashid-ud-din showed Murray a letter from Ellen Davidson in which she had requested Rs 1 lakh, ostensibly for urgent litigation over an estate in England. What was interesting about the letter was her promise that on receipt of the money, she would try to make him diwan in place of Salar Jung. Murray thought the letter a forgery and told the nawab as much. But Rashid-ud-din refused to believe him and gave Murray bills of exchange for Rs 50,000. These were returned with the demand for Rs 1 lakh being reiterated, since anything less would serve no purpose. The demanded amount was duly passed on to Murray who gave it to his wife, Mrs Davidson's ayah, to be delivered to her mistress.

When investigations started, Rashid-ud-din admitted he had received a letter from Mrs Davidson requesting the loan but was unable to produce the letter for scrutiny. He blamed Murray for its loss. When he realized that his political advancement was not likely, he panicked, and asked Murray for a receipt as evidence that it was a loan. He also doubted if the money had been delivered to Mrs Davidson. The receipt was also a cover in case the real purpose of the transaction was revealed. It was, of course, promptly declared a forgery by Mrs Davidson. Murray, for his part, claimed that the nawab had asked him to write a letter acknowledging the receipt of the money, which he had passed on to Mrs Davidson in response to her letter requesting the loan.

Major Thornhill passed on the details to Salar Jung, asking him to call Rashid-ud-din to account. Nothing happened, and in September 1863, an official request was made to Salar Jung asking him to bring the matter to the notice of the nizam, who it was presumed would ask Rashid-ud-din to explain his role in the affair. The explanation was to include a justification for attempting to conduct a secret correspondence with anyone in the residency without the knowledge of either the resident or the diwan. The usual mode of communication was through the vakil, Fyze Mahomed Khan, and the implication was that unless Rashid-ud-din knew that something underhand was involved, he would never have accepted the Murrays as intermediaries.

Rashid-ud-din's explanation that direct communication between his family and the residency had existed since the time of the late nizam was denied by Thornhill, who cited a brief, unrelated incident as the only exception. The fallout of this episode was that Rashid-ud-din was declared persona non grata at the residency, and the nizam was advised not to invite him to any durbar at which the resident was present. The *Englishman* noted the ban with approval: 'This is sufficient. It marks his Lordship's sense of this nobleman's conduct and will, I hope, be a warning to others, and put down the intrigues which it may almost be said pervade every minute of each day, and almost every great house in this capital.'[24] Rashid-ud-din had been banished from the scene, and this political extinction he blamed on Salar Jung for 'squealing' about the matter to the nizam. Later, he blamed him for not making vigorous enough efforts to lift the ban.

In her deposition, Mrs Murray pleaded for pity and leniency, maintaining that she had erred unconsciously and not from any wicked motive. But the Murrays were always going to be safe. Due to several technicalities, it would not have been possible for the Government of India to prosecute them; nor was there any way of making them return the money. Murray, who had been arrested pending a trial, was subsequently expelled from the nizam's dominions after spending eight months in custody.

Rashid-ud-din's versions of his role kept changing over the years, depending on the purpose they were supposed to serve. Initially, he admitted to Salar Jung that he had paid money to the Murrays who were supposed to pass it on to the resident to secure his appointment as diwan. After the nizam passed away in 1869, the explanation changed. He told Salar Jung that the bribe was not given *by* him but *through* him by the nizam. Since it was a well-known fact that both Afzal-ud-Daula, and before him his father, Nasir-ud-Daula, had often sought British permission to dismiss Salar Jung, this made it a very plausible story indeed. And since dead men tell no tales, there was no one to deny it. This was the story which was officially adopted during the time when Rashid-ud-din was to be appointed co-regent in 1877.

When Temple asked Salar Jung if he thought that Rashid-ud-din and his son Khurshed Jah were involved, Salar Jung said that he could not pin any intrigue on them but they were always exhibiting personal spite in petty ways. He told the resident that he had received a message from Rashid-ud-din to the effect that he should be readmitted to the resident's presence because the bribe had been given not by him but through him, the money being the nizam's. What is even more remarkable is that Salar Jung believed this to be true.[25] This was the version which the resident, Sir Richard Temple, recorded in his diary, even though during his tenure, Rashid-ud-din was still under the ban.

Just before Temple left Hyderabad in early January 1868, it was rumoured that Rashid-ud-din would try to bribe some of the residency servants to secure an interview with the next resident. Temple warned his servants against succumbing to temptation and refused to consider Rashid-ud-din's request for readmission. Rashid-ud-din had also requested that in case he was not readmitted, such kindness be shown to his son, Khurshed Jah. Nothing came of it, and he became increasingly bitter, holding Salar Jung responsible for his woes. Whatever his role in the Murray affair, Rashid-ud-din was now Salar Jung's implacable enemy.

The role of the former resident's widow, Ellen Davidson, is a little more difficult to understand, and there can, at best, be informed conjecture on the part she played. Salar Jung met her on his visit to England in 1876, and the two visited the opera together. There is epistolary evidence to suggest that she asked him for a loan of £2600 which she required most urgently, and which she promised to repay in annual instalments of £400 with interest at 5 per cent. Her security was to be her personal bond. What is relevant here is that there is much in common with the Murray case 'in both tone and content, that it is difficult not to suspect a connection between the two, despite earlier denials'.[26]

One possibility is that she was innocent, and her request to Salar Jung was a way out of a current financial difficulty. On the other hand, there is also the possibility that she did correspond with Rashid-ud-din, who, as we have seen, duly obliged with the money. With her husband's demise, any chance of her keeping her side of the bargain ended, and she bought the silence of the Murrays by sharing a part of the booty with them. Col. Thornhill indignantly asserted that 'no lady particularly the wife of a gentleman with such an outstanding reputation for probity as Col. Davidson enjoyed would stoop to seek a loan from a "native"'.[27] The truth was never known.

THE CONTROVERSY OVER THE VAKIL

In 1866, Salar Jung was made Knight Commander of the Most Exalted Order of the Star of India (KCSI), and the nizam was supposed to invest him with this honour at an appropriate ceremonial commanded by the queen. A new treaty concerning the extradition of prisoners was in the offing, and the suspicious nizam taunted Salar Jung about instigating the British to propose a clause in the treaty which required British criminals who took refuge in Hyderabad to be given up. Since every treaty with the British seemed to him to work against him, he accused Salar Jung of conspiring with the resident. However, it was another matter that had been simmering for a while which made Salar Jung tender his resignation on 21 January 1867.

The reason for the rift on this occasion was the appointment of a vakil whose choice was seen by many as a way of punishing Salar Jung. It was a characteristic of the Hyderabad political system to use vakils, or agents. The routine business between the nizam and his diwan was conducted through intermediaries called vakils who were confidential go-betweens. In accordance with etiquette, members of the nobility seldom met with the nizam or each other; they not only communicated through their vakils, but the vakil also served as a channel for a continuous ceremonial exchange of greetings and gifts between the nobles and the nizam. An able vakil could do much to enhance the position of his patron. The vakils worked in pairs so as to be a check on one another. Thus, all communication between the nizam and Salar Jung, except on durbar days (which did not occur oftener than once a week and seldom so often), was conducted viva voce through the vakils.

The office of the vakil was both well paid and respected. There were also a pair of vakils between Salar Jung and the resident of whom Raja Kandaswamy was the most famous. He belonged to a Tamilian family originally from Madras but which had migrated to Hyderabad in 1800. His father, Veeraswamy, is said to have supervised the construction of the Hyderabad residency. Kandaswamy was a close and trusted aide of Salar Jung and held a number of important positions. He was given the title of raja in 1869.

Server-ul-Mulk met him when he first came to Hyderabad and was looking for someone influential who could get him an interview with Salar Jung. Though his uncharitable and tasteless description of the man does him no credit, some of his observations may not be entirely off the mark.

This man was a contractor of the P.W.D. in the beginning, and was of Telugu nationality. Tall and exceedingly black—in fact, blacker than even the blackest negro—he had thick lips, and long ears in which he wore small ear-rings. His appearance invited laughter, and he conversed confusedly, but all the same he was the special favourite of the Minister for the reason that the Resident favoured him, and that he, the Prime Minister, wanted someone, who, while not possessing either much ability or capacity to intrigue or pervert facts, knew English, and would be a sort of intermediary (vakil) between the Resident and himself. Kundaswamy knew sufficient English for the purpose, but not a word of Persian or Arabic; and he knew only sufficient Telugu to carry on his work as a contractor. His ugly countenance was enough to frighten a Rustum, but as he was the pet of the Resident, he was useful to Nawab Mukhtar-ul-Mulk.[28]

Given the sensitive nature of the duties involved, it was natural for the vakils to enjoy the confidence of both the nizam and Salar Jung.

The nizam wanted to replace one of the vakils, and in his place he appointed Lashkar Jung, a man of bad character, and also an avowed enemy of Salar Jung. Lashkar Jung had previously been in charge of one of the nizam's personal talukas and in that capacity was guilty of embezzling Rs 5 lakh. Salar Jung had discovered the defalcation and made him return the money. He was also guilty of cruelty and oppression in his dealings in the villages under his charge.[29]

He was dismissed from service, and the villages were placed under Salar Jung's charge. Lashkar Jung repeatedly requested reinstatement but Salar Jung refused.[30] Expectedly, Lashkar Jung held a grudge; and Salar Jung, for his part, could hardly be expected to trust a man who, by his conduct, had forfeited his confidence, and was now his sworn enemy.

Salar Jung refused to recognize the nizam's nominee; he did not receive or even acknowledge him. This annoyed the nizam who voiced his irritation in language which Salar Jung found insulting. He immediately asked for permission to resign. The nizam neither accepted nor declined the resignation; he placed it in a kind of abeyance by asking the person who delivered it to keep it under his charge till a final decision was given. The nizam soon discovered that Salar Jung's replacement was hard to find, with all the noblemen, including the Paigah, refusing the high office in respectful but decided terms, their ostensible and, to all appearances, real reason being that they were unequal to the task.

Rashid-ud-din Khan, who was an unlikely candidate to advocate Salar Jung's case given the past history between them, told the nizam that he would be acting against the interest of Hyderabad if he did not reinstate Salar Jung. His absence would involve the country in endless troubles and eventually terminate in anarchy. In short, Salar Jung's removal would be a public calamity, and one that the nizam, on viewing the matter dispassionately, would regret.

The nizam, not a little surprised at this refusal from one of his premier noblemen, reminded him that the indignity of being prohibited from attending durbar when the resident was present was entirely due to the man whose cause he was so ardently advocating. Rashid-ud-din Khan then tried to convince the nizam that the prohibition was brought about by a set of peculiar circumstances in which both the resident and Salar Jung appear to have been misled in the Murray case. He used this opportunity to absolve himself of the charge that he had at that time coveted the post of diwan by saying that that assumption was nothing short of absurd, given the fact that he was now declining to accept it when it was vacant and offered to him.

The resident, Sir George Yule, had wanted to intervene, saying that the refusal of the nizam to invest Salar Jung with the KCSI would be viewed as an insult to the queen but was prevented from doing so by Salar Jung, who decided that he would fight this particular battle on his own. He realized that the resident's intervention would, in the long run, only make the nizam more antagonistic towards him. Though it was not true, many officials of the Government of India believed that Yule had saved Salar Jung by enlisting the services of the Paigah noble for this purpose. The matter, which dragged on for two months, was sorted out without the resident's active or open intervention.

The resident met the nizam to discuss the matter and recommended to him Salar Jung's continuance, not so much for the sake of favouring the minister, but for his own sake, and that of the welfare of his people. The nizam said that he was not satisfied with his minister but had never mentioned anything about changing him. The resident was told that Salar Jung was very proud and always threatening to resign. A servant should take orders from his master, not threaten him, the nizam said. As regards the investiture ceremony for the Star of India which was to be bestowed on the resident and Salar Jung, the nizam said that he would be happy to do so, even though he was displeased with Salar Jung.

The meeting ended with the nizam promising to grant another interview to the resident soon. It never materialized, and Fakhr-ud-din Khan Shums-ul-Umra II was despatched to discuss the issue with the resident. Yule impressed upon him that misgovernment by earlier ministers had cost the nizam dear but affected the British little by comparison; now the case was different, and the British would not look upon disturbances in the nizam's territories with indifference since the contagion could spread to their territories as well. When asked about the nizam's displeasure, the Paigah noble told him that the real gravamen against Salar Jung was his pride. He asked the resident to tell Salar Jung to send a representation 'in our Hindustani way', which meant a humble apology couched in flowery language. Salar Jung may have arrived at that conclusion too, since it was obvious that the nizam had taken some amount of personal offence, and until his feelings were appeased, there was little hope of reconciliation.

Salar Jung sent a representation to the nizam who indicated that he wanted certain clauses to be inserted which he thought essential for the vindication of his dignity. This was done, but still the nizam procrastinated. Salar Jung was asked to add an additional condition in the representation to the effect that he would not be unfaithful in future. How painful this must have been for him can easily be imagined but he had no choice but to comply. On 2 March 1867, Salar Jung was summoned to a durbar and was received by the nizam, and his nazar was accepted, ending the stand-off which had threatened the stability of Hyderabad.

In the end, a compromise was worked out where no one lost face. Salar Jung extracted a guarantee that Lashkar Jung would be privy to no confidential information and would fade out of the scene in a few weeks time. To certain conditions insisted upon by the nizam, Salar Jung wisely raised no objection, and when these documents were signed, the nizam fixed a day for receiving his minister in open durbar, a sign to all that peace had been restored. On 16 April 1867, Salar Jung was received at a public durbar by the nizam in which the customary etiquette was followed and he was presented with five pieces of khillat. The reconciliation was now complete.

In April 1867, the *Englishman* observed:

> ... The British Government is recognised as the supporter of the Minister on all occasions, and thus it comes to pass that in the eyes of the people these frequent insults heaped upon Salar Jung are regarded as proofs of the Nizam's independence and importance.[31]

Yule had written a long account of the dispute to the government, warning that the state would degenerate into anarchy if Salar Jung was removed since it was universally admitted that the ministership of Salar Jung had been a blessing to Hyderabad. An example will illustrate the point well enough. No sooner was it known that Salar Jung had resigned, a band of Rohillas seized a hill fort and rode freely over the country in the old Pindari fashion. When it was known that the diwan had been reinstated, they dispersed to their homes. Just the announcement was sufficient to convince them that the profession of a bandit was still an unsafe one.

Referring to a letter he had written to the nizam seeking a meeting and which Salar Jung was reluctant to deliver, Yule wrote:

> I consented however to repeated postponements of delivery of this letter, although I considered it advisable always to urge its being forwarded to His Highness. I was quite aware that the contents of the letter would get to His Highness's knowledge somehow or other, and might, in this way, probably lead His Highness to change his course without hurting his feelings to the degree compliance with my recommendations after a personal discussion would do.[32]

The secretary in the Foreign Department had acquiesced in this line of action and approved of postponing the 'actual presentation of such a demand as long as possible, in order that the Nizam might have time to change his mind and restore Sir Salar Jung to favour without any open interference from you'. As Harriet Ronken Lynton has observed, 'Over the years it became an item of received wisdom among British officials that Salar Jung owed his office to the continued support of the Residents . . . These repeated crises, together with repeated ambivalences by both the Nizam and his Minister, offered any Paramount power recurrent opportunities to influence the direction of events, to establish useful precedents, and to create obligations.'[33]

Did Salar Jung really mean to resign? Probably not. He had sent his letter at the insistence of the nizam but knew that he had Yule's backing. The resident, in turn, was confident of the viceroy, Sir John Lawrence's support on this issue. The nizam would have had to take him back, even if it was against his will. Salar Jung admitted as much when he wrote to Sir Richard Temple (who had succeeded Yule) in April 1867 describing the episode and admitting that external pressure had been brought to bear on the nizam even though he denied having invited or desired such interference. Salar Jung's statement in this regard must be taken with a pinch of salt since it is certain that he was in regular touch with Yule for the duration of the incident, and relied on his intervention. Hyderabad, it seems, was ruled by an ingenious mixture of British dictation and native intrigue.

Lawrence, while he was one with Yule on the subject that Salar Jung should not be allowed to resign, was a little more circumspect when it came to dealing with the minister. He did not want to encourage him against the nizam and was a little wary about supporting a minister who no longer had the affection of his master. In this case though, this sentiment was the result of his annoyance with Salar Jung who had recently asked for the restoration of Berar. It was necessary, he thought, to rein in Salar Jung. While, therefore, he sent a khareeta to the nizam asking him to retain Salar Jung, no copy of the khareeta was sent to the minister. Yule had been unwilling to leave Hyderabad till the matter was resolved, and Lawrence was a little peeved at the resident's unqualified and complete support on every issue to Salar Jung. Temple, the new resident, brought the khareeta with him to Hyderabad which was read out to the nizam by his secretary. He was silent when the complimentary opening sentences were read, but at the mention of Salar Jung's name, he expostulated in disgust, 'Oh! It's once more Salar Jung.'

Salar Jung was made to feel very uncomfortable in the nizam's presence. He told Temple that the real object of appointing Lashkar Jung was to harass him. He knew that the nizam could not afford to accept his resignation, and he had offered it as the only fair means he had of resisting.[34] Temple, who met Afzal-ud-Daula in the presence of Salar Jung, wrote about it in his memoirs.

The Minister Salar Jang accompanied us, and was made to feel thoroughly subdued in the presence of His Highness; the term 'presence' was to his ear an awe-inspiring sound, and for him his master had a quiet look of ineffable hauteur . . . Then in order to say something especially civil and polite I congratulated His Highness on the order and good government patent everywhere in his dominions. He replied, in a tone of slight displeasure that as there had during past times been good government in his dominions so there was still . . . He had however interpreted my compliment to be an indirect recommendation of his Minister and his susceptibility was aroused. This incident prepared me for finding him sensitively jealous in everything that concerned Salar Jang.[35]

Temple had also sized up the nizam, and his assessment of him is less than glowing.

He was addicted to superstition, and soothsayers or astrologers had power over his impressionable mind. If there was any idea in politics on which his thoughts fixed themselves it was this, that whatever thing had novelty must be evil, and that any so-called reform which the British Resident might suggest should be regarded with circumspection . . . For all that, he was loyal to the British Government which he felt to be his sole support. Only he wished that it would leave him to his own devices, and never interfere save to throw its aegis over him if he were threatened with insurrection, or to rescue him from his financial difficulties, should they prove otherwise insurmountable.[36]

This particular entente proved to be cordial, at least on the face of it. It was the last serious episode in which Salar Jung resigned or was threatened with dismissal. He survived, until in 1869, Afzal-ud-Daula died, and he became regent and diwan to the toddler nizam, who for obvious reasons, could not trouble him. But over a period of time, 'the British Resident assumed Afzal's mantle in that respect'.[37] But all the ill-treatment meted out to Salar Jung by successive nizams did nothing to his feelings of loyalty towards his sovereign. In Temple's words:

At the farewell interview, the Nizam seemed more distant and haughty than ever towards the Minister, whose nervousness was accordingly increased. I addressed to His Highness as many kind and respectful words as could be compressed into a few sentences of Hindustani, and he relaxed so far as to give quite a gracious answer. As we left His Highness's presence, the Minister expressed his satisfaction at my having spoken so respectfully to the Nizam. It was clear from the conversation that, despite the treatment he had so long been receiving from his master, Salar Jang felt to the full that affectionate veneration which all Muhammadans of the Deccan feel for the hereditary chief of their State.[38]

ANOTHER ASSASSINATION ATTEMPT

Temple's tenure in Hyderabad was a brief one, but it witnessed a significant rise in the power of the resident. He also shared a good understanding with Salar Jung, in whose abilities he had great faith. Salar Jung consulted him frequently and valued his advice greatly. He sent him detailed confidential reports about his own civil administration and the reforms he was trying to push through. Temple gave him 'excellent suggestions', and it was this period of the Temple–Salar Jung partnership which proved to be the springboard to real progress towards modernization. But the reforms were based on European principles, and the people of Hyderabad resented the changes made under British influence. There existed a deep-seated resentment not only against the foreign power, but also against Salar Jung who was seen as their chief ally.

This hostility came to light when on 27 January 1868, the last day of the feast of Ramzan, another attempt was made on his life. He was on his way to the palace of the nizam on 27 January on his *bocha* (a state palanquin), in order to be present at the customary Eid durbar, when he had a narrow escape. The palanquin surrounded by the diwan's attendants had almost reached the palace when two shots were fired in rapid succession from a distance of six or seven paces. There are differing versions of what really happened. One version holds that the first killed a guard, and the second injured one of the retinue after ricocheting off the bocha. In the confusion that followed, an Arab mercenary drew his sword and wounded the assassin on his arm. Another holds that the first shot missed Salar Jung and lodged in the framework of his palanquin, and the second struck a peon, wounding him mortally. He died, but not before he had inflicted an injury on the assassin's arm.

The man was overpowered and secured and owed his life to Salar Jung, who unruffled by what had happened, prevented any further act of violence by his attendants. Salar Jung continued on to the palace and assumed his usual place in the durbar. The nizam, who had been told about the incident, expressed his concern and congratulated him on his escape. After the durbar, Salar Jung mounted his elephant and took the same route (to show he was unafraid) by which he came to his residence. Shortly after, the assassin was handed over to the kotwal. He was later identified as a sentry at the mosque of Fakhr-ud-din Khan Shums-ul-Umra II, and popular opinion directed suspicion to his house because of its well-known dislike of the diwan.

However, it could have been equally possible that the assassin had been hired by the Arabs, who resented Salar Jung's resumption of lands held by them in mortgage, and for the payment of the wages of their mercenary bands. The motivation for his deed is bound to be mere conjecture since he went to his death without making a confession. Salar Jung had made a mercy appeal to the nizam to spare his life, but it was rejected, aggravated as the crime was, by the gravity of the probable political consequences should his attempt have succeeded.

Hyderabad in those days was a city seething with disaffection. It would have been difficult to find another city which contained a larger collection of fierce armed men ready for any kind of sanguinary affray. Groups of wild, ferocious-looking men armed to the teeth could be seen lounging about the palace gates of the different nobles or strutting around on their own account. One had only to gaze upon these men to form an idea as to the nature of the task Salar Jung's administration faced. Everyone above the social status of a coolie thought it necessary to carry with him a 'perfect museum of offensive weapons'.

The *Times of India* observed: 'Europeans often wonder what possible motive can induce men to burden themselves with the cartload of arms that these people carry as naturally and constantly as an Englishman sports a walking-stick.'[39] The English poet, Edwin Arnold, who visited Hyderabad in the 1880s, recorded his views in a witty fashion: 'This population goes armed, as has been said, to the teeth—to the stomach, to the back and the legs, to the neck and head. In truth, it is hardly less the fashion to wear pistols, sabres, daggers, guns, and spears in Hyderabad than to carry umbrellas in Piccadilly.'[40]

The *Pioneer* reported that in Hyderabad, arms and politics were the only professions, and the only thing that could be called an industry was the manufacture of swords and daggers. 'Every man has his waist belt full of weapons, with a flashing sabre or a rusty matchlock in his hand or on his shoulder.'[41] Considering that both these observations were made in the mid-1880s, after Salar Jung had met with significant success in taming the bellicose elements in Hyderabad, (and in fact, he himself had passed away), what the state of affairs must have been when he first became diwan can scarcely be imagined.

Soon after the failed assassination attempt, the nizam passed an order forbidding the carrying of arms within the city of Hyderabad by the unemployed. It was also announced that those who did not follow the provisions of the proclamation would be punished with a fine and imprisonment. Those who kept armed retainers would be held responsible for the conduct of their men, and it was further ordered that followers were to only bear arms when in actual attendance on their patrons; when off duty, the arms were to be deposited in the house of their employer. The order, even if it was enforced, yielded no results.

7

Berar: A Vexatious Issue

Berar was an issue which preoccupied Salar Jung throughout his life. To say that it was a preoccupation is to perhaps understate the case: it approached an obsession. In Berar, successive nizams inherited both a grievance and an ambition. One of the nizam's biggest complaints against Salar Jung was that his family was responsible for the cession of Berar. The latter, undaunted by opposition, and undeterred by refusal, tried all his life to have Berar restored to his sovereign. It is said that this was Salar Jung's only real ambition in life. Salar Jung had incurred the hatred of the turbulent portion of the population whose outbreaks he had repressed, and this feeling of hostility was greatly aggravated by his British sympathies. He hoped that the restoration of Berar would lessen his unpopularity with the people on this account.

Berar was the principal axis round which the relations between Hyderabad and the British revolved in the second half of the nineteenth century. It became a part of the subedari of the Deccan when Nizam-ul-Mulk Asaf Jah I killed Mubariz Khan in the battle of Shakhar Kheda in 1724. The Marathas raided it periodically but Asaf Jah's sovereignty was never in doubt. During Nizam Ali Khan's reign (1763–1803), territorial readjustments based on their respective fortunes in battle were made between the nizam and the Marathas. In 1822, the East India Company accepted the Wardha river as the eastern boundary of Berar.

Berar[1] consisted of six districts: Amravati, Akola, Buldana, Washim, Ellichpur and Yeotmal. The assigned districts comprised an area of 17,711 sq. miles and had a population of 26.72 lakh in 1881. Cotton cultivation was the main occupation and one which had made the region prosperous. There were coal deposits in Yeotmal which were also exploited. When Chandu Lal became diwan, he farmed out a substantial part of Berar to a moneylender from Hyderabad called Puran Mal. This arrangement soon ended under pressure from the resident, and in 1841, these districts came under the management of Messrs Pestonjee and Company, prosperous Parsi merchants, who in 1825–26 had exported large quantities of cotton from this area. The districts were assigned for reimbursing large advances made to the state by the Parsi merchants. They brought large tracts of land under cotton cultivation and had had a beneficial influence on the agriculturists in that region. This arrangement continued until 1845 when they were removed by coercive measures.

Berar was the richest part of the nizam's dominions. Renowned for its rich, black, alluvial soil, it was praised in the *Ain-i-Akbari*. The French traveller, Jean de Thévenot, described it as one of the richest parts of the Mughal Empire. Its strategic importance to the British lay in the cotton which it supplied to the factories of Manchester. Before the American Civil War, Britain received 80 per cent of its cotton supplies from America. This dropped drastically by 1862, and the deficiency was made good from Berar, where all other crops were discontinued so that the more profitable cotton could be grown instead.

Richard Cobden and John Bright, the most famous exponents of what came to be known as Manchester Liberalism,[2] were keenly interested in the stability of the supply of cotton to the mills of Manchester. They advocated expenditure on infrastructure works like canals, roads and railway lines. In July 1853, Sir Charles Wood, then president of the Board of Control for India, had stated that the objective of railway policy was, among other things, 'the commercial advantage of carrying products to and from the coast'. He also expressed a desire to open the great cotton districts of Berar to the western coast.

Although these districts had been assigned only temporarily by the treaty of 1853, it soon became obvious that the British had no intention of giving them back. While employment and the supply of raw cotton were important, an equally important motive was territorial expansion. Berar was both well-administered and prosperous. The efficient ryotwari system had replaced the cumbersome land revenue system which was still in existence in other parts. The Nagpur branch of the Great Indian Peninsular Railway ran from east to west, and roads connected the railways with important trade centres in the interior of Berar. The judiciary and police were effective and schools proliferated. The population increased, as did the area under cultivation. The cultivated area increased by 50 per cent and land revenue by 42 per cent.

In the last four decades of the eighteenth century, the nizam entered into a number of treaties with the East India Company. As a result of these treaties entered into by the nizam from 1759 to 1800, a British force called the Subsidiary Force came to be established at Secunderabad. In 1765 the British under Robert Clive had obtained the grant of five Northern Circars from the Mughal emperor, Shah Alam, without the knowledge of the nizam. Annoyed with this, the nizam challenged the British, who instead of facing him in battle, entered into a treaty with him in 1766 which confirmed Shah Alam's grant to the British as a free gift. In return, the British agreed to pay an annual quit-rent or peshkash of Rs 9 lakh. They also undertook to maintain a body of troops to settle the affairs of the nizam's government in 'everything that is right and proper', whenever required. The treaty was supposed to remove all 'doubts and suspicions' between the English and the nizam, and to establish 'a perpetual, just, and sincere confidence'.[3] This was the origin of the Subsidiary Force which was pledged to uphold the nizam's power and preserve internal peace, but in reality, served the purpose of maintaining British supremacy in the Deccan.

In 1800, the nizam, under the Treaty of Subsidiary Alliance, undertook to furnish 9000 cavalry and 6000 infantry to the English during times of war to augment the Subsidiary Force. This was the first of a series of alliances masterminded by Richard Wellesley, the Governor General, whose main aim was to end French influence. The nizam's main aim was protection from the Marathas, who posed a constant threat. The nizam never got the protection he wanted, but it ensured British influence in Hyderabad for the next 150 years.

Before the British came to India, the nizam's army consisted of the Paigah troops and those troops maintained by military commanders who had military jagirs given to them by the nizam. The Paigah troops were paid for by the grant of land in the form of jagirs, and formed the personal bodyguard to the nizam. The descendants of Tegh Jung, who came to be known as the Paigah family, were in charge of these troops. Both these categories were hereditary in nature, and it was no surprise that efficiency suffered. Apart from these troops, there was another category of troops, infantry and cavalry, which was paid in cash and could be said to be the real army of the state.

During the third Maratha war, this nizam's army performed very poorly. With the war against the peshwa looming, it was necessary to have an efficient fighting force to combat him. While we have already touched upon this issue in some detail in the Prologue, a quick recap is in order. The resident, Henry Russell, built up the infantry and cavalry at Berar and Aurangabad, and the remains of the old French Corps and the Finglas Brigade at Hyderabad, into a new armed force of about 7000 men. It was first known as the Russell Brigade after its founder, and later the Nizam's Contingent or the Hyderabad Contingent. It was initially paid for from the peshkash of Rs 9 lakh from the Northern Circars, but that soon proved to be inadequate since the cost of the Contingent ballooned to Rs 36 lakh as its size increased. This was when the financial problems of the state started, since the total revenue at that time was only Rs 1.5 crore.

Russell realized that it was impossible for the state treasury to pay the salaries of the Contingent given the precarious state of the government's finances. He came to an understanding with a commercial firm, William Palmer and Company, who was made responsible for the payment of salaries to the Contingent. From the time Russell made Chandu Lal enter into an agreement with this firm, it acquired an ascendancy and position which rivalled the British government in India. Palmer and Company figures prominently in the history of this period, and a narration in some detail of this 'scandalous' firm makes for interesting reading.

WILLIAM PALMER AND COMPANY

The founder, William Palmer, was the Eurasian son of General William Palmer by his second wife, Faiz-un-Nissa Begum. He came to Hyderabad in 1799 and became an officer in the nizam's army. Born in Lucknow, and educated in England where he attended the Woolwich Military Academy, he commanded cavalry forces for the nizam, winning victories in Berar. Equally at home in Mughal and English culture, he had 'a flair for entrepreneurial innovation that would later blossom into a banking fortune of almost unparalleled magnitude'.[4]

Early on, William realized that being a soldier was not what he wanted to do for the rest of his life. His service in Berar had made him realize its potential. Inspired by his elder half-brother John's entrepreneurial example, he dreamt of repopulating the area and growing indigo, cotton and opium there. In due course, he raised capital for a major logging and shipbuilding scheme to exploit the natural resources of the nizam's vast state. He had plans of opening a merchant house that would engage in banking and agency transactions since the restrictions of the two Acts of Parliament which applied to British subjects did not apply to him. In 1773, an Act of Parliament limited the rate of interest permissible in the East India Company territories to 12 per cent. In 1797, another Act prohibited British subjects in India from conducting financial transactions with Indian rulers without the permission of the Governor General. William Palmer was classified by the East Indian Company's bureaucracy as an 'East Indian' and not as a British subject, and Hyderabad was not part of the East India Company's territories. Both restrictions therefore did not apply to him.

In 1810, William Palmer left his position as brigadier general in the nizam's bodyguard to found William Palmer and Company with the Gujarati banker, Benkati Das. Palmer and Company seems to have first attracted the attention of the British government when it applied (in March 1814) for permission to open a banking agency in Hyderabad, and also to exploit the timber yields on the banks of the Godavari for building ships. The application, which was routed through the resident, Henry Russell, was viewed favourably, and the permission was received. At this time, the firm consisted of William Palmer, Benkati Das, Hastings Palmer, William Currie, the surgeon at the residency, and Samuel Russell, a friend of the resident to whom the latter had entrusted his money to invest in business. Samuel Russell lost no time in investing the resident's money in Palmer and Company. Apart from these, it was a closely guarded secret that members of the residency, including the resident, were also partners in the firm. Apart from Henry Russell, the resident, there was his brother Charles, Hans Sotheby, the assistant resident, and George Lamb, an Englishman. This fact was unearthed by Metcalfe who succeeded Russell. The former resident was thus an interested party when the application was forwarded to the government for permission to commence operations.

The patronage of the resident was a great advantage to the firm; its offices were located in the precincts of the residency, a fact which only added to its prestige. The firm prospered and soon attracted funds from many of the Europeans who worked for the East India Company. Chandu Lal and the other nobles curried favour with the firm, knowing that it enjoyed the support of the resident. But Russell, afraid that one day his chickens would come home to roost, and aware that the location of the firm within the precincts of the residency could not be reconciled with his position as a public official, asked the firm to find new premises. He also resigned as a partner of the firm. Just as it appeared that the prestige of the firm would be affected by this lack of support, in April 1815, William Palmer brought into the firm Sir William Rumbold, who was married to a ward of the Governor General, the Marquess of Hastings.

There were also investors, most of them British, who placed their funds at the disposal of the firm in return for a fixed annual interest rate of 12 per cent. Henry Russell had amassed a large fortune, and much of that wealth had come from his secret and illegal partnership in Palmer's firm, which by 1815 had become the most successful business in India outside British control. Palmer and Russell were friends, and the latter often dined at Palmer's mansion, known as Palmer's Kothi. But Russell, worried that his dealings with Palmer would be discovered, fell out with him. The firm ultimately collapsed, and in the inquiry that followed the failure of the firm, he disavowed Palmer completely and denied any links with the impugned firm. He even bribed the printers of the official inquiry report, *The Hyderabad Papers*, in order to ensure that the link between him and his erstwhile friend and business partner was never published. But we are getting a little ahead of our story.

Palmer and Company expanded rapidly, dealing in bills of exchange, Company bills and peshkash (charges on the revenues of specified districts). Within two years of starting business, it was loaning money to the diwan, Munir-ul-Mulk, and after that, government loans to Chandu Lal. These loans were repaid by tankhwahs drawn on designated revenue districts. The rate on the government loans was 2 per cent per month, or 24 per cent per annum, a rate which has been described as extortionate, but which appears to have been the usual rate in Hyderabad at the time. The high rate was also justified by the high risk involved and the inadequacy of the legal system to redress grievances.

The firm's first major loan to the nizam was to pay the salaries of the Hyderabad Contingent stationed in Berar. This was called the 'Aurangabad Arrangement' of 1818. The troops in Berar were paid through the agent in Aurangabad, Captain George Sydenham. Palmer's brother, Hastings, was deputed by the firm to Aurangabad. Govind Bakhsh, Chandu Lal's brother, who was sent to Berar as governor in 1806, had engaged to pay the Russell Brigade, as it was then known, from the revenues of Berar, but that arrangement failed. Govind Bakhsh continued to reside in Berar, but his role declined. In 1815, Palmer asked for an exemption for his firm from the provisions of the Act of 1797 forbidding loans to Indian rulers. This was necessary because William Rumbold, a British subject, had joined the firm. Hastings, the Governor General, granted the exemption in 1816; that Rumbold was married to a ward of his must certainly have helped.

The firm agreed to pay Rs 2 lakh per month for the pay of the Contingent, and in return, the nizam's government assigned to it the revenue of certain districts in Berar. The districts assigned yielded Rs 30 lakh annually; the remaining Rs 6 lakh were supposed to cover any contingency which might arise. It even opened a branch in Aurangabad to facilitate payment. The plunder of the nizam can be dated from this time onwards.

The Palmers soon controlled the financial system of the state. From a mere banking agency, it rose to the position of receiving commissions, and acted as an agency for the recovery of debts. It employed armed force to extort taxes from the villages and succeeded where even the nizam's government had failed in collecting taxes from the poor peasants. On account of its power and prestige, the firm was regarded as identical with the British government. Their oppressive methods made the people flee their homes, depopulating entire villages. Sensing that it would be wise to involve the government in Calcutta, the firm induced Chandu Lal to obtain the government's permission for taking a fresh loan of Rs 60 lakh. Chandu Lal applied to the Government of India to allow him to borrow that sum from the firm so that he might clear certain debts and also advance *taccavi* loans to cultivators.[5]

When Chandu Lal's request reached Calcutta, it created a stir. News about Palmer's transactions had reached some of the members of the council, and, led by John Stuart, they demanded a detailed account of the firm's transactions with the nizam's government. The firm, who corresponded with the government through Rumbold, replied that revealing the accounts of its constituents would be inconsistent with the confidence reposed in them, and asked the Governor General to relieve them from the anxiety which this request had caused. This cut no ice with the members, and Rumbold himself deposed at a meeting of the council and attempted to convince them of the bona fides of Palmer and Company. Stuart remained unconvinced and wanted Hastings to advance money to the nizam's government from the treasury. He was supported by John Adam, another member of the council. The accountant general also thought that Palmer's transactions were of a dubious nature.[6]

Stuart wanted a clarification on the rate of interest charged by the firm. His influence had convinced the other members of the council, including John Adam, and they all wanted to know why the loan could not be granted from the British treasury or floated elsewhere at a lower rate of interest. Despite the opposition, Hastings decided to grant the necessary permission to Chandu Lal to take the loan of Rs 60 lakh from the firm, having cast the deciding vote in favour of it. Meanwhile, the court of directors in England, who had come to know of the firm's dealings, strongly criticized the government for granting Palmer and Company the licence to commence monetary dealings with the nizam's government and questioned the actions of the Governor General.

Hastings was forced by the strongly worded letter from the court of directors to rethink his policy towards the firm. Realizing that a blanket ban on the firm's activities would ruin it, he decided to forbid Palmer and Company from any further financial dealing with the nizam's government. This ban came into effect in December 1820 after he had sanctioned Palmer's fresh loan of Rs 60 lakh, it being declared as essential to the financial health of the state by Chandu Lal, Palmer and Henry Russell.

The loan and the cancellation of the licence became a cause célèbre in India; in December 1920 Henry Russell resigned as resident after receiving intelligence that he was about to be sacked for his blatant involvement in corruption and bribe-taking. Even though his annual salary was only Rs 3400, he shipped home a fortune of Rs 85,000.[7]

He was succeeded by Charles Metcalfe, whose arrival spelled disaster for Palmer and his firm. Metcalfe was a man who was very different from Russell. He had been Wellesley's star pupil at his new college for civil servants at Madras, and had served as assistant to Colonel John Collins at the court of Scindia in Ujjain. Later, he was an assistant to the resident in Delhi. After his experience at Ujjain, where Collins moved around with a zenana, he developed a strong dislike for native courts.

On becoming resident, Metcalfe made diligent inquiries into Hyderabad's finances in an attempt to ascertain the causes of its chronic state of financial embarrassment. After making attempts to put a stop to 'back-stairs influence' and preventing the nizam from being 'fleeced by the fathomless cunning of the native underlings of the Residency',[8] he turned his eyes to what he thought was the main cause of the nizam's financial ruin, namely, the connection of the Hyderabad government with William Palmer and Co. 'It seemed to him that the State was lying prostrate and helpless at the feet of the English money-lenders.'[9]

Within a few months of his posting, Metcalfe accused Palmer of being in league with Chandu Lal in milking the exchequer for his own gratification:

> I do not object to merchants making good bargains for themselves. But when the resources of the State are sacrificed by a profligate servant, without any regard to the interests of his master, as the purchase of support of the Governor General through the influence of an individual, it is bribery in the most horrible degree and misery of it will be long felt by this suffering country.[10]

Metcalfe at once realized that there was much more than mere commerce in these transactions. The question had become a political one. Palmer and Company, armed with the double authority of the British and nizam's governments, had usurped the government of Hyderabad. It was fast becoming all-powerful in the state. It did not take Metcalfe long to realize that the safety of the nizam and the dignity of his own office could be maintained only by rescuing the nizam from the grip of the English company which had become completely identified in men's minds with the British government. Even Chandu Lal believed that so long as he had the support of the firm, he did not need to worry about the resident's opinion.

Large sums of money in the form of annual allowances were paid to members of the firm, or their near relatives. William Palmer's sons received annual stipends of Rs 1200 each when they were mere boys in school in England. Chandu Lal also paid a pension of Rs 1000 per month to Hastings Palmer, and William himself received a monthly gratuity of Rs 2000. It is said that the monthly pensions to the Palmer family amounted to a large sum, and the burden was borne by the exchequer. Apart from assiduously cultivating the friendship of the Palmers, Chandu Lal also kept the residency officials in good humour, sending them *dallies* of fruits and other provisions, prompting Metcalfe to remark that the vast quantity gave them the appearance of regular supplies, instead of being merely complimentary.[11]

This extraordinary influence was not merely the influence of a creditor over a struggling debtor, but drew its influence from extraneous sources. Sir William Rumbold had accompanied Hastings to India 'with the not very rare or unintelligible design of making as much money as he could', having 'passed the age at which the foot can be placed on the lowest step of the ladder of official promotion, and so with the aid of his friend, he had endeavoured to make for himself a shorter cut to fortune'.[12] Metcalfe said of him that he wanted to make a large and rapid fortune by means other than his own personal labour. When Rumbold joined the firm, he brought with him the Governor General's influence. 'He was just the man for the concern; and the concern was just the thing for him.'

It must have been with some reluctance that Metcalfe arrayed himself against the firm, since both William Palmer and Rumbold were no strangers to him. Rumbold had been a personal friend of long standing, and William Palmer was the half-brother of John Palmer of Calcutta, an intimate of Metcalfe for many years. He came to Hyderabad prepared to love William Palmer for his brother's sake, a resolve rendered easier by the amiable character of the man himself. Initially at least, it would seem that Metcalfe did not harbour any hostile feelings against the firm. Rumbold was married to a ward of Hastings, and Metcalfe knew that the Governor General, who was also his (Metcalfe's) patron and friend, was greatly interested in her welfare. All these factors would naturally predispose him in favour of the firm, and he was given a warm welcome in Hyderabad by all the principal partners of the firm. There are two schools of thought as to why Metcalfe acted the way he did. There are some who ascribe his actions to conscientiousness and others who attribute them to a sense of pique at having to play second fiddle to the firm. The truth may well lie somewhere in between.

Metcalfe greatly resented the key position Palmer and Company occupied in Hyderabad. He thought Palmer's activities illegal, at least in principle, if not the letter of the law, and wanted the nizam to borrow at lower rates of interest (6 per cent) but with territorial guarantees. He had formed a poor opinion of Russell and also came into conflict with Chandu Lal. He also insisted that Chandu Lal visit him, whereas previously it had been the other way around. A loner, Metcalfe also resented Palmer's central social position in Hyderabad. Perhaps, what really rankled was the considerable political power that Palmer exercised in Hyderabad.

Metcalfe wrote that the firm's activity 'tends to draw them quite out of their sphere of merchants . . . I lament the power which they exercise . . . in an authoritative manner not becoming their mercantile character, acting with the double force of the Nizam's Government and the British name.'[13] He was also peeved that he was not getting the importance due to a resident. 'They do not require my support. Their power here is far above it.

They have never, indeed, sought it . . . [the Palmers have] usurped power and authority no other merchants possess, and which no merchants ought to possess.'[14] He also resented the firm's direct communication with the Governor General. Edward Palmer, William Palmer's grandson, believed that Metcalfe opposed William Palmer because he was madly jealous of his power and influence in Hyderabad.

Metcalfe realized that the enormous clout which the partners of the firm wielded was likely to make them the paramount power in Hyderabad. Rumbold's connection with Hastings and the mounting indebtedness of the state made them all-powerful in the eyes of Hyderabad society. It was also apparent that many of the residency officials had a pecuniary interest in the firm and received high returns for their investment. Metcalfe decided to break the overpowering influence of the firm, even if it meant sacrificing his own prospects. Those who ascribe his acts to conscientiousness maintain that had he been self-seeking and selfish, he could easily have opted to keep quiet and support a firm which he knew had the support of the Governor General, a person from whom he had everything to expect.[15]

Metcalfe made a long tour of the nizam's dominions, particularly the parts of Berar which had become depopulated. The inhabitants had fled, and the lands which had been assessed at an exorbitantly high rate were left uncultivated. Metcalfe put in place a system where European officers were placed in charge of districts, the rates reduced, and cultivators invited to return with the promise of protection. This caused much resentment among the locals, who resented any measure to curb their habitual corruption. This system was abolished in 1829, and the old one, permeated by corruption, made a comeback.

Metcalfe's tour convinced him of the baleful influence of Palmer and Company, and of the drain their demands upon the government caused to the country. He proposed that the Government of India take steps to raise at a reasonable rate of interest a loan big enough to repay the firm. In the spring of 1821, Metcalfe suggested floating a 6 per cent loan in Calcutta guaranteed by the British government, from the proceeds of which he proposed to pay off the nizam's obligations to the House of Palmer. The proposal was made in an official letter, and before sending it to Calcutta, Metcalfe took the members of the firm into confidence. When this unwelcome announcement was made, the partners of the firm realized that easy money was no longer theirs for the taking. They represented to

Metcalfe that since the sudden liquidation of the loan would inflict huge losses, certain compensation should be made to them. Metcalfe consented to insert a clause conferring an additional gratuity of Rs 6 lakh on the firm. They also used the interval between their discussions with Metcalfe and the despatch of his letter to prevent the communication from succeeding in its aim. Rumbold wrote an urgent appeal to Hastings, and when Metcalfe's letter reached the Governor General, he chose to ignore it.

Rumbold convinced Hastings that Metcalfe was actuated by personal animus towards him and Chandu Lal, and as a result, Hastings entirely sided with the firm. Hastings also expressed his displeasure to his former protégé at not having consulted him on the subject. The proposal was shelved, and Hastings wrote privately to Metcalfe, pointing out what he considered to be his disloyalty. The influence of the firm only increased, and Chandu Lal even went so far as to ignore the resident and send a communication to the Governor General through Rumbold.

Metcalfe was both pained and embarrassed, but continued to persist in pointing out the political dangers of the firm's growing influence and the dangers of allowing so many officials from being associated with it. He also cautioned against the growing expenditure of the 'Resident's plaything', the Hyderabad Contingent, which was no longer needed since the Subsidiary Force was sufficient to protect the nizam within his territory. Outside it, there was no danger since Hyderabad was surrounded by British territory or that of allied princes. Metcalfe, aware that the estrangement between him and the Governor General was increasing, sent John Adam, a senior member of the council, a list of transactions of the firm and of the persons involved in them to show to Hastings privately. This paper vindicated his stand and justified all that he had done.

Hastings now realized that it would be untenable for him to support the firm. He wrote a letter of reconciliation to Metcalfe informing him that the proposed loan by which the liabilities to the firm would be paid had been sanctioned. Hastings left India on the completion of his tenure on 1 January 1823, and the matter was finally settled by John Adam as acting Governor General. The commission and compensation to the firm was disallowed. Metcalfe had come to know from Chandu Lal that the total debt to the company was Rs 83.5 lakh, and the state owed about Rs 17 lakh to native bankers. Adam cut down the debt to Rs 80 lakh and paid the money into the Hyderabad treasury. The loan thus advanced was subsequently liquidated by an arrangement under which the peshkash payable by the British for the Northern Circars was relinquished in perpetuity by the nizam.

With the departure of Hastings, who was seen to be the firm's chief supporter, the public lost confidence in the firm and withdrew its support and money. In 1824, Palmer and Company became bankrupt, 'not from any run upon it, but merely from want of funds to meet ordinary demands'.[16] While breaking the influence of the firm might have been politically expedient, the firm appears to have been treated with undue severity. There is no doubt that it had made a valuable contribution, and the safety of India in 1817–19 was due to the 'establishment and sanction of pecuniary transactions by Palmer and Company'.[17] The firm had rendered good service in advancing funds to equip and maintain the Contingent before and after the Pindari war. Had the supply of funds been left to the nizam, the soldiers would have, in all probability, remained unpaid, and 'it was entirely due to the manner in which William Palmer and Company came forward with the necessary funds that the Contingent was able to take the field at all'.[18] The firm made the advance without any guarantee that the loan would be repaid. Such services, it was thought, deserved more liberal treatment.

An aspect for which the firm was criticized pertained to the so-called extortionate rate of interest charged by it. But the 24 per cent charged by the firm was the ordinary rate which prevailed in Hyderabad and was what the Hyderabad government paid to the sahukars. When this matter came up for discussion in early 1824 at India House in the court of proprietors where the proposal for a testimonial for Hastings in recognition of the services he had rendered was being debated, Sir Charles Forbes, a leading banker in Bombay at the time, testified that the Government of India had actually paid 34 per cent for a loan in 1798, and that even now some firms in Calcutta were refusing money at 4 per cent per month while others were getting 12 per cent for three months.[19]

One of the grounds on which the testimonial was opposed was the interest Hastings had shown in Palmer and Company. Ultimately, the original proposition to give Hastings a further gratuity was defeated after six days of debate. The mutual attacks on Russell and Metcalfe fell through. In what was essentially a half-hearted measure, the court of directors sent a despatch conveying that if possible, the claims of William Palmer should be settled. This was never done, but the Hyderabad government continued to pay William Palmer and his family handsome allowances of Rs 45,000 per month.

Metcalfe had managed to paint the firm black, but insiders in Hyderabad, and even the court of directors in England, did not see it in that light. W.B. Martin, who succeeded Metcalfe as resident, staunchly defended the firm, and Palmer retained an honoured place in Hyderabad society. His relations with his own partners and constituents remained excellent, and immediately after the bankruptcy, the firm's trustees voted to give Palmer and his brother, Hastings, a monthly allowance of Rs 500, much to the annoyance of Metcalfe. Even those British constituents who had lost heavily lobbied in support of Palmer. Palmer had overextended his own bank to raise the Rs 60 lakh loan, borrowing heavily from local sahukars at very high rates. It was these creditors he first tried to repay when the firm became insolvent. After Rumbold's death in 1833, Palmer continued to try to recover what was owed to his firm, submitting claims by turns to a special court set up by Chandu Lal, a council of bankers, and to successive residents and Governors General. While most of the individual debts were settled, Palmer and Company was never repaid by the Hyderabad government.[20]

Palmer was given allowances and a pension by the nizam, but these were discontinued at the behest of Metcalfe. Chandu Lal then placed Palmer on his own payroll, paying him Rs 30,000 a year till his death. The nizam paid for the education of two of Palmer's sons in England, and at the time of his death in 1867, at the ripe old age of eighty-seven, Palmer enjoyed a pension of Rs 2000 per month from the nizam. Despite Metcalfe's successful prosecution of the firm, those connected with the firm continued to wield political influence. As Karen Leonard has pointed out, the Palmers' reputation rested on their local services and people's perception, and not on British support for the firm.[21]

The negative British view of the Palmer episode has remained the dominant narrative: Karen Leonard is of the view that Metcalfe's view has had an unfortunately long life in British historiography.[22] Recent studies have highlighted (what was known locally even at the time) that Palmer and Company was not the usurious monster it was made out to be. It was similar to the other firms operating in Hyderabad at the time; it was also typical in the political and financial role it played with respect to the Hyderabad government.

A TALE OF SHAME: THE ASSIGNING OF BERAR

Palmer and Company's insolvency did not bode well for the finances of Hyderabad. First Puran Mal, a Marwari banker, and then Pestonjee, a Parsi, took over the role of supplying loans to pay the Contingent, but payments were soon in arrears. By the 1840s, the East India Company had become a creditor as well; in 1845, the resident took over this role. The growing debt soon became a bargaining chip for the ceding of territory.

The payment of the Hyderabad Contingent soon became the single biggest cause for the financial ruin of the state. The Contingent virtually became part of the East India Company's army, and could be used by the nizam only with the consent of the resident. Faced with the unfortunate position of having to pay for something he could not use, the nizam built up his own forces as a counter, and a large part of Hyderabad's revenue was used for the upkeep of its military forces.

The importance given to the Contingent can be attributed to a variety of reasons. Chief among them was that the British government wanted to reduce the strength of the Subsidiary Force by maintaining another force at the nizam's expense. Also, there had been a strong French influence on the nizam's army in the late eighteenth century, and this was sought to be eradicated. Lastly, the Contingent gave employment to a large number of English and Eurasian officers.

The payment of the Contingent now devolved on Chandu Lal. He was unable to, or had no intention of saying no to the resident, who did as he pleased with the Contingent. Economy measures were unheard of and there were as many as five brigadiers who received special allowances, each with his own elaborate staff. Chandu Lal, both reckless and extravagant, resorted to large-scale borrowing from the sahukars at very high rates of interest. He assigned districts to them in return, and as a result, the revenue collection fell, making it even more difficult to raise the necessary finances. Chandu Lal had to meet the demands of the nizam on the one hand, and also meet the constant drain of Rs 3 lakh a month for the Contingent. The arrears kept growing, and by 1840, the amount owed was Rs 50 lakh.

Chandu Lal ceased to be diwan in 1843, and a rapid succession of diwans followed. For many months, the post remained vacant. Sporadic payments were made, but it was excuses and promises that were mostly on offer. No effort was made to scale down the Contingent or its expense. By 1849, the debt had risen to more than Rs 64 lakh, and Lord Dalhousie asked the resident, General J.S. Fraser, to insist on a settlement. Replying to a letter from the resident, Dalhousie made no secret of the fact that his patience was now at an end and that he disavowed 'the doctrine of our having any moral or political obligation to take the government of his country into our own hands, merely because he mismanages his own affairs'.[23]

Fakhr-ud-din Khan Shums-ul-Umra II, who had been appointed diwan in 1849, resigned in the same year, having found it impossible to carry on the government. All that he had been able to do was to keep up the current payment of the Contingent; the old debt continued to increase. The office of diwan was kept vacant, but Raja Ram Bakhsh was appointed peshkar. Dalhousie now sent the nizam an ultimatum that the whole amount should be discharged by 31 December 1850. It came with a threat. 'If on the arrival of that period the Governor General's expectations were disappointed, his Lordship would feel his duty to take such decided steps as the interests of the British Government demanded.'[24] These 'decided steps', it was well understood, would involve the exaction of territory as security for the payment of principal and interest.

The deadline passed with no repayment or any improvement in Hyderabad's finances. The resident busied himself in instructing those officers who were to be placed in charge of the districts to be held as security. They were Colonel Meadows Taylor, Henry Dighton and Mr Bullock. In the meantime, an event occurred which brought matters to a head. During the march of a detachment of British troops through the nizam's territory, a fracas occurred between them and the nizam's irregular troops. This, Dalhousie considered an affront to the Empire, and wrote a strongly worded letter to the nizam in which he dealt both with the incident and the repayment of the debt. The nizam was told that the former incident rendered him liable to the 'indignation of the Government of India, whose power can crush you at its will'. The Persian translation of this, which is by far the more famous quotation, was 'whose power can make you as the dust under foot, and leave you neither a name nor a trace'.[25] The letter then asked the nizam to cede a certain portion of his territory as repayment of the debt.

The letter had the desired effect. Never before had a communication from the Governor General been so strongly worded. The nizam knew that he had to take immediate steps, and one of the first was the appointment of Siraj-ul-Mulk as diwan in mid-1851. When the resident came to inquire which districts were to be handed over, he was told that the nizam would pay the whole debt and also make arrangements for the regular pay of the Contingent. Initially at least, he was as good as his word. In August, he paid the first instalment of Rs 34 lakh, leaving a balance of Rs 32 lakh to be paid on or before 1 October 1851. Faced with the alienation of some of the most fertile districts of his dominions, the nizam paid off half the debt by dipping into his own private treasury and by pledging some of his jewels to the sahukars.

But this was only a temporary measure, and soon matters were allowed to deteriorate as before. In time, the arrears increased, and it soon became obvious that the nizam would be unable to fulfil his promise. Lord Dalhousie sent him another letter in which the matter of assignment of territory was again broached. This letter, however, is remarkable for the sea change in Dalhousie's views regarding the status of the Contingent. In a complete turnaround from the past, he said that the nizam was not bound under treaty to maintain the Contingent. '. . . I could not argue that either the letter or the spirit of it bound the Nizam to maintain 9,000 troops of a peculiar and costly nature in peace because it bound him to give 15,000 of his troops on the occurrence of war.'[26] If the Contingent was to be continued, assignment of territory was a must. And even if it was to be disbanded, some assignment would still be required since such a large force could only be disbanded gradually and the debt also had to be repaid. Lord Dalhousie warned the nizam that if by the end of 1852 the matter was not resolved, he would press for obtaining a material guarantee not only for the debt, but also for the future payments of the Contingent.

Meanwhile, the nizam had resolved to pawn his jewels valued at £500,000 in order to pay off his debt. A state bank financed by the leading sahukars was proposed with Henry Dighton at its head. The nizam agreed to hand over his jewels to the bank and received an advance of Rs 40 lakh in return. Just as it seemed that this was a winning idea, Dalhousie played spoiler. He refused to sanction the formation of the bank, citing the Act of George III which prohibited financial transactions between Europeans and native princes. Nobody had expected this spanner in the works, and it created a panic in Hyderabad. The nizam, who had given his jewels, kept the money; the sahukars, for their part, wanted the jewels as security, given the fact that recoupment of their money was going to be difficult. Dighton found himself in a double bind: he was responsible to the nizam for the safety of his jewels on the one hand, and also responsible to the sahukars for repayment for the money they had advanced. He extricated himself from this delicate position in a remarkable manner.

Dighton deposited the jewels in a safe locked with three different keys, each held by one of the interested parties. The jewels were stored on different trays in the safe. Announcing that he needed to travel to Madras for a change of air and some business, he called for a meeting to make an inventory of the jewels to ensure that all was in order. At the meeting, the safe was opened, and each tray was brought before the shareholders and then carried back. But instead of being restored to the safe, they were secretly poured into a pair of jackboots before the tray was returned to the safe. The safe was then formally locked by all the stakeholders.

That same evening, Dighton left in a palanquin with a box marked 'medical comforts' which contained the precious cargo. He reached Madras, boarded a ship, and took the jewels with him to Europe where they were deposited with a banking firm in Holland. The firm advanced the money to pay off the sahukars, and eventually the jewels were redeemed by Salar Jung, who brought them back and returned them to the nizam.[27] The jewels, it is said, were almost sold when Siraj-ul-Mulk died, and it was Salar Jung, who acted with despatch in paying the interest immediately with a promise to pay the principal in a year's time, who saved them.

After the debacle of the bank, General Fraser resigned in November 1852. He did not assign any particular reasons for resigning beyond stating that 'private affairs required his presence in England'. He had recently received the news of his elder brother's demise and resolved to leave India for good. Also, the events of the recent past had brought the realization that he no longer enjoyed the Governor General's confidence. His successor, Colonel J. Low, was sent from Calcutta with a new treaty for the nizam to sign.

Low arrived in January 1853, fully aware of the role he was to play in the negotiations for the treaty which was to follow. Low advanced large sums from the Company's treasury to pay the Contingent, and by March 1853, the nizam's debt had crossed Rs 45 lakh. The resident's pleas for payment were 'met by evasions of the most vexatious nature'. It was obvious that perpetual remonstrance on the one hand, and undignified breaches of promise on the other, could not continue forever. In April, Low was directed to submit to the nizam a proposal for a new treaty on the basis of ceding territory in perpetuity to the British government.

The first demand was that the Berar provinces and Raichur Doab should be assigned in perpetuity to the British. In return, the debt would be cancelled and the Contingent would be maintained by the British. The nizam's response to ceding the districts was, 'God forbid that I should suffer such disgrace.'[28] Two acts of any sovereign were considered disgraceful at the time. The first was to part with hereditary territories, and the second was the disbanding of troops. It was only with difficulty that the nizam, succumbing to British Machtpolitik, agreed to cede territory, and that too, temporarily.

Initially, he tried to stall the issue by protracted negotiations and passive resistance. He, amongst other arguments, urged that there was nothing in the old treaty binding him to keep up the Contingent on its existing footing. Low acquiesced, remarking that the nizam was welcome to dispense with the services of the regular officers and resume immediate control of it himself. The nizam, a little taken aback at the suggestion, repudiated the idea at once. Low then asked the nizam if it was becoming the dignity of a sovereign like him to constantly keep his army in arrears and always clamouring for their pay. He told him that if he wanted to maintain the Contingent, he must make some definite arrangement for its support.

Lord Dalhousie had already intimated to the nizam that he would not hesitate to use military force to impose his will, but the nizam still continued with his resistance. Exasperated by a persistence which was born out of despair, the British resorted to deceit to achieve their end. On 14 May 1853, Davidson, then assistant resident at Hyderabad and not yet a colonel, wrote to Siraj-ul-Mulk asking him to meet the resident as the latter wished to inform him that his negotiations with the nizam were at an end, and he had applied to the government 'to move troops by today's post'. In the same letter, Davidson added that he had heard from his nephew in Poona that the European regiment there had been ordered to hold itself in readiness to march to Hyderabad.

Both the assertions in the letter regarding the movement of troops were absolutely false. But the British, not content to deceive by this misrepresentation alone, thought it necessary that the imminence of such action be impressed on the nizam's mind as truths by the nizam's own trusted advisers.

Siraj-ul-Mulk found in Burhan-ud-din, (the same confidential aide who had proposed Salar Jung for the diwanship), a willing conspirator who allowed his services to be purchased for the cause. Thus, with the connivance of the resident, the nizam was duped (and betrayed) into believing the contents of the letter. The next day, the resident received a note from Siraj-ul-Mulk that the nizam had at last consented to the treaty. He wrote, 'Booran-ood-deen and I persuaded him to accede to it. This was done when we were alone.'[29] The treaty was signed a week later on 21 May 1853. An article in the London *Statesman* written almost three decades later called it a 'tale of shame'.

Threat or not, there is no doubt that the nizam signed the treaty on the distinct understanding that the assigned districts would at some time distant be restored to him. Colonel Low had announced 'that if His Highness wished it the districts might be made over *merely for a time*, to maintain the Contingent *as long as he might require it*'. An eyewitness to the signing of the treaty was certain that it was very clear to all that the transfer was for certain specific purposes such as the expenses of the Contingent, the interest on the debt to the government, and the payment of Maratha chauth, and was terminable with the necessity.

At no time was the word 'perpetuity' used. The final treaty did not embody the points which the resident had led the nizam to suppose it would. By the time the nizam realized this, it was too late to retract. After having been humbugged into consenting to sign a treaty at all, he was subsequently bullied into giving his assent to what was placed before him. Given the unpleasant nature of the transaction, the nizam was surprisingly good humoured when the treaty was signed, something which can be attributed to his personal rapport with Low, who though firm, was most conciliating. As early as 1851, Lord Dalhousie, in his minute of 1851, had hinted at the use of force in acquiring the districts, asking the resident to 'state whether he will require any troops in addition to the Subsidiary and Contingent Forces for the purpose of enforcing the determination that has been announced'.[30]

The ironies in this are numerous. The very Contingent, for the punctual pay of which territorial security had been demanded, and which was maintained for the protection of the nizam, was now to be employed in arms against himself. The resident replied that he did not envisage armed resistance; in any case, the Subsidiary Force and the Contingent would be equal to the task if required. However, as a precaution, he requested the authority to summon the troops at Bellary and Nagpur in case of emergency.

Sir Charles Wood had wanted everything. 'Take the revenue, maintain the Contingent, and let us have no accounts.' Nevertheless, he was happy with Dalhousie's achievement and sent his congratulations. Dalhousie too seems to have been more than gratified at Low's performance which had exceeded his expectations. He wrote to Low: 'I consider the successful completion of this settlement with the Nizam as a feather in my cap.'[31]

The real interest involved in the case was the British need for cotton from Berar. The Lancashire-based cotton-textile industry depended almost entirely on the United States for its supply of cotton. The cotton from Berar was looked upon as a second source of supply to end this excessive dependence. All through the negotiations, it was neither the settlement of the nizam's debt, nor the payment of the Contingent, which agitated Dalhousie's mind but the British need for cotton. Dalhousie boasted that he had secured some of the finest cotton tracts in India which would make good a felt deficiency in that industry in Britain. Although Low had hoodwinked the nizam into thinking that it was only a temporary cession, it was apparent right from the beginning that Dalhousie intended it to be a permanent arrangement. He even added the revenue of Berar to the annual income of British India. He admitted to Low, 'Whatever may be the future surplus of revenue, these districts will never be returned to the Nizam's Government and we must therefore plan an arrangement on a footing of permanency.'[32]

What made the whole thing doubly humiliating for the nizam was the fact that the upkeep of the Contingent was not based on any treaty. The treaty of 1800 merely provided that the nizam would aid the Company in times of war. Nowhere did it say that he had to maintain 9000 troops of an extremely costly nature just because he was bound to provide 15,000 troops in the time of war. The British forced him to pay for an army deliberately imposed on him and took away his most fertile province to pay for something which no treaty had obliged him to keep. But Dalhousie, who represented a particularly aggressive form of imperialism, could hardly be bothered with basic norms of political morality. As he once said, it was not his mission to regenerate misgoverned states.

Colonel Davidson's choice of words in his letter written in August 1860 to the government is revealing and confirms the fact that the nizam was coerced into signing the treaty of 1853. 'We have now, however, obtained the material guarantee for the pay of the Contingent, &c., the fundamental principle of the treaty of 1853; and I cannot think, reviewing all the circumstances under which that treaty was *forced* on the Hyderabad Government . . .' This testimony from a person who succeeded the resident in that position, and who was present at all the negotiations that his predecessor conducted, is self-evident and requires no comment.

The British could well have taken Berar by physical force but chose to achieve their purpose by a little diplomatic dodging. In order to avoid an open rupture, they allowed the nizam to indulge in the pleasing fiction that the districts were not ceded, but only temporarily assigned, with the British holding them in trust. But the talk about eventual restitution was pure moonshine—the British never had any intention of restoring Berar to the nizam.

J. Bruce Norton, who served as advocate general of Madras from 1863 to 1871, remarked, 'Cotton stuffed the ears of justice, and made her deaf as well as blind.'[33] Even though Dalhousie fully recognized the nizam's unwillingness to cede the districts in perpetuity, in his farewell minute of 28 February 1853, he noted somewhat inaccurately that 'the Nizam has assigned in perpetual Government, to the Honourable East India Company, the Province of Berar and other districts of his State, for the permanent maintenance of the Hyderabad Contingent'.[34] The Indian government had forced a faithful ally to sign a treaty which could only have been wrung from a beaten foe. They had coveted Berar, and it was ultimately taken by an act of undisguised violence. Dalhousie had always intended that the cession would be a permanent one; and the Government of India too had quietly made up its mind that possession once obtained, restoration was out of the question.

The *Times of India* observed that 'the Nizam had been induced to assign to us what he considered the fairest portion of his dominions for a specific purpose, on the distinct understanding that it might some day or other be restored to him, well-knowing all the while that its restoration would never be consented to by us'.[35] It went on to add: 'If we do not intend to restore the Berars, do not let us try to persuade the world and the Nizam that we are holding them temporarily in trust . . . We ought not to be other people's agents, cultivating their acres, managing their property, and handing them the balance. Our position is a false one. Let us restore the Berars or keep them only as our own.'[36]

The treaty of 1853 stipulated that any surplus over expenditure on administration was to be handed over to the nizam, and that it would be incumbent on the British to maintain accounts. The objects of the expenditure were the maintenance of the Contingent at a strength of 7000 men; the liquidation of the debt of 48,00,000 hali sicca; and the payment to defray the cost of administration. It is interesting to note that the cost of maintaining the Contingent was substantially lower in the first year after the treaty was signed, reducing drastically from Rs 40 lakh to Rs 24 lakh. As soon as the Government of India was responsible for making the payment, the cost was immediately reduced to a reasonable figure. And no one could say that this reduction in cost came at the expense of efficiency since the Contingent acquitted itself most creditably during the Mutiny. It was only when the coffers of the government were threatened with loss that the reduction was both prompt and considerable. Clearly, the resident and the Governor General had been generous with someone else's money, in this case, the nizam's. Such a reduction effected five years previously would have wiped out the whole debt on account of which the assignment was made.

There was another reason why this debt was manifestly unfair. For a period of forty-one years (1812–53), the British had levied and retained the excise revenues of the cantonments at Secunderabad and Jalna. No accounts had been submitted for these, and in 1851, the nizam put forward a claim that these receipts should be adjusted against the debt. The resident, General Fraser, refused to allow what he called 'a problematic claim' to be credited in settling an actual debt. The treaty of 1853 admitted that these revenues properly belonged to the nizam, and indeed, from this year onwards they were collected by the nizam. Davidson, writing in 1860 about this debt, admitted, 'I have always been of the opinion that had the pecuniary demands of the two Governments been impartially dealt with, we had no just claim on the Nizam for the present debt of 43 lakh of Company's rupees.'[37]

As early as 1856–57, when Salar Jung had been in office for only a few years, he had attempted to negotiate, through his English friends like Colonel James Oliphant, a modification of the terms on which the districts were held. The revised terms would fetch the nizam a fixed sum, regardless of the gain or loss of the British government. The proposal, which was made in close consultation with Oliphant, was sent to the resident, Bushby, after taking the nizam's approval. Salar Jung urged the resident for a liberal settlement of the issue, pointing out the tremendous benefit which had already accrued to the British by maintaining a Subsidary Force which was considerably less in number than required by the treaty of 1800, for although the number of regiments was correct, the number of men was not. The treaty of 1853, by mentioning only the number of regiments which the Subsidary Force was to maintain, had made this gain a permanent one.[38]

Predictably, this request was ignored. When the British wanted to reward the nizam and Salar Jung after the Mutiny for their unflinching support during the upheaval, this issue came into focus once again when the treaty of 1860 was being negotiated. Salar Jung's own strong views on the Berar issue were formed only in the 1860s: during the negotiations of the 1860 treaty, he only echoed the views of the nizam. Colonel Davidson, as we have noted earlier, was a sympathizer with the nizam and Salar Jung in all this. He greatly angered his superiors in Calcutta when he pointed out that there were serious doubts about the debts (heavily loaded in favour of the British), which had formed the basis of the treaty of 1853. At one point of time, Lord Canning was so infuriated that he threatened to send Davidson back to his regiment.

EARLY ATTEMPTS AT RESTORATION

Salar Jung tried unsuccessfully all his life to ensure the restoration of Berar. The effort not only cost him a lot of money, but also earned him the enmity of the British. As noted before, Salar Jung's mission in life was the restoration of Berar, and he struggled to achieve this aim throughout his tenure in office. A deep sense of injustice to Hyderabad rankled: the scene of the nizam's humiliation in 1853 was indelibly imprinted on his memory. The issue had emotive overtones for both Salar Jung and the nizams he served. It was a stain on his family name which he was keen to obliterate. Both Nasir-ud-Daula and Afzal-ud-Daula repeatedly exhorted Salar Jung to recover Berar, and he tried everything in his power to do so. 'My first desire is to see Berar restored,' he wrote to a friend, H. Russell, in February 1877. A few months later in April, he wrote to Lord Northbrook somewhat dramatically, 'I shall go on bothering, bothering, until I get a favourable reply. It appears to me that there are three courses before me—either I must recover Berar, or I must be convinced of the justice of reasons for withholding Berar—or I must die.'[39]

There were also pragmatic considerations underlying Salar Jung's desire to regain the assigned districts. He needed money desperately to run the government, and if he secured Berar, its revenues could be used to meet the ever-increasing expenditure on administration and the railway line. When Raichur Doab was restored to the nizam, the expenditure on administration was halved, but the region yielded as much revenue as it did under British rule. Salar Jung no doubt realized that if he could recover Berar, he would halve its expenses while revenue would be maintained at its current level.

Salar Jung had hoped that the British would restore Berar in recognition of the nizam's loyalty during the Mutiny. His faith in the British sense of fair play and justice was now shaken, and in October 1866, he showed the first signs of discontent. Salar Jung wrote to the resident, Sir George Yule, on the subject of the restoration of Berar to the nizam. He pointed out that this territory had been assigned with great reluctance and had not been ceded in perpetuity. Although the treaty of 1860 had dispensed with the furnishing of accounts, the surplus still had to be paid, and the nizam had received nothing since the treaty had been signed. Thus, the surplus of the most productive part of the nizam's territory was spent on that area alone, depriving other less fertile areas of the nizam's dominions.

Salar Jung submitted that under the secret articles of the treaty of 1800, the nizam had a perpetual right to divide equally with the British any territory which was acquired by the joint military action of both powers. According to the partition treaty of 1799, he claimed Rs 41.5 lakh per year, half the revenues of Mysore state which was expected to lapse soon. (Under the Doctrine of Lapse, Lord Dalhousie's famous expedient, the government denied to a ruling family the right to adopt a male heir who would then continue the dynasty. A native state where there was no direct heir reverted to the Government of India.)

This, and other claims, amounted to Rs 60 lakh per year, and Salar Jung wanted Berar to be restored to the nizam in lieu of these claims. He argued that had Mysore been annexed immediately after the Mysore war, instead of the Wadiyars being reinstated on the throne, the nizam would have been entitled to a share of the spoils as per the treaty. If a Hindu raja had not been chosen in 1799, the nizam would have had a half share of the state as an ally of the East India Company in the joint conquest since the partition treaty declared that the cession of Mysore was an act of the nizam and the British government 'mutually and severally'.

Under the treaty of 1799, Mysore, which was conquered by the joint forces of the nizam and the British, was to be divided equally between the two victors. Later it was decided to hand over the state to the eight-year-old Krishna Raj Wadiyar, a member of the Hindu royal family that had ruled Mysore before Hyder Ali and Tipu Sultan. The boy assumed the direct administration of the state in 1810, but in 1831, the state was resumed by Lord Bentinck after a revolt of the Polygars, and was administered on behalf of the maharaja by a British commissioner. In 1862, the maharaja applied for the restoration of the state to him, but the case was rejected in

1863–64. However, in 1865 the maharaja pressed his claim once more. He was without issue and wanted to adopt a successor to his throne. He refused to accept the exclusive right of the British over his territories since the nizam was also a party to the conquest and could stake his claim if he was refused permission to adopt a successor. In June 1865, he adopted a two-year-old boy after being informed from London that Parliament was not going to discuss his case in that session.

Sir John Lawrence was a firm annexationist and wanted to make Mysore a British territory. Opposition from, among others, Sir George Clerk, former governor of Bombay, led the Secretary of State, Lord Cranborne, (later the Marquess of Salisbury), to decide against such a course of action. Lord Northcote, his successor, decided to restore Mysore to the adopted son of the maharaja.

In August 1866, Salar Jung had met Yule in connection with the nizam's claim on Mysore. He told Yule that he meant to go to England to raise this issue since that was where the matter was going to be settled. When the resident communicated this to the viceroy, Lord Lawrence, he was aghast. Yule was severely reprimanded and threatened with dismissal. The raising of the Mysore issue is significant because the maharaja had adverted to the nizam's claim to half the territory of Mysore when the British did not allow him to appoint a successor. Their agents were both active in London at the time and may have been in contact with each other. Salar Jung's claim to Mysore did nothing for the restoration of Berar, but it did have the effect of restoration of the Mysore dynasty since the British changed an earlier intention to absorb the state in order to prevent the nizam from claiming half of it.

Yule forwarded Salar Jung's letter of 27 October 1866 to the Foreign Department on 14 November. The viceroy was livid, and in his reply in February 1867 through J.W.S. Wyllie, officiating secretary to the Government of India, made his displeasure known in strong terms. Salar Jung was informed in a lengthy document that his claims were altogether baseless.

> It is painful to the Government of India to speak in harsh terms of any application from a Native State; but the *spirit of extravagant assertion* which pervades Sir Salar Jung's letter, unworthy alike of his princely master's dignity and of his own reputation for enlightened statesmanship leaves the Governor General in Council no alternative but to require that

the *future communications of the Hyderabad Durbar shall be framed in a tone more serious and circumspect.* [emphasis added].[40]

The final rap on the knuckles was delivered at the end of the communication when Yule was told, 'You will at the same time intimate to him that it is [a] matter of unfeigned regret to the Right Honourable the Viceroy and Governor General in Council to have been obliged to reject with censure an application proceeding from a Minister whose generally admirable conduct has merited the frequent thanks of this Government, and lately has even been distinguished by a high mark of royal favour from Her Gracious Majesty herself, the Queen of England and India.' The government also noted that in commenting on the cost of the Berar administration, Salar Jung had adverted to a subject which had been specifically 'removed by Treaty from the cognizance of the Court of Hyderabad'.

The Secretary of State agreed with the viceroy, Sir John Lawrence, and wanted Salar Jung to be told that the British government had no intention of giving up Berar. Salar Jung was upset at the rebuff but bided his time for a renewed effort. When Yule gently told him that his claims were not making him popular with the government, he said, but what could he do, 'he must do what seems right and as his master wished'.[41] The application of 1866–67 for the restoration of Berar showed Salar Jung for the first time in the role of a challenger to the British position on a major political issue and marked a major change in approach between the negotiations for the treaty of 1860 and the application of 1866–67.[42]

It was generally felt that Salar Jung had taken too much on himself by asking for restoration. Some years later, Lord Salisbury wrote to Lord Northbrook that Salar Jung was under the impression that Mysore was a precedent for Berar. What was noteworthy in this correspondence was the assertion that it was wrong for Salar Jung to imagine that the English would look upon a Mohammedan and a native state in the same way, implying that Hyderabad was not really Indian. It reflected the government's fears of an alliance between Hyderabad and the Middle East, since Lord Salisbury's mind was preoccupied with recurrent Islamic unrest in that sphere.

Salar Jung was greatly disappointed by this rejection of the nizam's claim to a share of Mysore. But his claim to Mysore was only a way of achieving his main objective which was the recovery of Berar. He would willingly withdraw any claims to Mysore if Berar was restored and the British agreed to pay the Contingent themselves. Yule told him that since the claim to Mysore had already been disallowed, his proposal would be quite pointless. In any case, by that time, the claim was no longer valid since the British had decided not to annex Mysore.

Apart from retaining Berar unfairly, the government did not fulfil its promise of making over the surplus from Berar to the nizam. It was not paid at all for the first six years since the treaty of 1860, and in 1867, only Rs 5 lakh was paid even though the surplus was in excess of Rs 17 lakh. Nor was there any attempt to curtail the expenditure on administration despite remonstrance from Salar Jung on the subject. Sir Stafford Northcote, the Secretary of State, conceded that Salar Jung had a valid point, and he wrote to Lawrence that while Berar's interest was not to be sacrificed, it would not be proper to spend everything on Berar, leaving the other provinces in need. The Duke of Argyll, who succeeded Northcote, was less understanding. He wanted larger sums to be spent on public works so that the surplus to the nizam was minimized. This, in fact, became the standing policy of the government, who ensured that not too much was left for the nizam's coffers.

For many Englishmen too, Berar was an injustice. In the words of Sir William Barton who was resident at Hyderabad during 1925–30:

> This much may be said, that Englishmen looking down the vista of years will not find it easy to condone the straining of a clause of the Treaty of 1800 in order to justify the raising of a large force, British in all but name but paid for by the Nizam, which practically doubled the Subsidiary Force and imposed such a heavy financial burden on the State that its budget was thrown out of equilibrium for seventy or eighty years.[43]

The British, by the treaty of 1860 and subsequent boundary adjustments, had secured a natural boundary except in the west of the dominions. The resident, Sir Richard Temple, had in 1867 pointed out the irregular nature of the line which separated the southern and south-western frontier of the assigned districts from territories directly administered by the nizam's government. The police officers complained of difficulties in jurisdiction, and in 1871 Salar Jung was persuaded to straighten out the frontier by an interchange of territory on the border, the understanding being that this would in no way affect the nizam's title over these areas.

Eighty-eight villages valued at Rs 19,628 were transferred from the unassigned to the assigned territory, and sixty-two villages whose value was assessed at Rs 21,253 were transferred to unassigned territory. It was ensured that the land revenue system introduced by the British in the villages transferred would be maintained by Hyderabad officials, following the transfer.[44]

8

The Child Nizam

On 26 February 1869, the nizam, Afzal-ud-Daula, died somewhat unexpectedly. He was only forty-four. It was thought that the luxurious retirement and passive indulgence in which he had lived for most of his twelve-year reign had contributed to a premature death. Undeniably, his last years had been spent in close seclusion and comparative inaction, but his physical characteristics and appearance gave promise of the biblical three score and ten years. Val Prinsep rather mysteriously, and without giving any details, observed:

> The late Nizam died in a singular and most distressing way. He had a disease, not dangerous of itself, but one which rendered a slight operation necessary; but he funked. He had all the people of the city who were afflicted with the same disease brought to him and operated on in his presence; yet he could not make up his mind, and at last mortification set in, and he died miserably.[1]

Sir Richard Temple was more explicit. It is almost certain that Afzal-ud-Daula died of complications from untreated hydrocele over an extended period of time. In August 1867 itself, Temple noted in his diary that Rafi-ud-din Khan Amir-i-Kabir II had told Lieutenant Tweedie that the nizam was suffering from hydrocele but would not submit to the treatment of the Muslim physicians from the medical school. Given Afzal-ud-Daula's highly suspicious nature, Temple wanted Salar Jung to intervene, but with caution.[2] Salar Jung told Temple that this suspiciousness extended only to political matters and he could offer advice on private matters without reserve. In this assertion, he was much mistaken. At the end of September, a physician told Temple that if left untreated, the nizam would be unable to walk. But the suspicious nizam still stubbornly refused to consult any medical officers employed under Salar Jung for fear of treachery.[3]

It is also certain that Afzal-ud-Daula, who had a sweet tooth, was diabetic. When his hakeems told him that he had a health problem involving sugar, the bewildered nizam refused to believe that something so tasty could be detrimental to his health. The story goes that Afzal relented after repeated entreaties from his doctors. His doctors wanted him to restrict his dessert to quarter of a laddoo and after some discussion it was decided that henceforth the nizam would consume only half a laddoo. But the apparent abstinence made no difference and his health continued to deteriorate. The perplexed hakeems finally had their answer a little later. One of the nizam's attendants hinted that it would be a good idea for them to check the size of the sweetmeat. To their horror the hakeems discovered that the laddoo was all of 5 kg, and half a laddoo in fact meant that the nizam was consuming two-and-a-half kilos of the sweetmeat on each occasion.[4]

In Hyderabad, Temple was succeeded as resident by C.B. Saunders, and in Calcutta, Lawrence was replaced by Lord Mayo. Lawrence's viceroyalty had proved to be a disappointing one. He knew India well, and was a hard worker, but narrow vision, a plodding mind, and a concern for detail made him more suited to the administration of a province than governing an empire. It was the mind of a first-rate subordinate, used to carrying out orders rather than formulation of his own policies. Rigid and obstinate, he had no talent for compromise, something which proved to be a disadvantage when dealing with colleagues.

He was dominated by the redoubtable Sir Charles Wood who was Secretary of State. Sarvepalli Gopal's description of Lawrence is worth noting: 'The Viceroy fainéant in India appeared to the Secretaries of State in London as a senior foreman awaiting orders. Lawrence had been too long a civil servant to be able to resist the directives of the home government.'[5] On his return to England in early 1869, Lawrence was raised to the peerage, but his 'reign only served to convince people that a civilian ought never again to occupy the Viceregal throne'.[6] But Lawrence's viceroyalty produced one measure for which the higher echelons of government had reason to be grateful. It was at his insistence that the annual hot-weather migration of the Government of India to Simla was instituted. From 1864 onwards, Simla became the hot-weather capital of British India; Peterhof, the house occupied by Elgin when he visited Simla, became the official viceregal summer residence.

The new viceroy, who arrived in India in January 1869, was Richard Bourke, sixth Earl of Mayo, a minor politician who had been chief secretary of Ireland. To many it seemed an eccentric choice, for Mayo knew nothing about India, but this dark horse proved to be a winner. Mayo was a tall, broad-shouldered, powerfully built man, with untiring energy and good sense. His kindness, cheerfulness, courtesy and enthusiasm gave him a personal magnetism which was irresistible, and won for him many friends. His charisma soon achieved for him popularity such as no previous viceroy had ever enjoyed.

Finance always occupied his closest attention. He also took personal charge of the public works department and foreign affairs, and took keen interest in agriculture and education. He governed India according to the needs of the people, and though he believed in Britain's imperial destiny, he held enlightened views on education and in people's participation in administration; the Mayo College in Ajmer to educate the sons of the ruling princes was started by him.

Mayo was tactful and conciliatory to the ruling princes who admired him for his debonair and dignified manner and courteous behaviour. He was able to assure them that annexation was a thing of the past. The British would interfere in instances of misgovernance, but those who ruled well would be subjected to the least possible control.

MAHBUB ALI KHAN

The young Mahbub Ali Khan, not yet three, was proclaimed as the new ruler by Salar Jung after consultation with the Paigah and other nobles. It was said that Afzal-ud-Daula, who had lost three sons before Mahbub finally survived, had at the bidding of a fakir never set eyes on him lest evil befall him. Salar Jung had despatched the Arab guards to all the city gates to ensure that no Englishmen entered the city at that time. Saunders, for his part, had telegraphed the viceroy for orders, and a reply ordering the immediate recognition of the young prince as nizam had been received. This decision was proclaimed by the beating of tom-toms, and allayed the apprehensions of the people who thought that the British were planning to occupy the city.

Saunders was a little miffed that he had not been consulted by Salar Jung, but the latter rightly pointed out that such permission was not required either by treaty or convention. In a fit of pique, the resident said that he and his party would attend the installation wearing their shoes and would sit on chairs rather than follow the old practice of sitting barefoot on the floor. For generations, the resident and his party sat on a carpet to the right of the masnad, barefoot and bareheaded, while the diwan and other attending nobles sat on the left, barefoot, but with heads covered. Saunders, like his predecessors, resented taking off his shoes in the presence of the nizam and squatting on the floor like the rest of the nobles.

He was probably not the first to protest though. There is a story that one of the earlier residents had requested Nasir-ud-Daula for the use of a chair as it was uncomfortable to sit cross-legged in the tight trousers which were in fashion at the time. Nasir-ud-Daula is said to have retorted, 'Let a pit be dug to dangle his feet in.'[7] General Fraser had made several attempts when he was resident but appears to have been successful only on one occasion when Nasir-ud-Daula received him at an encampment in which two chairs were placed, one for the nizam and the other for the resident.

There is an amusing anecdote which involves his son, Afzal-ud-Daula, when he was nizam. In Hyderabad, the expression for requesting an audience with the nizam involved the use of stylized phrases and florid Persian, and was, '. . . craves to see His Highness's feet.' The story goes that Afzal-ud-Daula was once annoyed with the resident, and when that official arrived for his interview, he was greeted by the nizam's feet stuck out from under a silken curtain. When they were withdrawn after a few moments, the audience was over.[8]

It was alleged that Lord Dalhousie had once remarked on the boot question to Davidson, 'Were I Resident at Hyderabad, catch me taking off my boots!' But Residents Colonel Low and Bushby took off their boots, and the same newspaper reported that it appears that 'Lord Dalhousie only cared for the degradation of the bootless feet in his own person, but not in that of his representative.'[9] Davidson, however, vehemently denied that Dalhousie had ever made such a remark: 'He never said anything of the kind, if he had wanted this he would have given his orders.'[10]

A change which had already taken place when Nasir-ud-Daula had ascended the masnad had to do with the way the nizam and the Governor General referred to themselves in official correspondence. It was conveyed to Nasir-ud-Daula that the Governor General would appreciate it if he stopped referring to himself as *ma badaulat*, the royal way of referring to oneself in the third person, in effect the Hyderabadi counterpart of the royal 'we'. On his part. he would stop calling himself *niazmand*, or petitioner, as previous Governors General had done in their correspondence with the nizam. It must be remembered that at the commencement of the nineteenth century, the Governor General was technically a tributary of the nizam, paying tribute for the Northern Circars. Forty years later, the position was entirely different: no tribute was paid, and the British had, in fact, become the paramount power in India. A change was therefore necessary. The nizam was also asked to stop the practice of conferring oriental titles on the residents and other British subjects.

A greatly agitated Salar Jung told Saunders that he would not be able to control the incensed nobles, Pathans and Rohillas if the nizam was thus insulted. But Saunders, set in his stirrups for war, refused to relent. He went as far as instructing the army to stand by and to sack Hyderabad if they should hear as much as a shot from the palace. He also established telegraph communications from his camp to the palace. It was a battle of wills, and in the end, Saunders had his way. He entered the durbar in his shoes and sat on a chair. Val Prinsep describes the incident in staccato sentences:

> The Resident insisted. He had a telegraph wire laid on from the Residency to the camp at Secunderabad; the troops were then kept under arms and an official left with orders if he heard one gun fired to give the signal to sack Hyderabad. Sir Salar, informed of this, said he would do what he could. He lined the streets with his own men. *The Resident left, paid his visit, sat on his chair, did not take off his shoes, and was not killed.* [emphasis added].[11]

However, in order to keep the level of the floor in line with the chairs, the floor was raised so that the resident would not (quite literally) look down on the young nizam. This gradually led to a change of dress amongst the Indian nobles too, who started wearing trousers and sherwani with shoes instead of the traditional neema jama. Saunders's action received praise from Lord Mayo, who was pleased that the resident had acted with much courage and succeeded in ending a practice which British officers had found most humiliating.

Sometime later, the resident summoned Salar Jung and also sent for two important Paigah nobles to discuss the future governance of the state. One of the nobles was Rafi-ud-din Khan Amir-i-Kabir II, son of the old Shums-ul-Umra II, whom earlier residents had greatly esteemed. Rafi-ud-din had inherited the titles from his father and become the premier noble of the realm, second only to the nizam in importance. The other noble who was invited by Saunders was Khurshed Jah, the eldest son-in-law of Afzal-ud-Daula, and the son of Rashid-ud-din Khan, who was still persona non grata after the Murray affair. The nobles indicated that they would attend, provided they got a personal invitation from the resident who duly obliged.

Khurshed Jah was a fair, thickset man of middle height, who, in the lifetime of his father, had separated from him with his share of the Paigah. He was a favourite of his grandfather, who showered him with gifts of money and jewellery without the knowledge of his father, who became jealous of him. He was also a favourite of the nizam, who bestowed his bounty on him. He was clever in accounts and proficient in Persian. His palace, like that of his father, was a haven for criminals. He ran a fiefdom of his own, and even the police could not enter it. Even Salar Jung's writ did not run here. It was a kind of independent state in itself, an *imperium in imperio*, with its own stamp, police and courts. The nizam had also given him the right to confer titles and to grant jagirs. As he was the favourite son-in-law, the nizam had conferred his own headdress on him. He met the Governor General on an equal footing and entertained the British officers with as much pomp and show as Salar Jung. Salar Jung had stationed a mukhtar—a kind of ambassador—at his durbar through whom he could get the orders of the civil courts and police carried out.[12]

Considering that Salar Jung had been a strong ally of the British, it would not have been unreasonable to expect that he would be installed as sole regent. But the government did not want to invest one man with too much power, and that too for a period of fifteen long years. The government thought it wiser to place two men in power who would act as a check on each other. This, and the fact that Salar Jung had made himself a little unpopular in official circles by posing the Berar question, convinced the British of the need for finding a co-regent. The Amir-i-Kabir II, who was the principal nobleman and the head of the Paigah family, was the obvious choice. It also suited Salar Jung well since the association of the Amir-i-Kabir II with his administration would help him win the support of both the populace and the nobility.[13]

After the discussions ended, Salar Jung drew up an agreement which both the Amir-i-Kabir and Khurshed Jah signed before it was sent to Saunders. According to the agreement, the state was to be administered jointly by Salar Jung and the Amir-i-Kabir II. Salar Jung would continue as diwan and directly administer the personal estate of the nizam but would consult the amir on matters of policy. The resident would be informed on all matters of importance. The infant nizam's grandmother, mother of the late nizam, Begum Sahiba Dilawar-un-Nissa, would also be kept in the picture. Salar Jung and the Amir-i-Kabir II agreed to consult with the begum at the palace on matters of state. It was agreed that these arrangements would end once the nizam attained his majority. Salar Jung was aware that only the full support and concurrence of the British government would enable the accession to be placed on a firm basis.

The dowager begum was given importance in the document as a mark of respect and as a way of ensuring her cooperation. As Salar Jung pointed out to Saunders, precedents existed in Hyderabad where mothers 'exercised openly and avowedly, direct control in the management and direction of public questions, though their sons, the reigning Princes, were not minors'.

The late nizam's younger brother, Roshan-ud-Daula, also threw his hat into the ring, laying claims to a share in the regency, but such pretensions were summarily rejected. Apart from his personal unacceptability, he was the next in line to the masnad, and 'the custom of this court has always condemned the heir apparent to spend his life in such strict surveillance as borders upon honourable confinement'.[14] Still, the two regents were taking no chances since 'the letter was better written than his education would justify', and, fearing a conspiracy, strengthened the guard at the nizam's palace after taking the dowager begum into confidence.

Saunders observed that the right of the British to interfere in case of marked or manifest misgovernment had not been in the document. While this was only to be expected, Salar Jung indicated that he was willing to go further than the terms of the statement by consulting the resident in all necessary and important matters as had been the policy of the state from the time of Mir Alam. In any case, the late nizam had never conferred the powers of regency on the co-regents, and therefore they had no official claim on their authority. It was derived from, or had the sanction of, the British.

Saunders advised the Government of India to accept the proposals. He paid a tribute to the ability and rectitude of Salar Jung, observing that he was as loyal to the British government as he was to his own. Saunders further observed, 'I have seen no other example of the Asiatic mind where subtlety of intellect blends so happily with honesty of heart and public integrity as in him.' The resident also praised the Amir-i-Kabir II as a highly respected nobleman whose 'character stands justly very high . . . [he has] political sagacity . . . probably has no ambition left unfulfilled and few personal ends to serve.' But Saunders was particular about one important point: he wanted the Government of India to supervise the education of the young nizam.

The young nizam's education received much attention and was the cause of some resentment. The government had advised the resident that the person to superintend his education should be 'an English gentleman of learning and ability' who would select any subordinate teachers who might be needed. Predictably, this did not find favour with anyone. This, it was argued, would interfere with the boy's religious education. Also, an English tutor could hardly be expected to be au fait with Hyderabad etiquette and customs. Ultimately, it was all about who would enjoy power and influence. The resident was aware that the real reason for wanting a Muslim as head tutor was to control an Englishman, who would then be in a subordinate position.

In the end, it was agreed that the selection would be left to the regents who would take the advice of the resident on the subject. For his part, Salar Jung procrastinated, saying that they should wait till the nizam was seven. The next year, he started the child's religious education with the Bismillah ceremony at the age of four years, four months, and four days. Moulvi Mohammed Zaman Khan, a Sufi of great erudition, was appointed to give lessons in the Koran.

A question which created some acrimony was whether the tutor should wear shoes or otherwise. The British saw the indigenous custom of removing shoes as a mark of respect, and by corollary, an act of subservience. Seven letters were exchanged between Saunders and Salar Jung between 3 May and 8 May 1869. Saunders did not mince his words, and said that it was infra dig for an English gentleman to 'pad about in his stocking feet' and considered the practice to be offensive to the government.

In his reply, Salar Jung bemoaned the constant infringement of local customs and manners, and offered to establish, if necessary, a schoolroom where shoes were allowed. However, he did not fail to point out that this would restrict the tutor in his attempts to teach the young nizam. As for the young boy, he was unaccustomed to wearing shoes indoors and would be uncomfortable doing so. This would certainly not conduce to attentiveness, and he would be tempted to exchange the classroom for more congenial surroundings, such as the palace. It also militated against the diktat of the government who wanted the tutor to also be responsible for his general upbringing and environment. If the tutor wore shoes, this would limit his access to only the classroom and preclude the possibility of such all-round mentoring.

Saunders' reply was patronizing and had an insulting tone. He called Salar Jung's proposal a 'retrogressive line of policy', and said that notwithstanding the 'national point of view', the crux of the whole issue was 'the bringing up of the Sovereign in such a way that when his minority is ended, he may rule the millions under his sway with true enlightenment and real greatness'. While he conceded the need for tact and caution, he thought it worthwhile to 'brush away if need be, a cartload of narrow prejudices, and . . . popular fancies held by a majority for the most part uneducated and entitled to little respect'.[15] He also claimed to have walked in Salar Jung's own home and garden without removing his shoes.

Salar Jung, who must have been irked by both the words and tone of the communication, merely responded by informing the resident that neither he nor anyone else, who had not removed their footwear, had ever gained access to where he lived, or for that matter, where Indian visitors, who observed the local custom, were admitted. The resident was told that he had been given access to only those rooms modified for the reception of westerners. There the matter seems to have ended, at least in official communication. It was quietly dropped since 'the real subject being discussed was not shoes but power'.[16]

SIR SALAR JUNG, GCSI

Regardless of all the disagreements, Salar Jung seems to have acquitted himself creditably in the eyes of the viceroy as far as the education of the young nizam was concerned. Mayo was pleased that Salar Jung had consented to the proposals with regard to education of the young nizam and the arrangements for administering the state during his minority. In a despatch to Saunders, Mayo had also expressed his keen interest in the good governance of Hyderabad, the reform of its administration, and its all-round development. One of the pillars of Mayo's India policy was the securing of a good local administration. He had the highest regard for Salar Jung's abilities, believing him to be 'one of the ablest and wisest men in India'. With Salar Jung at the helm, and a series of able residents, Hyderabad would get the good government it badly needed.

In August 1869, Mayo wrote to the Secretary of State, Lord Argyll, recommending Salar Jung for the first class of the Order of the Star of

India. 'I think therefore that your Grace might with advantage recommend him at a fitting opportunity to H.M. for the first class of the Order of the Star of India.'[17] When Saunders sounded Salar Jung about the honour, the latter was diffident about accepting it. On 8 June 1870, he wrote to the resident about his misgivings in this regard. He said that the young nizam's mother was very keen to get it for her son, and if he accepted the honour, he would 'be disrespecting my master for having accepted a thing which was conferred upon him, while the present Nizam was deprived of the same, and secondly, I am not the only manager of my master's country, I have also a colleague, and if he does not obtain similar marks of respect I shall be thought selfish . . . all will think that I did all this for my own personal aggrandizement and nothing else.'[18]

Saunders wrote back the next day telling him that he had not been taken into confidence about the honour to be conferred on Salar Jung or else he would have ascertained his views on the subject. As for the nizam, he did not qualify for the honour since he was still a minor. He ended with: 'As I would much like to have the opportunity of talking over the matters with you, I would be glad to have the pleasure of breakfasting with you tomorrow morning, if not inconvenient, as I do not like replying to the Viceroy's Private Secretary without first consulting you on the subject.'[19]

In reply, Salar Jung reiterated that he had no ambition and did not want it to appear that he was clamouring for higher honours. In case he was conferred the honour, he wanted that his views on its acceptance should be known so as to leave no doubt in anyone's mind. 'Notwithstanding that I mentioned yesterday that I have no ambition, I say now that I had and have no ambition, and that is that I should not be charged with disloyalty and faithlessness to my own Government, and to that Government which is the supporter of our Government . . .'[20]

In the end, Salar Jung accepted the honour. The ceremony of presenting Salar Jung with the insignia of a Knight Grand Commander of the Most Exalted Order of the Star of India took place in the residency on the evening of 5 January 1871. The residency was splendidly illuminated, and proceedings commenced with a state dinner to which not only the whole British community had been invited but also a large number of native nobles and high officials of Hyderabad. There were toasts to the health of the queen and the nizam after dinner.

The gathering then proceeded to the grand hall of the residency where a large party of invitees had already assembled. Huge chairs of state made of lead decked out in bright liveries of carving and gilding were placed on both sides of the hall, and each was ticketed in English and Persian with the name of the British officer or city noble who was to occupy it. In the centre of one row and slightly ahead of the other seats, was placed a chair for Salar Jung. On either side were his two sons aged eight and twelve respectively, with the elder, Mir Laik Ali, already bearing a striking resemblance to his father.

The resident's seat was just opposite the diwan's, and on a marble table in front of him, the collar and the badge were displayed. Salar Jung was then escorted from his temporary place of seclusion in one of the drawing rooms to his seat in the hall, the gathering all rising as he entered. Saunders congratulated Salar Jung on the fresh laurel added to his wreath, and then expatiated on the public qualities which had procured for him the crowning mark of the queen's approbation. Salar Jung, in his reply, expressed his gratitude and spoke of his earnest desire to strive for better results in his administration of the state.

SALAR JUNG ON TOUR

In February 1870, Salar Jung travelled out of Hyderabad for the first time in his life. The interdiction on leaving Hyderabad had ended with the death of Afzal-ud-Daula. Kandaswamy had told Temple that nothing would persuade the nizam that Salar Jung was not going to hatch mischief if he went on a tour of the interiors of the country. Never having left Hyderabad, he was at a great disadvantage, but he did not let this hamper him. Temple observed: 'Indeed, considering how restricted was his actual vision, I was surprised to find that he had so much liberality and comprehensiveness of view.'[21]

When Temple urged Salar Jung to try and make a tour of the country, he replied that the nizam would never willingly consent to it, since his prejudice in this matter was inflexible. It was also one of the conditions imposed on him when the rupture was patched up.[22] Afzal-ud-Daula went to the extent of refusing permission to even visit Bolarum. When Temple was to review the Reformed Troops at Fateh maidan, Salar Jung could not be present because he did not want to have to ask permission from the nizam. His military secretary, Major Proudfoot, attended in his stead.[23]

Salar Jung and his suite left Hyderabad on 14 February en route to Bombay and Berar. The journey to Gulbarga was covered in twenty-seven hours which included four short stoppages on the way. They arrived at Gulbarga railway station where they were received by a guard of honour consisting of a troop of the 4th Cavalry, Hyderabad Contingent, under the command of Lieutenant Talbot. The as yet unfinished station was decorated with flowers, and the railway employees had erected an arch at the entrance. On alighting from his carriage, Salar Jung was received by Captain A.F. Dobbs, the judicial superintendent of the railway, and conducted to the platform just as the locomotive, which was to take the party some 2 miles further where a large camp had been pitched for their stay, arrived at the platform. The locomotive was appropriately called 'Sir Salar Jung' and was driven by James Robertson, the managing agent, and on it, among others, were the resident, C.B. Saunders, and Captain G.H. Trevor, second assistant resident (who had arrived the evening before). The party then entered a carriage which had been placed at their disposal by Mr Middleton, the district traffic manager, and they proceeded down the yet unopened line to Naganhally where the camp had been pitched for their accommodation.

Salar Jung had expressed a wish to see the Shahabad station and the Caugnee viaduct, and accordingly the party departed at 7 a.m. the next day for the 16-mile journey. During the journey, the working of the engine was explained to Salar Jung, who evinced a lively interest. On arrival at Shahabad, they were conducted over the station. The train proceeded to the viaduct over the Caugnee, and then the party returned to Shahabad. At 5 p.m., the special train which was to take them to Bombay arrived, and they started for Poona at 6 p.m. where they had decided to break journey for a few hours before continuing their journey to Bombay.

The party arrived in Bombay on 18 February, and Salar Jung stayed with a Parsi friend, Muncherjee Bomanjee Panthakee, at his bungalow at Girgaum which had been renovated to welcome him in befitting style. Salar Jung visited Sir William Robert Seymour Vesey-FitzGerald, governor of Bombay, at Government House, Malabar Point, and was received by a guard of honour. On his return, he was entertained to lunch, along with the resident and other officials by his host. In the afternoon, the party visited the arsenal, the mint and the high court. There was also a visit to the Manockjee Petit Spinning and Weaving Company's mills at Tardeo, one of the largest mills in India at the time. Dinner was a sumptuous affair with the resident at the Adelphi Hotel in Byculla, famous as Pallonjee's hotel, after its owner. A few hours at the Grant Road Theatre rounded off the day's entertainment, and it was reported that Salar Jung was able to see the humour in many of Dave Carson's jokes.[24]

The next morning, the governor of Bombay returned Salar Jung's visit. The remainder of the morning was spent on a visit to the Crawford Market where Arthur Crawford, after whom the market was named, was there to welcome him. He was given a demonstration of a fire engine in action and also visited the municipal works. The same evening, he dined at Government House where a distinguished party had been invited to meet him. The next day, Sunday, was devoted to the reception of visitors who included the famous English educationist and social reformer, Mary Carpenter, who was visiting Bombay at the time.

On Monday morning, Salar Jung, accompanied by Saunders and other European officers, visited the Alexandra N.G. English Institution. The guests examined some of the girls in different branches of their studies and were much satisfied with the answers. Salar Jung was particularly impressed with the way the girls sang in English, and while leaving, expressed satisfaction at the fact that Indian girls were receiving an education in English.

On the same day, Salar Jung visited HMS *Forte* and was shown around the frigate and given explanations about everything of interest on board. After a befitting salute, the company then departed for the troopship, *Malabar,* where the troops had been mustered for inspection. Salar Jung had the novel experience of seeing a British regiment drawn up on the deck of a steamer. The interest and delight shown by Salar Jung was unmistakable, and the impression he created by his noble bearing and intelligence was a most favourable one. The party then proceeded to Elephanta. On their return, they were hosted for dinner by David Sassoon.

The next day, Salar Jung paid a return visit to Sir Jamsetjee Jejeebhoy (second baronet), at his residence, Mazgaon Castle. The baronet had called on him two days ago at his residence in Girgaum. At 3 p.m., Salar Jung left for Byculla station, and before taking leave of his host, presented him with a diamond necklace and a pair of diamond wristlets. The farewell party at the station included Dr Bhau Daji Lad, Manockjee Cursetjee, Cursetjee Cama and Sir Jamsetjee Jejeebhoy. Salar Jung left by special train at 4 p.m. for Aurangabad.

A TUTOR FOR THE YOUNG NIZAM

Salar Jung was forever trying to maintain the dignity of the young nizam. He also attempted to nullify the influence of the zenana and protect him from the dissolute ways of the court. He did this by instituting heightened levels of court etiquette, sometimes taken to absurd levels. He expected the nobles to show the utmost respect to the young sovereign and made use of every important ceremonial occasion to drive home the point.

On the nizam's birthday and on Eid days, custom and ceremonial usage demanded that nazars be presented by the diwan and the chief nobles at a formal durbar. But since Mahbub was a child and could not hold durbar, Salar Jung would go to the royal palace to pay homage. Mounted on a majestic elephant and surrounded by his armed retainers, he would arrive at the palace at the head of a long procession. Since etiquette forbade entry into the courtyard of the palace except on foot, he alighted at the outer gate and stood respectfully with his face turned towards the building where the nizam was supposed to be. There he made his salaams, his right hand touching the ground as he bent low, and then touching his forehead as he rose each time. This was repeated at the entrance of successive courtyards, until he arrived at the spot beyond which entry was barred to all. A female servant would convey his humble greeting to his royal master. The message was received by the nizam's grandmother, who acknowledged it by sending her blessings in return to Salar Jung. On his return, the same elaborate salaam ceremony was repeated until he reached the main entrance on the road.

Another incident makes a slightly different point. It is said that Nawab Fakhr-ul-Mulk II, one of the great nobles of Hyderabad, gave the young nizam a gift of a repeater watch in the 1870s. Mahbub was delighted with his new toy, but Salar Jung insisted that he return the gift. He also fined the nawab Rs 10,000 for teaching the nizam to take, when he should be learning to give. The huge fine recognized the substantial importance of the giver. With the money from the penalty, Salar Jung ordered 250 watches from England for the young nizam to give away![25]

One incident involved Mahbub and Salar Jung himself. It was strictly against the etiquette of the court to be inappropriately dressed in the presence of the sovereign. Two parts of the apparel were obligatory in the presence of the nizam: a *bugloos*, a belt often with an elaborate ornamental buckle, and a turban, called a *dastar*, of a shape unique to Hyderabad. (The nizam's dastar was often, but not necessarily, yellow, and embellished with a *toorah*, a stiff inverted tassel of gold thread which was also worn by others of royal blood. A few nobles were permitted to wear turbans of a different shape peculiar to their families.) On a visit to Golconda, the young boy ran into Salar Jung's room and found the diwan taking a nap. He had taken off his bugloos, and to be in the presence of the nizam without a girdle was most inappropriate. Salar Jung immediately paid the young nizam a penalty of fifteen gold mohurs. The next morning, he sent a further Rs 1500 to complete the fine.[26]

Yet another incident (which is part of the oral tradition) concerns an episode in which the young nizam broke an expensive pedestal chandelier in the hallway of the palace. A little later, Salar Jung walked in and asked the nizam if he was responsible for the destruction. The frightened young boy nodded without saying a word. Salar Jung is supposed to have said, 'I cannot tolerate such behaviour in the future Nizam of Hyderabad.' Asking for his walking stick to be brought to him, he asked the nizam to hold out his right hand. Not knowing what to expect, the boy held out a trembling hand into which Salar Jung thrust the stick with the words, 'You are the Nizam of Hyderabad. This palace and everything in it belongs to you. Be brave for you have nothing to be scared of. Now step forward and break every chandelier in this palace.' It is said that the boy gleefully broke every chandelier within reach. Chandeliers were very popular in Hyderabad, and Val Prinsep observed: 'Hyderabadists [sic] are, like all natives, mad on the subject of glass chandeliers. They have them even in the mosques, and when they are tied up in muslin bags they have anything but a religious look, but rather as if the family were out of town.'[27]

When the nizam was going to turn seven, the British reiterated the need for finding a suitable tutor. The Secretary of State, the Duke of Argyll, asked the Government of India to get a definite proposal from the co-regents for the nizam's education. Salar Jung once again tried to buy time by alluding to the toddler nizam's delicate health and the fact that he had yet to complete his basic introduction to the Koran. However, a little later, he yielded to the pressure and appointed a selection committee in England to find a suitable candidate. It comprised the former resident, Sir George Yule, Col. Thornhill and J.G. Cordery, former assistant residents in Hyderabad, his old friend, Col. J. Oliphant, and Col. Philip Meadows Taylor. When Saunders came to know of it, he seemed upset that Salar Jung had asked the committee to proceed further without consulting him on its composition or brief.

In his rejoinder, Salar Jung said that it was on British prodding that he was expediting matters. Salar Jung's promptness in the matter can be attributed to the fact that he wanted a tutor of his own choice rather than a nominee of the Government of India. Writing to Tom Palmer, one of his confidential agents, he said: 'I shall take care to insist on our right to nominate the tutor and not accept any officer nominated by the British Government for this important duty.'[28]

Saunders advised Salar Jung to increase the salary of the tutor so as to make him entirely immune to local intrigues and attempts to influence him with monetary inducements. In other words, the tutor might prove to be corruptible. This lack of faith in the future tutor's integrity was strange since the residents (and even some viceroys) had often boasted about the high moral fibre of Englishmen and the respect due to them. Salar Jung was willing to concede 'this comparatively trivial point'[29] but was categorical that the salary be definitively fixed before it was made public in England. He feared that if it was increased later due to British influence, the candidate would look to the British rather than to the nizam's government for future advancement.

On 8 September 1873, Salar Jung wrote to his secretary, Henry Bowen, who was on leave in England, asking him to 'tutor the tutor' about the practices of the court:

> I telegraphed to you the day before yesterday not to leave England before the selection was finally settled, and now write to say that whoever the gentleman selected may be, you will necessarily be in constant intercourse with him. I wish that you use your best endeavours to make him as nearly au fait with the practices and feelings of this Court as you yourself are, in fact I wish you kindly to tutor the tutor—so that he may come here feeling that his wishes and that of H.H. the Nizam's Govt are one and the same.[30]

The name the committee proposed was that of Captain John Clerk, late of the Rifle Brigade, and eldest son of Sir George Clerk, former governor of Bombay. The choice was a happy one, for Sir George had many Indian friends and was known to have a reputation for sympathy and understanding, and both his sons, John and Claude, were familiar with India from childhood. But Clerk's appointment was not without its share of uncertainty. The Duke of Edinburgh had made him his equerry, and he withdrew his candidacy. Since he was far superior to any of the other candidates, Salar Jung was very keen to get him to Hyderabad. Unaware of the reason for his withdrawal, he twice telegraphed Yule to try his utmost to secure his services, even offering an increase of Rs 500 per month to that already offered as an 'exceptional case'.

Captain John Clerk tried to explain the matter to Salar Jung through Col. J. Oliphant. He asked his father, who was friends with the colonel, to explain to Salar Jung the complication that had arisen. Oliphant wrote that while John Clerk was fully aware of the importance of the appointment he was about to receive, it was impossible for him to resist the pressure put upon him by the Duke of Edinburgh. However, the duke relented in the end. A compromise was reached by appointing Clerk honorary equerry, thereby freeing him to take up his appointment in Hyderabad. Clerk was provided with the necessary funds for travel and outfitting, and reached Hyderabad in January 1875.

Server-ul-Mulk, who was later appointed assistant to John Clerk, was initially appointed to the audit branch of the Public Works Department. When Salar Jung was convinced of his proficiency in Urdu and English, he made him assistant to a Mr O'Connor, who had recently arrived from England to tutor his sons, Laik Ali Khan and Saadat Ali Khan. O'Connor knew no Urdu and spent all his time amusing his young wife, so the whole burden fell on Server-ul-Mulk. Apart from Salar Jung's sons, there were also the sons of other nobles in the class. When O'Connor left, his place was taken by a Mr Krohn, who was an expert in Indian and English games.

Initially, the plan had been to get Syed Hossain Bilgrami (recently arrived from Lucknow) to teach the nizam English, but that fell through when John Clerk was appointed. Bilgrami, who came to Hyderabad in late 1873, was an Arabic scholar, having taught that language at Canning College, Lucknow. A Bachelor of Arts from Presidency College in Calcutta, he was also equally fluent in English, and was put in sole charge of the *Lucknow Times*, a biweekly paper of the talukdars of Awadh. In the Sarda Canal controversy that took place at that time, he sided with the talukdars, who were against its construction. A rival newspaper, the *Pioneer*, wrote in favour of the government.

According to Server-ul-Mulk, Bilgrami had angered the officials of Awadh by commenting on their arrogant behaviour, and this is said to have greatly angered the chief commissioner, Sir John Cooper, who was contemplating some action against him.[31] Lucknow had become an uncomfortable place for the young journalist, and if Server-ul-Mulk is to be believed, Syed Hossain sent him a letter asking him if he could come to Hyderabad.[32] Server-ul-Mulk intervened on his behalf with Salar Jung, and the permission was given. Salar Jung was impressed enough with the young man to appoint him as deputy to his private secretary, Henry Bowen, with a monthly salary of Rs 300 and lodging in the Lakkad Kot. Later, he was nominated to teach the nizam English, but this appointment fizzled out. Syed Hossain wrote elegantly in English, but Salar Jung never consulted him on matters of policy or entrusted any administrative work to him. He and Henry Bowen, in their capacity of private secretaries, were only entrusted with routine correspondence. After Bowen's death, Major Percy Gough, who was made military secretary on the recommendation of Clerk, was appointed private secretary, and Syed Hossain remained as an assistant during Salar Jung's lifetime.

Syed Hossain adopted the surname 'Bilgrami' at the suggestion of Salar Jung. He accompanied Salar Jung to England, and subsequently became education secretary in Hyderabad and also director of public instruction. He was also, for a time, private secretary to Mahbub Ali Khan, and after holding a number of high positions, including member of the Legislative Council and the first Muslim member of the India Council, on retirement, became adviser to Salar Jung III, grandson of his benefactor. He received the titles Nawab Ali Yar Khan Bahadur, Motaman Jung, Imad-ud-Daula and Imad-ul-Mulk.

It is as an educationist that Hyderabad owes Bilgrami a great debt. With the exception of the Osmania University, practically all the other educational institutions owe their existence to him. The State Library was also started by him, as was the Dar-ul-Uloom or Oriental College to encourage oriental learning and scholarship. A school was started which soon rose to become a college with Aghorenath Chattopadhyay as its principal. This college eventually became the Nizam College. At his instance, the Madrasa-e-Aizza was started for the education of the upper classes. By orders of Salar Jung, the *murshidzada*s (relatives of the nizam), who were hitherto brought up without any proper education, were compelled to go to this school. Recognizing the importance of industrial training, Bilgrami founded three industrial schools, one each at Aurangabad, Hyderabad and Warangal.

THE THREE Rs

John Clerk appears to have been impressed with Server-ul-Mulk's proficiency in both English and Urdu, and selected him as his assistant in the education of the nizam. He also received instruction in Urdu from him. Server-ul-Mulk describes his first meeting with the young nizam in his autobiography:

> After a short while I was summoned to appear before his Highness. I found myself in a small 'dalan' (covered verandah), with a small courtyard in front. A 'Masnad' was placed in the Dalan, and on that His Highness was sitting. He appeared to be about eight years of age. He had a gold embroidered cap on his head, and his hair, which he wore, plaited in Indian Fashion, fell down to his waist. He was wearing a Deccani Angarakka (a loose garment falling down to the ankles). Two or three 'Mamas' (female attendants), wrapped in snowy-white garments, stood behind him. Tahniyatt Yar-ud-dowlah and his son Mustakim Jung sat with folded hands in front of the Masnad. The first sentence which fell from His Highness's lips was 'What is the English language like? Let me hear it,' I said. 'I pray for your Highness's life and prosperity.' Immediately afterwards he rose and went away.[33]

The next day, Clerk arrived at the palace for his introduction to his young charge wearing the local dress, neema jama, thereby making the dispute about shoes irrelevant. They were anxious that the nizam be not overawed by his first meeting with the Englishman. A table and chairs were placed in a room on the right side of the palace, and there, Clerk and Server-ul-Mulk took their seats. Zaffar Jung, son of Khurshed Jah, who was to be the nizam's companion in his studies, was also present. The nizam arrived on an open palanquin, followed by female attendants. All the attendants were asked to leave. Mahbub betrayed no fear but seemed a little puzzled at the goings-on. Server-ul-Mulk pulled out two or three pictures from his pocket, and placing them before the nizam, made a funny little speech which amused both the children. The ice had been broken, and this marked the end of Clerk's first meeting with the nizam.

The next day, Server-ul-Mulk took a beautifully bound volume containing pictures of animals and short stories about them. He turned to the page with a tiger, and after reading it out in English, explained it in

Urdu. On a sign from Clerk, the lesson ended and the nizam was allowed to retire. The following day, Server-ul-Mulk arrived with a slate and a pencil. After reading out the stories, he purposely drew a defective picture of a tiger. The young nizam snatched the pencil from his hand and set about rectifying the defect in the picture. In a few days, they all became good friends. Salar Jung was much pleased and sent a watch and a chain to the nizam for the latter to gift it to Server-ul-Mulk.

Clerk and Server-ul-Mulk sat at the table with the nizam, while Zaffar Jung and other attendants sat on carpets on the floor of the courtyard. Work began soon enough on the English alphabet, and Server-ul-Mulk established his authority by a show of temper towards Zaffar Jung. But Zaffar Jung, who was Khurshed Jah's son, was, after all, a Paigah, and it would not have been possible to threaten him indefinitely. Since corporal punishment was out of the question, they resorted to an old English expedient called the 'whipping boy', where sons of a few mansabdars were also taught at the same time, and took the blows due to Mahbub according to the Victorian educational philosophy that knowledge entered a boy's head through the seat of his pants.[34] Whenever the nizam and Zaffar Jung were slack in their studies, it was the sons of the mansabdars who felt the weight of Server-ul-Mulk's displeasure. English was taught in the mornings and calligraphy in the afternoon. Later, grammar, geography and arithmetic from a regular 'Reader' were added to the daily syllabus. John Clerk, it appears, was more of a spectator than a tutor. Server-ul-Mulk said that 'at the time when lessons were given he sat quiet and never interfered in anything'.[35]

John Clerk, if Server-ul-Mulk is to be believed, was a bit of a snob, and considered himself superior to every British official, including the resident. He believed that the average Englishman was utterly ignorant of the ways of Indian nobility. He rarely met British officials, and when he did, met them with a degree of reserve. But Clerk's tenure proved to be short-lived. His wife died in April 1875 and was buried in the Christian cemetery in Hyderabad. The grief-stricken tutor resigned his position and went back to England with his infant son. Before that, Salar Jung conferred Hyderabadi titles on him as a token of respect for the tutor, unaware of the storm it would create. He became Istekamud-Daula-Mustekil Jung Captain John Clerk Khan Bahadur, commander of 500 cavalry, with a mansab of 7000. Such a step required the permission of the government, something which Salar Jung had failed to obtain. The resident ought to have warned him, but did not. He, however, was not slow in conveying the displeasure of the government to Salar Jung, something which resulted in hurt feelings on several sides.

Salar Jung said that he had no idea that a local distinction such as the one bestowed on Clerk was a matter of so much importance as to require the sanction of the queen. In any case, bestowal of Hyderabadi titles on Englishmen was not new, and there were several precedents, the most famous being that of James Achilles Kirkpatrick (Hashmat Jung). There is no mention if any prior permission was taken before conferring such titles on them. In all probability, the object of the title was to increase the tutor's prestige in the durbar. That such a harmless thing also led to unpleasantness greatly saddened Salar Jung.

Salar Jung delayed appointment of a successor in the hope that John Clerk would change his mind and return. He wrote to him in January 1876 about the difficulties in finding a successor who was as well liked by everyone as he was. Clerk did not return but recommended another Clerk to take his place: Captain Claude Clerk, his younger brother, a recommendation which was eventually accepted.

Salar Jung brought him back with him on his return from his European tour in August 1876. According to Server-ul-Mulk, Claude Clerk had lost the use of one of his legs and was also a lifelong sufferer from 'bladder complaints'. He says that Claude Clerk did not know how to teach; indeed, he goes on to say that his continued ill health made him unfit for any work. At the same time, he was very anxious about what people thought of him. Server-ul-Mulk's harsh opinion may perhaps have been influenced by the fact that 'he met me coldly, and maintained that attitude throughout his stay in Hyderabad'.[36] Also, Claude Clerk seems to have got the impression that Server-ul-Mulk was a man of lesser abilities than Syed Hossain Bilgrami, so Server-ul-Mulk's opinion was not without bias.

Claude Clerk, on his arrival, refused to be called tutor and styled himself as superintendent of education. He pestered Salar Jung for a qualified and experienced Englishman as his assistant. In the event, a Mr Davidson was appointed to the post. He was a 'sporting young man' who left all the work to Server-ul-Mulk, and also became his friend. Unfortunately, he passed away a few months after his appointment. There always seems to have been someone or the other who wanted to supplant Server-ul-Mulk, or at least share his duties. Since we only have Server-ul-Mulk's word for it, we must allow for an element of exaggeration. There was Moulvi Nazir Ahmed, a s*adar* talukdar, and an author of repute, who had ingratiated himself with Clerk. Server-ul-Mulk and the moulvi were supposed to divide the work between them, but fortunately, the Amir-i-Kabir II decided against his appointment. Clerk's next choice was Dost Muhammad Khan, who was employed in the educational department, and had a previous conviction of gambling against him. Clerk seems to have had a knack for selecting unworthy persons for the job. Mortality intervened on this occasion, and Dost Muhammad succumbed to an illness soon after. Server-ul-Mulk recounts with gratitude, 'God the merciful preserved me from this misfortune also.'[37]

Around this time, Clerk, whose contribution to the education of the young sovereign appears to have been negligible (according to Server-ul-Mulk), decided that the young nizam should be examined to see what progress he had made. Already prejudiced against Server-ul-Mulk, Clerk was in search of a new man. The test would be a foolproof way of discrediting Server-ul-Mulk should the nizam perform poorly in the examination. He was to meet with disappointment.

Salar Jung was anxious about the result. This was understandable, given the fact that the resident had openly declared that the minister was neglecting the education of the nizam and wished him to remain ignorant and illiterate so that he could enjoy his own power more. Server-ul-Mulk assured him of a positive outcome, asking only that honest men be selected as examiners. Accordingly, Mr Krohn was appointed to examine the nizam in English, and a Hindu gentleman who held a high position in the Public Works Department was sent to examine him in arithmetic.

The young nizam acquitted himself quite creditably, answering questions on grammar with confidence, and reading out a lesson with passable pronunciation. His companion, Zaffar Jung, did not fare as well: after a number of pauses, he got flustered and finally broke down. Both performed satisfactorily in history and geography. The next day, in the arithmetic test, the nizam answered all his questions correctly. Clerk's plan failed, but that did not prevent him from trying again. This time, Server-ul-Mulk himself requested an assistant, suggesting the name of Mirza Nasir Ali Beg, who had served in the educational department of Agra and had retired as deputy collector. The latter did not find favour due to his old age and bowed body, and Clerk managed to get Krohn appointed in the hope that Server-ul-Mulk and he would quarrel. That hope too was belied since the two got on very well: Krohn was only too happy to rid himself of work, and entrusted the entire burden of teaching to Server-ul-Mulk.

Server-ul-Mulk's and Salar Jung's greatest bête noire at this time was Moulvi Masi-uz-Zaman Khan, a partisan of Rashid-ud-din Khan Amir-i-Kabir III, who taught Arabic to the nizam. His elder brother, Moulvi Mohammed Zaman Khan, a pious and kind man who was the nizam's Arabic teacher before him, had written a voluminous work refuting the beliefs of the Mahdevis, a sect who believed that Mahdi, the Expected One, had come and gone in the person of their founder. The moulvi was assassinated by a young Pathan fanatic of the Mahdevi sect. He was caught and sentenced to death. A master of intrigue, Masi-uz-Zaman Khan missed no opportunity to try and discredit Server-ul-Mulk. Along with Shapurjee, a wily Parsee who had the complete confidence of the amir, the two wasted no opportunity in attempting to show Salar Jung and Server-ul-Mulk in bad light. The intrigues did not stop there, but suffice it to say that Server-ul-Mulk survived them all, ultimately even making his peace with Rashid-ud-din Khan before he died.

The nizam was soon able to read and write in Urdu, and made good progress in arithmetic as well. But it was not always smooth sailing. Like most children of his age, the young Mahbub did not like going to school. Mustaquim Jung, one of the other Indian teachers, would go to the palace, and with folded hands, request his young ward to attend class. On occasion, the young boy would, on sighting his teacher, immediately start running towards the zenana. Since the tutor could not enter the ladies' quarters, he would have to wait for the boy to be brought out. The boastful Server-ul-Mulk quoted the nizam as saying that had it not been for him, he would have remained illiterate. But the young boy at this stage never took to English habits or etiquette in his speech or dress, and he ate at a table only during the period set apart for his English education. He used to learn swimming in a small water tank in the company of his attendants.

AN INVITATION TO THE RESIDENCY

When the nizam was nearly eight, Saunders invited him to visit him at the residency. It was an invitation that could not be refused, and a state visit was duly arranged on 1 August 1874, shortly before the nizam's eighth birthday. Saunders sent out 400 invitations printed in letters of gold to both Indians and Europeans to attend the reception. The proposed visit sparked a wave of excitement in the city, and the entire route from the Purani Haveli to the residency was lined with people. The nizam's procession itself was nearly 2 kilometres in length and consisted of the infantry, cavalry, camels, elephants and state palanquins. All the animals were covered with silk drapes. The coats the soldiers wore, originally red in colour, had faded, and the weapons they carried were rusted, and the shields looked like lids of cooking pots.[38]

They were followed by numerous carts carrying tigers, leopards and cheetahs, all tethered with chains in carts which were also draped in silk. A group of half-naked stonecutters carrying their tools of trade followed the animals. At the end of this outlandish train was a fierce-looking executioner with a bare sword in his hand. If it was meant to be a show of strength, it failed, because it turned out to be more comedy than menace. The procession took more than two hours to reach its destination which was bedecked appropriately for the formal yet somewhat festive occasion. Entry was strictly by invitation, and the guests started arriving by 10.30 a.m. in all modes of transport. The noblemen were dressed in neema jama and wore jewelled belts from which were suspended swords with handles of pure gold, the scabbards being set with gems.

The nizam came riding an elephant covered in a yellow cloth. Behind him, separated by a partition, sat Salar Jung and Rafi-ud-din Khan Amir-i-Kabir II. He wore white, and his dress was thickly sewn with diamonds. There were many strings of pearls and diamonds around his neck and he sported a white turban. On entering the residency, the nizam was honoured with a gun salute, and the elephant stopped in front of the steps. The two regents hurriedly got down so that they could join the resident in the welcoming party. The young nizam was escorted to the masnad in the glittering hall by Salar Jung and the resident. It was 3 feet square and 2 feet high, covered with purple velvet and richly trimmed with gold. Above it, the Asaf Jahi and English flags crossed.

Salar Jung and other nobles took their seats to the right of the masnad, and the resident and his party sat on the left. Gifts were exchanged after expressions of friendship and goodwill had been voiced by both parties. From the gallery, European ladies dressed in their best finery watched the proceedings keenly. Women were normally not allowed to witness a durbar but an exception was made in this case, and the breach of etiquette condoned, since it was being held on 'foreign' soil.

After some time, the nizam retired for a rest, and members of his retinue were treated to a lavish meal. When the nizam completed his siesta at 4 p.m., the durbar was repeated, and shortly afterwards paan supari was served to the guests, indicating that the durbar was over. On a discreet signal from one of his courtiers, the young nizam stood up and looked around in a gesture of farewell. Salar Jung and the resident then held him by the hand on either side and walked to the exit. Booming guns could be heard in the distance as a salute to the departing royal.[39] The English ladies, realizing that it was a rare occasion, made full use of it. It was too early to retire for the day and much merrymaking followed.

9

The Nizam's State Railway

The idea of putting Hyderabad on the railway map seems to have first come from Sir Bartle Frere, when Afzal-ud-Daula was still the nizam. Earlier, it had been decided to connect Bombay and Madras on the Great Indian Peninsular Railway (GIPR) via Cuddapah and Bellary through Mudgal in the Raichur Doab. In 1860, Raichur and Dharaseo were restored to the nizam after seven years under British administration, and Salar Jung was persuaded to grant to the GIP Company land required to build the railway line. Frere, who became governor of Bombay in 1862, suggested that the proposed line should run from Shorapore to Cuddapah via Hyderabad instead of through Mudgal and Bellary. Apart from stressing its importance, Frere believed that it would be much cheaper.

He bounced his ideas off the then Secretary of State, Sir Charles Wood, who was quick to recognize the merit in Frere's suggestion, writing to him that the 'Nizam's Government will be more amenable when more accessible'.[1] But Sir William Denison, the governor of Madras, an old friend and confidant of Wood, told him that the nizam was a bigoted Muslim surrounded by a set of unruly tribes, and was likely to be an 'unquiet neighbour'. Wood, while convinced of the need for some line to Hyderabad, was now not so sure that he wanted to run it through the nizam's territories.

In Hyderabad, the resident, Sir George Yule, was trying his best to convince the viceroy, Lord Elgin, that the two lines should meet in Hyderabad. In this, he had Salar Jung's full support. In 1863, Yule recorded an exhaustive note on the relative merits of two alternative routes which could be adopted for connecting Madras and Bombay. His preference was for a longer route via Gulbarga and Hyderabad rather than a shorter route via Mudgal and Bellary. There was also an intermediate route which passed from Gulbarga to Raichur, joining the original line at Gooty. This was finally accepted and a branch line was later built from Gulbarga to Hyderabad.[2]

Before Yule could convince Elgin, the latter died, and he had to deal with his successor, Sir John Lawrence, who finally chose the direct route through Raichur and Gooty. Yule's arguments were based on military considerations. He pointed out that the Hyderabad line would make the troops at Secunderabad available at short notice to both Madras and Bombay, and also serve the cantonments of Poona and Bangalore which would otherwise remain isolated. In case of an emergency in Hyderabad, the troops from both these cantonments could easily be pressed into service.[3] In a minute on the proposed railway, he wrote that by connecting Secunderabad with Poona, Kamptee and Bangalore, they would quadruple the strength of each of these cantonments. 'We spent ten lakh of Rupees to house a few hundred soldiers permanently in one place; we refuse to spend the same sum to make the whole of our Army in the Peninsula ubiquitous.'[4]

In the same minute, he outlined the political advantages of the new branch line, saying that it would enlighten and awaken the people, and 'remove the isolation in which they stand to us . . . and open the door to education and general improvement in a way which no less material means could effect'.[5] There was also the advantage derived from having the stores for the Secunderabad troops conveyed by rail from Bombay rather than by cart from Madras. Apart from military reasons, Yule thought that the only way of infusing some life into Hyderabad was through the railway. He called Hyderabad a 'corpse', with all except Salar Jung having no life in them. He hoped that the railway would bring prosperity and hope to the lower classes whose rise would force upon the government ideas of an enlightened policy.[6]

Wood, for all his reservations, had recognized the value of a line connecting Hyderabad and conceded that such a line would ultimately have to be made. The motivation was almost entirely military, though the economic advantages of connecting Hyderabad with Bombay may have also contributed to the decision.

On 31 May 1864, Wood decided that a route via Raichur should be adopted for the main line, and a branch made from Gooty to Bellary. It was also decided that all efforts should be made to construct a line between Gulbarga and Hyderabad. Yule left Hyderabad in March 1867, and till then, little progress had been made on connecting Hyderabad with the main line. Six months later, in September, the residency reminded the government about the line and urged that a guarantee of 5 per cent interest be given by the British government so as to ensure the participation of a top-ranked company like the Great Indian Peninsula Railway Company in the tender.

Sir John Lawrence asked the resident, Sir Richard Temple, to obtain the consent of the nizam for the railway, and if possible, to get him to agree to finance half the guaranteed interest to the GIP Company which was to build the Hyderabad line. Temple was handed a telegram from the viceroy on the eve of his own departure from Hyderabad. The idea was to get the nizam to agree to defray half the interest guaranteed to the shareholders out of the surplus revenues of Berar, with the British government undertaking to defray the other half. The amount would be between Rs 3.5 lakh and Rs 5 lakh, and would decline as profits increased. It was estimated that the line would cost between Rs 1.2 crore and Rs 1.4 crore, with the principal being supplied by the GIPR Company.

At first, the nizam was completely opposed to the plan, regarding the railway as the forerunner of undefined evil in spite of Salar Jung's eloquent championing of the cause. He expressed his doubts about the increase in revenue and resented the loss of land for the line. But the financial and economic implications of the scheme were secondary; he was more concerned with the social and political impact of the introduction of the railway. When the enthusiastic Salar Jung pressed him for a quick decision, a very annoyed nizam observed that the diwan must have descended from British ancestors!

One fear which predominated was that his subjects and relatives would jump on to a train and flee the state without his permission. Ultimately, when the nizam's consent was given (just three days before Temple left Hyderabad), it was with the qualification that if any members of his family or his immediate servants or dependants left his territories without his permission, such absconders would be at once brought back on a simple request from him. Though the resident recommended that this condition be accepted, the government decided that they could not surrender any subject to the nizam unless he was charged with some crime. The nizam was, however, assured that he would enjoy jurisdiction over the railway in his own territory and would be able to stop any absconder by a telegraphic message. The nizam finally accepted, on the assurance that the resident would continue to support his authority over his own relatives and other subjects in Hyderabad.

It is interesting to read Sir Richard Temple's account of the episode. He said that his consent for the railway was difficult to obtain because he 'regarded the project with an undefined horror, as being likely to upset all orthodox notions' and bring him more into the ambit of the British. The financial part was of no concern to him, and his only two concerns were of upsetting the minds of his subjects and adding to British influence in his dominions. 'Afterwards, at the last moment, just before I left the Residency his permission was received. Though loyal at heart, he dreaded the British Government and disliked its civilization, yet he felt that it was the only strong tower where he could in extremity take refuge. So he reluctantly accepted its railway as a crowning evil.'[7]

The task of actual construction of the line fell on Lord Mayo. His arrival also heralded a major change in Lawrence's original proposal and one which Salar Jung opposed. Mayo was of the view that the state should build the railway line instead of the GIPR Company. By the late 1860s, the guaranteed-interest contracts had been discredited, and the next decade was one of state railways. Late in 1869, the Secretary of State decided that the railway would be built by the state as Mayo had decided, and that it would be standard gauge to allow the rolling stock of the GIP Company to pass over it. This change necessitated fresh negotiations with the nizam for the building of the Hyderabad railway.

Mayo took a personal interest in the whole affair, and when the final proposals unfolded, there was very little left of Lawrence's original scheme. Mayo decided that the junction of the Hyderabad line with the GIPR line would not be at Gulbarga, but at a place south of Caugnee. A major change, and one which put Salar Jung in a tight corner, was his insistence that the nizam bear the entire cost of the line. The Indian government would not bear half the cost. While the nizam was to pay for the line, the construction and the working of the line was to be entirely in the hands of the Government of India. Mayo wrote to the Secretary of State, the Duke of Argyll, 'I hope we shall get all the money we want for the Hyderabad railway from Sir Salar Jung.'[8] In the end they did, forcing him to acquiesce to a proposal he was most reluctant to accept. In the words of Bharati Ray, 'How the Nizam was gradually trapped into bearing the entire expense of the railway remains one of the most perfidious episodes of British political manoeuvrings in India.'[9]

In early 1870, Salar Jung drew up a draft of a detailed scheme for the proposed Nizam's State Railway. While he had all along been enthusiastic about the railway, he had not expected to foot the whole bill for it. He put before Mayo two alternative proposals for his consideration. In the first, he proposed that the nizam's government would provide, either from its own funds or with the help of capitalists, all the funds required for the railway, interest being paid at the rate of 4 per cent per annum on the whole sum from the revenues of Berar. In the second, he suggested that the Government of India participate in the provision of capital, with the sum subscribed by the Government of India being provided by the nizam's government against promissory notes, bearing interest at 4.5 per cent to be paid from the revenues of British India. Partial capital up to £500,000 of the entire outlay would be provided by the nizam's government at its own risk, but for any sum beyond this, interest would be paid from the Berar revenues.

Mayo rejected the first, and accepted the second with modifications which completely altered the character of the proposal. Mayo agreed with the contributions of the two governments as proposed by Salar Jung but wanted the interest on the British share of capital to be paid not from the imperial revenue but from the revenue of Berar. (To justify this decision, Mayo argued that one great advantage of the new line would be the increased efficiency of the Contingent and Subsidiary Force, a specious argument if ever there was one.) Other conditions included the provision of free land for the railway, suitable arrangements for the protection of British personnel involved in the construction, and adequate arrangements to cover the question of transit duties on imports and exports by the railway. While offending British subjects were to be surrendered to the Government of India, Mayo wanted some provision to be made to punish native Indian offenders who were not subject to British laws.

To add insult to injury, Mayo wanted a proposal to this effect from Salar Jung. He privately instructed Saunders to get Salar Jung to propose the terms of the agreement as if these were his own suggestions:

> I think it would be very desirable if the proposal in the terms in which I have now suggested could come from Sir Salar Jung himself. It should be in an official form and framed in such a manner that it would appear upon the proceedings of the Government of India and be published.[10]

After many interviews and much correspondence, Salar Jung reluctantly agreed. In the final proposal, it was decided that the nizam's government would provide all the capital for the railway. This would be financed from its own resources and from local capitalists. It would also pay all of the interest as long as the capital remained unpaid. The local capital market was to be tapped by issuing two kinds of shares: (1) those providing a guaranteed 6 per cent return, irrespective of profit or loss, and (2) those providing a guaranteed 5 per cent interest and a share in the profits. The shares were to be of the face value of Rs 1000 and would be transferable. The subscriber could not interfere with the construction or the working of the railway.

The final agreement for the railway was worked out after Salar Jung and Saunders visited Calcutta. That agreement, concluded on 19 May 1870, provided for the allotment of Rs 1 crore (British Indian rupees) by the nizam's government for the construction, maintenance and working of the railway, including provision of land and payment of necessary compensation. The railway would be constructed and managed through the resident at Hyderabad, with reports being furnished to the nizam. The resident would obtain approval of the plans and estimates from the Government of India, with Salar Jung being consulted on all important matters. The railway, to be called the Nizam's State Railway, would be the property of the nizam's government, but administrative control would vest with the resident and the staff appointed by him. The troops, police and stores of both the governments were to be carried at a concessional rate, and mails of both the governments were to be carried free. The Government of India would be free to construct a telegraph line along the railway route. The General Railway Act applicable to British India was to be made applicable to the railway and its management.

Mayo was overjoyed. The railway was entirely financed by the nizam but oriented to British needs. These were largely military; and since military considerations decided the route of the line, it soon became obvious that it would never be a commercially viable proposition. This did not worry Mayo, who by a few deft manoeuvres, had put the entire financial burden on the nizam. He told the Duke of Argyll that 'for the first time in the history of India a native Government has embarked a million of money in a State Railway of its own'. Also, because of the line's primarily military character, Mayo did not accede to Salar Jung's request for a narrow gauge line since it would isolate Hyderabad and not 'fulfil all that was expected of it'. However, Mayo had advocated the narrow gauge in other parts of India on grounds of economy. And both he and Argyll were generally in favour of a metre gauge in India as the costs were much lower, but defence needs triumphed over economy.

The line traversed unproductive and sparsely populated areas, bypassing big towns. Instead of Gulbarga, Wadi, an unimportant town, was chosen as the junction between the GIP Railway and the Nizam's State Railway, depriving Hyderabad of the commercial benefits of a connection with an important centre of trade and commerce. Salar Jung was against it, but a military line taking the shortest route to Secunderabad was for the mandarins in Calcutta the need of the hour. Salar Jung once again had to eat humble pie. Also, instead of being taken straight to Hyderabad, it was stopped short at Begumpet, some 6 miles away, from where one branch went to Hyderabad and the other to Secunderabad. A short branch line ran from Secunderabad to Trimulgherry for the exclusive use of the military.

Salar Jung watched helplessly as the nizam's money was used to serve the interests of the British. It would be wrong to say that he cooperated; he merely yielded when left with no choice. In the draft of a letter to Col. Oliphant available in the archives, he said, 'We were obliged to disburse more than one crore of rupees for the State Railway, to which I consented with great reluctance.'[11] But Mayo seemed to be very pleased with him. He praised him and recommended rewarding him with the GCSI, a fact we have noted in the previous chapter.

Apart from the pressure on Salar Jung, there may have been another reason which made him go along with the British without creating too much fuss. Reciprocity was normative in Hyderabadi culture. Salar Jung thought that if he acquiesced to British demands on the subject of the railway, they would respond with a favourable decision on Berar. In 1870, he wrote to Bowen how 'we did not like to remonstrate against it much more than what we did, only thinking that it would show as if we had no confidence in the British Government, and really I thought it as the most suitable reason for asking the Berars back'.[12] Saunders too had reported on this expectation in a report to the government in 1875, when he sarcastically said that, having met Mayo's views so fully regarding the Nizam's State Railway, 'he might wait for the day when the Assigned Districts would be restored to him for the asking by a pleased and propitiated Viceroy'.[13] Alas, reciprocity was not a mutually shared value. Giving in to the British did not lead to a reciprocal reward, but only resulted in greater control over Salar Jung.

Salar Jung realized that he had accepted an enormous financial burden for his state. With no control over its construction, it was bound to prove to be an expensive affair: the builders of the line had no reason to economize since they were not bearing the costs for it. Work on the new line began in 1871, and as the construction progressed, the financial burden soon came into sharper focus. While money was spent freely, nothing was flowing in. There was no public issue of shares till 1872, which in any case, were never considered a lucrative proposition by the local capitalists, who, used to quick returns, were unable to understand the nature of such an investment.

The shares were unsaleable except at a heavy discount, scrip certificates were non-existent, and the instalments called in remained unpaid or were paid with great reluctance. Salar Jung faced serious difficulties due to the inexperience of the Indian promoters and the lack of an individual with the necessary financial acumen. He needed someone who could steer the project through choppy financial waters and inspire enough confidence in the local moneylenders to get them to invest in it. To this end, Salar Jung offered employment to one J. Seymour Keay, who as his confidential agent, would help him raise money. It was an appointment that would cause him much heartache.

An optimistic Mayo had expressed the hope that he would be able to witness the opening of the new line before he left India, but destiny had other things in store. The viceroy was interested in prison reform, and on 8 February 1872 he visited the penal settlement at Port Blair in the Andaman Islands. In the evening as he was about to board the launch that was to carry him to his ship, he was stabbed twice between the shoulders by Sher Ali Afridi, an embittered Afghan convict. He collapsed soon after, and by the time the party reached the ship, Mayo was dead. His death seems to have been in no way connected with any action of his as viceroy, and is all the more tragic in its pointlessness.

This assassination, the only one of a British viceroy in 200 years, was deeply regretted both in India and in England. His appointment to India had invited criticism, but there was no doubt that his rule had been a success. The news was telegraphed direct to Windsor Castle four days after the attack, and Queen Victoria pasted the telegram into her journal. Mayo's widow, and his private secretary, Major O.T. Burne, who had been by his side when he died, recollected his dying moments to the queen. Queen Victoria described him as 'able, vigilant and impartial'.

Although Mayo had been extremely unfair to Hyderabad in the railway settlement, he had, on the whole, acquitted himself creditably as viceroy, combining 'the energy of a Dalhousie and the political sagacity of a Canning, and impressed people by his brilliance, his zeal and courteous behaviour'.[14] Since the last two years were traditionally considered the real testing time of a viceroy's term, Mayo's assassination certainly helped his posthumous reputation. It also won him tributes which were more glowing than if he had died in his sleep at a ripe old age. Moreover, the telegraph, still in its infancy, had yet to rob the viceroy of much of his freedom of action. Mayo was as an ideal viceroy at a time when it was ideal to be viceroy.[15]

His successor was Lord Northbrook, another of Wood's protégés, who had served under him as undersecretary and had filled the same place at the Home Office. Wood, who was now Viscount Halifax, Lord Privy Seal in Gladstone's cabinet, suggested Northbrook's name to the prime minister, who upheld his choice, even though the Secretary of State, the Duke of Argyll, had his reservations about the choice. Northbrook belonged to the famous Baring family which had made a name for itself in the field of banking. His father was a close friend of Wood. Northbrook lacked his mentor's quick mind and brilliance, and was as conservative as Mayo: his India policy was largely characterized by his wish to maintain the status quo.

When Gladstone selected Northbrook as viceroy, the latter already had some knowledge about India from his work at the India Office. He was the first viceroy to enter Calcutta by rail; the others had all come by sea and river. He took as his private secretary Captain Evelyn Baring, afterwards Lord Cromer, whom Curzon called the most famous of all private secretaries. Compared to the glamorous Mayo, Northbrook was rather colourless, shy and withdrawn. He had neither the personality nor charisma of his predecessor; his looks were decidedly unromantic, having been rather uncharitably described as 'just a nice, idiotic banker's clerk'[16] by a minister in Gladstone's government.

A JOB FOR SEYMOUR KEAY

The Scotsman, Seymour Keay, had worked as agent for the Bank of Bengal and was known to both Saunders, the resident at the time, and Salar Jung. According to an old ruling dating from 1798, but rarely invoked since, Salar Jung was in the habit of simply informing the resident when he was going to hire an Englishman. By an Act of British Parliament passed in

1797, British subjects could not make loans to native princes of India without the sanction of the Governor General in Council. This provision had been invoked in the case of Palmer and Company in the 1820s when the permission given to that company had been revoked.

Under the treaty of 1798, the nizam was prohibited from employing, or even allowing Europeans to remain in Hyderabad, without obtaining the permission of the British government. This was introduced with a view to checking the influence of the French, who enjoyed considerable influence in many Indian states at the time. It had not been invoked for many years, and Salar Jung had hired many Englishmen with no objection being raised by the British government. In 1870, the Government of India stipulated that a formal application for the employment of such persons should be submitted and a sanction for the same obtained from it. The rule appears to have been observed in its breach, with Salar Jung's verbal intimation to the resident being considered adequate.

Salar Jung duly informed Saunders that he proposed to hire Keay for financial advice on the railway project. Saunders said that the approval of the government would be required, but saw no reason why it should be withheld. Keay resigned his job and was on his way to Hyderabad when Salar Jung was informed that permission for his employment had been refused. In March 1872, the foreign secretary, Charles Aitchison, transmitted the orders of the acting viceroy, Lord Napier, to Saunders, which clearly said that if Salar Jung had any intention of hiring Seymour Keay as a confidential agent for raising funds, then this 'intention should be discouraged as soon as it manifested itself'. This embarrassed both Salar Jung, who had committed himself to Keay, and Saunders, who had implicitly authorized his employment.

Lord Northbrook also refused to sanction it. The excuse given was that it violated the spirit of the Act, though privately he agreed that this was not sustainable. The viceroy's objection seems to have been at the prompting of Sir Richard Temple (now finance member of his council) who opposed Keay's appointment vociferously. Northbrook's own inquiries had also led him to believe that Keay's appointment would not be in the interest of the government since they believed that it also had a political aim, namely, the restoration of Berar. (Though not entirely true at the time, it would become a self-fulfilling prophecy.)

Keay was also seen to be an intriguer who would get the government into difficulties. Northbrook examined the matter in some detail and decided to replace Saunders, who had applied for home leave, with Colonel P.S. Lumsden, quartermaster general of the Indian forces, who was believed to be a 'good and safe man'. Saunders rightly took this as an affront and asked that his leave be cancelled. Northbrook refused, and Saunders reluctantly proceeded on leave. It must be said in Saunders' defence, that he tried to justify the move to hire Keay, adverting to the financial pressure resulting from the railway project which Salar Jung had embarked on at 'our instance'. He even suggested that in case permission was refused, the Calcutta office should induce the Bank of Bengal to rehire Keay. This would also be a relief for Salar Jung who felt morally responsible for depriving Keay of his employment. Calcutta refused sanction, adding that Keay should have been aware of the rule, and Salar Jung was therefore under no obligation to him.

This was the first open crisis with the British, and Salar Jung decided to voice his resentment. He objected strongly to direct applications being required by the government since that would make his employees more loyal to the British than to himself. If this was to be the norm, he said, then he would employ no more Europeans. He was pursuing the matter, not with the hope of securing Keay's services, but to register his protest. Saunders had written to Calcutta about Salar Jung's complaints and extreme irritation on the matter, and urged that the reply of the government be couched in 'friendly and considerate terms' since Salar Jung was highly resentful, if not actually fuming. He maintained that the treaty provision about the employment of Europeans, which had not been invoked for many years, was meant to ensure that no Frenchman was employed in Hyderabad. The Government of India demurred. The word European 'included' Englishmen, asserting that the period of disuse was irrelevant, a kind of arrogance which only a government utterly certain of its power could indulge in. It absolved Salar Jung from all responsibility for the misunderstanding since he had made the offer only after the resident had assured him that no objection would be raised. The viceroy was prepared to consider favourably the removal of any difficulties which Salar Jung could face in the construction of the railway.

Lumsden did the job that was expected of him; he lost no time in getting Salar Jung to withdraw his appointment. Salar Jung expressed his appreciation of the viceroy's sentiments, simultaneously writing to Keay regretting his inability to employ him, and enclosing copies of the correspondence to justify his decision. A relieved Northbrook reported home the satisfactory settlement of the troublesome business and complimented Lumsden on his tactful handling of the affair. This was the last time that Saunders went out on a limb to advocate Salar Jung's point of view. In fact, he went to the other extreme, and in future disagreements we find him unduly harsh, no doubt with a view to demonstrating his loyalty to his superiors.

Salar Jung felt that the refusal of permission to employ Keay had adversely affected the prestige of Hyderabad and also affected the creditworthiness of the railway project. He told Saunders that the news of the refusal would spark rumours that the Indian government did not favour the railway line. 'Those who may be said to be vacillating now will at once say that it would be too hazardous risking their funds in an undertaking in which the British Government does not sympathize. The Sahookars here will be but too ready to catch any straw to avoid this matter.'[17] Similarly, while acquiescing to Lumsden on the Keay affair, he said that the episode would produce embarrassment for the nizam's government in its financial operations with the capitalists of the country.

Keay, however, was back in Hyderabad within two months as the manager of a local mercantile agency, Messrs W. Nicol & Co., something the authorities could not object to since it was not a government appointment. His subagent, Paterson, called on Major Tweedie, the assistant resident, who expressed the resident's surprise at Keay's return, given the circumstances of his departure. Keay wrote to the resident saying that he had intended no discourtesy to the residency and quoted a letter from Sir Richard Temple which made it clear that the objection of the government did not extend to commercial firms. He also pointed out (with a view to justifying his indecently early return), that he could only hope to expect employment in a place where he had mercantile contacts and influence; since he had all along served in Hyderabad, it was to Hyderabad that he had returned.

Salar Jung felt he had a moral obligation to Keay, and the latter did nothing to disabuse him of this idea. He entered into a secret contract with him to assist him in the business of the railway shares, and from March 1872, Keay received Rs 1500 per month from the diwan, an arrangement which lasted till 1877. Keay set about in earnest, securing legal advice about how to set up a railway company in a manner which would circumvent the earlier law which forbade English subjects from making loans to native princes.

At the same time, Salar Jung and Keay were enacting a little drama. The former made it known that Keay's return was extremely distasteful to him, and that as long as he (Keay) represented the firm, Salar Jung would have nothing to do with it. The righteous indignation exhibited by Salar Jung was a way of preventing the residency from insisting on Keay's removal from Hyderabad. That Salar Jung was still informally consulting Keay on many matters was known to the residency, at least later on, but there were no protests on this account.

Writing about the government's refusal on Keay to his friend and former resident, Sir George Yule, a few years later, Salar Jung wrote:

> I have very little confidence in the support and assistance of the Indian Government in enabling me to improve this country. A great deal is sometimes said about the necessity of Native States keeping pace with the advancements of the age, but this surely is said in mockery when uttered by the Indian Government, for every effort to advance is frustrated by that very Government by the interposition of obstacles to embarrass, and prevent the accomplishment of any measures undertaken for the improvement of the Government and people. In illustration I may allude to the case of the Nizam's State Railway undertaken at the instance of the British Government.[18]

FINANCING THE RAILWAY

The discovery of coal added a significant and new dimension to the railway question. In 1871, coal was found in the Madhavaram field in the Godavari area, and in April 1872, the Singareni coalfield, the richest coalfield in the nizam's dominion, was discovered. A report by the Geological Survey of India indicated that the coal was extensive and the field was favourably located for the export of coal. It was situated 52 miles from the town of Nagunpole, which was close to the right bank of the Godavari, and the area was reported to be suitable for the construction of a railroad.[19]

The demand for coal was rising with the expansion of the railway network. The GIPR Company depended on imported English coal, and Salar Jung recognized the advantages to be reaped from extending the line through the Singareni coalfields up to the Godavari in the south, and Chanda (modern Chandrapur) in the north, connecting the coalfield with the network of British Indian railways. Such a connection, he hoped, would also transform the loss-making railway into a profitable one. Salar Jung had broached the topic of constructing a narrow gauge line wherever he pleased in the state under the control of the Nizam's State Railway to Mayo. The late viceroy had been non-committal, and merely indicated that any future line might be a narrow gauge one. Keay advised Salar Jung that this should not be construed as a commitment, and wanted Salar Jung to keep the matter secret from the Government of India. They would, through their English contacts and friends, manage to procure the sanction of the Secretary of State to the scheme. Salar Jung accepted this advice and quietly had the area surveyed for a future extension of the railway.

Salar Jung's immediate concern, however, was how to raise more money for the railway. The final estimate for the railway was hali sicca 1,30,92,775, or British Indian rupees 1,11,99,380. While the nizam's government had paid 1,11,50,000 hali sicca, it had raised less than half of that amount from local financiers. The balance had come from the government's coffers, and there were still Rs 19,42,775 left to be paid.[20] Salar Jung desperately needed money, and he hit upon a new plan. Disappointed with the lukewarm response of the local financiers, he decided to tap the London market for funds.

An attempt had been made to raise a loan of Rs 50 lakh in Bombay through Nicol & Co. of Bombay and their senior partner John Fleming. These efforts, which began even as Keay's employment was still being debated, failed. Keay wanted Salar Jung to remit a sum of Rs 9 lakh, the equivalent of five years guaranteed interest on Rs 30 lakh, to enable the Mercantile Bank to advertise the issue. Salar Jung refused to provide the money. Keay opined that secrecy was all-important because the only thing that could ruin the scheme was the Government of India who could scare away potential investors if they heard of it before the advertisement appeared. Nothing came of this scheme, largely because none of the existing banks in Bombay were willing to advance money on the security of these shares.[21]

Salar Jung and Keay now turned with some hope to London to raise the necessary finance. Understandably, Salar Jung was none too keen to take a loan from the Government of India which would only result in ceding greater control to it. Since the government would not sanction this method, Salar Jung decided to form a joint stock company which would issue shares in its name. The Nizam's State Railway Company was thus constituted by an edict of the nizam issued on 18 October 1873. The company, with a capital of Rs 1 crore, was to provide capital for the construction of the railway, and to purchase or acquire all rights (excluding sovereignty) and liabilities of the nizam's government under the agreement of 19 May 1870. It was also empowered to make and maintain all necessary extensions and branches with the approval of the nizam's government.

There were to be five or more directors, two-fifths of whom would be nominated by the nizam's government and the rest elected by shareholders. The company was authorized to sell its shares outside the nizam's dominion to the extent of Rs 50 lakh, i.e., not more than 20,000 shares at Rs 250 each for a total of Rs 50 lakh. For these shares, the nizam was bound to pay a dividend at the rate of 6 per cent. To ensure this payment, the nizam would buy Rs 15 lakh worth of government securities which would be lodged with trustees as security.[22]

The Nizam's State Railway Company arranged to have its shares floated in the London market through the agency of the Hyderabad firm of Lachmi Das Lachman Das. In fact, this was actually arranged by Salar Jung for the company.[23] This firm, it will be recalled, was the one which had come to the rescue of Salar Jung when he needed to raise money as a young diwan in his attempt to break the stranglehold of the daftardars on the finances of the state. It was also the same firm which helped him falsify accounts[24] to hide payments made to his agents and others in London for the restoration of Berar, a subject which is discussed in the following chapter.

The firm of Lachmi Das Lachman Das was employed to overcome the provisions of the Act of 1797 which prohibited transactions between European firms and native princes: the actual transaction would be accomplished by a European firm, in this case Messrs Smith, Fleming and Company, the London financiers who were handling the share issue, with Lachmi Das Lachman Das as a front. In fact, it was a smokescreen for Keay, whose firm, W. Nicol & Co., had as its London counterpart Messrs Smith, Fleming and Company. It was on behalf of this firm that Smith, Fleming and Company approached the Secretary of State for permission for the public issue of shares in London. Great pains were taken to point out that the issue was not by the nizam's government but by the Nizam's State Railway Company.

Despite all efforts by Keay and others, the Secretary of State asked the Government of India for their observations. He was told that no such application had been received in Hyderabad, and the information furnished was not sufficient for an informed opinion on the subject. It was also pointed out that the government was opposed to large projects of such a nature being undertaken by European firms on a guarantee from native states. On the question of shareholders, the government gave a vague reply, saying that only local capitalists had been contemplated. Salisbury felt that 'shareholders' could not now be narrowed down to mean 'shareholders at Hyderabad' as an afterthought. Smith, Fleming and Company also sent him the legal opinion of a leading counsel to the effect that the loan was not prohibited by the Act of 1797, and also explained the facts at a personal interview. Salisbury gave permission for the public issue in England, with the qualification that the British government would undertake no financial liability in this case.

In spite of the happy tidings about the loan, Salar Jung seemed diffident about going ahead with it. Keay wrote in February 1875 that any further delay would make them vulnerable to fluctuations in the money market. He told Salar Jung that since he (Salar Jung) had no official dealings with any of the transactions, he could feign ignorance should the need arise about Lachmi Das's connection with him (Keay). As for Smith, Fleming and Company, it received no financial gains from the deal, and its participation appears to have been part of a bigger plan for greater political influence. By the middle of March, the arrangements for the loan were completed, and Keay arranged for the issue to be almost entirely underwritten by five large bankers at an additional 1 per cent to minimize risk.

Lawrence, the former viceroy, had been asked to be a trustee of the funds to be deposited by the nizam for the punctual payment of interest to shareholders. Before accepting, he made inquiries with the Secretary of State, who asked the viceroy in April 1875 to supply relevant details. The terms of the agreement, the Secretary of State was told, were that 'the Government of the Nizam will, with the aid of the shareholders, as already arranged, provide all the capital required for the construction of the Railway'. Aitchison said that he had all along been under the impression that the capital was to be raised only locally and not in England. A cable was accordingly sent to the Secretary of State.

At the end of it all, Keay sent a printed memorandum to Hyderabad announcing that subscriptions were open for £500,000, 6 per cent stock, being one-half of the capital of Rs 1 crore, the balance of which had been raised in India. It was secured by the nizam's guarantee to pay £6 per £100 per annum half-yearly in London. A deposit of Rs 15 lakh, equal to about five years' interest in securities of the Government of India in the name of the trustees at the Bank of England, was made as additional security. A committee consisting of Lord Sandhurst, Sir George Yule and Colonel H. Hopkinson was formed to oversee the issue. Efforts to discredit the issue by spreading rumours about the impermanence of the nizam's guarantee failed, and in the middle of June, Keay triumphantly reported that the issue had been a complete success. Salar Jung had won, albeit in a devious manner. He had created a company solely for the purpose of raising funds in England, an expedient to obviate the intermediation of the Government of India. Shorn of legal technicalities, the transaction was nothing more than a loan to the nizam's government.

A furious Northbrook first learnt of the public issue in England on 4 June from a Reuters telegram which solicited subscriptions for a loan of half a million sterling for the Nizam's State Railway. Bypassed and outsmarted by Salar Jung, he felt slighted by the Secretary of State, who he felt had damaged both his and the resident's position. Salar Jung would now believe that he could get his work done through his friends and agents in England, bypassing the Government of India. Northbrook believed Salar Jung to be a born intriguer, and he hoped that Salisbury would not willingly do anything to strengthen his hand. Northbrook held out the threat on the Berar question, warning Salisbury that he would have more trouble on that account in England than he (Northbrook) would in India.

The Government of India sent a cable to Salisbury objecting to the loan on political grounds and wanted it to be publicly repudiated. Salisbury explained that he had given the permission because he thought that the British government had no case and would lose if the question was debated in the House. He pointed out that it was difficult to politically justify the refusal when the funds were sought for improving public works. He stated that he had sanctioned the loan because the Government of India had been unable to justify that the loan was objectionable. 'A restriction so important in its operation and pecuniarily so detrimental to the Nizam, as that which you suggest, cannot now be imported into the agreement,' he wrote.[25]

The Government of India, however, were unconvinced by Salisbury's arguments. They believed, and with good reason, that Smith, Fleming & Co. was, to all intents and purposes, Salar Jung's agent, and the Nizam's State Railway Company was Salar Jung himself. Correspondence between the two continued till December 1875 when Northbrook finally threw in the towel. Salisbury placated the angry viceroy by assuring him that this would not be allowed to become a precedent for the future. Lord George Hamilton, undersecretary of state for India, told the House of Commons that this permission did not indicate any intention on the part of the British government to depart from the statute of 1797. Salar Jung was to be informed of the special nature of the permission which was granted 'solely in consequence of the desire of the Government to avoid even a semblance of neglect . . . but the permission implied no intention to depart from the policy of the Act of 1797.'[26]

The railway worked under the control of the British government, and the interest on the shares was paid for by the nizam's government, which in any case, owned nearly all the shares issued in India. The total value of the shares issued was £500,000 at 97 per cent. The sum realized was £485,000 of which £150,000 was invested in government bonds at 4 per cent and given to the trustees as a guarantee for the payment of interest to the shareholders. An amount of £335,000 was actually realized by the treasury, and a charge of £24,000 was incurred as expenses.

OPENING OF THE NIZAM'S STATE RAILWAY

The new line between Secunderabad and Wadi was inaugurated by Salar Jung on 8 October 1874 amidst festivities and celebration. A special train with Salar Jung and other nobles left the city terminus at 2 p.m. for Trimulgherry where the terminus for the military cantonment was established. On reaching, a salute was fired by a battery of the Royal Artillery, and then the party returned to the Hussain Sagar junction where they met the special train engaged to convey the guests invited from Bombay, Madras and intermediate stations along the GIPR and Madras lines.

Salar Jung's train was attached to the guests' special, and the united company (in forty carriages) reached Hyderabad terminus at 4 p.m. where it was received with a royal salute of twenty-one guns. The line was declared open by Salar Jung in the presence of an august gathering which consisted of judges, secretaries to the government, officers from Berar, railway engineers and officers of the public works department, apart from representatives of commerce and industry. A royal salute was fired by the Nizam's Artillery, and on conclusion of the ceremony, the guests repaired to the tents which had been provided for their accommodation in the public gardens.

In the evening, there was a grand banquet given in the public gardens. The gardens were beautifully lighted with a variety of oil lamps. At 9 p.m., dinner was served in a suite of tents pitched for the purpose, and Salar Jung personally received his guests at the entrance of the drawing-room suite. More than 300 guests sat down to dinner in a spacious marquee, where Salar Jung and the resident occupied the places of honour. Dinner was served in the best English style, and champagne and other wines flowed in profusion. After dinner, a toast was drunk to the queen and the royal family, as well as to the viceroy, Lord Northbrook. Speeches by the resident and Salar Jung followed.

The resident offered his congratulations and those of the viceroy. He read out a message from the foreign secretary on behalf of the viceroy 'on the completion of this important undertaking, which connects the capital of His Highness's dominions with the railway system of India, and brings it into direct railway communication with the three presidency towns'. He then proposed in a few words the health of Salar Jung. Salar Jung made a brief speech in reply, thanking the resident and the government for their good wishes for the success of the railway.

The stream of postprandial eloquence was brought to a conclusion by Major Tweedie, who proposed a toast to the health of the resident in a long and eulogistic speech. The guests then proceeded to the gardens where a display of fireworks in the best European style took place. Monsieur Deluny, a French artist settled in Hyderabad, was responsible for the fine show which included rockets, Catherine wheels, turbines, spirals, crosses and crescents, apart from a large number of balloons which floated away into the night. The pièce de résistance was a representation of a train in motion, the wheels and all the parts being represented by lines of light, which elicited universal praise. Since the display took place on the bank of one of the artificial lakes, the effect was greatly enhanced by the reflection of the pyrotechnics in the water.

Two days later, on 10 October, a durbar was held at the palace which had as its purpose the presenting of a letter to the nizam from the Government of India by the resident. It was reported that the nizam, who was only nine, performed his duties with a calm self-possession which belied his age. The resident read the viceroy's long letter of congratulations about how the new railway had connected Hyderabad with the rest of India. After the letter had been read, pen, paper and ink were brought to the nizam who signed his name on a paper to be conveyed to Lord

Northbrook, proof that his education in at least one of the 'three Rs' had not been neglected. Paan was handed around in small boxes, signalling the end of the durbar. When the resident gave the sign, everybody rose and bowed before the nizam before retiring.

In the evening, Rashid-ud-din Khan hosted a magnificent dinner at the palace for all those who had been present at the opening of the railway. He and his son received the guests on the steps of one of the pavilions of the palace. The pavilions and the grounds were beautifully illuminated with the outlines of the different pavilions, and the arcades which connected them marked out by rows of lamps. The banquet was spread in a hall where Parisian candelabra hung from the ceiling in such numbers that there was barely room for bouquets of flowers to be suspended between them. The tables were laid out in refined European style, and the dinner was served à la Russe. The elaborate meal, of which the menu is still available, consisted of soups, fish, jellies, entrees, cutlets, releves, pies and a variety of desserts. The festivities were unfortunately marred by an accident resulting from the fireworks display which followed dinner. A rocket mortar exploded, killing two men immediately, with two others succumbing to their injuries a little later. The night's gaiety underwent a total eclipse.[27]

A NEW VICEROY

Lord Northbrook left India in the spring of 1876, a year before his five-year term was to end. One of the main reasons for his premature departure was his incompatibility with Salisbury, who had become Secretary of State in 1874. He disagreed with his Afghanistan policy, and in September 1875, a controversy arose over tariffs as well. Salisbury wanted a reduction on the import duties on British cotton goods, while Northbrook, though a free-trader, wanted to promote Indian manufacturers. By now, the telegraph was sufficiently advanced to enable Salisbury to govern India by remote control, something which Northbrook deeply resented. Salisbury proceeded, as Northbrook put it, to rattle off orders from home, something Northbrook regarded as an unconstitutional exercise of home authority.[28] He resigned and was succeeded by Lord Lytton.

Lytton, the son of the bestselling novelist, poet, playwright and politician, Edward Bulwer-Lytton, was by temperament a poet. (As Robert Bulwer-Lytton, he was Queen Victoria's favourite poet.) A sensitive and delicate child, he had suffered from the turbulent break-up of his parents' marriage when he was only five. This emotional instability early in life took its toll, and Lord Lytton suffered all his life from uncertain health, much of which seems to have stemmed from emotional reasons.

Lytton had shown remarkable literary talents as a boy. Educated at Harrow and Bonn, he joined the diplomatic service and served in Paris, Athens, Vienna and Lisbon. He published his poems under a nom de plume, Owen Meredith, because his father thought that the world would not 'allow two of the same name to have both a permanent reputation in literature'. His verse novel *Lucile*, written under his pen-name, achieved wide popularity at the time, and American publishers printed it more than 2000 times between 1860 and 1938. He became a friend of Charles Dickens and other literary lights of London. He had also befriended the famous literary couple, Robert and Elizabeth Barrett Browning, in Florence when he had served as private secretary to his uncle, Sir Henry Bulwer, afterwards Lord Dalling, the British prime minister. In 1873, he succeeded his father as a peer, and two years later, refused the governorship of Madras on health grounds. Lytton, had he lived long enough, would have been father-in-law to a man famous for his India connection: his daughter, Emily, married Edwin Lutyens, colonial New Delhi's acclaimed architect.

Apart from being temperamentally unsuitable to the viceroyalty, and liable to fits of melancholy, he suffered from piles, a terrible misfortune for a viceroy, who had to spend much of his time sitting. When he consulted the eminent surgeon, Prescott Hewett, about the possibility of going to Madras, he was told that nothing could be worse for this complaint than the climate of India.[29] There is a photograph of Lytton on the viceregal throne in a lolling pose. To those unaware of the discomfort in the viceregal fundament, this gives the impression that he was an indolent or frivolous viceroy. This was a false impression; he took his work very seriously, and this pose can, with some certainty, be attributed to the distressing malady from which he suffered.

But it was not so easy to turn down a post as important as viceroy. Still, it is said that were it not for Lady Lytton, he would have declined the post. He had been minister of legation at Lisbon for only seven months when he received a letter from Disraeli in November 1875 offering him the viceroyalty of India and 'an opportunity, not only of serving your country, but of obtaining an enduring fame'.[30] Lytton, in his reply, thanked him for the great honour and went on to emphasize his complete ignorance not only of Indian affairs but also of administration.

More importantly, he adverted to his painful and distressing complaint which occasionally incapacitated him completely. He voiced fears about his health breaking down at some critical moment. Disraeli wrote back that his decision remained unchanged: Lytton was going to be the next viceroy of India.

The poetic viceroy and the practical diwan never really hit it off. Lytton seems to have developed an aversion to Salar Jung. He feared his strength and his fixity of purpose. They were, in any case, men of very different temperaments. The initial meeting itself set the tone of hostility which remained as long as Lytton was viceroy. Salar Jung sought a private interview with him just before his departure for England on 8 April 1876. (Salar Jung delayed his departure by a day so as to welcome the new viceroy who arrived on 7 April.) Lytton, who had himself only just arrived, granted it on condition that no official business would be discussed.

The meeting did not go well. Salar Jung had wanted to visit St Petersburg and Constantinople (on his way to England) which Lytton strongly disapproved of, given the fact that there were reports of Muslim rising in Turkey. Lytton had visions of Salar Jung building a hostile Muslim power in central India which would join the invading Turks as the advance wedge of a Russian army. (It mattered little to him that the Turks and the Russians were bitter enemies throughout the nineteenth century, and British policy had been to protect the Ottoman Empire against Russia.) Salar Jung was also guilty of 'sinister intercourse' with Arabia, and the paranoid Lytton was determined to foil what he thought were Salar Jung's attempts to enlist external support for the establishment of Muslim power in Hyderabad at all costs.

When it came to Salar Jung, the poet in Lytton vanished: he would be a thorn in the diwan's side as long as he was viceroy.

A FUTILE ATTEMPT

Salar Jung had tasted success with the loan floated in London in June 1875. He now sought to replicate that success with another loan for the extension of the railway up to the Godavari and Chanda. In October 1875, Salar Jung authorized the company to increase its capital to the extent of Rs 1 crore and to renew negotiations, with Keay's help, with foreign capitalists in England to raise money there. In March 1876, the company authorized a banker to represent it, who in turn appointed Smith, Fleming & Company for the purpose. The loan was for extension of the railway line up to the Godavari via Warangal and Singareni, with a northern branch to Chanda.

Even as Salar Jung was on his way to England (discussed in detail in chapter 12), Smith, Fleming & Company approached Salisbury once again for permission to raise money in England through a public issue. The senior partner, John Fleming, marshalled the relevant statistical data to convince the Secretary of State as to the value of the proposed extension. Even the GIP Railway would benefit since Singareni coal would be cheaper than the imported coal used by it. The claim was justified, but Salisbury refused to commit without referring the matter to the Government of India, suggesting that funds might be provided if the proposals were found beneficial to the country.

The resident, Sir Richard Meade, who had succeeded Saunders, proved to be the biggest hurdle in this affair. Privately, he was convinced of the benefits of the extension. However, he resented the fact that Salar Jung was advised by Keay, who, in his opinion, was only interested in feathering his own nest, and opposed relaxation of the Act of 1797. Salar Jung discussed the issue with Meade on his return from England. He told him that it had been decided in 1870, with Lord Mayo's concurrence, that the construction and working of future lines would be within the purview of the nizam's government, and that the narrow gauge would be the most suitable for future extensions.

Salisbury, who initially opposed the scheme, later revised his opinion on pragmatic grounds. He thought that it would make Salar Jung pledge, by way of interest, all his surplus revenue, and prevent him from using it for military purposes. Also, the creditors in England would back the Government of India if ever it became necessary to bring Hyderabad under direct control. Salisbury also reckoned that since Salar Jung's appeal for the restoration of Berar had been rejected, it would be a good idea to keep him happy with this small concession. Lytton held a similar view. He told Meade that since they had to suffer Salar Jung (since he could not be got rid of), it would be a good idea to humour him on matters of small consequence.

Meade said that since one-third of the loan money was to be deposited in London as a guarantee for the payment of 6 per cent interest, the nominal rate of 6 per cent would be increased. If Salar Jung ceased to be diwan, the nizam might refuse to pay the higher interest, and the shareholders would then force the Government of India to intervene. He also thought that

Salar Jung might use his shareholders' influence in England to reopen the Berar question. The Berar argument proved decisive: Lytton soon fell in line with Meade's thinking.

The Governor General's council discussed the matter and decided against allowing the nizam to raise money in England since it would reduce his dependence on the British government and allow him to seek support for the restoration of Berar through a powerful body of creditors in England. The government offered to loan the money or to construct the line on favourable terms. Salisbury was disappointed with the decision in Calcutta. He told Lytton that the refusal could result in sympathy for Hyderabad, since it was, in a sense, denying the state a chance to progress and prosper. Salisbury was also not sure that the matter could be defended in Parliament. In the end, Lytton had his way, and the secretary of state conceded half-heartedly that their arguments were probably valid.[31]

The decision was communicated to Salar Jung on 1 August 1877. Eight days later, he expressed his inability to accept either of the alternatives on offer. He said that it would weaken the credit of the state with sahukars and local capitalists, without whose loans it was impossible to run the government. The second offer was, in effect, an offer to lend material, again a different kind of loan, and therefore unacceptable. He urged the government to reconsider his request. Although Meade agreed with Salar Jung that the railway had been very expensive, the latter's request for reconsideration fell on deaf ears.

John Bright, a former cabinet member and an ardent advocate of British capitalists, brought up the matter in a debate in Parliament on 22 January 1878. He was highly critical of the government in resisting any investment of English money in India which it did not control. He called the refusal to allow Salar Jung to raise money in England an example of the 'narrow, jealous and miserable spirit' of the government.

Later, when an attempt was made by certain commercial firms to excite his interest once again, Salar Jung refused to deal with them, sending the entire correspondence to the resident. Ironically, the finances for the railway extension eventually did come from England, and on terms which were far more unfavourable.

10

La Revanche

In the ten years from 1867 to 1877, Salar Jung sent the British government nine petitions and numerous letters asking for Berar to be restored to the nizam. He stepped up his campaign during the period 1872–74, and five of the petitions were sent in this period. Salar Jung tried different approaches, including redemption of the mortgage, an escrow account for payment of the Contingent, and finally a demand to disband the Contingent.

In the spring of 1870, there was an unpleasant episode with Lord Mayo which led Salar Jung to doubt the future of his relations with British officials both in India and England. The viceroy was planning a visit to the west coast, and on his return, had planned a brief stopover at Berar. He invited Salar Jung to meet him there, and the diwan arranged entertainment and hospitality which he thought was befitting the status of the viceroy. But after the men and materials had been moved for the celebration, Salar Jung was peremptorily told by Charles U. Aitchison, the foreign secretary, who was part of the advance party, that Lord Mayo would not accept any entertainment from him, and it was Saunders, the resident, who was the proper person to entertain him.

Salar Jung correctly guessed that an acceptance of his entertainment would amount to a public acknowledgement of the nizam's sovereignty over Berar, and this was something the viceroy wanted to avoid. He recounted the incident to Sir George Yule four years later in a letter dated 16 October 1874. It seems to have made his resolve to restore Berar to the nizam even stronger. '. . . I said in reply that my feelings had been wounded sorely, however the course now adopted would not in any way affect the rights of my sovereign to the Province, and that it will one day be restored to him . . . This attempt to abrogate H.H. rights to the Districts I never forgot and I resolved that I should make the attempt to have its administration restored to our Government.'[1]

Deeply hurt after this episode, Salar Jung realized that it was necessary for him to feel the pulse in England on the Berar issue. In a letter to Henry Bowen, he expressed his reservations about support from the resident. '. . . Hence I fear that any discussion about the restoration of the Berars would be distasteful to the Resident, and under such circumstances it is natural to suppose that his sympathy would not be with us.'[2] This was one of the few occasions when Salar Jung had made a realistic assessment of the situation. Later, he was misled by his friends and agents in England into believing that the restoration was simply a matter of 'justice' being done; ostrich-like, he burrowed his head in the sand, unable to see, and not wanting to admit, that the British policy was against restoration, and his faith in the British sense of fair play was misplaced.

The English wanted Hyderabad to channel all outside business through the resident and other officials. They considered any outsiders as persons beyond their control, and therefore potential troublemakers to be viewed with great suspicion. Salar Jung, on the other hand, found himself suffocated and sometimes even slighted by petty officials in Calcutta. He reckoned that if he could commend to reflection, and if possible, active sympathy, his case on Berar directly to the statesmen and people of England where he was remembered fondly for his support during the Mutiny, his petitions would be more favourably received. To this end, Salar Jung hired confidential agents in England to tender 'expert advice' to help him get Berar back. Once started on this course, Salar Jung found it difficult to extricate himself from this network of secrecy which was of his own making. 'In doing so he began as the spider and only too late realized that he was the fly . . .'[3]

Even before he had hired Seymour Keay, Salar Jung had in his employ Thomas 'Tom' Palmer, a descendant of the House of Palmer, who was born of a Mughal princess of Delhi. Henry Mayers Hyndman, the prominent journalist, writer and English socialist who knew Palmer, was greatly impressed by him, and said that he was one of the most remarkable men he had ever encountered 'though few appreciated the great faculties which I believe were latent in him . . . Tall, powerful, and dark complexioned, keen eyes, a strong nose, magnificent teeth and a firm mouth and chin, his whole appearance was that of one who, in a stirring time, would be a capable and ruthless leader of men.'[4]

Palmer was a man of determined character, and Hyndman gives us an example of both his resolve and his ruthless streak. A certain colonel who was acquainted with Palmer had tricked him out of £800. When Palmer came to know that this colonel had received a large sum of money, he somehow contrived to inveigle him into his chambers. Once there, the colonel found himself looking into the muzzle of Palmer's revolver. It did not take long for Palmer to convince him to sign a cheque for the said amount; and the colonel, gagged and bound in Palmer's chambers, remained his prisoner till the cheque was cashed.

Such, then, was the man Salar Jung chose as his agent in London. What made him choose a man like him? Members of the Palmer family had been paid pensions by the nizam from the time William Palmer and Company had become bankrupt. Since they were dependants of the Hyderabad durbar, perhaps Salar Jung thought that they would be more loyal than others. As we have noted before, Salar Jung, as a young diwan, took the advice of the patriarch, William Palmer, in handling court intrigues and even in his relationship with the nizam. This pedigree, and Tom Palmer's own abilities, must have all played a role in his being picked by Salar Jung as a repository for his confidences. And since the House of Palmer still had claims pending against the nizam even in Salar Jung's time, it is likely that this fact also influenced the final selection.

Salar Jung outlined Palmer's brief in three letters dated 31 August 1871. In the first, he wrote, 'I wish you to undertake a journey to England, for the express purpose of obtaining the very best advice upon the course it will be desirable for me to take to enable me to recover that territory [Berar] for His Highness the Nizam, before moving politically in the matter.'[5] In the second, he said, '1. I wish you to assist me in recovering Berar for the Nizam. 2. For this purpose go to England and there secure the services of those you may consider most able to assist you in accomplishing this object both politically and legally.'[6]

The rewards he promised, should the end be achieved, were generous and covered various possible conditions of restoration. The highest reward of Rs 16 lakh would be given if Berar were restored and the Contingent disbanded or returned to the nizam; a lesser amount if the restoration took place with the Contingent being retained on its present terms; and the least (Rs 8 lakh) in case the Contingent was disbanded or returned to the nizam but the government demanded the payment of the Rs 50 lakh debt.

The last letter made it clear that the arrangement was a confidential one, and in case he (Salar Jung) was required to send an agent to advocate his claims before a tribunal, he would decline to do so. 'My particular desire is during the negotiations pending the settlement of the question to maintain the most friendly relations with Her Majesty's Government, this having since my accession to office always been my chief object after consulting the interests of my Royal Master His Highness the Nizam.'

Even though Keay's mandate when he was employed by Salar Jung had been finances for the railway project, the lines were soon blurred, and he also started helping Salar Jung with drafting petitions for Berar. When Henry Bowen, Salar Jung's private secretary, was on home leave in 1873, Salar Jung found that he had no one to help him with the Berar correspondence. Keay volunteered his services, and in a short time, had fully acquainted himself with the subject. Salar Jung confided to George Yule that the residency suspected that Keay was drafting his letters from the style of the correspondence 'but I have not avowed it to them'. That the roles of Palmer and Keay were not in watertight compartments was obvious, since as early as September 1871, we find Palmer writing to Salar Jung on international finance and how 'Your Excellency should not bind me to 5 per cent'. The two were soon in competition with each other, and Salar Jung had to also deal with this undercurrent of hostility between his two star agents.

In September 1872, Salar Jung submitted his petition on Berar which also had the signature of Amir-i-Kabir II. It proposed a permanent deposit of £8 million with the British government so that the Contingent could be paid from the interest. The money was to be raised by borrowing in the open market and would be repaid from the Berar revenues, profits of the proposed railway, and the sale of coal-rich deposits which had been found. At the time, Saunders was away on leave, and Lumsden was acting resident in his place. Lumsden sent an oral message through Kandaswamy to Salar Jung pointing out the absurdity of his proposal. He also urged the viceroy to refuse to discuss Berar until the nizam came of age.

The Calcutta office took a whole year to respond. The foreign secretary, Charles Aitchison, denied the application, saying that Hyderabad was not permitted to borrow money and that a 'territorial guarantee' was basic to the treaties of 1853 and 1860. This was bad news for Salar Jung since 'material guarantee', which the revenue from Berar was supposed to provide, was now replaced with 'territorial guarantee', which made the prospects of restoration even more remote. It was also bad timing on his part, coming as the application did, soon after all the fuss he had made about the financial burden of the railway.

Salar Jung sent another petition in November 1873 rebutting the view that a 'material guarantee' meant a 'territorial guarantee'. He went as far as saying that the nizam was under no treaty obligation to maintain the Contingent. He also repudiated the debt claimed on behalf of the Contingent on two grounds. First, the Subsidiary Force had for many years been kept below the strength specified in the treaty of 1800 (Palmer's research showed it was 47 per cent under treaty strength), with no saving having been credited to the nizam. Second, the *abkaree* revenues, the tax on liquor collected in Secunderabad, Bolarum and Jalna, had been retained by the British as imperial revenue. It was estimated that for forty-one years from 1812 to 1853, that revenue had averaged Rs 1 lakh annually.

There existed no legal or moral basis for claiming these revenues, and this had been brought to the notice of the government by Fraser and Davidson when they were residents. After the treaty of 1853, Dalhousie had implicitly admitted that this revenue belonged to the nizam by directing that it be paid to the nizam. He was, however, silent on the payment of arrears. These revenues were deposited in the treasury of the residency and used to pay for the building of roads and guarding British mail, activities which were paid for by the nizam, who refused to continue to do so except through these revenues. Had these revenues been paid, there would have been no question of the Rs 50 lakh debt.

Salar Jung, in his petition of November 1873, asserted that since the treaty of 1853 had been extracted under duress, it violated the treaties of perpetual friendship. Despite this, he offered to deposit £1 million, the equivalent of three years' pay, in advance for the Contingent as a perpetual guarantee against default. The petition was sent to Saunders who initially did not forward it to the Secretary of State, Lord Salisbury. Meanwhile, Palmer was continuing in his attempts to embolden Salar Jung still further. 'Your Excellency will raise the dignity of His Highness the Nizam's government by acting in the matter of Berar, and in all others, with quiet and firm resolution. Let the Resident, the Foreign Secretary and the Governor General see that you are not the timid statesman they take you to be.'[7] When Salar Jung pressed for a reply in a letter dated 8 March 1874, Saunders pointed out that the letter was not 'becoming' and had an inappropriate tone. However, he did forward it to Calcutta the next day with his own remarks, stating that the tone and the language of the petition was not respectful and that the extremely courteous official correspondence Salar Jung had received in the past had been interpreted as weakness by him.

Almost all his life, Salar Jung naively believed in the sense of justice and fair play of the English, even when events proved otherwise. But now, as his pleas fell on increasingly deaf ears, he was slowly beginning to doubt the bona fides of the British. In a despondent letter to Palmer, he wrote, 'My twenty years' experience in dealing with the British Government gives me little hope of our right being accorded. If otherwise, why have we not to this moment received an acknowledgement of our letters, and surely this is at least due to us in common courtesy from one government to another, but the application appears to be ignored.'[8]

'THE INFAMOUS BREAKFAST'

In March 1874, Salisbury did finally give a decision on the petitions. But he does not appear to have received Salar Jung's letter dated 24 November 1873. The correspondence on the subject moved very slowly, with Calcutta deciding whether to forward the petitions or deal with them directly without involving London. This delay rankled in Hyderabad, since Salar Jung realized that they were getting replies to older letters, with the Home Department not being updated with recent correspondence. Salisbury was categorical that territorial guarantees were integral to the treaties of 1853 and 1860, and declined any modification of the treaty of 1853. The decision was not unanimous. Sir George Clerk and Sir John Kaye, both members of the council, voiced their misgivings. Salisbury's decision, taken on 19 March 1874, was forwarded to Hyderabad on 13 May 1874. On 25 May, Saunders received a telegram confirming that the despatch was the final answer on the subject.

Northbrook confided his misgivings to Salisbury about dealing with the treaties during the minority of the nizam. 'It is perfectly impossible to say how the boy may turn out and in what condition the country may be in after he assumes the government. It is odd that this objection should not have occurred to Sir Salar Jung, for it was proposed by himself on a former occasion when he objected to concluding a treaty for the exchange of some territory in the minority of the Nizam . . .'[9]

If Salar Jung had entertained hopes of more sympathetic treatment by Northbrook on the Berar issue, he was soon disillusioned. As much an imperialist as Mayo, he lacked the latter's charisma and amiable manners. He considered Salar Jung to be a born intriguer and expected that Hyderabad would one day cause trouble to the British. He wanted the Berar question to be discussed only when the nizam attained majority, and that too on condition that all the treaties between the nizam and the British should be revised. Such revision, it was obvious, would benefit only the British. In many ways, it was the shrewd Northbrook, who behind a calm exterior, was the most implacable opponent of Salar Jung's ambitions, and engineered the policy which culminated during Lytton's viceroyalty.[10]

On 6 July, Salar Jung and the co-regent submitted a supplementary petition of forty-one printed pages. In this petition, Salar Jung argued that the Contingent was not necessary to ensure peace in the country, and that assent had been given to its maintenance by the nizam only after continuous meddling in the internal affairs of the state. Chandu Lal's maladministration of the state and diversion of the state revenue to the Contingent had resulted in great financial difficulties for Hyderabad. He held that the Contingent had been given an erroneous status by the British government, being unnecessary even in 1853, to say nothing of the present, and they were willing to ask for its disbandment if necessary.

In a despatch of 17 July 1874, Salisbury reiterated that the territorial guarantee could not be abandoned. Salar Jung's proposal to deposit one to three years' payment of the Contingent was also rejected. It was considered unfair to the people of Berar to transfer them from one system of administration to another, based on the finances of the nizam. Thus, there was to be no change in the treaties of 1853 and 1860. This was the final answer to all Salar Jung's petitions for the restoration of the assigned districts. Salisbury, in a private correspondence with Northbrook, said that he had made the refusal 'as stiff as is consistent with politeness' in accordance with his (Northbrook's) wishes. He drew his attention to a despatch asking him to collect facts for parliamentary discussion since the nizam had sent 'over 10,000 solid reasons to support his claim in the press and the House of Commons'.

Salisbury's decision was conveyed to Salar Jung by Saunders in a very strange and offensive manner. On 21 August 1874, he invited the leading nobles of Hyderabad to breakfast at the residency. The invitation was thought to be a social occasion, since the resident was scheduled to go to Bolarum to spend some time there. Among the guests were the Amir-i-Kabir II, his son Rashid-ud-din Khan, and other nobles inimical to Salar Jung. When the breakfast was over, Saunders announced in an arrogant speech that the petition on Berar had been rejected by the British government. It was the first time that Salar Jung had heard of this final decision of the government, and to hear it declared in such a peremptory manner must have been a rude shock for him. The news was received by all the nobles in silence. All except one, that is. The only noble who spoke was Rashid-ud-din Khan, who opined that there was no use in reiterating proposals which the British government had declined to entertain. Salar Jung must certainly have been much taken aback at this declaration. Saunders, for his part, was shrewd enough to see the opportunity that Rashid-ud-din provided, since he could now be counted upon to ingratiate himself with the British, and especially so, if it meant showing Salar Jung down.

Saunders's undiplomatic behaviour was condemned almost universally. Only Northbrook seems to have approved. Salisbury also disapproved, saying that Saunders had dealt with Salar Jung as a 'mere native', and had foolishly thought that he could suppress the minister 'with a frown'.[11] The press too was strident in its criticism. Perhaps Salar Jung was justified in taking offence at the way Saunders communicated the decision to him in the presence of a number of the nobility of Hyderabad. Did Saunders really mean to be insulting? An alternative view is that he had invited these nobles, not for the sake of wounding Salar Jung's pride, but to convey to them that Salar Jung had tried his utmost to get Berar back, even at the risk of quarrelling with the British government. It was supposed that Salar Jung would never have preferred the claim to Berar with such earnestness and persistence had it not been for the constant taunts and remonstrance of nobles who were averse to the British alliance.

Regardless of Saunders's true intention, Salar Jung felt deeply humiliated. He was also furious. The diwan requested a copy of the government order, or if that was not available, a copy of Saunders's speech at what Palmer christened 'the infamous breakfast'. He was denied the government order but was given a copy of the speech. Saunders's diplomatic gaffe had only further strengthened Salar Jung's resolve to keep trying for the restoration of Berar and confirmed the impression that he was being treated unfairly.

Salar Jung decided to ignore the resident's refusal to accept further petitions since the claims made in his repeated applications had not been declared invalid. While he anticipated suppression rather than consideration, within a month of the 'infamous breakfast' he sent another petition, observing that the Secretary of State had presumably not received the last petition of 24 November 1873 when he made his decision or 'he would have answered it in substance'. The rejection of a petition without discussing its validity amounted to suppression, something which he was confident that the British government, with its sense of justice and fair play, would not indulge in. Saunders refused to send the petition to Calcutta, and after the exchange of much correspondence between him and Salar Jung, the latter assured him that he would not send any more petitions in future: he would appeal directly to the Secretary of State for India.

On 1 October 1874, Salar Jung sent another long petition for submission to the viceroy and the Secretary of State. Meanwhile, Saunders had been instructed by the foreign secretary that he was not to receive any further communication on the subject from Salar Jung. Saunders returned the communication to Salar Jung, but he sent it back, urging its submission. The resident then asked the co-regents to consider the propriety of maintaining 'an attitude of persistent opposition' to a decision in which the government had already indicated its stand. That silenced Salar Jung for the time being, and he did not bring up the subject of restoration for the rest of Northbrook's term which ended in 1876.

In October 1874, the Government of India admitted that Col. Low had indeed told the nizam in 1853 that if he did not require the Contingent, it could be disbanded. But that statement was of no relevance since it was the words of the treaty which were binding. That remark had nothing to do with the treaty negotiations or with the nizam's decision to sign. Also, Salar Jung had not taken up this matter during the negotiation of the treaty in 1860, and a letter issued in September of that year clarified that the Contingent could be disbanded only with the consent of both parties.[12]

Salar Jung realized that his only hope was in educating the people of England and Parliament on the Berar issue. Through friends like Sir George Yule and the Duke of Sutherland, and his agents Keay and Palmer, he tried to create awareness about the Berar issue and instructed his agents to secure as much support as possible in Parliament. Salisbury was aware of the support that Salar Jung and his cause enjoyed among certain powerful people in England. He wanted to avoid any embarrassment in the House at all costs, and had instructed Northbrook in mid-1874 to be in readiness for a parliamentary debate. Northbrook prepared lengthy documents on the subject but voiced his fears that there were certain parts of the case which 'I fear neither look well nor be very easy to answer'. Luckily for them, the case generated little interest since the maladministration and the attempted assassination of the resident in Baroda took centre stage at the time. In any case, Parliament at the best of times had only a limited interest in Indian affairs.

THE CONFIDENTIAL AGENTS: TOM PALMER AND SEYMOUR KEAY

As we have seen, Tom Palmer first appeared on the scene when Salar Jung set out to retrieve Berar through efforts in England. Keay was added to help with the railway loan but was also helping Salar Jung to draft material on Berar. In fact, Keay knew as much as Palmer on the subject, and was also the abler of the two. Salar Jung was paying Palmer £1500 a quarter which was about Rs 5000 per month, a huge sum of money by any standards. It was therefore hardly surprising that Salar Jung made efforts to contain the growing expenditure on his agents in England.

In May 1872, Salar Jung told Palmer that in case he could do nothing to further the cause of the restoration of Berar through the influence of his friends it would be appropriate if he returned to Hyderabad. It was natural for Palmer to be alarmed. With his high salary and attractive expense account courtesy of Salar Jung, he had got used to living the good life, and was not about to give it up so easily. Salar Jung had confided in him about his alternative plan for redeeming Berar which involved a three-year deposit of Hyderabad Contingent salaries, a sum he was confident of procuring in India. Palmer preferred a scheme of raising the money through a loan in London, seeing in that alternative his chance of remaining in England.[13]

Palmer's correspondence with Salar Jung was carried on through Henry Bowen, the diwan's private secretary. He wrote to him in July expressing his unhappiness on Salar Jung wanting to recall him after all the efforts he had made. Apart from being a waste of money, it would also make Salar Jung look small 'in the highest quarters which have become interested in him'. Palmer wanted Salar Jung to make up his mind on the future course of action and stick to it. He was forever talking about his contacts in high places, including the palace.

> I have not had the heart to mention the Minister's last letter . . . to my friend in Windsor, for I fear that the Nawab's timidity and vacillation would pain him after all his repeated offers of support, and if he, as in duty bound, repeated it to the Queen, the Project might be considered at an end. He could not again approach the subject and ask for assistance if His Excellency changed his mind.[14]

He was in the habit of constantly raising Salar Jung's hopes, while at the same time having no scruples about lightening his pocket. It was not as if Salar Jung did not try to rid himself of Palmer. But life on expense accounts was an attractive proposition even at that time, and it was not so easy. Palmer said that securing intelligence cost money, and in a letter to Bowen, gave an indication of how some of the money had been spent. His contacts asked for money, and those who did not, were quite willing to accept expensive gifts like shawls and jewellery and even opera tickets. Palmer claimed to have spent £3800, more than half his yearly allowance, in such a manner.[15]

Meanwhile, even the queen seems to have been briefed on the Berar issue. This communication was arranged through one Lothrein, whom Palmer had befriended in Germany many years ago, and who had been an intimate of Prince Albert. Lothrein's influence over Queen Victoria may be judged by the fact that when all her councillors, and even the illustrious John Brown, her favourite Scottish attendant, failed to induce her to sign official papers (and they would sometimes be left to accumulate for months at a time), Lothrein was sent for as a last resort. He never failed by his 'personal influence and his touching appeals' to cajole her into the performance of her duties.

When Palmer put the Berar issue before Lothrein, the latter decided to help his old friend (or so Palmer wanted Salar Jung to believe). The actions of the Government of India in regard to Berar were put before Queen Victoria in all their iniquity, 'and everything goes to show she was personally strongly in favour of justice being done'.[16] Hyndman believed that when Salar Jung started from India for England, he had been given some assurance from the highest quarters that Berar would be given back and that he would return in triumph to Hyderabad as the benefactor of his country.

Palmer kept reinforcing Salar Jung's hopes as a way of keeping himself in business. He sent Salar Jung letters implying that he was on terms of secret intimacy with the court of St James. These letters were supported by enclosures, purporting to be written by Lothrein, who was made to report that he had laid the official despatches relating to Berar before Queen Victoria and that she was determined to see justice done. The letters were supported by original enclosures which were invariably written on the queen's own stationery. If the queen was at Balmoral, it was at once reported that a batch of Berar papers had been duly sent there, and the acknowledgement was written on stationery and envelopes emblazoned with the legend 'Balmoral Castle'.[17] Such evidence was indisputable, and Salar Jung can hardly be blamed for believing Palmer. But his dogged perseverance was to remain unrewarded: he waited patiently and sometimes impatiently for Berar, but it never came.

Palmer had allowed Salar Jung to believe that the restoration of Berar would be achieved with his influence in England, especially that of 'Mary' (code for Queen Victoria among Salar Jung's supporters advocating the Berar cause), but no progress was made. Salar Jung confided in Palmer when he was feeling depressed (which in those days was often enough), something which Palmer exploited to the full. But there were limits even to Salar Jung's optimism in the face of continuous disappointment, and in April 1874, he asked Palmer to confine himself to furnishing information and attending to the business of the railway loan since 'even the highest influence referred to has accomplished nothing'. Palmer was now to get only Rs 1500 a month, something which displeased him no end.

Palmer tried to justify his high allowances by adverting to his expenses at the India Office alone, which he claimed had amounted to more than £4300. Apart from encouraging Salar Jung in his false hopes, Palmer's other tactic was to tell him that if he gave up now, all the money that had been spent till then would be wasted. In reply, Salar Jung politely told Palmer that his information was not worth £1500 a quarter, and that he should confine his activities to the railway loan.[18]

Palmer, however, showed no signs of slowing down. Along with John Eldon Gorst, a lawyer and Conservative MP whom he had enlisted as a lobbyist, Palmer carried on with his old schemes and planned some new ones. Salar Jung seems to have reconciled himself to his agent's selfish enthusiasm since now there was no more talk of confining Palmer's activities to the railway loan. The requests for economy from Salar Jung and the resistance from Palmer were routine occurrences, as were the pleas from the agents to receive timely payment. Salar Jung, notwithstanding his efforts to prune expenditure on his agents, had not given up hope of the restoration of Berar. He continued to offer large bonuses to Palmer and Keay should they succeed. Keay was to share them with Gorst and four others he refused to name, citing confidentiality.

Adding to Salar Jung's troubles was the fact that Palmer and Keay were not the best of friends. Apart from the financial burden of paying his agents, the lack of cordiality between them was an added source of stress. Palmer considered Keay to be ill-mannered and inconsiderate. He neither liked nor trusted him, frequently undercutting his colleague, warning Salar Jung that his loyalty was only to himself. He claimed that Keay offended people whom he (Palmer) had carefully cultivated, and even went as far as doubting his reliability. John Fleming, who joined the group after 1876, seems to have similar views, calling Keay argumentative and troublesome, but softening the uncharitable assessment by granting that he was intelligent and his information was accurate. Of the two, Keay was the more capable, and the self-seeking Palmer knew it.

In July 1876, when Salar Jung was still in England, he asked Bowen to write on his behalf to Palmer severing the connection. On 28 July 1876, Bowen wrote to Palmer, telling him that since 'nothing has been effected through your exertions', all past arrangements were now cancelled and that he should do nothing more in the matter. The latter part of the letter showed that Salar Jung had not given up hope on Berar.

> . . . but for any information you may give or influence you may bring to bear in the question which is left to your pleasure, His Excellency will allow you a thousand pounds per annum and upon restoration of the Districts with or without the disbandment of the Contingent His Excellency will give you three lacs of Govt. Rupees or thirty thousand pounds as a bonus. In the payment of this amount all allowances and all connection . . . will terminate.[19]

The very next day, on 29 July 1876, Palmer wrote back with pained indignation that he had 'entirely devoted the past five years of my life, under His Excellency's continuous direction, to advancing the interests confided to me, in every way in my power, and have necessarily entered into engagements with others which are binding on me'. Palmer said that the fact that Salisbury had agreed to accept another petition on Berar, and that Disraeli had called upon Salar Jung, were entirely due to his efforts.

> . . . This success must equal His Excellency's highest expectations, and is entirely due to my exertions. Under these circumstances His Excellency will not expect me to accept any offer which changes the terms of the engagements by which he is bound to me, and I am bound to others. My reply to such an offer can only be that I decline to accept it. Unless therefore His Excellency is pleased before his departure from England, to

renew distinctly the engagements of 31 August 1871, I shall consider it to be his wish that the connection between us shall be henceforth at an end, and that therefore all allegiance from me to him and to HH the Nizam's Government terminates.[20]

Over a period of years, Salar Jung's circle of 'friends' in the Berar case increased. There was Sir George Yule, former resident, who gave encouragement and advice, and John Clerk, who despite his numerous visits overseas, carried on an active correspondence with Salar Jung. John Fleming, who had good connections and sound judgement, was another of Salar Jung's confidants till his firm went bankrupt in 1879 and he dropped out of the group. Others were Messrs Wilkinson, Hall and Maxwell all part of W. Nicol & Co. of Bombay, who started off by passing on messages to London, but later became involved in the Berar case as individuals and carried on an active correspondence with Salar Jung.

The details of Palmer's much-vaunted influence with the queen were revealed a few years later. Salar Jung had carried on a correspondence with John Clerk for some years, and the former nizam's tutor was one of his confidants. Clerk was in contact with Palmer in England and must have heard his tall claims about his connection in high places, including the queen. Palmer had also repeatedly led Salar Jung to believe that 'Mary' was au fait with the Berar case, and was sympathetically inclined to the cause. Palmer credited his contact at the palace with having spoken to Disraeli, and intervened in different ways with Salisbury and the Prince of Wales.

In 1880, John Clerk decided to verify these claims and learn the identity of Palmer's contact in the palace. He asked his friend, Sir Henry Ponsonby, who was private secretary to the queen about it. Lohlein (Hyndman calls him Lothrein and Ponsonby refers to him as Lohlein but they refer to the same person), it turned out, was a servant and not a secretary. He was Prince Albert's valet and was now the queen's personal servant with no role in public affairs. Palmer had given him some documents on Berar which he wanted laid before the queen. Ponsonby read them and asked permission from the queen to send them to Salisbury. The permission was given, and Ponsonby, in return, was given a large number of papers on the subject after the perusal of which he concluded that Berar should not be restored. Lohlein was told as much, and there the matter ended. The queen was never in the picture and nor did Salisbury ever submit the question of Berar before her.[21]

Ponsonby's version, in which the queen did nothing, needs some modification. Salisbury had observed to Northbrook way back in May 1874 that Salar Jung had 'powerful friends here', and, 'I think I told you the queen had interfered and questioned me about him.' As we shall see in a later chapter, when Salar Jung visited England in 1876, he met the queen, and though Berar was never discussed, Victoria had complained to Disraeli in late August of that year that it was 'unfortunate' that Salar Jung had not been allowed to state his case. Thus, the queen was certainly aware of both the Berar issue and Salar Jung's grievance. Her mild interest in the matter ultimately came to nothing, but it allowed Palmer to continue to raise false hopes in this regard, misplaced optimism which was costing Salar Jung a great deal of money.

Palmer, by the time this revelation was made, had ceased working for Salar Jung, having become an employee of Rashid-ud-din Khan, Salar Jung's sworn enemy. This, however, did not prevent him from claiming large bonuses from the treasury on Salar Jung's death, conveniently forgetting that these depended on the restoration of Berar. Palmer had received more than Rs 3 lakh (British government rupees) over the period 1871 to 1877, a sum which, in all probability, did not include expenses.

Keay had received Rs 1500 a month for three years from 1872. His assignment was renewed for a further three years in 1875. Keay had been employed with Nicol & Co., and it appears that his performance had not justified his high salary. When McIlwraith of the same firm inquired about Keay's remuneration over the years, Salar Jung gave a surprising answer. He said that apart from certain payments made to compensate him for the loss of the job he had promised him, no payments had been made to him (Keay) for a long time. The only explanation for this is that Salar Jung did not want to admit, even to a friend, that Keay was on his payroll. He certainly had very pressing reasons for this. Salar Jung was falsifying the accounts for the period from 1871 to 1877 to cover up the payments made in England for the restoration of Berar.[22] It was not something which anybody would have associated with him. It certainly did not accord with his code, but the facts are irrefutable.

FALSIFYING THE ACCOUNTS

One of Rashid-ud-din's constant complaints had been that Salar Jung never shared details of Hyderabad's financial condition, or what the funds of the nizam's government were being used for. He had always resented the 'autocratic handling of public funds' by Salar Jung. Salar Jung feared, and with good reason, the use Rashid-ud-din would make of such information. One of his officials, when questioned by Sir Richard Meade, the resident, had let slip that showing Rashid-ud-din the accounts would be to invite trouble, or words to that effect. Meade had reacted with great anger, and it was only after Salar Jung's intervention that his feelings were assuaged.

It appears that the accounts had been accommodated to circumstances for many years. Salar Jung had been keeping two sets of accounts to hide the payments made to his agents and others in England in connection with Berar. These false accounts covered the period from 1871 to 1877.[23] Salar Jung, as we have noted earlier, was in the habit of signing the accounts at the end of each day, and a great deal of his energy and time must have gone into fabricating fictitious entries. He had taken large sums of money from the public treasury in order to pay Keay, Palmer and others, and these amounts had originally been shown as *tahavilat*s, or advances, to the Salar Jung estate. The defalcation officially came to light in early 1890 when Hormusjee N. Vakeel, secretary of the Salar Jung Debt Commission, prepared a memorandum in which it was stated that in order to meet his heavy personal expenses, Salar Jung had introduced a system of tahavilats, or unadjusted advances from the government treasury to his personal estate. (The commission had been appointed to ascertain the public or semi-public debts of Salar Jung as the nizam had promised to pay them.)

It was discovered that more than Rs 41 lakh had been advanced from the treasury in this manner. The amounts relating to the period 1877 to 1881 were subsequently entered under various heads, with the largest sum being shown as a loan to the banking firm of Lachmi Das Lachman Das, Salar Jung's favourite banking firm from the time when he was a young diwan. In the false accounts, these sums were labelled 'loans to Luchmi Dass Sahoo'.[24] When Rashid-ud-din wished to see the accounts, Salar Jung removed the *seyaha*s (account sheets) for the years 1871 to 1877 and rewrote them in a manner which would account for the missing money, with large sums being shown as having been advanced by and repaid to local bankers.

In 1919, H.R. Lynch-Blosse, a young Indian Civil Service officer, wrote a 'Confidential Political Notebook' at the instance of the resident, Sir Stuart Fraser. The notebook, which is based on records of the Hyderabad residency from 1853 onwards, clearly brings out that Salar Jung, with the aid of Mahdi Ali, had rewritten the accounts for the period 1871–77 with fabrications. It also throws light on his motives for doing so.

The payments to those involved in the Berar case took the majority of the funds. Salar Jung had, after all, promised enormous sums of money to Palmer in his letter of August 1871 in case Berar was restored, and this is indicative of just how far Salar Jung was willing to go to achieve the return of the assigned districts. What is surprising is that, given his own code of conduct, he went to the extent of illegally diverting funds to make generous payments to his retainers Keay and Palmer, who had no compunction in bleeding him dry. What is equally surprising and revealing is the fact that Salar Jung was not above bribing those close to the nizam to buy, or retain their goodwill. When Sir Asman Jah, who became diwan in 1888, was criticized for bribing Server-ul-Mulk, he did not hesitate to mention in his defence that even the great Sir Salar Jung was a past master at the art. Lavish entertainment was another way in which part of the money was spent. It could also have been spent to bribe the press.[25]

This shows a slightly different Salar Jung from the one we have seen in the 1860s, one who was willing to resign on matters of principle. This 'pragmatic' side to him was on display in the 1870s. But there is a very thin line between pragmatism and dishonesty, and it appears that at least in this case, Salar Jung had decided to abandon both caution and his principles for achieving his idée fixe, sacrificing his better convictions to the necessity of the situation. His hold on reality and his moral sense seem to have been dislocated whenever his Berar loyalties were involved. Ostensibly, the ends justified the means in this case: Salar Jung seems to have forsaken his principles without even noticing that he was doing so.

The seyahas which Salar Jung had rewritten remained in his palace for some years before the matter became known. Even though the British came to know about it only in 1890–91, it had come to light in Hyderabad five years before that. His son, Laik Ali Khan Salar Jung II, placed these documents before the nizam and asked for his pardon. When he was questioned about the fabrications, he told the nizam that his father had told him that the original seyahas were in his custody, and he intended to place them before the nizam on his attaining majority, explain his actions, and ask for pardon.

Salar Jung's untimely death intervened, and it was left to his son to carry out his father's resolve. Mahbub ordered the destruction of the records and forbade any inquiry into expenditure under Salar Jung. It was the nizam's way of saying that whatever Salar Jung had done was in good faith and in the interest of Hyderabad. Salar Jung II, who seems to have continued some of those practices himself, was also pardoned for his past acts. The British saw no point in pursuing the matter, and there the matter ended in 1890.

Two years later in 1892, Asman Jah, who was diwan at the time, asked the advice of Sir Trevor John Chichele-Plowden, the resident, if any further action was necessary in the matter. Since Asman Jah's own position was very vulnerable at the time, the resident thought it prudent to let the matter rest. Regardless of the motives which led him to do so, this episode remains a blot on Salar Jung's name. He, however, did not personally benefit from this diversion of funds and died a debtor, owing some Rs 26 lakh at the time of his death.

11

'A Storm in an Indian Tea Cup'

In March 1875, it was announced that Albert Edward, the Prince of Wales (who became Edward VII in 1901), would visit India. This was not the first visit by a British royal nor would it be the last: Prince Alfred (the Duke of Edinburgh), Victoria's second son, had visited India in 1869–70. Prince Albert Victor, the Duke of Clarence, the eldest son of the Prince of Wales, would visit India in 1889. In the 1880s, Victoria's third son, Arthur, the Duke of Connaught, was resident for seven years. In October 1883, he took command of the army at Meerut and moved to Rawalpindi in October 1885, before his promotion as commander of the army in Bombay, a post he held from 1886 to 1890. Queen Victoria never visited India; the farthest east she travelled was Tuscany. These visits by her sons were important insofar that they made the British monarchy visible, 'bridging the divide between the virtual sovereignty of the queen and the proxy powers of the Viceroy'.[1]

The trip had been the prince's idea. Neither Disraeli nor Northbrook had suggested it. Queen Victoria, who had serious reservations on the subject, had not been consulted either. The prince had shared his wish with Disraeli, and *The Times* leaked the story on 20 March 1875. The queen's objections to the trip included a concern for the prince's health and the sheer intensity of the proposed itinerary. She also disapproved of some of those the prince wanted to take with him, singling out the Duke of Sutherland, Lord Carrington and Lord Charles Beresford as especially risqué. The prince enjoyed louche company, and the queen feared for the prince's morals. Fortunately, she approved of Sir Bartle Frere, the former governor of Bombay, who was organizing the whole trip. But her overriding concern seems to have been that the people in India might think that the Prince of Wales was the monarch and not she. She refused to allow any situation where the prince would take precedence over the viceroy: he was to travel not as her proxy but as a guest of the viceroy.[2]

'THE NIZAM WON'T ATTEND'

As soon as it became known that the prince would be visiting India, a number of Indian rulers had asked the government for an opportunity to pay their respects to the future king of England. They also requested the honour of hosting him. The nizam, however, was not one of them. However, it was well known that Salar Jung was in communication with the staff of the Prince of Wales about a possible visit to Hyderabad. The resident and the viceroy were never consulted. It was Northbrook who had to make the first move, asking Saunders to ascertain if the nizam would like to visit the prince at Bombay or Calcutta. Lord Northbrook had planned for the Indian princes to meet the English royal in Bombay. Salar Jung, after consulting with Rafi-ud-din Khan Amir-i-Kabir II, his co-regent, indicated that the delicate constitution of the nizam precluded such a visit.

On 3 August 1875, Salar Jung wrote to Saunders, giving reasons as to why he thought such a journey was inadvisable. He said that apart from his tender age, the nizam had a weak and excitable constitution which resulted in frequent indisposition. The fatigue of the journey and the unavoidable excitements connected therewith were likely to seriously affect the young sovereign's health.

> We have entered into these particulars because if anything occurred to His Highness during such a journey we should be blamed had we omitted this duty, not only by His Highness's own subjects, but by His Royal Highness the Prince of Wales and His Excellency the Viceroy, who, we have no doubt, entertain kindly feelings towards His Highness.[3]

Salar Jung agreed to lead a deputation composed of himself and Rashid-ud-din Khan, who would wait upon the Prince of Wales in Bombay. Predictably, the government took umbrage at what was seen as a slight and refused to entertain such a reply. What made matters worse was that the London *World* announced on 1 September that the nizam 'refused' to meet the Prince of Wales, and this erroneous version was promptly telegraphed to India by an overzealous correspondent. This mischievous invention was seized upon by the Indian press, 'for a series of those minatory diatribes which when directed against our feudatories are so eagerly welcomed by the despotic officials of the Indian Government'.[4]

On 19 August 1875, the foreign secretary, Charles U. Aitchison, had written to the resident expressing concern that the delicate health of the nizam would be affected by the trip to Bombay. 'The Viceroy had hoped that His Highness the Nizam would have been able to take the conspicuous place which belongs to him in connection with the visit of His Royal Highness the Prince of Wales. It will be a matter of regret to His Excellency if the state of His Highness's health should unfortunately exclude him from participating in the honour which is to be enjoyed by most of the Princes of India.'[5] Aitchison expressed his happiness to Saunders that the 'delicacy of His Highness's health is daily diminishing, and that the last time you met him you found him decidedly more vigorous than on any previous occasion'. He also voiced the hope that if the improvement continued at the same pace, there would be 'less ground than at present for the unfavourable anticipations which the Ministers entertain . . .'[6] Aitchison told Saunders to ask Salar Jung to consider the matter before an answer was sent to his letter.

The proposed deputation suggested by Salar Jung to wait upon the Prince of Wales in Bombay was dismissed out of hand by Aitchison 'as the duties of the occasion are not such as can be discharged except by His Highness the Nizam in person'.[7] He also indicated that the proposed visit of the Prince of Wales to Hyderabad would also be dropped if the nizam did not meet him in Bombay. Saunders was under the impression that Salar Jung was acting alone in the matter. He insisted on meeting the Amir-i-Kabir II, and wrote to Salar Jung on 1 September 1875, telling him of his resolve to communicate, in person, Aitchison's instructions regarding the Prince of Wales' visit to both him and the Amir-i-Kabir II. The interview was granted the same evening.

In his letter on 3 September 1875, Salar Jung reiterated to Saunders that the regents could not take upon themselves the responsibility of imposing such a tiring journey upon the weak and excitable child. He said that they would have been greatly honoured if the nizam could avail of the opportunity of waiting on His Royal Highness, and taken the 'conspicuous place' proposed for him in connection with the royal visit, but after taking the opinion of his medical officers (who had attended the nizam all his life and had obtained diplomas from the medical college at the residency), it had been considered most inadvisable to expose the nizam to the risks of such a journey. Salar Jung said that they could not ask 'any other doctors to give us their opinion as never having attended His Highness professionally they cannot be aware of the peculiar nature of his constitution'. All the doctors testified to the nizam's weak constitution and the inadvisability of such a long journey. Salar Jung wrote:

> We had previously acted on our own conviction as to the state of His Highness's health, founded on the reports of His Highness's hakeems; and now as suggested by Mr Aitchison we have taken the opinion of his medical officers . . . They all concur in saying that it would be most unadvisable to expose His Highness to the risks of such a journey.[8]

He further added that under the circumstances, 'we feel that we have no alternative left us but to rely upon the consideration and indulgence of His Royal Highness and His Excellency the Viceroy to excuse His Highness from undertaking a journey the responsibility of which we most sincerely regret we cannot incur'.[9]

Soon after this letter was despatched to the resident, Salar Jung received a visit from the assistant resident, Captain G.H. Trevor, who conveyed to the minister that his refusal was being viewed in a different light. There was a misconception that the nizam was not going because his dignity would in some way be compromised by his waiting on the Prince of Wales in Bombay. In a rebuttal of this view, Salar Jung, in a letter dated 4 September 1875, wrote to Saunders that such an idea had never entered their minds; or otherwise, they would have said so in their first letter on the subject.[10]

A greater honour than that of the nizam paying his respects to the heir to the throne could scarcely be conceived. Salar Jung reiterated this view and regretted that their motives were being impugned. There never had been any intention on their part of slighting the prince, he said; on the contrary, they considered his visit a great honour. While the delicate health of the nizam was a fact, Salar Jung would, in all probability, have opposed the visit in any case because he did not want the nizam to pay public homage to the Prince of Wales as his suzerain. He invoked the aid of the nizam's grandmother and the Paigah nobles to prevent the trip.

Salar Jung expressed the hope that in a few years' time, when the nizam was stronger and older, he would be able to pay his respects to the viceroy 'when the opportunity occurs of his doing so by a journey of two or three days, when the Viceroy happens to be within that distance; and perhaps ten years hence he will be able to proceed even to Calcutta for such a purpose'.[11] Salar Jung also enclosed a written opinion of the nizam's doctors who had not been told why such a report was needed.

> The constitution of His Highness the Nizam is very delicate and nervous, and apt to be affected by exertion, and though apparently strong is really weak. He has a scrofulous habit of body, in consequence of which his bones in infancy were so weak that the calves of his leg became bent (bandy-legged). His Highness is frequently subject to the ordinary diseases, such as fever, catarrh, and bowel complaints, which are easily overcome in other children; but with His Highness, when suffering from such diseases, his brain also suffers, and his whole system is affected. If he is obliged to keep awake on any occasion his heath suffers, as has frequently occurred. Even the exertion of a durbar, &c., affects him physically; and after every trip into the country some complaint or other generally follows. The change of seasons generally produces pain and soreness of the throat, which are with difficulty removed. For the above reasons it is not advisable to take His Highness out any distance, and doing so is not without risk. *It would be like walking on the parapet of a bridge.* [emphasis added].[12]

The resident responded by sending Salar Jung an extract of an article in the *Bombay Gazette* which called the nizam's refusal a display of pride and spite. He urged upon Salar Jung to silence all criticism by 'forthwith accepting in the most graceful and appropriate terms, on behalf of His Highness the Nizam, the courteous invitation given him by the Government of India'.[13]

Salar Jung's response was to say that they had told the plain, simple truth, giving in detail the reasons. He declared the assertions in the *Bombay Gazette* to be false, and its leading article not a subject for diplomatic correspondence.

> We have told you the plain, simple truth, and given in detail our reasons; and if we are disbelieved it will be a misfortune beyond our control. It would be impossible for us, I beg to repeat, to incur the responsibility of subjecting His Highness to the risk of the journey. We should incur the lasting reprobation of all His Highness's subjects should any evil

happen to His Highness, and not escape the censure even of the British Government. We do not say that His Highness *refuses* to go on any plea of his dignity or rank, or asks for any *condition* on which to go; but entirely on account of his tender years and delicate constitution, we solicit the British Government only to excuse his attendance for a time.[14]

Saunders' reply pointed out 'the gravity of the interests involved in your coming to a sound and judicious decision on the question, as already pointed out in the leading article of the *Bombay Gazette*'.[15] Salar Jung, in his reply, revealed a little more domestic detail for the information of the resident. He wrote about the difficulties he faced in convincing the zenana of the need for the nizam's journey, suggesting that if push came to shove, the nizam would have to be taken by force.

The matter stands thus: Supposing the Nizam is taken to Bombay, the question will be whether we should take him *alone*, or with his mother and grandmother. His Highness's attachment to his mother is so great that nothing but actual force would compel him to go without her. Any such force would cause the greatest excitement in the palace and outside, accompanied by great crying in the zenana; and this would make His Highness himself cry, as he is much given to crying when anything puts him out or his feelings are hurt, which might prove injurious, besides the after-effect of separation from his mother. In the other case, His Highness's mother is not in good health, having been suffering only a few days ago from scrofulous swellings. She is now better, but it is very doubtful whether she can be prevailed upon to go at all.

The grandmother is very old, and subject to rheumatism, from which she is always suffering. Besides, you are aware these ladies have never travelled out of the country and the very mention of the journey would fill them with the greatest alarm. The ladies cannot be compelled to go, even if we went to the length of forcing the Nizam. If threats or persuasion could prevail with the ladies, then all would be right except the risk to His Highness's health; but if they persistently refuse to go, then the only alternative would be to take His Highness by force, and of the consequences that may follow I leave you to judge yourself.[16]

Saunders, who had heard of the power of the ladies, softened his stand somewhat, suggesting that he could manage to persuade the nizam's mother but that the grandmother, with 'her age, her infirmities, and her rheumatic affections', had better be left alone. Salar Jung told Saunders that he would find the ladies more than a handful. He also clarified that when he spoke of the risks to His Highness's health, he meant *in* the company of his mother; without her, the risks would be greatly increased.

It soon became apparent to Salar Jung that the dignity of the government had been hurt, and they would, at some point, want to ascertain the veracity of his claims about the nizam's health. Saunders said as much when he wrote that Lord Northbrook would not be inclined to accept the reports on the nizam's health 'except under the guarantee of competent medical authority'. Salar Jung said he was sorry that despite the medical report furnished by him, the resident still entertained doubts about the state of the nizam's health. On 8 September 1875, Salar Jung opined that no reliance could be placed on the report of any doctor who was not familiar with the nizam's constitution. ('On the opinion of any doctor who has not been in attendance on His Highness we can place no reliance as he must necessarily be ignorant of His Highness's habit of body and antecedent medical history.'[17]) In the end, he communicated in no uncertain terms that if the viceroy still commanded the nizam's presence, then he would also have to take responsibility for any adverse consequences.

> If after perusing my explanations, all tendered in genuine good faith, His Excellency the Viceroy is of opinion that non-compliance with the proposal will prove detrimental to His Highness's interests, notwithstanding the possible risks to his health, and that he *must* undertake the journey for his own and his country's well-being, then his Highness must go to Bombay under any circumstances, and at all hazards.[18]

Saunders replied angrily that Salar Jung had, without consulting the co-regent, assumed the responsibility of declining, except under compulsion. He said that the viceroy had two courses open to him 'should he be called upon, under pressure of the responsibility which you most injudiciously and unbecomingly seek to impose upon him, to decide the question of His Highness's visit to Bombay', and both would prove to be detrimental and embarrassing, if not disastrous to the nizam and his government. He said that it was Salar Jung's duty to prevent 'the unpleasant consequence which a continued persistence in the line of conduct you have taken must entail upon the youthful Sovereign and his at present flourishing country'.

It was obvious that Saunders was uncomfortable with having this ticklish decision thrust on the viceroy by Salar Jung. 'You have deemed it becoming, in spite of what I have already written to you on that subject, to throw upon His Excellency the viceroy the invidious task of determining whether or not compulsion shall be brought to bear upon His Highness, by an order being issued directing the attendance of His Highness the Nizam at Bombay.'[19] Saunders was also 'grieved' to inform Salar Jung that his last letter was 'whether intentional or not, a slight on H.H. the Queen', and he wanted to meet the other nobles to ascertain if they shared the minister's views about the nizam's health and his inability to travel to Bombay to receive the English royal.

Salar Jung appeared to relent, but on 10 September, asked that the residency surgeon, Dr Wyndowe, examine the nizam before the invitation was finally accepted. Saunders insisted on an unconditional acceptance, assuring him that part of the responsibility would also be his. By now, it was amply clear that 'the issue was a political and not a medical one'.[20] The next day, Salar Jung accepted the invitation, and Saunders wrote him a warm letter assuring him of the services of the residency surgeon. It was Dr Wyndowe who ultimately conclusively settled the matter of the nizam's visit. On 21 October, he advised that the nizam was well enough to go to Poona but not to Bombay. Eight days later, he changed his opinion, saying that he was too unwell to go to Poona either.

Salar Jung was also being updated by Tom Palmer about developments in London regarding the proposed visit. He wrote about a contact called Russell, who was none other than the journalist William Howard Russell who accompanied the Prince of Wales, and later wrote an account of the trip in a book titled *The Prince of Wales' Tour: A Diary in India*. In an undated letter, Palmer wrote:

Mr Russell gave me the enclosed programme of the P of W's projected tour in India yesterday. He tells me that no Native Chief is to be visited. That HRH desired particularly to visit Hyderabad. The India Office said the city was not worth seeing and that it was full of disaffected ruffians, whom Sir Salar Jung himself could not control and who might endeavour to assassinate HRH.[21]

It was apparent that neither side involved could envisage the possibility that there was another way of approaching the question. Salar Jung saw only the justice of his position and the obstinacy of the British but 'failed to read in it the obituary of their trust in him'.[22] Dazzled by the splendour of the royal visit, and suspicious of Salar Jung, the British could interpret the nizam's absence only as an act of defiance on his part. There is no other reason why the attendance of an eight-year-old child who was known to be sickly should have provoked so much resentment.

In hindsight, the episode was entirely avoidable. It was a fact that the little nizam was a notoriously delicate and nervous child who had never been away from his mother or made a long journey in his life. Both his mother and grandmother were in indifferent health, and it was natural for those in charge of his well-being to not want to expose him to a fatiguing journey and also 'the anxieties and emotions consequent on maintaining the foremost position amongst the sovereigns of India in welcoming the Prince of Wales'. It was also a responsibility, which to put it mildly, Salar Jung would have found excessively difficult to bear. The *Times of India* wrote: 'To threaten a native sovereign with future mischief if he elects for good reason—or even for no reason at all—to remain away, is a coarse and clumsy way of promoting loyalty and affection amongst those who should be the pillars of our Empire of the East.'

THE ARRIVAL OF THE PRINCE OF WALES AND SALAR JUNG'S VISIT TO BOMBAY

In the end, the episode which the *Pall Mall Gazette* called 'A Storm in an Indian Tea Cup' ended with a deputation consisting of Salar Jung, Rashid-ud-din, Mohtasham-ud-Daula, Bashir-ud-Daula, and the peshkar, Maharaja Narayan Pershad Narender Bahadur, representing the nizam at Bombay in November 1875. The prince's suite consisted of the Duke of Sutherland (George Granville William Sutherland-Leveson-Gower, 3rd Duke of Sutherland, to give his full name), Sir Bartle Frere and his secretary Albert Grey, Lord Suffield, Lord Carrington, Lord Alfred Paget, Clerk Marshal, Major General Probyn, Lord Charles Beresford, Lieutenant FitzGeorge, Rev. Canon Duckworth, Dr Fayrer, Colonel Ellis, equerry to the prince, Francis Knollys, private secretary to the prince, and the journalist from *The Times*, William Howard Russell. *The Times* spent £10,000 on the trip, and other newspapers such as the *Illustrated London News* and the *Standard* ensured full coverage of the prince's progress in India. The prince's tour was to last five months, and the spectacle cost the British taxpayer £60,000, expenses which included the fitting out of his ship, the *Serapis*, and presents to native princes. The Government of India contributed £30,000, most of which was spent on special train carriages and the costs of security.

Salar Jung and suite arrived at Byculla station, Bombay, by a special train on 2 November 1875. Major Tweedie, first assistant resident, accompanied the party. A large gathering of influential persons in Bombay waited to receive him, many of them being persons who were known to him personally or were in communication with him. They included Mr Ravenscroft, acting chief secretary, Wilkinson, secretary, Public Works Department, Hyderabad, the agent of the G.I.P. Railway, the Parsi head priest from Poona, Khan Bahadur Nusserwanjee Jamaspjee, Muncherjee Bomanji Punthakee, agent to Salar Jung, and His Highness the Aga Khan's son, among many others. When Salar Jung alighted from the carriage, Major Tweedie introduced him to Ravenscroft who conducted him to the state carriage which was to convey him to the mansion of Sir Dinshaw Petit on Malabar Hill. His noblemen followed in other carriages. Salar Jung was escorted by a detachment of the bodyguard, and a salute of seventeen guns, in keeping with his status, was fired on his arrival.

The next day, Salar Jung called on the viceroy, Northbrook, at Government House, accompanied by Mohtasham-ud-Daula, Bashir-ud-Daula and others. Nazars were formally offered, and attar and paan distributed. Salar Jung and the viceroy had an animated conversation. In keeping with etiquette, the viceroy duly returned the visit, accompanied by the foreign undersecretary and his personal staff, where a similar ceremonial was enacted.

The Prince of Wales landed on 8 November and was given a civic reception by the Corporation of Bombay. He alighted in military uniform, wearing a pith helmet. When the strains of 'God Save the Queen' died away, Dosabhoy Framjee, the Parsi chairman, welcomed him with a formal address, to which the prince responded with a brief but warm speech. The prince, with Northbrook by his side, advanced slowly along the carpeted avenue, at the end of which a group of Parsi girls were waiting for him with garlands and baskets of flowers. He stopped from time to time to speak to the princes who were presented to him by the viceroy, and the first dignitary to be introduced to him was Salar Jung.

The Hyderabad party formally called on the prince at Government House the next day. It also happened to be his birthday, and he hosted a reception for the Indian princes. Russell, who described the visit, thought that Salar Jung appeared diffident, probably on account of the nizam's absence. 'His reserve may be accounted for by the apprehension that he would be regarded as a persona non grata on account of the inability of the young Nizam to appear, but there was nothing in his reception by the Prince after dinner last night, or in the manner of his Royal Highness to-day, which gave any outward sign of displeasure.'[23]

The Prince of Wales returned Salar Jung's visit on 11 November, when the royal, accompanied by Sir Bartle Frere, Ravenscroft, Major Tweedie and others, visited Salar Jung at the Petit mansion. The prince was escorted by a party of the Poona Cavalry and received a twenty-one-gun salute. The guard of honour presented arms, and Salar Jung received the prince as he alighted from the carriage. He escorted him to a seat to his right, where the prince had the Duke of Sutherland and Lord Carrington for company. The Hyderabadis sat to the left of Salar Jung according to their rank. After a short conversation, the Hyderabad nobles who had accompanied Salar Jung were introduced to the prince. Each presented the prince with a nazar of gold mohurs, which was touched and remitted by the prince. Salar Jung then presented the prince with attar and paan, with his nobles presenting the same to the British officers.

Salar Jung received some personal presents from the prince. They included a sword with a silver scabbard, its belt studded with jewels, a massive gold ring, a large gold medal with a medallion of the prince on one side, and on the other, three ostrich feathers, with the prince's motto beneath them; and three large books bound in red Morocco. The gifts given to Salar Jung, to be presented to the nizam on behalf of the prince, were a finely wrought silver flagon of the time of the Duke of Marlborough, a large gold medal attached to a broad blue ribbon, a massive gold ring, three finely finished rifles, and four books in red Morocco with the prince's monogram on the cover of each.[24] Salar Jung presented the prince with a gold scent bottle, and his nobles presented the prince's staff with similar gifts. More importantly, Salar Jung received invitations from both the duke and the Prince of Wales to visit England the next summer.

A LITTLE PUBLICITY

In what would prove to be a master stroke, Salar Jung ordered that copies of his correspondence with the resident on the subject of the Prince of Wales's visit be printed for circulation. Always convinced of the fair-mindedness of the Englishman, this is an indication that the limits of tolerance of even the loyal minister were being reached. The correspondence brought out clearly the bullying tactics employed by Saunders to achieve his aim of getting the invitation accepted. Copies of this correspondence were sent to Aden for submission to the Prince of Wales and his entourage when they arrived there. The resident was kept in the dark. Copies were also sent to Salar Jung's friends in England, requesting them to ensure that the prince learnt as much of the contents as they deemed proper. Thus, when the prince and his party landed, they were firmly of the opinion that Salar Jung was an innocent martyr to the brutality of Saunders. In a not so innocent move, he also sent the correspondence to friendly editors in England.

The correspondence soon found its way into the newspapers as Salar Jung, for all his subsequent protestations, must have intended. The *Pall Mall Gazette*, London, and the *Times of India*, Bombay, published all of it. An article in the *Pall Mall Gazette* under the pseudonym 'Deccaniensis', gave very unflattering descriptions of Hyderabad. The aim was to ensure that Hyderabad was excluded from the prince's itinerary. It was widely believed that it was the pen-name of Col. Bourke, a brother of Lord Mayo. Bourke, who later was to exercise considerable influence on government policy in India, was a known hardliner as far as India was concerned. In reply to 'Deccaniensis', Tom Palmer wrote refutations signed 'Hyderabadi' which were also published in the same paper. What greatly alarmed Calcutta was the possibility of the prince actually visiting Hyderabad. As a result of this fear, visits to all native chiefs were taken off his itinerary.

After reading the correspondence printed and circulated by Salar Jung, the Prince of Wales appeared to be aware of the way things were, since Russell wrote to Palmer in early September: 'Before I received your letter and copy of telegram PW had seen a letter containing some intelligence. I think he feels that the Nizam has been rather sat upon and he wants to visit Hyderabad if he can.'[25]

Northbrook had written to Salisbury in August 1875 saying that he had good reason to believe that Salar Jung had been communicating, either directly or through his staff, with the prince about a visit to Hyderabad. It was as if the government's amour propre would be severely tested if such a thing happened. 'I need hardly say that His Royal Highness could not, without seriously diminishing the position of the British government, visit Hyderabad territories unless the Nizam first visits and pays his respects to the Prince.'[26] Some weeks later, Northbrook advised Lord Salisbury to hint to the prince not to be 'over-civil' to Salar Jung. But that particular warning came too late. The prince had already been subject to pressure to do the opposite. Writing to the viceroy about it on 15 October, Lord Salisbury observed, 'Nothing is more remarkable than the influence which Salar Jung acquires over Englishmen with whom he came in contact and the fidelity with which they serve him after they have come home.'[27]

Salar Jung protested to the *Times of India* that he had not been taken into confidence. This was strange because there is little doubt that he must certainly have hoped for publicity in the press when he leaked the correspondence. It was believed in certain quarters that Salar Jung published the correspondence with the express object of ruining the resident's diplomatic reputation. While this was not true, there is no doubt that Salar Jung was looking to the press to support him in this case. One cannot say just how shocked he was at seeing the correspondence in the columns of the *Times of India*, but he did appeal to that paper not to publish any other letters that might be in its possession.

It would be fair to assume that he did not desire cheap publicity for the correspondence in the newspapers but was prompted by a sense of self-protection. When the London *World*'s publication of the nizam's 'refusal', (an assertion which Salar Jung described as a 'deliberate falsehood') was telegraphed to Bombay, he was forced, in self-defence, to send the correspondence to London, not so much for the press or the public, but for the perusal of Sir Bartle Frere and others so that they would be aware of the real facts. Salar Jung was protecting himself from the consequences of an audacious misrepresentation. But things printed for private circulation often find their way into the newspapers; and Salar Jung, with his experience, must have anticipated, and one would go far enough to say, even welcomed, such an eventuality.

The *Bombay Gazette*, a rival newspaper, pointed out that Salar Jung 'could not be very deeply grieved at the publication of a correspondence in which he makes so good a figure'. The paper also noted that the exchange hardly did the English any credit and that Salar Jung had won a diplomatic victory. He had managed to show both Aitchison and Saunders in a poor light and had the 'satisfaction of placing the Nizam before the British public in the now familiar character of the persecuted Indian Prince'.[28]

In blundering fashion, Saunders had cast doubts on the veracity of the nizam's illness. What was reflected in the correspondence between the diwan and the resident was that the nizam's presence was indispensable, no matter what the risk to his own life or those nearest and dearest to him. Saunders should not have insisted on the nizam's attendance but got the residency surgeon to certify his ill health to silence the critics. This was finally done, but it could not undo the damage. It was generally felt that Salar Jung had outwitted Saunders, who seems to have made a fatal mistake in doubting Salar Jung's assurance that the nizam was in delicate health. Salar Jung had never lost his temper or dignity, even when subjected to strong insinuations, and he certainly won an easy victory over a clumsy Saunders in the diplomatic controversy which had just concluded.

When the Prince of Wales finally came, he made it a point to discuss Hyderabad affairs with Northbrook on their first meeting. Some of his party, including the Duke of Sutherland, even visited Hyderabad. The duke, who became a lifelong friend of Salar Jung's, invited him to visit England. An unassuming man, the duke loved travelling, and thought nothing of gossiping with local policemen, stationmasters, coal miners and railway employees. A Liberal member of Parliament from 1852 until he succeeded his father as duke in 1861, he occasionally drove the engine of the prince's train like a consummate professional, often annoying the prince by appearing at the receptions on station platforms wiping the grease from his hands with an oily rag. He played a key role in the early history of the Highland Railway. He was a founder board member and contributed substantially towards the Sutherland Railway, providing the wherewithal for building the Duke of Sutherland's railway from his personal finances. He also supported the Sutherland and Caithness Railway. The Highland Railway operated these lines, absorbing them in 1884.

Salar Jung's step of printing the correspondence also did its work in another sense. In February 1876, the government absolved the two regents of disrespect to the Prince of Wales by their failure to arrange an opportunity for the nizam to meet him. The government wanted Salar Jung to withdraw the negative reply and indicate that the nizam would pay his respects to the prince when the time came and his health allowed him to do so. Salar Jung also seems to have earned the sympathy of the prince and his party. It was a happy ending for Salar Jung, who was received most cordially by both the prince and the viceroy in Calcutta. Writing to Col. Thornhill, he observed: 'My visit to Calcutta was most satisfactory as far as the Prince of Wales was concerned. H.R.H gave me a distinguished reception and treated me with remarked kindness. He even suggested my visiting England, which I told him I may perhaps be able to do in the summer of 1877.'[29]

A NEW RESIDENT

The notable casualty in all this was Saunders, who left Hyderabad soon after. Saunders had merely carried out the instructions transmitted to him, and in one of his letters to Salar Jung, had stated that he would act 'strictly and rigidly to the letter of his instructions in a case like the present to which the Government of India attached so much importance'. He, it was asserted, was only the medium through which the government made itself needlessly disagreeable to a friend and ally. Salisbury was upset at the resident's clumsy handling of the affair and felt that his uncouth behaviour had given Salar Jung a distinct diplomatic advantage. He wanted Saunders to go, but Northbrook seems to have resisted, at least initially, since after all, Saunders had only been carrying out his orders. In the end, Salisbury prevailed, and Saunders left Hyderabad.

However, well before this episode, Saunders had applied for six months' leave. His wife was ill, and he applied for leave to accompany her to England before the correspondence had been printed. Faced with the difficulty of finding a locum tenens of the requisite status for only a brief period, the government indicated that if he was unable to continue in his post, he must resign. The chief commissionership of Mysore was offered to him, which he ultimately accepted.

Saunders, however, did feel a little let down, both by Salar Jung and his own superiors. He may be forgiven for thinking that his confidence had been betrayed by Salar Jung, and his conduct misrepresented by the imperfect version published in the papers. He would never have suspected that the man to whom he had written with all the 'frankness of familiar intercourse' would use his letters against him in such a fashion. The government too appears to have sacrificed Saunders 'to the exigencies of the public service'. Nor was it keen to publish his justification, and the whole story of the negotiations carried on with reference to the nizam's journey. Saunders expressed his hurt and resentment by leaving Hyderabad without bidding farewell to Salar Jung or the other nobles of the court. But there seems to have been a happy ending for Saunders after all. In May 1876, he took charge as chief commissioner at Mysore, and was also permitted to retain a certain allowance which he had enjoyed as resident in Hyderabad but which was not, as a rule, given to the official in Mysore.

Saunders was succeeded by Sir Richard Meade in early December 1875. Meade had started his career in the Bengal Army, where he spent an uneventful twenty years. When the Mutiny broke, he was brigade-major of the Gwalior Contingent which mutinied, and he and his wife escaped with difficulty to Agra. Here, he raised a regiment of cavalry, which, under the name of Meade's Horse, did admirable service for four years. In June 1858, he escorted Maharaja Scindia of Gwalior (whose army had deserted) to the camp of Sir Hugh Rose, who after a brilliant campaign in central India, had marched from Kalpi to recapture Gwalior and reinstate the maharaja.

Meade distinguished himself by his bravery when he entered the palace at Gwalior which was still held by the rebels. After the recapture of Gwalior, he captured the famous rebel leader Tantia Tope, one of the chief agents of the massacres in Kanpur. In 1859, he came to the notice of Canning who appointed him political agent at Gwalior, and two years later, he became the Governor General's agent for the states of central India. Later, he was chief commissioner at Mysore and also conducted the inquiry into the maladministration in Baroda in 1873.

Meade was regarded by Salisbury as the man 'with the glove of velvet, and the hand of iron'. Northbrook was said to choose men who were reserved and cautious. But Meade turned out to be none of the above. His real intention was to show Salar Jung his place, and put an end to the stubborn resistance and show of independence with regard to, among other things, Berar. An observation made in one of his office notes accurately sums up his attitude to Salar Jung: 'This Salar Jung is only a Minister, and our obligations are to the Prince himself.'[30]

It is not known if Salar Jung knew what Meade thought about him, but the dinner chez Salar Jung to welcome the new resident and his wife in December 1875 was a grand affair. The numerous guests were mainly military officers, which is hardly surprising, since Secunderabad was a big cantonment. Mounted lancers were stationed inside the city gate to welcome the guests. The nizam's police maintained order as the guests drove up in their handsome carriages through the avenue of trees. They alighted at the foot of the terraced garden to be received by Salar Jung.

The garden and baradari were decorated with oil lamps, flowerpots and festoons of various kinds. The oil lamps were arranged to read 'In Honour of Sir Richard and Lady Meade'. The gravelled walks had white dhurries, and numerous lights in globes of coloured glass were placed along the flower beds. Fountains of water made a pleasant sound, and coloured lights on the copings of buildings which overlooked the garden added to the visual appeal of the reception. At 7.00 p.m., a band played 'God Save the Queen' after which the dancing girls entered. On completion of the dinner, which was a sit-down affair, the company retired to the upper part of the building to view the fireworks, followed by a mini naval battle conducted from the opposite sides of the garden reservoir.[31]

Towards the end of 1875, Salar Jung travelled to Simla to meet Northbrook. The two had a free and frank discussion on 30 December on the Berar issue. The viceroy, in a letter written to Meade on the same day, recounted what had transpired. He told Meade that he had communicated to Salar Jung that he (Northbrook) could not accept the accuracy of the historical review of the relations between the nizam and the British government which Salar Jung had sent. He emphasized to Salar Jung that the question of Berar was to be considered in reference to the treaties and the entire military status of Hyderabad. Northbrook ended by saying that he could not say what effect the conversation had had on Salar Jung. In this he was entirely accurate since his words were like water off a duck's back. Nothing daunted, Salar Jung continued to petition for the restoration of Berar.

12

The European Sojourn

After his meeting with Northbrook in Simla, Salar Jung was in Calcutta in early January 1876 to attend a meeting of the Chapter of the Star of India. On his return, he gave the Duke of Sutherland's invitation to visit England serious thought. He decided to accept the offer and wrote to the duke on the subject.

> . . . Upon further enquiry into matters of the administration here after my return I have come to the conclusion that it will be much better for me to leave this year than in all probability it would be next, and as I do not on my account [wish] that both seasons should pass without my taking advantage of the opportunity with which H.R.H. has honoured me. I would beg to ask Your Grace would do me the favour of kindly communicating the purport of this note to His Royal Highness and stating that it is agreeable to H.R. Highness I would like to leave India about the 11 April next returning to India in three months' time provided nothing unforeseen occurs to prevent it.[1]

A DECISION TO TRAVEL

By the time Meade arrived in Hyderabad, Salar Jung had made the arrangements for his tour. On meeting the diwan, the resident found him determined to make the trip which Northbrook believed would be used to push the Berar case. The viceroy was also annoyed at the fact that Salar Jung had informed the government of his trip instead of asking for permission. He had also made arrangements for the administration of the state in his absence without taking the government into confidence, a position of independence which the viceroy thought inappropriate.

Meade was asked to remind Salar Jung that permission of the government was necessary for both before he left the shores of India. Salar Jung readily agreed to obtain such clearance from the authorities. The government soon realized that the arrangement suggested by Salar Jung, i.e., that Bashir-ud-Daula and Mukaram-ud-Daula would look after the state in his absence with the assistance of the Amir-i-Kabir II, was the only practicable arrangement. Northbrook wanted it made clear to Salar Jung that all the arrangements were to have the sanction of the government.

Salar Jung's proposed visit caused much excitement, especially in England. The question on everyone's lips was if he would use this opportunity to bring up the Berar question before Parliament, or at least, the India Office. This was a mistaken expectation because Salar Jung had always maintained that he would never appear before Parliament as a petitioner. He was, however, not without the hope that 'some public spirited MP would be so stirred by the dishonour to England in the treatment of this staunch ally that he would then on his own initiative cause the question to be agitated in the House of Commons'.[2]

An issue which was the subject of some debate in Hyderabad was whether Salar Jung should agree to Meade's proposal to send a member of his staff on the trip. The fact that this was the resident's way of keeping an eye on Salar Jung was not lost on anybody. Salar Jung's friends argued that the designated officer would act as a spy, and the press would get the impression that Salar Jung was visiting England as a dependant of the Indian government. Seymour Keay, writing to Henry Bowen in January 1876, made his point somewhat more dramatically by calling it 'simply madness' and asserting that if any residency staff accompanied Salar Jung, the public would assume that since he was not the minister's servant, he must be his master.[3] Salar Jung, unable to withstand the pressure from Meade, agreed to take Captain G.H. Trevor, first assistant resident, with him to Europe.

In Paris, en route to India, Lytton had received a bundle of papers from Salar Jung which contained confidential correspondence and notes on conversations with Saunders concerning the Berar question, along with copies of secret documents. This was a diplomatic impropriety which could not be allowed to pass unnoticed. When Meade came to know about it, he told Salar Jung that this was a breach of confidence, which, if repeated, would render friendly conversations on pending questions difficult, if not impossible.[4]

Apprehensive that Salar Jung would want to discuss what had now long become his idée fixe, the return of Berar, the Government of India sounded Lord Salisbury about not talking politics with Salar Jung. Salisbury said he would receive the Indian noble with every courtesy, but political issues would be taboo. News of this resolve was soon public and caused consternation among the well-wishers of Hyderabad in England. One of them, Sir George Bowyer, a Quaker and a respected MP who had been recruited to the Berar cause by Sir John Gorst, was appalled, and after verifying the authenticity of the assertion observed, 'No Indian Prince, though the ruler of millions and though his ancestors were sovereigns when England was a Roman Province, can approach the Throne on appeal for justice except at the will and pleasure of the Indian Government and when the Indian Government refuses to forward their appeal, the Secretary of State shuts the door in their faces if they appeal direct to the Queen through him.'[5]

Bowyer was also not slow in bringing this to the notice of the prime minister, Benjamin Disraeli. The Duke of Sutherland too responded with expected indignation, reminding the government that had Salar Jung turned against the British during the Mutiny, they would, in all probability, have lost India. He agreed to speak to Queen Victoria, who 'expressed herself deeply interested in Salar Jung'.[6]

Salar Jung's entourage consisted of fifty-two people, including Major Neville, commandant of the Reformed Troops, his surgeon Major Williamson, a number of nobles including two Arab chieftains, and several officials. They were given a festive send-off, and the station was overflowing with well-wishers from all walks of life, and included merchants and court officials. A brightly coloured shamiana was put up at the railway station which was festooned with buntings. Many brought the embroidered armbands into which a coin was stitched, the traditional way of wishing a traveller a safe return.

CELEBRITY DU JOUR

Salar Jung sailed for Europe on 8 April 1876, aboard a chartered Rubattino steamer, the *Asia*. His departure was delayed from Bombay by a day in order to take part in the reception of the newly arriving viceroy, Lord Lytton, who landed on 7 April at the dockyard, and who, as we have seen, met Salar Jung before the latter's departure for England.

The party arrived at Rome on 5 May, and the next day Salar Jung paid a visit to the Quirinal Palace and had a private audience with King Victor Emmanuel II of Italy. Major Neville played the role of translator to perfection, and the king could hardly believe that he was not a native-born Italian. On 9 May, Salar Jung met Pope Pius IX who expressed his gratitude for the protection afforded by the nizam to Roman Catholics in his territories and expressed the hope that it would continue. The pope also conversed with the other members of the party, and gave them his hand to kiss and promised to pray for them.

There is an amusing story that one of the Arab chiefs accompanying Salar Jung was unable to grasp the subtle nuance of the pope giving him his hand to kiss. He grabbed his hand and gave his holiness a hearty handshake. Salar Jung also called on the Crown prince (who later became King Umberto I) and Princess Margherita. It was during this trip that he acquired two of the most famous pieces of the Salar Jung museum: The *Veiled Rebecca* by Giovanni Maria Benzoni and the woodcarving, *Mephistopheles and Margaretta*, by an artist who remains unknown.

After Rome, Salar Jung visited Florence, reaching Paris on 13 May. Rooms had been booked for the party at the Grand Hotel des Capucines. On the evening of his arrival, Salar Jung met with an unfortunate accident, slipping on the stairs and injuring his femur. His travelling medical attendants, Dr Williamson and one of his hakims Syed Ali, were on hand to attend to him. Salar Jung fainted due to the pain during the medical examination, and the best surgeons in Paris were called in. This injury was troublesome, not only because of the bodily agony and enforced inactivity, but because it upset Salar Jung's carefully planned programme. He bore the pain stoically and was always in good humour. The pope's reputed 'evil eye'[7] was sometimes mentioned, but the pain or inconvenience was never adverted to.

Salar Jung reclined on a double mattress in the middle of his hotel room, his legs stretched towards the right so as not to put any pressure on the injury. According to the original plan, Salar Jung was to spend only one night in Paris. He was to reach Boulogne on 15 May, and then take the special steamer to Dover, from where he was to board the special train placed at his disposal, and start his England sojourn on 16 May. The hotel in Paris had expected the party to stay only for a night. In the event, they found that their clients stayed for much longer, and Salar Jung's friends worried about the practical implications of his injury.

While he was in Paris, Salar Jung received almost twenty letters a day. Written in French and in English, some begged for alms, while others offered merchandise and luxury goods. Some asked for an interview, and yet others offered him amusements and recreations of all kinds. Tailors, shoemakers and the like, forced their cards and prospectuses on to the servants in the hope of making a big sale. Salar Jung was much amused by it all but was relieved to learn that he would be spared all this soon, since it was a 'Parisian persecution from which he would be free in London'.

By the end of May, Salar Jung had recovered sufficiently to continue his journey, arriving at Folkestone on 1 June and reaching London the same night. (Lord Northbrook also arrived in London on the same day but his arrival went unnoticed.) The Duke of Sutherland had written to Salar Jung urging him to come to England where he would be more comfortable in the accommodation arranged for him. Salar Jung crossed the Channel aboard the SS *Alexandra* in a tent set up on deck. He gifted the ship's captain with a gold ring and asked that £15 be divided between the ship's crew. The duke was the first to board the steamer to welcome his Indian guest. Since he was still unable to walk, Salar Jung was carried ashore in an armchair by English sailors.

He was received, among others, by the mayor of Folkestone who read an address of welcome. Salar Jung responded in kind, apologizing for not being able to stand, and for a reply which had been hastily prepared. He thanked the mayor for his welcome, and told his audience of the pleasure it gave him to carry out his long-cherished desire to visit England. In conclusion, he referred to the visit of the Prince of Wales and said that the royal visit 'has very materially strengthened the affections and developed the loyal feelings of the Native Princes and people of India to the British Crown and to the Empress of India'.[8]

The Duke of Sutherland had arranged carriages in advance after consulting Palmer on the subject. Palmer had advised him to buy three new carriages for Salar Jung which he could also use in Hyderabad, and hire the rest. Since he was still unable to walk, Salar Jung used a wheelchair to get around. The doctors in Paris had misunderstood the nature of his injury, and two eminent English surgeons, Sir James Paget and Prescott Hewett, were invited to give their opinion. The French doctors in Paris had given an incorrect diagnosis, pronouncing it to be an oblique dislocation of the hip joint. The medical examination in London revealed that the head of the thigh bone had received an impacted fracture at the point where it is secured in a socket on the pelvis.

Salar Jung received a letter from Lord Salisbury dated 3 June 1876 inquiring after his health.

> I have the honour to acknowledge with many thanks your courteous letter of yesterday. I am very glad to know from you that the arrangements which have been made have proved convenient. But it is a source of great and sincere regret to me to learn that the accident which in Paris was thought to be a slight contusion has in closer examination turned out to be much more serious. I earnestly hope that the skill of the surgeons which are now attending you may ensure for you an early and complete recovery.[9]

Salar Jung received a most enthusiastic welcome from all classes of people in England. Lionized by the press, he was also awarded temporary memberships of clubs. Some of the clubs which made him a temporary member included the Travellers Club, Junior United Service Club, Navy Club and the Athenaeum at Pall Mall. Salar Jung visited mines and factories, and spoke to people from all walks of life. He received many visitors. They included the Prince of Wales, the Marquess of Salisbury, Lord Northbrook, distinguished politicians and some of his old friends from Hyderabad days.

Salar Jung seems to have carried on a regular correspondence with persons back home, and one of them was Meade. The friction in their official relationship would come later. For now, all seemed happy and cordial. On 9 June 1876, he wrote:

> Since my arrival here I have received a great deal of kindness and attention. Her Majesty, the Prince of Wales and several other people among the nobility and gentry have been most kind in their inquiries, and I have had over 100 visitors. No one could have been kinder and more attentive than Lord Northbrook. He lives nearly opposite to me, and has been in two or three times and comes again tomorrow. This attention on the part of Lord Northbrook is very gratifying to me.
>
> . . . I am engaged to dine with the Prince of Wales on the 20th, with the Duke of Sutherland on the 22nd and Mr Disraeli on the 24th, and on the 21st the Hebdomadal Council of the University of Oxford have

invited me to Oxford to receive the Honorary Degree of D.C.L. . . . but I am not quite sure yet that I shall be able to be present at Oxford on the Commemoration Day.[10]

On 20 June, the Prince of Wales gave a banquet in his honour at Marlborough House. It had been postponed on account of Salar Jung's accident. The guest list included the Dukes of Connaught and Cambridge, Prime Minister Benjamin Disraeli, the Duke and Duchess of Sutherland, the Marquess and Marchioness of Salisbury, Lord Napier of Magdala, Lord and Lady Lawrence, Sir Bartle and Lady Frere, and Sir Stafford Northcote, Bt, Chancellor of the Exchequer and his wife Lady Northcote. Nizam Yar Jung and Captain John Clarke were in attendance on Sir Salar Jung.

On the next day, Salar Jung was conferred an honorary degree by Oxford University. They had wanted the usual public ceremony, but Salar Jung declined since his health would not permit it. The citation was read at a public convocation, but the degree was actually conferred at a much smaller private gathering at the Sheldonian Theatre. The proceedings were opened by the vice chancellor, and Salar Jung, who had been wheeled on a couch to the entrance of the theatre, walked slowly with the help of crutches across the floor. Salar Jung's contribution to Hyderabad, especially during the Mutiny, was praised, and after the degree had been conferred, the proceedings ended. Salar Jung and the others left the theatre accompanied by loud and repeated applause. Salar Jung had gone to Oxford by a special train which departed from London in the morning and returned in the afternoon. The cost was £24, in addition to the twelve first-class tickets at 18s 6d, and five second-class tickets at 14s, for the rest of the party accompanying Salar Jung. In Hyderabad money, the trip cost less than hali sicca 485.

Salar Jung was presented to Queen Victoria on 3 July at Windsor Castle by the Marquess of Salisbury, and offered his nazar as a token of allegiance. This had a comic aside: nazar was distorted into *nugger* and then into *mugger*,[11] and then finally into crocodile, in which form it appeared in the papers to the utter bewilderment of the public. He dined with the queen and spent the night at the castle. Guests at the dinner thrown in his honour included Princess Beatrice, Prince Leopold and the Marquess and the Marchioness of Salisbury. Victoria presented an autographed copy of her book *Leaves from the Journal of Our Life in the Highlands from 1848 to 1861* to Salar Jung.

On his return to London, Salar Jung accompanied the Duke of Sutherland to the Woolwich Arsenal and also the London Docks. On 5 July, he received a visit from the secretary of the Manchester Chamber of Commerce, who had come to invite him to visit that city. Citing his semi-invalid status, Salar Jung politely refused. That same evening, Salar Jung and suite attended the state ball at Buckingham Palace.

On 6 July, Salar Jung attended a dinner given by the Marquess of Salisbury in his honour. The next day, Salar Jung hosted a dinner at his residence, 140, Piccadilly, for the Prince of Wales. The thirty guests included the Marquess of Salisbury, Lord Northbrook, Lord Lawrence and Maharaja Duleep Singh. (Salar Jung had gifted Duleep Singh a carpet. The prince wrote to him on 30 July 1876 thanking him for it.) Before the dinner, there was an Eastern-style durbar at which Salar Jung offered a nazar of 101 gold mohurs to the prince.

Shortly after, Salar Jung arrived at Trentham Hall on a visit to the Duke of Sutherland. After spending a few days there, the party proceeded to the duke's Scottish residence, Dunrobin Castle. The magnificent Dunrobin Castle stands on a prominent bluff set a little back from the shore a mile north-east of Golspie and 4 miles south-west of Brora.Laid out below it, between the foot of the bluff and the sea, are extensive formal gardens. The castle underwent a major expansion which was completed in 1851. The end result was described by Queen Victoria as 'a mixture of an old Scotch castle and a French chateau'. Both Trentham and Dunrobin were used as a base by Salar Jung from which sorties to places of interest were made. These included trips to collieries, railway centres, steelworks, a china factory, a brick and tile factory, and a textile mill. Salar Jung did not let his injury stand in the way of his exploring England and enjoying the generous hospitality of his hosts.

At the Dunrobin Castle on 15 July, Salar Jung received addresses presented by deputations from the town halls of Inverness, Dingwall, Tain and Wick. He gave a long reply to the deputation from Inverness, which was the first to present its address, and briefly acknowledged the others. He expressed his pleasure at his visit to England and appreciated the warm hospitality of his hosts. With regard to the compliment paid him as to his contribution at the time of the Mutiny, he modestly said that he was only doing his duty. The deputations were then entertained to lunch, where a toast to Salar Jung's health was drunk with loud applause. Salar Jung, in turn, proposed a toast to the duke's health and that of his son and affianced bride. Salar Jung had gifted a carpet embroidered in gold as one of the presents to the duke who was delighted with it and wrote to say that he had hung it over the stair railings since 'we do not walk upon so much beauty in this country'.[12] The duke's son, the Marquess of Stafford, received a shawl.

A few days later, Salar Jung, accompanied by the lord provost and members of his own entourage, visited the principal places of interest in Edinburgh, driving through the town in open carriages and predictably attracting much attention. The party departed for London that same evening.

On 25 July, Salar Jung was presented with the honorary Freedom of the City of London—a signal honour—at a special meeting of the Court of Common Council, held at Guildhall and presided over by the mayor. The formal ceremony was conducted in the council chamber, where at 1 p.m., Salar Jung took his place on the dais as the guest of the day. After the town clerk had read the resolution conferring the Freedom, the chamberlain of London, Benjamin Scott, gave his address. He said that this was the first time that 'the Minister of a Native Indian Ruler has received the honorary Freedom of this ancient city', and its bestowal on Salar Jung was also 'the expression of a desire on the part of this Corporation for a closer intimacy between this country and the independent Native Princes of the East who are Her Majesty's valued allies'. He referred to Salar Jung's stellar role during the Mutiny and his many reforms which had materially benefited the people of Hyderabad. He ended with the hope that Salar Jung would soon recover his health, and 'be long spared to benefit your fellow-countrymen by your wise administration'.[13]

Sir Salar Jung, in reply, said that he was 'placed under peculiar obligation to this great city for being made the recipient of such a high mark of distinction, one which, I think, cannot fail to encourage my contemporaries in India, whose efforts, like my own, are directed to the performance of loyal and honourable duty'. He went on to add that he had full confidence that the alliance between Hyderabad and the British would be maintained as before, and 'the bonds of amicable relationship between the people of England and India will be daily strengthened'. In conclusion, he said that he would prize the honour 'not merely because it is a distinction most complimentary in itself, but because it will convey to my countrymen . . . the assurance that the public of this great country, no less than its Government, can cordially recognize their fidelity as allies and appreciate their labours as statesmen.'[14]

After the ceremony ended, Salar Jung was escorted to Mansion House, where a select company of some 300 persons had been invited to lunch at the Egyptian Hall to meet the Indian dignitary. An excited crowd lined the route from Guildhall to Mansion House, eager to catch a glimpse of the extravagantly feted Indian. In his address, the Lord Mayor, after calling him a wise, intelligent and penetrating man, adverted to his role in siding with the British during the Mutiny and doing so much towards a resolution of that difficulty. Salar Jung, he said, would return to India with the feeling that 'we looked to him as a man of the future destined to take a prominent part in the government of the great Empire to which we owed so much'.[15] Salar Jung made a brief reply in which he thanked his hosts for the 'honour and kindness you have done me to-day'.[16] The visits and functions continued throughout Salar Jung's stay, and on 26 July, he received deputations from the Manchester Corporation and the Manchester Chamber of Commerce at his residence, 140, Piccadilly.

His visit to England had been an unqualified success. No native of India had ever elicited so much admiration from London society. 'His manner is so like that of a well-bred English gentleman that many people cannot understand how or where a native of India who has never been in England can have picked up what seems to have been a kind of second nature with Sir Salar.'[17] Salar Jung even had a play written in honour of his visit. Joseph Turnley dedicated his play on Henry II, *The King, or the First Plantagenet*, to him on the occasion of his visit to England. In his dedication, he heaped much praise on Hyderabad's prime minister, ending with, 'In Sir Salar Jung heroism itself seems gracefully ennobled and magnificently enshrined.'[18]

All the adulation naturally excited the envy of the native chiefs back home, and a strange story appeared in the press.

> It appears that certain Rajahs and Nawabs, sorely vexed and envious at the high honour which H.E. Sir Salar Jung has received in England, have determined upon making pilgrimages to Mecca and Benares 'to calm their perturbed spirits.' Our contemporary adds: 'Our informant leads us to believe that these self-same worthies would have been better pleased had the accident which His Excellency recently sustained terminated less favourably.'[19]

But it was obvious from the style of entertainment and the speeches that Salar Jung was treated not so much as a friend, but as a novelty in England.

Under the ducal auspices, Salar Jung was the celebrity du jour, and the *Deccan Herald* observed somewhat uncharitably:

> The Duke of Sutherland is an extraordinary nobleman. He has patronised
> fire engines and wicker coffins ere now, and Salar Jung may be happy in
> belonging to the category of distractions which His Grace from time to
> time takes up; but, whatever the Nizam's Minister may think in his heart
> on the matter, it cannot fail to be a feather in the Duke's cap that he was
> showman to so distinguished a foreigner as his guest.[20]

Commenting on the fact that Salar Jung kept harping on the fact that Hyderabad was an ally of the British in his speeches, the same newspaper observed, 'The alliance is so much between the immense and the infinitesimal that it suggests the flea claiming equality with the lion because he lives in the noble beast's coat.'[21] It noted that apart from this, Salar Jung's speeches were graceful enough, and he was wise enough to make no ante- or postprandial allusion to his mission—Berar.

SMOKE AND MIRRORS

Lord Salisbury had declared that he would not discuss political issues such as Berar with Salar Jung. A few hours before Salisbury was to call on him in London, his aide de camp, Fitzgerald, told him that he should make no reference to either Berar, or the railway loan, in his conversation with the Secretary of State. He assured Salar Jung that Salisbury had had nothing to do with the prohibition on submitting a petition on Berar, and that a new one would receive consideration if he sent it on returning to Hyderabad.[22]

When Salar Jung asked him if this was an authorized statement, Fitzgerald assured him that it originated from Salisbury himself, allowing Salar Jung to nurse a consolatory hope of some future change in circumstances more favourable to his wishes. A newspaper report in the *Statesman* said that Salar Jung was under the surveillance of Fitzgerald for his entire stay in England. It was Fitzgerald who decided whom Salar Jung would see. He was not allowed to meet anyone unless the individual had been approved by Fitzgerald. The two categories especially interdicted from meeting the diwan were journalists and Indians residing in England. As a result, Salar Jung refused to see many persons, often giving offence.[23] Salar Jung, however, never mentioned this fact in his correspondence.

The Duke of Sutherland too had been canvassing on behalf of Salar Jung, and at his behest the prime minister, Benjamin Disraeli, came to call on him. Salar Jung described the visit to the duke in a letter dated 30 July 1876.

> . . . On my telling him that of the permission I received from Lord Salisbury to open my case again—and on my hazarding an opinion that I ought to do more than obtain this permission, Mr D. said there's only one thing to be done—to bring the case before Parliament—because public discussion would often bring justice—but as there is no time for that I should on my return act through proper channel [sic] in bringing my case forward, and that as my visit has had an excellent effect here morally speaking he had no doubt that justice would be [done] me—and when I told him and [sic] sometimes policy is allowed to interfere with justice he said that the best policy was justice.[24]

Salar Jung, greatly buoyed after this interview, thought that finally Berar would be returned after due process. Salar Jung seems to have laid great store by the influence of the Duke of Sutherland, but this faith appears to have been misplaced. The duke not only belonged to the Tory party which at that time was out of power, but he was a peer who was greatly disliked by Salisbury. He had spoken privately in favour of the Royal Titles Bill but voted against it in the House of Lords under party pressure. He was greatly disliked by the party in power. About him, the *Bombay Gazette* observed somewhat uncharitably: '. . . a man whom nature intended for an engine driver, but changing her mind at the last moment, transformed into a Duke. His Grace is a good-natured man with a small allowance of brains and no political influence, but of course his rank and intimacy with the Royal Family give him great social weight.'[25] Salar Jung thought he held a court card but discovered only later that it did not belong to the trump suit.

RETURNING HOME

Henry Mayers Hyndman, the English socialist, wrote about Salar Jung's visit to England in his reminiscences. According to Hyndman, the India Office did its best to make Salar Jung politically uncomfortable. Salar Jung felt this, and remarked sadly, 'I am not the man in London that I am in Hyderabad.'[26] However, in spite of all the intrigues, it was understood and agreed that when, at the close of his visit, the diwan went to Osborne House to take his leave of the queen, he would formally ask for, and Victoria would herself concede, the restoration of the assigned districts.

Salar Jung went to the Isle of Wight, arrived at Osborne House, and was ushered into the royal presence as arranged. The queen, it was reported, went forward three steps to meet him. Salar Jung was so overwhelmed by this gesture that he forgot to ask for Berar. The story may be apocryphal, but Hyndman believed that Salar Jung had been threatened in London as to the evil that would befall Hyderabad if he ventured to take advantage of the good disposition of the queen. At the last moment, his nerve failed him, and he left England empty-handed.[27]

Salar Jung departed from London on 31 July1876. Since his injury had far from healed, he had to be lifted and lowered through a skylight to an inside cabin of the ship for the Channel crossing. The party had ninety pieces of luggage which needed to be reinforced to withstand the rigours of the journey. They included wines and four English typewriters inlaid with pearl. A letter from the manager of the Remington Sewing Machine Co. dated 21 June 1876 to Arthur Oliphant requested information on the type of the typewriters required and if the machines were to be packed for shipment. After suggesting that three extra ribbons for each machine would suffice, the company offered its machines inlaid with pearl at £31. 'These are very handsome, and we think His Excellency might like one or two of these as well.'[28] The typewriters appear to have been only of ornamental value since the draft letters dated after 1877 in the Telangana State Archives and Research Centre are in longhand.

His first halt on the return journey was Paris where he took in at a glance the principal sights of the city. He also visited the Notre Dame cathedral and was shown the coronation robe of Napoleon I. When told that Napoleon IV, at present in England, would wear the same for his coronation, Salar Jung philosophically remarked: 'One must never say this or that will occur, nor call any one King who cannot dwell in his own country.'[29] In the evening, he enjoyed an outing at the Paris opera and witnessed the performance of Fromental Halévy's *La Juive*.

The Hyderabadi party turned many heads at the opera, and it was on them that the principal attention of the public was fixed. Someone went as far as saying that Salar Jung was an Oriental prince who had revolted, escaped from Turkish captivity, and been wounded in the process! The

Paris papers called him 'H.E. Salard-Yung' and thought he was an Indian prince. The *Figaro*, in fact, called him the nizam himself, a misconception which seems to have travelled to Italy as well, for when Salar Jung had landed at Naples, artillery guns boomed, and the British vice consul went on board the steamer to welcome him.

Salar Jung also seems to have found time to visit the famous French jeweller, Oscar Massin, asking him to make a piece of jewellery for the nizam. The piece of jewellery was none other than the famous golden yellow diamond belt of Mahbub Ali Khan. Massin recorded in his diary that one day, an aristocratic man had walked into his workshop in Paris with a wooden bowl full of diamonds and asked him to make a special piece of jewellery. There is little doubt that this could only have been Salar Jung.[30]

On 3 August, Salar Jung left Paris. A large crowd of Parisians had assembled to see him start from the Rue de l'Arcade. He asked for 600 francs to be distributed among the waiters, and the party set off in ten landaus, six omnibuses and nine wagons. The party travelled via Mont Cenis to Turin, Milan and Brindisi, where they embarked for Bombay on 8 August. Salar Jung had cabled Hyderabad that they were sailing from Brindisi, and that the welcoming party should not meet him in the western part of the nizam's dominions as earlier planned, but only at Hyderabad. On the homeward journey, Salar Jung paid a flying visit to the Khedive at Cairo.

On the way, he received letters from his wife and his daughter in English. The letters show them to be intelligent women who seemed to share a bond of genuine affection with Salar Jung. It is not known if his wife could indeed write as well as her letter leads us to believe, but it is not improbable since her husband and his sons and daughters were all proficient in the language.

His daughter, Noor-un-Nissa Begum, sent him a letter on 11 July, telling him that it had just rained and how the weather was cooler. 'I suppose you have found the European climate much colder than ours, but I hope it will have done you some good and you will come back to us with fat rosy cheeks, so that we will hardly recognise you, darling father. We are well, with the hope of seeing you soon.'[31]

On 8 August 1876, his wife Aziz-un-Nissa Begum wrote to him acknowledging his note from Dunrobin Castle but voicing her disapproval on his silence on the state of his health and if he had 'recovered from the effects of your accident and if you walk as gracefully as before'. After inquiring about his travel plans, she ended with, 'I am anxious to see you, my darling, and hope your trip over Europe will have greatly contributed to improve your precious health. With my best and earnest wishes for your safe arrival in Bombay.'[32]

She also added a PS: 'By the last two mails, why did you not write to your Mother? She has felt this negligence rather deeply, although she did not mention it to anyone.' This communication between a Muslim noble and his wife in purdah, which resembles that of a European couple, is remarkable for its time. It shows the easy, close, affectionate and equal relationship Salar Jung shared with his wife.

On the voyage home, their steamer passed a ship carrying English troops. When the soldiers and sailors knew who was on board, they swarmed on deck and on to the rigging, and cheered him. There were cries of, 'Three cheers for Salar Jung, the Saviour of India.' Salar Jung reached Bombay on 24 August 1876. In Bombay too, the crew and passengers cheered him on his arrival. The next day he reached Hyderabad after an absence of four and a half months, where, predictably, he was given a rousing and affectionate welcome by all classes of people.

SALAR JUNG'S REMOVAL CONTEMPLATED

Salar Jung returned to Hyderabad greatly pleased with all the adulation he had received. In every formal address, his faithfulness and that of the nizam during the Mutiny had been a subject of comment, and confirmed to him that the British public remembered his great contribution in saving India for the British at that time. Even though he had been received with great civility and perfect courtesy everywhere, there had been no progress on the political front. He even complained to Salisbury that his discussions with people seemed to be limited to the weather. It was reported to the queen that he had not been allowed to discuss anything 'but the heat of the weather', and she seemed inclined to offer Salar Jung the chance of another visit. It was ruled out. At the end of August, she complained to Disraeli that it was unfortunate that Salar Jung had not been given the chance to state his case, something which each one of her subjects had the privilege of doing.[33]

Still, there was a glimmer of hope when he received Salisbury's permission to renew his petition: it served as a defensive consolation, a carapace for his irredeemable optimism on Berar. He thought that

Salisbury's assurance meant that the matter would be considered on its merits, and restoration would follow. In this he was much mistaken, and would suffer the deepest disappointment. One of the reasons for Salisbury's assurance through Fitzgerald was that the press, both in England and in Hyderabad, had revived the Berar question. Anxious that Salar Jung might raise the issue in England, Salisbury was keen to avoid embarrassment to his government, and this explained the empty reassurance given to Salar Jung. It was, as Salar Jung discovered, a mere blind, disguised as a favour. Whether as a grievance-monger or as a supplicant for the restoration of Berar, all Salar Jung got was more trouble and a vexation of spirit. Apart from enjoying the sweetness of a social triumph over his enemies in the Government of India, his trip achieved little.

Salar Jung now had an implacable enemy in the viceroy. Lytton seems to have developed a dread of Salar Jung's ability, independence of spirit and fixity of purpose almost as soon as he landed in India, and his resentment grew when he read about Salar Jung's 'imprudent utterances' in England. What irked Lytton no end was Salar Jung's portrayal of Hyderabad as an independent power in alliance with England, when in reality, it was, like the other states, for all practical purposes, only a feudatory[34] of the British. He suspected his moves to secure support for Berar in high official and aristocratic circles in England. He observed: 'The intrigues of Sir Salar Jung were regarded by me as the greatest danger to which the British power in India was exposed during my viceroyalty—a danger far greater than any which was involved in war or famine.'[35]

According to him, Salar Jung had arranged three personal appeals to Queen Victoria for the restoration of Berar. He had urged the Prince of Wales not to encourage Salar Jung in his petition for the restoration of the districts and importuned the queen not to receive any private communication in this regard. It is said that Salar Jung had taken a large amount of money and some extremely valuable state jewels with him to England. According to Lytton, he had spent over Rs 70 lakh in England on corrupting the press and Parliament.

Lytton had been briefed in full by Northbrook before his arrival in India. His predecessor had indicated that it might be necessary to consider the possibility of removing Salar Jung from his post. This idea greatly appealed to Lytton, and it soon became an obsession. Writing to Salisbury in April 1876, he said that it was a matter of serious consideration 'whether we should not upset Salar Jung during his absence or at least allow his own colleagues to upset him'. He felt removing Salar Jung from his post would be the best way forward. 'I fear that Salar Jung is too far gone in a wrong groove to be now got back into a right one by anything we can do and as long as he is in power he is likely to give us a great deal of trouble.'[36]

The 'best practical solution' of the Salar Jung problem, he wrote in early May 1876, even before Salar Jung had departed for England, 'might be the fall and removal from the office of that Minister, if it can be effected by the spontaneous action of his own colleagues'.[37] In a confidential letter to Meade, Lytton inquired about the desirability and practicality of such a step. He also wanted to know if Meade could prepare the ground for such an event without appearing to play any part in it, and more importantly, without compromising his own position.

Meade advised against any such move because Salar Jung not only enjoyed great influence and authority in the state, but was also the only one capable of running it efficiently. His colleagues were loyal to him and would not support any move to replace him. In any case there was no one who could take his place: Salar Jung, at least for the moment, was indispensable, and there was no saying what would happen if he were replaced. Meade added, 'Whatever trouble he may give the government, I must frankly state that I would bear it rather than see him vacate office.'[38] All in all, Lytton's suggestion was both impolitic and undesirable since it would have disastrous effects.[39]

Salisbury concurred with Meade that removing Salar Jung was not such a good idea. It would shock opinion in England, and if matters deteriorated in Hyderabad as a result of the removal, the complaints would be embarrassing to all, and render any other similar interference involving another prince difficult for the viceroy. Salar Jung survived the threat which remained unknown to him at the time. This, however, was only the thin end of the wedge. Worse was to follow. Salar Jung may not have sensed it then, but there was much disappointment and frustration in store for him.

Salar Jung's first few weeks after his return to Hyderabad passed peacefully enough. He still experienced pain in the hip, but it had healed enough for him to get around with a cane. He had a wooden horse built, on which he practised mounting. As he told John Clerk, riding was the only pastime he enjoyed heartily, and he was soon riding twice a week with the young

Mahbub. He wrote to the former tutor: 'I sometimes find myself playing with him as if I were a boy and I feel that the occupation does me good and I hope His Highness also.'[40] The young Mahbub's chief delight was a pony which he rode to his heart's content when he was not obliged to sit in durbar; so in all probability, he enjoyed the sessions with Salar Jung as much as the minister did.

13

Lytton's Grand Durbar

In April 1876, the Royal Titles Bill received assent. Despite strong Liberal opposition, it had been passed by Parliament, now dominated by Prime Minister Disraeli. By this Act, the queen became the Empress of India, Kaiser-i-Hind. On 28 April 1876, Queen Victoria issued a proclamation adding this title to her existing titles. The prime minister was of the view that it had been a serious omission not to have added a new title to the Crown in 1858, and 'therefore persuaded Parliament to endow Her Majesty's title and authority in India as the paramount power with a new adornment'.[1] Great political importance was attached to these titles since it enabled the British government to claim a succession to the Mughal throne.

Prince Albert had first raised the issue of making Victoria Empress of India in 1858, and he proposed that her formal designation should be 'the Great Mughal', making her the symbolic heiress of the Mughal dynasty. Luckily, good sense prevailed at the time, and the matter seems to have been dropped. When the Conservative government proposed the bill which would make Victoria Empress of India, Disraeli's opponents assailed it as a 'grotesque capstone' to his imperialist foreign policy. The bill was passed by Parliament with a comfortable majority, but not before it had triggered unexpected controversy both in Parliament and the press.[2]

PLANS FOR AN 'IMPERIAL ASSEMBLAGE'

Lytton was equally enthusiastic about the new title. Since he had always maintained that the way to hold India was to secure the loyalty of the princes, he saw in this a great opportunity. When Disraeli had steered the bill through Parliament, Lytton had written to him that it would be 'ridiculous' to proclaim the new title merely through official circulars when 'a few acts of liberality' would be received 'throughout the whole of India with energetic demonstrations of enthusiasm'.[3] It would be neither becoming, nor politic, to give currency to the new title by a mere notice in the official gazette. It would, Lytton said, give the feudal aristocracy of India an opportunity to rally round the British Crown, and also rebut the Liberals in Parliament who thought that the title 'had been created out of caprice or as a covert design' against the native princes.

Given his predilection for pomp and pageantry, Lytton embraced the scheme with great enthusiasm, even if it appeared blatantly opportunistic in many quarters. He began planning the first of a series of ceremonies which were intended to symbolize India reunified under a new ruler. As ardent an imperialist as Disraeli, he unveiled his plan for a special durbar, a magnificent 'Imperial Assemblage' in which he proposed to announce the new title and dazzle the princes. It was a tradition inspired by Mughal durbars, and Lytton adopted this tradition with a view to inspiring loyalty in Indian subjects by using a symbolic language that they were familiar with. It would not only stamp the authority of the queen upon the throne of the Mughals but also inaugurate 'a policy of identifying the Crown of England with the hopes and aspirations, sympathies and interest of the Indian aristocracy, and of defining more distinctly the subordinate position of the Indian states'.[4] It would be described later by Bernard Cohn as 'a ritual . . . of subordination' on the part of the Indian princes as the British appropriated some of the feudatory ceremonials of the Mughals and added some of their own.

A controversial and unconventional viceroy, Lytton was at heart a romantic poet, a Bohemian, drawn to symbols of medieval ceremony, ritual and exotic costumes. He hoped that the assemblage would have the practical effect of making Queen Victoria paramount among the Indian princes, and cement the Indian system of governance around her. The princes, with their formal professions of fealty, would confirm the role of the Crown as the basic source of symbolic legitimation. He took special pains to ensure that the 'great feudal aristocracy' of India was honoured appropriately at the assemblage, and that they, in turn, formally deferred to the Raj.

There was also a more practical reason for the ostentation. Britain appeared to be on the verge of a war with Russia in Central Asia, and it was important to have the loyalty of the native princes of India. Lytton

considered the people of India to be 'dumb' in political matters, and as a
body politic, the seat of its motive power was in its head, the aristocracy.
'As the head wills, so the body will move. If we have with us the Princes, we
shall have with us the people.'[5] Lytton's plan was to reach out to the princes
and chiefs who he thought had been greatly neglected by the British. The
idea was to flatter this 'feudal aristocracy' into loyalty by appropriate gifts
and titles. He also wanted to make an ostentatious display of the military
might of British India to send a message to European powers in general,
and to Russia in particular, who were looking to exploit the weakness of
the Ottoman Empire to further their spheres of influence in that region.[6]

Lytton spared no expense and brooked no obstacle as he set about
organizing a ceremony which he intended to be a great historical event in
itself. He worked obsessively to create an imperial spectacle which would
cement British rule over diverse elements by invoking ancient forms and
ceremonies. In Lytton's opinion, the presentation of salutes and banners
would be more effective than any political concessions. Aware that what he
was proposing would be condemned as a gimmick, he wrote to Salisbury
that 'the further east you go, the greater becomes the importance of a bit
of bunting'.[7]

Salisbury supported Lytton in this display, recognizing the need to win
over the aristocracy and the princes. But he expressed his doubts about the
huge expenditure on the proposed durbar when a famine was raging in the
Bombay and Madras presidencies. The press was strident in its criticism
of this heartless expenditure when thousands were starving. Given its bad
timing, it was rumoured that the princes too were not favourably disposed
to the durbar. Lytton had no qualms about being a little economical with
the truth when he assured the Secretary of State that public opinion
strongly favoured the durbar, and the princes were so taken with the idea
that it was difficult to curb their enthusiasm.

After the cabinet gave its approval, Lytton notified (in August 1876)
that the 'Imperial Assemblage' (better known as the 'Delhi Durbar') would
be held at the old imperial capital of Delhi on 1 January 1877. All the
principal princes were expected to attend the assemblage, which would
afford them a chance to formally acknowledge the authority of the queen
as also to render homage to her. It was proposed to abolish the system
of exchanging gifts between the viceroy and the Indian princes, but the
presentation of nazar by the princes would be retained as a 'salutary symbol
of feudal allegiance'.[8]

Commemorative medals with the effigy of the queen on one side and 'Victoria, Empress of India' on the reverse would be presented by the viceroy on the occasion. The queen approved of the idea and even sent Salisbury a drawing of her profile to ensure that it was rendered accurately on the medal. A commemorative coin, minted in gold and silver, was also distributed. It bore the queen's image and her new designation 'Kaiser-i-Hind' in Persian and Hindi and 'Empress of India' in English. Special currency comprising annas of the smallest denomination were also issued. The title 'Kaiser-i-Hind' was not without its share of controversy. It was pointed out that it was a male title, not a female one. But Salisbury, ever the pragmatist, pointed out that this was because the government did not wish to change the gender on the coin from one reign to another. The queen was less concerned about the name and more interested in her image on the coin, rejecting two versions of the coin before accepting the third.[9]

Lytton also asked the Home Department for permission to present banners to the princes, who he claimed were 'easily affected by sentiment' and 'susceptible to the influence of symbols'. He also proposed a privy council for India, which would have as its members the important princes and members of the viceroy's council. This was at first rejected and later modified beyond recognition by London. But Lytton was letting his imagination run wild. He dreamed up a scheme for a new imperial crown with the princes contributing the jewels for it. He wanted a philanthropic fund announced in London for hospitals and leper asylums in India, with a target of £1,00,000. Disraeli observed that Lytton's schemes were now sounding like the Arabian nights.[10]

Hyderabad was the foremost among the princely states, and the viceroy was naturally very keen that the nizam attend. The refusal by any prince would be an inappropriate slight to the British government. Given the fact that Salar Jung, on his recent visit to England, had projected Hyderabad as an independent state in alliance with England, Lytton was all the more keen that the nizam should appear in Delhi in his 'proper character as feudatory'. Lytton was aware that Salar Jung would have grave reservations in the matter since it involved the nizam publicly acknowledging the queen's sovereignty over him. He also categorically asserted to Meade that under no circumstances would he allow Salar Jung to represent the nizam at Delhi.

The invitation received in Hyderabad soon became the subject of animated discussion. As expected, Salar Jung was not keen that the nizam attend. Left to himself, he would probably have declined the invitation, but the young nizam's grandmother and mother were keen that the young sovereign attend the durbar. Hyderabad had always considered itself an independent ally of the British, and in no treaty were the words 'subsidiary' or 'paramount' status mentioned. It was a dilemma which Salar Jung found hard to resolve. He had saved Hyderabad during the Mutiny only to have Lord Canning declare Britain the heir to the Mughal Empire, and the paramount power in India. Whether the nizams had ever become sovereign or remained titular feudatories of the Mughals was a separate issue. The British flaunted their power but knew that in Salar Jung they had a shrewd and strong challenger.

Meade explained to Salar Jung that the nizam was duty-bound to attend. According to Meade, it was after a prolonged discussion that Salar Jung accepted the invitation. Whatever Salar Jung's reasons for accepting, Lytton was now very pleased that all the princes, including the nizam who had been considered doubtful, would attend the durbar. As a precaution, the residency surgeon was asked to examine the nizam twice a week to ensure that he did not fall ill. The nizam remained healthy, and preparations were made for his and Salar Jung's departure for Delhi.

AN ILL-TIMED APPLICATION

Just before his departure, Salar Jung earned the ill will of both the resident and the viceroy by submitting a fresh application for the restoration of Berar. He could not have chosen a less appropriate time for his new petition. Lytton was furious. He objected not only to the tone, but also the timing of the new petition. Also, the serious imputations made in earlier petitions had not been withdrawn, and Lytton wanted Salar Jung to withdraw all previous communications on the subject. Salar Jung's defence was that he had been authorized to do so by Salisbury in a confidential oral message through his aide de camp, Fitzgerald. As for the timing, Salar Jung rather naively asserted that it was appropriate as his visit to Delhi would afford him a suitable opportunity to discuss the issue with the viceroy.

At a time when the durbar was the only thing on everyone's mind 'that rascal',[11] as Lytton wrote to Salisbury, was queering the pitch. Raising the Berar question was bound to result in unpleasantness in Delhi. The last thing Lytton wanted was that someone, or something, should spoil his very special party. Salar Jung was brusquely told to withdraw his petition and submit a fresh one after the durbar. He should have known by then that the British had no intention of restoring Berar, but he still chose to submit the new petition at the time that he did. Had he not done so, he would have spared himself the humiliation and frustration which resulted from a series of incidents following its submission.

The viceroy was incensed over the fact that Salar Jung had chosen to make his fresh submission at a time when all the other princes were about to assemble at Delhi to testify their loyalty to the queen. The foreign secretary sent Meade a telegram on 22 December 1876 communicating Lytton's extreme displeasure, questioning Salar Jung's timing 'for re-opening a question on which the final decision of Her Majesty's Government has been communicated to him'. It went on to add: 'Unless His Excellency receives without delay such reassurances from the Minister as will satisfy him of the loyalty of the Nizam's Government, he fears he will be unable to receive Sir Salar Jung with the cordiality he would otherwise have wished to do.'[12]

This telegram is quoted in the memorandum Salar Jung distributed to his friends about his experience in Delhi. In it, he had also written, 'I am certain I have in no way merited the expressions therein used.' Stung to the quick about the aspersions on his loyalty, he confided in the Duke of Sutherland: '. . . I will only remark on the question of loyalty referred to by the Viceroy that I am quite confident my loyalty to Her Majesty the Queen and Empress of India is not exceeded by that of any of Her Majesty's subjects.'[13]

Salar Jung was told that unless the 'offensive imputations' in the previous representations on Berar were withdrawn, no further correspondence from him on the subject would be entertained. Lytton also wanted the diwan to assure him personally of the nizam's loyalty to the queen. Stung by this demand, Salar Jung adverted to Salisbury's permission to reopen the Berar issue, and wrote a long letter summarizing all the details of the Berar case for the viceroy's perusal. He also withdrew all previous applications for the restoration of Berar as desired by the viceroy. Lytton, however, insisted on the explicit acknowledgement of the queen's supremacy over the nizam. This insistence on a written recognition of the nizam's subservience to the queen appears to have originated from Lytton. Meade was of the view that the nizam's presence in Delhi was itself an acknowledgement of the queen's supremacy.

On Lytton's order, Meade asked Salar Jung to withdraw the earlier letter for necessary alteration. Meade suggested that Salar Jung insert the word 'suzerain' in the letter. When Salar Jung wanted to know the meaning of the word, he was told by his private secretary, Arthur Oliphant, that it was a synonym of sovereign. While Salar Jung admitted the queen's sovereignty verbally to Meade, he showed a marked disinclination to put it in writing. In this he was technically right, since the nizam had at no time, or by any treaty, surrendered his internal autonomy to the British, or accepted that he was a feudatory of the queen. Given the great changes in the relative power of the two governments, it was the Government of India which was trying its utmost to relegate the nizam to the position of a vassal. After further discussion, he agreed to insert words to the effect that he fully recognized the supremacy of the queen over the nizam. However, in his draft the next day, Salar Jung excluded all mention of the queen's supremacy.

Lytton expressed his disappointment at Salar Jung's evasion and returned the draft to Meade. It was only after Lytton met the nizam on 30 December that Meade managed to get an acceptable draft from Salar Jung. He stated that he would protect the interests of the nizam and his country by supporting 'the dignity of Her Majesty the Empress of India whose entire supremacy *of position* over His Highness the Nizam *according to existing Treaties* I have never called in question, and I most fully recognise, and I do most conscientiously assure His Excellency the Viceroy that this is my desire'.[14]

The words in italics were not included in the original draft, and Lytton, after some deliberation, decided to accept the changes as sufficient acknowledgement of the queen's supremacy. Meade sought to disabuse Salar Jung of the notion that the nizam was an equal ally of the British government. He pointed out to him the 'absurdity of any such pretension', and hoped that the nizam's attendance at the durbar would remove any doubts as to the nizam's real status vis-à-vis the queen.

In fact, even before the correspondence about the sovereignty or suzerainty of the queen had been concluded, the nizam had already acknowledged such overlordship, at least in practical terms. He met the viceroy on 26 December, and accepted a silk banner and a gold medal bearing the queen's portrait from him as tokens of feudal allegiance. Such a visit to the representative of the queen could only be construed as a public act of obeisance to the paramount power.

Salar Jung had requested a private interview with Lytton in Delhi. A time was appointed for it, but when Salar Jung arrived, he found that

Meade was also going to be part of the interview. If ever an example was needed of the lack of trust between the diwan and the resident, this was it. In his dialogue with the viceroy, Salar Jung was given to understand that a fresh letter would be accepted, but that it should be sent only after 15 January 1877.

THE GRAND DURBAR

The durbar was not held within the walls of Delhi but on the surrounding plain which transformed itself into a city of pavilions and tents. The site of the camp was on a plain 4 miles north-west of the city, running beside the ridge from which the British troops had besieged the rebels during the Mutiny. The English camps were mostly on the site which was occupied by the British army in 1857. Just twenty years later, Englishmen and natives were meeting as friends on the very spot where they had met in battle.

The English camps consisted of two rows of tents forming a wide street with a pavilion at one end. The pavilions and tents varied in size and appearance depending on the importance of the individual. In the viceroy's camp, the tents were canvas houses and the pavilion a canvas palace. At the end of the street was a big durbar tent with the viceroy's throne at one end, with a life-size portrait of Queen Victoria hanging behind it. The camp was lit with gas made from castor oil supplied free of charge by the maharaja of Jaipur, whose camp was similarly illuminated. In the durbar tent there were triple cast-iron lamps grouped on a standard designed by Lockwood Kipling, principal of the Mayo School of Art at Lahore, and father of Rudyard, who was at the time a ten-year-old schoolboy in England.

Banners displaying the shields and colours of each ruling house were initially ordered from Calcutta but later this task was given to Kipling, who was seconded to the viceroy's staff for the duration of the preparations.[15] One of the ladies who had helped to embroider these banners in Simla was Alice Macdonald, Rudyard's mother. The camps of lesser officials were on a smaller and less grand scale. The governor of Bombay, the governor of Madras (the Duke of Buckingham), the lieutenant governor of Bengal (Sir Richard Temple) and the commander in chief, all had their own camps.

The camps of the Hindu and Muslim chiefs were of a different nature, and spaces had been set apart for each to arrange his camp after his own fashion. Some were radiant in blue and scarlet, surmounted by gold knobs and other ornaments. Most of them were surrounded by walls of coloured cloth supported by bamboo canes, tipped with golden knobs or steel spearheads.[16] Each ruler had brought his own troops, and his own band, to say nothing of the hundreds of attendants who looked after the elephants and camels. Only the khan of Khelat had asked the British to provide him with tents, elephants and camels for 100 men. When they were sent a ready-cooked dinner on the day they arrived, they seized the cutlery, ate the cakes of Pear's soap, and used the basins and jugs to eat and drink.[17]

The location of the assemblage where the proclamation was to take place was a grassy plain about 2 miles north of the viceroy's camp. Two thousand labourers had worked for weeks to level the ground. Three structures had been set up on the turf-covered plain for the ceremonial to proclaim Queen Victoria Empress of India: a throne pavilion for the viceroy; an amphitheatre for the princes and high officials; and blocks for representatives of foreign governments and spectators. The throne pavilion was a splendid hexagonal structure of red, blue and gold near the centre of the plain, each of its sides being 40 feet long. It resembled a glorified bandstand, rising 10 feet from the ground, its conical roof capped with an imperial gold crown. The amphitheatre for the reception of the princes and high dignitaries was a pavilion of blue, white and gold which stretched out for nearly 800 feet in front of the throne pavilion. It was divided into thirty-six compartments. The floor was covered with red cloth, and the chairs were blue. Behind the throne pavilion was a stand for guests, staff and minor British officials.

Lytton had commissioned Val Prinsep to paint the Imperial Assemblage as a present for the queen. He was to receive £5000 for the painting, along with return fare and expenses while in India. This money was to be collected from the princes who had expressed a desire to send a present to the queen. Contributors were to have their portraits recognizably painted into the picture, and to receive a lithograph of it.[18] Prinsep was, however, less than impressed at the scene he was supposed to reproduce on canvas, deploring the atrocious taste and calling it the 'kind of thing which outdoes the Crystal Palace in "hideousity" . . . all iron, gold, red, blue and white . . . The Viceroy's dais is a kind of scarlet temple 80 feet high. Never was there such Brummagem ornament, or more atrocious taste . . . The size . . . gives it a vast appearance like a gigantic circus and the decorations are in keeping.'[19] Prinsep felt that it was going to be impossible to paint the scene because of the size, and was relieved to find that Lytton was anxious that he paint a rather 'fanciful picture' with the Jumma Masjid in the background.

All the invitees had assembled in Delhi before Lytton's arrival. Altogether, there were a lakh of people assembled on the plain, which included sixty-three rulers and their retinues, including the begum of Bhopal; about 800 titular princes and nobles; the khan of Khelat, the prince of Arcot and the princess of Tanjore; ambassadors from Siam, Burma and Nepal; all the foreign consuls and senior British officials; the Governors General of Goa and Pondicherry; 15,000 troops; and the editors and reporters of native and European newspapers. In a curious coincidence the three princes who represented three important native states were all young boys: the nizam, the Gaekwar of Baroda and the maharaja of Mysore. On more than one occasion, the three sat on a sofa and talked together in the manner of boys.[20] The nizam was given Metcalfe House, the former home of the British agent in Delhi, as his residence in Delhi for the duration of the durbar.

The viceroy made his public entry into Delhi on the afternoon of 23 December 1876. The route was lined with British troops. The princes had also been invited to station their troops at intervals on either side of the road according to their fashion. Long lines of elephants, in magnificent trappings and howdahs which were like thrones of gold and silver, could be seen all along the route. The retinues of the Punjab chiefs were posted outside the Lahore gate, and the troops of Baroda, Mysore and Hyderabad were drawn up on both sides of the road which ran along the ridge.

The war elephants mounted by warriors in chain mail and armed from head to foot provided a grand spectacle. The elephants had steel points on their tusks, shields of steel on their foreheads, and chain mail hanging down their trunks. The howdahs were of shot-proof steel, and the warriors sat in the howdahs in complete armour, carrying weapons of every description— spears, swords, battleaxes and muskets. There were also bands of horsemen in medieval chain armour. The officers wore plumes on their helmets, some of feathers, and some of gold and silver, while their horses were bedecked in gold and silver trappings. Of particular interest were the gold and silver six-pounder cannons of Baroda. The gold cannon was drawn in a carriage of silver, and the cannon of silver was drawn in a carriage of gold. The carriages were drawn by enormous cattle from Gujarat whose horns were tipped with silver and gold. The most crowded place was the Jumma

Masjid whose towers and terraces were full of the foreign dignitaries and guests of the different governments in British India.

Lytton, accompanied by his wife, arrived at the railway station at 2 p.m. and was greeted with a gun salute. He was greeted at the station by the lieutenant governors of Bengal, Punjab and the North-Western Provinces; the commander-in-chief of India; high officials and the sixty-three ruling princes who had come to attend the durbar. He welcomed the princes with a short speech, thanking them for the cordiality with which they had responded to his invitation, and expressed the hope that 'the close of our proceedings will confirm the auspicious character of this commencement'.[21]

The princes were then introduced to the viceroy who shook hands with all of them. He spoke separately to the nizam, Scindia, Holkar, the Gaekwar of Baroda and the maharajas of Jaipur and Kashmir. Lytton then mounted his elephant, and the procession 'began to pour through the streets of Delhi in a continuous stream of British majesty and Indian splendour'.[22] (The elephant has for long been the symbol of sovereignty in India.) As the viceroy moved along the route, the British troops presented arms, and the bands played the national anthem. The retinues of the princes paid ceremonial homage according to their own custom, coming to attention and saluting in oriental fashion.

First came the 11th Hussars followed by a battery of the Royal Horse Artillery and the 3rd Bombay Cavalry. The personal escort of the viceroy and his aides-de-camp (ADCs) followed on elephants, two abreast. After them, rode the chief herald of the assemblage, who was followed by twelve trumpeters on horseback. The remainder of the procession consisted of a long line of elephants carrying the commander-in-chief, lieutenant governors, chief justices and secretaries to the Government of India. Another procession of elephants bore native noblemen and personages of high rank dressed in bright Oriental costumes. The procession lasted three hours and traversed 6 miles before it reached the viceroy's camp. It moved from the railway station towards the Jumma Masjid before turning round the mosque, traversing Chandni Chowk, and leaving Delhi via the Lahore gate.

Lytton was feeling ill the next day but had sufficiently recovered by the morning of Christmas Day to hold discussions with Sir Philip Wodehouse, the Duke of Buckingham and Sir Richard Temple about the famine in Madras. Lytton spent the next day, 26 December, in receiving visits from the princes. Each ruling chief with his suite was received on arrival by mounted officers. As his party advanced to the reception pavilion, a salute was fired. A British guard of honour presented arms, and the prince was then conducted into the inner reception pavilion by the foreign secretary or undersecretary, and presented with ceremony to the viceroy. The viceroy cordially received each chief and offered him a seat to his right, and then took his own seat on the throne immediately below a full-length picture of Queen Victoria.

After the exchange of pleasantries, each prince[23] was presented with a coloured satin banner fastened to an elaborately worked brass pole and embroidered in coloured silks with his titles on one side and his armorial bearings on the other. The banner was brought in by Highland soldiers and placed in front of the viceroy. The viceroy descended from the dais and presented the prince with the banner after a brief speech in which he hoped that 'it may never be unfurled without reminding you, not only of the close union between the Throne of England and your loyal and princely house, but also of the earnest desire of the Paramount Power to see your dynasty strong, prosperous and permanent'.[24]

A gold medal was also presented to the prince which bore a portrait of the queen, and which the viceroy said should be preserved as an heirloom 'in remembrance of the auspicious date it bears'. (Lytton lost his medal in the mud. He had also ordered too many medals, and years later, the Calcutta mint melted down the unused stock.) The princes viewed the banners with great favour, and they were displayed with great pride on subsequent occasions throughout the assemblage.

The banners formed a striking picture on proclamation day, and were also carried in procession on the last day of the durbar. The only problem was their weight. Each banner needed two Highlanders to carry it, and the princes had to hoist them on top of the elephants when taking them in procession. The khan of Khelat provided some unwitting amusement when he insisted on being given a banner, in spite of being told that he was an independent prince and the banner was meant only for feudatories. He said that he didn't want to be an independent prince and wanted a banner like all the rest. Sadly for him, his request was turned down.[25]

Lytton received twenty-one ruling princes in this manner, and the next day, 27 December, he received sixteen, and returned fifteen visits to those who were entitled to that honour, who included the nizam. At the meeting with the nizam, there was further unpleasantness with

Salar Jung. Lytton was upset that Salar Jung had wrongly translated his (Lytton's) words to the nizam, substituting 'friendship' and 'alliance' when the words used by Lytton were 'loyalty' and allegiance'. Lytton asked the government translator to tell the nizam that what he really meant was 'obedience' and 'fidelity'.[26]

This carried on for the next two days. There was only one episode which struck a jarring note. Scindia had been kept waiting for two hours outside the durbar tent through a mistake on the part of the British officer in charge of him. His sulky demeanour during the audience showed his deep resentment at the treatment he had received. His feelings were assuaged by Lytton's brainwave of telegraphing the queen and obtaining her permission to make Scindia (who was already a G.C.S.I.) a Grand Commander of the Order of the Bath and informing him immediately. Amour propre was respected: Gwalior and Kashmir were made honorary generals in the Indian army at the durbar.

Lytton also decided to increase the number of guns in the salute of some of the more important princes. Three were raised to twenty-one guns—the nizam, the Gaekwar of Baroda and the maharaja of Mysore. Seven others which included Scindia, Jaipur and Kashmir had their personal salutes raised to twenty-one. (Salar Jung was given seventeen). But the joy of the princes was short-lived; their dreams of parity with the viceroy ended when they discovered that the viceroy's salute was now thirty-one and that of the queen 101.

PROCLAMATION DAY

The New Year's Day, 1 January 1877, had been declared a public holiday, and every soldier in the Indian army had received an extra day's pay. Nearly 16,000 prisoners were released and amnesty extended to all those exiled after the Mutiny with the sole exception of Feroze Shah, a relative of Bahadur Shah Zafar, under whose leadership an uprising was still feared. A new order, the Order of the Indian Empire, was instituted, and the Order of the Star of India was enlarged. (In Nagpur, a certain Jamsetji Tata named his new cotton factory 'Empress Mills'. The name brought bad luck because the mill was badly damaged by a fire later that year. He had better luck when he named his new premises in Bombay 'Swadeshi Mills' in 1886.)

The scene on the morning of the proclamation was a dazzling one. Oriental costumes and insignia mixed with British uniforms and banners in a manner never seen before. Every prince, and every governor and lieutenant governor sat under his own banner surrounded by his nobles and officers. The bright satin and velvet of the princes and their retinues mingled with the red and dark-blue uniforms of the Europeans.

In the centre of the amphitheatre were the three boy princes, the nizam, the Gaekwar of Baroda and the maharaja of Mysore. On the right were the ruling chiefs of Rajputana, and on the left were Maharaja Scindia, and the maharaja of Holkar. At the extreme left were the chiefs of Punjab and the maharaja of Kashmir. The others were minor chiefs who were feudatories of the local governments rather than the Government of India.

At noon, trumpets announced the arrival of the viceroy and his wife. It had been announced that Lady Lytton would attend the formal proclamation ceremony—the first time that a female member of the viceroy's family would take part in a public function which Indians attended. With memories of 1857 still fresh, and with racism very much in evidence in the Western world, many Anglo-Indians saw this participation as highly inappropriate. While most Europeans in India derided Lytton including his wife and daughters in the ceremonies, it was his fond hope that this inclusion would help bridge 'the inconvenient and deplorable gulf existing between English and native society'.[27]

The military bands played a grand march. Later, the bands struck up the national anthem, and the guards of honour presented arms as the viceroy took his appointed seat upon the throne. The chief herald then read the proclamation in English. It was then read in Urdu by T.H. Thornton, the officiating foreign secretary to the Government of India. The royal standard was then hoisted, and a grand salute of 101 salvoes of artillery was fired. After the salutes and feux de joie had ended, the viceroy rose to make his speech. In a long address, he addressed each section of the empire: British administrators, members of the civil and military services, officers and soldiers of the army both British and native, volunteer soldiers, princes and chiefs and native subjects of the empire. He ended with:

> We trust that the present occasion may tend to unite in bonds of yet closer affection [between] ourselves and our subjects; that from the highest to the humblest all may feel that under our rule the great principles of liberty, equity, and justice are secured to them; and that to promote their happiness, to add to their prosperity, and advance their welfare, are the ever present aims and objects of our Empire.[28]

At the end of the viceroy's speech, Scindia rose and congratulated the queen as the Empress of India with the power to give the absolute order or *hukumat*. The maharajas of Kashmir and Udaipur expressed similar sentiments, and there was a very pregnant pause when the assembly waited for a brief address from the principal Muslim prince, the nizam, or his diwan. Salar Jung, who had no desire to speak, did not stir. Rashid-ud-din then nudged the nizam and whispered in his ear. The nizam turned to the resident who exchanged a few words with Salar Jung. In the end, Salar Jung rose and gave a short speech in English after which the viceroy left the dais.

> I am desired by His Highness the Nizam to request your Excellency to convey to her Majesty, on the part of himself and the chiefs of India, the expression of their hearty congratulations upon her assumption of the title of Empress of India, and to assure her that they pray for her long life and for the enduring prosperity of her empire both in India and England.[29]

Lytton's speech had nothing of real value to offer and was 'a tissue of carefully and beautifully woven platitudes'. Robert Knight of the Calcutta *Statesman* had given half-hearted support to the durbar, questioning the huge expenditure at a time of famine. He wanted the British to reciprocate with some measure which would benefit the populace and not just the princes. He wrote: We think we have had enough and more than enough of stars and ribbons, banners and medals, certificates of merit, and all such cheap and meaningless vanities . . . The people and Princes of India, are to be forever treated as children, to be put off with pattings and praises, and kept from sulkiness by such toys as stars and medals, and parchment certificates. It is not statesmanship: but Beaconsfield "fireworks".'[30]

In fact, most newspapers saw Lytton's address as a wasted opportunity. There was no mention of representative government, and it was generally felt that it had failed to uphold the principles and hopes of the transfer of power in 1858. Rabindranath Tagore composed a song condemning the princes for participating in such festivity at a time of famine. The *Indian Charivari* depicted Lytton as a fairground attendant, the provider of an imperial peep show.[31] It was the Indian bureaucracy who benefited the most, with engineers, magistrates, police inspectors, surgeons, clerks and builders featuring prominently in the honours list. Hundreds of Indians were rewarded with titles and other new forms of status. As noted, the ghost of the Mutiny was also finally laid to rest, with almost 16,000 prisoners released, including those who had not been freed in 1858.[32] The banquet in the evening of proclamation day was a stag affair attended by both Indian and European gentlemen. The three days following the banquet were taken up with receptions, visits, dinners and the distribution of medals.

On 3 January, a delegation from the Aligarh Muslim University comprising Moulvi Cheragh Ali, Moulvi Muhammed Karim and Moulvi Samiullah Khan had an audience with the nizam and conveyed to him their decision to name the college museum after him. Mahbub appreciated the efforts of the founders and promised further financial aid. (In 1882, when Sir Syed Ahmed Khan visited Hyderabad for the first time, the nizam made a permanent settlement of Rs 2000 to be managed by Sir Syed himself. Permanent endowments of land revenue income were set aside by both Hyderabad state and Salar Jung's estate. A large dining hall was named Salar Manzil after the diwan.)[33]

On 5 January, the last day of the assemblage, Lytton reviewed a march-past of native and British troops. The viceroy then left for Patiala by a special train. Soon after his departure, there was a tremendous downpour that lasted all night, reducing the camp to a sea of red mud. The heavens had been kind to Lytton, for the ensuing chaos would have ruined the event. Lytton wrote to the queen about how the durbar had been a triumph of organization and logistics, 'an achievement highly creditable to all concerned in carrying it out'. But not all were terribly happy at Lytton's efforts to dress everyone in the colours of medieval feudalism. British ladies arriving in Delhi with trunks of new dresses were mortified to learn that they would be sharing space with 'dark gentlemen' who would be present at balls and parties as part of Lytton's way of honouring the Indian potentates. Their anger was shared by the Anglo-Indians who also excluded Indians from their social life.

This attempt to unduly accommodate Indian potentates led Anglo-Indians to label Lytton's viceroyalty the 'Black Raj'. Lytton found himself in a heavy crossfire of criticism, with many foreigners and Indians appalled by the 'raw gaucherie' and pointless flummery of the assemblage. Educated Indians and journalists were aghast at the extravagant spectacle and questioned this wasteful expenditure at a time of famine. There had been no balls for the ladies and no parties without 'dark gentlemen' present.[34] The preponderance of Indians in the New Year's Honours list was another cause for resentment. Whatever his other shortcomings, Lytton was perhaps the least racially prejudiced viceroy to have come to India.

It is interesting to note, though, that Simla's reputation for amorous immorality (gambling, drinking and adultery) is said to have been acquired during Lytton's regime. A flirtatious viceroy, he is alleged to have had affairs with the wives of two of his ICS subordinates. Whatever his other dalliances, this was not true, since it was his two ADCs who were the lovers of these women. This reputation of Simla endured even afterwards thanks to the writings of Rudyard Kipling.[35]

A BITTER AFTERTASTE

The assemblage left Salar Jung with a very poor taste in the mouth. His 'fidelity as an ally and his labours as a statesman' had always been recognized by the British, and this shabby treatment left him feeling humiliated and belittled. In retaliation, he printed his version of his conversations with Meade (as he had done in the past with Saunders at the time of the visit of the Prince of Wales) and sent it to his friends in England. The Duke of Sutherland was requested to place the notes before the Prince of Wales. But in this, Salar Jung was much mistaken. It was naive of him to imagine that any help would come from England. It proved to be a futile effort which only served to alienate Lytton and Meade even further. The resident's discreet inquiries revealed that Salar Jung had been fraternizing with Scindia and Holkar during the durbar and had held several private interviews with both. On his return, he had sent them copies of his petition on Berar and notes on his conversations with Meade.

Scindia was known to watch developments on Berar with keen interest since he had a grievance against the British regarding Gwalior fort. If Salar Jung succeeded with Berar, he could press his claims once again. Meade concluded that if Salar Jung had sent the papers to Holkar and Scindia, there was no way of knowing if he had not sent them to other native princes as well. Lytton reported to the queen that Salar Jung was behaving 'abominably', and trying to incite Holkar and Scindia to support him on Berar and also press their own claims. An irate Lytton wrote to Salisbury, 'Salar Jung will, I suspect, be a thorn in our flesh till he reaches the world where the wicked cease from troubling.'[36] Salisbury agreed that some mischief was 'brewing' in Salar Jung's 'dreamy brain', and he would give them incessant trouble as long as he lived.[37] Salar Jung, in a span of a decade, had gone from being the poster boy of the British to public enemy number one.

On 7 February 1877, Salar Jung submitted another letter to the resident, which even after six weeks was not sent to Calcutta. The excuse was that the government was waiting for the return of all previous applications from the India Office since these had now been withdrawn by Salar Jung in his Delhi letter. It was a bitter pill for Salar Jung to swallow. He complained to Claude Clerk that he had never received such treatment before, and nor had he heard of any of the nizam's ministers being subjected to such humiliation. To make matters worse, Meade wanted Salar Jung to send a formal communication withdrawing all the earlier petitions on Berar. Salar Jung refused, saying that his letter of 27 December in which he had already done so should suffice. It was obvious that the resident did not show the sympathy and support that Salar Jung's past history justified, and which the minister expected from him.

Salar Jung was not the only one to feel humiliated at the durbar. Claude Clerk, who had taken up his position in November 1876, found himself continually ignored and bypassed by British officials. During his brother's brief incumbency, his title had been guardian of the nizam, and the agreements of 1869 had called this position 'superintendent of the nizam's education'. Meade must have been aware that Salar Jung and Clerk were on good terms, and therefore decided that Clerk too needed cutting down to size. He demoted him to tutor, even though there were tutors for the different subjects. Clerk, for his part, had taken a dislike to Meade and his protégé Rashid-ud-din, and voiced it in Hyderabad and in England through his letters to his brother.

The *Bombay Review* noted this fact a few years later when reporting on the education of the nizam. It observed that 'the superintendent of his education, who accompanied him, came in largely for a share in the slights and indignity with which it was thought proper to treat the Minister, Sir Salar Jung'. It further noted that 'Captain Clerk's existence was simply ignored, because he had been selected not by the Foreign Office but by Sir Salar Jung'.[38]

Meade was not satisfied with the nizam's progress as shown in Clerk's report for 1877 and 1878. He viewed both the Clerk brothers with suspicion. He was convinced that John Clerk had been appointed by Salar Jung with a view to influencing powerful persons in England on his behalf. As for Claude Clerk, he believed that he was in cahoots with Seymour

Keay for private aims of his own. Meade's suspicions that Salar Jung had ulterior motives in appointing his tutors were confirmed when Salar Jung tried to get Major Percy Gough appointed as tutor under Claude Clerk. Lytton refused permission. Gough had never been to university and was a military man with some influence in England, and this attempt only confirmed Lytton's suspicion that Salar Jung's motives lay elsewhere.

Lytton and Meade both believed that Salar Jung's aim was to reduce the nizam to 'a cipher' so that he could enjoy untrammelled power. They felt that the seclusion of the nizam in the palace was not conducive to the development of a sound body and mind. Salar Jung visited him daily, but almost everyone else was excluded from his presence and he was rarely allowed to leave the palace. It was therefore decided that a qualified tutor would be appointed after government approval. Salar Jung was not in favour of such a proposal, but Meade managed to get his approval for the appointment of J.F. Dowding, at that time the principal of Rajshahi College in Bengal, as the assistant tutor.

THE GREAT FAMINE

The year 1877, however, will probably be etched in the memory of Indians not so much for Lytton's durbar but for the great famine of 1876–78. 'As drama, the famine would endure better than the durbar.'[39] Starting with the failure of the monsoon in southern India in the summer of 1876 as well as that of the retreating monsoon, the famine was made more acute by the failure of the monsoon in the summer of 1877 as well. It would take a toll of 5 million lives, and both the administration in Madras and in Calcutta were shown in a poor light. William Digby, the twenty-eight-year-old editor of the *Madras Times*, highlighted the callous response to the tragedy in his book on the subject.[40]

Even as the famine had just begun, the governor of Madras, the Duke of Chandos, sailed on a tour of the Andamans, Rangoon and Ceylon. On his return, he was preoccupied with making the trip to Delhi for the great durbar. To his credit, he described the scale of the crisis in telegrams to Lytton, who dismissed him as alarmist. By the time he started for Delhi, 65,000 had died in the presidency and 13,000 in Mysore. Bellary, Kurnool and Cuddapah were the worst-hit districts, but the situation in the far south was not much better. People ate poisonous roots and leaves, and there were the dead and the dying everywhere. Cholera and malaria added to the toll.

One would have thought that hunger and pestilence would prevent such a grand event, but Lytton seemed quite immune to the suffering.

Relief was crippled by the rigid application of conservative dicta: distribution of food was said to create dependency, and free trade was best, with merchants being allowed to move grain across the land. Amazingly, the wage was reduced from two annas per day to one and a half. Lytton only made matters worse by issuing orders prohibiting any reduction in the price of food during the famine. He discouraged relief works since mere distress was not enough reason for doing so. He accused his British critics of indulging in 'humanitarian hysterics' and invited them to foot the bill if they wanted to save Indian lives. He dispatched Sir Richard Temple to Madras with instructions to ignore 'humanitarian humbugs' and to reduce the cost of relief measures.

Temple's watchword was parsimony. While 'work camps' were created so as to enable those afflicted to earn something, the wage called the 'Temple wage' provided less sustenance than that received by those at the Buchenwald concentration camp during World War II.[41] The daily supplements were reduced, and no attempt was made to bring in emergency supply of grain. Temple's own colleagues protested against the severity of the measures taken. Digby remarked that Temple wrote 'numberless memoranda and very long minutes' and took a 'rose-coloured view' which the death rate contradicted.[42] The famine received better coverage than any previous outbreak, and he was criticized both in the press and in lectures. The *Pall Mall Gazette* despatched Henry Hyndman to cover the crisis, and at home, even Florence Nightingale voiced her protest.

After persistent requests, Lytton finally decided to see for himself, arriving in Raichur on 27 August, and two days later in Madras. The report of the Indian Famine Commission published in 1880 admitted that the government was blameworthy. 'It can scarcely be asserted that the system adopted was altogether satisfactory or efficient.' It was the understatement of the decade.

14

An Army for the Nizam

Apart from serious disagreements on Berar, a bone of contention between Meade and Salar Jung was the enlarging and maintenance of the so-called Reformed Troops. This body of men had its origins in the period after the Mutiny when it was agreed by the British government that the organization and equipment of a portion of the nizam's troops should be put on a different footing as compared to the rest of the forces. This was done in order to prevent mutineers from entering the state from British India, and also to subdue the turbulent part of the population. The task was assigned to the raja of Wanaparthy, who already had under him a small body of troops.

Raja Rameshwar Rao I of Wanaparthy had imported Siddis from Somalia and Abyssinia, and organized them into two regiments—one of Siddi soldiers called the African Bodyguard and another regiment of Siddi cavalry known as the Wanaparthy Lancers. On account of skirmishes between the raja's troops and the nizam's, the resident engineered a tripartite arrangement by which the raja presented his African Bodyguard and Wanaparthy Lancers to the nizam, and he in turn was appointed the inspector general of 'His Highness the Nizam's Field Force'. They were given the duties of escort and became the nizam's African Bodyguards. This force, which rendered good service and constituted the nucleus of the 'Reformed Troops', ceased active service in 1858 itself, but the salutary effect it had had on bringing peace in certain districts made it evident that increasing its strength and extending it to the whole territory, would yield very favourable results.[1]

This force served the nizam well during the Mutiny, and later continued to take part in subduing Afghans and dacoits in the Deccan. The African cavalry, later renamed as the Golconda Lancers, became part of the nizam's regular forces. When the raja died, all his personal forces and troops, including the African cavalry, were gifted to the nizam.[2]

In 1859, there was an attack on the diwan deodi, which housed the treasury and the revenue offices, by the henchmen of a refractory noble. Repulsing this attack necessitated the use of another body of troops since the raja of Wanaparthy's troops were camped some distance from Hyderabad. Infantry was withdrawn from the city levies and placed under the command of a European officer. This infantry, together with the raja of Wanaparthy's troops, and Nawab Nizam Yar Jung's cavalry, was located in Hyderabad, and in June 1862, the whole of these troops were termed the 'Reformed Troops' and placed under the command of Major Rocke who was called inspector general. In August 1866, his designation was changed to commander, and the designation of the troops altered to 'His Highness the Nizam's Regular Troops' in December of the same year.[3]

THE REFORMED TROOPS

It was Salar Jung's intention to neutralize the menace of the Arabs, Sikhs and Rohillas by using the Reformed Troops. His idea was to control this lawless class by enrolling them in this force. In this, he had the support of the resident, Col. Davidson, and later also made it clear to his successor Sir George Yule, that he required a body of troops to counter any outbreak. Prior to 1862, Hyderabad had no army of its own, and there was total dependence on the British forces. Salar Jung realized that he could not indefinitely rely on the whims and fancies of the military chiefs and of the irregular levies, and needed an efficient force to maintain peace.

In 1862, Salar Jung entrusted the task of organizing the Reformed Troops to Raja Girdhari Pershad, better known as Bansi Raja. Bansi Raja was a trusted aide of Salar Jung. A Persian, Hindi and Urdu scholar, he was also conversant with Sanskrit and Arabic. He was also a fine poet in Persian, a chronographer, and a master in the art of rhetoric. He made arrangements for special durbars, both Mughlai and English. In addition, he was *serishtadar* of the troops, apart from setting up and controlling factories which manufactured a variety of goods, including a munition factory.

Bansi Raja was a key figure in the nizam's court and attended to the arrangements for durbars, festivals and all ceremonies connected with birth, marriage and death in the nizam's palace. He acted as an adviser to the nizam and was much respected as a trustworthy companion and mediator, apart from being regarded a noted literary figure. He was in charge of the various departments of the nizam's palace, a delicate task requiring talent, maturity and tact since he had to deal not only with the nizam, but also keep the begums and the nobles happy. A long associate of Salar Jung, his selection was proof, if ever any was needed, of Salar Jung's unerring instincts in judging character. Bansi Raja owed everything to Salar Jung, a fact he acknowledged in his poems on various occasions. He was also on good terms with the Paigah nobles and served as a mediator between Rashid-ud-din Khan and Salar Jung when the former was appointed co-regent in 1877.

Bansi Raja reorganized the troops, taking into consideration aspects such as the recruitment of able-bodied men and the retirement of the old and the infirm. He also provided uniforms and arms and equipment to the troops, and arranged for their daily training under European officers. In 1864, he was made the head serishtadar of the regular forces. On Salar Jung's prompting, he established a gunpowder factory in 1864, and an ordnance factory in 1868, and it was from these factories that the troops were supplied arms and ammunition. He also set up a leather factory to supply leather goods to the force. He asked the government to give him grass plots for the supply of grass, grain and gram to the cavalry. It was Bansi Raja who maintained a record of annual expenditure and the disbursement of monthly salaries to the armed forces.[4]

The regular forces of Hyderabad consisted of the regular troops, the Golconda Brigade and the nizam's Jamiat-i-Nizam-i-Mahbub or Myseram Regiment. The regular troops, as we have noted, consisted of the African Cavalry Guard, originally formed during the time of the raja of Wanaparthy in 1858. There were also three lancer regiments. The infantry consisted of the first, third, fourth and sixth regiments. The Golconda Brigade was formed during Salar Jung's time with the intention of escorting distinguished guests and was named the Golconda Lancers. It consisted of a regiment of cavalry, infantry and a battery of artillery stationed at Malakpet.

The Jamiat-i-Nizam-i-Mahbub consisted of two battalions of infantry, one each at Keshavgiri and Myseram. It was manned by Arabs and Rohillas. The brainchild of Bansi Raja, it was a way of ridding Hyderabad of turbulent Arabs and Rohillas by offering them regular employment. Many years ago, Bansi Raja had played a major role in divesting the Arab jemadars of the districts and placing them under the government. He had also ended the practice of paper recruitment and ensured that payment was made only to those who were actually on the rolls. The first assistant resident, Major Euan Smith, commented on Bansi Raja's contribution:

> He is in many ways, I am told, a remarkable man, and has been often made use of by the minister to carry through many delicate and confidential transactions. One of these occurred some two years ago, when the Arabs were to be a [sic] great extent deprived of their Jagirs and enrolled into Jamiat-i-Mahbub. Sir Salar Jung entrusted the conduct of this delicate affair to Bansi Raja, and he carried it through to a successful conclusion. It is also said and believed that to his initiative is due the establishment of the Reformed Troops in their present footings.[5]

The task of organizing the irregular troops, including enlisting and training, was given by Salar Jung to his special protégé, Moulvi Mahmud, an enterprising thirty-five-year-old, who was energetic and industrious, but also overbearing and harsh. Moulvi Mahmud also started a factory which manufactured excellent swords, muskets and carbines. It also manufactured cartridges on a small scale. The idea was to bring the irregular levies under the Arab chiefs under his control and transform the *risala khas* or state levies, an irregular and undisciplined force of sixteen to twenty regiments of infantry of 300–500 men and cavalry of 500 which were scattered over the districts, into a disciplined army.

Salar Jung also wanted to transform the sarf-i-khas, the personal troops of the nizam, consisting of five regiments of infantry and 1200 cavalry, into two regiments, one of infantry and the other cavalry, with the cavalry forming the nizam's bodyguard. The noblemen maintained armed retainers who had no respect for the law, and whose ranks seemed to constantly swell with a fresh influx of Arabs and Rohillas into Hyderabad. The British were very keen that this lawless element be curbed and their numbers controlled. The irregular troops, which, apart from the Arabs, also consisted of Rohillas, Sikhs, Rajputs, Baluchis and other tribes, were used for guard and escorting duties, and assisting the police in preventing dacoity.

By the mid-1970s, Salar Jung's efforts in building up an arsenal and the development of a trained force had begun to be highly suspect in the eyes of the British, but back in the late 1850s, when this exercise first started, it had the support of the British. In 1859, a request was made to supply old muskets from British arsenals for the use of the state troops. This request was granted on Davidson's recommendation. The arms were given on the understanding that there would be a reduction in the irregular troops, which were a burden on the finances and administration of the state. This reorganization elicited praise from Calcutta, who thought that it achieved the twin objectives of efficiency and economy.[6]

In 1866 Salar Jung had sent Yule a statement of the strength of the Reformed Troops. A total of 24,000 foot soldiers and 4700 cavalry had been reduced to about 14,000 foot soldiers and 3200 cavalry after the reduction, including 1700 soldiers and 380 cavalry which had been transferred to the police. Yule had no objection to donating old and obsolete muskets to the troops. The supply of rifles from England was, however, not permitted. He also allowed Salar Jung to horse his field batteries since the task could not be efficiently performed by bullocks.

It is clear that Salar Jung was thinking of replacing the Hyderabad Contingent with an efficient body of troops to suppress internal revolt. He asserted that if the nizam did not have an efficient body of troops to quell internal disturbances, he would be perceived as impotent and weak. The Hyderabad Contingent could not be used for trivial reasons, and its use, as noted earlier, required a request made in advance with reasons as to why it was needed, an arrangement which was altogether useless in times of an emergency. Salar Jung had for long been pointing out that neither the Subsidiary Force (for which the Northern Circars had been ceded in perpetuity as advance payment) nor the Hyderabad Contingent (for which Berar had been assigned) were available to the nizam when he needed them. The British maintained that it was incumbent on them to investigate the situation behind each request before 'our own troops' entered the fray.

Yule thought that it was better to run the slight risk of the force turning against them, rather than keep it in such a state of inefficiency as to render it useless in critical situations. Salar Jung's honeymoon with the British had not yet ended, and Yule wanted to support Salar Jung so that 'his power is not weakened by intrigues or his time entirely occupied in counteracting them'. When Sir Richard Temple became resident, he was a little alarmed at this trend and wanted to review the Reformed Troops. Salar Jung excused himself, unwilling to ask the nizam for permission to attend, but declared himself delighted at the resident's intention.

Temple reviewed the troops on 30 May 1867 and found their movements smartly conducted, firing rapid and precise, and cavalry well-mounted. Temple doubted if such a force was required in Hyderabad. 'The general result of the review, as regards the troops, was satisfactory, but whether such a body was wanted at all in the place it then was, was quite another question.'[7] Temple had been warned by General (Sir John) Grant, who commanded the Subsidiary Force, of the danger of allowing Salar Jung to organize the Reformed Troops, 'which in time of peace were useless, and in time of trouble would be a source of anxiety'.[8] This was in keeping with the prevailing thinking on the subject where the military power of the princes was viewed with suspicion; while a rising of the princes was not feared, there remained a cautious attitude towards their military power.

By the mid-1870s, as we have already noted, Salar Jung's repeated petitions for the restoration of Berar had greatly soured relations between him and the paramount power. What had been allowed, and even supported earlier, was now suspect. In 1875, Saunders voiced his concern to the Government of India about the great proliferation of these troops, which he said had swelled to more than double the number authorized in 1862.

In August 1875, Saunders sent a confidential note to Salar Jung, inquiring about the regular troops and the state's arsenal. He was questioned about the source of the guns and ammunition. Saunders also wanted him to provide a break-up of arms supplied by the British and those manufactured in the local workshops. Salar Jung, in his reply, said that the guns had been obtained from the Secunderabad arsenal; and since the supply of old muskets of the Contingent had been stopped many years ago, old ones had been refurbished. Some new ones which had been made by hand were also being used by both the troops and the police.

Meade suggested that this was Salar Jung's way of adding weight to his demand for the restoration of Berar. Salar Jung responded by telling Meade that the facts had been known to all the successive residents, and from Davidson's time, the troops had been given the hand-me-downs of the Contingent and new guns manufactured by the Gunfoundry, Hyderabad. It was the political officers who appeared to be far more agitated about these troops than the military, and Salar Jung believed that this was only one more way of harassing him. An inspection of the weapons by the British military officers had revealed that most of these weapons were in such poor condition that they were considered more hazardous to the user than to the enemy. They also believed that there was no real depth to the reorganization of the army, and therefore it was not much of a threat. 'The Indian Government had long played a kind of catch-22 with the Minister:

if he left the Arabs with their own chiefs, the British complained about their lawlessness, whereas if he brought them under control they complained that he was forming an army loyal to himself.'[9]

In mid-1876, Salisbury had voiced his concern to Lytton about curbing the military power of Hyderabad. Although Northbrook was aware of the situation, he did little to counter it during his viceroyalty. It again fell to Lytton's lot to rein Salar Jung in. There were alarming reports of the manufacture of breech-loading rifles in the state. Lytton also referred to the large number of private troops, reportedly 60,000, maintained by the nobles. If the regular troops were being used as an excuse for training and equipping these irregular troops, then the nizam would be in 'possession of a tolerably powerful army'. The panicky Lytton even wrote to the queen. 'Salar Jung keeps a large arsenal for the manufacture of all kinds of arms, quite out of all proportion to the legitimate wants of a state protected by British troops.'[10]

In 1876, the Government of India ordered that while the troops could be maintained at the current level, there was to be no addition to their strength. Furthermore, no European was to be employed without the permission of the government. Any improvement in armaments and measures for the manufacture of arms and ammunition could only be undertaken with the specific permission of the government. The resident was also empowered to order the inspection of any factories where arms were manufactured.

When these orders were communicated to Salar Jung, he received their import without comment or the slightest display of annoyance or disappointment. It was as if he knew what was coming beforehand, and accepted the news with passive indifference. He was still hoping for the restoration of Berar and preferred to avoid another flashpoint. As for Rashid-ud-din, he had been active in poisoning the ears of the resident, telling him that Salar Jung's ultimate aim in this military reorganization was the restoration of Berar. Meade required little convincing since he too had long viewed the entire exercise as one which had the potential to menace British supremacy in India.

BANSI RAJA'S ARMS FACTORY

In 1868, Bansi Raja started an ammunition factory in Hyderabad. He wrote in his book, *Kalam-i-Mutafarikhat*, that it was on the prompting of Salar

Jung that he had started this and many other factories. As the relations between Salar Jung and the British deteriorated, this factory attracted the attention of the paramount power. On 1 August 1876, Salisbury sent Lytton a telegram in which he said that he had received information about a munition factory in Hyderabad under a Scotsman called Graham, and he wanted him to ascertain the truth about it. Meade was asked to report expeditiously on the matter. The fact that many telegrams were exchanged on the subject between the foreign secretary and the resident is indicative of the great alarm Bansi Raja's factory had caused.

In an interim report telegraphed to Simla, Meade said that Colonel H. Cadell, officiating inspector general of ordnance in Madras, had reported this matter officially and had wanted to inspect the factory but failed to obtain access to it. Another British officer who had wanted to see the arsenal, but could not, had written that the manufacture of breech-loaders had begun in the city for arming the Reformed Troops, and this would demand corresponding action because 'our Native Troops are armed with the Enfield'.[11] He also suspected that Salar Jung had a major role to play in establishing the factory. On receiving Meade's telegram dated 7 August 1876, the Foreign Office scoured its files for any previous report on the subject. It was discovered that the matter had been mentioned in a confidential report from Hyderabad in 1875: 'Muskets, and, it is believed, rifles can now be manufactured at Hyderabad as well as gunpowder and ammunition. Excellent swords and lances can also be turned out by numerous artificers in the service of the Government and private persons.'[12]

Meade asked Major Euan Smith, first assistant resident, to inspect Bansi Raja's factory, and on 9 August 1876, Major Smith, accompanied by Captain Wynter, visited the arms factory situated in the heart of the city. He was received by Bansi Raja whom he described as 'a most talkative and courteous kayastha Hindu who showed the most willingness to show me everything that there was to be seen'.[13]

According to Smith, the facility employed about 500–600 persons, and there were two sheds in which production took place. He reported that since everything was made manually, the arms turned out were very rough in appearance. Bansi Raja told him that at full capacity, they could manufacture five muskets a day, but Smith though that the correct estimate was closer to twice that number. An old and highly skilled artificer, originally from Jaipur, was also capable of making a Martini-Henry rifle, one of which was shown to Smith, who observed later that though at first glance it 'would pass muster anywhere', a closer examination would reveal that it had not been made by European workers.

Smith also reported that he saw no signs whatsoever of any equipment for the casting of guns, but Bansi Raja had told him with disarming candidness that there would be no difficulty in casting any number of guns. The Scotsman Graham's role was confined to inspecting the muskets on behalf of the government, something which he did on a weekly basis. Bansi Raja, in what must certainly be considered prevarication, told Smith that he had received no support from anyone in the government to set up the factory. He said that he was treated only as a contractor by the government. The contracted price for the muskets with sword, bayonet and scabbard was 44 hali sicca rupees, and his profit per item was in the range of Rs 12 to 15 hali sicca rupees. It is obvious that Bansi Raja was keen to hide the trail which led all the way to Salar Jung.

Major Smith further observed:

Bansi Raja has a monopoly of almost all the supplies for the army including the Reformed Troops and the Police. He supplies all their accoutrements, and has a large buff and leather manufactory in another part of the city. He supplies grass and grain to the cavalry. He has the monopoly of supplying powder and ammunition and is also employed in many offices about the Nizam's palace, and has the monopoly of supplying itr and pan at the Darbars and is always present at the palace on the occasion of the visit of the Resident.[14]

Meade forwarded Smith's report to the Government of India with his own remarks. He said that he would 'not be inclined to pass its existence over as a matter of no importance'. He said that the inspection had been cursory and unprofessional, and things which would have been suggestive to an ordnance officer may have escaped observation. Later, Meade deputed his military secretary, Col. Fraser, to inspect the two military workshops said to be active in the city. In the workshop of Bansi Raja, he found a steam engine adapted for the manufacture of rifles, but it had yet to be used. The introduction of steam machinery in workshops had been specifically prohibited by the Government of India in November 1876.

At the other factory under Moulvi Mahmud, he found a small engine at work and a breech-loading ordnance which was only a model. If some breech-loading rifles had been made, they must have been made by hand.

Salisbury was somewhat relieved but wanted a close watch to be kept since it was no trifling matter. He was clear that native princes must not be allowed to manufacture arms of precision. As for the size of the troops, he wanted the limits to be defined precisely and adhered to.

When Meade asked Salar Jung to explain the moulvi's activities, the latter denied that the moulvi had been made all-powerful. He said that the moulvi had been appointed as a judge of a court for the settlement of disputes when the Arab and Rohilla regiments were set up, as it had been decided to control the abuses of the Arab chiefs regarding the disbursing of salaries. His powers were later extended to allow him to institute an inquiry into any matter concerning the whole of the troops, except the sarf-i-khas, the Jamiat-i-Nizam-i-Mahbub and the regular troops.

Salar Jung believed that the transfer of men from their own chiefs to officers in the nizam's service was a good thing since it brought them directly under his control. Meade, while admitting this, was worried about the enormous increase in Salar Jung's power. The resident had also been told that at two parades, Moulvi Mahmud had exhorted the troops and officers to achieve greater efficiency, and more importantly, had made inflammatory references about the assigning of Berar. Salar Jung denied this, saying that the parades were mere roll-calls.

When Meade questioned Salar Jung about the arms factories, the latter denied having any knowledge about them. This barefaced lie shows that Salar Jung now no longer believed that the British deserved the gentlemanly treatment he had been giving them. Meade made it amply clear to Salar Jung that he would not allow the taking up of any military measures without the sanction of the government. Moulvi Mahmud's overenthusiasm also elicited comment, and at Salar Jung's behest, a meeting was held on 13 August 1877 to discuss these issues. Salar Jung was told that he was not at liberty to establish an arsenal without the permission of the government, and that he should curb the moulvi, who appeared to have gone beyond his instructions in several matters.

It is not difficult to understand what Salar Jung was trying to do. He wanted to build a disciplined armed force under his control as a counter to other centres of power such as the Paigahs and the Arabs. The desire for administrative reform was, in all probability, secondary. Given that the restoration of Berar was at the top of his agenda throughout his life, it was Salar Jung's desire to have an efficient and effective force to maintain order in the state, thereby obviating the need to maintain the Hyderabad

Contingent. The British, who had realized what Salar Jung was up to, were naturally very uncomfortable with his actions: they were never going to let one man become too powerful. As for Berar, it was obvious to all except Salar Jung that they had no intention of restoring it.

Lytton set up a committee, the Native States' Armament Committee, to shape the Government of India's policies towards the armies of the Indian states in general. The seven-member committee, which submitted its report in October 1877, questioned the need for permitting the states to maintain military establishments which were in excess of their internal needs, since the excess would always be a source of anxiety. The committee was strongly against giving arms of precision to the states. It was also opposed to the employment of Europeans in a military capacity.

As far as Hyderabad was concerned, it felt that the Reformed Troops were far in excess of what was required, considering that the state was protected by the Subsidiary Force and the Hyderabad Contingent. It suggested that the Reformed Troops and the reorganized city regiments be disbanded and the irregular levies reduced. The arsenal could remain, provided it was inspected from time to time. No arms of precision were to be manufactured there. It was the closure of Bansi Raja's workshop which seems to have hurt Salar Jung the most. He expressed his resentment at the disloyalty of the Hyderabadis who had reported the matter to the residency officials.

Lytton accepted the report, and Meade, with great alacrity, demanded limitation of the strength of the troops and reduction in the irregular levies. The former was to be restricted to 240 men in the artillery, 1000 in the cavalry and 2000 in the infantry. The number in the reorganized city regiments was to be limited to 2000. Tired of resistance at every stage, and on every issue, Salar Jung accepted the order, knowing that there was little headway he could make against the combine of a ruthless Meade and the hostile viceroy.

When war against Sher Ali, the Amir of Kabul, was imminent in November 1878,[15] Salar Jung, in a letter to Meade, offered all help to the British in this military venture. Undoubtedly, the aid volunteered was more of a moral than material nature, but the very fact that Hyderabad, the chief of the Muslim states, had made common cause with the British on this issue, would carry 'considerable weight in St Petersburg and Constantinople' and have a 'tranquilizing effect on the feelings of the great body of Indian Mussalmans'.[16] What added to the importance of Salar Jung's declaration of goodwill was the fact that now he had no hesitation in speaking of the British government as the 'Paramount Power,' something he had found so objectionable two years ago. The *Bombay Gazette* remarked that Salar Jung 'now appears to have forgotten his old grudges, and to be eager to seize an opportunity of showing how loyal he has always been at heart'.[17] It summed up the feelings of the British to the regular troops most pithily when it noted that Salar Jung had created an army which, while useless for active service, could not be left unwatched by the Government of India since it could work great mischief in troubled times. It added, 'In fact, the best proof of his sincerity Sir Salar Jung could give in offering to assist the Paramount Power would be to disband these ragamuffins.'[18]

HYDERABAD'S INFLUENCE IN SOUTH ARABIA

The British fear of a revival of Muslim power was a source of constant discomfort to them. Another issue on which Meade thought Salar Jung had not cooperated was in preventing Hyderabadi influence in the Hadhramaut region of South Arabia.

We have already noted in a previous chapter the sizeable Arab presence in Hyderabad. The Hadhrami diaspora was linked to India via family ties, trade and politics. British Indian subjects of Arab Hadhrami origin had family and property in this area of the Arabian Peninsula. This connection offered Britain a justification to intervene in the region: they were protecting the interests of their Arab Muslim subjects. In 1869, the opening of the Suez Canal strengthened British control over commerce in the Persian Gulf region. It now wanted to control not just the Gulf but also the entire rim of the Arabian Peninsula. British interest in the south-west rim of the Arabian Peninsula brought it in direct contact with the Arab traffic across Asia.

The British Muslim subjects became the chief agents via whom British imperial rivalries were played out. Ever since the British had gained control of Aden harbour in 1829 and created a post of resident there, the relatively weak Ottoman political sovereignty in these areas was dented. In fact, it was the issue of Ottoman political sovereignty that had brought Britain into the region. As imperial contestations over the Persian Gulf ports intensified, Britain turned its attention to the south-west rim of the Arabian Peninsula, hoping to tame the ambitions of Russia, Germany and France as it secured treaties with the smaller emirates in the area. The administrative ambit of the Bombay government was extended to cover the Gulf so as to oversee and protect British interest in the region. The political agent at Aden now also monitored tribal activities in Muscat, Yemen and the Arabian Peninsula.

Saunders, in his political report for the year 1872, had outlined the activities which had enabled the Arabs in Hyderabad to grow rich, often through underhand means. 'They roll property, lend money at enormous rates of interest, and indulge in all kinds of petty and illicit traffic with the result of growing rich and respectable fast.'[19] As we have seen, the nizam's government was often a debtor, and many influential Arabs had risen high in the nizam's service, chiefs like Ghalib Jung, Mukaddam Jung, Barak Jung and his half-brother, Al Bin Umar, serving as good examples. Several of the army commanders were Arabs from Arabia, and some were, in fact, from the families of the ruling chiefs in Hadhramaut. Salar Jung himself had a body of Arab infantry in his service who were stationed some 24 miles from Hyderabad and kept separate from the regular army. It was this power and influence which prevented summary deportation of the Arabs, since both the resident and the diwan were tired of the plunder by roving groups of Arabs.

In 1872, special identity passes were issued to Arabs in Hyderabad. To control the hitherto unrestricted entry of Arab immigrants, the permission of the Hyderabad government conveyed through the resident as well as the sanction of the political agent in Aden became necessary for travel to India. These provisions, however, merely remained on paper. In practice, not a single Arab ever applied for a passport via this method. The introduction of the new railway also made illegal Arab immigration easier. In any case, there was little support for such regulations from the nizam, who saw the Arabs as an integral part of Deccani society, recognizing their special status in the political economy of Hyderabad.[20]

The Indian Arabs were gradually drawn into the factional politics and wars in their homeland. Arms, money and supplies were being sent from Hyderabad by the Indian Arabs to fight factional wars in south-west Arabia, particularly in Mukalla and Shehr in the Hadhramaut area. Mukalla and Shehr were two important port cities in south-west Arabia bordering Yemen in the Dhofar area. They were important depots for the lucrative slave trade, and Mukalla was also important as a coal depot. Therefore, these cities were important, both from the Ottoman and the British points of view. Indian Arabs with political ambitions sought to exploit these rivalries and establish themselves in positions of power.

Among the nizam's Arab commanders was the mowullud Barak Jung who hailed from a place called Shibam. Shibam was connected to the sea via Shehr which had fallen into the hands of Sultan Ghalib-bin-Mohsin who belonged to the Kathiri tribe. The deposed *nakeeb* of Shehr, Ali Najee, had friendly relations with Barak Jung's family which was now headed by Hakeem Abdulla-bin-Umar, his elder brother. There was also a third brother, Awadh-bin-Umar, better known as Sultan Nawaz Jung, whose career and ambition are central to this discussion. Shehr's occupation by Ghalib-bin-Mohsin deprived Shibam of access to the sea. It was thought that the other point of access to the sea, namely the port of Mukalla, was also likely to fall into his hands. This would deprive Barak Jung's family of its customary intercourse with India which had continued for generations. It was therefore decided that his brother, Nawaz Jung, would take a party of 200 armed Rohillas to aid the rightful nakeeb of Shehr.[21]

In 1866, Salar Jung forwarded a request from Barak Jung to the resident, Sir George Yule, in which the former wanted the Government of Bombay to supply arms on payment to his family, and sought the government's intervention in the reinstatement of the nakeeb of Shehr. Salar Jung, while forwarding the letter to the resident, adverted to the long service of Barak Jung's family to the nizam's government but stopped short of recommending the case. He wanted the Bombay government's decision to be based on its own judgement. Nawaz Jung, armed with an introduction from Yule, met the governor of Bombay who declined to equip the Arabs with weapons or stores but referred him to the commissioner of customs who was authorized to permit the export of military stores after submitting each individual case to the government for orders.[22]

Nawaz Jung had ambitions of ruling Shehr and had cast his eyes on Mukalla as well. The British wanted to have the sole right of controlling Nawaz Jung's activities; it did not suit their imperial purpose to have his brother, Barak Jung, or the nizam interfere in the war at Shehr. Nawaz Jung meanwhile continued to maintain his Hyderabad links, occupying a position in the Arab force there. He depended on monetary support from Indian Arabs to pursue his ambition of becoming the ruler of Shehr and then expanding his sphere of influence to Mukalla as well.

By the end of 1874, Nawaz Jung was well ensconced as the jemadar of Shehr. Saunders reported that he and his brother had been using their wealth and influence derived by association with the nizam for the purpose of territorial expansion. The resident at Aden sent a report in which he wrote that forty Rohillas had left for Shehr under the garb of pilgrims. It was also stated that a steamer and a brig had been acquired by the Hyderabadis to be sent to Shehr for use against the nakeeb of Mukalla. Saunders expressed his concern at these happenings, and wrote to Salar Jung in 1874 asking him to inquire into the departure of the Rohillas and the acquisition of the vessels, and to fix responsibility for these acts. He expressed dissatisfaction at the factional feud between Barak Jung and Mukaddam Jung, and wanted Salar Jung to ensure that the money and influence acquired by the parties concerned under the protection of the nizam should not be used for private wars and disturbing the balance of established power in Arabia. He also told him that he was aware that the steamer was carrying arms and not engaged in peaceful trade as had been made out earlier.[23]

It was known to all that it was Hyderabad's financial muscle which was keeping the conflict alive. In March 1875, it became known to the resident at Aden, General Schneider, that the two chiefs, the jemadar of Shehr and the nakeeb of Mukalla, had blockaded each other's ports. Schneider despatched his assistant, Captain Prideaux, to both ports, and he discovered that neither chief was able to effectively blockade the port of the other. The resident at Aden said he feared that Shehr would soon triumph over Mukalla, and the result would be a powerful Muslim chief allied with the nizam, understandably a most undesirable state of affairs. Northbrook gave instructions to Schneider that while both warring parties were to be called to account for all acts prejudicial to British interests, the British would not interfere in the marine warfare between the two.

The British were upset that Nawaz Jung had the temerity to become an independent ruler outside British territory and retain his rights in India as well, maintaining family ties and managing property. Seema Alavi has observed: 'British notions of territorial-framed subjecthood and neat ethnic categorizations had no space for such extraterritorial forays of subject people . . . Indeed, the porous borders and the fluid and well-knit political economies of the premodern world encouraged multiple identities. While this seemed natural to Indian Arabs it was unacceptable to the British government.'[24] Initially the British pressurized Salar Jung, asking him to ensure that Barak Jung sever all ties with Hyderabad. Salar Jung deflated some of that pressure by saying that Barak Jung knew nothing of the political ambitions of his brother, and he was merely residing in Shehr with his elder brother, Abdulla, who was chief there. While the nizam refused to take action against Barak Jung, he did, under British pressure, agree to remove Nawaz Jung from the rolls of the Arab force in Hyderabad.

Barak Jung was asked to stop encouraging his brother's political ambitions and to provide any related information to the nizam. Barak Jung, for his part, refuted all charges against his brother, especially the one relating to monetary assistance from Hyderabad. He, in fact, blamed the aggression of the chief of Mukalla for the unrest. The British resident promised not to interfere in the region but at the same time offered to mediate. Barak Jung, however, always viewed the nizam and his government as central to the resolution of the dispute, thinking that his personal status would rise if the nizam was involved. But the nizam refused to oblige and ordered that Nawaz Jung be removed from the official roll of the military, and asked Barak Jung to sever all connections with him, in keeping with the orders of the British government.[25]

Nawaz Jung was not going to give up so easily though. Backed by his brother in Hyderabad, he tried to buy time with the resident at Aden, seeking permission to visit Hyderabad to wind up his affairs and bring his family back to Shehr. He said that all he wanted was to profit from his gains in the war against Mukalla, and he was in no way opposed to the British. Meade, who feared the political ramifications of Indian Arabs becoming political chiefs in Arabia, remained unconvinced. He made it plain to Salar Jung that Barak Jung could not enjoy the best of both worlds: if he wanted to retain his influence in Arabia, he should withdraw from his position in Hyderabad. He was also told that only the British resident at Aden was to be used as a mediator, and that the Hyderabad government could not intermediate in the dispute. Barak Jung was very keen to involve Hyderabad in the resolution of the dispute and wanted the Hyderabad resident to mediate. He suggested that Nawaz Jung visit Hyderabad to explain his actions.[26]

However, despite the demands for Nawaz Jung to relinquish his official position in Hyderabad and unhappiness at his challenging their political sovereignty, the British were happy to use him to challenge Ottoman political sovereignty in the region. It was believed that Ottoman expansion in the southern rim of Arabia could be controlled by propping up independent Arab chiefs like Nawaz Jung who was seen as a potential ally. The latter was aware of this political agenda and played along as long as it suited his purpose. The British offered him assistance in his local battles for supremacy in Shehr. However, it was Nawaz Jung's invasion of Mukalla that triggered British intervention in his affairs.[27]

Salar Jung, who was caught in a balancing act, evaded questions inquiring about the aid given to Nawaz Jung. There is no doubt that he did try to help the interests of Barak Jung's family in Arabia. It is also probable that he wanted to divert the attention of some of the refractory elements of the state by allowing them an outlet for their pugnacity in Arabia, while adding to the anxiety of the British. However, it is unlikely that he was attempting to set up a sphere of influence there. Relations with the British were still quite cordial at the time (1874–75), and he scrupulously observed all the formalities of sending these matters to the resident. Meade's accusations that he had acted at variance with the views of the Government of India, and that he would have had a commanding position in Arabia had the British not intervened, appear a little extreme.[28]

15

A Fait Accompli

It was when the subject of the Reformed Troops was generating much heat over a period of many months that Salar Jung's co-regent, Rafi-ud-din Khan Amir-i-Kabir II, died on 6 April 1877. It was to be both a personal and official loss for Salar Jung. It was also just the chance Lytton had been waiting for to cut Salar Jung down to size. Although the amir's presence had been a nominal one, and his role in matters of policy and practical government had been negligible, Salar Jung had found it difficult to ignore him completely. His had been a voice of support, and at times, of caution, and although they had not always agreed, Salar Jung respected him and valued their relationship. His mere presence provided that fine balance which prevented Salar Jung from assuming the position of sole ruler of Hyderabad.

A question which had occurred to both Salar Jung and the resident was what would happen when the amir was no longer there. Meade had made inquiries about the arrangements for administering the state should anything happen to the Amir-i-Kabir or the nizam during Salar Jung's visit to the Continent. In February 1876, Salar Jung wrote to Meade that since the amir took no active part in the executive work of the administration which was carried out by himself and his nephew, Mukaram-ud-Daula, in consultation with Bashir-ud-Daula, if anything happened to the amir, it would not interfere with the administration of the country, and it 'could be carried on as hitherto by the two gentlemen I have mentioned'.[1]

On the death of his colleague, Salar Jung proposed to the British that he be made sole regent. He would run the administration with the advice and assistance of the resident. Even though it appeared that Salar Jung wanted to assume supreme power, it was a perfectly logical decision since the late Amir-i-Kabir had never concerned himself with day-today administration; no one doubted that Salar Jung could man the shop himself. The peshkar, Maharaja Narayan Pershad Narender Bahadur, lacked administrative experience, and Rashid-ud-din Khan Vikar-ul-Umra, the younger brother of the late co-regent, was Salar Jung's sworn enemy. Also, a new colleague would mean restriction of power and even a lack of cooperation in the important reforms which Salar Jung was proposing.

The British did not see it that way. Indeed, it was naive of Salar Jung to believe that the British would agree to put him in sole charge after all that had transpired in the past few months. As far back as 1874, long before the unpleasantness with Lytton, the Government of India had made up its mind that Salar Jung was not to be trusted since his aims were incompatible with those of the Government of India. By 1877, Salar Jung had given enough 'trouble' to the British, and it was natural that they would vehemently oppose any plan of making him the sole regent or encourage his belief that he could dictate his decisions to the government. As for Lytton, the prospect of appointing this 'slippery customer' as sole regent was unthinkable.

A series of memoranda exchanged between Hyderabad and Calcutta emphasized the undesirability of giving sole power to Salar Jung because of his disinclination to recognize 'the true position of the British Government, and the objectionable means adopted by him for obtaining political influence in England, also to the fact that he has no large following in Hyderabad save amongst the officials (chiefly foreigners) he has appointed'.[2]

AN ENEMY FOR A COLLEAGUE

Lytton's plan was to support Rashid-ud-din Khan for the co-regency. Rashid-ud-din would obey the British out of gratitude for their support, and more importantly, would be a permanent thorn in Salar Jung's flesh. Rashid-ud-din had lived in the shadow of his elder brother who had inherited the titles and the power. Unlike his elder brother who was born of a princess, he was the offspring of a commoner. In Hyderabad such things made a difference. He was also the younger sibling. Even though it was rumoured that he was his father's favourite, Rashid-ud-din laboured under these twin disabilities, and it was no surprise that he lusted after power all his life.

Rashid-ud-din's unsavoury past was common knowledge. Davidson had reported that common rumour attributed the instigation of the attack on the residency during the Mutiny to Rashid-ud-din. The moulvi who led the attack on the residency was a friend of Rashid-ud-din. When an attempt was made on the lives of Salar Jung and the resident two years later, the assassin, Jehangir Khan, was identified as Rashid-ud-din's son's standard-bearer. Davidson described Rashid-ud-din as 'that most pernicious and factious intriguer . . . who seemed to care little what occurred if he was able to thwart Mookhtar-ool-Mulk Salar Jung'. Yule had described him as 'able but incorrigibly corrupt', and Temple had suspected that he was responsible for stirring up trouble between the British and the Hyderabadis.

After the Murray affair, this 'notorious and dangerous intriguer of Hyderabad' was banned from the residency and found himself a political pariah. For this disgrace, he blamed Salar Jung; and even during the period of the ban, he held him responsible for not doing enough to get it lifted. This was not true, for it was not in Salar Jung's power to lift the ban; he could at best advocate its removal, and this he did. In 1867, when Temple had just taken over as resident, Salar Jung spoke to him about Rashid-ud-din's request, and on receiving his agreement, sounded the nizam about it. The nizam said that he would think about it and send a reply a week later. When none came, Salar Jung made another attempt, saying that Rashid-ud-din had been sufficiently punished. The nizam promised to reply in a few days' time, but he never did.

When Rashid-ud-din raised the matter with the nizam again, the enraged sovereign accused him of conspiring with Salar Jung against him. Again, he refused to give a clear answer. Nor was it ever forthcoming since he passed away in February 1869. This assumes significance since it was only after Afzal-ud-Daula's death in 1869 that Rashid-ud-din asserted that the Murray scheme had originated from the nizam and he had agreed to take responsibility for it. The British believed this version in 1877 since it now suited them in their efforts to thwart Salar Jung. In fact, Rashid-ud-din's hostility to Salar Jung was one of his chief recommendations for a post he was intellectually and morally unsuitable to occupy, the high position being foisted on him by Lytton's animosity towards Salar Jung.

The British were well aware of the continual jockeying for power that went on between Salar Jung and the Paigah nobles. The rivalry was inherent in the social system of Hyderabad, and it was only his official position that enabled Salar Jung to take precedence over a Paigah nobleman. Precedence was all-important in society, and it was something which was jealously guarded: Hyderabad etiquette demanded a show of cordiality, but hostility and intrigue lay just beneath the surface.

After the nizam's death, Rashid-ud-din had petitioned Saunders, the resident, for the lifting of the ban, or at least its temporary suspension, so that he could witness the installation of the child nizam to the masnad. Saunders sought permission from Calcutta, indicating that Salar Jung also supported the removal of the ban. It was finally granted. Rashid-ud-din even had the gall to immediately propose himself as a member of the administration, a suggestion which was summarily rejected by the resident.

But Rashid-ud-din's shady past had not prevented Saunders from cultivating him with the idea of neutralizing Salar Jung. Given his restless ambition and personal disgrace, Rashid-ud-din was longing to be recalled to public life, and Saunders saw in this a great opportunity. It was something Salar Jung also realized, since he told Col. Thornhill that Saunders's aim had been 'to threaten me by assuming intimacy with this nobleman'.[3] The British at first banned Rashid-ud-din. Later, they excused his actions in the bribery case by believing his story that he had been a mere cat's paw, a shield for the nizam. They then used him repeatedly after 1877 for the discomfiture of Salar Jung.

Rashid-ud-din, for his part, had realized that the future belonged to the British and tried his best to ensure that his sons learnt their ways. He converted a part of the mardana of his home to Western style and later hired an English tutor for his sons, Khurshed Jah and Fazal-ud-din Khan Vikar-ul-Umra II. When the ban was lifted, he had no intention of being found wanting. The youths were dressed in European clothes and were taught to eat at a table with crockery and cutlery. Special kitchens were built and Goanese cooks employed to prepare the bland cuisine for which the young men were supposed to cultivate a taste.

Rashid-ud-din himself refused to change, being too old and too set in his ways. He had even refused to accept a knighthood, contemptuous of the notion that anyone other than the nizam could either ennoble or demean him.[4] (The apogee of this European embrace can be seen in Falaknuma Palace built by Vikar-ul-Umra II, and Erram Manzil built by Fakhr-ul-Mulk II. It is said that the situation reached a stage where a nobleman's son who grew up in England, on his return, greeted his father by shaking hands with him!)

Meade, aware of Salar Jung's resistance to working with Rashid-ud-din, had in his letter of 28 May 1877 proposed Salar Jung as sole regent.

He was no friend of Salar Jung but realized that if the diwan resigned consequent to Rashid-ud-din's nomination, it would be unfortunate for Hyderabad, to say nothing of the howl of protests in the press and potential trouble at home. But Lytton would have none of it. He got Meade to alter his letter and recommend the Vikar-ul-Umra's nomination. In his thinking, if Salar Jung resigned, they would be rid of a redoubtable foe. If not, Salar Jung would find his powers restricted by his colleague who had been put there to frustrate him.

The British metanoia on Rashid-ud-din is not difficult to understand. Lytton was hoping that Rashid-ud-din's appointment would provoke Salar Jung's resignation. He felt it would be a 'Godsend' if he voluntarily resigned. The viceroy knew that he could not dismiss Salar Jung without proof of his misconduct. He had scrutinized Salar Jung's letters to Rashid-ud-din and to Scindia on the subject of Berar and the queen's suzerainty but could find nothing incriminating. Scindia denied receiving any communication from Salar Jung, and Rashid-ud-din could not produce any convincing evidence. Lytton fervently hoped that Salar Jung would oblige with a voluntary resignation. The timing was also just right. Parliament was not in session, and Salar Jung's friends in England would be unable to help him. Salisbury also wanted to see Salar Jung's back but wanted Rashid-ud-din's appointment to be handled with 'utmost civility' and 'expressions of goodwill' towards Salar Jung. He did not want Salar Jung's admirers to allege that the diwan had been insulted into resigning.

But Salar Jung did not budge. He refused to accept Rashid-ud-din as his colleague. Nor did he resign. Meanwhile, relations between Meade and Salar Jung had deteriorated to the extent that the resident had demanded to see the notes Salar Jung had sent to his friends on the events at Delhi during the durbar to check if they were correct, since he did not consider the minister capable of making an accurate note of conversations. As Harriet Ronken Lynton observes: 'To say to a man of Salar Jung's standing that he was not trusted to make an accurate report, and to put it in terms of his not being competent to understand enough English for the purpose, was to offer a double insult, totally gratuitous, and to violate everything Salar Jung believed about the way gentleman treated one another.'[5]

In the end, the Government of India communicated to Meade their decision to force Rashid-ud-din on Salar Jung.

By that arrangement [1869] the present Minister—a distinguished member of the official class—was associated in the Government with the head of the nobility [Amir-i-Kabir], who was also connected by descent and marriage with the ruling family; thus, in the persons of the Co-Administrators, the three principal interests of Hyderabad—the dynastic, the departmental, and the landed—were duly represented.[6]

Two important changes in the language used above need to be noted. First, Salar Jung was no longer co-regent but was now a co-administrator, a change which was made at Meade's suggestion. Second, Salar Jung, who hitherto had always been referred to as a 'nobleman', was now demoted to a mere 'official' in government terminology. When Lord Hartington, the Secretary of State, was replying to a question in 1881 on the appointment of the co-regent, he said that 'it was decided to associate with the regent, who was a very distinguished representative of the official classes at Hyderabad, a representative of the Hyderabad nobility'. This was almost the exact language used by Lytton's government to justify their choice of Rashid-ud-din as co-regent. The phrase 'representative of the official classes', as applied to Salar Jung, was intended as a slight and was taken as such by the diwan who was of much nobler descent than the Paigah noble. In fact, Salar Jung's ancestors were nobles when those of Rashid-ud-din were still commoners. The latter's claim to be a premier noble was based on his relationship by marriage with the nizam.

Salar Jung still stubbornly refused to accept his bête noire as his colleague. He told Meade that he had been appointed minister by the grandfather of the present nizam, and to resign his present position of trust was not an option. He was the nizam's minister and not a minister of the Government of India. He would resist the decision of the government which was an insult to him, and he would not be responsible for the consequences. Taken aback at Salar Jung's courage, Meade reminded him that he owed his position as co-regent not to the nizam but to the Government of India whose diktat he was bound to obey. He asked Salar Jung not to create a situation which would imperil the independence of Hyderabad and create a scandal which would ruin himself and his family.

One can sense a new strength in Salar Jung's approach. Gone were the days when he wrote to earlier residents asking for their support. Bharati Ray has observed: 'He now stood proudly on his own strength and his own ability, and asserted spiritedly his position as the guardian of the state during the minority of his master. In this, he was also indirectly asserting the authority and independence of the Nizam whose servant he declared he was. The Nizam's Minister was bound to serve his own master, and not the foreign rulers of India.'[7]

Lytton realized that Salar Jung had now taken the bit between his teeth. Any hesitation now would weaken their position throughout India. He decided to enforce the decision immediately, and with that aim, asked Meade to summon the Hyderabadi noblesnobles, Major Neville, the nizam's commandant, and Captain Gough, the military secretary. Salar Jung was to be asked to accept the order of the government in their presence or else resign. In case he refused to do either, Meade was to request Rashid-ud-din to form a ministry and choose his own colleague. He was also to prevent Salar Jung from seeking the support of influential people, to take the force at Secunderabad into confidence, and strengthen the security at the residency. Salar Jung, unaware of the plot being hatched behind his back, sent two letters to the resident refusing to accept Rashid-ud-din as co-administrator.

On 22 September 1877, Meade had travelled on the railway to meet Lytton at Shahabad. (The viceroy was on his way to Mysore to superintend the famine operations there.) In all probability, the modus operandi on how to deal with Salar Jung's intransigence was decided at this time. Salar Jung's obstinacy seems to have driven Meade into a state of near panic, for he sent a telegram to the viceroy the very next day asking for authority to remove Salar Jung if he refused to yield, and to notify the measure to the nobles of Hyderabad. On the same day, Lytton sent a reply with very precise orders. He asked Meade to proclaim Rashid-ud-din as the co-regent. In case Salar Jung refused to act with him as colleague, he was to immediately announce the appointment of Mukaram-ud-Daula, his nephew, as diwan, if he (Meade) approved of him and if the nephew was willing. In case he refused, then Meade was to make his own recommendation, but in no case was he to delay the announcement of Rashid-ud-Din as co-regent. The communication ended with: 'Be careful to treat Sir Salar Jang with all courtesy and consideration compatible with circumstances. Personal force towards him should be avoided if possible but you should take such precautions, military and other, as you may deem expedient. It is undesirable to inform Sir Salar Jang beforehand what you will do if he resists. In any conversation with him assume that his loyalty and good sense will ensure his obedience.'[8]

On the same day, Meade sent a final letter with his first assistant, Major Euan Smith, asking him to end his fruitless resistance. That same evening, Smith returned with a message from Salar Jung accepting the viceroy's decision. Rashid-ud-din had also visited the residency on the same day, and Meade and he had a long conversation as to the measures required if Salar Jung persisted in his dogged refusal to accept him as a colleague. Meade wrote to Lytton that Rashid-ud-din seemed unsure of himself and was unable to gauge the reactions of the people in case Salar Jung resigned or was removed. He also appeared clueless as to who would fill the vacant post in case it fell vacant.[9]

Notwithstanding the fact that he had finally relented, Salar Jung still dragged his feet when Meade sent him a formal announcement of the appointment with instructions that it should be published in the state gazette and preparations made for a special durbar. Sensing that Salar Jung was disinclined to act, Meade took the initiative. He sent a private letter to Rashid-ud-din and announced the appointment to the nobles. Bypassed, Salar Jung now had no choice but to accept the fait accompli.

Soon after the appointment of Rashid-ud-din Khan, Salar Jung had written to Captain John Clerk on 28 September 1877 informing him of the decision to foist Rashid-ud-din on him, and how, faced with no choice, he had decided to cooperate as far as possible. That Lytton and Meade had terrorized Salar Jung into submission is apparent from the latter part of his letter. 'I am not writing to the Duke nor any of my friends, please inform them of this if you think proper. I find that the Government of India dislikes my writing to my friends in England and the results are exceedingly unpleasant to me, so I am not writing. You will see the difficulties of my position. I suppose I must make the best of what cannot be avoided.'[10]

The limits of Salar Jung's endurance had been reached. The man who had pulled out all the stops in his attempts to recover Berar was now so unsure of himself that he did not even want to inform his friends of the great injustice done to him by the appointment of his enemy as co-administrator. If Lytton had read this letter, he would have realized that his victory was complete. He had succeeded in breaking Salar Jung's spirit, and the tired diwan had lost the will to resist. Resigned to his fate, Salar Jung was now a beaten man and appears to have had no hesitation in admitting as much to his friends.

Lytton's letter to Salisbury on 24 September 1877, just one day after Salar Jung had finally thrown in the towel, is revealing. 'If he resigned, either on the Railway question, or the Berar question, the barking of his English kennel might be rather embarrassing to us; but on the

Regency question, so far as I can yet judge, we stand on impregnable ground, and he is in a thoroughly false position. I have long been convinced . . . the sooner we suppress Salar Jung, the better. He is the most dangerous man in all India; and, like a horse, or a woman that has once turned vicious, thoroughly irreclaimable.'[11]

What caused Salar Jung to finally give in? Salar Jung maintained that although his views were unchanged, he was powerless to resist and considered it his duty to remain by the side of the nizam during his minority. In a letter to John Fleming, almost a year later, on 20 August 1878, Salar Jung explained his action, saying that he resisted till the very last and only gave in when 'the Resident took the extraordinary step of announcing the appointment of the Ameer-i-Kabir and others independent of myself'. He said that further resistance would have been futile since they would have 'set me aside altogether, if I had not given in then or, worse still, made that a pretext for assuming the Government'. Aware that Parliament would have been able to do nothing, he ended by saying, 'For the present I believe it would be wise to keep quiet and let the ill blood and bitterness be laid to rest before taking any fresh step in the matter.'[12]

SALAR JUNG THREATENED?

Salar Jung's version was the only one for a few years after the episode, but in July 1881, Robert Knight's *Statesman* in London published reports of threats that had been made to Salar Jung to get him to fall in line. The English journalist, Robert Knight, was the principal founder and the first editor of the *Times of India*, Bombay, and the *Statesman*, Calcutta. He fought for a press free of government control or intimidation, and was an ardent critic of colonial rule. Knight's dissenting views on current events dispelled the halo of omnipotence associated with the empire, and the papers which he founded strongly criticized the Raj as long as he controlled them.

The newspaper report in the *Statesman* maintained that Salar Jung had been threatened with arrest and deportation to Madras or Bangalore (depending on the version).[13] If this was indeed the case, then a joining of the dots would indicate that this threat was in all probability made by Major Euan Smith on 23 September. This would explain Salar Jung's sudden volte-face on the evening of the same day. Still, any conclusion in this regard must remain in the realm of speculation. What seems certain, however, is that Salar Jung was convinced about the imminence of some action against him which had been conveyed to him either directly or indirectly.

One of the final instructions given by Lytton in his telegram points in this direction: 'It is undesirable to inform Sir Salar Jang beforehand what you will do if he resists.' An oral tradition also corroborates this version of the story. Salar Jung therefore yielded to a necessity he could not control, being unwilling to push resistance to a point which might endanger those very establishments he wished to defend. 'To retrace his steps when further opposition reached a point of no return and presaged a break-down of relations was a technique used by Salar Jung on more than one occasion. This popular version of the episode therefore seems believable.'[14]

The newspapers soon got wind of this juicy titbit and gave it wide publicity. The *Delhi Gazette* wrote about 'The Hyderabad Sensation'.

> Among the most startling revelations that have come to light through Mr Knight's attack on the Co-Regent is the fact that the seizure and imprisonment of Sir Salar Jung was actually contemplated by Lord Lytton's Government! . . . That Sir Salar averted the blow by yielding to the appointment of a Co-Regent is said to have been due to the advice of his personal friends . . . the public has every right to know the causes which led the Government of India even to contemplate the taking of so serious a step as the seizing of the Minister of a friendly Power and imprisoning him in a British fortress.[15]

Almost two weeks later, the *Delhi Gazette* quoted at length from the *Statesman* of London.

> At this very critical conjuncture (about the 22nd September 1877) Sir Richard Meade took a trip by railway to a junction-station about 120 miles from Hyderabad, to pay a flying visit to Lord Lytton, who was on his way to Mysore. On the Resident's return a message was conveyed to Sir Salar Jung—we may be sure by an indirect channel—to the effect that, full powers having now been obtained from the Viceroy, if he again refused to acquiesce in the 'final orders', his arrest and deportation to Madras by a special train on the Nizam's own State Railway would follow . . . We are not, therefore, in a position to give absolute proof of the authenticity or authority of this disgraceful threat, the reality of

which was widely talked of in Hyderabad; but although we do not believe the actual perpetration of the outrage to have been intended, Sir Salar Jung himself undoubtedly believed it.[16]

Salar Jung denied the assertions made in the newspaper article. He informed Meade that he had received no threat, directly or indirectly, from anyone regarding deportation and also authorized the publication of his statement. The Foreign Office lost no time in taking advantage of the permission. The *Bombay Gazette* observed: 'Misfortune makes strange bedfellows, and it must be with a feeling of carefully suppressed satisfaction that Sir Salar Jung finds the Foreign Office of Calcutta covering the Indian newspapers with certificates of character obtained from himself.'[17]

Salar Jung wanted to avoid a durbar, but that was not to be. A special durbar was held on 29 September in Secunderabad at which Meade arrived, accompanied by two generals and some fifty officers. Clearly, he was taking no chances, but the durbar went off smoothly. Salar Jung's defeat was final and his surrender unconditional. Lytton, whose aim had always been the removal of Salar Jung, agreed that this victory had greatly weakened the diwan's position and strengthened that of the resident. Salisbury wrote in congratulatory terms to Lytton, invoking once again an equine simile. 'In such a context there is no question you did right not to yield one inch. It would be as dangerous as yielding to a restive horse.'[18]

One of Salar Jung's correspondents during this period was none other than Lady Salisbury. After thanking her for the pretty piece of English China she had sent him as a souvenir of his visit to England, Salar Jung seems to be confiding in her.

> . . . Your kind letter has come to me at a time when I seem to have more trouble than on any previous occasion—more trouble I must honestly say than has fallen to my lot during the whole of my past career . . . I do not intend troubling you with my troubles and politics, as I have no doubt that you have enough of political trouble in England, but I must candidly tell you that I believe the treatment I have received since my return to India has arisen solely from jealousy of the kindness and attentions I received in England . . . Since the receipt of your letter I have wished so much that England and India were not so far apart, for the feeling often comes over me that I should be quite contented if I could from time to time have little conversations with Lord Salisbury—where one feels that

trust is mutual the thoughts of the heart are so easily communicated and mutual satisfaction is the result.[19]

Salar Jung, no doubt, was being polite in his reference to Lord Salisbury. It would have been a little too naive of him to not know that Salisbury was as much an accomplice in plotting his downfall as were Meade and Lytton.

The new arrangement was a totally unworkable one. The two co-administrators hated each other, and there was no question of any cooperation between them. Meade kept encouraging Rashid-ud-din to take a greater part in the administration, and the latter did not miss any chance to oppose Salar Jung at every turn. This interference naturally dampened his enthusiasm for improving the administration. Sir Steuart Bayley, who succeeded Meade, realized the damage done by his predecessor when he wrote to Ripon on the subject. He said that the double arrangement had more evil consequences than Meade had anticipated, since it had seriously hampered Salar Jung's internal policy and curbed his enthusiasm to introduce new reforms and to complete old ones.[20]

Lytton justified this interference in the internal affairs of Hyderabad by arguing that the treaties with Hyderabad had made the Government of India the supreme protector of the state, and that it was in the exercise of such a power that they had assumed the guardianship of the young nizam. This, however, was not true. No treaty had ever given the guardianship of Hyderabad to the British. If anything, the treaties had debarred them from interfering in the internal administration of the state. It was Lytton who had imposed his will on the state with no pretence to any civility.

16

C'est La Vie

Lytton had forced Salar Jung to accept Rashid-ud-din as co-regent but he wasn't finished with him just yet. He again targeted the minister, this time by asking for the dismissal of his private secretary, Arthur Oliphant. In 1876, Henry Bowen, who had been Salar Jung's private secretary, retired to England, and Salar Jung was faced with the task of finding a suitable candidate to fill that post. His choice fell on Arthur Oliphant, son of his old friend, Col. J. Oliphant. Arthur had already served for several years in Bombay Presidency and was no stranger to India. Even if he did not actively lobby for the post, he seems to have been interested enough to visit Hyderabad to be considered for that position. Salar Jung wrote to his old friend about his son's visit, expressing his happiness at making his acquaintance. He narrated the unpleasantness that occurred between the assistant resident, Major Tweedie, and Arthur when the former wanted to know why Arthur had corresponded with him (Salar Jung) without routing it through the resident.

> Your son of course told him that he was not a Government servant and therefore did not see the necessity of applying for the Resident's sanction to see me, to which Major Tweedie replied that for that reason the necessity was greater for his going through the Resident. You will perceive from this the evident desire of Major T. to cut off all intercourse between me and my European friends and others unless it is done with the sanction of the Residency authorities, a restriction which neither justice nor any antecedents at all warrant, and in justification of which no Treaty or any engagement can be pleaded.[1]

Saunders forwarded Arthur Oliphant's appointment to the viceroy who approved it. He was hired in May 1876 and joined Salar Jung in Naples en route to England. Almost immediately, he came into conflict with Captain G.H. Trevor, who it will be recalled had been included as a last-minute addition to the party on Sir Richard Meade's insistence. On being joined by his own private secretary, Salar Jung used him in preference to Captain Trevor, and this was resented by the assistant resident. It was not Arthur Oliphant's fault, but the fact remains that once again, he found himself at the receiving end of a residency officer's antagonism. Trevor was not slow in communicating his feelings to Meade, and this served only to harden the resident's attitude towards Salar Jung on his return from England and during the Delhi durbar. In any case, Lytton was convinced that the employment of Europeans by native states was 'purely mischievous in its effects' and decided to reduce the large number employed by Salar Jung, of which Arthur Oliphant was the most visible example.[2]

L'AFFAIRE OLIPHANT

In the autumn of 1877, the government moved for the dismissal of Arthur Oliphant from his post. Oliphant was accused of encouraging Salar Jung to secure English influences for support against the Government of India. It was alleged that he had written the applications for the restoration of Berar, and was also the channel for transmitting Salar Jung's grievances against the resident and the Government of India to England. Meade had warned him about his activities but Oliphant felt that he was only being true to his employer. The resident felt that European officials dabbling in political questions violated the implied condition in which their employment was sanctioned.

The Government of India brought a number of charges against him. These included the fact that he knew about the Berar application of December 1876 and had, in fact, written the letter Salar Jung sent the resident. He had also failed to persuade Salar Jung to bow to the resident's influence. Other charges accused him of explaining to Salar Jung that 'suzerain' meant 'sovereign' but failing to persuade him to acknowledge the queen as the nizam's suzerain. He was also supposedly guilty of encouraging and assisting his employer in resisting the appointment of Rashid-ud-din Khan as co-administrator.[3] All in all, it was generally held that he had been instrumental in prolonging controversies which had been very embarrassing to the British government.

The assistant resident, Major Euan Smith, wrote disparagingly to Meade that Sir Salar Jung used to be satisfied with a Eurasian but now he wanted an English secretary who could influence matters in which he differed with the Government of India. Meade echoed a somewhat similar view when he said that with Oliphant as his secretary, Salar Jung was under the impression that he could bring his grievances directly to the secretary of state, bypassing the resident. Smith, in his letter, listed some of Oliphant's crimes of omission and commission. He was accused of corresponding with persons in England to put pressure on the Government of India; Salar Jung, it was said, was so much under his private secretary's influence that it was affecting the good relations between Hyderabad and the government. Smith also claimed that Oliphant was much hated by the native officers since he was trying to control everything, and he had come to India with political ambitions.

All these charges were made with the intention of proving that Salar Jung was attempting to circumvent the viceroy's office. But there is a considerable difference between fact and inference, a distinction which became blurred during Meade's time where motives were imputed with a dangerous freedom and without any corroborating facts. Earlier residents had taken care to document what they reported, but Meade supported his charges with newspaper articles or vague statements averring that something was the opinion of 'all classes' in Hyderabad.

Apart from a few Paigahs, Meade had no contact with any of the other nobles of Hyderabad, but this did not prevent him from 'professing to converse with a broad spectrum of the court'. Meade even went to the extent of compiling a list of all the complaints the British government had against Salar Jung for the past twenty years, interpreted them in his own way, and called his list, 'Note illustrative of the various occasions on which His Excellency the Minister Sir Salar Jung has acted at variance with the views and opinions held by the Government of India.'

Regardless of the merits of the case, the sanction of the government for the employment of Arthur Oliphant was withdrawn, and the decision was conveyed verbally to the co-administrators by Meade. Salar Jung, while accepting full responsibility for his secretary's activities, asked the government to reconsider its decision. Meade firmly said that the decision was final and admitted of no discussion. His co-administrator, only too pleased to show his old adversary down, and revelling in Salar Jung's discomfiture, immediately stated that the nizam's government had no choice but to accept and give immediate effect to the orders. That was the end of Arthur Oliphant's career in Hyderabad. The viceroy also administered a stern warning to two other Europeans in the service of the nizam and issued new instructions that future European applicants were to sign a declaration that they would not be a party to any measures or proceedings opposed to the views or policy of the Government of India. A jubilant Lytton wrote to Disraeli: 'In India at least the power and prestige of that restless schemer are now completely extinguished.'[4]

Meade received instructions from the viceroy asking him to inform the co-administrators that they would be held jointly responsible for every rupee spent by either of them beyond the nizam's dominions. If Oliphant were employed as an agent in England by Salar Jung, it would be seen as an act of disloyalty incompatible with his position as diwan and co-administrator.

Lord Salisbury was unhappy with the way Oliphant had been treated and cabled Lytton asking for a suspension of the orders, but the former private secretary had already left Hyderabad. Salisbury felt that a strong warning would have been adequate since there was no proof of Oliphant advising Salar Jung to be antagonistic to the government. Later commenting on 'poor Oliphant's doom', Salisbury said, 'I think you have been Draconic; but it is clear that no backward step could now be taken without an exhibition of weakness. He I fear will be ruined but we must console ourselves with the reflection that his fate will be a salutary warning to other amateur English politicians in India . . .'[5]

From the correspondence available, it is apparent that Oliphant harboured hopes of an inquiry in England on the subject of his dismissal and of being reinstated. On 30 November 1877, he wrote to Salar Jung from Bombay.

> . . . I have only to say that if I am reinstated and then an order in Council is published prohibiting British subjects from doing anything opposed to the views of that held by the Resident or the Indian Government, my services to you would in that case not be available even in the most unimportant matters—and of course I could not help you in any important matters where your views differ with those of the Resident or Indian Govt . . .[6]

In the same letter, he sent Salar Jung two coded messages, one of which he was expected to telegraph, depending on what he thought was the better course of action. 'If you prefer that a Parliamentary Inquiry should take place unless friends can procure for me an unconditional reinstatement, please tell Mr. W to telegraph number one message . . . If on the other hand you prefer to leave the matter to the discussion of me and my friends in England, then tell Mr. Wilkinson to telegraph number two message . . .'[7] There is no further correspondence available so we do not know which message Salar Jung chose to send.

It was generally believed that the 'extraordinary civilities' lavished on Salar Jung by the Prince of Wales, Lord Salisbury and other high dignitaries in England had created the problem because this treatment suggested to Salar Jung that he might at any time bring to bear powerful influence in England to secure his own objects over the head of the Government of India. Many believed that it was the 'ill-judged meddling of the Prince of Wales and other high personages at home in Indian politics' that had led to the dismissal of Oliphant, who was perceived by the resident and the government as being too clever for his own good when all he was doing was the bidding of his master, Salar Jung. It was alleged that the Prince of Wales had used his personal influence on Salar Jung's behalf and had also received valuable presents from the diwan, a charge which he later denied.

The press, both in India and in England, commented adversely on Oliphant's dismissal. The *Bombay Gazette* wrote that it was certainly objectionable that native princes or ministers should secretly correspond with high personages at home for the purpose of upsetting the Government of India, but unless it could be shown that Oliphant did more than conscientiously fulfil the instructions of Salar Jung, he should not personally be blamed for this correspondence. 'The letters were Sir Salar Jung's, not Mr Oliphant's. It is not as if the latter gentleman had personally set on foot an agitation against the Government; he was merely an instrument and it should have been foreseen, when his engagement as Private Secretary was sanctioned, that he would necessarily have work of this kind to do.'[8]

Referring to Oliphant's influence on Salar Jung's decisions, it went on to add that, given the fact that Salar Jung was a man of strong character and clear intellect, it would be very surprising if Oliphant 'ever went beyond his duty of putting his master's instructions into decent English'. His treatment was both unjust and cruel if he had been dismissed on the 'mere suspicion that he may have been the contriver of some of the Government of India's embarrassments'.

The *Times of India,* writing in a similar vein, inquired with some sarcasm if the government expected Oliphant to pocket Salar Jung's money without rendering proper service or to work in the interests of the British. 'We cannot but say that in removing this able gentleman from his post the Government of India have shown strange childishness. If Sir Salar Jung's arguments were strong, it was not the writer's fault. Sir Salar Jung is responsible for them, not the Secretary. He was simply his master's servant and should not have been reprimanded for doing his work.'[9] It added, 'Government looks with suspicious eyes towards educated natives who set their feet in Native States, but this is the first time we see the authorities suspecting a brother Englishman.'[10]

On 21 December 1877, Oliphant wrote to Salar Jung about the advance of £5000 made to him by the diwan. 'As you gave me £5,000 in advance in Nov. in anticipation of settling my account and as according to my official letter to you of today it is postponed for the present I hereby guarantee to retain the same untouched until such time as my claim is settled.'[11]

Oliphant's removal gave rise to protests in England. There was a good deal of private agitation, and Salisbury had to answer several awkward questions from the queen herself. When the matter came up for discussion in Parliament, Salisbury took 'high ground' and refused to submit the relevant papers or discuss the issue on grounds of public interest.[12]

In early 1878, Lord Salisbury indicated that though he could not write anything to vindicate Oliphant's character, if Oliphant would refer people to him, then he would be happy to tell them that his removal was occasioned by political reasons alone and that there was nothing against him personally. Such a flimsy reassurance did little to save Oliphant's career, and he spent the next several years living on the income of the settlement Salar Jung had made on him. He worked with the Oriental Bank in England for a while, and in 1887, after the death of Maharaja Duleep Singh and his father, Col. Oliphant (who had been equerry to the maharaja), Arthur was entrusted with the upbringing of the maharaja's five children, including Sophia Duleep Singh who later became famous for her fight for female suffrage and the welfare of Indian soldiers in World War I.

THE NEPHEWS AND THEIR TITLES

Rashid-ud-din had become Amir-i-Kabir III and was now officially the head of the Paigah family. He lost no time in trying to enlarge his properties at the expense of his nephews, contrary to the settlement reached earlier in 1877. The dispute had started the moment his brother, Rafi-ud-din, had died. Rafi-ud-din was one of four sons of his father by different wives. One son had died in childhood, and the others were Rashid-ud-din and Sultan-ud-din, the latter also dying early leaving two sons, Bashir-ud-Daula (the future Sir Asman Jah) and Mohtasham-ud-Daula. Since he himself was childless, Rafi-ud-din had adopted his two nephews when their father died. The 'Nephews', as they came to be known, were to inherit all Rafi-ud-din's titles and estates according to his will. When he was on his deathbed, Rafi-ud-din had sent for Salar Jung, and with his household as witnesses, requested him to be the executor of his will. He was also told that Rashid-ud-din should be forbidden from interfering with his family or its property.

The nephews were not merely the adopted sons of Rafi-ud-din but were related to the nizam through their father. Bashir-ud-Daula was the elder one and had been minister of justice (Sadr-ul-Maham) and had also deputed for Salar Jung (Madr-ul-Maham) in his absence, including acting together with Mukaram-ud-Daula when Salar Jung was touring the Continent in 1876. Notwithstanding Rafi-ud-din's will, Rashid-ud-din advanced his claim on the titles and estates bequeathed to the nephews. In his mind, he had a rightful claim on all the titles and properties.[13]

Salar Jung, who became the mediator in this dispute, kept Meade informed. As far as he was concerned, this was a part of the internal affairs of Hyderabad, and the British had no role to play in disagreements between Hyderabad nobles. Meade's letter to him from the hill station of Mahabaleshwar where he was spending the summer seemed to confirm that opinion.

> I do not feel called on to offer here any opinion regarding these claims, and feel sure that Your Excellency will deal with them in a just and impartial manner, both as regards the two Nawabs and Rashid, whose rights in the matter have I know been receiving your special consideration.[14]

In an official letter on the subject, Meade had reported that it was finally decided that no action would be taken till he returned from his summer break, something which he claimed was understood by all the stakeholders. He later claimed that he had been misunderstood, saying that the word 'here' in his letter meant while he was at the hill station, and italicized the word in all subsequent quotations even though he had not done so in the original communication. Salar Jung said that he interpreted 'just and impartial manner' to indicate the resident's faith in his judgement and willingness to abide by his decision. As it turned out, even the words 'special consideration' appeared to have a different meaning. For Meade, who was siding with Rashid-ud-din, it meant settling the dispute in a way he wanted.[15] Meade's duplicity and arrogance must have stunned Salar Jung.

Salar Jung proposed that the highest titles of Shums-ul-Umra and Amir-i-Kabir be given to Rashid-ud-din. The nephews were to get the lesser titles and the estates. There was a precedent of separation of titles, and Salar Jung argued that many people were unaware of the existence of the lesser titles. Rashid-ud-din, who wanted all the titles and the lands, took his grievance to Meade who gave him his support. In the end, after prolonged negotiation, he agreed to accept only the titles, provided they were not separated, and to leave the estates with the nephews. But this proved to be a false dawn. A person aspiring for public office in Hyderabad had first to settle any disputes (especially if it included subordinates over whom he would have authority) in which he was involved so as to start with a clean slate. This was the reason Rashid-ud-din acquiesced in the decision to give him all the titles but no estates.

Rashid-ud-din now had all the power of the state, and he soon began to use it. The estates in the possession of the nephews yielded a total income of about Rs 20 lakh. His own estates yielded much less, about Rs 1.25 lakh. In a period of just six months from September 1877 to March 1878, he made a number of demands, all of which were met. The first demand was for the transfer of estates yielding Rs 3 lakh which Meade urged them to agree to for the sake of peace. Soon after, there was another demand for estates yielding Rs 6 lakh and again it was agreed to.

One of his demands was for Rs 5 lakh in cash to free him from monetary entanglements, which, according to him, did not befit the recognized head of a great family. He also wanted the nephews to endow his younger son with immovable property bringing in a sum of Rs 254,000 per annum. Yet another demand was for the Jehan-numa Gardens for his own use. The nephews flatly refused, but the demands were renewed periodically 'until at length, without the pretence of any legal claim, they assumed the form of positive demands'. Later, he demanded the Jehan-numa Gardens for the use of his younger son instead of his own use on the plea that his elder son already owned a handsome garden and pleasure house.[16]

The nephews still firmly refused. They were threatened with the displeasure of the nizam's government, a threat which soon bore fruit. They were debarred from attending the nizam's durbars, and after some time, concluded that it would be prudent to buy peace at a price. They agreed to pay Rs 5 lakh in cash and assign jagirs yielding Rs 2,54,000 on condition that there would be no further demands. Rashid-ud-din persisted with the demand for the Jehan-numa Gardens which was refused. Finally, on 9 April 1878, with the mediation of Major Euan Smith, it was decided that the Jehan-numa Gardens would be given to the Shums-ul-Umra as 'an appanage of the title'.[17] When Meade was given the news about the happy termination of the affair, he is said to have exclaimed, *Allah-il-illillah*. But the celebrations proved to be premature.

Only four days later, Rashid-ud-din was up to his tricks again. While retaining the jagirs and the cash, he returned the letter relating to the Jehan-numa Gardens, declaring that he would accept it only if it was given unconditionally. The nephews refused to alienate this property, and there the matter seems to have rested for the next eight months. But the ravenous appetite of the rapacious co-administrator knew no limit. Hasnabad and Narainkhera were two of the most important jagirs still with the brothers. In January 1879, Rashid-ud-din turned his attention to them.

The properties and private affairs of the nephews were in the hands of Mohammed Shakoor, a steward who was a notorious intriguer and an enemy of Salar Jung. He was also a signatory to the will of the late Amir-i-Kabir. Temple, who had met him, described him as a great drawback on the otherwise good management of the late Amir-i-Kabir, a great enemy of Salar Jung and an inveterate fomenter of intrigue. 'The man, though all smiles before me, looked the character given him.'[18]

On 10 January 1879, without warning, Shakoor suddenly changed sides, taking up employment under Rashid-ud-din. The jagirs of Hasnabad and Narainkhera were at the time in actual charge of Shakoor's son, Muhammed Jamal-ud-din, whose fidelity the nephews now had every reason to suspect. Alarmed at these developments, the nephews raised a relief party of their own retainers to defend their property the next day, and sent a trusted aide to supersede Shakoor's son. They were advised by the nizam's government (read Salar Jung) to do nothing before meeting their uncle, Rashid-ud-din.

A meeting was arranged between uncle and nephews on 12 January in which the former gave them the false assurance that he had no intention of interfering with their possessions, and all he wanted was the respect due to the head of the family. On the same evening, however, a proclamation under his seal was issued to the effect that Hasnabad and Narainkhera now belonged to him, and that Shakoor's son, who was now in his employ, was authorized to collect the revenue on his account.

The nephews appealed to the resident but he declined to receive their protest, asking them to take their grievance to the nizam's government who only asked them to listen to their uncle. On 23 January 1879, Rashid-ud-din ordered his armed levies under the command of Muhammed Shakoor to take the jagirs by force. Left with no choice, the nephews sent their own retainers to protect their property. This was just the kind of situation Salar Jung had feared and wanted desperately to avoid. Greatly alarmed at the probability of civil war, he persuaded the nephews to recall their troops. At the back of his mind was Berar: Parliament would scarce consider its restoration to a ruler who was unable to maintain peace in the territories he already possessed. He also suspected that the reason for Meade's interference in the dispute was to create so much unrest that the question of the restoration of Berar could be countered by adverting to incompetent rule, of which the current situation was a perfect example. That Meade, who was greatly threatened by an increase in the number of Reformed Troops, seemed quite unconcerned about a situation of near civil war only confirms that things were going as he had planned.

Meanwhile, Rashid-ud-din's henchmen were indulging in plunder and rapine. The affected villagers sent a petition to the resident, describing their plight and asking for his help. After five days, Meade replied that he would not interfere and that redress lay with the nizam's government. The balance of power had now swung in Rashid-ud-din's favour, a fact not hidden from the populace. They realized that any appeal in this regard would be futile and the idea was dropped. The ladies of the zenana (whose signatories included the young nizam's grandmother and mother) also chipped in with a petition to the viceroy, asking for justice for the nephews. Unsurprisingly, Lytton ignored the appeal. Salar Jung, petrified at the thought of civil war, continued to advise his nephews against an armed defence of their properties. And with no restraint from Meade, Rashid-ud-din continued to gobble up properties unchecked. Meade countenanced Rashid-ud-din in these spoliations, and succeeded in dragging Salar Jung himself into seeming complicity, since the minister did not dare to openly oppose the alliance between the resident and Rashid-ud-din.

Meade asked Salar Jung to convene a court of inquiry to establish when and how Hasnabad and Narainkhera had been granted, and Rashid-ud-din's claim to them. A little later, the resident wanted the nephews to establish their claim to these jagirs, not only against Rashid-ud-din, but also against the state. Salar Jung denied that the state had ever come into the picture as far as these territories were concerned. He appointed his nephew and son-in-law, Mukaram-ud-Daula, to conduct the inquiry. The inquiry, which started in May, ended in August, the intention always being that it should be a short affair. The nephews were at a distinct disadvantage because the entire inquiry was controlled by Meade who passed on instructions through a very unwilling (but helpless) Salar Jung. Evidence which the nephews claimed was vital to the case was not admitted because it would delay the case, nor was a postponement of even a week allowed for their convenience. When Meade came to know that the nephews had engaged an English barrister, Tyrrell Leith, to represent them, he directed Salar Jung to ensure that no European lawyer was allowed in the court. A lawyer who was a citizen of Hyderabad was sent instead, and their plea that such a person would be vulnerable to pressure from Rashid-ud-din fell on deaf ears.[19]

Rashid-ud-din produced a document which, according to him, justified his claim on the estates. It was part of a group of five papers which related to the grant of estates, and he claimed that the first one gave him the ownership after his brother's death. This was immediately challenged by the nephews, but instead of asking Rashid-ud-din to prove its authenticity, Meade (through Salar Jung) asked the nephews to disprove it. The nephews were not allowed to examine the original document but were provided with relevant extracts. They asserted that the other four papers be admitted as evidence claiming that a later seyaha gave the estate to the late Amir-i-Kabir, with no restrictions as to the next owner. This was refused.[20]

The charges and countercharges of forgery so sickened Salar Jung that he finally threw in the towel. He wrote to Meade on 13 August asking that the two estates be transferred to Rashid-ud-din according to the purport of the seyaha. Meade wrote back confirming that Mukaram-ud-Daula's opinion was clear that the seyaha was genuine and the latest word of the nizam on the subject. Salar Jung, who had all along fallen in line with the resident's wishes, 'experienced a last flicker of independence'. 'He now refused to bear the odium of a decision his conscience would not support: he denied that Mukaram-ud-Daula's opinion had said that the seyaha was the latest the Nizam had executed on the subject and went on to say, somewhat belatedly, that the rest of the case could not be conducted by either Mukaram-ud-Daula or himself.'[21]

Salar Jung should never have nominated Mukaram-ud-Daula for the inquiry because it effectively ended his nephew's career in public life. As we have already noted, Bashir-ud-Daula had been Mukaram-ud-Daula's colleague. Moreover, he was torn between loyalty to his own uncle and pressure from the most powerful noble in the state, to say nothing of the resident, who was openly siding with Rashid-ud-din. Regardless of his verdict, he would have a Paigah for an enemy. Mukaram-ud-Daula withdrew from public life, ostensibly on health grounds. It was announced that he was going to England for treatment. A rumour was rife that he was impotent. There was also talk in Hyderabad that he had been deliberately driven to lose his mind by those who wanted him out of the way. Though it was not described as such in those days, it seems certain now that he had suffered a nervous breakdown. The tragedy of it was that Salar Jung had once considered him the only person capable of succeeding him. He lived on in Hyderabad as a harmless recluse.[22]

The dispute never died down during the lifetime of the disputants. Salar Jung, for his part, had stopped opposing Rashid-ud-din, since he was by now a beaten man and prudently refused to invite more humiliation by further resistance. The last few years were the nadir of his career, and he was never the same man again. Lytton resigned in 1880 and was succeeded by Lord Ripon. The new viceroy instructed Sir Steuart Bayley to negotiate a new and more amicable settlement. While the compromise failed, he and Salar Jung did decide on the broad outlines of a new settlement on the lines of the 1877 agreement where the titles would be with Rashid-ud-din and the estates with the nephews. By that time, Mohtasham-ud-Daula had died, leaving Bashir-ud-Daula to inherit the lands. But before this scheme could yield any results, Rashid-ud-din passed away on 12 December 1881, having divided the estates he had wrested from the nephews between his sons, Khurshed Jah and Vikar-ul-Umra II. The squabbling started afresh, and in the end, Salar Jung proposed a scheme which divided the Paigah into three parts: the Khurshed Jahi Paigah, the Vikar-ul-Umrahi Paigah and the Asman Jahi Paigah (Bashir-ud-Daula).

According to the new arrangement, the estates and jagirs which Bashir-ud-Daula had inherited from his adoptive father were given back to him. He also inherited his brother's share of properties. Rashid-ud-din's properties were divided between his sons with those associated with titles going to Khurshed Jah. The Paigah talukas, which carried service commitments, were divided equally among the three. Khurshed Jah became Shums-ul-Umra V and Amir-i-Kabir IV. Vikar-ul-Umra inherited the lesser titles. Since there was no title for Bashir-ud-Daula, a new one, Asman Jah was created for him.

The origin of the name is associated with an interesting story. When Salar Jung sat pondering a title for Bashir-ud-Daula, a Parsi gentleman with him said, 'Sir, do you know where the sun comes from? It comes from the sky [asman]. The sun is sometimes there and sometimes not, but the sky is always there.'[23] Inspired by this remark (even if it was completely unscientific), Salar Jung came up with the title of Asman Jah. Ironically, only a few years after Salar Jung's demise, Asman Jah became diwan and ended up outranking his cousin Khurshed Jah, who was the head of the Paigah family. The latter never entered public life and devoted himself to his private interests all his life. In hindsight, all the ugly wrangling had been entirely pointless.

THE PLEDGE

In March 1878, a year after Salar Jung's petition on Berar, a reply arrived from Calcutta. The resident forwarded it to Salar Jung and Rashid-ud-din, and also volunteered to clarify any doubts which they might have. Salar Jung politely refused the offer, but Meade insisted on a meeting with the two co-administrators.

Meade emphasized that the Government of India would be very put out if the co-administrators attempted to raise the Berar matter in Parliament. Rashid-ud-din immediately volunteered to give the government a written undertaking, assuring the viceroy that no such action was contemplated. Salar Jung was left with no choice but to agree. This pledge was to be communicated to the viceroy by Meade, but later he wanted the co-administrators to put it in writing. Salar Jung was happy to record his own version rather than leave his verbal statement at the mercy of the resident's interpretation. But as it turned out, even that freedom was denied him. The co-administrator rejected four successive drafts, leading to the suspicion that he was showing them to the resident. While sending the fifth draft, Salar Jung sent Rashid-ud-din a note saying that he had asked the assistant resident, Major Euan Smith, to call on him. In reply, Rashid-ud-din told him that anything Smith agreed to would also have his approval.

The fifth draft too did not find favour, and ultimately, Salar Jung signed a new one dictated by Smith. Confiding to Hall of W. Nicol & Co., he wrote:

> . . . Not to mention my own reluctance to appeal to Parliament it would have been futile, nay, ruinous, to have shown any spirit of resistance. There is nothing, as you know, to prevent the Resident taking the most arbitrary and iniquitous measures in order to circumvent the purposes of Government and we are quite defenceless against him, as experience has already shown. He will moreover have the assistance of my colleague who has been raised up on purpose, and who would not scruple to lend himself to any intrigue that promises him an accession to power or increase of favour.[24]

These are the words of a defeated man. Salar Jung's friends in England protested the giving of the pledge and thought that Parliament would protect him if any injury was threatened. Notwithstanding their righteous indignation, by now Salar Jung had learnt to view things in a more realistic manner, even if he still believed in the innate sense of justice of Parliament and the British people. He knew that the resident had the power to ruin him long before the matter reached Parliament. In what must rate as one of his most realistic assessments of his own position, Salar Jung wrote to John Fleming in July 1878 about the problems he was facing. He had now come to terms with the vulnerability of his position.

> It must always be borne in mind that it is possible for the Indian Government at any time to bring irresistible pressure on me. Before Parliament has made any progress with the inquiry, they have it in their power to bring irretrievable ruin on me and on the State. With a ready tool in my colleague, they may at any moment cause a mutiny, disorganize the administration or do any other mischief they like to ruin my character and that of my Government.[25]

Salar Jung also told him that ever since the pledge, the disparaging of senior officials which he had appointed had stopped.

My colleague . . . began to find fault with my higher grade officials who are mostly men of enlightened views drawn from other parts of India. Without openly or officially supporting my colleagues, the Resident followed his example by repeating similar disparaging opinions against my officials . . . Since the pledge . . . these intrigues have ceased and things are falling into a smoother groove.[26]

Salar Jung, at the best of times, was never a popular ruler. His desire to carry out reforms and correct abuses had deeply affected and offended many of the nobles. It was therefore no surprise that these men should readily welcome another power which they could employ against him. It was normal for Rashid-ud-din to hold daily durbars at his palace where all discontented and disaffected persons assembled and steps were taken to disconcert Salar Jung's politic and wisely conceived measures. They often told Salar Jung to his face that they would complain against him to the co-administrator. Rashid-ud-din was the willing recipient of the confidences of these persons, who for one reason or another, held a grudge against the minister.

One of Rashid-ud-din's constant complaints was that Salar Jung did not involve him with administrative decisions or part with important information. On one occasion, fed up with Rashid-ud-din's constant carping on the issue, Salar Jung decided to deal with it in his own manner. He loaded a large quantity of official records, documents and correspondence on a huge twelve-wheel cart drawn by four oxen and sent it to Rashid-ud-din. When the cart reached the Paigah noble's residence he was told that these were the documents he had shown a desire to peruse. Horrified, Rashid-ud-din immediately sent the cart back to Salar Jung, his ardour for seeing official documents having cooled somewhat.[27]

Salisbury's message to Salar Jung in London had only raised false hopes since it was now amply clear that there had never been any intention of reconsidering the case. Fleming wrote to the diwan: 'And one time I would have ridiculed the idea of an English official lending himself to intrigues for the deliberate object of destroying the credit of a friendly State, but I am compelled by recent events to believe such a thing possible.'[28]

THE RESIDENT GETS A SCARE

According to Server-ul-Mulk, the old, established rule that no person from the city could visit Secunderabad without Salar Jung's permission was after great efforts set aside at about this time. It was reported that Meade had summoned some of the Arab jemadars to the residency and 'specially tutored' them. He claims that Meade asked him to call on him every Saturday to present a weekly report on the progress of the nizam's education. But since Salar Jung had the loyalty of those under him, the old rule continued to be observed.[29]

Server-ul-Mulk also narrates an incident where Meade had visited Salar Jung to convey the contents of a communication from the viceroy. Though he does not mention the contents of the letter or even the year of the incident, it is obvious from the description of events that Meade had come with the intention of telling him that his days as diwan were numbered or something to that effect. If this was indeed the case, this incident would in all probability have taken place in mid- or late 1877. Meade had summoned Salar Jung to the residency, but news of the contents of the letter seems to have leaked to Salar Jung who feigned indisposition and invited Meade to his deodi instead.

On the day of the meeting, the courtyard was full of Arab and Pathan troops, and the ainakhana was full of Arab jemadars, all armed to the teeth. Meade was greatly alarmed at the sight of the armed men, and when Salar Jung asked to see the contents of the docket from the viceroy, the resident said that, since he was unwell, he (Salar Jung) could visit him at the residency where everything would be explained to him. Salar Jung smiled and told Meade that he knew all the facts, and throwing his handkerchief on the floor, said that he had as much respect for office as for the handkerchief but that he (Meade) could not snatch it away from him, 'even at the risk of losing my head'. Salar Jung was supposed to have said: 'The Government has not appointed me, nor am I subordinate to it. You certainly have the power to arrest and carry me away, but the responsibility for bloodshed in, disaster to, the State, will rest with the Government before God and Man.'[30] When this conversation was taking place, the Arab jemadars barged in and said: 'Nawab Sahib, we are prepared to lay down our lives—we await your command.'

Meade was by now in a blue funk. Salar Jung, feigning displeasure, sent the men away and apologized for their behaviour to the resident. He then asked to be shown the contents of the communication, but Meade, who presumably had had enough for one day, beat a hasty retreat, saying that the matter could be postponed till Salar Jung had recovered his health and was less upset and angry. A frightened resident was then escorted out by

Tehvur Ali, Salar Jung's foster-brother, with an assurance from the diwan that no one would dare lay a finger on him without his orders. Server-ul-Mulk quoted as his source, Riasat Ali, the son of Tehvur Ali.[31] There is no mention about what happened next, but Salar Jung's show of strength seems to have worked.[32]

Even though Salar Jung and Meade had serious differences in political affairs, this does not seem to have affected their personal relations. Their relationship was marked by great courtesy and friendliness, even if their political views were diametrically opposed to one another. Salar Jung corresponded with him even after he had left Hyderabad, and as we have already noted, corresponded with him when he visited England and the Continent in 1876. They also interacted socially, sometimes sharing a game of billiards in Salar Jung's deodi. T.H. Thornton, who wrote Meade's biography, observed:

> And here it may be stated that, in spite of all that subsequently happened, Sir Richard Meade's relations with the Minister were always of a most friendly character. At times . . . when differences threatened to be critical, the two statesmen would often enjoy a game of billiards together as if nothing had happened.[33]

Thornton also narrates a somewhat amusing anecdote involving Lady Meade and Salar Jung. This took place soon after the co-administrator crisis when Salar Jung was showing his guest around the deodi. Thornton included it in his narrative, presumably, to show with what good humour Salar Jung had taken his political defeat. He showed her, among other things, the private room in which his interview with Meade had taken place and where the ultimatum regarding the manufacture of arms and the appointment of a co-administrator had been conveyed to him. When Lady Meade admired the room, Salar Jung observed with mock solemnity: 'I don't like that room. That is the dentist's room, where all my teeth have been pulled out.'[34]

Lady Meade's maiden name was Emily Malcolm, and she was the second daughter of Colonel Duncan Malcolm, who for long had been assistant to the resident at Hyderabad and subsequently became resident at Jodhpur. He died in 1854 at the early age of forty-seven when he was resident at Baroda.[35] Emily was born in Hyderabad, and according to Server-ul-Mulk, she was the lady Siraj-ul-Mulk, Salar Jung's uncle, had wished him to marry.[36] It is difficult to ascertain if this was just bazaar gossip or fact. It seems that Lady Meade was annoyed at the fact that Salar Jung did not leave his retainers near the gate the way the Amir-i-Kabir III did when he visited the residency. The tom-toms, she said, gave her a headache. There also seems to have been another cause for complaint which is ironic. She said that Salar Jung did not remove his shoes and walked all over her carpets when he visited the residency. The boot was now well and truly on the other foot!

Even if he chose to make light of his political defeat on that occasion, Salar Jung was now a different person. Energetic and optimistic all his life, he was now a sour, bitter and disillusioned man, his enthusiasm for administration all but gone. In December 1881, he wrote to Yule in despair: 'I have long ago given up every hope not only of the restoration of Berar, but even of the possibility of our being able to improve and embellish the territory that is left still or of long preserving the internal autonomy of the State.'

The Berar question did come up for discussion in Parliament, thanks to the articles which appeared in Robert Knight's London *Statesman* which highlighted in 1881 Salar Jung's unfair and humiliating treatment, on both the question of the co-regency and Berar. But by then, Salar Jung had admitted defeat and refused to be drawn in again by the pugnacious editor of the *Statesman*.

THE NIZAM'S EDUCATION

At the end of 1879, a scrutiny of Mahbub's report card showed that he was making good progress in geography, arithmetic and Urdu. In English, he had finished reading all of *Little Facts for Little People*, almost all of *Odd Stories about Animals*, and was studying the chapter on verbs in his *Grammatical Primer*. Clerk's assistant tutor, J.F. Dowding, noted that the nizam had also learnt by heart William Wordsworth's poem, 'We Are Seven'. The nizam, however, showed no interest in history, not even the history of his own dominions.[37]

Meade reported to his superiors in Calcutta on the nizam's progress. 'His Highness appears to have a fair ability to learn where the subject interests him, but where this is not the case, he is undoubtedly slow and his progress is backward.' He also observed, 'He is gradually acquiring a colloquial knowledge of English and his pronunciation is unusually good.'

The only impediment to his progress, according to Clerk, was an excess of female company, 'After twelve the Azure retires to the zenana, and tyrannises over 400 women, who spoil and pet him as a matter of course. Zenana influence is the principle thing against which the tutor of one of these boys has to contend.'[38] In 1880, the resident had reported to the Government of India about 'unfortunate irregularities' which assumed great seriousness due to some inmates of the palace encouraging the nizam's 'boyish follies'.[39]

One of the rumours which Masi-uz-Zaman Khan had spread was that the young nizam was suffering from a 'certain illness'. Salar Jung was blamed for allowing him to be kept in the mahallat where he could not be supervised by him. The resident subjected the diwan to some severe epistolary scrutiny in this regard. There was a protest from the ladies against these shameful accusations, and the residency surgeon, Dr Law, was deputed to corroborate the existence of the supposed disease. Dr Law reported that there was no disease but found the nizam weak and thin, and blamed the court physician Bakar Ali Khan for it.

The object of the whole exercise by Masi-uz-Zaman Khan was to relocate the nizam away from the mahallat to the Mahtab Mahal so as to be able to continuously influence his young mind. In this he succeeded admirably since he and his supporters put up at the palace with the nizam and controlled him throughout the day, apart from lesson hours where he came to Server-ul-Mulk at the Suleman Jah Haveli. Quick to realize what had happened, Salar Jung ordered Server-ul-Mulk to stay at the palace with a view to neutralizing some of the baleful influence of the moulvi and his supporters. He granted a mansab of Rs 200 from the diwani to his father-in-law, so as to free Sever-ul-Mulk from financial worries for his family.

After some time, the resident was not happy with even the Mahtab Mahal arrangement. Salar Jung suggested that the resident should shift from the building at Chadarghat, which was only for temporary use, and move to Bolarum, which was where the residency was housed. The nizam could then reside in this building. Sir Richard Meade agreed but this was not liked by the zenana. The nizam's grandmother, on the advice of the Amir-i-Kabir III, refused. Some intriguers with an overactive imagination saw this as a move by the diwan to remove the young nizam from the city and usurp all power. As a compromise, he was shifted to the Purani Haveli (old palace) which was then readied as a school for the royal student. His progress improved and Meade observed, 'The measure was rendered very desirable by circumstances into which I need not enter, and was certainly attended with benefits to the young Nizam.'[40]

As the nizam grew older, Salar Jung's opponents, and there were many, took advantage of Rashid-ud-din's and Meade's dislike of the diwan to poison the nizam's ears against him. If Server-ul-Mulk is to be believed, they succeeded in this for a time. One day Clerk sat at the breakfast table with an album and began to show the nizam photographs of various persons. When he came to Salar Jung's photo, he lavished praise on him. At this, the nizam threw aside the album. The Amir-i-Kabir and Shapurjee, the Parsi steward of Rashid-ud-din, tried their best to discredit Salar Jung in the eyes of the nizam. They bought off the female attendants of the palace (Mahtab Mahal) with presents 'so that praises of the Amir-i-Kabir and blemishes of the Minister could be carried by men and women alike to the Royal Ear'.[41]

One of the issues concerning the nizam's education had to do with the *musahib*s, middle-aged and elderly courtiers who were attached to the nizam. They made a thorough nuisance of themselves, hanging around the nizam, constantly interrupting his education in the classroom, and corrupting his mind with 'obscene jest and gross flatteries'. They served as irritants in other aspects of his training as well. The young nizam displayed a talent for tennis but lost interest since he was never allowed to lose. If he was unsuccessful at a high jump, they asked for the bar to be lowered. Clerk tried to rid himself of them, but neither Salar Jung nor Rashid-ud-din Khan obliged. The latter, while trying to take credit for getting rid of them, actually added four more.

Salar Jung did not feel strongly enough about the matter. In any case, he knew that Meade would support Rashid-ud-din against him and saw no need to stick his neck out on this occasion. Also no one, not even Clerk, seems to have given much thought to the fact that the young boy needed playmates of his own age. Salar Jung sometimes sent his sons and other boys to the palace, but most of the time Mahbub was surrounded by fawning adults, divorced almost entirely from children of his own age.

In June 1880, Clerk managed to get three young musahibs appointed, but it proved to be a short-lived arrangement since it was realized that it would be necessary to remove them all. By 1882, the eleven musahibs were removed and replaced by Zaffar Jung, son of Khurshed Jah and grandson of Rashid-ud-din Khan; Mir Saadat Ali, younger son of Salar Jung; and Hugh Gough, son of an English family with old military connections in India.

Young Mahbub seems to have been a shy and somewhat diffident child with fragile health. Claude Clerk's wife told Wilfrid Scawen Blunt when he visited Hyderabad what she believed was the reason for the young nizam's diffidence.

> She says the young Nizam's extreme shyness and frightened manner are due to an accident which happened in his zenana. While playing with a pistol he accidentally shot a child, and he has been made to believe that the English Resident has power at any time to imprison him for this. He is, however, she says, talkative enough with her, and declares his intention of managing everything at Hyderabad himself as soon as he gets on the throne.[42]

Such an incident did indeed take place. Returning home from an outing at Rashid-ud-din's garden, the young nizam went into the zenana from where a shot was heard. Investigation revealed that he had been given a loaded pistol belonging to M. Shapurjee. Young Mahbub took it into the zenana, and when he and a servant child were alone together, it went off, accidentally killing the child instantly. Shapurjee admitted ownership of the pistol but denied giving it to the young nizam.

Salar Jung, who immediately wrote to Meade about the incident, mentioned the ban on arms in the zenana which Clerk had insisted on some two years ago. But he gave a different twist to the story. He said that the young nizam had laid down the gun, and it had been picked up by the servant child who accidentally shot himself. Salar Jung's version stretched credulity, and Clerk wanted an investigation which would pin responsibility on Rashid-ud-din and his steward. This was exactly what Salar Jung wanted to avoid, since he was almost sure that Meade would side with Rashid-ud-din, and Clerk would be made the scapegoat. Meade greatly disliked the tutor and was looking for an excuse to dismiss him.

V.K. Bawa has observed that the education of the young nizam was important because of its implication for the time when the nizam assumed charge at the helm of affairs. 'Salar Jang was ranged with the forces of conservatism against the British on this point. The British wanted the Nizam to be oriented towards their modes of behaviour, while Salar Jang wanted to isolate him from British influences.'[43] Even before Salar Jung's death, the nizam was under 'the influence of the less attractive aspects of court life, and this became a cause of deep regret to Salar Jang'.[44]

On one occasion, Meade made it known that he would like to visit the nizam in his private capacity and without notice. This was contrary to the established rule of the durbar, and the nobles were appalled at the suggestion. But then it was not so simple to refuse the resident. Salar Jung outsmarted him by hastily assembling an impromptu durbar. He was warned of the impending arrival of the resident by the *harkaras* posted by him on the Afzal Ganj Bridge. When Meade galloped in, he was greeted by troops who saluted him. A bit taken aback, he asked the arzbegee on whose authority they were there. He was told that they were only doing their duty and required no special orders. In the meantime, Salar Jung, Rashid-ud-din and other nobles arrived.

The resident was in the room along with the nizam, Clerk and Zaffar Jung. The nizam, a little wonderstruck at the turn of events, looked silently into the resident's face when the latter started a conversation with him. After some time, all the nobles and Salar Jung were also invited into the room and sat down at the breakfast table. Meade, who had been effectively foiled by the 'wily Asiatic'[45] Salar Jung, was more than a little put out and made an abrupt exit.

Salar Jung's policy of isolating the residency had been commented on by many residents. He was anxious not only to protect himself (and the administration) from intrigues, but also preserve the internal autonomy of Hyderabad by preventing any day-to-day interference from the residency. Throughout Chandu Lal's long administration, the residents and the staff dealt only with the de facto diwan, and not with other nobles. A limited interaction had taken place between the late Shums-ul-Umra II after he had been diwan for five months when he met the resident, General Fraser once. Sir Richard Temple, though he wanted to encourage interaction between British officers and Hyderabad nobles, found it difficult to even get an audience with the nizam. Sir George Yule had no truck with any native nobleman, and many important reforms were carried out in his time with no opposition. Many thought that all Salar Jung was interested in was clinging on to power; in fact, all he wanted was to be obstructed as little as possible in the discharge of his duties as long as he was in office.

When Val Prinsep visited Hyderabad in 1877, the young nizam sat for him. His account is of interest since it tells us something about the personality of his young subject. The time allotted to him was early in the morning, and he found the boy playing tennis. Prinsep thought he would make a good player since he hit straight and volleyed well. But the young boy proved to be a most fidgety subject, sitting at times on the arm of the chair and sometimes at the back, anywhere but in the right position. A chamberlain tried to keep him occupied by telling him stories but in vain. He exhibited a child's curiosity, asking Prinsep about his colours and soon asked for some brushes. ('. . . I perceive that the Azure wants my brushes, which I gave him, and sends for a paint-box and commences a picture of the chamberlain . . . it is against etiquette to refuse the Azure anything and it was this that Mustafun Jung had whispered.'[46])

The young boy was of an acquisitive turn of mind and extremely careful and meticulous in the arrangement of his personal belongings. Prinsep found his books and papers beautifully arranged in his desk. After the first sitting, he called for a cloth and himself folded his newly acquired brushes carefully. When Prinsep told Salar Jung about the brushes, he said that the nizam always took all the nazars presented to him. Salar Jung had initially thought that this was done on the prompting of the zenana but later discovered that he locked away all he got himself.

Prinsep observed that the influence of the zenana was the main influence which any tutor of a prince had to counteract, and Captain Claude Clerk was no exception. He commented on the greatly improved health of the young boy whom he describes as a 'weakly specimen of scrofulous childhood' before Captain Clerk undertook his education. Surrounded by domestics and constantly fed unwholesome food, it was no wonder that his health suffered. Little by little, this influence was overcome, and the young boy was also made to take an interest in sports. He rode well and was also anxiously preparing to learn cricket.

The upbringing of the nizam became the source of much jealousy in Hyderabad. The conservative lobby wanted him to be brought up much like themselves—in their eyes, the English tutor was simply an 'invention of the English devil'. The more liberal party, with Salar Jung at its head, wanted to give the nizam every opportunity of becoming a thoroughly enlightened prince with knowledge of all things English. It was feared that the period of greatest danger was when he got into the zenana. It was hoped that he would not emerge from it a vicious and effeminate rake, a slave to passion, and unmindful of the good of his people. But it was realized that it would require an exceptionally strong mind to resist the blandishments of a score or two of beautiful young women in his seraglio. There was an apprehension that all the careful tuition would be undone by the intrigues of the zenana, with his mind being led by women attached to old-fashioned institutions rather than to the English codes of integrity and education. But by the time Mahbub was fifteen or sixteen, the damage had already been done. Claude Clerk had been known to comment, 'He must occasionally "visit his mother" as it is called, and we wink hard as to his doings with women.'

One of the reasons for locating the nizam to the Purani Haveli was his penchant for wine and for women. A high wall separated the bachelors' quarters from the ladies' section in the Purani Haveli. Besides the nizam, his companions included Salar Jung's two sons, Kishen Pershad, the grandson of Maharaja Narayan Pershad Narender Bahadur, and the sons of some other nobles lived in the bachelors' quarters. Mahbub was allowed to spend one night a week in the ladies' quarters.

On one occasion, Mahbub wanted to spend an extra night in the ladies' quarters. This was not so easily arranged since special permission would be required. Also, they were closely guarded. Mahbub asked Kishen Pershad to get a ladder, and it was placed against the wall adjoining the female quarters. Laik Ali, who was the strongest of all the boys, scaled the wall and pulled out one of the maids from the other side. When Salar Jung came to know about the incident, he told the peshkar, Maharaja Narayan Pershad Narender Bahadur, about it. The raja said that his grandson was duty-bound to carry out the orders of the sovereign. In any case, it was Salar Jung's own son, Laik, who had actually used the ladder. The matter was dropped, but the young nizam had made a note about all the fuss and it must have rankled.[47]

17

Robert Knight and the *Statesman* Libel Case

The English journalist, Robert Knight, was the principal founder and the first real editor of the *Times of India*, Bombay, and *Statesman*, Calcutta, which, under him, grew into the foremost newspapers of western and eastern India respectively. He truly believed in the adage that journalism consists of printing what someone else does not want printed, the rest merely being public relations.[1] His attack of the Raj alienated many of his countrymen, but his critical attitude spread to English-speaking Indians. He, more than anyone else, made the press a 'fourth estate' in India, and a part of the political process. Knight's challenges of official policy and conduct gave Indians a sense of grievance and paved the way for the development of Indian nationalism.[2] Much like Salar Jung, whose name carries little resonance for today's generation, Knight, despite his importance, fell into obscurity and seems to have been ignored by history.

It is not clear when or how Knight made Salar Jung's acquaintance, but the two seemed to be good friends, or at least sufficiently well acquainted for Knight to seek financial help from Salar Jung to fund his ventures. Knight had intended to found a London journal in 1865, but a lack of finances prevented it. By December 1878, he had completed the prospectus for a London *Statesman*, to 'awaken the conscience of the English people to the real character of our rule in this country'.[3] In a letter to Salar Jung in December 1878, he claimed the full approval of Gladstone and other Liberal leaders, and then made his request for financial aid:

> It is almost useless for me to go on writing in India as I have done for the 20 years past. The Government simply becomes more despotic every year, and less capable of dealing with the condition of the people . . .

I feel sure that in London, we could awaken a conscience amongst the people that would put an end once for all to the injustice, oppression, neglect, and cruelty with which all classes from the native Prince down to the ryot are now treated by our Government without hope of redress. The Statesman here has become a valuable property but it has cost us Rs. 1,00,000 [sic] and I want you to help me start this London paper. It would injure the scheme, if it were to be known that any native gentleman was assisting me but our financial agents here Messrs. Nicholls & Co. could manage the matter entirely. What I wish you would do is lend me at a mild rate of interest—say 8 per cent, Rs 10,000 or 20,000 for say three years. That money need only be deposited with Nicholls & Co. as brokers in any name you liked, and they would be responsible for its repayment . . .

P.S. If you have any hope at all of getting justice done to the Nizam, believe me it is through our influence with Mr. Gladstone, and the great Liberal leaders who will soon be in power.[4]

But Salar Jung, who had burnt his fingers with Lytton and Meade a year before, naturally wanted to avoid any further controversy. He wished Knight all success but politely refused to finance the paper because if the matter were to be made public, 'it would be very disastrous to me'.[5]

A year later, Knight still needed money, and we find him again knocking on Salar Jung's door for funds.

Our expenses are heavy, and I cannot afford to carry on the paper for any great length of time unless the people and Princes of India help me by contributing liberally as subscribers. Thus you should take copies of the Statesman for all your officials and for your schools. No one will blame you for doing this. We have already nearly 1,000 subscribers in India, but we ought to have 3,000.[6]

A couple of days later he proposed that subscriptions bought by Indians should be sent to MPs and other men in public life in Britain. He told Salar Jung: 'It would be of no use for you to hire an agent here or to spend a *lakh* of rupees. It is public opinion only that will insist on your being treated with the honour and consideration overdo [sic] you.'[7] A fortnight later, he made a request for 200–300 subscriptions.

> For the first time in the history of our rule, is there now an opportunity
> of making the leading men in Parliament and the reading public of
> England, acquainted with what our rule really is . . . If the Princes and
> People of India will but help now, we will change the whole system of
> English rule within a year or two.[8]

Salar Jung granted his request and sent him a draft for £280, the money
equivalent of 200 subscriptions. But the weekly soon changed into a
monthly due to Knight's health problems and, in fact, closed down till
June 1880. By that time, Gladstone and the Liberals had been voted into
power, and Knight was very hopeful that the new dispensation would treat
Salar Jung and the nizam with justice. In letters to Salar Jung, he voiced his
optimism about the future.

> Our turn is now coming for the institution of a wiser and juster rule
> of India than has ever yet been seen. I cannot tell you my feelings of
> indignant shame at the treatment which you *personally* and H. H. the
> Nizam as a Prince have received at the hands of our Foreign Office in
> India. Having Mr Gladstone's ear and the confidence of the great Liberal
> leaders, I will take that the quarrel about the Berars, and the petty insults
> offered to yourself, are fully known and understood.[9]

He expressed his hopes of a royal commission to look into the working
of the Indian government, one which he hoped would set the system
to rights. Once again, there was a request for money. He said that his
personal friends like the maharaja of Jaipur had promised funds, and
Travancore had already provided £80. Salar Jung sent him another £200.
These loans and donations by the native states to Knight led J.G. Cordery
who succeeded Meade as resident to assert that the *Statesman* had been
in Salar Jung's pay. But there is no evidence to support such an assertion
since these appear to be in the nature of one-time subsidies to maintain
his paper and not part of a permanent arrangement.

Gladstone had named the Marquess of Hartington as his S S and Lord
Ripon, viceroy. Knight was angling for an appointment to the viceroy's
legislative council and had sounded Gladstone about it. Hartington wrote
to Ripon about Knight calling him 'clever and energetic' but that he could
also be troublesome. He said that if it was well-informed, outside criticism
which he wanted, then Knight was his man. Ripon was not particularly
enthused by the idea and said as much.

Knight's hopes of a significant personal role in Indian political affairs ended with the publication on 1 October 1880 of an explosive exposé of the intrigues of Rashid-ud-din Khan. It was the second of a three-part series called 'Restoration of the Berars', the first part, which traced the history of the British takeover, having appeared in July of that year. After giving gossipy details of the Murray case, the article said that the government, irritated with Salar Jung's repeated pleas for the restoration of Berar, had foisted his rival, Rashid-ud-din Khan, on Salar Jung.

These passages from the *Statesman* created a storm:

> But as no loyal or honourable opponent of the Nawab Salar Jung could be found in Hyderabad it was necessary to secure for the purpose one that was disloyal and dishonourable. Such a person was found in the Nawab Wikar-ool-Oomra . . . In 1861 the Nawab Wikar-ool-Oomra was detected, described, and denounced by the British authorities as a disloyal and dishonourable person, the chief contriver and agent in a fraudulent and corrupt conspiracy, whereof the Nawab Salar Jung was to have been the principal victim, and the Nizam the principal dupe.[10]

Quoting from the administration report of the government, the article went on to add:

> The Nawab Wikar-ool-Oomra having been pronounced guilty, some eight years ago, of lending himself to intrigue, the object of which, it was believed, was to procure for himself the office of Minister, had been prohibited, under the orders of the Supreme Government, from appearing on any public occasion, the Nizam's own durbar not excepted, when the British representative was present.[11]

The article continued in its hard-hitting vein:

> It was notorious that the Nawab Wikar-ool-Oomra . . . could not and would not cooperate harmoniously with the Minister. His character was bad. He had robbed and deceived his master; he had insulted the British Government and slandered its representative. But now he was fully available *for the discomfiture of Salar Jung*, and the infamy of his antecedents only made him the more subservient.

The article, written by Major Evans Bell, put the responsibility squarely on the Hyderabad residency and its bosses in Calcutta, and demanded an inquiry into the facts. 'We charge Lord Lytton's Foreign Office with this crime, and demand an inquiry into the facts.'

The establishment was not going to be a mute spectator. Knight was stopped by a court summons from returning to Calcutta in mid-December. A criminal libel suit had been filed against him in the name of Rashid-ud-din, the work, in all likelihood, of John Gorst, who represented the plaintiff in all hearings. The case was transferred to the Queen's Bench, and Knight, set in his stirrups for war, prepared for a sensational defence in which he hoped to get witnesses from Hyderabad to show Rashid-ud-din's evil influence. But an elaborate defence needed money, and he appealed 'to the people and Princes of India' through his Calcutta paper to contribute to a *Statesman* defence fund since the 'opportunity of bringing home to the conscience of England the faults of our Government of India under the late regime, that they shall be made impossible in the future, may never occur again . . .'[12] He asked Salar Jung to help set up such a fund with the help of the maharajas of Indore and Travancore, and requested him for a personal donation of £500.

But Knight had shot his last bolt, at least as far as Salar Jung was concerned. The latter responded with a letter which must have come as a huge shock to Knight. Salar Jung said that he did not want to get mixed up with the case. He said it had never been his intention to encourage Knight in bringing Hyderabad affairs before the public, and in his letter, he made it very plain that he wanted to have no role in the whole affair.

> You are well aware that ever since I have known you it has been far from my desire to encourage you in bringing Hyderabad affairs before the public . . . neither directly nor indirectly have I been any party to the publication of the article on which the libel was based . . . [as] this case concerns my colleague, approved by the British Government, the Resident, and the Calcutta Foreign Office, my position prevents my being mixed up with it all, as *I ought not and cannot come* into collision with those authorities . . . [emphasis added]
>
> When you first asked me, as you may remember, on your first starting the *Statesman* as a weekly journal, to afford you some pecuniary aid in your undertaking, I felt very loathe to refuse you, not merely as the editor of a paper, but as you were my personal friend . . . It was therefore

a relief to my mind to be able on two later occasions, when you appealed to me for aid in your difficulties, to meet your wishes as far as was in my power. I hope that my having thus come to your aid did not lead you to think that I wished you to give any special prominence to Hyderabad affairs, or indeed publish anything concerning them.[13]

Salar Jung ended his letter hoping that their friendship would continue and that he would not take this refusal amiss. Knight had volunteered to break a lance in Salar Jung's defence, but the cautious diwan turned him down. In Salar Jung's defence, it can be said that he really had no choice. Tired of the constant bickering about Berar, and of being ganged up against by Rashid-ud-din Khan and the resident, it is no wonder that he took the path of least resistance. There is no evidence to suggest that he encouraged, or was responsible for, Knight's crusade on his behalf, which it appears was entirely the reforming editor's own quest for justice, and also presumably, personal glory. There is no record of any further communication between Salar Jung and Knight.

THE LIBEL SUIT

The suit became a topic of lively interest in the Indian press. Several papers carried Knight's appeals for funds, and fundraisers were held to raise money for the defence. The case was heard in early February, and Knight's lawyers argued that there was no question of criminal libel as there was no intention to disturb the peace. A civil action would require witnesses and archives from Hyderabad, and hence the case could only properly be heard in India. Tom Palmer, who was now no longer in Salar Jung's employ, wasted no time in accepting Rashid-ud-din's brief. The presiding officer agreed, and Knight was discharged in the case. The pugnacious editor promised that the allegations would be printed in Calcutta, but Rashid-ud-din's death on 12 December 1881 ended the case.

But before that, the third part of the series appeared on 1 July 1881 in the London *Statesman*. The fifty-page essay attacked the resident, Sir Richard Meade, and his staff, and was also highly critical of the Hyderabad Contingent which was described as an utter scandal for the extravagance of the pay of its officers and their opulent lifestyle, all paid for by the nizam. It narrated in detail the lurid story of how Rashid-ud-din had usurped the title from his nephew and how the residency staff had colluded with him in the spoliation of his nephews. It also showed how Lytton had rehabilitated Rashid-ud-din as a counter to Salar Jung, and how Salar Jung, threatened with arrest and deportation, had been forced to accept his rival and enemy as co-regent.

Knight said that it was Lord Northbrook who had selected Meade for suppressing Salar Jung. Meade was one of 'those serviceable officers who understood what it is to simply obey orders'.[14] The instructions were never reduced to writing, but Meade understood perfectly well what he had been sent to Hyderabad for. His predecessor, Saunders, had been removed because his grip was not tight enough for the pressure to be put on Salar Jung. 'The man to snub Sir Salar Jung and to make iron enter his soul was Sir Richard Meade. He fulfilled his orders so thoroughly, but so coarsely, that he at last produced a scandal . . .'[15]

Meade, who had only recently retired to England, was stung to the quick. He denied the accusations and wanted to vindicate himself. He told Hartington that many of the statements were false and others were 'gross misrepresentations'. Hartington and Ripon were both of the opinion that all the charges against Meade were without foundation. The viceroy wanted criminal libel charges to be brought against Knight, and at the same time, warned the Secretary of State about Rashid-ud-din Khan whom he described as 'a stupid, blundering, and not very clean-handed individual'. T.H. Thornton, who had been aide to Meade at Hyderabad, said the article was full of outrageous misstatements and abounding in 'disgraceful innuendoes and other productions of malevolent bazaar gossip'. Thornton, while crediting Knight with some ability, especially in economics, also thought that he displayed a genuine sympathy with the native princes and people of India but called him the 'ready dupe of slanderers and not very scrupulous in his methods'.[16]

Questions were asked in the House of Commons in August 1881, and Hartington wanted to know which official papers could be produced as evidence. He told Ripon that most of Meade's reports discussed Salar Jung's character and conduct very freely and could not be published. Also, most of the confidential papers were already in the hands of the opposing party, having been obtained, he said, by bribery. Ripon sent the papers to England, admitting that some of the revelations had shocked him. Meade had initially opposed the appointment of Rashid-ud-din Khan and was forced by Lytton to recommend it. This was explosive stuff, and it was decided not to allow Meade to sue for libel. Meade, for all his sense of outrage, knew that the account in the newspaper which acknowledged that he was only following orders from Calcutta was correct, but the proof lay buried in confidential archives. Lytton and Salisbury maintained a studied public silence, with their Liberal successors covering up for them.

When the matter came up before the House of Commons again in February 1882, Hartington acknowledged receipt of a letter from the Government of India in October which conclusively proved that Meade had acted under orders and in entire accord with the wishes of the government. They retained an unshaken confidence in his integrity and honour, and considered the allegations of corrupt conduct against him to be totally without foundation. With this ringing endorsement of Meade's character, the Secretary of State very conveniently skirted the question of whether the charges in the *Statesman*'s article were indeed accurate.

Meade had sought legal proceedings to clear his name, but since the court was likely to ask for the production of confidential papers concerning this episode, this would not be in the public interest. A request to publish the inquiry report by a backbencher, D.R. Onslow, was also declined on the same ground. There is no doubt that a full disclosure would have resulted in a scandal and seriously embarrassed the government and also Meade. Wilfrid S. Blunt, globetrotter and author, reported that two years later, Gorst told him something similar. Blunt was travelling from Hyderabad to Calcutta and found Gorst in the same train and had a long conversation with him.

It seems that Gorst formerly brought the matter of Berar before Lord Salisbury, and interested him in the right way, but Lytton was adverse, and afterwards it was Gorst who prosecuted the 'Statesman' newspaper on the part of the Government for its publication of the facts relating to Salar Jung's attempted arrest, and the bribe taken by Sir Richard Meade. He told me the prosecution was dropped in consequence of representations from the Calcutta Foreign Office that a scandal would be created, and he himself was of opinion that Sir Richard Meade would have come badly out of the affair.[17]

The former resident, Sir George Yule, had also written to Knight supporting him. His letter only confirmed the opinion held by many that Salar Jung had been ill-used by the Government of India.

It is, I think of very great importance that the suit which has been brought against you by the Amir-i-Kabeer, Wikar-ool-Oomra, Co-Regent of Hyderabad, should go to trial. It would be a public misfortune were it to be compromised; for, in common with many others who know the facts, I have long been anxious to see the treatment which Sir Salar Jung has of late years received at the hands of the Government of India (particularly in the appointment of Wikar-ool-Oomra as Co-Regent with him) brought to the notice of the Home Government in such a way as to compel it to make a full inquiry.[18]

Yule said that he would have liked to address the matter to the Secretary of State but an inquiry in the usual way by 'officials' would have been futile and could have resulted in making Salar Jung's position worse (if such a thing were possible) than it was at present. It was also futile, he said, to look for cooperation from Salar Jung because, given his treatment over the years, he had lost faith even in his right to remonstrate. 'His natural caution and modesty have, under the treatment he has received, become developed, I fear, into absolute fault; and anything like co-operation from him, in these circumstances, is not, I am persuaded, to be looked for.'[19]

He proceeded to say that he was overjoyed because he saw the libel suit as a way of exposing Salar Jung's wrongs without implicating him.

When, therefore, I saw in the *Times* a brief report of the prosecution entered against yourself by the Ameer, I rejoiced at it as an opening that might lead to the exposure of Salar Jung's wrongs without implicating him, and I resolved to offer you such help as I might feel justified in giving towards exposing the character of the Co-Regent, regarding whom you have, to the best of my knowledge and belief, said in your article nothing but the truth, *and even less than you would have been justified in saying* [emphasis added] . . . Although I have not referred in this letter to the other matters discussed in your two articles on the Restoration of Berar, I may say that I believe every word in them to be true, and that the main facts are susceptible of complete proof from the reports of our own officers.[20]

This was an endorsement from a person who knew Hyderabad well, and was even more familiar with its intrigues. What is interesting is that Yule feels that the pugnacious editor has pulled his punches in revealing the truth about the amir. But in a sense, it was never about the amir. Knight was targeting the Government of India, which he accused of restoring a discredited man accused of base conduct to favour for no other reason than to utilize his 'audacious unscrupulousness' to thwart Salar Jung. If he was used as a tool to destroy Salar Jung, then it was hoped that he would prove no less effective in the destruction of the *Statesman*. However, the belief that the amir was instigated by the government to undertake his prosecution, as Knight believed, may not have been true. The co-regent consulted legal advisers on his own account, and it was their advice which led him to give his assent to legal proceedings against Knight in England.

The opinion on Knight was mixed. He was considered an earnest man of great ability and considerable experience, often lacking tact and erring in judgement, but imbued with the honest conviction that the special mission of righting all Indian wrongs had been entrusted exclusively to himself. But a good cause may be considerably injured by want of tact and judgement, and by advocacy which is 'unjustifiably violent', something which the press in India accused Knight of. The *Delhi Gazette* thought that the issue was more about Robert Knight and self-projection, and less about India and how it had been wronged.

> If Mr Knight, the self-commissioned Champion of India, were actuated by any other than selfish motives, he would not be so violent, and would not so persistently mar a good cause by his ill-judged advocacy. We cannot avoid the conclusion that it is not India to which he is devoting his time and talents, but Robert Knight . . . He had a good opportunity of doing India a service which would have won for himself a name in history. He has lost it by a too free indulgence in self-glorification, and the display of a much too keen desire to sacrifice everything and everybody to personal conceit.[21]

18

The Reformer

The idea of an organized system of government owes its birth to the vision of Salar Jung. Before him, all power was centralized in the diwan, there being no concept of a regular and systematic form of government with separate departments and secretariats. As Cheragh Ali has observed, 'It was altogether a new idea, an element foreign to the old conservative mind of Hyderabad, to have anything like an organised system of government.'[1] We have already noted the reforms introduced by Salar Jung in the early part of his tenure which were in the nature of setting up basic institutions. They met the crying need of the hour, and materially improved the administration, but much more needed to be done. There was a need for uniformity in the administration, and with the exception of the restored districts, the system of administration in the mofussil had great room for improvement.

The changes described in the following pages have reference to the reforms introduced during the period 1864–80, in which Salar Jung attempted to continue the good work he had set in motion soon after he took over as diwan. While it will be impossible to do justice to all his reforms in the compass of a few pages, the following account provides the flavour.

REFORMS IN ADMINISTRATION: GOVERNMENT DEPARTMENTS

A board of revenue was established in 1864 to supervise and direct the revenue administration, including that of the restored districts. This made the Munshi Khana and the Kacheri-Azla-e-Mustarida—the separate office established for the administration of the restored districts—unnecessary, and both of these were abolished. The board was also given the task of creating uniform civil divisions of the diwani territory. One of the problems faced was that while the number of talukas was fixed, the number of talukdars was subject to an increase or decrease every year. Some talukdars held only a few villages, while others held a number of talukas.[2] It was this disparity which the board of revenue was tasked with eradicating, and this important work of zillabandi started in 1864.

Zillabandi

The unit of administration was the village, and these were united according to convenience into talukas, which again were formed into districts and further into subas or provinces. Before Salar Jung's time, there were five subas: Hyderabad, Aurangabad, Bidar, Bijapur and Berar. After the cession of Berar in May 1853, four remained. But the assigning of territory, granting of jagirs and farming out lands for revenue collection without properly defined limits resulted in the obliteration of territorial boundaries. This made it difficult to collect land revenue. Under zillabandi, the country was divided into well-defined districts called zillas, subdivided into talukas with definite boundaries administered by a regular establishment working under the direct control of the government.

After redistribution was completed in 1867, the whole of the dominions were divided into five divisions, fourteen districts and seventy-four talukas. A sadar talukdar was in charge of each division. The talukdar who was in charge of the district was assisted by two subordinate talukdars, and all three officials had well-defined civil, criminal and executive powers. Talukdars were of three classes, and each class was divided into three grades. At the head of each taluka was a *tehsildar* whose principal duty was to collect land revenue. The talukdars were the superiors of the tehsildar and supervised his work. The lowest official in the village was the patel. There were generally two patels in each village, one for revenue and the other for police purposes. The patwari was the clerk and accountant. The district treasuries were under the talukdar. An establishment of clerks was placed under these officials to assist them in their work. All the officers exercised judicial powers in varying degrees until the time the judiciary was separated from the executive. The munsifs and mir adals appointed for the administration of justice in the districts were abolished.[3]

Since the talukdars of the districts were subordinate to the sadar talukdars, the court of the sadar talukdar also became the court of appeal. They also tried criminal cases which were beyond the powers of talukdars. A few years later, judicial assistants were appointed to help them in the discharge of their judicial duties. Government treasuries were established in each taluka and district, and placed in charge of their respective tehsildars and talukdars. A regular system of assessment and survey and settlement was introduced. Instead of making assessments at harvest time when the peasant was not allowed to touch his crops, assessment was made on a fixed scale once in a year, and the peasant could dispose of his harvest whenever he chose.

The field was the unit of survey, and settlement was made with due regard to climate, proximity of markets, condition of the cultivators and other factors. The term of settlement was thirty years, the same as in British India. A revenue survey school was established at the suggestion of Syed Mahdi Ali, then commissioner of survey so as to obtain the services of trained men. Recognizing the fact that the economic condition of the country depended on the prosperity of the agricultural class, Salar Jung granted further concessions to the peasantry. Land attached to the peasant's house was exempted from assessment, and a proprietary right to his holding was conferred upon him.

Regarding the new system of assessment, the annual report of 'Moral and Material Progress' for the year 1867–68 stated: 'Pains have been taken more and more to render the annual settlements equitable and moderate' so 'that all classes high and low connected with land or trade continue to flourish'.[4] Meade, after an inspection of the public offices in Hyderabad in 1880, observed: '. . . The work and records of the Survey Department appear to me to be admirable and leave nothing to be desired, and the care that has been bestowed on everything in this department was very striking.'[5] Equally striking was the increase in revenue, which had trebled in three decades.

Many years ago, Saunders had been similarly appreciative when he observed: 'Owing chiefly to the abolition of the baneful system of former times, by which the collection of revenue was farmed out to contractors, disturbances in the interior of the country became rare. The Hyderabad Contingent has not fired a shot, except on their own parade ground, since the suppression of the Mutinies. In no respect does the recent administration of His Highness's country contrast more favourably with the state of things prevailing twenty years ago than in the regard to revenue matters.'[6]

Revenue Department and Finance

In 1864, the office of the accountant general was established which was charged with keeping the accounts of the entire territories of the nizam. He was empowered to correspond directly with the talukdars and to introduce the new tabular statement of accounts, similar to the accounts maintained in the restored districts. The talukdars sent him a number of monthly and annual reports. At the end of the year, the accountant general submitted the annual accounts, along with his suggestions to improve the system. The new system was calculated to bring about uniformity in the statement of accounts. In the same year, a Daftar-i-Tankih was placed under the charge of an auditor general whose duty consisted of auditing accounts and all pay bills before money was disbursed from the government treasury.[7] In the metropolis, a separate office was established for the state treasury.

A revenue secretary was appointed under Salar Jung in 1864. Apart from issuing his orders on revenue-related matters, he also attended to correspondence with the board of revenue, the accountant general and the auditor general. The revenue secretary also took over the functions of the administration of the restored districts, and the Kacheri-Azla-e-Mustarida was abolished. Salar Jung was personally in charge of all revenue reforms, the revenue payable by a village, appointments of talukdars, police, stamp paper and taxes.[8] In revenue matters, Salar Jung was assisted by his nephew, Mukaram-ud-Daula. The accountant general's office was asked to give its views on financial matters, and, in time, it developed into the finance department.

In 1864, a separate office called the Daftar-i-Mulki was established, which eventually became the political department. It dealt with transactions with the British government and the talukdars. It issued orders for the grant of jagirs, and crimes such as conspiracies against the state, robbery of mail and dacoity, were also under its purview. In the same year, an office was created under a secretary and an assistant to attend to all matters concerned with the regular forces. While there was no separate office for matters connected with the irregular troops, there was an officer who looked after the roll of establishment and other matters connected with these forces. In 1876, a military secretary was appointed. The office which looked after the distribution of mansabs, hitherto under the revenue secretary, was now transferred to the military secretary in 1877.

In the period 1864–66, Salar Jung established the nucleus of a secretariat, with a number of secretaries directly reporting to him. His reforms during this period followed the model of the restored districts (which had been under British administration from 1853–60), and Berar. The next phase of reforms saw the abolition of the board of revenue. Since many of the duties which had hitherto been performed by the board of revenue were assigned to the sadar talukdars, that body was left with a much-diminished workload. Salar Jung decided to appoint three of the board members as sadar talukdars, and in place of the board, a central revenue department, Sadar Mahakma-i-Malguzari was established under the control of two officers. But this proved to be a short-lived experiment, and in 1868, four Sadar-ul-Mahams or ministers of department, were created.

The four ministers were from noble families, and there was a Sadar-ul-Maham for each of the functions of revenue, judicial, police and miscellaneous matters. Mukaram-ud-Daula was appointed the minister for revenue, and was responsible for agriculture and commerce, stamp paper, customs, forests and excise. In 1869, Bashir-ud-Daula was appointed the first minister of justice with powers to supervise the courts, and Shamsher Jung became minister for police. The post of inspector general of police, created in 1867, was under him, but it was soon abolished. Shahab Jung Bahadur was appointed minister for miscellaneous affairs and was given charge of public works, education, medical, municipalities and village roads. The chief engineer of public works reported to him.

Regardless of the creation of the Sadar-ul-Mahams power remained centralized in the office of the diwan. A number of secretaries dealt directly with Salar Jung, and these included those of the political and legal departments and the military secretaries of the regular and irregular troops. Salar Jung retained direct control of the central treasury, mint, post office and railways, and post and telegraphs. Even in the subjects transferred to the ministers, Salar Jung exercised considerable authority. The power to sanction the budget and all public expenditure vested with him. Thus, rather than full-fledged policymakers, the ministers were little more than high-ranking executives. All the real power was centralized in the office of the diwan and the person of Salar Jung.

The posts of Sadar-ul-Mahams were created not so much for the sake of better administration, but because Salar Jung discovered that his attempts to dissociate the nobility from the new administration jeopardized its public acceptance by them. A nominal association of a few influential nobles with some of the new departments as 'ministers' helped win their support as also that of the public. Administration was not hampered in any way since it was in the hands of competent secretaries. This measure also served the goal of educating the younger nobility.[9]

In 1871, mines and quarries were placed under the charge of the superintendent of forests, and rules were framed for charging duty on persons working the mines and quarries. In 1875, a survey and settlement department was organized and placed under the charge of a commissioner. Initially started as a small experiment in Pattan taluka, its success was the reason it was extended to the whole of Aurangabad, and a superintendent of revenue survey was appointed with four or five assistant superintendents under him. He was further assisted by a deputy who was entrusted with the supervision of the accounts, stores, printing and mapping branches. In 1877, this was also extended to Naldurg district, with a similar administrative structure. In 1878, an irrigation department was formed for the purpose of carrying out minor irrigation works under the Sadar-ul-Maham. The next year, a department for the settlement of boundary disputes was formed, and a settlement officer was appointed with seven assistants under him.

The person Salar Jung entrusted with the post of commissioner of the survey and settlement department was Syed Mahdi Ali. Salar Jung had a peculiar insight into the character of men, and his discerning judgement seldom failed to form a correct estimate of a man's worth. With the help of this remarkable ability, he was able to gather around him some of the ablest minds of northern India, of which Mahdi Ali was undoubtedly one of the most gifted. He had been tehsildar of Etawah, where he attracted the attention of Sir Allan Octavian Hume who was the collector of Etawah at the time. He passed the exam for deputy collectorship and was posted as deputy collector of Mirzapur.

Salar Jung brought him to Hyderabad in 1867, and he was appointed inspector general of revenue and later commissioner of the settlement and survey department. A friend and disciple of Sir Syed Ahmed Khan, he subsequently became Salar Jung's revenue secretary. After Salar Jung's death, he was ennobled and received the titles of Munir Nawaz Jung, Mohsin-ud-Daula and finally Mohsin-ul-Mulk, a title by which he was known to the world for the rest of his life. He was also responsible for the introduction of Urdu in place of Persian as the court language in the capital and the mofussil.

Judicial Reforms

The Sadar Adalat-e-Azla-Mustarida, which had been established to hear appeals from judicial officers in the restored districts and to decide references made by talukdars, was converted into a court of appeal with jurisdiction over the entire diwani territory and was renamed Mahakma-e-Sadar Murafa.

In 1872, a court of appeal, Mahakma-e-Murafa-e-Azla, was established which heard civil and criminal appeals from all the metropolitan courts and also from the mofussil. It consisted of a chief justice and four associate justices. Cheragh Ali described it as an appellate court of judicature. It was also empowered to frame rules of procedure for all the courts of justice. But the diwan and the minister for justice could order a retrial, a power which could be abused by either of them. In 1874, Salar Jung agreed to regard the decision of the court as final, but the people were not pleased with this decision and he continued to interfere, contrary to his own order. A list of thirty-four heinous crimes was prepared over which the court was to have original jurisdiction. The diwan retained the death sentence and life imprisonment in his hands.

In 1872, a new court called the Adalat-ul-Aliyah was set up which consisted of a chief justice and four associate judges. It entertained appeals from the Dar-ul-Qaza, Diwani-e-Buzurg, Faujdari-e-Buzurg and Adalat-e-Murafa-e-Azla. Appeals above Rs 5000 were entertained by Salar Jung himself. It had original jurisdiction within the city limits in civil suits involving more than a certain minimum amount, but it had no jurisdiction over the lower courts as its counterpart in British India had, even though it was styled as a high court. The Sadar-ul-Maham adalat supervised the administration of justice in the entire diwani territories. He controlled all the courts, whether civil or criminal, in the metropolis and the mofussil. He also issued stamp paper used by the courts. He could also order a retrial in exceptional cases, with the sanction of the diwan.

An interesting innovation was the establishment of the panchayat system in the city which was later extended to the villages. This differed from the panchayat which settled disputes among the Hindus and whose members were drawn from among the village elders. The Dar-ul-Infasalath, or panchayat, had a statutory basis, unlike the panchayat which was based on custom and usages. It was presided over by an arbiter appointed by the government who could either be a Muslim or a Hindu. It settled both civil and criminal cases, and administered both Muslim and Hindu law. The new experiment was announced through a notification in 1875, and the rules of proceedings were transmitted to all panchayats through a circular, with the high court ensuring that the proceedings were conducted in accordance with the rules. It proved to be a success, with residents of other localities also submitting petitions for the extension of the scheme. The success of the new panchayats was largely due to the able persons who acted as arbiters (*hakam*s). This gradually led to the decline of the old panchayat system.

We have already noted the setting up of a judicial secretariat in 1862. Moulvi Moiduddin Khan was the first judicial secretary. The most famous judicial secretary was Moulvi Mushtaq Hussain, who assumed charge in 1876. A former sadar talukdar of Gulbarga, he was a supporter of the separation of the judiciary from the executive. In 1880, he drew Salar Jung's attention to the steps required to be taken in this regard. He suggested that the office of minister of justice be abolished, and an all-powerful high court be established. Salaries of the judicial officers were to be increased, and revenue and judicial functions separated, with judges and sub-judges appointed in the districts and talukas. It is said that the history of judicial administration from 1883 to 1921 is the history of the implementation of his proposals.

In 1875, Salar Jung established a legal department tasked with the framing of rules and regulations for the guidance of courts. A *nazim* was appointed to supervise the department. Two years later in 1877, a legal secretary was appointed who was to assist the government in the formulation of rules and regulations for the courts.

Police Reforms

The police administration was reorganized in 1865, and this year marks the beginning of modern police administration. A separate police force was created for the city and the suburbs and for the districts. A superintendent of police was in charge of a district, and each functionary had his own separate establishment. A code of rules was framed to define the powers and duties of the new functionaries. An inspector of police (*amin*) was appointed for every two talukas. The superintendents were divided into three grades and the inspectors into two classes, each class having three grades. With the appointment of a separate superintendent of police, the expenses of the police office establishment increased considerably.[10]

A Police Act was passed which defined the powers of the force. The police force was now under a legal obligation to assist the judicial department in the dispensation of justice. The entire police force was under the talukdars of the district, and the police was bound to execute any order issued by any of the talukdars and the tehsildar in their official capacity. A police code drawn up in 1865 by the board of revenue contained details about the discipline and dress of the force. It also enumerated a list of offences in which the police could or could not interfere, and a set of detailed rules as to the manner in which the police was to carry out its duties.

In 1867, the police department was separated from the revenue department. A sadar *muhtamim* was put in charge of the police department, and the whole state was divided into divisions with each division being headed by a *naib* sadar muhtamim of kotwali, or deputy inspector general of police who was subordinate to the sadar muhtamim kotwali, the inspector general of police. When the post of Sadar-ul-Mahams kotwali or minister of police was created with Shamsher Jung Bahadur as its first incumbent, it had under its control the entire police administration in the metropolis and the mofussil. With the exception of a few large jagirs, the jurisdiction of the police included jagirs. In cases where the big jagirdars had their own police force, this force was expected to help the diwani police when necessary. The railway police, which was introduced later, was under the supervision of the resident.

Miscellaneous Reforms

A public works department was set up in 1867, with a sadar muhtamim, or chief engineer, in charge. When the office of Sadar-ul-Maham mutafarrikat, or minister for miscellaneous affairs, was appointed, this department along with education, medical and municipality, and village roads were under his supervision. The office of chief engineer was retained but was subordinate to the minister. In 1869, a workshop as a department of the public works department was established, as was a public works department store. In 1875, a geological survey department was started with a superintendent in charge.

Postal services had existed in a very rudimentary form when Salar Jung assumed office. There were a number of post offices operated by the British which were primarily for correspondence to and from British territory. Mail between the districts and Hyderabad also passed through these post offices till regular communication between Hyderabad and the districts was set up in 1862. In 1871, a postmaster general was appointed, with post offices now springing up in the districts and talukas. The mail was delivered through a system of daily runners.[11]

Other changes included the establishment of a Persian private secretary to the diwan and the creation of a secretary to the diwan in the miscellaneous department to deal with official business connected with the educational and medical departments. These duties were added to the revenue secretary and later to the office of the Persian private secretary. On similar lines, the public works department and the department of public education had sadar muhtamims, or divisional engineers, and muhtamim talimat, or inspectors of education respectively.

Salar Jung's tenure as diwan was also witness to technological advances in communication such as the electric telegraph. Hyderabad was connected with Bombay and Kurnool in 1856–57, and Salar Jung used the new device for official purposes as well as for personal reasons. The telegraph, which owed its existence in India to Lord Dalhousie, often faced problems from lawless elements: Salar Jung once complained to the raja of Wanaparthy about the lines being cut in his jurisdiction.[12]

Educational Reforms

The modern system of education in Hyderabad owes its origin to Salar Jung. He established schools and colleges, and lent his support to medical and engineering colleges. His primary aim appears to have been the supply of competent personnel to man government posts. He regarded the state as the chief means of social change, and seems to have been less aware of the importance of education and technical expertise in fostering a scientific temper and effecting change. He thought it necessary to train the nobility in Western tradition because he expected them to be in the vanguard of progress and development of Hyderabad.

When Salar Jung first became diwan, everything was in a deplorable condition, and the education system was no exception. The madrasas had declined due to lack of government patronage, and the curriculum seems to have been restricted to the Koran, and some penmanship. Subjects like philosophy, law and logic were not taught at all. Such learning, it appears, was confined to the nobility, who appointed tutors for their children.

In 1834, an English public school was opened by a clergyman of the Church of England. Soon after he became diwan, Salar Jung established the Oriental College (Dar-ul-Uloom) at Hyderabad in 1853–54, where the medium of instruction was Arabic, Persian and English, and where Marathi and Telugu were also taught. It had about 160 students, and it was Salar Jung's aim to produce 'young men of superior attainments for the service of the state'. By 1860, a school had been opened in each district headquarter and taluka. When the Sadar-ul-Mahams were appointed, education was placed under the minister for miscellaneous affairs, and an officer was appointed as education secretary and director of public instruction in 1869–70. The curricula were revised, and the educational services were reorganized.[13]

In 1860, a college for civil engineering was established to which a school for teaching English was also attached. In 1872, this school became the Chadarghat Anglo-Vernacular School which later served as the nucleus of the Hyderabad College, which was affiliated to Madras University in 1884. In 1878, Salar Jung established the Madrasa-i-Aliya for the education of his sons and those of other nobles. It operated from Rumbold's Kothi at Chadarghat, and Mr Krohn was its first headmaster.

Western medicine was introduced in Hyderabad in 1846, thanks to the vision and ability of the residency surgeon, Dr W.C. Maclean, who set up a medical college when General Fraser was the resident. He was encouraged by Siraj-ul-Mulk, and in 1853, eighteen candidates were examined by a committee, of which ten passed at the first attempt, and eight were declared successful the next year. Some of the graduates were appointed in government posts and designated hakims; others carried on private practice. The residency surgeon was also the head of the medical department of the nizam's government.

The atmosphere in Hyderabad was not conducive to the spread of Western medicine. The nizam never took recourse to it, nor did Salar Jung. The latter, in fact, was averse to taking any medicine at all, and refused to take treatment of any kind, even when he was near prostrate from diarrhoea on one occasion. He did, however, intervene in 1856, when Dr George Smith, the residency surgeon, reported that some of his Muslim students had refused to dissect a dead body. Salar Jung spoke to one of the objectors himself, and asked him to waive all religious scruples in the study of his profession.[14]

An Unfinished Agenda

Unfortunately, Salar Jung died before he could witness the completion of the edifice whose foundations he had laid in very trying circumstances. The events after his death were only a confirmation of his reforms, and a consolidation of his policies on broader and deeper lines. In fact, he had proposed a complete reorganization of the administration in 1882, but it could only be partially implemented before mortality intervened. Mahdi Ali had drawn up a confidential paper bringing attention to the defects in the administrative machinery, especially the Sadar-ul-Maham system. Salar Jung agreed with him but said that he had implemented the Sadar-ul-Maham scheme so as to avoid the accusation that he was not training the nobles of Hyderabad for high positions in government. In any case, so many conflicting interests had to be conciliated in the late 1870s that he had been unable to put pressure on the Sadar-ul-Mahams—who were in the hands of their subordinates—to perform better.

Salar Jung had planned that the powers exercised by the Sadar-ul-Mahams would be transferred to a board of revenue, a high court and committees. The Sadar-ul-Mahams would now be assistants to the Madar-ul-Maham, the diwan. The board of revenue, abolished in 1867, was reconstituted, and all revenue offices, with the exception of the commissioner of revenue survey and settlement, were placed under it. A number of important departments such as the mint, post office, stamps, treasury, accountant general, and revenue survey and settlement, were to be supervised directly by the diwan's revenue office that would also prepare the budget and report on general administration.

An inspector general of police was to be created, but he would have no jurisdiction over the city or suburban police and the city jails. A reorganization of the judiciary with a separation of civil and criminal powers was planned. The high court was to be given increased powers, and a supreme judicial council would supervise the working of the high court.

Salar Jung's reforms thus envisaged a further centralization of power in the hands of the diwan. However, only the board of revenue could be established before his death in February 1883.

SOCIAL AND CULTURAL CHANGE IN HYDERABAD

Salar Jung changed the face of Hyderabad by making numerous improvements, but he was conservative when it came to the social sphere. He mistakenly believed that age-old usages and customs could be continued forever, regardless of the change in other aspects of society. He thought that he could modernize the administration, the army and the education system but still freeze social customs in the Mughlai pattern, not realizing that it was impossible to prevent changes in one sphere from affecting the others. This was a misconception he laboured under all his life. He was determined not to disturb the old Mughlai way of life, the most sacrosanct being the etiquette to be observed in the presence of the nizam.

But change was inevitable. With constant exposure to Europeans, and also visits to England by the nobles, it was only a matter of time before there were changes in clothing, language, education, transportation, furniture and even the status of women. It was a top-down process. The changes first appeared among the nobles and then slowly filtered down to all levels of society. We have already noted the squabble over shoes and sitting on the floor in a previous chapter. The custom in Hyderabad was to spread white sheets over the carpets and to sit on them in the lotus position. The nizam sat on an arrangement of pillows and bolsters covered in the royal yellow colour. On ceremonial occasions, velvet with gold embroidery was used, transforming the gaddi into a masnad. Saunders had made a big fuss about removing his shoes and sitting on the ground. Later, Salar Jung acquiesced and started providing chairs for the resident and his party. But he took care to arrange the masnad on a raised platform so that everyone was at the same level. When Mahbub was older, he made a throne for himself and chairs for his court. (Chairs and western furniture were now common in the houses of the nobles.)

The changes in the style of sitting affected in turn the style of dressing. The neema jama and angharka looked awkward and clumsy in a chair. They were best suited for sitting on the floor, where they also looked graceful. The pyjama and the sherwani now took centre stage, and Mahbub was the first nizam to wear this garment on official occasions. It was also a favourite with Salar Jung. With the change in sitting and dressing, the need to proceed barefoot due to reasons of hygiene disappeared, since it was now clear that the floors were meant only for walking on. Gradually, this custom, which had for long been a source of great annoyance, disappeared.

It had also been a highly misunderstood custom which had acquired implications of status for the British. They equated discalceation with inferior status, whereas in the past, there had been no such association. In a later development, servants and tradesmen entering British homes observed the traditional custom, and ironically discalceation acquired validity as indicative of relative status. The British went into society bareheaded but with shoes; the Hyderabadis covered their heads but removed their shoes. In Hyderabad, removing footwear was not a matter of dignity, but of politeness. But as in other spheres, change was inevitable here as well: within a decade and a half, Mahbub and his entire court were wearing shoes.

Shoes and discalceation seem to have been rather important to the British. Unhappy at having to remove their own footwear, they had no compunction about enforcing this rule when it suited them. In March 1862, long before Saunders' successful protest at the time of Mahbub's accession to the masnad, an incident occurred in Bombay which became famous as 'the Shoe Question'. Nusserwanjee Byramjee, a Parsi cabinetmaker, was barred from appearing before the income tax commissioners at the Town Hall in Bombay till he removed his native-style shoes at the entrance of the room. Byramjee objected on the grounds that such removal was contrary to his faith, while the British officials maintained that the gesture was an established and expected mark of respect. If Byramjee had chosen to wear Western-style shoes or worn stockings with his traditional footwear, he would have been allowed to enter. Simin Patel observes, 'The colonial imagination condensed, though not consistently, the complex codes of dress in India into the categories of native and western wear, demanding from the wearer bodily deportments associated with each style. The observance of "shoe respect", as the Indian tradition of removing shoes at various thresholds came to be called, was expected particularly of native citizens who wore indigenous footwear in official settings.'[15]

The chairs led to a different and less elaborate style of dressing and eliminated the need to discalceate. The increased contacts between the British and the native people also influenced a gradual shift in language from Persian to the vernacular Urdu, and then to English. But Persian had the blessings of Salar Jung, and Persian remained the language of the Hyderabad durbar till the last quarter of the nineteenth century, even though in British India, English had replaced Persian in the second quarter of that century.

The establishment of railway communication between Hyderabad and the outer world contributed powerfully to the completeness of the change which came over the spirit and methods of Hyderabad politics. Nobles, who formerly never travelled beyond the limits of the nizam's dominions and rarely left the city, now visited Bombay and Calcutta, and even crossed the seas to distant Europe. The notion of resisting reforms merely because of the changes they would engender had grown fainter: the sense of inability to stop the clock and force back the hands increased with the passage of time.

THE MULKI–NON-MULKI CONFLICT

We have already noted how Salar Jung as a young diwan had to modernize the revenue system and the bureaucracy to achieve financial stability. For this purpose, he utilized British administrative practices and advice while recruiting qualified personnel from outside Hyderabad. While he did attempt to introduce new, and at the time modern, administration, he ensured that the old Mughlai institutions, their personnel and the nobility of Hyderabad were preserved. He used them to counter British interference, and also to curb the power of the new class of outsiders who had been imported to run the diwani administration.

When Salar Jung became co-regent in 1869, the minority of the heir gave him a free hand to make the changes he wanted. Indians with British training and experience were inducted into the administration after 1869. Salar Jung took personal interest in this endeavour, and many were personally selected by him. Perhaps the best example of his personal interest is the selection of first John Clerk, and then his brother Claude Clerk, to superintend the education of the young nizam. On occasion, he took the advice of the resident or the Government of India.

The bias seems to have been in favour of recruiting Muslims from north India. After the Mutiny, Mughal administration in Delhi ended, and many Delhi Muslims took employment in Hyderabad. Others, recently retired from service under the British, also came to Hyderabad. In 1872–73, Salar Jung had written to Sir Syed Ahmed Khan to obtain the services of civil servants from north India. Aligarh became a major source of recruitment in the 1870s, with many of those who took jobs in Hyderabad being associated with Sir Syed Ahmed Khan and the fledgling Aligarh Muslim University. The family of Sir Syed had a long association with Hyderabad, and Sir Syed visited Hyderabad, as we have already noted, in 1882 when Salar Jung was still diwan. He visited Hyderabad again in 1891, bringing with him his disciples who included the poet, Hali. His son, Syed Mahmood, was appointed a judge of the Hyderabad High Court.

It was to these persons that the term 'non-Mulki' was applied; they were also called 'Hindustani' since the majority were from north India. Apart from these, there were Parsis and Hindus and some Europeans as well.[16] This started a process which led to a scenario where the Mulkis (old residents of Hyderabad who considered themselves to be sons of the soil) were pitted against the non-Mulkis. But this was not the first time that outsiders had entered the state, and the entry of these on Salar Jung's invitation was not unique. Karen Leonard's study of the kayasthas shows that such a migration continued for many generations, and that Hyderabad had always been regarded as fertile ground for employment by the Mughals and other good families from Delhi.

The persons brought in from Awadh and Lucknow were regarded with jealousy by the natives of Hyderabad, 'and created a sense of grievance among the local population who felt that they were unfairly excluded from the loaves and fishes of office'.[17] These men drew high salaries, and the avenues of promotion were entirely under their control. The natural-born Hyderabadi, 'uneducated and useless despaired of obtaining employment or enjoying the consideration and honour which was the portion of their forefathers'. The discontent, which had confined itself to the detestation of the instruments, was later extended to the head of the administration, Salar Jung. The appointment of Syed Mahdi Ali and Fida Hussain as revenue secretary and chief justice caused much resentment. The vast power wielded by the former was viewed with great jealousy, particularly since he had the power to make appointments. He was supreme in his own department, the survey department, and Salar Jung also consulted him on the working of the others. It is said that Salar Jung was led by him in almost all matters.

Another associate of Sir Syed Ahmed Khan was Moulvi Cheragh Ali, whose book *A Critical Exposition of the Popular 'Jihad'*, published in 1885, is still relevant today. A man of keen intellect and great learning, he was, in a sense, more radical than his mentor Sir Syed to whom the book was dedicated. His work was more than just a refutation of myths about jihad: it was a powerful plea for a rational understanding of the Koran and Hadith.[18] Cheragh Ali was also responsible for the multi-volume *Hyderabad (Deccan) under Sir Salar Jung*, which is an indispensable guide to the administration under Salar Jung.

The *Bombay Gazette* noted that Salar Jung's task was an extremely difficult one, and in an observation which still resonates with the India of today, observed:

> Like all native States, Hyderabad contains plenty of intriguers and malcontents who are always ready to give trouble if they cannot get into Government employment. The ambition of most people who live under native rule is not to work honestly for a living, but to live at the expense of other people by currying favour with the Prince or his courtiers and getting a public situation from them. This fact represents one of the greatest difficulties which Salar Jung has to contend with.[19]

The same newspaper also noted the resentment of the Hyderabadis towards Salar Jung for importing personnel to man the administration:

> One of the greatest bones of contention in Hyderabad is the employment of foreigners and men from Oudh and the North-West Provinces. Sir Salar Jung prefers to choose his own men to carry out the work for which he is responsible, and he chooses these outsiders evidently because he thinks he cannot get the talent and ability he constantly requires about him in Hyderabad. His colleague in the Government, an old-fashioned Mahomedan, who loves his own people and the pleasure of patronizing them, not so much for the service they are able to do the State as for the amount of private satisfaction they are able to afford him, either by obsequious conduct or by zeal in obstructing a rival . . . and by doing so has gained considerable popularity. It would appear as if nothing had done so much to weaken the hold which Sir Salar Jung undoubtedly had at one time upon the affections of his people as this preference for foreigners to the exclusion of Hyderabadees.[20]

Later, during the time of Salar Jung II, the change of the official language from Persian to Urdu gave an advantage to the migrants from North India, especially to the kayasthas and Muslims who were fluent in that language.

Salar Jung realized that the importing of British practices and outside personnel could have a serious cultural and political impact on Hyderabadi society. In order to ensure that this did not happen, he developed policies which were designed to isolate the new administrators and the British officials, not only from each other, but also from the nizam and other important nobles in Hyderabad. The diwans preceding Salar Jung had denied the resident access to the nobles of Hyderabad to prevent intrigue, and Salar Jung continued with this policy till his death in 1883.

Afzal-ud-Daula had wanted the Paigah nobles to have little interaction with Salar Jung. His suspicious nature visualized the ridiculous combine of the latter with the former, against him. He also wanted the nobility to have no truck with the residency, something Temple thought absurd, but which Salar Jung approved of. Temple observed: 'I again pointed out the absurdity of the notion, but I rather feared that the Minister seemed to think it was reasonable.'[21] Salar Jung had promised Temple that he would help in the matter but did nothing. He was almost as keen as the nizam that there should be no interaction with the resident and the nobles so as to preclude intrigue, something which was already in great abundance in Hyderabad. Temple may have realized this when he remarked: 'The Minister promised that this should be done. I was by no means sure, however, that it would, for this was the one, and so far only point on which I was dissatisfied with the Salar Jang. It is . . . bad policy to keep the Resident secluded and in the dark as regards the real character, individually and collectively, of the upper classes. I feared that the Salar Jang either gave in to the prejudice, or else concurred in it.'[22]

Salar Jung also sought to prevent access to traditional sources of power and tried not to draw too many recruits from the same source. The diwani employees had no status in court and received salaries. They received no jagirs or titles, nor any hereditary stipends or mansabs. If diwani officials wanted to visit the resident or any important noble, they had to take special permission from Salar Jung. He viewed them as mere employees, who, on no account, were to have any connection with either his private affairs or with the royal palace. Their usefulness started and ended with their role in administrative matters.

Even in administrative matters, only Hyderabadis were entrusted with sensitive posts. Thus, men from Salar Jung's own jagir headed the accountancy and treasury department, where they worked under his close supervision. Similarly, another Hyderabadi was chosen for the reform of the customs department, which was an influential and important post. Salar Jung was aware that there was a predominance of north Indians in his administration, and selected as a counter, Kandaswamy, a Tamilian, as his English-speaking vakil to represent him to the resident, fully aware that the man was intensely disliked by many north Indians. He vigorously opposed the suggestion from the north Indian Muslims that Urdu replace Persian as the language of administration.

It must be remembered that Salar Jung, for all his reforming zeal, was a conservative at heart, and therefore his vision of society was also a conservative one. Two essential points were always given importance before any administrative decision was taken. Firstly, there was to be no violation of the precepts of Muslim law. Secondly, there was to be no abrupt change which affected the customs and rules followed by the people. Salar Jung was guarding against any sudden discontinuity since he maintained that all the people 'require is that they shall be left in the enjoyment of their old established customs and usages, any disruption of which is sure to be felt by them as hurtful'.[23] Salar Jung, writing to an English friend, outlined his views on this subject. He said that he liked to be liberal as far as improvement of the people and advancement of public life was concerned, but was a conservative when it came to the question of national usages and customs so long as they did not impede progress. His idea was to continue to enjoy the sympathies of both the progressive and conservative parties.[24]

It is therefore clear that Salar Jung was conciliatory in his approach: he wanted to ruffle as few feathers as possible so that he could continue unhindered in his agenda of improving the administrative machinery of Hyderabad. He also tried to minimize the opposition from the nizam, the nobles and the old Mughlai officials. He took particular care not to antagonize the nobles, who if they wanted, could make trouble for him and were also his rivals for power. Karen Leonard maintains that Salar Jung believed that the nobles were the living representatives of the court culture and political traditions of Hyderabad, and he wished to preserve them in that role.[25] The policy of separation between the new administrative personnel and the nobles kept the diwani administrators free from intrigue and under his control, while also preserving the values and traditions of old Hyderabad. 'Thus the social and ceremonial life of the court continued to flourish, despite a demonstrable and increasing erosion of the nobles' political power in the state.'[26]

The restriction on political and social contacts led to the development of two separate societies. This was in contrast with the social life before the 1820s, where there were cases of individual Europeans and even early

British residents who had successfully become 'White Mughals'. Another area where the British could not go was the old walled city. The reason given was that the presence of armed and dangerous irregular forces presented a danger to their safety. If the British did not enter the old walled city, then the nobles too seldom ventured out. This suited Salar Jung well, since he sometimes presented the conservatism of the zenana and the Paigah nobles as an excuse for denying the resident. According to Server-ul-Mulk, by consulting the nizam's grandmother and other ladies of the zenana 'in certain important political matters . . . [Salar Jung] was able to protect himself from the unreasonable interference of the Resident, by the use of her ladyship's name'.[27] 'On several controversial issues during his thirty-year tenure, Salar Jung forestalled reform measures urged by successive Residents by citing cultural backwardness on the part of the Nizam or nobles.'[28]

While Salar Jung wanted to keep the political distinct from the social, there were exceptions. He subscribed generously towards the cost of what is now the Secunderabad Club on the understanding that a certain number of nobles and high officers would be admitted as members. This helped promote intimate relations and a feeling of friendship and goodwill with the British.[29] The building of the club which he donated was at one time his hunting lodge, and the land, part of his jagir. To this day, his descendants are given immediate and free membership of the club. Today, Salar Jung's marble bust, which looks benevolently on all those who sit in the colonnade, is the only artefact which links him to the club. His son, Laik Ali Khan Salar Jung II, founded the Nizam Club in Hyderabad, which till Independence had the prime minister of Hyderabad as its president.

Many of Salar Jung's reforms started in the 1870s. Karen Leonard identifies two important turning points in the pace of his reforms. The first was in 1869 when Afzal-ud-Daula died and Salar Jung became the co-regent. The second came in 1877 when Rashid-ud-din Khan died, and Salar Jung was finally freed from his baleful influence. Both these deaths allowed him to centralize the evolving administration under himself and freed him from the need to conciliate the Mughlai nobles.[30] But perception of these changes was slowed by his attempt to preserve traditional structures and personnel, especially those close to the nizam. This also helped conceal the passing of political power to the new structures which he had centralized under himself. It was this tendency which made Salar Jung vulnerable to the charge that he was 'power hungry' and was only interested in the aggrandizement of his own position.

19

An Era Ends

In April 1878, Lord Salisbury, who had given unqualified support to Lytton, became foreign secretary in England. His departure was a personal loss to the viceroy. Salisbury's successor, Viscount Cranbrook, gave him full freedom but Lytton's own days as viceroy were numbered. In April 1880, Gladstone came back to power and Lytton resigned. There was no question of any cooperation between Lytton and the new prime minister or, for that matter, his secretary of state, Lord Hartington. The latter had, in fact, openly declared in Parliament that Lytton was unfit to hold the post of viceroy.

RIPON'S ARRIVAL

The new viceroy, Lord Ripon, who assumed charge in June 1880, was a good choice for India. He had been undersecretary (1861) and Secretary of State for India (for a few months in 1866), and was no stranger to Indian affairs. Of sound pedigree, he was the son of a prime minister,[1] being born in 10, Downing Street when his father was in office. He was a wise administrator, closely interested in the people's welfare, and although he never exhibited any outstanding brilliance or ability, he never deviated from a high code of honour and duty throughout his life. His appointment as viceroy gave him the distinction of becoming the first Catholic to occupy a high office of state since the seventeenth century.

Ripon resembled Lytton in being a short man with a large beard, but there any similarity ended. In other respects, he was Lytton's antithesis. Lytton was handsome, whereas Ripon was decidedly plain. Lytton was a brilliant speaker; Ripon was 'prosaic, endowed with neither grace nor sparkle',[2] and an altogether dull speaker. Lytton was bright but tended to be volatile; Ripon was steady but something of a mediocrity. Whereas Lytton was a bit of a dandy when it came to dressing, Ripon was known for his total disregard for sartorial elegance. There was also one other important difference: Ripon was by far the wealthier of the two; in fact, he was probably the wealthiest of all the viceroys, not counting two of his successors who had married into great wealth.

Sarvepalli Gopal has remarked that while British policy was in essentials decided by the government of the day, there were times when the personal touch of understanding made a world of difference.[3] While general policy directives came from London, a great deal depended on the attitude of the viceroy—whether he had decided to understand and conciliate, or divide and manipulate, the people he governed. A man noted for his sincerity and moral earnestness, Ripon was far more tactful and diplomatic than his predecessor. He disapproved of Lytton's treatment of Salar Jung, calling it 'foolish and violent to a high degree'. He was, from the start, anxious to forge a better relationship with the minister. Ripon disapproved of Lytton's India policy and was determined to convince Indians that he wanted to govern them in their own interest, rather than any narrow, selfish objectives of the British. On the subject of British paramountcy, however, there was no difference of opinion between him and his predecessor.

Lytton had warned Ripon about Salar Jung before he left India. He believed Salar Jung to be 'positively dangerous', his paranoia once again on display when he warned his successor about a strong Muslim state. In the final analysis, the fight between the viceroy and the minister only served to alienate the people of Hyderabad and destroyed the friendship between the two governments. Lytton derived great pleasure from getting the better of Salar Jung in a fight which he seems to have made a personal one. But Salar Jung was labouring under many disadvantages, and the contest could hardly be called an equal one. In the end, after all the fuss and fury, it was also entirely pointless.

Ripon was eager to establish a better relationship with Salar Jung but without letting down his guard. In a private letter to Hartington, he wrote: 'The true way to deal with the subject is . . . to take a new departure in regard to British relations with Salar Jung, without of course abandoning the watchfulness which it is necessary to maintain in the case of a person who is evidently so prone to intrigue as Sir Salar Jung, or allowing him to assume the uncontrolled power at which it seems evident that he formerly aimed.'[4]

Meade's successor was Sir Steuart Bayley, in whom Ripon reposed great trust, and whose tact and diplomacy could be relied upon to smooth things out. The new resident was cut from a cloth entirely different from that of Meade. He was sympathetically inclined to Hyderabad and was able to establish a good rapport with Salar Jung, a relationship which the bullying Meade had completely destroyed. Meade had, in fact, proposed to leave Hyderabad well before the completion of his term as he thought that he deserved a well-earned rest. But his financial resources were so greatly reduced by a bank failure, and a general depreciation in securities, that he was obliged to ask that his proposal for premature retirement be kept in abeyance. Lytton was more than happy to retain him. 'A change in the important post you now hold would have been to me just at the present moment rather embarrassing. The longer you hold it the better pleased I shall be . . .'[5]

In spite of all that had passed between them on the political front, Salar Jung corresponded with Meade after he had left Hyderabad, an epistolary connection that ended with Salar Jung's sudden demise in February 1883. On 27 March 1881, soon after Meade had left Hyderabad, Salar Jung wrote him a brief letter:

> I write a few lines to wish you good-bye and God-speed home, which the sudden movement of the train and the hurried manner in which you were obliged to take your place prevented my doing at the station on Wednesday. As you said in your speech at the dinner given by the Hyderabad Club we have had many official differences during your career as Resident of Hyderabad but I am sure our private relations have always been and will continue to be friendly as long as we are spared. On hearing from you of your safe arrival in England I hope to have the pleasure of writing to you, and I hope our correspondence will never be interrupted.[6]

In Hyderabad, the thaw in relations with the arrival of the new resident showed results almost immediately. Bayley got the co-administrators to sign a formal resolution regulating the education of the nizam. The superintendent of the nizam's education was invested with greater powers. It was he who decided the place, hours of study, and recreation of his young ward, as also the number and composition of the nizam's attendants. The ticklish issue of the nizam's education had finally been settled to the satisfaction of all concerned.

Yet another matter which was sorted out was the question of the production of, and the import duty on opium, in Hyderabad. Hyderabad imported opium from British India but levied no duty on the import. The difference in price gave rise to smuggling. Lytton had wanted the state to prohibit the cultivation of poppy, but Salar Jung had not agreed. Now, with relations greatly improved, he gave his approval. The production of opium in Hyderabad was prohibited: it was to be imported into Hyderabad after obtaining a licence through the resident from the opium agent at Malwa after paying the stipulated duty. The smuggling soon stopped.

SOLE ADMINISTRATOR

On 12 December 1881, Rashid-ud-din, whose intrigues and machinations had troubled Salar Jung for many years, breathed his last. He had been suffering from a wasting disease which had reduced him to a skeleton. It is said he was addicted to opium which he consumed in large quantities. A visit to Bombay for treatment had proved futile. A newspaper reported with typical British understatement that 'his removal from the scene was not altogether a regrettable occurrence'.[7]

The government now had to decide if they wanted to leave Salar Jung as sole administrator or elect another successor. The correspondent of the *Bombay Gazette* reported:

> As regards the question of the appointment of a co-regent I believe I am correct in saying that it is very improbable that any nomination will be made to the vacant office . . . The general feeling is that the Government of India owe some sort of reparation to the Minister for the unhandsome treatment he received at the hands of the late Viceroy. Lord Ripon could not signify his approval and confidence in Sir Salar in a more graceful manner than by allowing him to retain sole charge of the State whose fortunes he has virtually guided for the last seven-and-twenty years.[8]

The report in the press proved to be accurate. In the end, the government wisely decided to leave Salar Jung as sole administrator, a decision in which Bayley played a major role. Now that the British had cut him some slack, Salar Jung's relations with the paramount power greatly improved, thanks to the excellent rapport between the chastened minister and the tactful and gentler resident. The reconciliation, which was begun with the appointment of Bayley, was completed with Salar Jung's installation as regent. It was clearly seen as a repudiation of Lytton's policy towards Salar Jung and was accepted as a guarantee of cordial relations between the nizam's government and the British.

But Salar Jung was now a different person. Embittered and unhappy, he had reconciled himself to the fact that none of his pet schemes would ever reach fruition: it was futile and silly to continue to be at loggerheads with the paramount power. The British too had realized that the scene had now changed completely: the reasons which had led to Rashid-ud-din's appointment no longer existed. Salar Jung had fallen in line with regard to the nizam's education, and the expansion of the Reformed Troops was no longer on the agenda. Berar was now only a distant dream for which Salar Jung had stopped lobbying for support in England. The practical diwan must also have realized that the nizam would be a major in three years' time, and there was no telling how things would be under him. He had required the British to survive under his father and might need them again.

With Bayley's arrival, relations between Salar Jung and the residency became once again cordial and collaborative. The persecution, which virtually took its departure with Meade, now utterly disappeared with Rashid-ud-din's death. It ended the adversarial relationship which Meade had forced on Salar Jung by his overbearing behaviour. The tone of the correspondence reflected once again the mutual respect and trust which had been the norm in the past. It was now hoped that Salar Jung, untrammelled by official fussiness, and untroubled by the intrigues of his discontented colleague, would continue with his reforms. Ripon wrote to his friend Lord Northbrook on the subject.

> I have just taken a rather important step in regard to Hyderabad affairs; we have determined not to appoint a successor to the late Amir-i-Kabir and to allow Salar Jung to be sole Regent until the Nizam comes of age. In taking this course I have acted in accordance with the advice of Sir Steuart Bayley, the Resident, and I am confident that we have done right. In fact there is nobody at Hyderabad fit for the office of Co-Regent. This step will, I hope, put our relations with Sir Salar Jung upon a better footing than we have been on of late years and will pave the way for the negotiations which must inevitably take place before the Nizam attains

his majority, which he will do in 1884. I am glad to say the Council were unanimous in accepting Bayley's recommendations.[9]

Ripon was certainly right about the effect it would have on Salar Jung. For Salar Jung, it was less about being restored to favour than about being vindicated. Two weeks later, Ripon again wrote to Lord Northbrook, describing the minister's pleasure at being appointed sole regent. Northbrook grudgingly agreed, adding a word of caution because the 'gentleman wants looking after'.

Salar Jung was ready to face reality and collaborate with the resident for the betterment of Hyderabad. Many schemes which had been in abeyance were once again undertaken. For a while, at least, he seemed like the dynamic diwan of old. But there is no denying that the pressure and tensions of the last few years had taken their toll. Submissive and indecisive, he also displayed diminished vigour. Perhaps he just wanted to enjoy the new peace, apprehensive that any show of independence would reopen old wounds. It had been said that Salar Jung had become swollen-headed and assumed so defiant an attitude towards the Indian government that it was found necessary to teach him a lesson. In reality, apart from his annoying persistence on the Berar issue, he was always friendly, courteous and deferential.

An example of Salar Jung's changed attitude towards the British and his acceptance of British supremacy is the permission he sought in connection with the acceptance of the Order of the Medjidie, an award he had received from the Turkish government. He had been an honorary member of the relief committee organized in London for the Turks during the Russo-Turkish War of 1877-78. In April 1878, the *Pioneer* of Allahabad had made some scurrilous observations, alleging that Salar Jung had received the award by resorting to unfair means. Salar Jung represented to the government, and Meade, who was resident, received a communication from the foreign secretary that the viceroy had accepted Salar Jung's disclaimer and had no objection to his accepting the award. Lytton appreciated Salar Jung's expressions of loyalty and was confident that cordial cooperation would be maintained, which for Lytton meant that now Salar Jung's uncritical collaboration with colonialism would continue.

The foreign department had always held that the Indian states could not deal with foreign powers on their own, since for international relations, the native states were regarded as British subjects. The existing rules did not permit the wearing of foreign orders, the exception being Major Evelyn Baring, who had been on actual service under the Khedive of Egypt, a subordinate of the Sultan of Turkey, who was permitted to wear the Order by a notification in the *London Gazette*. Even though he had been allowed to accept it, Salar Jung had never worn the Order, and it was only when he saw Major Baring wearing it in Simla in 1882 that he asked for permission to wear it. Ripon consulted the Secretary of State and permission was given. The queen even permitted him to wear the insignia of the Order in England. The fact that Salar Jung had accepted that he was a British subject for dealing with a foreign country and his applying for permission must have pleased the foreign office no end. The viceroy, in turn, responded with cordiality and generosity. Relations were now again on an even keel.[10]

ABDUL HAQ AND THE RAILWAY SWINDLE

The Nizam's State Railway showed a loss of Rs 65,887 in the first half of 1875. The expenses per train-mile were Rs 4.35 as against Rs 2.20 on the GIP Railway. This was not entirely unexpected. The unfavourable terms of the agreement were to blame, but the main culprit was the excessive charge for maintenance which was Rs 1.58 per train-mile as against Rs 0.63 per train-mile on the GIP Railway.[11] The agreement with the GIP Railway was terminated, but the railway was still making losses in July 1877.

The entire expenditure on the line up to the end of 1877–78 was 1,90,00,075 hali sicca, and the total receipts were to the tune of 26,39,187 hali sicca, leaving a liability of 1,63,60,888 hali sicca. Of this, 1,10,72,977 hali sicca had been provided by the issue of shares, and the balance had been paid from the treasury. Naturally, Salar Jung wanted to be rid of this incubus.

In 1881, Abdul Haq, an official under Salar Jung, put forward a proposal from a friend in Bombay and an agent of a syndicate of capitalists in England for the extension of the line. The syndicate would form a company in London which would buy the Nizam's State Railway for Rs 2 crore and raise capital for the construction of a new broad gauge line from Hyderabad to Chanda in the north and to Godavari in the south. It was estimated that this extension would cost Rs 2.4 crore, and the nizam's government would have to guarantee interest of 4 per cent for five years. On the face of it, the terms were very favourable for Hyderabad, but the catch was that that the syndicate was to be granted the mining lease for all mines, known and unknown, for ninety-nine years.

Salar Jung was in favour of the plan at first, but later his inherent caution made him take a closer look at the offer. He realized that it was the mining lease and a monopoly over the precious mines, and not the railway, which motivated the capitalists. Jones, the officiating resident in Bayley's absence, questioned the bona fides of the promoters and deplored the haste with which matters were being pushed through. But later, an interview with Abdul Haq changed his mind, and he withdrew his objections to the proposal.

Bayley, on his return, opposed the mining scheme but was in favour of the railway proposal, which apart from relieving the nizam's government of a permanent liability, was also of strategic importance to the Indian government as a means of exploiting the mineral wealth of Hyderabad, as a means of communication, and a way of making the present line up to Wadi remunerative. While the foreign secretary recognized that the new line would become the main line of communication between Calcutta and Madras upon completion of the Nagpur–Calcutta line, and vital for the movement of troops, Sir Evelyn Baring, the finance member, had misgivings about the financial position of the promoters and their true intentions. He was not against the extension of the railway but was opposed to those who were to implement it. Ripon agreed with Baring and thought that the syndicate making the offer was not to be trusted, saying that it would not be right for Hyderabad 'to be pigeoned by a set of speculators'.[12] The proposal of the syndicate was rejected, but the government informed the resident that it was in favour of the extension, provided it was implemented by persons whose financial position was sound enough to complete the assignment.

Abdul Haq was again tasked with arranging matters in England. His mandate included the formation of a suitable company who would undertake the two schemes. He was to keep in touch with the Secretary of State and also consult with Salar Jung on all important matters. The mining scheme was to be kept separate from the railway one, though Salar Jung had softened his stand and was now willing to make a concession with regard to the mines already known. Haq first contacted the Rothschilds, who were the nizam's agents in London, but they showed no interest. He then approached Messrs Morton, Rose and

Company who submitted a proposal which Salar Jung rejected out of hand as being unfavourable to Hyderabad.[13]

They then submitted a second proposal which envisaged the formation of a joint stock company with a share capital of £300,000 and the power to float debentures of £15,00,000. This company would construct a broad gauge railway from Hyderabad to Warangal and from there to a place near Chanda, and to the banks of the Godavari or the Krishna in the south-east. It would purchase and work the existing line and pay the purchase money through £500,000 fully paid-up shares, £1,091,666 in cash and £75,000 deposit to form a security for payment of interest. The nizam's government would pay 5 per cent interest for twenty years on all money paid towards capital as well as the purchase money for the line. Land would be granted free for railway construction, and all materials for the line would be allowed free of duty.[14]

Simultaneously, a proposal was mooted by Messrs Watson and Stewart of London for the mining rights throughout the state of Hyderabad. They undertook to form a company with a share capital of £10,00,000, to work the mines in existence and also those which would be registered in the next five years. The company would immediately spend £1,00,000 in the development of mines, and on the completion of the railway, would guarantee a minimum traffic equal to 1 per cent on the capital of the railway company. The concession was to run for ninety-nine years and stipulated royalties paid on gold, silver, coal and iron. The concession would be declared null and void if the concessionaires failed to fulfil their obligations. Salar Jung approved of this proposal.

The terms of the railway scheme proposed by Morton and Rose were worse than that of the syndicate, and Bayley, who had by then left Hyderabad to become a member of the viceroy's executive council, recognized that the dice was loaded against Salar Jung and Hyderabad. He wrote to Ripon that as a private adviser, he would advise against the scheme. However, as a member of the government, he realized that he should refrain from giving advice to Salar Jung on financial matters. He was, however, concerned that Salar Jung should fully comprehend what he was getting into. Salar Jung was being pressurized to accept by Abdul Haq and Major G.H. Trevor, first assistant resident, who was almost the de facto resident.

A weary Salar Jung gave his approval. Col. Hastings Fraser, military secretary, thought that Salar Jung had yielded because of the pressure put upon him by Haq and Major Trevor. Keay thought that Salar Jung had also been deceived about the commercial prospects of the undertaking. Robert Knight, in a letter to the House of Commons, wrote that Haq had been brought to Hyderabad by Meade from a subordinate position in the British Indian Service 'as the instrument that was required for outraging Sir Salar Jung into retirement'. He had for long exercised great influence at the residency. One of his brothers was the head of the Hyderabad police, another of the cantonment police, and his nephew worked at the residency itself. Haq thus knew all the secrets of both court and residency, being described as both 'the tool and terror' of the residency and therefore of the state. 'There is not a native subordinate in the Residency who is not under his orders. No dispatch from the Government of India to the Residency, however secret or confidential it may be, is 24 hours in the Residency before Abdul Haq or his brother has read it.'[15]

Salar Jung may have realized the possibility of financial bankruptcy, but with pressure also from London in the form of the Secretary of State, Hartington, there was little he could have done. Hartington had taken an unusual interest in this business from the start. When Salar Jung rejected the first proposal from Morton, Rose and Company and recalled Abdul Haq, he was very upset, and in an unprecedented move, met Abdul Haq before his departure from London to know Salar Jung's reasons for rejecting the scheme. Hartington seems to have been very impressed with Haq and wrote to Ripon about how he had made a very favourable impression on all who had seen him and 'watched his proceedings here'.[16]

Hartington laid the blame entirely on Salar Jung, though Ripon thought that Salar Jung had valid reasons for rejecting the first proposal. Haq had told Hartington that Salar Jung would not take any important step without the approval and encouragement of the Government of India; silence on the part of the resident was interpreted as disapproval by Salar Jung. Hartington suggested to Ripon that it would be nice if the resident could persuade Salar Jung to accept the second scheme. And in the end, Salar Jung did.

Hartington's interest in the matter is inexplicable. In all probability, he was influenced by English capitalists and middlemen since it is difficult to believe that it was only Haq's charm that was responsible. (Haq was later implicated in shady deals with the promoters of the railway and mining schemes.) It was no secret that the British business houses and finance companies had long influenced Indian administration, both through

Parliament and through direct communication with the India Office. Ripon too, despite his doubts, played the role of a passive spectator, too busy perhaps with his local self-government scheme to take much interest in Hyderabad affairs.

THE NIZAM ON TOUR

Always ready to break new ground, Salar Jung took the nizam on the first tour of his dominions in January 1883. Attempts had also been made to give the young boy an insight into administrative affairs. Pleased with these developments, the government had expressed its satisfaction at the measures taken and hoped that 'if the present discipline can be maintained with requisite elasticity during the next three years . . . that His Highness will have moulded into a very favourable specimen of an Indian Chief, and will be able to stand comparison with the Princes of Mysore and Baroda.'[17]

It was the first tour for a nizam in more than a hundred years, and the tour included Raichur, Gulbarga and Aurangabad. It was as much an educational tour as a ceremonial one. The people could catch a glimpse of their young ruler, and the ruler could learn how his state was administered. Aspects of the administration were explained to him, and it was also a learning experience for his schoolmates who accompanied him. His party included the grandson of the peshkar, who later also occupied the same post, and courted fame under the title of Maharaja Kishen Pershad.

The tour of Aurangabad district started on 12 January, and it had been arranged that the nizam would reach Aurangabad in the evening at 5 p.m. But the preparations for the visit had started weeks before, and the traffic on the roads was extraordinary: elephants with shining howdahs; camels carrying enormous loads; pack bullocks; horses and ponies and vehicles of all descriptions were all headed one way—Aurangabad. Hundreds of white tents came up on the maidan, and the area where the nizam was to stay was soon occupied by tents. Indeed, the logistics involved in the trip resembled the movement of an army.

Claude Clerk arrived as part of the advance party to inspect the arrangements for the royal visit. The nizam's suite consisted of some twenty-four chief officials who included Salar Jung and his two sons, the Vikar-ul-Umra II, Mr Krohn and Hugh Gough. Salar Jung was accompanied by his two secretaries, Mahdi Ali and Syed Hossain Bilgrami. The nizam, his mother and his grandmother accounted for thirty riding horses, twenty pairs of carriage horses, 290 servants and 100 troops. In addition, the trip involved hundreds of others, and supplies were imported on a daily basis. At each stop, the stations were adorned with flags and bunting and floral decoration.

As there was no railway link from Ahmednagar to Aurangabad, that part of the journey had to be covered by carriage. The nizam was in an irritable mood since they had to cross a difficult stream. He asked Salar Jung's sons and Kishen Pershad to inform Salar Jung that he would spend the night at the camping site and proceed to Aurangabad only the next day. Both Clerk and Salar Jung were united in the view that there should be no change in the royal orders as far as possible, to maintain the prestige of the state. But the nizam was in no mood to relent, and angrily turned on Clerk and said, 'Salar Jung and you want to compel me. I will not go. Let us see how you will make me go.' A humiliated Salar Jung observed with great regret, 'His Highness did not appreciate my petition,' and looking heavenward, exclaimed, 'Oh God! Please grant that Salar Jung may not live to see his reign.'[18]

The nizam soon realized that his petulance was unwarranted and had caused hurt. He invited Salar Jung to lunch with him. During the course of the repast, he admitted that Salar Jung was right in asserting that unnecessary changes should not be made in timetables, and gave him his jewelled pocket watch as a token of affection. Salar Jung used this episode to instruct his sons and Kishen Pershad on the respect owed to the nizam, regardless of his age.

> If the welfare of the sovereign or the state or the people be at stake or the right of any man be imperilled by an order which the sovereign uttered in anger, then it is the duty of a subject to tell him so, but with refinement and tact. For the sovereign's anger is like a storm at sea; when the storm has abated he should be told that his orders will be carried out, but that the circumstances being what they are, the matter should perhaps be reconsidered. And that is the practical thing to do, for if harm should result from obedience to an order given in anger, then the sovereign will say, 'With full knowledge and for his own advantage the ingrate did not warn me of the danger.' Familiarity between sovereign and subject is most dangerous and should be avoided at any cost, for it is impossible to maintain due respect and honour under such circumstances.[19]

Once Aurangabad was reached, the nizam's itinerary included a visit to Mokhunda, an ancient building a little outside the city in which his ancestor, the first nizam, had lived for some years. The nizam left in state for the residence of his ancestors, and the procession was a very striking one. The nizam, borne on the back of one of the finest elephants in the world, was seated in a magnificent *ambari* (howdah) covered with yellow cloth. He was attired in a yellow silk robe and a yellow turban with a golden plume but wore no jewels. Behind him on the same howdah were Salar Jung and the Vikar-ul-Umra II. On reaching the seat of his ancestors, he was ushered into the old palace and made to sit on the same gaddi and under the same canopy on which the first Asaf Jah had sat more than a hundred years ago. He then received the nazars of his chief officials and subjects. This was followed by an inspection of the general illumination throughout the city in his honour.

The next day, a visit to the shrine of Hazrat Baba Shah Musafir, who was Aurangzeb's spiritual guide, took place. On his return, he rode through the streets which were lined with police. After lunch, he received a lesson in practical administration from Mahdi Ali, the revenue secretary, who explained the zamindari and ryotwari tenures, the manner in which the annual settlement was made with the cultivators, and the way the land revenue was realized. A set of taluka papers were explained, and the young nizam was receptive, asking pertinent questions. He was also shown the treasury and the records maintained there. The next day, the nizam visited Salar Jung's ancestral house in the heart of the city. He presented the nizam a valuable nazar consisting of a sword inlaid with jewels, two gold watches, a whip and some jewels. The evening's repast too was a lavish affair. The illuminations were beautiful, and the entertainment ended with a grand display of fireworks.

The following day started with a ride and was followed by a lesson in the system of revenue administration, once again conducted by Mahdi Ali. In the afternoon, the nizam visited the Anglo-Vernacular School and distributed prizes. He made a brief public speech on this occasion, possibly the first time he had made a formal address in public. The next day was declared a holiday, a popular idea which was received with a round of applause.

After a visit to the shrine of Hazrat Nizamuddin Aulia, Mahdi Ali explained the revenue work of the talukdars, and a detailed account was given of the system on which the annual budgets were prepared. The nizam was also shown the revenue accounts of the district for the past year. In the evening, the nizam entertained W.B. Jones, the resident at dinner which was followed by the customary fireworks. During the course of the trip, papers regarding judicial work were also shown to the nizam, and he was told about the progress made in the judicial field in the last twenty years. Bilgrami then explained the municipal institutions in the country. Visits to Roza, Daulatabad and Ellora caves rounded off the trip. The nizam returned to Hyderabad via Poona, where he was the guest of Khan Bahadur Dastur Nosherwanjee Jamaspjee who spared no effort or expense to give his royal guest a befitting reception.

MARRIAGE PLANS?

It was around this time that the issue of the nizam's marriage cropped up. The teenage Mahbub, who was old enough to assert himself, was now creating quasi-parental difficulties for Salar Jung. He had developed an adolescent infatuation for a girl to whom he was writing love letters. Clerk, who was worried that he might be 'running amok' in the zenana, suggested that the solution to the young sovereign's raging hormones was marriage. Mahbub was only sixteen when he met a young girl, Amat-uz-Zehra Begum, in the zenana. Salar Jung was against a nikah marriage with any lady residing in the zenana.

Shortly before his death, Salar Jung had carried on correspondence with the Government of India about the marriage of the nizam. Mahbub had expressed a desire to marry before his eighteenth birthday as custom forbade him to do so for one year after the birthday. Now the British suddenly turned into matchmakers. Should the bride be the daughter of a Hyderabad nobleman or from another princely state? If so, which one, given the internal political repercussions of such an alliance? Another alternative was a simple nikah marriage to a girl of no social importance. The girl would stay with the nizam's mother at Chowmahalla Palace, and the nizam would continue to reside with his tutors at Purani Haveli, the main British concern in all this being the nizam's education. An unwanted pregnancy was also a concern since Mahbub was, to put it mildly, fond of the pleasures of the zenana.

For Salar Jung, who was just recovering from years of acrimony over Berar with the British, a royal wedding must have been the last thing on his mind, and he voiced his opposition to it. The British were worried about the possibility of an illegitimate heir if the nizam did not marry, inviting a comment from Salar Jung that, by European standards, many of the previous nizams too were illegitimate. He also pointed out that after marriage, the nizam would have a palace of his own, over which Clerk would have no control. In the end, Mahbub decided against a marriage as the family tradition did not require it. The heirs to the masnad were generally not the offspring of royal wives: legal fiction imputed legitimacy to all the children of the nizam, regardless of their mother's status.

Server-ul-Mulk told Meade that there was a rumour in Hyderabad at the time that Salar Jung had ambitions of marrying one of his daughters (who was said to be very beautiful) to the nizam and that 'conversations' had proceeded through Tahniyat-Yaver-ud-Daula (the Vakil-e-Sultanat) with the nizam's grandmother. Meade is said to have remarked that Salar Jung, who was de facto ruler, would now become de jure sovereign.[20] If this was indeed true, Salar Jung's opposition to the nizam's marriage must be seen in a different light.

Amat-uz-Zehra Begum, who was Mahbub's sweetheart in the zenana, was, in fact, none other than the mother of the seventh nizam, Mir Osman Ali Khan. As her name suggests, she was a Shia. But who was she? According to Kazim Nawaz Jung, Salar Jung's grandson and the son-in-law of the seventh nizam, she was Salar Jung's granddaughter through his *mutah nikah*[21] to a Hindu lady called Pritamji Sahiba. Osman Ali Khan referred to Pritamji as his mother's *munh boli nani*. The fact that Osman Ali Khan gave his daughter in marriage to Kazim Nawaz Jung, Salar Jung's great-grandson, lends credence to this connection with the Salar Jung family.[22] Talk about Mahbub's marriage was shelved, but Salar Jung soon had to deal with another issue, and this was the proposed trip of the nizam to England the next year.

THE NIZAM'S PROPOSED TRIP TO EUROPE

Salar Jung's sons were leaving on a trip to Europe, and the nizam expressed a desire to travel to England the next year, making grand plans to return by way of the United States, China and Japan. On 1 April 1882, the nizam wrote to Salar Jung suggesting the trip. Bayley welcomed the idea, saying that this would be welcome exposure for the young sovereign. Naturally, Salar Jung would accompany the nizam, even though Claude Clerk thought that Hyderabad would be better served if he remained while the nizam was away. Salar Jung was so fearful of intrigues against himself (and with good reason) that he trusted nobody and ensured that the nizam never went anywhere without him.

Claude Clerk had discussed the possibility of such a trip with his young ward but had seemed to think that it would materialize only after the nizam attained his majority. He thought him to be an observant boy who would benefit from the trip, but believed that it would be best if he waited for a few years after he had assumed charge before he made the trip. According to Server-ul-Mulk, the proposal originated from Clerk, who tricked the nizam into writing letters to the resident and to Salar Jung suggesting a trip to the Continent and England, the ostensible purpose of the letters being to show how well he could write. Salar Jung was said to have remarked that it was not within his power to reverse the opinion of the nizam, and that 'this letter in the hands of the Government of India will be like a coconut in the hands of a monkey', and that the trip to England could not be stopped.[23]

Salar Jung was caught in a bind. He was unhappy at the thought of the nizam being away for an extended period without his watchful eye. On the other hand, he was equally worried about what could happen back home if he was away for such a long period of time, the duration of the trip being estimated anywhere between three and eight months. There was also Berar at the back of his mind. In case he went to England and the Berar issue cropped up, of which there was every chance, he may have to repudiate it in public, ending any chance, however slim, of its restoration. In any case, he had pledged not to raise the Berar issue during the minority of the nizam.

Keay, even though he was no longer on Salar Jung's payroll, had been sporadically active on this front, no doubt still hoping to get that pot of gold at the end of the Berar rainbow. It suited him well to have Salar Jung visit England again. Salar Jung's old friend, Sir George Yule, had hinted at the dangers of agitation if the nizam visited England. Salar Jung was ambivalent on the subject: he feared spoiling relations with the British now that they were on much more pleasant terms, but at the same time could not be 'entirely deaf to the old siren song'.[24]

When the proposal was placed before the Governor General in Council in May 1882, it was approved with the proviso that the trip was not to be used as an opportunity for discussing political questions (read Berar). Salar Jung gave an assurance to this effect, and the correspondence after November 1882 had to do with details of the itinerary, the composition of the accompanying party, and the rank of the political officer accompanying the nizam. But in December of that year, Salar Jung seems to have had second thoughts about the tour. He confided in W.B. Jones, the new resident, the misgivings of certain friends about the high cost of the tour, the immaturity of the nizam, and the rumours that the trip was about the restoration of Berar.

Calcutta had secured the approval of the India Office and deputed the resident at Indore to accompany the nizam. Any change in plans was not going to be countenanced easily. Jones had replaced Bayley, but after only a short stay in Hyderabad, there was talk of his being shifted on considerations of health. When Salar Jung protested that he could not leave Hyderabad in the hands of a new resident, Calcutta agreed to make the change only on Salar Jung's return. Meanwhile, the news that the tour might be called off seems to have reached Calcutta, causing consternation. The queen had been informed of the trip, and it could not be abandoned at this stage. Jones wrote to Salar Jung on the subject.

> I have received an urgent telegram from Mr Grant [GOI Foreign Department] deprecating in the very strongest way even the rumour of the abandonment of His Highness's trip to Europe. The project has proceeded so far it has been regarded as a such a settled thing that it has been submitted to H.M. the Queen that [sic] the mere rumour of its abandonment will . . . produce a most unfortunate impression . . . It is really important that the unfortunate impression which unless instant contradiction is given will go abroad, should be prevented . . .[25]

In another twist, an impression was created by Claude Clerk that the nizam was no longer interested in the trip. Salar Jung, who by now was himself completely disinterested in the trip, gave the half-hearted assurance that, though the nizam was now less keen to go, he was still interested since it would hurt his pride to abandon a project he had himself set in motion. Salar Jung's remembrance of old humiliations and slights, and the possibility that he would have to completely and publicly disavow the Berar cause if he went to England, made him more reluctant with each passing day. He could not refuse because he no longer had the courage to oppose, but his dithering on the issue showed his disinterest.

Clerk wrote to Bayley in Calcutta about the impasse, and the latter responded in a very reasonable manner. 'I feel confident that if Sir Salar Jung would face the difficulty of having to put on record the fact that he had changed his mind, and that the Nizam had changed his, Lord Ripon would be the first to recognise that as a sufficient reason for postponing the trip, or rather suppressing it (for it is useless to talk of postponing) . . .[26] But Salar Jung was unable to muster up the courage to cancel the trip. Destiny would take that decision for him.

EVENTIDE

On 5 February 1883, Duke John Albert of Mecklenburg-Schwerin arrived at the residency for a brief visit. Salar Jung made arrangements to show him all the sights of Hyderabad and had planned a grand banquet in his honour. That had to be cancelled owing to the demise of the wife of Khurshed Jah Shums-ul-Umra V, who was the daughter of the fifth nizam, Afzal-ud-Daula. It was decided to have a smaller dinner restricted to about sixty guests on 8 February.

On the morning of 7 February, Salar Jung had breakfast with the duke and Evelyn Baring, (later the 1st Earl of Cromer), who had first come to India in 1872 as private secretary to his cousin, Lord Northbrook. In the evening, he took his guests to the Mir Alam Tank, where they, along with other guests, spent some time sailing on the lake. According to Server-ul-Mulk, Salar Jung then came to the royal palace. Server-ul-Mulk was also there, and when he inquired if the diwan wanted to meet the nizam, Salar Jung said that he did not want to trouble His Highness who was then in the zenana. He, however, pointed to some marble tables of excellent workmanship and said that he would be glad if they were presented to the nizam on his behalf. According to Server-ul-Mulk, Salar Jung was in the pink of health at that time.

Salar Jung returned to the deodi and started a game of billiards with his marker at around 6.45 p.m. and continued playing till 7.30 p.m. There seemed to have been some early symptoms of nausea, but these were ignored, and he dined at 8 p.m. as usual. After some time, he seems to have vomited, but there were no clear signs of what ailed him. He checked the cash books and signed them before retiring for the day.

Salar Jung was a firm believer in astrology and appears to have been quite knowledgeable on the subject. Two astrologers, Gulab Shah of the Punjab and Gothsi Pandit, were in his employ and had been given a fixed day and time for meeting him. There was also Pandit Mohan Lal, who had been employed on the recommendation of Server-ul-Mulk. On the night of 7 February, it was Mohan Lal's turn to meet the diwan. Salar Jung, after signing the papers put to him by Pattapi Rama Rao, the accountant, attended to his correspondence and issued urgent orders. He then summoned the astrologer and asked him to draw up the horoscope of the hour.[27] When the horoscope was drawn, it showed prosperity and success, and the astrologer said as much. But Salar Jung knew enough about astrology not to be taken in by such an interpretation. He smiled and remarked, 'Panditji, the house reserved for life is vacant.'

Mortality seems to have always been on his mind. Whenever Salar Jung went on a long trip, he carried with him all the material required for a funeral, should he pass away during the course of the journey. The astrologer passed the matter off as of no consequence. However, when he was allowed to depart, he rushed in panic to Server-ul-Mulk to inform him of what had just transpired. Since it was the middle of the night, the latter was annoyed at having his rest disturbed and said as much. The astrologer only said, 'I wish to God that my horoscope is wrong.'

At about 2 a.m., Salar Jung took ill and sent for Dr Bakar Ali, who on arrival, said that it was cholera. After administering some medicine, he sat down and read the Koran to Salar Jung. On the doctor's arrival, Salar Jung left the zenana and lay on a bed in a room near his office. It was the last time any of the female members of his family saw him alive.

At 5 a.m., his sons, who were to accompany the duke on a panther hunt, came to see him, and on finding him ill, proposed a cancellation of the hunt. Salar Jung assured them that he was only slightly indisposed and asked them to keep their appointment with the duke. When Dr Bakar Ali returned to Salar Jung's room about half an hour later, he found him in some pain and administered some morphine which brought temporary relief. Salar Jung still did not think he was very ill and refused to postpone the dinner in honour of the duke. He said that his sons would be present in case he had not recovered fully to attend.

His sons returned from the hunt and told him that the duke had drawn first blood. But as the day advanced, Salar Jung's condition worsened: his weakness increased and his voice sank to a whisper. Mahdi Ali, who visited the deodi at around 9 a.m., realized that the matter was more serious than previously thought and wanted to summon the residency surgeon. By 11 a.m., Salar Jung was near prostrate. He still stubbornly refused to send for Dr Beaumont, the residency surgeon. It was only at 2 p.m. that Laik Ali Khan, after discussions with Mahdi Ali, sent for him without his father's knowledge. The resident drove to the deodi but desisted from seeing Salar Jung for fear that an interview might worsen his already delicate health. Dr Beaumont, accompanied by the military secretary, Major Gough, and the secretary for public works, Mr Wilkinson, arrived, and the three stayed till the very end.

But it was already too late. Salar Jung was in a state of collapse, and the end was visibly near. Dr Beaumont pronounced the case to be a hopeless one. Salar Jung's calmness and serenity in the face of death was made even more remarkable by the fact that the certainty of his death was realized very unexpectedly. Till the end, he exhibited perfect self-control and firmness. He had made a will when he had visited Calcutta, but he now gave no instructions of any kind, either as to private or state affairs. He had always expressed his disapproval of men giving instructions from their deathbeds. Such persons, he believed, did not have the full use of all their faculties and were likely to err and only confuse matters for the survivors. He now acted upon this principle with great consistency. He did not utter a single word about what he wanted done in the future, nor did he send a message to the nizam.[28]

The word soon spread that the diwan was seriously ill, and the courtyard in front of the deodi was full of carriages of those who had come to make inquiries. Hundreds from more humble backgrounds came on foot asking after Salar Jung's health. The corridors were crowded with officials, all anxious about the health of their diwan. Till 5 p.m., he retained full command of his faculties, speaking in English to Dr Beaumont, in Persian to Dr Mirza Ali, and in Hindustani to Dr Bakar Ali. But from here on, it was all downhill. It soon become obvious that the end was near, and all hope of his recovery was abandoned.

Perhaps the saddest part of this whole sad business was that the ladies of the house could not take their leave of him, even though it was certain that the end was very near. If they had entered, the doctors would have had to leave the patient, which presumably would have hastened the end. Messages came and went with increasing frequency from and to the zenana. The agony of his mother, wife and daughters can only be imagined. A son, a husband and a father lay dying under the same roof, but they were denied one last meeting. It seems odd that since the doctors had already declared his case as a hopeless one, no one questioned their right to preclude a family farewell.

Just before the end came, Laik Ali Khan, who was already overcome with grief, was gently pushed into the room. It was thought that Salar Jung might have some parting words of advice or a blessing for him. The dying man gave him an affectionate look but said nothing. All day long, the Angel of Death had been hovering over the deodi, and one could almost hear the beating of his wings. Shortly after 7.15 p.m., those wings were folded, and Salar Jung exited this world. A cramp seized him. He put his hand slowly under his ear and said softly, 'Allah! Allah!' Finally, at 7.18 p.m.,[29] Salar Jung drifted out of the harbour on a silent tide. End of an era is a trite saying, but there is no other way to describe his passing: Salar Jung had guided the fortunes of the state for three decades, and it was difficult to believe that Nawab Sahib, as he was known, was no more.

A crowd of women, friends and relations, some eight hundred in number, had collected at the house, and when they heard of his death, they shrieked and cursed and screamed and rolled on the floor, tearing their clothes, breaking their bangles and behaving like insane persons. The news of his passing was at first received with incredulity, but the tumult caused by the mourners soon convinced people that the news was true. A great cry of sorrow from those assembled in the courtyard was followed by a deep silence, punctuated by the sobs of those who could not control their grief. Bilgrami and Wilmott describe the scene as follows:

> As the news spread through the city, men and women mourned as for the loss of a dear relation, for to many of them he had filled the place of one. His Highness the Nizam, when told of the fatal termination of the Minister's illness, burst into tears, refusing to be comforted. Those who visited the city that night describe it as wearing the appearance of a city of the dead. There was no life, no noise, no bustle in the streets. But few people were about, and those that were looked like men stricken with some sudden and most terrible calamity. All that night and for days after Haiderabad was clothed in sorrow, such as it had never known before, for the death of him who had been the guiding star of the fortunes of the State for nearly a third of a century. In the morning the sullen boom of the minute guns from the British Cantonments at Sikanderabad and Bolaram announced the melancholy news there.[30]

There has always been an air of mystery surrounding his death. The French governess, Mademoiselle Gaignaud, told Wilfrid Scawen Blunt, the author of *India under Ripon*, that she thought that Salar Jung had been poisoned. She said that some sweets had been sent to him on the afternoon before the onset of his illness. He had complained of nothing till late Wednesday evening (7 February), but he passed away less than twenty-four hours later the next day. The symptoms were not of cholera, and there was no vomiting except that which he himself caused by putting his fingers in his throat. He complained of a burning in his throat and chest, and great thirst. His colour remained unchanged after his death.

Of the two residency doctors, Dr Beaumont said it was cholera and immediately signed the death certificate to that effect; the other demurred, but there is no evidence to suggest that he put his dissent on record. No one thought it necessary to conduct an autopsy. The diwan had been plied with potions mixed by two holy men who wrote words in Arabic, Persian and Sanskrit on leaves, of which they then made an infusion. Mademoiselle Gaignaud said that the English doctors were only summoned after 3 p.m. when all others had lost hope.[31]

An English lawyer told Blunt that he was in Hyderabad when Salar Jung died, and had had an appointment to see him on business that very morning. He was of the opinion that it was not a natural death, even though the residency doctor had certified it was cholera. Some had attributed the illness to tinned oysters, and several persons present at the picnic had been unwell but recovered. A newspaper later reported that several other people who were guests at the Mir Alam picnic had been ill briefly but had soon recovered without any ill effects. Salar Jung's collapse was so sudden and complete that he hardly spoke, and left no orders or directions on any subject.[32]

The use of poison was not unknown at the time in India or in Hyderabad. Sir Thomas Metcalfe, agent at the court in New Delhi, was said to have been poisoned at the instance of Zeenat Mahal, Bahadur Shah Zafar's favourite queen. When Harriet Tytler[33] asked Hakim Ahsanullah Khan, Zafar's personal physician, if he could poison ad libitum, he said: 'I can. Show me your victim and tell me when you want him to die. In a year? Six months? One month or a day? He shall die, and what is more, your physicians will never find out the real cause of his death.'[34] The poison used was said to have a vegetable base and was common knowledge among famous hakims of the time. Claude Clerk had suspicions that he had been poisoned during one of his illnesses but had survived. Indeed, the residency surgeon had died of poison in 1869, according to the inscription on his gravestone.

It is possible that Salar Jung had kept such a poison in readiness to be consumed by him should he get fed up with it all. This is, of course, mere conjecture, but there was a story at the time which held that Salar Jung, disappointed with the way the nizam was shaping, killed himself rather than serve him as diwan.[35] Talk of poison in the zenana reared its head again many years later when Prince Moazzam Jah, Osman Ali Khan's younger son through his eldest wife Dulhan Pasha, feared that he and his elder brother, Prince Azam Jah, might be poisoned by their own mother. Mother and sons shared an antagonistic relationship, and the resident, T.H. Keyes, recalled that Moazzam Jah used to tell his guests that his mother wanted to become regent. When told that this was impossible since both the brothers had attained their majority, he replied: 'We won't be here. Mother is always experimenting with poisons, and there are no cats left in King Kothi.'[36] Their fear is all the more understandable in light of the fact that it was widely believed that Dulhan Pasha was of unsound mind. Shops in the Abids area used to down their shutters when they saw her car coming as she was in the habit of running up huge bills which remained unpaid.

Given the freedom with which poison was employed for nefarious purposes at that time, it is not too far-fetched to attribute Salar Jung's death to its use. He had long been out of favour with the government, and his death would not be greatly regretted. Nor would it be closely investigated. Salar Jung was by now a very tired man. The recent talk of the nizam's marriage and visit to Europe must have exhausted him. This, coupled with a fatalistic attitude, may have led to his passive acceptance of the illness that had struck him. As Harriet Ronken Lynton put it, 'He was tired. He was burned out. He was ready to give up. Death if it came, was an honourable way out. And so he went.'[37]

'LECTOR, SI MONUMENTUM REQUIRIS, CIRCUMSPICE'

The funeral procession started from the deodi at 9 a.m. It was headed by elephants from which cakes and money were distributed to the poor. Thousands joined the procession, and the vast sobbing, surging crowd was proof enough, if ever any was needed, of the popularity and stature of the departed noble. At the casements above, women sobbed and beat their breasts while the Arabs, Rohillas and Pathans, who were part of the procession and 'who had known his bounty, wept bitterly for their benefactor'.[38] The nizam too was quite overcome with grief and witnessed the passage of the procession. The mourners were on foot, and many were bareheaded. A steady influx of mourners resulted in the funeral procession becoming more than a mile long by the time it reached the Daira Mir Momin, the burial ground of the family.

Located about a mile from the Charminar, the land for this burial ground was purchased by Mir Momin, Muhammad Quli Qutub Shah's prime minister. Mir Momin, who is considered the architect of Hyderabad, had migrated to Hyderabad from Astrabad (in Persia), and is said to have converted the plot into a sanctified necropolis by mixing the soil from the battlefield of Karbala, the site of the martyrdom of the Prophet's grandson Imam Husain. After Mir Momin's death in 1625, he was buried in this necropolis which he bequeathed as a free burial ground for the Muslims.

The procession reached the burial site at 10.30 a.m. at which hour the minute guns from Chadarghat started. The troops fired three volleys of musketry as the body was lowered into the grave. In contrast to the imposing tombs of other kings and nobles, Salar Jung's grave makes no demand that he be remembered. He was buried, according to his wish expressed many years before, in a simple grave with only a headstone. He certainly got his wish. To tread the ground where history was made is always a powerful motivator, but when I visited his grave, I found it to be austere to the point of being utterly nondescript. It is difficult to believe that the founder of modern Hyderabad is buried here. The graves of his son and grandson which lie in close proximity are also as austere.

The *Times of India* correspondent described the funeral as follows:

In the court-yard there were three or four of the City regiments, and from the Regular troops the 3rd Regiment of Infantry was drawn up in line. The crowd was immense. Never have I before beheld such a large crowd in Hyderabad; nor such a sad crowd. Every face wore a settled look of grief, and many strong men were weeping like children. Soon the body, borne on a fret-work bier and covered with cloth of gold, entered the gateway of the court. The Infantry 'presented arms', 'reversed arms', and wheeling into [a] column of half companies, preceded the coffin, which was followed by thousands all the way to the grave . . . the coffin passed through, and the last solemn services over, three volleys were fired by the 4th Regiment Infantry over the grave, and the crowd which was most orderly slowly dispersed. His Highness the Nizam's Artillery fired from the saluting battery 54 minute guns. His Excellency's age . . . stalwart Arabs and Rohillas were so moved that they wept and cried out from the anguish of their hearts to their 'Malick'.

What Sir Salar Jung's care, treatment, and love for his Royal Master was can perhaps be realized from the effect his death has had on His Highness the Nizam, who is stated to have shown as much grief as the members of His Excellency's family.

A day after the funeral, the resident paid condolence visits to Salar Jung's sons and also to the nizam. On the third day after the burial, members of the family, as well as a great number of the citizenry, visited the grave for the performance of certain ceremonies as also to place wreaths and flowers on it. The next day, it was found that not a single flower was left since the people were so anxious to possess some memento of the departed statesman that they even collected a pinch of earth from the grave to treasure as a remembrance. Vast crowds continued to visit his grave till long after his death. Prayers were offered, and in some instances, petitions placed on his tomb. Some refused to believe that he had died. For years after his death, mullahs used to read the Koran near his grave. Such was the respect he commanded during his lifetime, that people left behind petitions seeking a miraculous intervention from the grave.

On 12 February, the nizam presented a mourning khillat to Salar Jung's sons, Mir Laik Ali and Mir Saadat Ali, at a durbar. Genuinely grief-stricken at the demise of the man, who in a sense had been like a father to him, the nizam broke down while placing the white shawls on their shoulders. Public offices throughout the nizam's dominions were closed for three days. The news of Salar Jung's demise was published by the Government of India in the government gazette extraordinary, edged with a deep black border.

With a feeling of deep regret the Governor-General in Council announces the death on the evening of the 8th instant from cholera of His Excellency Nawab Sir Salar Jung, G.C.S.I., Regent and Minister of the Haidarabad State. By this unhappy event the British Government has lost an experienced and enlightened friend; His Highness the Nizam a wise and faithful servant; and the Indian community one of its most distinguished representatives.[39]

The following, taken from a letter written by the resident to the Government of India immediately after his death, shows the esteem he was held in by all classes of people:

> I do not know how to express the concern and sorrow which Sir Salar Jung's death has caused to everyone here. At present the sense of personal bereavement seems to outweigh the feeling of public loss. Every British officer who has had the honour of his acquaintance feels his death as he would that of a friend of many years. Those who had the pleasure to serve under him will mourn the kindest, the most considerate of masters. The British Government will lament the death of one whose loyalty and attachment to it, based as they were on an intelligent appreciation of the true interests of the Haidarabad State, were only second to his loyalty and attachment to his own Sovereign. Most of all His Highness, for whom Sir Salar Jung had so laboured, must grieve his loss. No master had ever a more devoted servant. It seems so hard that he should have passed away before he could see the Sovereign whose interests he had so striven for on the throne.[40]

Condolences poured in from all parts of India and also England. The viceroy telegraphed a message from Queen Victoria and also offered his own condolences. Similar messages were received from the Secretary of State, the Duke of Sutherland and the maharaja of Holkar. Indore was in mourning for three days as a mark of respect.

It was decided to perpetuate his memory by erecting a suitable memorial, a water supply for the city, and any surplus which would remain from the funds subscribed would be used for education. A sum of Rs 1 lakh was subscribed, and a public meeting was held on 12 March presided over by the resident for this purpose. Jones paid Salar Jung a rich tribute in his oration:

> On the public career of the late Regent there is but little necessity for me or for any one of us to dwell long. His fame has transcended the limits of Haidarabad . . . Those of us who are Englishmen mourn for one who, while true to his religion and country, and ever feeling that his first duty was to his own Sovereign, was for thirty years the loyal friend, and often the trusted adviser of the Government of Her Majesty the Queen-Empress, gave us his entire and devoted support at the time of danger,

and has extended to us personally a thousand kindnesses . . . He was emphatically, and in the best sense, and not merely by his official rank, the foremost gentleman in the place. His hospitality and liberality were, as we all know, unbounded. And equally remarkable was his liberality of thought.

. . . In his personal relations he was eminently just, humane, and truthful . . . Of him it may truly be said that he endeavoured to give every man not only his due, but always much more than his due. He was extremely sensitive as regards the honour of his word, and people have sometimes taken advantage of this trait of character by straining a careless expression to serve their own object. He very seldom, however, pledged his word, and in this respect was habitually on his guard.

Visitors to St Paul's Cathedral in London will find its architect Sir Christopher Wren's epitaph in a great circle in the floor directly under the dome. It is in Latin, *Lector, Si Monumentum Requiris, Circumspice*, which translates as 'Reader, if you seek his memorial, look around you.' If a visitor looks around, he will see not only the Wren crypt but also the glorious monument he created. The same would apply to Salar Jung, except that for him, the whole of Hyderabad was his monument.

Epilogue

When Salar Jung died, the nizam had yet to attain the age of majority. A council of regency was formed with the young nizam as president, Mir Laik Ali Khan as secretary, and Bashir-ud-Daula, Khurshed Jah and the peshkar Maharaja Narayan Pershad Narender Bahadur as members. Mir Laik Ali Khan and Maharaja Narayan Pershad Narender Bahadur, his father's old friend, were appointed as joint administrators for the purposes of day-to-day administration. A board was set up to administer the sarf-i-khas lands, with the nizam, Vikar-ul-Umra II and Saadat Ali Khan (Salar Jung's younger son) as members. With Salar Jung's death, all hopes of any opposition to the British grip on Hyderabad ended. The nizam was still a callow youth, and Salar Jung II, who became his diwan, was not very much older. As T.H. Thornton put it, 'all questioning of British suzerainty in India is buried (we hope for ever) in Sir Salar Jung's grave . . .'[1] And indeed so it was.

SALAR JUNG II

Mir Laik Ali Khan, who was born on 13 November 1861, was educated first at home, and then at the Madrasa-i-Aliya. He and his brother were sent to England for higher education. He was a competent marksman, and a good billiards and lawn tennis player. An intelligent man with a very retentive memory, he was also an excellent speaker. However, he was inexperienced and also very indecisive. At a durbar held in October 1883, he was given the tile of Salar Jung, thus becoming Salar Jung II.

Maharaja Narayan Pershad Narender Bahadur, was keen to become diwan. He had retained the services of Sir John Gorst hoping that the English lawyer would help him do so. The peshkar's legal adviser in India was Tom Palmer. When Gorst came to India, he visited Calcutta with Palmer for company. In Calcutta, they met the nizam, Laik Ali and the peshkar. Gorst found the nizam to be intelligent but shy. He seems to have formed a very poor opinion of Laik Ali, calling him 'tipsy and depraved', his influence on the nizam stemming from the fact that he was his drinking partner and supplier of liquor. He also described him as 'a clown' of no ability who used violent language against the British government. Gorst found it hard to believe that he could be the next diwan.[2]

Meanwhile, Seymour Keay, who was supporting Laik Ali's candidature, was writing, according to Gorst, 'scurrilous' articles in the *Statesman*. He accused Gorst of robbing the treasury of Rs 75,000 (£5300), something which Gorst denied, saying that his legal fees amounted to £1000 per month. It was reported that a sum of Rs 82,000 had been withdrawn by the Hyderabad treasury for payment to Palmer. The *Pioneer* observed that this was, in fact, 'a fee for Mr Gorst', a statement which was never contradicted.[3]

The peshkar's efforts were in vain. Lord Ripon decided to agree with the nizam's recommendation to appoint Laik Ali Khan to the post. The peshkar lost face (and his money). Gorst pocketed the money, and after returning to England, wrote a philippic in the *Fortnightly Review* in April 1884, the chief aim of which was to decry the work done by Salar Jung by 'a combination of faint praise and undisguised abuse'. In his article called 'The Kingdom of the Nizam', he said that Salar Jung's attempts to establish a sound system of administration had failed completely, and if at all he had succeeded in anything, it was in hoodwinking the British government. These accusations provoked much indignation. What Gorst hoped to achieve is not clear. It is possible that he wrote the article in a moment of pique, miffed at being unable to secure the post of diwan for his client.

On 5 February 1884, when Mir Mahbub Ali Khan was formally installed on the masnad by Lord Ripon, Laik Ali Khan became diwan of Hyderabad. It was a logical choice. He was the son of Salar Jung, a class-fellow, and a boon companion of the nizam. His accession to the post of diwan was marked by great warmth, and for a while, the two shared the most cordial relations. But the honeymoon didn't last long. Laik Ali Khan made himself extremely unpopular with his sovereign. He forgot that there is a wide gulf which separates a noble from a ruler, and presumed too much about his friendship with the nizam. The nizam felt terribly slighted by the breach of court etiquette of which Laik was routinely guilty. His impudent familiarity prompted the nizam to complain about his behaviour. Server-ul-Mulk, who was a repository of the nizam's confidence, tells us how in this case, familiarity, quite literally, bred contempt:

> He will sit on a chair, with legs straightened out, while I stand; he will take out cigarettes and smoke without hesitation in my presence; and in spite of strict orders, he wears whatever dress he likes at Court functions, and will sit with his back turned towards me, laughing and joking with others. He did not consider me even equal in rank, but lower.[4]

An incident seems to have brought the simmering resentment to a boil, finally provoking a break. The diwan had been reading aloud to the nizam when the latter demanded to see the article being read out to him. Salar Jung II, who had been drinking, threw the paper across the table.[5] Mahbub, who had been groomed to be a stickler in etiquette by Salar Jung—who if anything, had been the other extreme—was stunned at this impertinence and resolved to dismiss him.

Another incident, which took place in March 1884 when the nizam had an attack of cholera, also contributed to the increasing trust deficit between the two. Fearing the worst, and believing that a council of regency would again be established, Salar Jung II sent Syed Hossain Bilgrami to Khurshed Jah Amir-i-Kabir IV for consultation and future action. But the nizam recovered, and Salar Jung II tried to cover up the indiscretion by attributing the action to Server-ul-Mulk and the Amir-i-Kabir IV, saying that it was their idea to approach the resident for the succession of Zaffar Jung, the nizam's cousin. The nizam was soon told the truth, and this hardly helped Salar Jung II's cause.

The relationship turned extremely sour, often prompting harsh criticism from the nizam. In March 1887, Laik Ali Khan began to act strangely. He was paranoid about being assassinated and neglected his duties. He applied for leave and left the city without seeing the nizam. Such indefensible behaviour could not be countenanced, and his resignation on grounds of ill health was accepted by Mahbub in April 1887, after taking the viceroy into confidence.

Salar Jung II made some superficial administrative changes in his short tenure of three years. The change from Persian to Urdu as the official language took place when he was diwan, a change which his father had resisted because Persian for him 'symbolized the victory of Islam in India'. The seeds of a 'Mohammedan University' were sown by him, even though the Osmania University was established at the time of the seventh nizam, Mir Osman Ali Khan. The office of arzbegee was replaced by an aide-de-camp, and the daily court circular, *Siahah*, abolished. Correspondence with the residency was seldom brought to the notice of the nizam, and when it was, it was only for information.

Salar Jung II went on a European tour in 1887. He was honoured with the K.C.I.E. by Queen Victoria. He returned to India, settling in Poona where he died on 7 July 1889 at the age of only twenty-seven. No notice of his passing was taken by the Government of India. His body was brought to Hyderabad, and he lies buried close to his father. Left with no suitable alternative, the nizam selected Bashir-ud-Daula Asman Jah as his successor. Asman Jah, even though he had served as Sadr-ul-Maham under Salar Jung, and had also officiated for him on occasion, was not known to have any talent for administration. His candidature was reluctantly agreed to by the viceroy as a pis aller.

THE RAILWAY SCHEME: POSTSCRIPT

Salar Jung died before the railway scheme was finalized. The resident passed the buck, and no one wanted to study the details of the project. This, however, did not prevent the Government of India from approving it. The council of regency which was administering Hyderabad was persuaded to accept the proposal after some initial misgivings. The Government of India, in approving the proposal, washed its hands of the whole affair, accepting no responsibility for the end result. It claimed that the decision was primarily that of the Hyderabad government. Opposition for the scheme came from the people who believed that it was a rip-off. They started an organized movement against the railway scheme, and a committee consisting of many noblemen, merchants, bankers and government officials was formed.

The leaders of the agitation, a Parsi by the name of Dastur Asaji Hoshang, one of the secretaries of the committee, and Aghorenath Chattopadhyay, principal of Hyderabad College, were arrested and deported to British India. Aghorenath, who was something of a radical, was a remarkable figure in the intellectual life of Hyderabad. A student of Oxford when Salar Jung visited England in 1876, he attracted the minister's attention, who prevailed upon him to settle in the nizam's dominions. (He also had a famous daughter: Sarojini Naidu.) The agitation was discussed in the British Parliament, and no satisfactory answer was given as to why the resident had intervened on behalf of an English group of railway promoters.

Morton, Rose and Company withdrew from the scheme, saying that it would not be possible for them to raise money on the terms offered by Haq. Haq then persuaded William Clarence Watson, who was also a promoter of the mining scheme, to float the company which came to be known as the Nizam's Guaranteed State Railway Company. Haq received full support from the resident, J.G. Cordery, who was certainly in cahoots with him. Under pressure from the resident, the council of regency also succumbed, and the agreement was signed in December 1883, with both Calcutta and London giving it their seal of approval.

The terms were even more unfavourable than the Morton, Rose and Company proposal. Under it, a new company would buy out the Nizam's State Railway Company for £1,666,000 but the nizam was obliged to take £500,000 of that in company shares. The new company paid only £341,666 in cash, and left the nizam to buy off the Indian shareholders at £625,000. The nizam had to guarantee a 5 per cent profit (for which £200,000 was deducted in advance) on £4,500,000 for twenty years, a crushing financial liability of approximately Rs 32 lakh every year, far in excess of any surplus realized by Hyderabad. Attempts to get the newly installed nizam to quash the agreement failed, and in 1886, the first section of the new line was completed. The swindle by a few adventurous businessmen, with the collusion of the British government, was now complete. As Bharati Ray has observed: 'It is evident that railway development in Hyderabad constitutes one of those episodes in which political manipulation, selfishness and profiteering are inextricably intermingled.'[6] The aims of the Government of India in this respect seem to have 'coincided happily with the pecuniary interests' of a section of the queen's British subjects.[7]

The scent of lucre was in the air, and it was strong. Abdul Haq, though negotiating from the Hyderabad side, secretly deducted £83,000 for himself as a 'sales commission' as testified by J.G. Cordery to a parliamentary committee. Haq's associate, William Clarence Watson, received £100,000 as 'promotional expenses'.[8] It was now that Seymour Keay appeared on the scene as a whistle-blower, writing to the viceroy, with a copy to the *Statesman*, that the proposal with the 5 per cent guarantee and the interest payments would put ruinous pressure on the Hyderabad treasury, while the anticipated gains from the extension to Chanda rested on 'unfounded assumptions'. But Calcutta was at the time obsessed with the climax of the Ilbert Bill controversy, and the railway deal was quietly signed on 27 December 1883. Robert Knight, who had always considered Haq to be a shady wheeler-dealer, observed that he had long had a profound distrust of the whole business as a mere job of the 'promoters', and that both the nizam and the British investors were going to be duped. Knight wrote to the House of Commons urging an investigation into the railway scam to save the young nizam and Hyderabad from financial ruin.

Knight, meanwhile, unleashed a series of articles which, according to him, told the whole sordid Hyderabad story. 'Beginning on 21 December, a century of tawdry linen was strung out across eight rambling articles within sixteen days, an indictment of British encroaching, bullying, cheating and exploiting the dynasty of the Nizams and their officials.'[9] Knight blamed the residency and its corrupt officials for the political mess. Since 1881, there had been a parade of residents, with three residents having served there in two years. The real power lay with the first assistant resident, Major G.H. Trevor, but his position had been compromised. His brother, who had been appointed tutor to the nizam, lacked teaching qualifications. Salar Jung had given this brother a lucrative sinecure to keep Trevor happy. After seven years of doing nothing, the brother retired on a generous pension which the council of regency had recently doubled.

Knight sent Ripon secret papers which allegedly proved that the railway extension scheme had been forced on Salar Jung by Haq and the residency, but these the viceroy was quick to disbelieve and discard. Knight later published excerpts from a secret memo by Colonel Hastings Fraser which allegedly showed that Salar Jung had been coerced into accepting the Chanda extension plan, the real purpose of which was the enrichment of Haq and 'to provide a lot of Civilians in London with large salaries at the expense of the Nizam's treasury, under the pretence of their acting as a Board of Directors'.[10]

Ripon, even though he had repudiated Knight's 'evidence', used his visit to Hyderabad at the time of the nizam's installation, to corroborate the details which Knight had shared with him. He found Hyderabad to be 'a mass of intrigue and corruption which it is not easy to exaggerate'. He gave as examples the case of Trevor's brother and that of the peshkar who had admitted to falsifying the accounts to hide Hyderabad's deep debt. As we have already noted, one withdrawal of Rs 82,000 went to

John E. Gorst for his influence-peddling on behalf of the peshkar. Ripon found Hyderabad to be full of shady Europeans living off the nizam or some wealthy noble, claiming influence in the residency or in Westminster which they did not have.

Regardless of all the accusations, Haq continued to prosper. Laik Ali Khan, now officially Salar Jung II, endorsed the railway deal, and Haq was ennobled (he became Sirdar Diler Jung) by the nizam for his successful negotiations in the matter. Knight bemoaned the fact that he had 'all the proof in my hands of the scoundreldom of Abdul Haq', but then 'that fatal memorandum of the young Diwan's appeared justifying and condoning all'.[11]

In October 1885, Knight was vindicated when the Secretary of State, Lord Randolph Churchill, and his India Council, discovered the massive commission Haq had paid to himself and chided the Government of India for approving such a deal. But Abdul Haq and his associates continued to flourish. They formed the Hyderabad Deccan Mining Co. on 1 January 1886, and personally obtained the concession of all mineral rights in Hyderabad for a pittance. They then sold the concessions to their company for £850,000, of which Haq's share was £120,000. He even persuaded the nizam to invest a similar sum in the company, but instead of sending the order to London, pocketed the money and gave the nizam some of his own unissued shares. When this was discovered by the nizam in April 1888, he was livid. He dismissed Haq and demanded the return of his funds.[12]

These and other details of the great swindle came to light at the hearings of a select committee of the House of Commons which began its deliberations on 1 June 1888. The mendacious Cordery, who was resident since April 1883, completely disavowed Haq, and denied having any knowledge about the goings-on. He claimed not to know that Haq was a partner in the railway company, or that the mining concessions were in any way linked with the railway project. The select committee concluded that the interests of Hyderabad had been injured by the concessionaires, but there was no talk of criminal proceedings, only 'more effective and direct British assistance to princely states'. Haq tried to regain his position at the Hyderabad court but was rebuffed by the nizam.

While apologists of the Raj point to the Indian Railways as one of the ways in which British rule had benefited India, the truth is that 'in its very conception and construction the Indian Railways was a big British colonial scam'.[13] The government guaranteed returns on capital of 5 per cent per annum, a very high rate of return unavailable on any other safe investment.

This was possible only because the government made up any shortfall by payments which came from Indian taxes. British shareholders made huge amounts of money by investing in the railways.

This assured payment meant that there was no incentive for the companies constructing the railways to economize, since bigger outlays meant a higher return. Also, guaranteed railway shares absorbed up to a fifth of British portfolio investment in the twenty years to 1870. The first line started in 1853, but only 1 per cent of it originated in India. The British supplied all the equipment, and controlled all the technology, which meant that all the profits were repatriated. It has been aptly described as 'private enterprise at public risk'.[14]

The railway also provided a much-needed market for the overpriced steel manufactured in England. While each mile of railway cost the dollar equivalent of £2000 in the United States, the corresponding cost in India in the 1850s and 1860s was £18,000. It was twenty years before a 5 per cent return could be achieved. Even after the government took over railway construction in the 1880s, the cupidity of the private contractors ensured that a mile of Indian railway still cost nearly twice as much as in Canada and Australia.[15]

INTRIGUE AND MISMANAGEMENT

J.G. Cordery, who was resident till 1889, seemed quite at home in the world of Hyderabadi intrigue, and may not have been entirely above board in his own dealings. His successor, Sir Dennis Fitzpatrick, was uncomfortable in the environment he found himself in and avoided getting involved in Hyderabad politics. Fitzpatrick left Hyderabad to become lieutenant governor of Punjab in 1891. By then, the finances of the state were in a precarious condition, and he wrote a friendly letter to the nizam, warning him of the impending financial catastrophe.

But the nizam was addicted to alcohol and opium, which he consumed in large quantities, and was hardly out of the zenana. He took no exercise, ate irregularly and had no fixed sleeping hours. By 1889, he had come increasingly under the influence of his former tutor, Server-ul-Mulk, who many thought was usurping the nizam's powers. After Salar Jung's death, intrigues amongst the nobles and high officials flourished unhindered. Hyderabad had always been a hotbed of intrigue, but Salar Jung, with his great talents, had managed to keep things under control. Matters reached such a sorry pass that Asman Jah felt obliged to bribe Server-ul-Mulk to put in a good word about him to the nizam.[16]

According to Server-ul-Mulk, he received Rs 80,000 out of an amount of Rs 1 lakh of the bribe money. He gave the money to the nizam as a nazarana, and told him about the attempt to buy his support.[17] Sir Trevor John Chichele-Plowden, who had succeeded Fitzpatrick as resident, was asked to conduct the inquiry. Mahdi Ali Khan Mohsin-ul-Mulk, whose aide had taken the bribe money to Server-ul-Mulk, found himself banished by the nizam. Part of the reason for this attempt to bribe appears to be the drafting of the *Quanuncha Mubarak* or 'auspicious code' which was being drafted by Server-ul-Mulk in which the powers and duties of all officials, including the diwan, were to be prescribed. The coterie around Asman Jah feared that if the nizam took the reins of government in his hands, their influence would end quite precipitately. They saw Server-ul-Mulk as the key figure in all this, and hence the need to buy his services. But it all ended quite badly.

In 1893, the council of state was replaced by a consultative body called the cabinet council with the diwan as president, Vikar-ul-Umra II as vice president, and Maharaja Kishen Pershad and three other ministers as members. But the nizam was unhappy with his diwan, who had handed over the reins of government to subordinates. It was the secretaries who ruled the roost, and Asman Jah's tenure was marked by grave financial mismanagement and public scandals. It was time for him to go, and go he did. His successor in November 1893 was Vikar-ul-Umra II, the builder of Falaknuma Palace which he famously gifted to the nizam.

The change did not lead to any substantial improvement in the administration. It was too much to expect, given the fact that Vikar-ul-Umra II had much less experience in public affairs than his predecessor. Server-ul-Mulk's influence continued to grow, as did the charges of nepotism against him. He soon became more powerful than the diwan. Despite attempts by Plowden to rid Hyderabad of his influence, it was only at the end of January 1897 that he succeeded. The charges against him, apart from nepotism, were constant interference in the affairs of state, including the high court. Finally, the nizam ordered Server-ul-Mulk to leave Hyderabad for Delhi, never to return.

But ironically, Plowden, an ICS officer who was resident for nine long years, does not seem to have enjoyed a good reputation. He was accused by Seymour Keay, by then a member of Parliament, of supporting Server-ul-Mulk for corrupt motives.[18] (It was Plowden's daughter, Pamela, with whom the young Winston Churchill fell in love when he first met her in 1896. She rejected his advances and married Sir Victor Lytton who was the son of the former viceroy, Lord Edward Lytton. Sir Victor became governor of Bengal (1922–27) and also held charge of the post of viceroy briefly.)

The finances of Hyderabad went from bad to worse, the nizam's personal expenditure being a major reason for the crisis. In 1900, a serious famine added to these financial woes, and the crisis was tided over by recourse to a loan of Rs 2 crore from the British government by hypothecating part of the Berar surplus. Plowden left Hyderabad and was replaced by Sir David Barr. In 1901, Kishen Pershad became diwan, and the next year Lord Curzon came to Hyderabad and the British finally got what they had always wanted—the leasing of Berar in perpetuity.

BERAR: THE BRITISH FINALLY PREVAIL

The English had long wanted Berar to be assigned in perpetuity, and in December 1902, they finally had their way. The final act of the Berar drama was played out nearly twenty years after Salar Jung's death. Mahbub Ali Khan had, in a sense, grown up with the Berar issue and abhorred the idea of leasing the assigned districts in perpetuity. The subject was brought up by the viceroy, Lord Curzon, who wanted a permanent cession from the nizam in return for a fixed annual rent of Rs 25 lakh. The nizam refused categorically, ending his discussion with the resident, Lt Col. David Barr 'with an absolute refusal unattended by any argument or reasons'. Curzon also wanted to get rid of the Hyderabad Contingent altogether. The Secretary of State, Lord George Hamilton, didn't think the nizam would agree and was emphatic in his opposition to Curzon visiting Hyderabad. He did not want him to be in any way associated with a failed negotiation or one which was concluded by 'exercising personally upon the Nizam the authority and coercion of a Viceroy'.[19]

Ignoring the advice, Curzon met the nizam on 30 March 1902 in Hyderabad, and within a day's time, had secured the settlement he wanted. The viceroy observed that as long as the nizam felt that he had a chance of getting Berar back, he was unlikely to consider any other solution. Curzon wrote to the Secretary of State, Hamilton, 'Nizam accepted my Berar proposals . . . As long as he thought that he had a chance of getting back

Berar in complete restitution he said that he would naturally prefer not to consider any other solution . . . If I could tell him that the chance were so remote as to be unworthy of serious consideration, then he would not only accept my proposal with pleasure, but he was so grateful for the generosity of its terms.'[20]

Things didn't quite turn out the way the nizam wanted. At the interview, he had intended to present to the viceroy a letter requesting restoration, not as a matter of right, but as a favour, on the occasion of the coronation of Edward VII. The nervous and shy nizam, overwhelmed by the personality[21] of the viceroy, could not get himself to deliver the letter. In the course of the interview, Curzon told him that the confirmation of Maharaja Kishen Pershad as diwan was subject to his own sanction, and the condition for such confirmation was that Sir George Casson Walker, who had been loaned to the nizam, should have his status raised from secretary to adviser.

Curzon told Mahbub that the restoration of Berar was unlikely since its retention was a policy common to both Liberal and Conservative parties. The viceroy was adamant. Mahbub, left with no choice, was forced to do the unthinkable: he accepted the proposal of a lease in perpetuity offered by the viceroy. Aware that such a complete turnaround would be considered highly suspicious, Curzon assured Hamilton that he had convinced the nizam, who had yielded, not from weakness, but from conviction. In his anxiety to prove his point, Curzon made the nizam sign a document declaring a voluntary cession. Such a volte-face was impossible without coercion. Though the exact nature of Curzon's 'convincing arguments' are not known, Wilfrid Scawen Blunt, in his diary, said that the nizam surrendered after threat of deposition, and was so overwhelmed with grief that he refused to eat for four days.

Twenty years after Lord Ripon's visit another viceregal visit was paid to Hyderabad, and the Nizam was pressed by Lord Curzon at the close of the entertainment at the palace to accord him a perpetual lease of the Provinces for the Indian Government, and the Nizam, in deference to his guest, verbally consented. In the morning, however, he would have recalled his promise, and it was only on compulsion, and on threat of deposition, that he signed the treaty laid before him as a binding document by the Resident . . . The Nizam, my informant added, refused for four days to take food after this occurrence.[22]

Curzon's assurance to Hamilton 'that at this moment, he [the nizam] is the most contented man in Hyderabad' can only be seen as a way of assuaging his own guilty conscience. It is ironic that in a communication to the Secretary of State in September 1901, Curzon had observed: 'We all have a sub-latent consciousness that the Berar question has not been tackled in strict accordance with the most scrupulous standards of British honour.'[23]

From 'exclusive management' in 1853 and 'trust' in 1860, Berar was now leased in 'perpetuity', and was to be administered by the chief commissioner of the Central Provinces. As per the treaty signed between the nizam and the British government in December 1902, Berar was leased in perpetuity for a fixed and perpetual rent of Rs 25 lakh per annum. The British were given the right to redistribute, reduce and control the Hyderabad Contingent as they saw fit. The British gained on two accounts. It would allow them to administer Berar as a part of the Central Provinces instead of as a separate unit, i.e., Central Provinces and Berar. It also enabled the government to reduce the size of the Contingent and merge it with the Indian army. After signing the agreement with Curzon, Mahbub was made a Knight Grand Cross of the Bath (G.C.B.), an honour he sarcastically referred to as 'Gave Curzon Berar'.[24] Mahbub had a sense of humour and was not above schoolboy pranks. A flock of birds flew out of a pie being served at the state banquet, one landing on Lady Curzon's tiara and another on Curzon's head![25] Curzon's views on this are not available to posterity.

SALAR JUNG III

When Salar Jung II died, his son, Yousuf Ali Khan, the future Salar Jung III, who was born on 13 June 1889 in Poona,[26] was only twenty-four days old. His widow returned to Hyderabad with her infant son. Yousuf grew up under the watchful eyes of his mother and a few faithful retainers. His health, like that of his grandfather, was delicate in the early part of his life. The nizam, Mahbub Ali Khan, did not allow his differences with the infant's father, Salar Jung II, to affect his relationship with the child. He took the child under his personal care and protection, and gave special attention to his education. Private tutors were appointed to teach him. He also attended the Madrasa-i-Aliya. The nizam was given regular reports about his progress, and even the Government of India was kept informed about the education of the young child through the resident.

Yousuf Ali Khan was a bright child who was tutored at home. A bibliophile, he was one of the most widely read nobles of Hyderabad. The physical side of Salar Jung III's development was also given special attention. After the early phase of delicate health, he regularly played cricket, football and tennis. He had his own cricket team, in which he also played, along with Nawab Moin-ud-Daula. He became a good swimmer despite the fact that he nearly drowned at the age of five. He liked riding, tent-pegging and polo. He had his own polo team (the Salar Jung polo team), owning fifty to sixty polo ponies.

Since Yousuf had lost both his father and his uncle by the time he was one year old, the estate was looked after by Salar Jung I's mother. On her death in 1895, the estate was handed over to a committee appointed by a royal mandate. Since the nizam was unhappy with the functioning of the committee, the management of the estate was entrusted to Raja Lalta Pershad, and the revenue secretary, A.J. Dunlop. Since the estate was deeply in debt, the nizam paid off half the debt from his personal finances. In 1898, on the occasion of the nizam's birthday, Yousuf was conferred with the titles of Khan, Bahadur, and Salar Jung. He was also given a mansab of 2500, cavalry of 1500, an *alam* (flag) and a *naqqara* (kettledrum).

'THE DAYS OF THE BELOVED'

Mahbub Ali Khan passed away on 29 August 1911, aged forty-five, his premature demise being brought about by his erratic and unhealthy lifestyle. The end came in Falaknuma Palace after a drinking binge lasting three days. Mahbub, 'marinated in alcohol' for many years, would not emerge from this health crisis alive. He slipped into a coma and died without saying a word. His reign is still considered Hyderabad's golden era, and was labelled the 'The Days of the Beloved'. (The word Mahbub literally means beloved.)

Mahbub had been a popular ruler and was widely mourned. His reign had seen a degree of communal harmony that many feel will never be achieved again. The famous Ganga-Jamuna tehzeeb of Hyderabad was fully on view: festivals were celebrated across communal lines, and people took considerable trouble to indicate their respect of others' religious beliefs and sentiments.[27] During the devastating flood of 1908 when the Musi broke its banks killing many thousand, the nizam took the advice of the Hindu pandits and donned a sacred thread to appease the river goddess.[28]

Mahbub was famous for both his munificent charity and reckless extravagance. His charities were legendary. He gave so much, and so consistently—often in unsolicited succour—that his unceasing benevolence put considerable strain on his resources. Luckily for him, the line between a ruler's private expenses and public expenditure was blurred: he earned Rs 1 crore from his crown lands alone, and also had the liberty of dipping into the treasury whenever he wanted. His penchant for buying up all the contents of a shop if he learnt that the owner was going through a lean phase is well known. There are also numerous stories of how he went to the aid of indigent parents who were facing difficulty in getting their daughters married. The aid was both generous and prompt: among deserving worldly causes, financing a wedding ranked second only to financing a pilgrimage to Mecca. Those were times of amazing individual generosity, and what is significant is that the benefactors believed in charity with dignity—on no occasion was the recipient's self-esteem hurt.

Mahbub was famous for spending money on a scale which defied belief. He would discard clothes and accessories after using them just once. His 176-foot wardrobe at Purani Haveli is testimony to the fact that he acquired garments on a scale not seen, before, or since. The contents of the wardrobe would be distributed to the poor on his birthday. Mahbub also ended up making his chamberlain, Albert Abid, a very rich man. A Persian-born Armenian Jew, Abid gave Hyderabad its first department store and a new name to an abandoned locality. Mahbub did not like to repeat his silk socks, and the enterprising valet would put them back in the packet they came in and sell them once again to his trusting master. There were also rumours about how he removed Mahbub's rings when he was in a drunken stupor and thanked him profusely the next morning for his generous gifts.[29] It was the most lucrative position in the palace, and Abid certainly exploited its full potential. D.F. Karaka observed: 'Every time Mahbub Ali Pasha unfastened a button or changed a garment, Abid was there. He had to be there. His Highness could not do without him.'[30] Abid was married to Annie Evans who had worked as a governess for Meade's wife. The couple invested in a shop run by Annie that catered mainly to the Europeans and the Muslim nobility, as well as a dressmaking business. Abid also charged a hefty commission from traders on any transaction.[31]

It is said that though Mahbub owned more precious stones than all the other Indian princes put together, his appetite for what Sir Dennis Fitzpatrick, the resident, called 'pieces of sparkling vanity'[32] was insatiable.

(His son and successor, Mir Osman Ali Khan, considered at one time to be the world's richest man, would swing to the other extreme, practising a frugality considered by many as a comical miserliness.)

Mahbub had inherited the largest hoard of jewels ever amassed in India: diamonds from Golconda, Colombian emeralds, Burmese sapphires and rubies, and ropes of Basra pearls. His vaults were overflowing with diamond-encrusted turban ornaments, necklaces, armbands and bracelets. One vault contained a dinner-plate-sized gold mohur that had once belonged to Emperor Jehangir, which at 12 kg, is said to be the largest coin ever minted.[33] But he wanted more. Those charged with husbanding the finances of the state had a hard time in keeping the exchequer solvent, given the fact that enormous amounts were being depleted at an alarming rate. Mahbub loved diamonds, but his acquisition of the Jacob diamond (named after the dealer who sold it to him), the world's fifth-largest diamond, and the most famous in the nizam's collection, caused him a great deal of discomfiture. It was the reason for his appearance in a court of law as an ordinary deponent in what came to be known as the 'Imperial Diamond Case'.

Alexander Malcolm Jacob, the diamond dealer, claimed to be a Turk born near Constantinople but remained, for the most part, a man of 'mysterious origins and colourful infamy'. He was sold as a slave to a rich pasha who educated him, and he is said to have acquired wide knowledge of Eastern life, language, literature, art, philosophy and occultism. Arriving penniless in Bombay, he travelled to Hyderabad sometime in 1867–68 where it is said he spent a year working for Rafi-ud-din Khan Amir-i-Kabir II, as a scribe. He then moved to Calcutta where he worked for a jeweller before setting up a flourishing business in gems, jewellery and curios in Simla. The lure of profiting from the vast sums Mahbub was spending on jewellery drew him back to Hyderabad. His intention was to sell the 184-carat Imperial diamond, as it was then called, to the nizam for Rs 46 lakh.

The deal went horribly wrong. Mahbub had agreed to buy the stone on the condition that the real diamond was brought to him for approval. By this time, the resident, Dennis Fitzpatrick, had heard about the deal and resolved to stop it on the grounds that the nizam's government was near bankrupt, and Mahbub, who already possessed the best collection of jewels in the world, did not need one more extravagantly priced bauble. When Jacob came to Hyderabad, he faced great disappointment. Mahbub refused to buy the diamond and wanted the Rs 23 lakh he had given Jacob to be returned to him. But Jacob had used that money to pay a jewellery firm in London. He was now left with the diamond and a debt of Rs 23 lakh. He asked for time to repay the nizam but was arrested in September 1891 and charged with misappropriation and criminal breach of trust. The 'Imperial Diamond Case', which came before the Calcutta High Court, ultimately resulted in Jacob being exonerated. The nizam deposed as a witness at Saifabad Palace where he was cross-examined for several days. A cross-examination of Albert Abid, who appeared as a witness, revealed that he had been promised a commission of Rs 5 lakh by Jacob if the deal went through.

Jacob never saw the diamond again. After an out-of-court settlement, in another civil case, the nizam was given ownership of the diamond. Jacob received only his legal costs and died a broken man in Bombay in 1921 where he is buried. The diamond, which Mahbub considered unlucky, was wrapped in a rag and tucked away in a drawer of his writing table. It was reportedly found in the toe of a slipper during Osman Ali's reign, and the seventh nizam is alleged to have used it as a paperweight. The diamond was involved in further legal wrangles in 1972, a round of litigation that lasted three decades. This time it was Mahbub's grandson, Mukarram Jah, who faced the music.[34] The Jacob diamond is now the property of the Government of India, and is held in the vaults of the Reserve Bank of India in Mumbai where it is the centrepiece of any exhibition of the nizam's jewels.

A NEW DIWAN

Mahbub's son, Mir Osman Ali Khan, became the seventh nizam in 1911, and it was during his reign that Salar Jung III was invested with full powers to administer his estate comprising 1480 sq. miles and a population of nearly 2 lakh people. When Maharaja Kishen Pershad, the diwan, resigned in 1912 citing health grounds, the nizam decided to appoint Salar Jung III in his stead. His appointment was received with delight and high expectations by the people of Hyderabad. Given his youth and inexperience, he was assisted by Syed Hossain Bilgrami, who by now had held many important posts in government.

Given his qualities of head and heart, it was expected that he would be at least equal to, if not outshine, his worthy grandfather. But fate decreed otherwise. History repeated itself when he resigned in 1914 after only two and a half years, due to personal differences with the nizam. Apparently, he had never been popular with the seventh nizam, who resented his popularity and his friendship with the resident, A.F. Pinhey. S.M. Fraser, who succeeded Pinhey as resident, said that there was no doubt that the nizam had grown bitterly jealous of his popularity, and went out of the way to treat him as a boy.

His mother, who had seen a similar fate befall her husband, and witnessed the tragedy of his early demise, was naturally worried about her son. A depressed Salar Jung III was referred to the family physician, Dr Hunt, for treatment. Hunt suggested that Salar Jung III should amuse himself like the European nobility by collecting art objects. This struck a receptive chord in the young nawab. The loss of premiership was put at the back of his mind, and in time, modern India gained a magnificent collection of art objects.

Salar Jung III, however, did accomplish some notable tasks during his short tenure as diwan. It was in his time that the department of archaeology and a small causes court were set up. A large number of scholarships were given to deserving students for studies both in India and abroad. He also contributed his own money to this end. Like his father, Salar Jung III also travelled to England and the Continent after he resigned as diwan. In February 1921, he returned after a stay of many months, laden with rare objects and numerous books. Again, in May 1927, he left for England. On his return, he followed this up with trips to Japan and the Middle East.

BERAR AGAIN

Generations of nizams had been smarting under the humiliation of the cession of Berar, and Osman Ali Khan was no exception. When he was made Knight Grand Cross of the British Empire or a G.B.E. in 1917, he is said to have wryly commented (probably drawing inspiration from a similar remark made by his father), that GBE stood for 'Gave Berar to the English'.

In October 1923, Osman Ali Khan reopened the question of Berar in a letter to the viceroy, Lord Reading, his remonstrance covering 150 years of the relationship. It was accompanied by a voluminous memorandum of forty-three pages and eighteen appendices, and traversed the entire history of relations between the British and the nizam. It ended with a peremptory demand asking for the complete restoration of Berar and the removal of the Contingent from Hyderabad.

In reply, Reading sent a semi-official letter dated 11 March 1925 in which he expressed reluctance to engage in a controversy over the past and politely denied his charges and rejected his demands. Osman Ali Khan followed it up with another letter on 20 September 1925 in which he asked for the restoration of Berar and also asserted that 'save and except in matters relating to foreign powers and policies, the Nizams of Hyderabad have been independent in the internal affairs of their State just as much as the British government in British India'. In his application, he put forth the view that the Berar question was an issue between 'two independent governments having mutual relations with each other', and there was equality between the nizam and the British on this question.

Lord Reading, in his reply of 27 March 1926, strongly asserted the supremacy of the British, and disabused the nizam of his independence in the internal affairs of Hyderabad. The British imperial tradition had been nurtured on the feeling that territory once gained should never be surrendered. Though Lord Reading was a former chief justice of England, he was not predisposed to looking into the legal merits of the case. The Berar case would neither be reopened nor referred to a court of arbitration.[35] His scathing reply, now a part of Raj folklore, is often quoted as the classic statement of the role of British paramountcy in the Indian states:

> The sovereignty of the British Crown is supreme in India, and therefore no ruler of an Indian State can justifiably claim to negotiate with the British Government on an equal footing. Its supremacy is not based upon treaties and engagements, but exists independently of them and, quite apart from its prerogatives in matters relating to foreign powers and politics, it is the right and duty of the British Government, while scrupulously respecting all treaties and engagements with the Indian State, to preserve peace and good order throughout India . . . The right of the British Government to intervene in the internal affairs of Indian States is another instance of the consequences necessarily involved in the supremacy of the British Crown . . . Where imperial interests are concerned, or the general welfare of the people of a State is seriously and grievously affected by the action of its Government, it is with the Paramount Power that the ultimate responsibility of taking remedial action, if necessary must lie.[36]

The nizam had also enlisted the help of the maharaja of Patiala in this matter. The latter, in his capacity as the chancellor of the Chamber of Princes, wrote to Reading's successor, Lord Irwin, pleading the nizam's case. In his reply, Irwin snubbed the maharaja politely and said that the internal matters of a state could not be discussed by members in session. He also sent a copy of the maharaja's letter to Hyderabad where the nizam was asked to explain his conduct. The nizam panicked and came out of the episode rather poorly. He claimed that he had been asked by the resident, T.H. Keyes, to respond in the negative to both the questions put to him, namely, whether he had authorized the maharaja to advocate his case, and if he was aware that such a letter was being sent to the viceroy before it was despatched.

The Government of India Act, 1935, contained a constitution for the federation of India, and provision was made in it for the joint governance of the Central Provinces and Berar as one governor's province, provided an agreement was signed between the two governments. In October 1936, such an agreement was entered into providing for the accession of the nizam to the federation of India to the extent of the territories known as Berar, and for their joint administration with the Central Provinces. The nizam was reaffirmed as the sovereign of Berar, and he was given the right to fly his flag alongside the British flag, to confer Hyderabad titles on Berar inhabitants, and to have the khutba read in his name in any mosque in Berar. It is also from this time onward that the heir apparent of the nizam was granted the title of His Highness and Prince of Berar.[37]

For all his miserliness, Osman Ali Khan acquitted himself very creditably when Prime Minister Lal Bahadur Shastri visited Hyderabad in 1965 and asked him to contribute to the National Defence Fund. He promptly announced that he would contribute five tonnes of gold to the war fund, in today's gold price about Rs 1500 crore. He was known to have a wry sense of humour and said that he was not donating the empty iron boxes in which the gold coins were being transported and wanted them back. The boxes were duly returned.[38]

SALAR JUNG III'S COLLECTION AND THE MUSEUM[39]

Salar Jung III had inherited the *Veiled Rebecca*, the wood carving *Mephistopheles and Margaretta*, priceless oriental manuscripts of the Koran, and an illustrated anthology of Muhammad Quli, among other items, from his grandfather and father. He added to these over the years and built a huge collection which filled his palaces. His passion for collecting art and curios became an all-absorbing obsession. There was a big oval table in the ainakhana where the pieces brought by merchants would be placed and their prices displayed. He would select the pieces, write down the offer price and initial it. The paymaster would later pay for it. The art pieces in the deodi were arranged in seventy-seven rooms.

When the deodi could accommodate no more, he stocked his art objects in his other palaces. Over the years, the collection assumed alarming proportions. His city palace and his country mansion at Saroornagar were full to overflowing with art objects. He knew the value of each piece in his collection and kept a vigilant eye on their preservation and location. It is said that he knew exactly where each piece had been stored or exhibited.

Salar Jung III's collection was the result of not only his travels in India and abroad, but also from purchases made on his behalf by agents of auction houses. Art dealers from all around the world sent him catalogues and kept him abreast of the new pieces available with them. Auction houses Christie's and Sotheby's sent him their catalogues. Besides having agents in the principal Indian cities, he also used to participate in auctions in Hyderabad, and J. Moosa, Rahim Khan and Abdul Aziz, the owners of the local auction halls, became his agents. His favourite jeweller in Bombay was Gazdar, who helped him evaluate foreign jewellery. His collection boasted of Emperor Jehangir's wine cup and Aurangzeb's dagger, to mention only two notable objects in this enormous collection.

Families selling their heirlooms gave Salar Jung III the right of first refusal. A kind-hearted man, he sometimes allowed himself to be duped because 'the man needed the money'. He was an expert in judging calligraphy and could identify the handwriting of any great writer of the past. His knowledge of paintings was exceptional, and he could identify the country of origin of a carpet by simply looking at the stitching and knots.

Salar Jung III had plans to set up a museum either at Khwaja Pahadi near the Mir Alam Tank or at Moula-Ali. Poona and Ooty were also considered as likely locations. He devoted a lot of time, energy and resources on the designs, but unfortunately, death claimed him suddenly on 2 March 1949, before work could commence. His last purchase—a set of ivory chairs gifted to Tipu Sultan by Louis XVI—arrived after his death. They can be seen in the Salar Jung Museum today. The military governor declared a public holiday as a mark of respect, and the Hyderabad Art Society passed a resolution of condolence. The society also resolved to start a museum associated with his name.

Salar Jung III left behind more than 40,000 art objects, and a large number of books and manuscripts. The example of duty has often been set to the government by individual effort and private enthusiasm; and the government, which is almost always a tardy learner, has warmed to its task by slow degrees. In this case, however, it acted swiftly. Since Salar Jung III was a bachelor, the Government of India appointed a committee by virtue of a special ordinance to administer the affairs of the Salar Jung Estate. M.K. Vellodi, the then chief civil administrator of Hyderabad, approached Dr James Cousins, a well-known art critic, to organize the various objects into a museum. Since Cousins was engaged, he suggested the name of G. Venkatachalam. The venue of the proposed museum was to be the diwan deodi, Salar Jung III's residence when he was alive. This new museum was controlled by the Salar Jung Estate Committee and was declared open to the public on 16 December 1951 by Prime Minister Jawaharlal Nehru.

Since Salar Jung III had no direct heirs, his property had to be divided among a large number of his relations. There were 114 claimants to the property who formed themselves into different groups and filed five different compromise memoranda in the court between 1956 and 1958. The Government of India and the government of Andhra Pradesh passed a decree on 5 March 1958 considering all these compromise memoranda. By virtue of the compromise deed dated 2 December 1958 and the high court decree thereon, all parties to the suit agreed to relinquish their rights in all art objects and books in the museum and library in favour of the Government of India. The compromise deed was largely an outcome of the patience and diligence of Nawab Mehdi Nawaz Jung, chairman of the Salar Jung Estate Committee.

The museum then came to be administered by the Government of India as a subordinate office under the then ministry of scientific research and cultural affairs. This arrangement continued till 1 July 1961, when the administration of the museum was transferred to the Salar Jung Museum Board—an autonomous body formed by an Act of Parliament. On 1 July 1961, the Salar Jung Museum, together with its library, was declared to be an institution of national importance by an Act of Parliament known as the Salar Jung Museum Act, dated 19 May 1961.

Under the Act, the Government of India vested the ownership of the collections, and transferred the administration of the museum and library to a board of trustees consisting of eleven members (five ex officio, and six nominated), with the governor of Andhra Pradesh as its ex officio chairman. Being autonomous, the board is self-governing. However, the Government of India has retained powers to exercise overall control over the museum in matters pertaining to policy and finances. The Salar Jung Museum has a unique status insofar as it is the only museum in India which is fully autonomous but is wholly financed by the Government of India.

The collection was first housed in the diwan deodi where the Oriental and the Western collections were displayed in seventy-seven rooms of the palace. (The deodi was demolished in the 1970s, and the city civil courts are located in the area now.) However, this was always going to be a temporary location, and a master plan for the construction of a new building was submitted at an estimated cost of Rs 97.05 lakh. The first phase was to construct a central block with the remaining two blocks, one on each side, to be taken up at a later stage. The bulk of the expenditure was to be borne by the Government of India, through the state government.

The Salar Jung Estate Committee donated 5.8 acres of land situated on the southern bank of the Musi river and Rs 5 lakh. A piece of land measuring 4.75 acres was purchased and added to the plot donated, thereby making sufficient provision for the future expansion of the museum. The state government provided a grant of Rs 5 lakh, and also consented to construct the building through its public works department. In view of the high cost, it was decided to proceed with the construction in a phased manner. The cornerstone of the new building was laid by Pandit Nehru on 23 July 1963, and the central block of the new building was completed on 16 January 1968. The library was the first section to be shifted. The work of shifting and rearranging was done simultaneously, and the museum was opened to the public on 1 June 1968. It was officially inaugurated on 24 July 1968 by the President of India, Dr Zakir Husain.

The objects on display have now been systematically classified and displayed. In view of the vast collection, it was proposed to construct two more blocks on either side of the existing building. These two blocks, namely, Turab Ali Khan Bhavan (western block) and Laik Ali Khan Bhavan (eastern block) came up in 1999. The plan is to ultimately house all the Western art in the Turab Ali Khan Bhavan and all the Eastern art in the Laik Ali Khan Bhavan. The central block will exhibit the entire Indian collection.

At present, there are thirty-eight galleries in the museum in three blocks: the Indian block (thirty galleries), the western block (seven galleries) and the eastern block (two galleries) in which more than 13,000 objects are on display. (This is a little more than about a fourth of the collection. Most museums display only a certain percentage of the objects in their possession. The Salar Jung Museum is no exception—there are a large number of chandeliers and exquisite period furniture, among other artefacts, still waiting to be displayed.) The exhibition hall in the Turab Ali Khan Bhavan, named after the late Abbas Yaar Jung, a descendent of the Salar Jungs, and a former member of the museum's board for many years, was inaugurated in October 2007. There is also a founders' gallery where the portraits and personal belongings of the family attempt to recreate for the viewer the life and times of the Salar Jungs.

The museum has been acquiring art objects to augment the existing collection and fill gaps in the evolutionary sequence. It has also received gifts from various sources. Endowments from celebrities include a diamond-studded watch from Pandit Nehru and a bequest comprising paintings, porcelain, furniture and bronze pieces from Padmaja Naidu in September 1976. The museum has also played host to the exhibition of the nizam's jewellery. The exhibits of the museum can be broadly divided into Indian art, Persian art, Nepalese and Tibetan art, Sino-Japanese art and Western art. A discussion on the exhibits of the museum is beyond the scope of this book. Suffice it to say that they never cease to leave the viewer awestruck. And a source of perpetual wonder is the fact that most of it is the collection of one man.

While it is the museum's collection of art objects that is always in the limelight, Salar Jung III's collection of books and manuscripts rivals his enormous collection of antiques and objets d'art. The library consists of more than 62,000 printed books in English, Urdu, Hindi, Telugu, Persian, Arabic and Turkish. The English books include journals and albums of rare photos and engravings. The majority of the English books were added by Salar Jung III. However, the collection of books, which had been acquired by several preceding generations, was given the form of a library by Salar Jung. There are 8556 manuscripts in Arabic, Persian, Urdu and other languages, and 1450 calligraphic panels in the collection. The museum's manuscript collection is remarkable both for its quality and quantity.

The statue of Salar Jung III faces the museum building as if guarding
his exhibits. One wonders if the spry nawab would have approved of
what posterity has done with his magnificent collection. Harindranath
Chattopadhyay described the museum as 'India's finest liberal university',
and wrote a poem called 'The Museum?' in March 1953, the first lines of
which are:

> This is no Museum—as it is said
> For, as you know, a Museum is dead . . .
> And this which millions shall come to see
> Is all alive with immortality.

The poet also hit the nail on the head with the last lines of the same poem:

> Prince of Collectors; you have come to stay
> You are immortal and shall never pass away.[40]

Notes and References

Introduction

1. Urdu-speaking Pathans who had migrated to Hyderabad from the Rohilkhand region of present-day Uttar Pradesh.
2. The Vidarbha region of Maharashtra, is the eastern region of the Indian state of Maharashtra, comprising Nagpur Division and Amravati Division.
3. Sir William Barton, *The Princes of India*, Nisbet & Co. Ltd, London, 1934, p. 211.
4. Sir Richard Temple, *Men and Events of My Time in India*, London, John Murray, 1882, p. 294.
5. Karen Leonard, 'Hyderabad: Mulki–Non-Mulki Conflict', in Robin Jeffrey, ed., *People, Princes and Paramount Power*, Oxford University Press, New Delhi, 1979, p. 66.
6. Bharati Ray, *Hyderabad and British Paramountcy, 1858-1883*, Oxford University Press, New Delhi, 1988, p. 173.
7. Harriet Ronken Lynton and Mohini Rajan, *The Days of the Beloved*, Orient Longman Ltd, New Delhi, 1987, p. 29.
8. Harriet Ronken Lynton, *My Dear Nawab Saheb*, Disha Books, New Delhi, 1993, p. 3.
9. Sir Richard Temple, *Men and Events of My Time in India*, p. 288.
10. Ramachandra Guha in the Fifth Sharda Prasad Memorial Lecture, New Delhi, 16 April 2016.

Prologue

1. Narendra Luther, *Hyderabad: A Biography*, Oxford University Press, New Delhi, 2006, p. 102.

2.   Ibid.

3.   The rank was always expressed in military terms as a commander of so many cavalrymen, even if the holder was not from the military. The generic term, *mansabdar*, by which Mughal officers were known, meant 'holder of rank'. The mansabdari system was created by Akbar, who grouped imperial officers into thirty-three ranks (zat) from commanders of ten to 10,000. The ranks above 5000 were generally reserved for princes, and those below the rank of 500 were simply called mansabdars. Each rank of mansabdar was further divided into three classes (first, second and third), on the basis of whether the cavalrymen a mansabdar was required to maintain were equal to, half or less than half of the number indicated by his zat rank. The zat rank indicated an officer's grade in the hierarchy, whereas his *sawar* rank indicated his trooper ranking which specified the number of cavalrymen he was required to maintain.

4.   Yusuf Husain Khan, *Nizam-ul-Mulk Asaf Jah I*, The Basel Mission Press, Mangalore, 1936, p. 42.

5.   Swapna Liddle, *Chandni Chowk: The Mughal City of Old Delhi*, Speaking Tiger, New Delhi, 2017, p. 47.

6.   Syed Hossain Bilgrami and C. Wilmott, *Historical and Descriptive Sketch of His Highness the Nizam's Dominions*, Vol. 2, Times of India Steam Press, Bombay, 1884, pp. 60-61.

7.   Swapna Liddle, *Chandni Chowk*, pp. 51-52.

8.   Bilgrami and Wilmott, *Historical and Descriptive Sketch of His Highness the Nizam's Dominions*, pp. 62-64.

9.   Ibid., p. 65.

10. Asaf the Seer, was the prime minister of the Biblical ruler Solomon and the title signified wisdom of a high order.

11. Quoted in Narendra Luther, *Hyderabad: A Biography*, p. 103.

12. Yusuf Husain Khan, *Nizam-ul-Mulk Asaf Jah I*, p. 289.

13. William Irvine, *Later Mughals*, Vol. II, M.C. Sarkar & Sons, Calcutta, 1922, p. 346.

14. Ibid., p. 353.

15. Yusuf Husain Khan, *Nizam-ul-Mulk Asaf Jah I*, pp. 229-30.

16. William Dalrymple and Anita Anand, *Koh-i-Noor*, Juggernaut, New Delhi, 2016, pp. 54-55.

17. Irvine, *Later Mughals*, Vol. II, p. 371.

18. Yusuf Husain Khan, *Nizam-ul-Mulk Asaf Jah I*, p. 287.

19. Ibid., pp. 284-90.

20. Henry George Briggs, *The Nizam: His History and Relations with the British Government*, Vol. I, London, 1861, pp. 54-55.

21. Sarojini Regani, *Nizam-British Relations, 1724-1857*, Concept Publishing Company, New Delhi, 1988, p. 41.

22. Ibid., pp. 42-43.

23. Ibid., p. 46.

24. William Dalrymple, *White Mughals*, Penguin India, New Delhi, 2004, p. 87.

25. Syed Husain Bilgrami and C. Wilmott, *Historical and Descriptive Sketch of His Highness the Nizam's Dominions*, p. 131.

26. John Zubrzycki, *The Last Nizam*, Picador India, New Delhi, 2006, pp. 35-36.

27. Quoted in Harriet Ronken Lynton, *My Dear Nawab Saheb*, Disha Books, New Delhi, 1993, p. 12.

28. Ibid.

29. Edward Thompson, *The Making of the Indian Princes*, Oxford University Press, 1943, p. 6.

30. Ibid., p. 15.

31. Sarojini Regani, *Nizam-British Relations, 1724-1857*, p. 169.

32. Sir Richard Temple, *Journals Kept in Hyderabad, Kashmir, Sikkim, and Nepal*, Vol. 1, W.H. Allen & Co., London, 1887, p. 50.

33. William Dalrymple, *White Mughals*, p. 204.

34. Ibid.

35. Ibid., pp. 205-06.

36. Harriet Ronken Lynton, *My Dear Nawab Saheb*, p. 15.

37. Henry George Briggs, *The Nizam: His History and Relations with the British Government*, Vol. I, p. 84.

38. Ibid., p. 71.

39. *Englishman*, 11 June 1853, quoted in Maulvi Syed Mahdi Ali, *Hyderabad Affairs*, Vol. 3, Bombay, 1883-86.

40. Edward Thompson, *The Making of the Indian Princes*, pp. 15-16.

41. *Times of India*, 12 July 1867, quoted in Maulvi Syed Mahdi Ali, *Hyderabad Affairs*, Vol. 3, Bombay, 1883-86.

42. Bharati Ray, *Hyderabad and British Paramountcy, 1858-1883*, Oxford University Press, New Delhi, 1988, p. 7.

43. Ibid.

44. Sir Richard Temple, *Journals Kept in Hyderabad, Kashmir, Sikkim, and Nepal*, Vol., p. 111.

45. Ibid., p. 184.

46. Ibid., pp. 113-14.

47. Ibid., pp. 129-30. A nazar was a gift from an inferior to a superior (usually the nizam). It was given whenever someone came with a petition or to mark a special occasion. Nazars ranged from gold coins and precious stones to horses and elephants, daggers and swords, and even eunuchs and dancing girls.

48. Ibid., p. 130.

49. Ibid., p. 136.

Chapter 1: The Heritage

1. M.A. Nayeem and Dharmendra Prasad, *The Salar Jungs*, Salar Jung Museum, Hyderabad, 1986, p. 3.

2. Ibid., p. 4.

3. He was technically Munir-ul-Mulk II since this title had first been given to Sheikh Shams-ud-din Muhammed Hyder, but in keeping with convention, he has been called Munir-ul-Mulk.

4. V.K. Bawa, *The Nizam between Mughals and British: Hyderabad under Salar Jung I*, S. Chand & Company, New Delhi, 1996, p. xviii.

5. *Bombay Gazette*, 10 February 1883, quoted in Maulvi Syed Mahdi Ali's *Hyderabad Affairs*, Vol. 3, Bombay.

6. Syed Hossain Bilgrami, *A Memoir of Sir Salar Jung, G.C.S.I.*, Times of India Steam Press, Bombay, 1883, p. 15.

7. *Bombay Gazette*, 10 February 1883, quoted in Maulvi Syed Mahdi Ali's *Hyderabad Affairs*, Vol. 3, Bombay.

8. *Times of India*, 2 March 1867, quoted in Maulvi Syed Mahdi Ali's *Hyderabad Affairs*, Vol. 3, Bombay.

9. *Bombay Gazette*, 10 February 1883, quoted in Maulvi Syed Mahdi Ali's *Hyderabad Affairs*, Vol. 3, Bombay.

10. Server-ul-Mulk, *My Life*, translated by Nawab Jivan Yar Jung, London, undated, p. 90.

11. *Athenaeum*, 22 June 1876, quoted in Maulvi Syed Mahdi Ali's *Hyderabad Affairs*, Vol. 3, Bombay.

12. Salar Jung to Dighton, 1 June 1853, quoted in Syed Hossain Bilgrami, *A Memoir of Sir Salar Jung*, pp. 18-19.

Chapter 2: The Diwan and His Deodi

1. *Madras Spectator*, 8 June 1853, quoted in Maulvi Syed Mahdi Ali's *Hyderabad Affairs*, Vol. 3, Bombay.

2. *Englishman*, 8 June 1853, quoted in Maulvi Syed Mahdi Ali's *Hyderabad Affairs*, Vol. 3, Bombay.

3. *Englishman*, 8 June 1853, quoted in Maulvi Syed Mahdi Ali's *Hyderabad Affairs*, Vol. 3, Bombay.

4. Narendra Luther, *Hyderabad: A Biography*, Oxford University Press, New Delhi, pp. 134-35.

5. *Englishman*, 11 June 1853, quoted in Maulvi Syed Mahdi Ali's *Hyderabad Affairs*, Vol. 3, Bombay.

6. *Madras Spectator*, 8 June 1853, quoted in Maulvi Syed Mahdi Ali's *Hyderabad Affairs*, Vol. 3, Bombay.

7. Salar Jung to Dighton, 1 June 1853, quoted in Syed Hossain Bilgrami, *A Memoir of Sir Salar Jung, G.C.S.I.*, Times of India Steam Press, Bombay, 1883, pp. 19-20.

8. *Englishman*, 20 June 1853, quoted in Maulvi Syed Mahdi Ali's *Hyderabad Affairs*, Vol. 3, Bombay.

9. 'Administration Report of the Dominions of H. H. the Nizam, by Salar Jung', quoted in Maulvi Syed Mahdi Ali's *Hyderabad Affairs*, Vol. 3, Bombay.

10. V.K. Bawa, *The Nizam between Mughals and British: Hyderabad under Salar Jung I*, S. Chand & Company, New Delhi, 1996, p. 90.

11. Ibid.

12. Rani Sarma, *The Deodis of Hyderabad*, Rupa & Co., New Delhi, 2008, p. 23.

13. Ibid., pp. 21-22.

14. Ibid., p. 50.

15. Ibid., p. 51.

16. Ibid., p. 52.

17. Lady Isabel Burton, *The Romance of Lady Isabel Burton*, ed., W.H. Wilkins, Vol. II, Dodd Mead & Company, New York, 1897, pp. 581-82.

18. Monier Williams, later Sir Monier Monier-Williams, who studied and taught Sanskrit, Persian and Hindustani, was the second Boden professor of Sanskrit at Oxford University, beating Max Müller to the post. Both candidates had to emphasize their support for Christian evangelization in India since that was the basis on which the chair had been funded by its founder. Williams was selected since his dedication to Christianization was never in doubt, while Müller was more of a liberal. After his selection, he declared that the conversion of India to Christianity should be the aim of orientalist scholarship.

He was made KCIE in 1887, after which he adopted his given name of Monier as an additional surname.

19. Monier Williams, *Modern India and the Indians*, Trubner and Company, London, 1878, p. 147.
20. Ibid.
21. Server-ul-Mulk, *My Life*, translated by Nawab Jivan Yar Jung, London, undated., pp. 89-90.
22. Ibid., p. 91.
23. Narendra Luther, *Hyderabad: A Biography*, p. 156.
24. Server-ul-Mulk, *My Life*, p. 96.
25. Harriet Ronken Lynton, *My Dear Nawab Saheb*, Disha Books, New Delhi, 1993, pp. 35-36.
26. Server-ul-Mulk, *My Life*, p. 104.
27. Ibid., p. 105.
28. Rani Sarma, *The Deodis of Hyderabad*, p. 66.
29. Ibid., p. 26.
30. Server-ul-Mulk, *My Life*, p. 104.
31. *Times of India*, 21 December 1875, quoted in Maulvi Syed Mahdi Ali's *Hyderabad Affairs*, Vol. 3, Bombay.
32. Lady Isabel Burton, *The Romance of Lady Isabel Burton*, pp. 583-84.
33. Mir Moazam Husain in his introduction to Rani Sarma, *The Deodis of Hyderabad*, Rupa & Co., New Delhi, 2008, p. xxiv.
34. Ibid., p. xxvii.
35. Val C. Prinsep, *Imperial India*, Chapman and Hall, London, 1879, quoted in Maulvi Syed Mahdi Ali's *Hyderabad Affairs*, Vol. 3, Bombay.
36. Ibid.

Chapter 3: Early Reforms

1. The Paigah jagirs were first assigned by Asaf Jah I to Abul Khair Khan and his son Abul Fateh Khan, Tegh Jung, the first Shums-ul-Umra, for the purpose of the maintenance of a body of horse called His Highness's household troops.
2. Moulavi Cheragh Ali, *Hyderabad (Deccan) under Sir Salar Jung*, Vol. 1, Bombay, 1884, p. 74.
3. Karen Leonard, 'Banking Firms in Nineteenth-Century Hyderabad Politics', *Modern Asian Studies*, 15, 2 (1981), pp. 178-79.
4. Ibid., p. 179.

5. Ibid., p. 187.

6. Ibid., pp. 186-89.

7. Karen Leonard, *Social History of an Indian Caste: The Kayasths of Hyderabad*, Orient Longman Limited, Hyderabad, 1994, pp. 23-24.

8. Ibid., p. 62.

9. He never actually held the title of daftardar, being the second of four sons. His elder brother, Ujagar Chand, held the official designation.

10. *Englishman*, 1 May 1849, quoted in Maulvi Syed Mahdi Ali's *Hyderabad Affairs*, Vol. 3, Bombay.

11. Karen Leonard, *Social History of an Indian Caste*, p. 64.

12. Harriet Ronken Lynton, *My Dear Nawab Saheb*, Disha Books, New Delhi, 1993, p. 31.

13. Seema Alavi, *Muslim Cosmopolitanism in the Age of Empire*, Harvard University Press, 2015, p. 93.

14. Sir Richard Temple, *Journals Kept in Hyderabad, Kashmir, Sikkim, and Nepal*, Vol. 1, W.H. Allen & Co., London, 1887, p. 22.

15. Seema Alavi, *Muslim Cosmopolitanism in the Age of Empire*, p. 94.

16. Sir Richard Temple, *Men and Events of My Time in India*, John Murray, London, 1882, p. 292.

17. Ibid.

18. Ibid.

19. Sir Richard Temple, *Journals Kept in Hyderabad, Kashmir, Sikkim, and Nepal*, Vol. I, p. 16.

20. Sir William Barton, *The Princes of India*, Nisbet & Co. Ltd, London, 1934, p. 197.

21. Quoted in Shanti Sadiq Ali, *The African Dispersal in the Deccan: From Medieval to Modern Times*, Orient Longman Limited, Hyderabad, 1996, p. 194.

22. *Englishman*, 20 June 1853, quoted in Maulvi Syed Mahdi Ali's *Hyderabad Affairs*, Vol. 3, Bombay.

23. *Madras Spectator*, 25 July 1853, quoted in Maulvi Syed Mahdi Ali's *Hyderabad Affairs*, Vol. 5, Bombay.

24. *Englishman*, 6 August 1853, quoted in Maulvi Syed Mahdi Ali's *Hyderabad Affairs*, Vol. 5, Bombay.

25. Mir Osman Ali Khan, the seventh nizam, had perfected the art of squeezing out as much as he could by way of nazaranas. The offerings were no longer token amounts, and large amounts of cash and even jewellery were expected and accepted. A time came when the very sight

of Osman Ali Khan or the prospect of his visit created a sense of dread in the family whom he was to visit. When the nazar was associated with the expectation of an appointment, it was expected to be in direct proportion to the importance of the post. Osman Ali Khan sullied both his hands and his reputation. In contrast, his father, Mahbub Ali Khan, had refrained from using any of the nazars for his personal needs.

26. Salar Jung, 'Hyderabad State, Miscellaneous Notes on Administration (Hyderabad 1856), Salar Jung Library, Hyderabad.

27. Sir Richard Temple, *Journals Kept in Hyderabad, Kashmir, Sikkim, and Nepal*, Vol. 1, pp. 120-21.

28. Karen Leonard, 'Banking Firms in Nineteenth-Century Hyderabad Politics', *Modern Asian Studies*, 15, 2 (1981), p. 195.

29. Karen Leonard, *Social History of an Indian Caste*, p. 67.

30. Ibid.

31. Ibid., p. 82.

32. Ibid., p. 83.

33. Karen Leonard, 'Banking Firms in Nineteenth-Century Hyderabad Politics', *Modern Asian Studies*, 15, 2 (1981), p. 191.

34. Ibid., p. 198.

35. *Madras Spectator*, 16 February 1855, quoted in Maulvi Syed Mahdi Ali's *Hyderabad Affairs*, Vol. 5, Bombay.

36. Colin Mackenzie, *Storms and Sunshine of a Soldier's Life*, Vol. 2, David Douglas, Edinburgh, 1884, pp. 112-13.

37. Karen Leonard, 'Banking Firms in Nineteenth-Century Hyderabad Politics', *Modern Asian Studies*, 15, 2 (1981), p. 197.

38. Sir William Barton, *The Princes of India*, p. 203.

39. 'Translation of a Representation (*urzee)* from Salar Jung to the Nizam in 1856', quoted in Maulvi Syed Mahdi Ali's *Hyderabad Affairs*, Vol. 3, Bombay, p. 179.

40. 'Administration Report of the Dominions of H.H. the Nizam, Salar Jung', quoted in Maulvi Syed Mahdi Ali's *Hyderabad Affairs*, Vol. 3, Bombay, p. 178.

41. 'Translation of a Representation (*urzee)* from Salar Jung to the Nizam in 1856', quoted in Maulvi Syed Mahdi Ali's *Hyderabad Affairs*, Vol. 3, Bombay, p. 179.

42. V.K. Bawa, *The Nizam between Mughals and British: Hyderabad under Salar Jung I*, S. Chand & Company, New Delhi, 1996, pp. 64-65.

43. M. Fathulla Khan, *A History of Administrative Reforms in Hyderabad State*, New Hyderabad Press, Secunderabad, 1935, p. 59.

44. V.K. Bawa, *The Nizam between Mughals and British*, p. 64.
45. 'Administration Report of the Dominions of H.H. the Nizam by Salar Jung', quoted in Maulvi Syed Mahdi Ali's *Hyderabad Affairs*, Vol. 3, Bombay, p. 163.
46. *Englishman*, 11 August 1855, quoted in Maulvi Syed Mahdi Ali's *Hyderabad Affairs*, Vol. 4, Bombay.
47. Ibid.
48. V.K. Bawa, *The Nizam between Mughals and British*, p. 65.

Chapter 4: 'Our Faithful Ally'

1. William Dalrymple, *The Last Mughal*, Penguin Viking, New Delhi, 2006, p. 16.
2. Ibid., p. 20.
3. Quoted in Miles Taylor, *The Indian Maharani*, Penguin Random House, Gurgaon, 2018, p. 71.
4. Syed Hossain Bilgrami, *A Memoir of Sir Salar Jung, G.C.S.I.*, Tomes of India Steam Press, Bombay, 1883, p. 36.
5. *Times of India*, 30 August 1876, in quoted in Maulvi Syed Mahdi Ali's *Hyderabad Affairs*, Vol. 3, Bombay, p. 121.
6. Harriet Ronken Lynton, *My Dear Nawab Saheb*, Disha Books, New Delhi, 1993, pp. 49-50.
7. V.K. Bawa, *The Nizam between Mughals and British: Hyderabad under Salar Jung I*, S. Chand & Company, New Delhi, 1996, p. 35.
8. *Times of India*, 15 March 1869, quoted in Maulvi Syed Mahdi Ali's *Hyderabad Affairs*, Vol. 3, Bombay.
9. Syed Hossain Bilgrami, *A Memoir of Sir Salar Jung*, p. 37.
10. V.K. Bawa, *The Nizam between Mughals and British*, pp. 38-39.
11. Rajendra Prasad, *The Asif Jahs of Hyderabad: Their Rise and Decline*, Prachee Publications, Hyderabad, 2010, p. 77.
12. Harriet Ronken Lynton, *My Dear Nawab Saheb*, p. 50.
13. Quoted in Harriet Ronken Lynton, Ibid., pp. 50-51.
14. Syed Hossain Bilgrami, *A Memoir of Sir Salar Jung*, p. 39.
15. Quoted in Harriet Ronken Lynton, *My Dear Nawab Saheb*, p. 52.
16. Ibid., p. 53.
17. A popular tank used during the hot weather for drawing water.
18. Quoted in Harriet Ronken Lynton, *My Dear Nawab Saheb*, p. 52.
19. Ibid., p. 54.
20. Ibid.

21. Quoted in Henry George Briggs, *The Nizam: His History and Relations with the British Government*, Vol. 2, B. Quaritch, London, 1861, pp. 76-77.

22. Quoted in Harriet Ronken Lynton, *My Dear Nawab Saheb*, p. 56.

23. Ibid., p. 55.

24. Ibid., p. 57.

25. Ibid., p. 58.

26. Syed Hossain Bilgrami, *A Memoir of Sir Salar Jung*, p. 40.

27. Quoted in Henry George Briggs, *The Nizam*, p. 87.

28. Ibid., pp. 85-86.

29. Hastings Fraser, *Our Faithful Ally, the Nizam: An Historical Sketch of Events*, Smith, Elder, London, 1865, p. 291.

30. J.D.B. Gribble, *History of the Deccan*, Vols. 1 & 2, (reprint) Rupa & Co., New Delhi, 2002, p. 239.

31. K.S.S. Seshan, 'The Hyderabad Connect', *The Hindu*, 29 October 2015. Taylor was also an accomplished painter, and his series of paintings on the sculptures in the Ellora Caves established his reputation as an artist. After he returned to England in 1860, he devoted his time to writing novels on Indian themes. In 1875, he came and stayed in Hyderabad as a guest of Salar Jung. He passed away the next year, at Menton in southern France, while sailing back to England.

32. J.D.B. Gribble, *History of the Deccan*, Vols. 1 & 2, p. 241.

33. Ibid., pp. 243-44.

34. Swapna Liddle, *Chandni Chowk: The Mughal City of Old Delhi*, Speaking Tiger, New Delhi, 2017, p. 107.

35. Syed Hossain Bilgrami, *A Memoir of Sir Salar Jung*, p. 42.

36. *Morning Post*, 3 June 1876, quoted in Maulvi Syed Mahdi Ali's *Hyderabad Affairs*, Vol. 3, Bombay.

37. Syed Hossain Bilgrami, *A Memoir of Sir Salar Jung*, pp. 40-41.

38. Ibid., p. 41.

39. Ibid., p. 42.

40. *Times*, 26 May 1876, quoted in Maulvi Syed Mahdi Ali's *Hyderabad Affairs*, Vol. 3, Bombay, p. 71.

41. Rajendra Prasad, *The Asif Jahs of Hyderabad*, p. 97.

Chapter 5: After the Mutiny

1. Miles Taylor, *The English Maharani*, Penguin Random House, Gurgaon, 2018.

2. Penny and Roger Beaumont, *Invisible Empresses of the Raj*, Jaico Publishing House, Mumbai, 2011, p. 356.

3. S. Gopal, *British Policy in India, 1858-1905*, Orient Longman, 1992, p. 1.

4. Viscount Mersey, *The Viceroys and Governors-General of India, 1757-1947*, John Murray, London, 1949, p. 76.

5. S. Gopal, *British Policy in India*, p. 2.

6. Quoted in Christopher Lee, *Viceroys: The Creation of the British*, Constable, London, 2018, p. 90.

7. William Dalrymple, *The Last Mughal*, Penguin Viking, New Delhi, 2006, p. 124.

8. Bernard S. Cohn, 'Representing Authority in Victorian India', in E. Hobsbawm and Terence Ranger (eds), *The Invention of Tradition*, Cambidge University Press, Cambridge, 1983, p. 180.

9. Bharati Ray, *Hyderabad and British Paramountcy, 1858-1883*, Oxford University Press, New Delhi, 1988, p. 30.

10. Ibid.

11. Ibid., p. 36.

12. A khareeta was a letter, almost always in Persian, enclosed in a bag of rich brocade, which was contained in another of fine muslin. The seal of the sender was suspended from the mouth of the bag which was tied with a string of silk. This was the kind of letter which was exchanged between princes of great rank in India, and between them and the government.

13. Hastings Fraser, *Our Faithful Ally, The Nizam: An Historical Sketch of Events*, Smith, Elder, London, 1865, pp. 302-303.

14. *Englishman*, 2 April 1859, quoted in Maulvi Syed Mahdi Ali's *Hyderabad Affairs*, Vol. 3, Bombay.

15. Harriet Ronken Lynton, *My Dear Nawab Saheb*, Disha Books, New Delhi, 1993, p. 69.

16. Syed Hossain Bilgrami, *A Memoir of Sir Salar Jung, G.C.S.I.*, Times of India Steam Press, Bombay, 1883, p. 44.

17. Ibid.

18. Harriet Ronken Lynton, *My Dear Nawab Saheb*, p. 64.

19. James Oliphant to Salar Jung, 21 May 1858, Telangana State Archives and Research Centre.

20. James Oliphant to Salar Jung, 9 August 1858, Telangana State Archives and Research Centre.

21. James Oliphant to Salar Jung, 18 January 1860, Telangana State Archives and Research Centre.

22. James Oliphant to Salar Jung, 26 July 1860, Telangana State Archives and Research Centre.
23. Harriet Ronken Lynton, *My Dear Nawab Saheb*, p. 72.
24. Ibid., p. 79.
25. James Oliphant to Salar Jung, 1 October 1859, Telangana State Archives and Research Centre.
26. Bharati Ray, *Hyderabad and British Paramountcy*, p. 24.
27. Miles Taylor, *The Indian Maharani*, Penguin Random House, Gurgaon, 2018, p. 84.
28. Ibid., pp. 84-85.
29. Rajendra Prasad, *Asif Jahs of Hyderabad: Their Rise and Decline*, Prachee Publications, Hyderabad, 2010, pp. 87-88.
30. *Englishman*, 7 December 1861, quoted in Maulvi Syed Mahdi Ali's *Hyderabad Affairs*, Vol. 3, Bombay.
31. Harriet Ronken Lynton, *My Dear Nawab Saheb*, p. 86.
32. Bharati Ray, *Hyderabad and British Paramountcy*, pp. 40-41.
33. Mark Bence-Jones, *The Viceroys of India*, Constable, London, 1982, p. 46.
34. Ibid., p. 51.

Chapter 6: The Nizam's Perpetual Displeasure

1. Sir Richard Temple, *Journals Kept in Hyderabad, Kashmir, Sikkim, and Nepal*, Vol. 1, W.H. Allen & Co., London, 1887, p. 126.
2. Ibid., p. 128.
3. Ibid.
4. Ibid., p. 163.
5. Ibid., p. 258.
6. Ibid., p. 245.
7. Ibid., p. 104.
8. Ibid., p. 87.
9. Ibid., p. 92.
10. Ibid., p. 101.
11. Quoted in V.K. Bawa, *The Nizam between Mughals and British: Hyderabad under Salar Jung I*, S. Chand & Company, New Delhi, 1996, p. 35.
12. Sir Richard Temple, *Journals Kept in Hyderabad, Kashmir, Sikkim, and Nepal*, p. 94.
13. Ibid., p. 42.

14. Sir Richard Temple, *Men and Events of My Time in India*, John Murray, London, 1882, p. 288.

15. Ibid., p. 289.

16. Ibid., pp. 288-89.

17. *Englishman*, 23 April 1859, quoted in Maulvi Syed Mahdi Ali's *Hyderabad Affairs*, Vol. 3, Bombay.

18. Hastings Fraser, *Our Faithful Ally, The Nizam: An Historical Sketch of Events*, Smith, Elder, London, 1865, pp. 306-07.

19. Ibid.

20. Harriet Ronken Lynton, *My Dear Nawab Saheb*, p. 101.

21. *Englishman*, 10 June 1861, quoted in Maulvi Syed Mahdi Ali's *Hyderabad Affairs*, Vol. 3, Bombay.

22. William Dalrymple, *White Mughals*, Penguin India, New Delhi, 2004, p. 197.

23. *Englishman*, 5 December 1862, quoted in Maulvi Syed Mahdi Ali's *Hyderabad Affairs*, Vol. 3, Bombay.

24. *Englishman*, 14 November 1862, quoted in Maulvi Syed Mahdi Ali's *Hyderabad Affairs*, Vol. 8, Bombay.

25. Sir Richard Temple, *Journals Kept in Hyderabad, Kashmir, Sikkim, and Nepal*, Vol. 1, p. 244.

26. Harriet Ronken Lynton, *My Dear Nawab Saheb*, p. 98.

27. Ibid., p. 99.

28. Server-ul-Mulk, *My Life*, translated by Nawab Jivan Yar Jung, London, undated, pp. 80-81.

29. Syed Hossain Bilgrami, *A Memoir of Sir Salar Jung, G.C.S.I.*, Times of India Steam Press, Bombay, 1883, p. 53.

30. Ibid.

31. *Englishman*, 6 April 1867, quoted in Maulvi Syed Mahdi Ali's *Hyderabad Affairs*, Vol. 8, Bombay, p. 30.

32. Yule to Secretary, Foreign Department, 2 February 1867, No. 137, National Archives of India.

33. Harriet Ronken Lynton, *My Dear Nawab Saheb*, p. 105.

34. Sir Richard Temple, *Journals Kept in Hyderabad, Kashmir, Sikkim, and Nepal*, Vol. 1, p. 107.

35. Sir Richard Temple, *Men and Events of My Time in India*, pp. 286-87.

36. Ibid., p. 287.

37. Harriet Ronken Lynton, *My Dear Nawab Saheb*, p. 108.

38. Sir Richard Temple, *Men and Events of My Time in India*, p. 300.

39. *Times of India,* 4 February 1868, quoted in Maulvi Syed Mahdi Ali's *Hyderabad Affairs,* Vol. 3, Bombay.

40. Quoted in John Zubrzycki's, *The Mysterious Mr Jacob,* Random House India, New Delhi, 2012, p. 41.

41. *Pioneer,* 8 February 1884.

Chapter 7: Berar: A Vexatious Issue

1. Also referred to as the Berars, since Berar was divided into East and West Berar. East Berar had its headquarters at Amravati and West Berar at Akola. We shall refer to it as only Berar as has been done in the earlier narrative.

2. Manchester Liberalism, or the Manchester School as it was also called, are terms for the political, economic and social movements of the nineteenth century that originated in Manchester, England. Led by Richard Cobden and John Bright, it expounded the social and economic implications of free trade and laissez faire capitalism. It took the theories of economic liberalism advocated by classical economists such as Adam Smith and made them the basis for government policy.

3. Narendra Luther, *Hyderabad: A Biography,* Oxford University Press, New Delhi, p. 111.

4. William Dalrymple, *White Mughals,* Penguin Books, New Delhi, 2004, p. 145.

5. Sarojini Regani, *Nizam-British Relations, 1724-1857,* Concept Publishing Company, New Delhi, 1988, pp. 226-27.

6. Ibid., pp. 228-29.

7. John Zubrzycki, *The Last Nizam,* Picador India, New Delhi, 2006, p. 62.

8. John William Kaye, *The Life and Correspondence of Charles, Lord Metcalfe,* Richard Bentley, London, 1864, p. 40.

9. Ibid., p. 41.

10. Quoted in John Zubrzycki, *The Last Nizam,* p. 63.

11. Sarojini Regani, *Nizam-British Relations,* p. 226.

12. John William Kaye, *The Life and Correspondence of Charles, Lord Metcalfe,* p. 46

13. Karen Leonard, 'Palmer and Company: An Indian Banking Firm in Hyderabad State', *Modern Asian Studies,* 47, 4 (2013), p. 1172.

14. Ibid.

15. John Kaye in his biography of Lord Metcalfe takes this view.

16. Sarojini Regani, *Nizam–British Relations*, p. 236.

17. Karen Leonard, 'Palmer and Company: An Indian Banking Firm in Hyderabad State', p. 1178.

18. J.B.D. Gribble, *History of the Deccan*, Vols. 1 & 2, Rupa & Co., New Delhi, 2002, pp. 168-69.

19. Ibid., p. 169.

20. Karen Leonard, 'Palmer and Company: An Indian Banking Firm in Hyderabad State', pp. 1180-81.

21. Ibid., p. 1182.

22. Ibid., p. 1162.

23. Hastings Fraser, *Memoir and Correspondence of General James Stuart Fraser*, Whiting & Co. Ltd, London, 1885, p. 291.

24. J.B.D. Gribble, *History of the Deccan*, p. 204.

25. Ibid., pp. 207-08.

26. Ibid., p. 211.

27. Ibid., pp. 213-14.

28. Ibid., p. 220.

29. *Statesman* (London), 1 July 1881, quoted in Maulvi Syed Mahdi Ali's *Hyderabad Affairs*, Vol. 2, Bombay.

30. *Times of India*, 3 August 1868.

31. Dalhousie to Low, 28 and 30 May 1853, Dalhousie Papers, National Archives of India.

32. Dalhousie to Low, 30 May 1853, Dalhousie Papers, National Archives of India.

33. Quoted in Sarojini Regani, *Nizam–British Relations*, p. 299.

34. Ibid.

35. *Times of India*, 3 August 1868, quoted in Maulvi Syed Mahdi Ali's *Hyderabad Affairs*, Vol. 2, Bombay.

36. Ibid.

37. J.B.D. Gribble, *History of the Deccan*, p. 226.

38. V.K. Bawa, *The Nizam between Mughals and British: Hyderabad under Salar Jung I*, S. Chand & Company, New Delhi, 1996, p. 147.

39. Salar Jung to Northbrook, 27 April 1877, Northbrook Papers, National Archives of India.

40. J.W.S. Wyllie to Yule, 13 February 1867, Foreign Department, Political No. 145, quoted in Maulvi Syed Mahdi Ali's *Hyderabad Affairs*, Vol. 2, Bombay.

41. Yule to Lawrence, 1 December 1866, Lawrence Papers, National Archives of India.
42. V.K. Bawa, *The Nizam between Mughals and British*, p. 155.
43. Sir William Barton, *The Princes of India*, Nisbet & Co. Ltd, London, 1934, p. 196.
44. Bharati Ray, *Hyderabad and British Paramountcy, 1858-1883*, Oxford University Press, New Delhi, 1988, p. 113.

Chapter 8: The Child Nizam

1. Val C. Prinsep, *Imperial India*, Chapman and Hall, London, 1879, pp. 316-17.
2. Sir Richard Temple, *Journals Kept in Hyderabad, Kashmir, Sikkim, and Nepal*, Vol. 1, W.H. Allen & Co., London, 1887, p. 190.
3. Ibid., p. 215.
4. Interview with Ahteram Ali Khan.
5. Sarvepalli Gopal, *British Policy in India, 1858-1905*, Cambridge University Press, Cambridge, 1965, p. 61.
6. Mark Bence-Jones, *The Viceroys of India*, Constable, London, 1982, p. 58.
7. Harriet Ronken Lynton and Mohini Rajan, *Days of the Beloved*, Orient Longman Ltd, New Delhi, 1987, p. 53.
8. Ibid., p. 29.
9. *Englishman*, 5 August 1862, quoted in Maulvi Syed Mahdi Ali's *Hyderabad Affairs*, Vol. 4, Bombay.
10. Ibid.
11. Val C. Prinsep, *Imperial India*, p. 308.
12. Server-ul-Mulk, *My Life*, translated by Nawab Jivan Yar Jung, London, undated, p. 111.
13. Bharati Ray, *Hyderabad and British Paramountcy, 1858-1883*, Oxford University Press, New Delhi, 1988, p. 60.
14. V.K. Bawa, *The Nizam between Mughals and British: Hyderabad under Salar Jung I*, S. Chand & Company, New Delhi, 1996, p. 54.
15. Harriet Ronken Lynton, *My Dear Nawab Saheb*, Disha Books, New Delhi, 1993, p. 114.
16. Ibid., p. 115.
17. Mayo to Argyll, 12 August 1869, Mayo Papers, National Archives of India.

18. Salar Jung to Saunders, 8 June 1870, Telangana State Archives and Research Centre.

19. Saunders to Salar Jung, 9 June 1870, Telangana State Archives and Research Centre.

20. Salar Jung to Saunders, 10 June 1870, Telangana State Archives and Research Centre.

21. Sir Richard Temple, *Journals Kept in Hyderabad, Kashmir, Sikkim, and Nepal*, Vol. 1, W.H. Allen & Co., London, 1887, p. 45.

22. Ibid., p. 166.

23. Ibid., p. 126.

24. A form of American entertainment that found its way to India in the mid-nineteenth century was blackface minstrelsy, in which white performers painted their faces black to enact insensitive stereotypes of black folk for the entertainment of white audiences. Dave Carson was a popular minstrel whose San Francisco Minstrels ran to full houses at the Grant Road Theatre. One of his characters was a foppish Parsi gentleman, Davejee Carsonbhoy, who was a big hit with his Hindu audiences. Blackface representation has now been wiped off the American stage and screen, being an uncomfortable reminder of slavery in the years gone by.

25. Harriet Ronken Lynton, *My Dear Nawab Saheb*, pp. 1-2.

26. Val C. Prinsep, *Imperial India*, p. 317.

27. Ibid.

28. Salar Jung to Palmer (draft letter), 11 August 1873, Telangana State Archives and Research Centre.

29. Harriet Ronken Lynton, *My Dear Nawab Saheb*, p. 116.

30. Telangana State Archives and Research Centre., 8 September 1873.

31. Server-ul-Mulk, *My Life*, pp. 116-17.

32. Another version holds that when Salar Jung visited Lucknow in 1872, he was greatly impressed with Syed Hossain and invited him to come to Hyderabad.

33. Server-ul-Mulk, *My Life*, p. 130.

34. Harriet Ronken Lynton and Mohini Rajan, *Days of the Beloved*, p. 33.

35. Server-ul-Mulk, *My Life*, p. 146.

36. Ibid., p. 153.

37. Ibid., p. 157.

38. Narendra Luther, *Hyderabad: A Biography*, Oxford University Press, New Delhi, pp. 159-60.

39. Ibid., p. 161.

Chapter 9: The Nizam's State Railway

1. Wood to Frere, 25 July and 4 October 1862, quoted in Bharati Ray, 'The Genesis of Railway Development in Hyderabad State: A Case Study in Nineteenth Century British Imperialism', IESHR, 21, 1, (1984) p. 46.

2. V.K. Bawa, 'Salar Jung and the Nizam's State Railway, 1860-1883', *IESHR*, p. 309.

3. Ibid.

4. 'Minute by Sir G.U. Yule on the Proposed Railway to Hyderabad', 18 October 1867, Maulvi Syed Mahdi Ali's *Hyderabad Affairs*, Vol. 4, Bombay.

5. Ibid.

6. V.K. Bawa, 'Salar Jung and the Nizam's State Railway, 1860-1883', p. 309.

7. Sir Richard Temple, *Men and Events of My Time in India*, London, John Murray, 1882, pp. 299-300.

8. Mayo to Argyll, 29 October 1869, Argyll Papers (microfilm), National Archives of India.

9. Bharati Ray, *Hyderabad and British Paramountcy*, Oxford University Press, New Delhi, 1988, p. 138.

10. Mayo to Saunders, 18 October 1869, Mayo Papers, National Archives of India.

11. Salar Jung to Oliphant, 16 June (year not available), Telangana State Archives and Research Centre.

12. Salar Jung to Bowen, 30 July 1870, Telangana State Archives and Research Centre.

13. GOI Abstract of Saunders' Confidential Report, Secret 453-84, 12/1879, National Archives of India.

14. Bharati Ray, *Hyderabad and British Paramountcy*, p. 67.

15. Mark Bence-Jones, *The Viceroys of India*, Constable, London, 1982, p. 75.

16. Ibid., p. 76.

17. Salar Jung to Saunders, 7 April 1872, Foreign Gen. A Proceedings, September 1875, 54-70, National Archives of India.

18. Salar Jung to Yule, 16 October 1874, Telangana State Archives and Research Centre.

19. Bharati Ray, *Hyderabad and British Paramountcy*, pp. 144-45.

20. Ibid., p. 146.

21. V.K. Bawa, 'Salar Jung and the Nizam's State Railway, 1860-1883', pp. 322-23.

22. Ibid., p. 324.

23. Bharati Ray, *Hyderabad and British Paramountcy*, p. 147.

24. Karen Leonard, 'Banking Firms in Nineteenth-Century Hyderabad Politics', *Modern Asian Studies*, 15, 2 (1981), p. 195.

25. Secretary of State to GOI, 21 October 1875, Foreign Gen. A Proceedings, March 1876, 9-12, No. 9, National Archives of India.

26. Ibid.

27. Parties at Rashid-ud-din's palace seem to have been predisposed to some tragedy or the other. In 1863, when he gave a party in honour of the resident, Sir George Yule, there was an accident involving the fireworks in which one of the set pieces known as a *taramanden* exploded and hit the stock of lemon bottles, and pieces of glass flew around. Upset that the resident might think that the incident was design and not by chance, Rashid-ud-din, along with Salar Jung, called on Yule the next day to offer an explanation with his apologies.

28. Mark Bence-Jones, *The Viceroys of India*, p. 85.

29. Mary Lutyens, *The Lyttons in India*, John Murray, London, 1979, p. 2.

30. Ibid., p. 1.

31. Bharati Ray, *Hyderabad and British Paramountcy*, p. 151.

Chapter 10: La Revanche

1. Salar Jung to Yule, 16 October 1874, Telangana State Archives and Research Centre. and Research Centre.

2. Salar Jung to Bowen, 30 July 1870, Telangana State Archives and Research Centre.

3. Harriet Ronken Lynton, *My Dear Nawab Saheb*, Disha Books, New Delhi, 1993, p. 134.

4. Henry Mayers Hyndman, *The Record of an Adventurous Life*, Macmillan and Co., London, 1911, p. 168.

5. Salar Jung to Palmer, three drafts, of which only one is dated, 31 August 1871, Telangana State Archives and Research Centre.

6. Ibid.

7. Palmer to Salar Jung, 31 October 1873, Telangana State Archives and Research Centre.

8. Salar Jung to Palmer, 22 July 1873, Telangana State Archives and Research Centre.
9. Northbrook to Salisbury quoted in V.K. Bawa, *The Nizam between Mughals and British: Hyderabad under Salar Jung I*, S. Chand & Company, New Delhi, 1996, p. 163.
10. Bharati Ray, *Hyderabad and British Paramountcy, 1858-1883,* Oxford University Press, New Delhi, 1988., p. 166.
11. Ibid., p. 119.
12. V.K. Bawa, *The Nizam between Mughals and British*, p. 166.
13. Harriet Ronken Lynton, *My Dear Nawab Saheb*, p. 159.
14. Palmer to Bowen, 12 July 1872, Telangana State Archives and Research Centre.
15. Palmer to Bowen, 10 June 1873, Telangana State Archives and Research Centre.
16. Henry Mayers Hyndman, *The Record of an Adventurous Life*, p. 171.
17. 'The Scandal at Hyderabad: The Palmer Influence', *Statesman*, 8 January 1884.
18. Harriet Ronken Lynton, *My Dear Nawab Saheb*, p. 162.
19. Bowen to Palmer, 28 July 1876, Telangana State Archives and Research Centre.
20. Palmer to Bowen, 29 July 1876, Telangana State Archives and Research Centre.
21. This is based on a letter dated 23 April 1880 (in the Claude Clerk collection) from Ponsonby to Claude Clerk. The letter was addressed to Claude, even though it was his brother John who had written the letter. Quoted in Harriet Ronken Lynton, *My Dear Nawab Saheb*, pp. 257-58.
22. V.K. Bawa, *The Nizam between Mughals and British*, p. xvii.
23. Ibid., p. xvii.
24. Karen Leonard, 'Banking Firms in Nineteenth-Century Hyderabad Politics', *Modern Asian Studies*, 15, 2 (1981), p. 195.
25. V.K. Bawa, *The Nizam between Mughals and British*, p. xvii.

Chapter 11:'A Storm in an Indian Tea Cup'

1. Miles Taylor, *The Indian Maharani*, Penguin Random House, Gurgaon, 2018, p. 139.
2. Ibid., pp. 149-50.
3. *Statesman*, 16 November 1875, quoted in Maulvi Syed Mahdi Ali's *Hyderabad Affairs*, Vol. 3, Bombay.

4. *Vanity Fair*, 23 October 1875, quoted in Maulvi Syed Mahdi Ali's *Hyderabad Affairs*, Vol. 3, Bombay.

5. *Statesman*, 16 November 1875, quoted in Maulvi Syed Mahdi Ali's *Hyderabad Affairs*, Vol. 3, Bombay.

6. Ibid.

7. Ibid.

8. Ibid.

9. Ibid.

10. Salar Jung to Saunders, 4 September 1875, Telangana State Archives and Research Centre.

11. *Statesman*, 16 November 1875, quoted in Maulvi Syed Mahdi Ali's *Hyderabad Affairs*, Vol. 3, Bombay.

12. *Pall Mall Gazette*, 27 October 1875, quoted in Maulvi Syed Mahdi Ali's *Hyderabad Affairs*, Vol. 3, Bombay.

13. Ibid.

14. Ibid.

15. Ibid.

16. Ibid.

17. Ibid.

18. Ibid.

19. Ibid.

20. V.K. Bawa, *The Nizam between Mughals and British: Hyderabad under Salar Jung I*, S. Chand & Company, New Delhi, 1996, p. 179.

21. Palmer to Salar Jung, undated letter of 1875, Telangana State Archives and Research Centre.

22. Harriet Ronken Lynton, *My Dear Nawab Saheb*, Disha Books, New Delhi, 1993, p. 122.

23. William Howard Russell, *The Prince of Wales' Tour: A Diary in India*, 2nd ed., Sampson Low, Marston, Searle & Rivington, London, 1877, pp. 140-41.

24. Syed Hossain Bilgrami, *A Memoir of Sir Salar Jung, G.C.S.I.*, Times of India Steam Press, Bombay, 1883, p. 81.

25. An enclosure of a letter from Palmer to Salar Jung, Telangana State Archives and Research Centre.

26. Quoted in Harriet Ronken Lynton, *My Dear Nawab Saheb*, p. 126.

27. Ibid., pp. 126-27.

28. *Bombay Gazette*, 20 November 1875, quoted in Maulvi Syed Mahdi Ali's *Hyderabad Affairs*, Vol. 3, Bombay.

29. Telangana State Archives and Research Centre., 8 January 1876.

30. Quoted in Bharati Ray, *Hyderabad and British Paramountcy, 1858-1883,* Oxford University Press, New Delhi, 1988, p. 72.

31. Rani Sarma, *The Deodis of Hyderabad*, Rupa & Co., New Delhi, 2008, p. 65.

Chapter 12: The European Sojourn

1. This quotation is from an undated draft, but as subsequent events showed, the final version must have conveyed something very similar (Telangana State Archives and Research Centre.)

2. Harriet Ronken Lynton, *My Dear Nawab Saheb*, Disha Books, New Delhi, 1993, p. 175.

3. Keay to Bowen, 31 January 1876, Telangana State Archives and Research Centre.

4. T.H. Thornton, *General Sir Richard Meade and the Feudatory States of Central and Southern India,* Longmans, Green and Co., London, 1898, p. 291.

5. Copy forwarded to Salar Jung by Tom Palmer, 3 March 1876, Telangana State Archives and Research Centre.

6. Harriet Ronken Lynton, *My Dear Nawab Saheb*, p. 176.

7. It is said that Pope Pius IX possessed the ability to cast the evil eye involuntarily. He was thought to have this ability after he glanced at a nurse holding a child in an open window and the child supposedly fell to its death moments later. After this incident, legend has it that everything he blessed ended in some kind of misfortune. Pope Leo XIII was also believed to have suffered from the same affliction. Salar Jung may have been very inclined to believe this myth after his accident.

8. Syed Hossain Bilgrami, *A Memoir of Sir Salar Jung, G.C.S.I.,* Times of India Steam Press, Bombay, 1883, p. 87.

9. Salisbury to Salar Jung, 3 June 1876, Telangana State Archives and Research Centre.

10. T.H. Thornton, *General Sir Richard Meade and the Feudatory States of Central and Southern India*, p. 295.

11. *Mugger* means crocodile in Hindi.

12. Harriet Ronken Lynton, *My Dear Nawab Saheb*, p. 178.

13. Syed Hossain Bilgrami, *A Memoir of Sir Salar Jung*, p. 99.

14. Ibid., pp. 99-102.

15. Ibid., p. 103.

16. Ibid., pp. 103-04.

17. Ibid., p. 109.
18. Joseph Turnley, *The King, or the First Plantagenet*, A.H. Bailey and Co., London, 1876.
19. *Times of India*, 7 August 1876, quoted in Maulvi Syed Mahdi Ali's *Hyderabad Affairs*, Vol. 3, Bombay.
20. *Deccan Herald*, 23 August 1876, quoted in Maulvi Syed Mahdi Ali's *Hyderabad Affairs*, Vol. 2, Bombay.
21. Ibid.
22. V.K. Bawa, *The Nizam between Mughals and British: Hyderabad under Salar Jung I*, S. Chand & Company, New Delhi, 1996, p. 168.
23. *Statesman*, 28 November 1876, quoted in Maulvi Syed Mahdi Ali's *Hyderabad Affairs*, Vol. 3, p. 127, Bombay.
24. Salar Jung to the Duke of Sutherland, 30 July 1876, Telangana State Archives and Research Centre.
25. *Bombay Gazette*, 17 August 1876, quoted in Maulvi Syed Mahdi Ali's *Hyderabad Affairs*, Vol. 3, Bombay.
26. Henry Mayers Hyndman, *The Record of an Adventurous Life*, Macmillan and Co., London, 1911, p. 172.
27. Ibid.
28. Letter to Arthur Oliphant, 21 June 1876, Telangana State Archives and Research Centre.
29. Syed Hossain Bilgrami, *A Memoir of Sir Salar Jung*, p. 110.
30. Shalini Sharma, 'The Jewellery Chasers', *Deccan Chronicle*, 23 September 2018.
31. Noor-un-Nissa Begum to Salar Jung, 11 July 1876, Telangana State Archives and Research Centre.
32. Aziz-un-Nissa Begum to Salar Jung, 8 August 1876, Telangana State Archives and Research Centre.
33. Miles Taylor, *The Indian Maharani*, Penguin Random House, Gurgaon, 2018, p. 112.
34. Technically, the nizam was never a feudatory or a tributary to the British government. The nizam paid subsidy for services to the British government, and received from it a tribute for provinces held in feudal tenure under it. These relations were modified by time and circumstances, but the nizam's position, at least nominally, was that of a sovereign prince and a protected ally of the British.
35. Quoted in Rajendra Prasad, *Asif Jahs of Hyderabad: Their Rise and Decline*, Prachee Publications, Hyderabad, 2010, p. 98.

36. Lytton to Salisbury, 14 April 1876, quoted in V.K. Bawa, *The Nizam between Mughals and British*, p. 167.
37. Lytton to Meade, and to Salisbury, 2 May 1876, Lytton Papers, National Archives of India. He wrote to both on the same day.
38. Quoted in V.K. Bawa, *The Nizam between Mughals and British*, p. 167.
39. Meade to Lytton, 9 May 1876, Lytton Papers, National Archives of India.
40. Salar Jung to John Clerk, 13 June 1877, Telangana State Archives and Research Centre.

Chapter 13: Lytton's Grand Durbar

1. Bharati Ray, *Hyderabad and British Paramountcy, 1858-1883*, Oxford University Press, New Delhi, 1988, p. 77.
2. Penny and Roger Beaumont, *Invisible Empresses of the Raj*, Jaico Publishing House, Mumbai, 2011, p. 225.
3. Edwin Hirschmann, *Robert Knight: Reforming Editor in Victorian India*, Oxford University Press, New Delhi, 2008, p. 151.
4. Bharati Ray, *Hyderabad and British Paramountcy*, p. 78.
5. Lytton to Salisbury, 11 and 25 May 1876, quoted in Bharati Ray, ibid., p. 78.
6. Miles Taylor, *The English Maharani*, Penguin Random House, Gurgaon, 2018, p. 173.
7. Edwin Hirschmann, *Robert Knight*, p. 151.
8. Bharati Ray, *Hyderabad and British Paramountcy*, p. 79.
9. Miles Taylor, *The English Maharani*, p. 176.
10. Ibid.
11. Quoted in Bharati Ray, *Hyderabad and British Paramountcy*, p. 80.
12. Salar Jung's 'Memorandum of Delhi Correspondence and Interviews', No. 336, National Archives of India.
13. Salar Jung to the Duke of Sutherland, 20 January 1877, Telangana State Archives and Research Centre.
14. V.K. Bawa, *The Nizam between Mughals and British: Hyderabad under Salar Jung I*, S. Chand & Company, New Delhi, 1996, p. 189.
15. Miles Taylor, *The English Maharani*, p. 175.
16. J. Talboys Wheeler, *The History of the Imperial Assemblage at Delhi*, Longmans, Green, Reader and Dyer, London, p. 47.
17. Mary Lutyens, *The Lyttons in India*, John Murray, London, 1979, pp. 74-75.

18. Ibid., p. 75.

19. Val C. Prinsep, *Imperial India: An Artist's Journals*, Chapman and Hall, London, 1878, pp. 20, 29.

20. J. Talboys Wheeler, *The History of the Imperial Assemblage at Delhi*, p. 67.

21. Ibid., p. 53.

22. Ibid., p. 54.

23. Banners were only presented to those princes of superior rank who were entitled to a salute. Ruling chiefs not entitled to a salute were given gold medals and other gifts.

24. J. Talboys Wheeler, *The History of the Imperial Assemblage at Delhi*, pp. 58-59.

25. Mary Lutyens, *The Lyttons in India*, p. 80.

26. Miles Taylor, *The English Maharani*, p. 177.

27. Penny and Roger Beaumont, *Invisible Empresses of the Raj*, p. 232.

28. J. Talboys Wheeler, *The History of the Imperial Assemblage at Delhi*, p. 87.

29. Ibid., p. 88.

30. *Statesman*, 6 January 1877.

31. Miles Taylor, *The English Maharani*, p. 180.

32. Ibid., p. 179.

33. A.G. Noorani, *The Destruction of Hyderabad*, Tulika Books, New Delhi, 2013, pp. 6-7.

34. Mary Lutyens, *The Lyttons in India*, p. 87.

35. David Gilmour, *The British in India*, Allen Lane, Penguin Random House, London, 2018, p. 315.

36. Lytton to Salisbury, 12 April 1877, Lytton Papers, National Archives of India.

37. Salisbury to Lytton, 9 March and 11 May 1877, Lytton Papers, National Archives of India.

38. *Bombay Review*, 22 May 1880, quoted Maulvi Syed Mahdi Ali's *Hyderabad Affairs*, Vol. 3, Bombay.

39. Rajmohan Gandhi, *Modern South India: A History from the 17th Century to Our Times*, Aleph Book Company, New Delhi, 2018, p. 213.

40. William Digby, *The Famine Campaign in Southern India, 1876-1878*, Vol. 1, Longmans, Green and Co., London, 1878.

41. Shashi Tharoor, *An Era of Darkness: The British Empire in India*, Aleph Book Company, New Delhi, 2016, pp. 182-83.

42. Quoted in Rajmohan Gandhi, *Modern South India*, p. 214.

Chapter 14: An Army for the Nizam

1. Syed Hossain Bilgrami and C. Wilmott, *Historical and Descriptive Sketch of the Nizam's Dominions*, Bombay, 1884, p. 214.
2. Shanti Sadiq Ali, *The African Dispersal in the Deccan: From Medieval to Modern Times*, Orient Longman Limited, Hyderabad, 1996, p. 196.
3. Ibid., pp. 214-15.
4. Sheela Raj, *Portrait of an Era: Hyderabad in the Days of the Nizams*, 1828-1896, Minerva Press, London, 1996, p. 90.
5. Ibid.
6. V.K. Bawa, *The Nizam between Mughals and British: Hyderabad under Salar Jung I*, S. Chand & Company, New Delhi, 1996, p. 130.
7. Sir Richard Temple, *Journals Kept in Hyderabad, Kashmir, Sikkim, and Nepal*, Vol. 1, W.H. Allen & Co., London, 1887, p. 111.
8. Ibid.
9. Harriet Ronken Lynton, *My Dear Nawab Saheb*, Disha Books, New Delhi, 1993, p. 203
10. Lytton to Queen Victoria, 20 August 1876, Lytton Papers, National Archives of India.
11. Sheela Raj, *Portrait of an Era*, p. 109.
12. Ibid., p. 109.
13. Memorandum by Major Euan Smith, 10 August 1876, National Archives of India, Foreign Department, No. 476.
14. Ibid.
15. In November 1878, Lytton launched the invasion of Afghanistan with the aim of replacing the Afghan amir, Sher Ali, who was reputed to harbour pro-Russian sentiments, with a ruler more favourable to Britain. Lytton was severely criticized for the errors of fact and judgement which he made in pursuit of his 'forward' policy towards Afghanistan. He was accused of misleading Parliament and the British public about the situation in the country. He exaggerated the threat posed by Sher Ali, and underestimated the duration and ferocity of the resistance the invasion was likely to provoke. The conflict dragged on until September 1880, with rising human, financial and political costs, till the Battle of Kandahar ended what is known as the Second Anglo-Afghan War.
16. *Bombay Gazette*, 5 November 1878, quoted in Maulvi Syed Mahdi Ali's *Hyderabad Affairs*, Vol. 3, Bombay.
17. Ibid.
18. Ibid.

19. Quoted in Seema Alavi, *Muslim Cosmopolitanism in the Age of Empire*, Harvard University Press, 2015, p. 98.
20. Ibid., pp. 98-99.
21. V.K. Bawa, *The Nizam between Mughals and British*, p. 183.
22. Ibid.
23. Ibid., pp. 184-85.
24. Seema Alavi, *Muslim Cosmopolitanism in the Age of Empire*, p. 103.
25. Ibid., pp. 102-03.
26. Ibid., pp. 103-04.
27. V.K. Bawa, *The Nizam between Mughals and British*, pp. 106-07.
28. Ibid., p. 187.

Chapter 15: A Fait Accompli

1. Salar Jung to Meade, 28 February 1876, Telangana State Archives and Research Centre.
2. Secret 328-60; K.W.1 signed by H.T. Thornton, December 1879, National Archives of India.
3. Harriet Ronken Lynton, *My Dear Nawab Saheb*, Disha Books, New Delhi, 1993, p. 209.
4. Harriet Ronken Lynton and Mohini Rajan, *The Days of the Beloved*, Orient Longman Ltd, New Delhi, 1987, p. 88.
5. Harriet Ronken Lynton, *My Dear Nawab Saheb*, pp. 210-11.
6. Quoted in ibid., p. 213.
7. Bharati Ray, *Hyderabad and British Paramountcy, 1858-1883*, Oxford University Press, New Delhi, 1988, p. 88.
8. Message from Viceroy to Resident, Salisbury Papers Bundle XX, India Office Library, M/2/123, quoted in V.K. Bawa, *The Nizam between Mughals and British: Hyderabad under Salar Jung I*, S. Chand & Company, New Delhi, 1996, p. 196.
9. Meade to Lytton, 26 September 1877, Lytton Papers, National Archives of India.
10. Salar Jung to John Clerk, 28 September 1877, Telangana State Archives and Research Centre.
11. Quoted in V.K. Bawa, *The Nizam between Mughals and British*, p. 200.
12. Salar Jung to John Fleming, 20 August 1878, draft of a letter in the Telangana State Archives and Research Centre.
13. *Delhi Gazette*, 7 September 1881, quoted in Maulvi Syed Mahdi Ali's *Hyderabad Affairs*, Vol. 3, Bombay.

14. V.K. Bawa, *The Nizam between Mughals and British*, p. 197.

15. *Delhi Gazette*, 27 August 1881, quoted in Maulvi Syed Mahdi Ali's *Hyderabad Affairs*, Vol. 3, Bombay.

16. *Delhi Gazette*, 7 September 1881, quoted in Maulvi Syed Mahdi Ali's *Hyderabad Affairs*, Vol. 3, Bombay.

17. *Bombay Gazette*, 9 September 1881, quoted in Maulvi Syed Mahdi Ali's *Hyderabad Affairs*, Vol. 3, Bombay.

18. Salisbury to Lytton, 25 October and 9 November 1877, Lytton Papers, National Archives of India.

19. Salar Jung to Lady Salisbury, 17 July 1877, Telangana State Archives and Research Centre.

20. Bharati Ray, *Hyderabad and British Paramountcy*, p. 91.

Chapter 16: C'est La Vie

1. Telangana State Archives and Research Centre., undated draft.

2. Bharati Ray, *Hyderabad and British Paramountcy, 1858–1883*, Oxford University Press, New Delhi, 1988, p. 92.

3. Harriet Ronken Lynton, *My Dear Nawab Saheb*, Disha Books, New Delhi, 1993, p. 216.

4. Lytton to Disraeli, 20 December 1877, Lytton Papers, National Archives of India.

5. Quoted in V.K. Bawa, *The Nizam between Mughals and British: Hyderabad under Salar Jung I*, S. Chand & Company, New Delhi, 1996, p. 203.

6. Oliphant to Salar Jung, 30 November 1877, Telangana State Archives and Research Centre.

7. Ibid.

8. *Bombay Gazette*, 17 November 1877, quoted in Maulvi Syed Mahdi Ali's *Hyderabad Affairs*, Vol. 3, Bombay.

9. *Times of India*, 19 November 1877, quoted in Maulvi Syed Mahdi Ali's *Hyderabad Affairs*, Vol. 3, Bombay.

10. Ibid.

11. Oliphant to Salar Jung, 21 December 1877, Telangana State Archives and Research Centre.

12. Bharati Ray, *Hyderabad and British Paramountcy*, p. 93.

13. Harriet Ronken Lynton, *My Dear Nawab Saheb*, p. 241.

14. Quoted in ibid.

15. Ibid., p. 242.

16. *Times of India*, 16 July 1879, quoted in Maulvi Syed Mahdi Ali's *Hyderabad Affairs*, Vol. 3, Bombay.

17. Ibid.

18. Sir Richard Temple, *Journals Kept in Hyderabad, Kashmir, Sikkim, and Nepal*, Vol. 1, W.H. Allen & Co., London, 1887, p. 178.

19. Harriet Ronken Lynton, *My Dear Nawab Saheb*, pp. 246-47.

20. Ibid., p. 247.

21. Ibid., p. 248.

22. Ibid., p. 250.

23. Ibid., p. 254.

24. Salar Jung to Hall, 15 June 1878, Telangana State Archives and Research Centre.

25. Salar Jung to Fleming, 30 July 1878, Telangana State Archives and Research Centre.

26. Ibid.

27. Interview with Ahteram Ali Khan.

28. Fleming to Salar Jung, 9 August 1878 and 5 September 1878, Telangana State Archives and Research Centre.

29. Server-ul-Mulk, *My Life*, translated by Nawab Jivan Yar Jung, London, undated, p. 148.

30. Ibid., pp. 149-50.

31. Ibid., p. 150.

32. Given the importance of what had happened, it is strange that there is no reference to such an episode in either Salar Jung's or Meade's correspondence or writings or in any secondary source consulted in my research.

33. T.H. Thornton, *General Sir Richard Meade and the Feudatory States of Central and Southern India*, Longmans Green, London, 1898, p. 283.

34. Ibid., p. 350.

35. Ibid., p. 14.

36. Server-ul-Mulk, *My Life*, p. 266.

37. Statement of His Highness's Studies at the End of the Year 1879 by J.F. Dowding assistant tutor to His Highness the Nizam, Simla Records, Political A, August 1881, Nos 105-12, National Archives of India.

38. Quoted in John Zubrzycki, *The Last Nizam*, Picador India, New Delhi, 2006, p. 92.

39. V.K. Bawa, *The Nizam between Mughals and British*, p. 110.

40. Meade to Lyall, Secretary, Government of India, 1 September 1880, Simla Records, Political A, August 1881, Nos 105-12, National Archives of India.
41. Server-ul-Mulk, *My Life*, p. 162.
42. Wilfrid Scawen Blunt, *India under Ripon: A Private Diary*, T. Fisher Unwin, London, 1909, p. 67.
43. V.K. Bawa, *The Nizam between Mughals and British*, p. 111.
44. Ibid.
45. He was described in this manner by the viceroy, Lord Northbrook, to Lord Salisbury, Secretary of State.
46. Val C. Prinsep, *Imperial India*, Chapman and Hall, London, 1879, quoted in Maulvi Syed Mahdi Ali's *Hyderabad Affairs*, Vol. 3, Bombay.
47. Narendra Luther, *Hyderabad: A Biography*, Oxford University Press, New Delhi, pp. 162-63.

Chapter 17: Robert Knight and the *Statesman* Libel Case

1. An anonymous quote, often misattributed to George Orwell.
2. Edwin Hirschmann, *Robert Knight: Reforming Editor in Victorian India*, Oxford University Press, New Delhi, 2008, pp. 2-3.
3. Knight to Salar Jung, 20 December 1878, Telangana State Archives and Research Centre.
4. Ibid.
5. Salar Jung to Knight, 3 January 1879, Telangana State Archives and Research Centre.
6. Knight to Salar Jung, 18 December 1879, Telangana State Archives and Research Centre.
7. Knight to Salar Jung, 20 December 1879, Telangana State Archives and Research Centre.
8. Knight to Salar Jung, 3 January 1880, Telangana State Archives and Research Centre.
9. Knight to Salar Jung, 2 April 1880, Telangana State Archives and Research Centre.
10. *Statesman* quoted in *Delhi Gazette*, 4 February 1881, quoted in Maulvi Syed Mahdi Ali's *Hyderabad Affairs*, Vol. 4, Bombay.
11. *Delhi Gazette*, 4 February 1881, quoted in Maulvi Syed Mahdi Ali's *Hyderabad Affairs*, Vol. 4, Bombay.
12. *Statesman* (Calcutta), 3 February 1881.

13. Salar Jung to Knight, 13 January 1881, Telangana State Archives and Research Centre.

14. *Statesman*, 22 January 1884, quoted in Maulvi Syed Mahdi Ali's *Hyderabad Affairs*, Vol. 5, Bombay.

15. Ibid.

16. T.H. Thornton, *General Sir Richard Meade and the Feudatory States of Central and Southern India*, Longmans Green, London, 1898, pp. x and 351-52.

17. Wilfrid S. Blunt, *India under Ripon: A Private Diary*, T. Fisher Unwin, London, 1909, p. 84.

18. Yule to Knight, 22 February 1881, quoted in Maulvi Syed Mahdi Ali's *Hyderabad Affairs*, Vol. 4, Bombay.

19. Ibid., Vol. 4.

20. Ibid., Vol. 4.

21. *Delhi Gazette*, 13 August 1881, quoted in Maulvi Syed Mahdi Ali's *Hyderabad Affairs*, Vol. 4, pp. 167-68, Bombay.

Chapter 18: The Reformer

1. Moulavi Cheragh Ali, *Hyderabad (Deccan) under Sir Salar Jung*, Vol. 1, Education Society's Press, Bombay, 1884, p. 111.

2. Ibid., p. 81.

3. Ibid., pp. 83-84.

4. Quoted in M. Fathulla Khan, *A History of Administrative Reforms in Hyderabad State*, New Hyderabad Press, Secunderabad, 1935, p. 64.

5. Ibid., p. 65.

6. Ibid., p. 67.

7. Moulavi Cheragh Ali, *Hyderabad (Deccan) under Sir Salar Jung*, pp. 101-02.

8. Ibid., p. 100.

9. Karen Leonard, *Social History of an Indian Caste: The Kayasths of Hyderabad*, Orient Longman Limited, Hyderabad, 1994, p. 85.

10. Moulavi Cheragh Ali, *Hyderabad (Deccan) under Sir Salar Jung*, pp. 88-89.

11. Syed Hossain Bilgrami and C. Wilmott, *Historical and Descriptive Sketch of the Nizam's Dominions*, Vol. 2, Bombay, 1884, pp. 229-30.

12. Ibid., p. 92.

13. V.K. Bawa, *The Nizam between Mughals and British: Hyderabad under Salar Jung I*, S. Chand & Company, New Delhi, 1996, pp. 86-88.

14. Ibid., p. 88.

15. Simin Patel, 'Cultural Intermediaries in a Colonial City: The Parsis of Bombay c. 1860-1921', unpublished DPhil dissertation submitted to the University of Oxford, 2015, p. 21.

16. Karen Leonard, 'Hyderabad: The Mulki–Non-Mulki Conflict', in Robin Jeffery, ed., *People, Princes, and Paramount Power*, Oxford University Press, New Delhi, 1979, p. 66.

17. V.K. Bawa, *The Last Nizam: The Life and Times of Mir Osman Ali Khan*, Penguin Books, New Delhi, 1992, p. 59.

18. A.G. Noorani, *The Destruction of Hyderabad*, Tulika Books, New Delhi, 2013, p. 7.

19. *Bombay Gazette*, 18 June 1878, quoted in Maulvi Syed Mahdi Ali's *Hyderabad Affairs*, Vol. 3, Bombay.

20. Ibid.

21. Sir Richard Temple, *Journals Kept in Hyderabad, Kashmir, Sikkim, and Nepal*, Vol. 1, W.H. Allen & Co., London, 1887, p. 172.

22. Ibid., p. 173.

23. Hastings Fraser, *Memoir and Correspondence of General James Stuart Fraser*, Whiting & Co. Ltd, London, 1885, p. 439.

24. Quoted in V.K. Bawa, *The Nizam between Mughals and British: Hyderabad under Salar Jung I*, p. 234.

25. Karen Leonard, 'Hyderabad: The Mulki–Non-Mulki Conflict', p. 70.

26. Ibid.

27. Server-ul-Mulk, *My Life*, translated by Nawab Jivan Yar Jung, London, undated, p. 98.

28. Karen Leonard, 'Hyderabad: The Mulki–Non-Mulki Conflict', p. 71.

29. Sir William Barton, *The Princes of India*, Nisbet & Co. Ltd, London, 1934, p. 200.

30. Karen Leonard, *Social History of an Indian Caste*, p. 68.

Chapter 19: An Era Ends

1. Viscount Goderich who was prime minister for only 144 days in 1827–28.

2. Mark Bence-Jones, *The Viceroys of India*, Constable, London, 1982, p. 111.

3. S. Gopal, 'Drinking Tea with Treason', in William Roger Louis, ed., *Adventures with Britannia:* Personalities, Politics and Culture in Britain, University of Texas, 1995, pp. 145-58.

4. Quoted in Bharati Ray, *Hyderabad and British Paramountcy, 1858–1883,* Oxford University Press, New Delhi, 1988, p. 99.

5. T.H. Thornton, *General Sir Richard Meade and the Feudatory States of Central and Southern India*, Longmans, Green, London, 1898, p. 344.

6. Ibid., p. 348.

7. *Bombay Gazette*, 5 May 1882, quoted in Maulvi Syed Mahdi Ali's *Hyderabad Affairs*, Vol. 3, Bombay.

8. *Bombay Gazette*, 20 December 1881, quoted in Maulvi Syed Mahdi Ali's *Hyderabad Affairs*, Vol. 4, Bombay.

9. Quoted in Bharati Ray, *Hyderabad and British Paramountcy*, pp. 279-80.

10. V.K. Bawa, *The Nizam between Mughals and British: Hyderabad under Salar Jung I*, S. Chand & Company, New Delhi, 1996, p. 206.

11. V.K. Bawa, 'Salar Jung and the Nizam's State Railway', *IESHR*, Vol. II, No. 4, October 1965, p. 332.

12. Ripon to Hartington, 27 January and 7 June 1882, quoted in Bharati Ray, *Hyderabad and British Paramountcy*, p. 155.

13. Bharati Ray, *Hyderabad and British Paramountcy*, p. 155.

14. Ibid., pp. 155-56.

15. *Statesman*, 1 January 1884.

16. Bharati Ray, *Hyderabad and British Paramountcy*, p. 157.

17. Political A Branch, May 1882, Nos 215-23, Feb. 1882, Nos 460-65, National Archives of India.

18. V.K. Bawa, *The Nizam between Mughals and British*, p. 212.

19. Quoted in Harriet Ronken Lynton and Mohini Rajan, *The Days of the Beloved*, Orient Longman Ltd, New Delhi, 1987, p. 110.

20. Server-ul-Mulk, *My Life*, translated by Nawab Jivan Yar Jung, London, undated, pp. 263-64.

21. A mutah nikah is recognized as a temporary marriage among the Shias.

22. V.K. Bawa, *The Last Nizam: The Life and Times of Mir Osman Ali Khan*, Penguin Books, New Delhi, 1992, pp. 38-39.

23. Server-ul-Mulk, *My Life*, pp. 186-87. This stretches the imagination somewhat, and it is difficult to believe that a trip of such importance could originate in such a manner.

24. Harriet Ronken Lynton, *My Dear Nawab Saheb*, Disha Books, New Delhi, 1993, p. 283.

25. Quoted in ibid., p. 284.

26. Ibid., p. 286.

27. Horary astrology is an ancient branch of astrology in which an astrologer attempts to answer a question by constructing a horoscope for the exact time at which the question was received by the astrologer.

28. *Bombay Gazette*, 14 February 1883, quoted in Maulvi Syed Mahdi Ali's *Hyderabad Affairs*, Vol. 3, Bombay.

29. Some sources give the time of death as 7.25 p.m. In any case, it seems certain that he died between 7.15 p.m. and 7.30 p.m.

30. Syed Hossain Bilgrami and C. Wilmott, *Historical and Descriptive Sketch of the Nizam's Dominions*, Times of India Steam Press, Bombay, 1884, pp. 181-82.

31. Wilfrid Scawen Blunt, *India under Ripon: A Private Diary*, T. Fisher Unwin, London, 1909, pp. 200-01.

32. Ibid., p. 173.

33. Harriet Tytler was the only woman present at the siege of Delhi in 1857, the most crucial encounter of the Mutiny. Married to Captain Robert Tytler, she gave birth to a son at this time, christening him Stanley Delhiforce. Her memoirs tell a fascinating personal story, and her unique eyewitness account of the siege is both compellingly readable and historically significant.

34. Harriet Tytler, *An Englishwoman in India: The Memoirs of Harriet Tytler, 1828-1858*, ed., Anthony Sattin, Oxford, London, 1986, p. 143.

35. Oudhesh Rani Bawa told the author what the grandson of the kotwal during Salar Jung's time had narrated to her. The gist of the story is that on one occasion, Salar Jung went to meet Mahbub Ali Khan at the palace, and he was received by the nizam in a state of dishabille; in fact, he was half-naked, and had his arms around two of his concubines. It was after this that Salar Jung decided that he had lived long enough.

36. 'Of Power and Poison', *Deccan Chronicle*, 1 June 2014.

37. Harriet Lynton Ronken, *My Dear Nawab Saheb*, p. 287.

38. Syed Husain Bilgrami and C. Wilmott, *Historical and Descriptive Sketch of the Nizam's Dominions*, p. 182.

39. Quoted in ibid., p. 184.

40. Quoted in ibid., pp. 184-85.

Epilogue

1. T.H. Thornton, *General Sir Richard Meade and the Feudatory States of Central and Southern India*, Longmans Green, London, 1898, p. 349.

2. Archie Hunter, *A Life of Sir John Eldon Gorst: Disraeli's Awkward Disciple*, Routledge, London and New York, 2013, pp. 160-61.

3. Archie Hunter, *A Life of Sir John Eldon Gorst*, pp. 162-63.

4. Server-ul-Mulk, *My Life*, translated by Nawab Jivan Yar Jung, London, undated, p. 228.

5. Harriet Ronken Lynton and Mohini Rajan, *The Days of the Beloved*, Orient Longman Ltd, New Delhi, 1987, p. 48.

6. Bharati Ray, *Hyderabad and British Paramountcy, 1858-1883*, Oxford University Press, New Delhi, 1988, pp. 162-63.

7. Ibid.

8. Edwin Hirschmann, *Robert Knight: Reforming Editor in Victorian India*, Oxford University Press, New Delhi, 2008, p. 205.

9. Ibid., p. 206.

10. *Statesman*, 3 and 4 April 1884.

11. Knight to Claude Clerk, 10 June 1884, quoted in Edwin Hirschmann, *Robert Knight*, p. 209.

12. Edwin Hirschmann, *Robert Knight*, p. 225.

13. Shashi Tharoor, *An Era of Darkness: The British Empire in India*, Aleph Book Company, New Delhi, 2016, p. 208.

14. Ibid., pp. 208-09.

15. Ibid., p. 209.

16. V.K. Bawa, *The Nizam between Mughals and British: Hyderabad under Salar Jung I*, S. Chand & Company, New Delhi, 1996, p. 219.

17. Server-ul-Mulk, *My Life*, p. 278.

18. V.K. Bawa, *The Nizam between Mughals and British*, p. 220.

19. Hamilton to Curzon, 13, 20 and 25 March 1902, Curzon Papers, National Archives of India.

20. Curzon to Hamilton, 20 and 27 March and 2 April 1902, Curzon Papers, National Archives of India.

21. Curzon was a supremely confident and arrogant man who believed in his destiny to rule. A famous sardonic doggerel about Curzon was as follows: My name is George Nathaniel Curzon, / I am a most superior person. / My cheeks are pink, my hair is sleek, / I dine at Blenheim once a week.

22. Wilfrid Scawen Blunt, *India under Ripon: A Private Diary*, T. Fisher Unwin, London, 1909, p. 207.

23. Zubaida Yazdani and Mary Chrystal, *The Seventh Nizam: The Fallen Empire*, Cambridge University Press, 1985, p. 28.

24. Harriet Ronken Lynton and Mohini Rajan, *The Days of the Beloved*, p. 47.

25. John Zubrzycki, *The Last Nizam*, Picador India, New Delhi, 2006, p. 106.

26. Salar Jung III was born in 'Gladhurst Estate' on Bund Garden Road in Poona (now Pune), a property he acquired in adult life from the Dorabji Tata Trust in 1937. It was the summer home of Sir Dorabji Tata and his wife Lady Meherbai, and it is said that one of the reasons Salar Jung III bought the property was to acquire its grand collection of crystal and other curios. It is currently known as the 'Dutch Palace'.

27. Harriet Ronken Lynton and Mohini Rajan, *The Days of the Beloved*, p. 77.

28. John Zubrzycki, *The Last Nizam*, p. 103.

29. 'Of Power and Poison', *Deccan Chronicle*, 1 June 2014.

30. D.F. Karaka, *Fabulous Mogul: Nizam VII of Hyderabad*, D. Verschoyle, London, 1955, p. 42.

31. John Zubrzycki, *The Mysterious Mr Jacob*, Random House India, New Delhi, 2012, p. 138.

32. Quoted in ibid., p. 134.

33. Ibid., p. 135.

34. John Zubrzycki, *The Last Nizam*, pp. 96-99.

35. V.K. Bawa, *The Nizam between Mughals and British*, p. 175.

36. Quoted in A.G. Noorani, *The Destruction of Hyderabad*, Tulika Books, New Delhi, 2013, pp. 36-37.

37. V.K. Bawa, *The Nizam between Mughals and British*, p. 175.

38. 'The Rich Legacy of Nizams', *Deccan Chronicle*, 1 June 2014.

39. This section draws heavily on and is based on Bakhtiar K. Dadabhoy, 'Three Salar Jungs and a Museum', in Vanaja Banagiri, ed., *Hyderabad Hazir Hai*, Rupa & Co., New Delhi, 2008.

40. Bakhtiar K. Dadabhoy, 'Three Salar Jungs and a Museum', in Vanaja Banagiri, ed., *Hyderabad Hazir Hai*, Rupa & Co., New Delhi, 2008, p. 45.

Glossary

Abkaree	Tax on liquor (literally, 'hard water')
Alam	Flag; standard
Amari	Howdah
Angharka	Upper garment
Anglo-Indians	British who made their careers in India
Amir-i-Kabir	The great noble
Arzbegee	An officer of the court who receives and presents petitions to the ruler
Arzee	Petition
Baradari	A Mughal-style open pavilion with three arches on each side. Literal meaning: twelve doors
Begum	Indian Muslim noblewoman; a title of rank and respect
Bibi	Indian wife or mistress
Bismillah	The Muslim ceremony to mark the beginning of a child's initiation into religious studies
Bugloos	A ceremonial belt required to be worn in the presence of royalty. A local adaptation of 'buckle'
Chauth	One-fourth of the revenue paid as tax
Chobdar	Ceremonial mace bearer
Council for India	Advisory body to Secretary of State for India after transfer to the Crown
Court of Directors	Directors of East India Company, London
Circar	Government
Crore	100 lakh
Daftar	Office
Daftardar	Record-keeper
Durbar	A public reception at Court; the Court of a ruler

Danga	Riots by which military chiefs tried to ensure payment of arrears
Daroga	Officer, overseer or superintendent
Dargah	Sufi shrine; burial place of a saint
Dastar	Turban
Deodi	Courtyard house or *haveli*
Din	Faith (for Muslims)
Diwan	The prime minister of a state or province
Diwani	Of or relating to the Diwan; same as *Khalisa* and opposed to jagir
Fakir	Religious mendicant
Eurasian	Person of mixed European and Asian blood
Governor General	Head of the East India Company in India
Governor General in Council	Decision making body of the Government of India
India Office	Office of the Secretary of State for India in London
Fasad	Riots
Fauj	Army
Firangi	Foreigner
Firman	A written order from the ruler
Gaddi	Throne
Ghadr	Mutiny
Hakim	Physician of traditional medicine
Hali Sicca	Hyderabad currency
Harkara	Runner or messenger; in some cases a newswriter or spy
Howdah	The seat on an elephant's back
Hundi	A bill of exchange
Jagir	Landed estate, granted for service to the State and whose income belonged to the *jagirdar*
Jehad	Holy war or struggle
Jemadar	military commander
Kafir	Infidel
Karkhana	Workshop or factory
Khansama	Butler in the eighteenth century; nowadays it usually means cook
Khanum	A concubine or junior wife

Khareeta	Sealed brocade bag used to send letters instead of an envelope
Khillat	Symbolic dress of honour gifted by the ruler as a mark of patronage
Khutba	Primary formal occasion for public preaching in the Islamic tradition such as at the noon prayer on Friday
Kothi	A large town house with a succession of courtyards
Kotwal	The police chief
Kotwali	The office of the *Kotwal*
Kulcha	A baked bread
Kummerbund	Broad waist sash
Lakh	One hundred thousand
Madrasa	Traditional Islamic school or college
Mansabdar	A Mughal nobleman and office holder, whose rank was decided by the number of cavalry he would supply for battle
Mardana	Men's section in a house
Masnad	The arrangement of cushions and bolsters which formed the throne of the Nizams
Moulvi	Scholar who interprets Islamic law
Mir	A title usually signifying that the holder is a Sayyed
Mirza	A prince or gentleman
Mofussil	Rural areas; originally the area outside the three capitals of Bombay, Calcutta and Madras
Mohur	A gold coin
Mujtahid	A person accepted as an authority on Islamic law
Mulki	Native Hyderabadi
Munsif	Judicial officer in the district
Munshi	Indian private secretary or language teacher
Naqqara	Kettle drum
Nawab	The term originally referred to a governor but in later usage was used as a grand title
Nazarana	Symbolic gift given in court to a feudal superior
Neema jama	Traditional Mughal dress
Nikah	Marriage
Paan	A preparation of betel nut
Padshah	Emperor

Paigah	Family appointed by Asaf Jah I to maintain a body of troops; premier nobles
Palki	Palanquin or litter
Patel, Patwari	village land revenue official
Peshkar	Deputy Diwan
Peshkash	Offering given by a subordinate to a superior, more specifically the money paid to the Marathas by subordinate powers such as the Nizam
Peshwa	Prime Minister to the Maratha ruler
Peshwaz	long outer garment worn by a lady
Purdah	Literally, a curtain, signifying the concealment of women within the *zenana*
Qasida	Ode, usually a poem in praise of a patron
Qizilbash	Name given to Safavid soldiers due to the tall red cap worn by them; literal meaning: 'redheads'
Resident	The East India Company's ambassador to an Indian court. As British power increased Resident's increasingly assumed the role of regional governors controlling the court and the city they were sent to
Risaldar	Senior Indian officer in a cavalry regiment
Ryot	Farmer; cultivator
Sahukar	Bankers, moneylenders
Samasthan	An ancient Hindu principality which existed before the time of the first Nizam
Sanad	Certificate
Sarf-i-Khas	Office managing Nizam's personal estate, administered by the Diwan on behalf of the Nizam
Sarpeche	Turban jewel or ornament
Sati	The practice of burning widows or the burned widow herself
Sebundy	Revenue instalment or sepoys employed to collect it
Serrishtadar	Record keeper
Seyaha	Accounts, vouchers
Sayyed	A lineal descendant of the Prophet Mohammed
Sepoy	Indian infantry private in the employ of the East India Company
Shamiana	Indian marquee
Shikar	Hunting

Sowar	Cavalry trooper
Suba	A province; one of the subdivisions of the Mughal empire
Subedar	Viceroy or provincial governor
Sufi	Muslim mystic
Taccavi loans	Short-term agricultural loans
Taluka	Sub-division of a district
Talukdar	Chief collector of revenue in a *taluka*, a sub-division of a district
Tehsildar	District official in charge of revenue collection and taxation
Thana	Police station
Tehzeeb	A composite of etiquette, good manners, refinement, urbanity and culture
Toorah	A stiff inverted tassel of gold thread worn in a dastar
Umra	High nobleman
Unani	Ionian (or Byzantine Greek) medicine still practiced in India
Vakil	Ambassador or representative; in modern usage lawyer
Viceroy	Head of the Government of India after 1857; Queen's representative
Zat	Mansabdars were known by two ranking numbers known as the *Zat* or personal rank and the *Sawar* or troop rank. *Zat* was a number which represented the rank or status of a Mansabdar in the military system.
Zamindar	Landholder or local ruler
Zenana	Harem or women's quarters
Zilladar	Officer responsible for maintaining law and order in the districts

Appendices

Appendix I

SECRETARIES OF STATE FOR INDIA, 1858–85

Lord Stanley (afterwards 15th Earl of Derby)	1858–59
Sir Charles Wood (afterwards Viscount Halifax)	1859–65
Earl de Grey and Ripon (afterwards Marquess of Ripon)	1866
Viscount Cranborne (afterwards Marquess of Salisbury)	1866–67
Sir Stafford Northcote (afterwards Earl of Iddesleigh)	1867–68
Duke of Argyll	1868–74
Marquess of Salisbury	1874–78
Viscount Cranbrook	1878–80
Marquess of Hartington (afterwards 8th Duke of Devonshire)	1880–82
Earl of Kimberley	1882–85

Appendix II

VICEROYS AND GOVERNORS GENERAL OF INDIA, 1858–84

Earl Canning	1858–62
Eighth Earl of Elgin	1862–63
Sir Robert Napier (Acting)	1863
Sir William T. Denison (Acting)	1863
Sir John Lawrence (afterwards Lord Lawrence)	1864–68
Earl of Mayo	1869–72
Sir John Strachey (Acting)	1872
Lord Napier of Merchistoun (Acting)	1872

Earl of Northbrook	1872–76
Earl of Lytton	1876–80
Marquess of Ripon	1880–84

Appendix III

RESIDENTS AT HYDERABAD, 1857–1884

Colonel C. Davidson	1857–62
Major A.H. Thornhill	1862–63
Sir George Yule	1863–67
Sir Richard Temple	1867–68
J.G. Cordery	1868
A.A. Roberts	1868
J.G. Cordery	1868
C.B. Saunders	1868–72
Colonel P.S. Lumsden	1872
C.B. Saunders	1872–75
General Sir Richard J. Meade	1875–81
Sir Steuart C. Bayley	1881–82
Major G.H. Trevor	1882
W.B. Jones	1882–83
J.G. Cordery	1883–84

Appendix IV

RULERS OF THE ASAF JAHI DYNASTY

Qamr-ud-din Nizam-ul-Mulk Asaf Jah I	1724-48
Ahmed Khan Nasir Jung	1748-50
Hidayat Mahi-ud-din Khan Muzaffar Jung	1750-1
Sayyid Muhammad Khan Salabat Jung	1751-61
Nizam Ali Khan Asaf Jah II	1761-1803
Sikander Jah Asaf Jah III	1803-29
Farkhunda Ali Khan Nasir-ud-Daula Asaf Jah IV	1829-57
Tahniat Ali Khan Afzal-ud-Daula Asaf Jah V	1857-69
Mahub Ali Khan Asaf Jah VI	1869-1911
Osman Ali Khan Bahadur Asaf Jah VII	1911-50

Appendix V

CHRONOLOGY OF RULERS AND OFFICIALS
DIWANS OF HYDERABAD, 1781–1914

Ghulam Syed Khan Aristu Jah	1781-1804
Raja Raghutam Rao	1804
Abul Qasim Mir Alam	1804-1808
Nawab Munir-ul-Mulk	1808-1832
Maharaja Chandu Lal	1832-1843
Raja Ram Bakhsh	1843-1846
Alam Ali Khan Siraj-ul-Mulk	1846-1848
Amjad Ali Khan Saif Jang Amjad-ud-Daula	1848
Fakhr-ud-din Khan Shams-ul-Umra II Amir-i-Kabir I	1849
Raja Ram Bakhsh	1849-1850
Raja Ganesh Rao	1851
Alam Ali Khan Siraj-ul-Mulk	1851-1853
Turab Ali Khan Mukhtar-ul-Mulk Sir Salar Jung I	1853-1883
Council of Regency	1883-1884
Laik Ali Khan Salar Jung II	1884-1887
Mazhar-ud-din Khan Bashir-ud-Daula Asman Jah	1888-1894
Fazal-ud-din Khan Iqbal-ud-Daula Vikar-ul-Umra II	1894-1900
Maharaja Kishen Pershad	1900-1912
Yusuf Ali Khan Salar Jang III	1912-1914

MINISTERS OF HYDERABAD, 1869–1883

1. 1869 to 1882

Name	Designation	Department
1. Turab Ali Khan	Diwan (Madur-ul-Maham)	Sir Salar Jung I
2. Mahdi Ali Khan	Sadr-ul-Maham	Police
3. Mazhar-ud-din Khan Bashir-ud-Daula	Sadr-ul-Maham	Judicial
4. Yawar Ali Khan Shahab Jung	Sadr-ul-Maham	Miscellaneous
5. Parwarish Ali Khan Mukaram-ud-Daula	Sadr-ul-Maham	Revenue

2. 1882 to 1883

Name	Designation	Department
1. Turab Ali Khan Sir Salar Jung I	Diwan (Madur-ul-Maham)	
2. Mahdi Ali Khan Shamsher Jung	Sadr-ul-Maham	Police
3. Mazhar-ud-din Khan Bashir-ud-Daula	Sadr-ul-Maham	Judicial
4. Yawar Ali Khan Shahab Jung	Sadr-ul-Maham	Miscellaneous

Bibliography

PRIMARY SOURCES

Archives

Telangana State Archives and Research Centre

Salar Jung Papers

National Archives of India, New Delhi (microfilm copies of private papers)

Argyll Papers
Dalhousie Papers
Lawrence Papers
Lytton Papers
Mayo papers
Northbrook Papers
Salisbury Papers

The Records of the Government of India in the Foreign Department, 1858-84.
Despatches to and from the Court of Directors, 1858.
Despatches to and from the Secretary of State, 1858-84.

Nehru Memorial Museum and Library, New Delhi

Syed Hossain Bilgrami Private Papers

Theses and Dissertations

Imadi, A.K., 'The Nobles of Hyderabad: A Study in Social Change', PhD, Osmania University, Sociology, 1977.

Patel, Simin, 'Cultural Intermediaries in a Colonial City: The Parsis of Bombay c. 1860-1921', DPhil, University of Oxford, 2015.

Compilation of Source Materials

Maulvi Syed Mahdi Ali's *Hyderabad Affairs*, vols 1-7; Index volume and vol. 8 (supplementary volume), Bombay, 1883-86; vols 9-10, London, 1889.

A comprehensive collection of newspaper extracts, official reports, books and articles dealing with the political and economic developments in Hyderabad in the nineteenth century compiled by Salar Jung's revenue secretary.

Vol. I   Physical Features of Nizam's Dominions; Natural Phenomena; Mining, Agriculture, etc.

Vol. II   Treaties; The Hyderabad Contingent and Subsidiary Force; The Berar issue.

Vol. III Salar Jung I; Revolt of 1857; Prince of Wales' Tour; Politics (1850s to 1880s); Palace Affairs.

Vol. IV State Debt; Loans to State; Arrears of Pay; Currency; Railways and Public Loans; Miscellaneous.

Vol. V   Administration; Frequent Changes of Diwan and Consequences; Disorders in the State.

Vol. VI Memorandum by Salar Jung I and Financial Statements 1878-1881; Revenue Survey Report by Mahdi Ali.

Vol. VII History of the Famine in the Nizam's Dominions, 1876-1878.

Vol. VIII Administration; Hyderabad Contingent and the Subsidiary Force; Disorders; Salar Jung I and II; Miscellaneous; Railway and Public Loans.

Vol. IX English Newspaper Comments on the Hyderabad (Deccan) Mining Company and other matters; Report of the House of Commons' Committee.

Vol. X Indian Newspaper Comments; Reports of Evidence on the Hyderabad (Deccan) Mining Company and other matters.

Newspapers

Bombay Gazette
Bombay Telegraph and Courier
Deccan Chronicle
Deccan Herald
Englishman
Friend of India and Statesman
Madras Spectator
Pall Mall Gazette
Pioneer
The Hindu
The Statesman
The Times
Times of India

SECONDARY SOURCES

Books

Alavi, Seema *Muslim Cosmopolitanism in the Age of Empire*, Harvard University Press, 2015.

Ali, Moulavi Cheragh *Hyderabad (Deccan) under Sir Salar Jung*, Vol. 1-IV, Bombay, 1884-86.

Ali, Shanti Sadiq, *The African Dispersal in the Deccan*, Orient Longman Limited, Hyderabad, 1995.

Argyll, 8th Duke of, *India Under Dalhousie and Canning*, London, 1865.

Ashton, S.R., *British Policy Towards the Indian States, 1905-1939*, London, 1982.

Balfour, Lady Betty, *The History of Lord Lytton's Indian Administration*, 1876 to 1880, London, 1899.

Barton, Sir William, *The Princes of India*, Nisbet & Co. Ltd., London, 1934.

Barnett, Richard, *North India Between Empires: Awadh, the Mughals and British, 1750-1801*, Berkeley, 1979.

Bawa, V.K., *The Nizam Between Mughals and British: Hyderabad Under Salar Jung I*, S. Chand & Company, New Delhi, 1996.

Bawa, V.K., *The Last Nizam: The Life and Times of Mir Osman Ali Khan*, Penguin Books, New Delhi, 1992.

Bearce, George D., *British Attitudes Towards India*, 1784-1858, Oxford, 1961.

Beaumont, Penny and Roger, *Invisible Empresses of the Raj*, Jaico Publishing House, Mumbai, 2011, p. 232.

Bell, Major Evans, *Retrospect and Prospects of Indian Policy*, London, 1868.

Bilgrami, Syed Hossain, and C. Wilmott, *Historical and Descriptive Sketch of the Nizam's Dominions*, 2 Vols, Bombay, 1884.

Bilgrami, Syed Hossain, *A Memoir of Sir Salar Jung, G.C.S.I.*, Times of India Steam Press, Bombay, 1883.

Bence-Jones, Mark, *The Viceroys of India*, Constable, London, 1982.

Blunt, William Scawen, *India Under Ripon: A Private Diary*, T. Fisher Unwin, London, 1909.

Briggs, Henry George, *The Nizam: His History and Relations with the British Government*, 2 Vols, London, 1861.

Burton, Lady Isabel, *The Romance of Lady Isabel Burton,* ed. W.H. Wilkins, Vol. II, Dodd Mead & Company, New York, 1897.

Burton, Major Reginald George, *A History of the Hyderabad Contingent*, Calcutta, 1905.

Campbell, Claude A., *Glimpses of the Nizam's Dominions*, C.B. Burrows, London, 1898.

Chaudhury, N.G., *British Relations with Hyderabad*, 1798-1843, Calcutta, 1964.

Copland, Ian, *The British Raj and the Indian Princes: Paramountcy in Western India, 1857-1930*, Orient Longman Ltd., New Delhi, 1982.

Dalrymple, William, *The Last Mughal*, Penguin Viking, New Delhi, 2006.

Dalrymple, William, *White Mughals*, Penguin India, New Delhi, 2004.

Fraser, Hastings, *Memoir and Correspondence of General James Stuart Fraser,* Whiting & Co. Ltd., London, 1885.

Fraser, Hastings, *Our Faithful Ally, The Nizam: An Historical Sketch of Events*, London, 1865.

Gandhi, Rajmohan, *Modern South India: A History from the 17th Century to Our Times*, Aleph Book Company, New Delhi, 2018.

Gilmour, David, *The British in India*, Allen Lane, Penguin Random House, UK, 2018.

Gopal, S., *British Policy in India, 1858-1905*, Orient Longman, 1992.

Gopal, S., *The Viceroyalty of Lord Ripon*, 1880-1884, Oxford, 1953.

Gribble, J.D.B., *History of the Deccan*, Vol 1 &2, Rupa & Co. New Delhi, 2002.

Hirschmann, Edwin, *Robert Knight: Reforming Editor in Victorian India*, Oxford University Press, New Delhi, 2008.

Hobsbawm, E. and Terence Ranger (eds.), *The Invention of Tradition*, Cambridge, 1983.

Hyndman, Henry Mayers, *The Record of an Adventurous Life*, Macmillan and Co. London, 1911.

Imam, Syeda, ed., *The Untold Charminar: Writings on Hyderabad*, Penguin Books, New Delhi, 2008.

Jeffrey, Robin (ed.), *People, Princes and Paramount Power*, Oxford University Press, New Delhi, 1978.

Karaka, D.F., *Fabulous Mogul: Nizam VII of Hyderabad*, D. Verschoyle, London, 1955.

Kaye, John William, *The Life and Correspondence of Charles, Lord Metcalfe*, Richard Bentley, London, 1864.

Khan, M. Fathullah, *A History of Administrative Reforms in Hyderabad State*, Secunderabad, 1935.

Khan, Yusuf Husain, *Nizamu'l-Mulk Asaf Jah I*, The Basel Mission Press, Mangalore, 1936.

Krishnaswamy, Mudiraj K., (compiled), *Pictorial Hyderabad*, (Hyderabad, 1929-34), 2 Vols.

Lee, Christopher, *Viceroy: The Creation of the British*, Constable, London, 2018.

Lee Warner, Sir William, The Protected Princes of India, London, 1894.

Liddle, Swapna, *Chandni Chowk: The Mughal City of Old Delhi*, Speaking Tiger, New Delhi, 2017.

Low, Sir Sydney, *The Indian States and the Ruling Princes*, London, 1929.

Luther, Narendra, *Hyderabad: A Biography*, Oxford University Press, New Delhi.

Lutyens, Mary, *The Lyttons in India*, John Murray, London, 1979.

Lynton, Harriet Ronken and Mohini Rajan, *The Days of the Beloved*, Orient Longman Ltd., New Delhi, 1987.

Lynton, Harriet Ronken, *My Dear Nawab Saheb*, Disha Books, New Delhi, 1993.

MacKenzie, Colin, *Storms and Sunshine of a Soldier's Life*, Vol 2, David Douglas, Edinburg, 1884.

Mersey, Viscount, *The Viceroys and Governors-General of India 1757-1947*, John Murray, London, 1949.

Mullick, G.B., *Lord Northbrook and His Mission in India*, Calcutta, 1873.

Noorani, A.G., *The Destruction of Hyderabad*, Tulika Books, New Delhi, 2013.

Panikkar, K.M., *Introduction to the Study of the Relations of Indian States with the Government of India*, London, 1927.

Prasad, Rajendra, *Asif Jahs of Hyderabad: Their Rise and Decline*, Prachee Publications, Hyderabad, 2010.

Prinsep, Val. C., *Imperial India: An Artist's Journals*, Chapman and Hall, London, 1878.

Raj, Sheela, *Portrait of an Era: Hyderabad in the Days of the Nizams*, 1828-1896, Minerva Press, 1996.

Ray, Bharati, *Hyderabad and British Paramountcy,1858-1883*, Oxford University Press, New Delhi, 1988.

Regani, Sarojini, *Nizam-British Relations, 1724-1857*, Concept Publishing Company, New Delhi, 1988.

Russell, W.H., *The Prince of Wales' Tour: A Diary in India*, (2nd ed.), London, 1877.

Sajanlal, K., *Studies in Deccan History*, Madras, 1951.

Sanyal, N., *Development of Indian Railways*, Calcutta, 1930.

Sarma, Rani, *The Deodis of Hyderabad*, Rupa & Co., New Delhi, 2008.

Server-ul-Mulk, *My Life*, translated by Nawab JivanYar Jung, London, undated.

Singh, K Natwar, *Magnificent Maharaja*, Rupa & Co. New Delhi, 2005

Taylor, Col. Meadows, *The Story of My Life*, London, 1877, 2 Vols.

Taylor, Miles, *The Indian Maharani*, Penguin Random House, Gurgaon, 2018.

Temple, Sir Richard, *Journals Kept in Hyderabad, Kashmir, Sikkim, and Nepal*, Vol. 1, W.H. Allen & Co., London, 1887.

Temple, Sir Richard, *Men and Events of my Time of India*, London, John Murray, 1882.

Tharoor, Shashi, *An Era of Darkness: The British Empire in India*, Aleph Book Company, New Delhi, 2016.

The Chronology of Modern Hyderabad from 1720 to 1890, The Central Records Office, Hyderabad, 1954.

Thompson, Edward, *The Making of the Indian Princes*, Oxford University Press, London, 1943.

Thornton, T. H., *General Sir Richard Meade and the Feudatory States of Central and Southern India*, Longmans, Green, London, 1898.

Tytler, Harriet, *An Englishwoman in India: The Memoirs of Harriet Tytler 1828-1858*, ed. Anthony Sattin, Oxford, 1986.

Wheeler, J.Talboys, *The History of the Imperial Assemblage at Delhi*, Longmans, Green, Reader and Dyer, London.

Yazdani Zubaida and Mary Chrystal, *The Seventh Nizam: The Fallen Empire*, Cambridge University Press, 1985.

Zubrzycki, John, *The Mysterious Mr Jacob*, Random House India, New Delhi, 2012.

Zubrzycki, John, *The Last Nizam*, Picador India, 2006.

Articles

Cohn, Bernard S., 'Representing Authority in Victorian India', in E. Hobsbawm and Terence Ranger (eds.), *The Invention of Tradition*, Cambridge, 1983.

Bawa, V.K., 'Salar Jang and the Nizam's State Railway', *The Indian Economic and Social History Review*, Vol. II, No. 4, October 1965.

Dadabhoy, Bakhtiar K., 'Three Salar Jungs and a Museum', in Vanaja Banagiri ed. *Hyderabad Hazir Hai*, Rupa & Co., New Delhi, 2008.

Leonard, Karen, 'Banking Firms in Nineteenth-Century Hyderabad Politics', *Modern Asian Studies*, 15,2 (1981), p. 178-179.

Leonard, Karen, 'Palmer and Company: an Indian Banking Firm in Hyderabad State', *Modern Asian Studies* 47, 4 (2013) pp. 1157-1184, Cambridge University Press 2013.

Leonard, Karen, 'The Hyderabadi Political System and its Participants', *The Journal of Asian Studies*, Volume XXX, Number 3, May 1971.

Leonard, Karen, 'The Deccani Synthesis in Old Hyderabad: An Historiographic Essay', *Journal of the Pakistan Historical Society*, Reprint.

Neogy, Ajit, 'British Role in the Selection of the Nizam's Dewan in the 19th Century', *The Quarterly Review of Historical Studies*, Vol. XI, No. 3, 1971-72.

Ray, Bharati, 'The Genesis of Railway Development in Hyderabad State: A Case Study in Nineteenth Century British Imperialism', *The Indian Economic and Social History Review*, Vol. XXI, No. 1.

Ray, Bharati, 'Salar Jung, Berar and the British', *The Calcutta Historical Journal*, Vol. 2, No 1 (1977).

Ray, Bharati, 'The Politics of Imperialism: Lord Lytton and Sir Salar Jung', *Bengal Past and Present*, Vol. C II, January-June, 1983.

Ray, Bharati, 'The Politics of Paramountcy: Lord Northbrook and Hyderabad State, 1872-1876', *The Quarterly Review of Historical Studies*, vol. 24, no. 1, 1984-85.

Ray, Bharati, 'A Reward That Was Not: An Examination of the Anglo-Nizam Treaty of 1860', *The Calcutta Historical Journal*, vol. 8 nos. 1-2, July 1983 – June 1984.

Regani, Sarojini, 'The Appointment of Diwan in Hyderabad State (1803-87)', *Andhra Historical Research Society Journal* (1958-60), Vol. 25.

Sajanlal, K., 'Sir Salar Jung's Visit to England and the Berar Question', *Journal of Osmania University, Golden Jubilee Volume* (1968).

Seshan, K.S.S., 'The Hyderabad Connect', *The Hindu*, 29 October 2015.

Sharma, Shalini, 'The Jewellery Chasers', *Deccan Chronicle*, 23 September 2018.

Tomlinson, B.R., 'India and the British Empire, 1880-1953', *The Indian Economic and Social History Review*, vol. 12, 1975.

'The rich legacy of Nizams', *Deccan Chronicle*, 1 June 2014.

Websites

https://www.archive.org
www.royalark.net
www.wikipedia.org
www.salarjungmuseum.in

Index

Acknowledgements

A book is made possible by many institutions and people. Although in the usual author-fashion I speak possessively of this as my book, it is in truth the product of collaboration: the joint efforts of persons and institutions even though the cover proudly proclaims only my name. Inevitably, in a venture such as this, one is indebted to those who have gone before. This biography of Salar Jung is based on the work of a large number of scholars and authors, apart from of course his own correspondence and archival records. My bibliography illustrates the full scale of my debt but certain books belong on a personal roll of honour since my debt to them has been especially heavy, and among whose pages I have pillaged, précised, and paraphrased shamelessly. It is only appropriate that I acknowledge these to whom I owe the greatest debt of gratitude with a special mention.

Harriet Ronken Lynton's *My Dear Nawab Saheb*, was the book which in a sense started it all since the seed for writing this biography was sown after I read this book. If it was involved in the seeding of this book, it has also been one of the foundations for this work. Apart from giving me my first glimpse into Salar Jung's life and work, it has proved to be immensely useful in pointing the way to relevant correspondence and documents connected with the great Diwan. I can only hope that the end product is worthy of the inspiration.

Bharati Ray's *Hyderabad and British Paramountcy, 1858-1883* is another book which was of immense help given that it is a commentary on the legal, political, administrative and economic implications of the application of the policy of paramountcy to Hyderabad in the second half of the nineteenth century. It is also an important source of material on the political aims and stratagems of Salar Jung who paradoxically was both principal collaborator and chief opponent of the British. This book too

473

has been a goldmine in pointing the way to archival sources. In many cases I have resorted to taking a shortcut and quoted from it where I did not have access to the original archival material. I have had no compunction in précising and paraphrasing with what I believe to be a judicious licentiousness, but hopefully not unforgiveable promiscuity, and can only hope that this acknowledgement is adequate recompense for the author's intellectual labour.

V.K. Bawa's *The Nizam Between Mughals and British: Hyderabad Under Salar Jung I*, based on his doctoral thesis, also smoothed the way considerably since it is a fairly comprehensive account of Salar Jung's career and also includes some personal details unavailable in the work of Ray and Lynton. I also had the pleasure of personally interacting with him and his wife Dr Oudhesh Rani Bawa on a number of occasions. Alert and sharp with perfect recall, even though he is almost a nonagenarian, I have greatly benefited from my conversations with the eminence grise of historians on Hyderabad.

Thanks are due to those who oiled the wheels of progress and it gives me great pleasure to acknowledge the large cast of characters and celebrate the friendships that helped me realize a complex project. I would like to thank Vaishali Patil, for her help in typing out my research notes. She converted the cursive script of letters written more than a century-and-a-half ago into Times New Roman and must have often wondered what other torture I was going to inflict on her, and when it would all end. On occasion I despatched her to libraries to procure books and material which has proved to be crucial in the writing of this book. Her efficient and cheerful assistance contributed greatly to the progress of this venture. I suspect she has become a fan of Salar Jung herself. For many miscellaneous kindnesses my thanks go to C.S. Rao, Subash Nair, Devendra Bisht and V. Chandrasekar. They provided significant assistance along the way and deserve my warmest thanks. I would also like to thank R.C. Nair for the author photo.

Kiran Misra, a friend from college days, cheerfully assisted me in my research in the National Archives at New Delhi. Her help has been inestimable and I really cannot thank her enough. My gratitude also goes to the staff at the National Archives of India, New Delhi, for their cooperation and support. Dr Zareena Parveen, director of the Telangana State Archives and Research Centre, provided all assistance from the beginning. The Archives which she heads is the repository of Salar Jung's correspondence and the Mecca for researchers on Hyderabad's great diwan. Thanks are also due to Praveen Kumar, G. Prabhakar, Sai Leela at the Archives library and the indispensable M. Khaleel who dug out and produced the requested records with great alacrity.

I would like to thank my friend Anuradha Naik for accompanying me to the Paigah tombs, and the Daira Mir Momin, Salar Jung's final resting place. Serendipity also played a role. My chance meeting with Numan Khan, in the Archives at Secunderabad proved to be nothing short of a godsend for me. He supplied photographs without stint and his kindness to a complete stranger is much appreciated. I wish him all success in the making of his documentary on the Paigahs.

Milee Ashwarya who commissioned this book was as usual unflagging in her enthusiasm and was personally committed to the book. This is our third book together. It is important for a writer to have his text checked by a discerning editor for quite often what appears to be crystal clear to the author is confusing to the reader. In this I was lucky to have Saksham Garg's comments who proved to be an excellent sounding board. He shared my enthusiasm for the book and was invaluable in offering useful perspectives and making insightful suggestions. However his attempts at reducing the size of the book met with very limited success.

Shantanu Ray Chaudhuri and Clare Stewart expertly copy-edited the text and their conscientious and diligent copy-editing has added polish and clarity to many rough edges. While all efforts have been made to ensure the accuracy of facts, and also to ensure that I did not inadvertently fail to give due citations, I will be happy if errors and omissions are brought to my notice.

My friend, A. Nagender Reddy, the director of the Salar Jung Museum, proved to be invaluable, providing information, reference material and photographs on tap. It is a huge advantage to have the head of an institution from which you hope to get substantial help on your side. Soma Ghosh, the librarian at the Museum library, went out of her way to provide photographs and material and made valuable suggestions. She cheerfully clarified doubts and sent material requested by me with great despatch. Thanks are also due to M. Krishnamurthy and Bahadur Ali of the Salar Jung Museum for their help in providing the requested photographs.

Ahteram Ali Khan, the great grandson of Bairam-ud-Daula and Sultan Bakht Afroz Begum (Salar Jung's youngest daughter), was kind enough to speak at length about his illustrious forbear and some of the amusing anecdotes in the book are his contribution. He shared photographs generously and allowed me to photograph the painting of Salar Jung in his possession.

Perhaps my biggest debt is to information technology: had it not been for the Internet, and that wonderful initiative encapsulated in a website called https://archive.org the writing of this book would have become infinitely more difficult, laborious, time-consuming and expensive. The facility of accessing material with the click of a mouse is best appreciated by those who have had to encounter delay and frustration due to non-availability of material or bureaucratic obstruction. It was indeed reassuring and a huge relief to know to know that even a book published in the mid-nineteenth century was only a few clicks away. All the books published in the nineteenth and early twentieth century which I have used in researching this book have been taken from this website.

It is customary to acknowledge the support of friends and family when putting a book to bed. Thanks are due to my friends Devendra Singh and Dakshita Das for their hospitality in New Delhi and to Anupam Kapoor for his assistance in Secunderabad. As always my mother, Rati, and my sister Tushna, brother-in-law Phiroze and nephew Navroz, provided important moral support, celebrating the highs and sympathizing with the lows. This book is dedicated to my uncle and aunt Noshir and Nawsha Jalnawala, and was intended to commemorate their sixtieth wedding anniversary in April 2019 but my tardiness precluded such a possibility. It is also dedicated to the memory of Feroz Shapurji who over the years has read all my books. His sudden demise before this book could go to press has deprived me of a friend, benefactor and well-wisher.

Copyright Acknowledgements for Photographs

Grateful acknowledgement is made to the following for permission to reprint copyright material:

The Salar Jung Museum for photographs 1, 5, 12, 25, 26, 27, 28, 35, 37, 39 and 40.

Claude A. Campbell, *Glimpses of the Nizam's Dominions*, C.B. Burrows, Bombay and London, 1898 for photographs 2, 3, 4, 6, 8, 9, 10, 11, 13, 14, 19, 20, 22, 23, 29, 31, 32, 33, 34 and 36.

Numan Khan for photographs 7, 21, 24 and 30.

The author for photograph 38.